(Continued on back endsheets)

German Writers from the Enlightenment to Sturm und Drang, 1720-1764

Dictionary of Literary Biography • Volume Ninety-seven

German Writers from the Enlightenment to Sturm und Drang, 1720-1764

8339

Edited by
James Hardin
University of South Carolina
and
Christoph E. Schweitzer
University of North Carolina, Chapel Hill

A Bruccoli Clark Layman Book
Gale Research Inc.
Detroit, New York, London

Manufactured by Edwards Brothers, Inc.
Ann Arbor, Michigan
Printed in the United States of America

The paper used in this publication meets the minimum requirements
of American National Standard for Information Sciences—Permanence
Paper for Printed Library Materials, ANSI Z39.48-1984. ∞™

ISBN 0-8103-4577-3 ·
90-3466 CIP

Contents

Plan of the Series

. . . Almost the most prodigious asset of a country, and perhaps its most precious possession, is its native literary product—when that product is fine and noble and enduring.

Mark Twain*

The advisory board, the editors, and the publisher of the *Dictionary of Literary Biography* are joined in endorsing Mark Twain's declaration. The literature of a nation provides an inexhaustible resource of permanent worth. We intend to make literature and its creators better understood and more accessible to students and the reading public, while satisfying the standards of teachers and scholars.

To meet these requirements, *literary biography* has been construed in terms of the author's achievement. The most important thing about a writer is his writing. Accordingly, the entries in *DLB* are career biographies, tracing the development of the author's canon and the evolution of his reputation.

The purpose of *DLB* is not only to provide reliable information in a convenient format but also to place the figures in the larger perspective of literary history and to offer appraisals of their accomplishments by qualified scholars.

The publication plan for *DLB* resulted from two years of preparation. The project was proposed to Bruccoli Clark by Frederick G. Ruffner, president of the Gale Research Company, in November 1975. After specimen entries were prepared and typeset, an advisory board was formed to refine the entry format and develop the series rationale. In meetings held during 1976, the publisher, series editors, and advisory board approved the scheme for a comprehensive biographical dictionary of persons who contributed to North American literature. Editorial work on the first volume began in January 1977, and it was published in 1978. In order to make *DLB* more than a reference tool and to compile volumes that individually have claim to status as lit-

erary history, it was decided to organize volumes by topic, period, or genre. Each of these freestanding volumes provides a biographical-bibliographical guide and overview for a particular area of literature. We are convinced that this organization—as opposed to a single alphabet method—constitutes a valuable innovation in the presentation of reference material. The volume plan necessarily requires many decisions for the placement and treatment of authors who might properly be included in two or three volumes. In some instances a major figure will be included in separate volumes, but with different entries emphasizing the aspect of his career appropriate to each volume. Ernest Hemingway, for example, is represented in *American Writers in Paris, 1920-1939* by an entry focusing on his expatriate apprenticeship; he is also in *American Novelists, 1910-1945* with an entry surveying his entire career. Each volume includes a cumulative index of subject authors and articles. Comprehensive indexes to the entire series are planned.

With volume ten in 1982 it was decided to enlarge the scope of *DLB*. By the end of 1986 twenty-one volumes treating British literature had been published, and volumes for Commonwealth and Modern European literature were in progress. The series has been further augmented by the *DLB Yearbooks* (since 1981) which update published entries and add new entries to keep the *DLB* current with contemporary activity. There have also been *DLB Documentary Series* volumes which provide biographical and critical source materials for figures whose work is judged to have particular interest for students. One of these companion volumes is entirely devoted to Tennessee Williams.

We define literature as the *intellectual commerce of a nation*: not merely as belles lettres but as that ample and complex process by which ideas are generated, shaped, and transmitted. *DLB* entries are not limited to "creative writers" but extend to other figures who in their time and in their way influenced the mind of a people. Thus the series encompasses historians, journalists, publishers, and screenwriters. By this means readers of *DLB* may be aided to perceive litera-

*From an unpublished section of Mark Twain's autobiography, copyright © by the Mark Twain Company.

ture not as cult scripture in the keeping of intellectual high priests but firmly positioned at the center of a nation's life.

DLB includes the major writers appropriate to each volume and those standing in the ranks immediately behind them. Scholarly and critical counsel has been sought in deciding which minor figures to include and how full their entries should be. Wherever possible, useful references are made to figures who do not warrant separate entries.

Each *DLB* volume has a volume editor responsible for planning the volume, selecting the figures for inclusion, and assigning the entries. Volume editors are also responsible for preparing, where appropriate, appendices surveying the major periodicals and literary and intellectual movements for their volumes, as well as lists of further readings. Work on the series as a whole is coordinated at the Bruccoli Clark Layman editorial center in Columbia, South Carolina, where the editorial staff is responsible for accuracy of the published volumes.

One feature that distinguishes *DLB* is the illustration policy–its concern with the iconography of literature. Just as an author is influenced by his surroundings, so is the reader's understanding of the author enhanced by a knowledge of his environment. Therefore *DLB* volumes include not only drawings, paintings, and photographs of authors, often depicting them at various stages in their careers, but also illustrations of their families and places where they lived. Title pages are regularly reproduced in facsimile along with dust jackets for modern authors. The dust jackets are a special feature of *DLB* because they often document better than anything else the way in which an author's work was perceived in its own time. Specimens of the writers' manuscripts are included when feasible.

Samuel Johnson rightly decreed that "The chief glory of every people arises from its authors." The purpose of the *Dictionary of Literary Biography* is to compile literary history in the surest way available to us–by accurate and comprehensive treatment of the lives and work of those who contributed to it.

The *DLB* Advisory Board

Foreword

DLB 97: German Writers from the Enlightenment to the Sturm und Drang, 1720-1764 includes articles on thirty-four literary figures whose first printed works appeared in or after 1721 and before 1765, linking at the latter date with *DLB 94: German Writers in the Age of Goethe: Sturm und Drang to Classicism.* The editors are well aware that neither literary labels nor chronological divisions provide clear-cut demarcations in the history of a literature; but of the two, the chronological division seemed preferable, and it has guided us in placing authors in specific *DLB* volumes.

Since there is a significant break in the tradition of German letters just before the period covered by this volume, it was felt that an essay dealing with the changes that took place on the German intellectual scene between the late seventeenth and early eighteenth centuries would be helpful to the reader. Professor P. M. Mitchell's "The German Transformation from the Baroque to the Enlightenment," in the appendix, provides an introduction to the literary trends represented by the authors in the volume. Mitchell stresses the importance of other European countries, especially France and England, for Germany's progress during this time of transition. These influences are most visible in the areas of philosophy and aesthetics, and they can also be seen in the development of such genres as bourgeois tragedy, the fable, Anacreontic poetry, the novel, and the essay. As Mitchell points out, Johann Christoph Gottsched set the tone for the aesthetic orientation and the literary practice of the beginning of the eighteenth century.

The time span covered by this volume is generally known as the Enlightenment. The writers treated in the volume were instrumental in preparing for the late eighteenth-century blossoming of German literature, philosophy, and culture called Classicism. But it should not be forgotten that German (or Weimar) Classicism was itself in many respects a continuation and refinement of the ideas of the Enlightenment. Furthermore, we do not do justice to the many accomplishments of the period if we view it only in light of what follows. Rather, we should recognize the immense achievements brought about by the writers included in this volume: in this period German was finally accepted as the standard literary language, critical journals were established, and basic concepts of democracy were widely discussed. We must also remember that side by side with the Enlightenment, Pietism was a strong force in Germany in this period. Friedrich Gottlieb Klopstock's poems and many other literary works owe their peculiar vitality to the individualism associated with Pietism. Its voice was heard throughout the Age of Goethe.

Included in this volume are such seminal figures as Gottsched, Klopstock, Johann Georg Hamann, Johann Gottfried Herder, Christoph Martin Wieland, Gotthold Ephraim Lessing, and Johann Joachim Winckelmann, as well as lesser known authors who have been unduly neglected and have heretofore not found a place in English-language reference books. Authors and editors have taken pains to make the primary bibliography of each figure as complete as possible, so that the user will find reliable lists of first editions together with the first English or American translation of the work. We have also attempted to provide listings of modern translations. Since *DLB 97* was conceived with the English-reading user in mind, we have provided translations of the titles and quotations cited in the text. To facilitate further research a critical bibliography follows each entry, together with information on the location of the extant literary remains of the author in question. Finally, the reader will find at the end of the volume a list of books that we recommend for further reading. Most are in English, but we have also included a few important recent publications in German.

The editors are grateful to the contributors and to the publisher for their efforts to provide interesting illustrations for this volume.

–James Hardin
Christoph E. Schweitzer

Acknowledgments

This book was produced by Bruccoli Clark Layman, Inc. Karen L. Rood is senior editor for the *Dictionary of Literary Biography* series. Philip B. Dematteis was the in-house editor.

Production coordinator is James W. Hipp. Systems manager is Charles D. Brower. Photography editor is Susan Brennen Todd. Permissions editor is Jean W. Ross. Layout and graphics supervisor is Penney L. Haughton. Copyediting supervisor is Bill Adams. Typesetting supervisor is Kathleen M. Flanagan. Information systems analyst is George F. Dodge. Charles Lee Egleston is editorial associate. The production staff includes Rowena Betts, Anne L. M. Bowman, Teresa Chaney, Patricia Coate, Sarah A. Estes, Mary L. Goodwin, Cynthia Hallman, Susan C. Heath, David Marshall James, Kathy S. Merlette, Laura Garren Moore, John Myrick, Cathy J. Reese, Edward Scott, Laurrè Sinckler, Maxine K. Smalls, John C. Stone III, Jennifer Toth, and Betsy L. Weinberg.

Walter W. Ross and Parris Boyd did the library research with the assistance of the following librarians at the Thomas Cooper Library of the University of South Carolina: Gwen Baxter, Daniel Boice, Faye Chadwell, Cathy Eckman, Gary Geer, Cathie Gottlieb, David L. Haggard, Jens Holley, Jackie Kinder, Thomas Marcil, Marcia Martin, Laurie Preston, Jean Rhyne, Carol Tobin, and Virginia Weathers.

The editors are grateful for the biographical work of Valerie M. Bernhardt, Jeffrey Lopes, and William N. Wallace. The University Research Council of the University of North Carolina at Chapel Hill provided a grant which was instrumental in the completion of this book.

German Writers from the Enlightenment to Sturm und Drang, 1720-1764

Dictionary of Literary Biography

Johann Jakob Bodmer

(19 July 1698 - 2 January 1783)

Arthur D. Mosher
University of South Carolina

BOOKS: *Von dem Einfluß und Gebrauche der Einbildungs-Krafft: Zur Ausbesserung des Geschmackes; oder, Genaue Untersuchung aller Arten Beschreibungen worinne die außerlesenste Stellen der berühmtesten Poeten dieser Zeit mit gründtlicher Freyheit beurtheilt werden*, anonymous, by Bodmer and Johann Jakob Breitinger (Frankfurt am Main & Leipzig [actually Zurich], 1727);

Anklagung Des verderbten Geschmackes; oder Critische Anmerkungen über den Hamburgischen Patrioten, und die Hallischen Tadlerinnen, anonymous (Frankfurt am Main & Leipzig [actually Zurich], 1728);

Evergetae: Die Wohlthäter des Stands Zürich (N.p., 1733);

Character der teutschen Gedichte, anonymous (Zurich, 1734);

Brief-Wechsel von der Natur des poetischen Geschmackes: Dazu kömmt eine Untersuchung wie ferne das Erhabene im Trauerspiel Statt und Platz haben könne; wie auch von der Poetischen Gerechtigkeit, by Bodmer and Pietro di Calepio (Zurich: Orell, 1736; reprinted, with afterword by Wolfgang Bender, Stuttgart: Metzler, 1966);

Critische Abhandlung von dem Wunderbaren in der Poesie und dessen Verbindung mit dem Wahrscheinlichen: In einer Vertheidigung des Gedichtes Joh. Miltons von dem verlohrnen Paradiese; der beygefüget ist Joseph Addisons Abhandlung von den Schönheiten in demselben Gedichte (Zurich: Orell, 1740; reprinted, with afterword by Bender, Stuttgart: Metzler, 1966);

Johann Jakob Bodmer; painting by J. C. Füeßli (from Gero von Wilpert, Deutsche Literatur in Bildern, *1965)*

Critische Betrachtungen über die poetischen Gemählde der Dichter, mit einer Vorrede von Johann Jakob Breitinger (Zurich: Orell, 1741; reprinted, Frankfurt am Main: Athenäum, 1971);

Schreiben an die critickverständige Gesellschaft zu Zürich, über die Critischen Beyträge Hrn. Prof. Gott-

scheds, anonymous (Zurich: Heidegger, 1742);

Critische Betrachtungen und freye Untersuchungen zum Aufnehmen und zur Verbesserung der deutschen Schau-Bühne: Mit einer Zuschrift an die Frau Neuberin, anonymous (Bern, 1743);

Aufrichtiger Unterricht von den geheimsten Handgriffen in der Kunst Fabeln zu verfertigen: Dem Hr. Johann Wursten von Königsberg mitgetheilt von Hr. Daniel Stoppen aus Hirschberg in Schlesien, und Mitgliede der deutschen Gesellschaft in Leipzig, anonymous (Breslau [actually Zurich]: Korn, 1745);

Beurtheilung der Panthea, eines sogenannten Trauerspiels: Nebst einer Vorlesung für die Nachkommen und einer Ode auf den Nahmen Gottsched, by Bodmer and Breitinger (Zurich, 1746);

Critische Briefe, by Bodmer and Breitinger (Zurich: Heidegger, 1746; reprinted, Hildesheim: Olms, 1969);

Der Mahler der Sitten: Von neuem übersehen und starck vermehret, 2 volumes, by Bodmer and Breitinger (Zurich: Orell, 1746; reprinted, Hildesheim & New York: Olms, 1972);

Critische Lobgedichte und Elegien, anonymous, edited by Johann Georg Schultheß (Zurich: Orell, 1747); republished as J. J. Bodmers Gedichte in gereimten Versen mit J. G. Schuldheißen Anmerkungen: Dazu kommen etliche Briefe (Zurich: Orell, 1754);

Der gemißhandelte Opiz in der Trillerischen Ausfertigung seiner Gedichte, by Bodmer and Breitinger (Zurich, 1747);

Pigmalion, oder Die belebte Statüe, anonymous (Hamburg: Martini, 1748); republished as Pygmalion und Elise, anonymous (Berlin, 1749);

Neue critische Briefe über gantz verschiedene Sachen, von verschiedenen Verfassern, anonymous (Zurich: Orell, 1749); revised as Neue critische Briefe über gantz verschiedene Sachen, von verschiedenen Verfassern: Neue mit einigen Gesprächen in Elysium und am Acheron vermehrt, anonymous (Zurich: Orell, 1763);

Noah, ein Heldengedicht, anonymous (Frankfurt am Main & Leipzig: 1750);

Die unschuldige Liebe, anonymous (N.p., 1750);

Jacob und Joseph: Ein Gedicht in drei Gesängen, anonymous (Zurich: Orell, 1751); revised as Jacob und Joseph: ein Gedicht in vier Gesängen, anonymous (Zurich: Orell, 1754);

Die Synd-Flut: Ein Gedicht. Erster und Zweyter Gesang, anonymous (Zurich: Heidegger, 1751); enlarged as Die Synd-Flut: Ein Gedicht. In fynf

Gesaengen, anonymous (Zurich: Heidegger, 1753);

Jacob und Rachel: Ein Gedicht in zween Gesaengen, anonymous (Zurich: Orell, 1752); republished as Jacob und Rahel: Ein Gedicht in zween Gesängen (Zurich: Geßner, 1759);

Der Noah: In Zwölf Gesängen, anonymous (Zurich: Gessner, 1752); revised as Die Noachide in zwölf Gesängen, as Bodmer (Berlin: Voß, 1765; revised edition, Zurich: Bürgkli, 1772); translated by Joseph Collyer as Noah: Attempted from the German of Mr. Bodmer. In twelve books, 2 volumes (London: Collyer, 1767); translation revised as The History of Noah and His Family: Being in the manner of, and a sequel to the celebrated Paradise lost, of Milton, and the Death of Abel, by Gessner. Written originally in the German language by M. Bodmer, and freely translated by Joseph Collyer. In twelve books (Newcastle upon Tyne: Printed by W. Thompson, 1790);

Die Columbona, ein Gedicht in fynf Gesaengen, anonymous (Zurich: Orell, 1753);

Dina und Sichem: In zween Gesaengen, anonymous (Trosberg: Wachsmuth [actually Zurich: Orell], 1753);

Jacobs Wiederkunft von Haran, ein Gedicht, anonymous (Trosberg: Wachsmuth [actually Zurich: Orell], 1753);

Joseph und Zulika, in zween Gesaengen, anonymous (Zurich: Orell, 1753);

Der Parcival, ein Gedicht in Wolframs von Eschilbach Denckart: Eines Poeten aus den Zeiten Kaiser Heinrichs VI., anonymous (Zurich: Heidegger, 1753);

Der erkannte Joseph, und der keusche Joseph: Zwei tragische Styke in fynf Aufzygen, von dem Verfasser des Jacob und Josephs, und des Joseph und Zulika. Samt verschiedenen Briefen yber die Einfyhrung des Chemos, und den Character Josephs, in dem Gedichte Joseph und Zulika, anonymous (Zurich: Orell, 1754);

Edward Grandisons Geschichte in Görlitz, anonymous (Berlin: Voß, 1755);

Fragmente in der erzaehlenden Dichtart: Von verschiedenem Innhalte. Mit einigen andern Gedichten, anonymous, by Bodmer and Christoph Martin Wieland (Zurich: Orell, 1755);

Die gefallene Zilla: In drei Gesängen, anonymous (Amsterdam: Sinwel [actually Zurich: Orell], 1755);

Arminius-Schönaich, ein episches Gedicht von Hermannfried (Frankfurt am Main, 1756);

Inkel und Yariko, anonymous (Lindau, 1756);

Das Banket der Dunse, anonymous (N.p., 1758);

Die Larve, ein comisches Gedicht, anonymous (N.p., 1758);

Electra, oder die gerechte Uebelthat: Ein Trauerspiel. Nach einem neuen Grundrisse (Zurich: Orell, 1760);

Lessingische unäsopische Fabeln: Enthaltend die sinnreichen Einfälle und weisen Sprüche der Thiere. Nebst damit einschlagender Untersuchung der Abhandlung Herrn Lessings von der Kunst Fabeln zu verfertigen, anonymous, by Bodmer and Breitinger (Zurich: Orell, 1760);

Polytimet: Ein Trauerspiel. Durch Lessings Philotas, oder ungerathenen Helden veranlasset, anonymous (Zurich: Orell, 1760); reprinted in Gotthold Ephraim Lessing's *Philotas,* edited by Wilhelm Grosse (Stuttgart: Reclam, 1979), pp. 63-79;

Ulysses, Telemachs Sohn: Ein Trauerspiel. Nach einer neuen Ausbildung, translated by Bodmer (Zurich: Geßner, 1760);

Drey neue Trauerspiele. Nämlich: Johanna Gray; Friederich von Tockenburg; Oedipus, anonymous (Zurich: Heidegger, 1761);

Gespräche im Elysium und am Acheron, anonymous (N.p., 1762);

Julius Cäsar, ein Trauerspiel; herausgegeben von dem Verfasser der Anmerkungen zum Gebrauche der Kunstrichter, anonymous (Leipzig: Weidmann & Reich, 1763);

Marcus Tullius Cicero: Ein Trauerspiel, anonymous (Zurich: Orell, Geßner, 1764);

Gottsched, ein Trauerspiel, oder: Der parodirte Cato, anonymous (Zurich, 1765);

Die Töchter des Paradieses, anonymous (Zurich: Orell, Geßner, 1766);

Calliope, 2 volumes (Zurich: Orell, Geßner, 1767);

Archiv der schweitzerischen Kritick: Von der Mitte des Jahrhunderts bis auf gegenwärtige Zeiten. Erstes Bändchen, anonymous (Zurich: Orell, Geßner, Füßli, 1768);

Die Grundsätze der deutschen Sprache. Oder: Von den Bestandtheilen derselben und von dem Redesatze, anonymous (Zurich: Orell, Geßner, 1768);

Neue theatralische Werke, von Herrn Professor Bodmer in Zürich. 1. Band (Lindau: Otto, 1768)–comprises *Der Vierte Heinrich, Kaiser; Cato der Aeltere oder der Aufstand der römischen Frauen; Atreus und Thyest;* "Eindrücke der Befreiung von Theben, eines leipzigischen Trauerspieles auf einen Kenner der Griechen"; republished as *Politische Schauspiele, von verschiedenen Verfassern* (Lindau & Chur: Typographische Gesellschaft, 1768);

Politische Schauspiele: Marcus Brutus; Tarquinius Superbus; Italus; Timoleon; Pelopidas (Zurich: Orell, Geßner, 1768);

Politische Schauspiele: Aus den Zeiten der Cäsare (Lindau & Chur: Typographische Gesellschaft, 1769)–comprises *Octavius Cäsar, ein Drama; Nero, ein politisches Drama; Thrasea Pätus, ein Trauerspiel;*

Politische Schauspiele: Von griechischem Innhalt (Lindau & Chur: Typographische Gesellschaft, 1769)–comprises *Die Tegeaten; Die Rettung in den Mauern von Holz; Aristomenes von Messenien;*

Von den Grazien des Kleinen, anonymous (Biel, 1769); reprinted in *Die deutsche anakreontische Dichtung,* edited by Friedrich Ausfeld (Strasbourg: Trübner, 1907), pp. 152-162;

Historische Erzählungen die Denkungsart und Sitten der Alten zu entdecken, anonymous (Zurich: Orell, Geßner, 1769);

Der Hungerthurm in Pisa: Ein Trauerspiel, anonymous (Chur & Lindau: Typographische Gesellschaft, 1769);

Der neue Romeo: Eine Tragicomödie, anonymous (Frankfurt am Main & Leipzig, 1769);

Die Botschaft des Lebens: In einem Aufzuge. Der zärtlichen Unschuld gewiedmet, anonymous (Zurich: Bürgkli, 1771);

Conradin von Schwaben, ein Gedicht, mit einem historischen Vorberichte; Die Gräfinn von Gleichen, ein Gedicht mit einem historischen Vorberichte, anonymous (Karlsruhe: Macklot, 1771);

Karl von Burgund: Ein Trauerspiel, anonymous (N.p., 1771); edited by Bernhard Seuffert (Heilbronn: Henninger, 1883; reprinted, Nendeln, Liechtenstein: Kraus, 1968);

Der neue Adam, anonymous (Bern, 1771);

Anleitung zur Erlernung der deutschen Sprache: Für die Real-Schulen. Mit hoher Approbation, anonymous (Zurich: Bürgkli, 1773);

Die Biegungen und Ausbildungen der deutschen Wörter: Für die Real-Schulen. Mit hoher Approbation, anonymous (Zurich: Bürgkli, 1773);

Cajus Gracchus: Ein politisches Schauspiel, anonymous (Zurich: Bürgkli, 1773);

Der Fußfall vor dem Bruder: Ein Trauerspiel. In drey Aufzügen. Der blühenden Unschuld gewiedmet, anonymous (Zurich: Bürgkli, 1773);

Geschichte der Stadt Zürich: Für die Real-Schulen. Mit hoher Approbation, anonymous (Zurich: Bürgkli, 1773);

Sittliche und gefühlreiche Erzählungen: Für die Real-Schulen. Mit hoher Approbation, anonymous (Zurich: Bürgkli, 1773);

Unterredung von den Geschichten der Stadt Zürich: Für die Realschulen. Mit hoher Approbation, anonymous (Zurich: Bürgkli, 1773);

Wilhelm von Oranse in zwey Gesängen, anonymous (Frankfurt am Main & Leipzig, 1774);

Arnold von Brescia in Zürich: Ein religiöses Schauspiel, anonymous (Frankfurt am Main, 1775);

Das Begräbniß und die Auferstehung des Messias: Fragmente. Mit Vorbericht und Anmerckungen des Herausgebers, anonymous (Frankfurt am Main & Leipzig [actually Tübingen], 1775);

Der Haß der Tyranney und nicht der Person, Oder: Sarne durch List eingenommen, anonymous (N.p., 1775);

Schweitzerische Schauspiele: Wilhelm Tell; oder der gefährliche Schuß; Geßlers Tod; oder das erlegte Raubthier; Der alte Heinrich von Melchthal; oder die ausgetretenen Augen, anonymous (N.p., 1775);

Arnold von Brescia in Rom, samt Überbleibseln von seiner Geschichte, anonymous (N.p., 1776);

Hildebold und Wibrade; Maria von Braband (Chur: Otto, 1776);

Der Tod des ersten Menschen; und die Thorheiten des weisen Königs: Zwey religiöse Dramen (Zurich, 1776);

Evadne und Kreusa: Zwey griechische Gedichte (Zurich: Bürgkli, 1777);

Telemach und Nausikaa (Zurich, 1777);

Die Cherusken: Ein politisches Schauspiel (Augsburg, 1778);

Drey epische Gedichte: Makaria; Sigowin; und Adelbert (Zurich: Orell, Geßner, Füßli, 1778);

Odoardo Galotti, Vater der Emilia: Ein Pendant zu Emilia. In einem Aufzuge; und Epilogue zur Emilia Galotti. Von einem längst bekannten Verfasser (Augsburg: Mauracher, 1778);

Patroclus: Ein Trauerspiel nach dem Griechischen Homers. Von einem längst bekannten Verfasser (Augsburg: Mauracher, 1778);

Der Vater der Gläubigen: Ein religiöses Drama (Zurich: Orell, Geßner, Füßli, 1778);

Literarische Denkmale von verschiedenen Verfassern (Zurich: Orell, Geßner, Füßli, 1779);

Der Gerechte Momus (Frankfurt am Main & Leipzig, 1780);

Brutus und Kaßius Tod: Von dem Verfasser der Noachide (Basel: Serini, 1782);

Der Levit von Ephraim aus dem Französischen des Rousseau in dem Plane verändert von Bodmer (Zurich: Orell, Geßner, Füßli, 1782);

Bodmers Apollinarien, oder Nachgelassene Gedichte, edited by Gotthold Friedrich Stäudlin (Tübingen: Cotta, 1783);

Vier kritische Gedichte von J. J. Bodmer, edited by Jakob Baechtold (Heilbronn: Henninger, 1883; reprinted, Nendeln, Liechtenstein: Kraus, 1968);

Joh. Christoph Gottsched und die Schweizer J. J. Bodmer und J. J. Breitinger, edited by Johannes Crüger (Berlin & Stuttgart: Spemann, 1884; reprinted, Darmstadt: Wissenschaftliche Buchgesellschaft, 1965);

Johann Jacob Bodmer: Schriften, edited by Fritz Ernst (Frauenfeld: Huber / Zurich: Corona, 1938);

Schriften zur Literatur, by Bodmer and Breitinger, edited by Volker Meid (Stuttgart: Reclam, 1980).

OTHER: *Die Discourse der Mahlern,* 4 volumes, edited by Bodmer and Johann Jakob Breitinger, 3 volumes (volumes 1-3, Zurich: Lindinner, 1721-1722; volume 4, Zurich: Bodmer, 1723)–volume 4 published as *Die Mahler. Oder: Discourse von den Sitten der Menschen;*

John Milton, *Johann Miltons Verlust des Paradieses: Ein Heldengedicht. In ungebundener Rede übersetzt,* 2 volumes, translated anonymously by Bodmer (Zurich: Rordorf, 1732); revised as *Johann Miltons episches Gedichte von dem Verlohrnen Paradiese. Uebersetzet und durchgehends mit Anmerckungen über die Kunst des Poeten begleitet* (Zurich: Orell, 1742; reprinted, Stuttgart: Metzler, 1965);

Pietro dei Conti di Calepio, *Paragone della poesia tragica d'Italia con quella di Francia,* edited by Bodmer (Zurich: Rordorf, 1732);

Gotthard Heidegger, *Gotthard Heideggers kleine deutsche Schriften,* edited by Bodmer (Zurich: Rordorf, 1732);

Johann Jakob Lauffer, *Thesaurus Historiae Helveticae continens lectissimos scriptores,* edited by Bodmer (Zurich: Orell, 1735);

Helvetische Bibliothek, bestehend in historischen, politischen und critischen Beyträgen zu den Geschichten Des Schweitzerlands, edited by Bodmer and Breitinger, 6 volumes (Zurich: Orell, 1735-1741);

Karl Friedrich Drollinger, *Elegie an Herren Doctor Haller, auf das Absterben seiner Mariane,* edited by Bodmer (N.p., 1737);

Samuel Butler, *Versuch einer deutschen Uebersetzung von Samuel Butlers Hudibras, einem satyrischen Gedichte wider die Schwermer und Independen-*

ten, zur Zeit Carls des Ersten, translated by Bodmer (Frankfurt am Main & Leipzig [actually Zurich], 1737);

Friedrich Rudolf, Freiherr von Canitz, *Des Freiherrn von Canitz satirische und sämmtliche übrige Gedichte, mit einer Vorrede von der Dichtart des Verfassers,* edited by Bodmer (Zurich: Däntzler, 1737);

Johann Jakob Lauffer, *Historische und Critische Beyträge zu der Historie der Eidsgenossen,* 4 volumes, edited by Bodmer and Breitinger (Zurich: Orell, 1739);

Breitinger, *Critische Abhandlung von der Natur, Den Absichten und dem Gebrauche der Gleichnisse: Mit Beyspielen aus den Schriften der berühmtesten alten und neuen Scribenten erläutert,* edited by Bodmer (Zurich: Orell, 1740);

Breitinger, *Critische Dichtkunst,* 2 volumes, edited by Bodmer (Zurich: Orell, 1740);

Sammlung critischer, poetischer, und andrer geistvollen Schriften, zur Verbesserung des Urtheils und des Wizes in den Wercken der Wolredenheit und der Poesie, 5 volumes, edited by Bodmer and Breitinger (Zurich: Orell, 1741-1744); republished as *Sammlung der Zürcherischen Streitschriften zur Verbesserung des deutschen Geschmacks wider die Gottschedische Schule, von 1741 bis 1744: vollständig in XII Stüken. Neue Ausgabe,* 2 volumes, edited by Christoph Martin Wieland (Zurich: Orell, 1753);

Freymüthige Nachrichten von neuen Büchern, und andern zur Gelehrtheit gehörigen Sachen, 20 volumes, edited by Bodmer and Breitinger (Zurich: Heidegger, 1744-1763);

Ein halbes Hundert neuer Fabeln: Durch L. M. V. K. Mit einer critischen Vorrede des Verfassers der Betrachtungen über die poetischen Gemählde, edited by Bodmer (Zurich: Orell, 1744);

Martin Opitz, *Martin Opitzens Von Boberfeld Gedichte: Von J. J. B. und J. J. B. besorget. Erster Theil,* edited by Bodmer and Breitinger (Zurich: Orell, 1745; republished with new preface, 1755);

Jacob Immanuel Pyra and Samuel Lange, *Thirsis und Damons freundschaftliche Lieder,* edited by Bodmer (Zurich: Orell, 1745);

Johann Adolf Schlegel, *Vom Natürlichen in Schäfergedichten, wider die Verfasser der Bremischen neuen Beyträge, verfertigt vom Nisus, einem Schäfer in den Kohlgärten, einem Dorfe vor Leipzig, zweyte Auflage, besorgt und mit Anmerkungen vermehrt von Hans Görgen, gleichfalls einem Schäfer daselbst,* edited by Bodmer and Breitinger (Zurich: Heidegger, 1746);

Alexander Pope, *Alexander Popens Duncias mit historischen Noten und einem Schreiben des Uebersetzers an die Obotriten,* translated by Bodmer (Zurich: Orell, Füßli, 1747);

Neue Erzählungen verschiedener Verfasser, edited by Bodmer (Frankfurt am Main & Leipzig, 1747);

Proben der alten schwäbischen Poesie des dreyzehnten Jahrhunderts: Aus der Maneßischen Sammlung, edited by Bodmer and Breitinger (Zurich: Heidegger, 1748; reprinted, Hildesheim: Gerstenberg, 1973);

Christian Wernicke, *N. Wernikens, ehemaligen Königl, Dänischen Staatsraths, und Residenten in Paris, poetische Versuche in Ueberschrifften: Wie auch Helden- und Schäfergedichten. Neue und verbesserte Auflage,* edited by Bodmer (Zurich: Geßner, 1749);

Crito: Eine Monat-Schrift, edited by Bodmer (Zurich: Geßner, 1751);

Johann Caspar Hirzel, *Empfindungen bei Betrachtung der Werke des Schöpfers,* edited by Bodmer (Zurich, 1751);

Eberhard Friedrich Freiherr von Gemmingen, *Poetische Blicke in das Landleben,* edited by Bodmer (Zurich: Geßner, 1752);

Thomas Parnell, *Der Eremite, von Dr. T. P.,* translated by Bodmer (Hamburg: Geisler, 1752);

Die geraubte Europa von Moschus; dieselbe von Nonnus, translated by Bodmer (Zurich, 1753);

Die geraubte Helene von Coluthus, translated by Bodmer (Zurich: Orell, 1753);

Christoph Martin Wieland, *Erinnerungen an eine Freundin,* edited by Bodmer (Zurich, 1754);

Wieland, *Der geprüfte Abraham: Ein Gedicht in vier Gesängen,* edited by Bodmer (Zurich: Orell, 1754);

Wieland, *Hymnen: Von dem Verfasser des gepryften Abrahams,* edited by Bodmer (Zurich, 1754);

Johann Caspar Hirzel, *Die Seligkeit ehelicher Liebe,* edited by Bodmer (Zurich, 1755);

Heinrich Brysacher, *Ode von dem Erdbeben,* edited by Bodmer (Zurich, 1756);

Ulrich Boner, *Fabeln aus den Zeiten der Minnesinger,* edited by Bodmer and Breitinger (Zurich: Orell, 1757; reprinted, Leipzig: Zentralantiquariat der Deutschen Demokratischen Republik, 1973);

Chriemhilden Rache, und die Klage: Zwey Heldengedichte aus dem schwaebischen Zeitpuncte. Samt Fragmenten aus dem Gedichte von den Nibelungen und aus dem Josaphat. Dazu koemmt ein Glossarium, edited by Bodmer and Breitinger (Zurich: Orell, 1757);

Sammlung von Minnesingern aus dem schwaebischen Zeitpuncte CXL Dichter enthaltend: Durch Ruedger Manessen, weilend des Rathes der uralten Zyrich. Aus der Handschrift der Königlich-Französischen Bibliothek herausgegeben, 2 volumes, edited by Bodmer and Breitinger (Zurich: Orell, 1758-1759);

Homer, *Vierter Gesang; und sechster Gesang der Ilias. In Hexametern übersetzt*, translated by Bodmer (Zurich: Orell, 1760);

Homer, *Homers Werke: Aus dem Griechischen übersetzt von dem Dichter der Noachide*, 2 volumes, translated by Bodmer (Zurich: Orell, Geßner, Füßli, 1778);

Apollonius, *Die Argonauten*, translated by Bodmer (Zurich: Orell, Geßner, Füßli, 1779);

Altenglische Balladen: Fabel von Laudine; Siegeslied der Franken, translated by Bodmer (Zurich: Füßli & Steiner, 1780);

Francesco Lemenes *Jakob beym Brunnen: Ein Schäferspiel des Lemene*, translated by Bodmer (Zurich: Orell, Geßner, Füßli, 1780);

Altenglische und altschwäbische Balladen in Eschlibachs Versart: Zugabe von Fragmenten aus dem altschwäbischen Zeitalter, und Gedichten, translated by Bodmer (Zurich: Füßli & Steiner, 1781);

Litterarische Pamphlete: Aus der Schweiz, edited by Bodmer (Zurich: Bürgkli, 1781).

PERIODICAL PUBLICATIONS: "Der gestäubte Leipziger Diogenes, oder kritische Urtheile über die erste Speculation des Leipziger Spectateurs," by Bodmer and Johann Jakob Breitinger, *Historischer und politischer Mercurius* (Zurich: Lindinner, 1723);

"Von den vortrefflichen Umständen für die Poesie unter den Kaisern aus dem schwäbischen Hause," *Sammlung critischer, poetischer, und andrer geistvollen Schriften*, no. 7 (1743): 25-36;

"Klopstocks Messias," *Freymüthige Nachrichten*, 5 (25 September 1748);

"Das Nibelungenlied," *Freyüthige Nachrichten*, 13 (1757): 92-94, 381;

"Die Rache, ein Heldengedicht aus dem schwäbischen Zeitpunkte," *Freymüthige Nachrichten*, 14 (1757): 74-76, 83-85, 94-96;

"Über das dreyfache Gedichte des Dante," *Freymüthige Nachrichten*, 20 (1763): 268-270, 276-278;

"Cimon: Ein Schaferspiel," *Schriachs magazin der deutschen Critik*, 2, no. 2 (1773): 101ff;

"Auszüge aus meinem Tagebuch, 1752-1782," edited by Jakob Baechtold, *Turicensia: Beiträge zur Zürcher Geschichte* (1891): 190-216;

"Mein poetisches Leben," edited by Theodor Vetter, *Zürcher Taschenbuch*, n.s. 15 (1892): 123-131;

"Persönliche Anekdoten," edited by Vetter, *Zürcher Taschenbuch*, n.s. 15 (1892): 91-122.

At least as prolific as Goethe but rarely read today, Johann Jakob Bodmer was one of the most influential critics of the first half of the eighteenth century. Bodmer and his friend Johann Jakob Breitinger are usually seen as the victors in their famous literary dispute with Johann Christoph Gottsched because of their emphasis on the imagination in the process of literary creation. Bodmer's name attracted young talent to Zurich during much of the eighteenth century. Goethe referred to him as a "Henne für Talente" (a hen for talent, that is, one who "hatches" new talent) and as the "Hebamme des Genies" (midwife of genius). Friedrich Gottlieb Klopstock and Christoph Martin Wieland each resided in his home, the latter for several years. His professional life included the publication of the works of several other poets. His mind eagerly extended its grasp to many diverse fields: into historiography, particularly that of Switzerland, he introduced a contemporary, pragmatic approach that eventually overcame the mere chronological listing of facts; his studies of ancient and medieval philology led to his discovery and publication of several significant works of medieval German literature; in politics he disseminated Jean-Jacques Rousseau's republican ideas in German-speaking Switzerland; and in literary criticism eighteenth-century Germany owed much of its awareness of Milton and Dante to Bodmer.

Bodmer was born in Greifensee, Canton Zurich, to a reformed clergyman, Hans Jakob Bodmer, and Esther Orell Bodmer, the daughter of a wealthy merchant family. His father wanted him to become a clergyman, but early negative experiences at a Latin grammar school and at the Collegium Carolinium in Zurich resulted in abandonment of these plans. Bodmer was sent to Lyons and Geneva during the spring of 1718 and to Lugano and Bergamo several months later to learn the business of his mother's family, silkspinning. His literary interests, however, had already surfaced in his youth: he had read the Old Testament; Ovid's *Metamorphoses* both in Joerg Wickram's 1545 revision of Albrecht von

Title page for the first volume of the journal edited by Bodmer and Johann Jakob Breitinger from May 1721 until January 1723

Halberstadt's German translation and in the original; Pierre Bayle's *Dictionnaire historique et critique* (1697-1706); and the works of the influential early seventeenth-century German poet Martin Opitz. In Wickram, Bodmer found "Geschmack an dem Wunderbaren und Abentheuerlichen" (taste for the marvelous and the adventurous). His stays in France and Italy resulted in the acquisition of the French translation of Joseph Addison and Richard Steele's *Spectator*, several humanistic Latin works, and Torquato Tasso's *Gerusalemme liberata* (Jerusalem Delivered, 1581). On his return to Zurich in 1719 he became a volunteer scribe in the chancery of the Canton Zurich, where he had access to the rich historical documents of the city and canton.

Influenced by the *Spectator* and the concept of a moral weekly, Bodmer, Breitinger, Johannes Meister, Daniel Cornelius Zollikofer, Dr. Laurenz Zellweger, and Johann Jakob Lauffer founded the Gesellschaft der Mahler (Society of Painters) in February 1720. The new society sought "die Tugend und den guten Geschmack in unsern Bergen einzuführen" (to introduce virtue and good taste into our mountains). On 3 May 1721 the first issue of the society's journal *Die Discourse der Mahlern* (The Discourses of the Painters) appeared; publication was suspended with the ninety-fourth issue at the end of January 1723. The contributions, signed with the names of famous painters to signify the idea that each author was "painting" ideas on the imagination of the reader, sought to describe the Swiss and German peoples and their customs as precisely as possible in order to improve them by enlightened thinking. Never particularly successful and always subjected to censorship, the journal served at least to provide a forum for Bodmer and Breitinger to express much of their later literary thinking in seminal form. In his contributions, which made up approximately sixty percent of the articles published, Bodmer addresses both literary and aesthetic questions and human faults. Rhetoric and poetry have essentially the same purpose and goals, he says. The artist's–specifically, the poet's–task is to imitate nature as precisely as possible; while this may not seem an original concept, Bodmer emphasizes the act of observing rather than the artistic rendering. The "Einbildungs-Kraft" (imagination) absorbs and recalls the impressions of the natural world; it is only receptive. Poetry must, however, produce a lively effect in the reader, a much more lively effect than that of pure fantasy. This effect arises not through the beauty of the portrayed object but through the accuracy of the imitation. This interpretation of the poetic effect forms the basis for Bodmer's critique of the Daniel Casper von Lohenstein school of baroque poetry, with its alleged inability to mention anything without a metaphor. Lohenstein's supposed overuse of metaphor is mere decoration.

Made aware of Milton through the *Spectator*, Bodmer received a copy of an English edition of *Paradise Lost* and taught himself English in order to read it. He then began to translate the work into German. The translation was completed by May 1725 but did not appear until 1732, primarily because of religious censorship in Zurich. As was his wont, Bodmer continually revised the text; three subsequent editions appeared.

In 1725 Bodmer became a teacher at the Collegium Carolinium; in 1731 he was named professor of Swiss history. His students later remembered that he was different from the other teachers, most of whom were clergymen, in that he never taught with an authoritative tone but rather sought to find cause-and-effect connections between events. Although his lectures were not well attended and the clerical instructors viewed him with skepticism, he can be credited with the introduction of historical pragmatism into Swiss historiography, which until that time had been chiefly concerned with the chronicling of names, places, and dates. The devotion of his students earned him the title "Vater der Jünglinge" (father of the youths). In 1727 he helped found the Helvetische Gesellschaft (Swiss Society), and together with Breitinger and other members edited and published many original historical documents and essays with explanations and interpretations: the *Thesaurus Historiae Helveticae* (1735), the *Helvetische Bibliothek* (Swiss Library, 1735-1741), and the *Historische und Critische Beyträge zu der Historie der Eidsgenossen* (Historical and Critical Essays on the History of the Confederates, 1739).

On 1 April 1727 Bodmer married Esther Orell. The couple had four children, all of whom died young. At first the couple lived in the Neumarkt section of old Zurich, moving in 1739 to the Landhaus zum oberen Schönberg (Country House on the Upper Schönberg), which overlooked the city and lake. Bodmer purchased the house in 1756 and lived there for the rest of his life. He traveled occasionally during the summers to Trogen, Canton Appenzell, to visit Zellweger, who had become the center of an influential group of Zurich intellectuals that included Johann Caspar Hirzel and Salomon Gessner.

Bodmer's business ventures met with limited success. After disputes with the Heidegger publishing house, in which he had invested, Bodmer financed Markus Rordorf as a printer in 1731. This enterprise failed, and Bodmer invested in a publishing firm owned by his nephew Konrad Orell and Konrad von Wyss. Orell und Compagnie became the parent firm of the still extant Swiss company Orell Füßli Verlag. In 1737 Bodmer became a member of the Great Council (also known as the Council of the Two Hundred) in Zurich.

Bodmer corresponded with many European literary figures. The most significant correspondence began in 1728, when Bodmer wrote to Count Pietro di Calepio of Bergamo after reading Calepio's essay on Italian customs. Bodmer arranged for the publication of some of Calepio's writings, most notably *Paragone della poesia tragica d'Italia con quella di Francia* (A Comparison between Italian and French Tragic Poetry, 1732). The letters center on three major topics: the basis of literary taste, the nature of tragedy, and the freedom of poetic fantasy. For Bodmer, taste is totally objective and rationally describable, while Calepio argues for a combination of subjective and objective elements; poetic pleasure is derived for Bodmer from reflection on the agreement between the artist's image and the original object, while Calepio sees it as primarily sensual. In tragedy, Bodmer's exemplary hero portrays a general truth and thus educates the audience through reflection; Calepio sees as the primary element an emotional upheaval which results from the audience's total identification with the hero—catharsis in the Aristotelian sense. Bodmer argues in the letters that such creations of fantasy as Milton's angels and demons have a rational basis because of the significance of the truth which stands behind the fiction and the ease with which the reader can penetrate the surface story; Calepio counters that the way the truth is clothed, that is, the way the author portrays the truth, is critical in the evocation of the desired result in the reader. The correspondence continued until shortly before Calepio's death in 1761. Bodmer published an edited and translated version of several of the early letters in 1736 as *Brief-Wechsel von der Natur des poetischen Geschmackes* (Correspondence on the Nature of Poetic Taste).

The results of Bodmer and Bretinger's collaboration, which had continued since the publication of their journal *Die Discourse der Mahlern*, were set forth in the four critical works of 1740-1741 for which they are best known today: Bodmer's *Critische Abhandlung von dem Wunderbaren in der Poesie* (Critical Treatment of the Fantastic in Poetry, 1740) and *Critische Betrachtungen über die poetischen Gemählde der Dichter* (Critical Observations about the Poetic Paintings of the Poets, 1741) and Breitinger's *Critische Abhandlung von der Natur, Den Absichten und dem Gebrauche der Gleichnisse* (Critical Treatment of the Nature, the Purposes and the Use of Parables, 1740) and *Critische Dichtkunst* (Critical Poetics, 1740). It is difficult to separate their

Bodmer's house near Zurich; drawing by an anonymous artist, circa 1750 (Universitätbibliothek, Heidelberg)

individual contributions to these works. Breitinger wrote a preface to Bodmer's *Critische Betrachtungen über die poetischen Gemählde der Dichter*, while Bodmer probably contributed several chapters to Breitinger's *Critische Dichtkunst*. Bodmer seems to have functioned as the stimulus, Breitinger as the cautious critic and theoretician, but the fruitfulness of their collaboration lay in their ability to develop their concepts together. After Breitinger's death Bodmer wrote: "Der Mitdenker meiner Gedanken, der Gesellschafter meines Lebens, der Zeuge meiner Handlungen hat mich verlassen" (The co-thinker of my thoughts, the companion of my life, the witness of my actions has left me).

Bodmer stressed the relationship between poetry and rhetoric, although the former is seen as much more effective because it can delight the reader. Since the days of the *Discourse der Mahlern* the political, moral, and religious effects of poetry on a wide public had been the guidelines for Bodmer's aesthetic judgments. The poet transmits philosophical and moral truth in a way that the public at large can comprehend it. The im-parted images should awaken the same sensations in the reader as the natural objects did in the poet. With his active imagination the poet observes closely, yet selectively, choosing individual characteristics from what is observed and recombining them in novel ways to capture the attention and to enrapture the senses of the reader. The possibilites for recombination lead so far from the true and the possible, as they are commonly recognized, that the appearance of contradiction arises, which Bodmer and Breitinger call "das Wunderbare" (the marvelous), because it captivates the reader. The penetration of the truth behind the illusion is the principal act of artistic reception.

Bodmer's aesthetic theory had a strongly theological basis. He classified *Paradise Lost* as the work of a modern Homer and later enthusiastically received early fragments of Klopstock's *Der Messias* (The Messiah, 1751-1773) at least partially because of their religious content and the moral effect that that religious content was intended to have on the reading public. Although somewhat at odds with the prevailing Protestant

Brief-Wechsel
Von der
Natur
Des
Poetischen
Geschmackes.
Daju kömmt eine
Unterfuchung
Wie ferne das Erhabene im
Trauerfpiele Statt und Platz
haben könne;
Wie auch von der
Poetifchen Gerechtigkeit.
Zürich,
Bey Conrad Orell, und Comp. 1736.

Title page for Bodmer's edition of the correspondence between himself and Count Pietro di Calepio on literary taste

Gottfried Wilhelm von Leibniz's ontology and in Wolff's own emphasis on empirical observation. Beginning with the publication of *Von dem Einfluß und Gebrauche der Einbildungs-Krafft* (Concerning the Influence and Use of the Imagination, 1727), Bodmer and Breitinger sought to establish poetics on the firmly scientific model proposed by Wolff. They borrowed the Leibnizian idea that the existing world is but the best of many possible worlds; there are other logically possible worlds which, though nonexistent, still provide objects for poetic observation. A second creator after God, the poet makes his own logically consistent world. Bodmer and Breitinger sought to provide an "empirical" source for poetic images which could be used to critique what they felt to be the excesses of the baroque, especially as represented by the ornate, but ponderous, style of late seventeenth-century Silesian poets, but which also liberated the poet from the restrictions of the "rational" approach to poetic creation proposed by Gottsched and his followers.

Bodmer's *Critische Abhandlung von dem Wunderbaren in der Poesie* provided his defense of Milton and his visions of angels and demons against attacks by Voltaire and Constantin Magny. His earlier work on a translation of Milton had led to a theoretical formulation of the proper use of metaphor to heighten the effect of poetic imitation. Shakespeare is held up as the poet most worthy of imitation. This justification of what Johann Christoph Gottsched considered baroque excess contributed substantially to the literary feud between Gottsched, on one side, and Bodmer and Breitinger, on the other. Prior to the appearance of this work Bodmer had carried on a friendly correspondence with Gottsched, and, even more surprising in view of their later animosity, Gottsched republished Bodmer's verse history of German literature, *Character der teutschen Gedichte* (Character in German Poems, 1734), in his journal *Beyträge zur Critischen Historie der Deutschen Sprache, Poesie und Beredsamkeit*, in 1738. In 1742 Gottsched published an essay in the *Beyträge* that was highly critical of Shakespeare and marked the beginning of the literary feud.

Bodmer and Breitinger's dispute with Gottsched can be seen as a collision between English and French influence. Gottsched, influenced by French criticism, stressed correct form; Bodmer and Breitinger, with English models in mind, were more interested in the subject matter of poetry. Gottsched sought rules according to

orthodoxy, Bodmer retained from his childhood a fascination with the images of the Old Testament and the book of Revelation. Those images were the proper object of epic representation, the most sublime poetry. The recombinations of observed elements are limited by what is believable in any given society; hence, Homer could use pagan mythology because it reflected the belief system of his day. Since Christianity represented the true divine revelation, it provided the primary source for knowledge of the world beyond direct sense perception.

Besides religion, the other dominant influence in Bodmer's thinking can be found in the philosopher Christian Wolff's interpretation of

Title page for Bodmer's book on the fantastic in poetry, in which he defends irrational elements in literature

which anyone could write a poem; Bodmer and Breitinger rejected a priori rules and stressed the creative imagination of the artistic personality. A work of art, they said, is not derived from rules; it makes its own rules. Bodmer and Breitinger recognized the powerful effect of true poetry, an effect that went beyond the rational but not counter to it; true poetry, they held, should not only edify and instruct but must move the reader. Gottsched stressed the rational side of the human being as the faculty to which poetry must appeal. For Gottsched, literary style should be clear, natural, close to prose; Bodmer and Breitinger advocated metaphorical, symbolic writing, which leads the reader to imagine the described objects as if they were actually present. The dispute was at its height during the 1740s, when Bodmer and Breitinger published several satirical essays in the journals they edited, the *Sammlung critischer, poetischer, und andrer geistvollen Schriften* (1741-1744) and the *Freymüthige* (1744-1763). Gottsched and his followers responded in his journal, the *Critische Beyträge zur Geschichte der Historie der deutschen Sprache, Poesie und Beredsamkeit* (1732-1744). By mid century Bodmer and Breitinger had emerged victorious,

as more and more writers distanced themselves from Gottsched. In another sense, German literary criticism had begun to reject the premises of both Gottsched and Bodmer. Gotthold Ephraim Lessing, for example, attacked Gottsched in defense of Shakespeare in his "17. Literaturbrief" (Seventeenth Literary Letter, 1759) but also distanced himself from Bodmer through his emphasis on action in drama rather than on the description of a morally exemplary character in *Laokoon: oder Über die Grenzen der Mahlerey und Poesie* (Laocoön; or, Concerning the Boundary between Painting and Poetry, 1766).

Nowhere do Bodmer and Breitinger provide a coherent exposition of their model for poetic creation. Much of their writing seems inconsistent and even self-contradictory, as Bodmer rarely develops a thought through to its logical conclusion and freely borrows from various sources without attempting to reconcile them or to determine the meaning in the original context. He bases his arguments primarily on examples drawn from Milton, Opitz, the Middle High German poets of the thirteenth century, and Homer.

In the German-language literature of the thirteenth century Bodmer found the simplicity and sublimity of the *Iliad* and the *Odyssey*. Such works assumed the accepted value system of the society in which they arose and were dependent on it. They used it to instruct, to promote political and moral lessons. In 1743, prior to his inspection of the so-called Manessische Handschrift (The Great Heidelberg Codex of the German Minnesingers), Bodmer anticipated the discovery of such poetic genius because the social and political situation of the Hohenstaufen dynasty of the late twelfth and early thirteenth centuries reminded him strongly of the social and political upheavals of Homer's time. The publication of the essay "Von den vortrefflichen Umständen für die Poesie unter den Kaisern aus dem schwäbischen Hause" (Concerning the Superb Conditions for Poetry under the Emperors from the Swabian Dynasty, 1743) marks the beginning of Bodmer's lifelong search for medieval literary documents, a search which resulted in editions and modern renditions such as *Proben der alten schwäbischen Poesie des dreyzehnten Jahrhunderts* (Samples of the Old Swabian Poetry of the Thirteenth Century, 1748), *Chriemhilden Rache, und die Klage* (Chriemhild's Revenge, and the Lament, 1757), and his hexameter version of Wolfram von Eschenbach's *Parzival*, titled *Der Parcival, ein Gedicht in Wolframs von Eschilbach Denckart: Eines*

Poeten aus den Zeiten Kaiser Heinrichs VI. (Parcival, a Poem in the Mode of Thinking of Wolfram von Eschilbach [*sic*]: A Poet of the Times of Emperor Henry the Sixth, 1753). Although these editions and free adaptations did not stimulate the interest of the literary world of the mid eighteenth century, they paved the way for early-nineteenth-century philological work on medieval texts. Some patriotic interest motivated Bodmer's interest in German literature of the thirteenth century as a model for contemporary creations: since Middle High German is much closer to Bodmer's Swiss dialect than to modern standard German, and since Bodmer believed that the Heidelberg Codex had originally been transcribed in Zurich, its discovery was interpreted to support his and Breitinger's viewpoint in their controversy with Gottsched. In their *Der Mahler der Sitten* (Painters of Customs, 1746) Bodmer and Breitinger even advocated the creation of an Upper-German / Swiss literary standard language to compete with the East Middle German standard promoted by Gottsched and the Leipzig school. Bodmer also found in the literature of the German Middle Ages an originality of expression and a firmly based moral order that he considered an illustration of how culture and history cooperated in great literary achievement.

Bodmer did not concern himself only with the publication of medieval German literature. His collaboration with Breitinger on an edition of the poems of Opitz (1745), who was considered exemplary of their poetic thinking, provided the first modern critical edition of contemporary literature.

Bodmer's reputation grew to the point that young poets sent him their work for criticism. In May 1747 he received several lines of a poem, written in hexameter by an anonymous poet, which treated the life of Christ. What was to become Klopstock's *Messias* so excited the Swiss critic that he made inquiries about the identity of the young poet and subsequently invited Klopstock to come to Zurich and live in his house so that Bodmer could supervise his work and provide for him, and thus help him finish work on the epic more quickly. In the *Messias* Bodmer found his theories on the role of the imagination in poetic creation confirmed; an author had been discovered to silence the hostile criticism from Leipzig. On 23 July 1750 Klopstock arrived in Zurich and moved into Bodmer's house overlooking the city. Eight days later, Klopstock went sailing on Lake Zurich with several companions, including

some attractive young women. This outing resulted in his poem "Von der Fahrt auf der Zürcher See" (About the Excursion on Lake Zurich, 1750), but such preoccupations severely alienated him from his rather ascetic host, who could not reconcile the verse of this "seraphischer Jüngling"(seraphic youth) with his worldly behavior. On 3 September Klopstock left Bodmer's house for good. Only a formal reconciliation ever came about; but Klopstock's influence had already stimulated Bodmer to resume work on his own Biblical epic in hexameter verse, *Die Noachide* (1765; translated as *Noah*, 1767), the first version of which was completed in 1749 and published in 1752 as *Der Noah*.

Bodmer's attempts to write epics, fables, and dramas have been the object of much ridicule. His verse is certainly uneven and demonstrates a lack of skill, and much material was borrowed, as was the custom of the age, from other sources without acknowledgment. His major literary creations can be classified as biblical epics, such as *Die Noachide*; historical and legendary epics, such as *Die Columbona* (1753); historical and patriotic plays, such as *Wilhelm Tell; oder der gefährliche Schuß* (William Tell; or, The Dangerous Shot, 1775); religious and biblical plays, such as *Der erkannte Joseph, und der keusche Joseph* (Joseph Recognized and Chaste Joseph, 1754); plays based on antiquity, such as *Octavius Cäsar* (1769); parodies of the works of others, such as *Gottsched, ein Trauerspiel, oder: Der parodirte Cato* (Gottsched, a Tragedy; or, The parodied Cato, 1765); and satires, such as *Das Banket der Dunse* (The Banquet of the Dunces, 1758). Bodmer's translations into German were more successful: his Homer translation (1778) remained a classic well into the nineteenth century.

While Bodmer was still mourning the loss of Klopstock, Wieland anonymously sent him a fragment of his epic "Hermann" (1882) for critique in summer 1751. On 29 October 1791 Wieland revealed his identity in a letter to Bodmer that included his curriculum vita. After some inquiries about his character, Wieland was invited to live in Bodmer's house and arrived in Zurich on 25 October 1752. Wieland was only nineteen at the time, neither drank nor smoked, and adapted himself to the ascetic rules of his host much better than Klopstock had. A close relationship developed. The two men worked at the same table, wrote notes to one another, and praised each other's work. Wieland remained until 25 June 1754, when a position was found for him as a tutor; by that time some friction had developed between him and Bodmer because of Wieland's turn toward a more frivolous, anacreontic style and the increasing amount of time he was spending in the company of other literary friends, particularly women.

Bodmer's house became an almost obligatory goal for literary visitors to Zurich. During Wieland's residence Christian Ewald von Kleist visited Bodmer, albeit for a short time because of his dislike for Wieland. Kleist was amazed at the intellectual climate in the somewhat provincial town: "statt daß man im großen Berlin kaum drei bis vier Leute von Genie und Geschmack antrifft, findet man in dem kleinen Zürich mehr als zwanzig bis dreißig derselben" (whereas one hardly meets three or four people of intelligence and taste in the large city of Berlin, one finds in the little city of Zurich more than twenty or thirty such people).

In 1762 Bodmer founded the Historischpolitische Gesellschaft (Historical-Political Society). The simplicity and purity of the ancient Swiss confederacies, Bodmer believed, provided a model for his contemporaries, which he applied in his efforts to educate the youth as citizens of a democratic republic. His historical and patriotic plays can be viewed as part of this program to promote in Switzerland his and Rousseau's republican ideas and patriotic thinking. In his later years, he prepared several textbooks for the newly reformed Zurich secondary schools on German language and on Swiss history, folklore, and legends. Bodmer retired from his teaching post at the Collegium in 1775. Goethe visited Bodmer in June 1775 along with Christian and Friedrich zu Stolberg and Johann Kaspar Lavater, and in November 1779 in the company of Duke Karl August of Weimar. In his autobiography, *Dichtung und Wahrheit* (Poetry and Truth, 1811-1833), Goethe seems to remember the beautiful scenery more than the meeting with the "munterer Greis" (lively old man).

Toward the end of Bodmer's life his reputation in the literary world was elevated again through the publication of his Homer translation, a task on which he had worked since the mid 1760s. In his translation of Old English ballads (1780-1781) he abandoned his beloved blank verse in hexameter, adopting a line with four stresses and end rhyme. He almost eagerly approached death in the hope of a reunion with his former working companions, such as Breitinger, who had died in 1776, but he continued writing al-

Bodmer, circa 1781; painting by J. H. W. Tischbein (Dithmarscher Landesmuseum, Meldorf)

most until the end. He arranged for the transfer of his extensive medieval manuscript collection to his student Christoph Heinrich Müller, who prepared an edition, the *Sammlung Deutscher Gedichte aus dem XII., XIII. und XIV. Jahrhundert* (Collection of German Poems from the Twelfth, Thirteenth, and Fourteenth centuries, 1782-1785). Bodmer died on 2 January 1783.

Letters:

Leonhard Meister, *Über Bodmern: Nebst Fragmenten aus seinen Briefen* (Zurich, 1783);

Briefe berühmter und edler Deutschen an Bodmer, edited by Gotthold Friedrich Stäudlin (Stuttgart: Mäntler, 1794);

Briefe der Schweizer Bodmer, Sulzer, Geßner: Aus Gleims literarischem Nachlasse, edited by Wilhelm Körte (Zurich: Gersner, 1804);

Friedrich von Hagedorn, *Poetische Werke,* edited by J. J. Eschenburg, volume 5 (Hamburg: Campe, 1825);

Bodmer in old age; engraving by J. F. Bause, after a painting by Anton Graff

Josephine Zehnder-Stadlin, *Pestalozzi: Idee und Macht der menschlichen Entwicklung* (Gotha: Thienemann, 1875), pp. 318-573;

Eduard Bodemann, *Johann Georg Zimmermann: Sein Leben und bisher ungedruckte Briefe an denselben von Bodmer, Breitinger, Gessner, Sulzer, Moses Mendelssohn, Nicolai, der Karschin, Herder, und G. Forster* (Hannover: Hahn, 1878);

"Johann Christoph Gottsched und Johann Jakob Bodmer: Briefwechsel," edited by Eugen Wolff, *Zeitschrift für den deutschen Unterricht,* 11 (1887): 353-381;

Harold Thomas Betteridge, "Klopstock's Correspondence with Bodmer and Breitinger," *Modern Language Review,* 57 (July 1962): 357-372;

Wielands Briefwechsel, edited by H. W. Seiffert, volume 1 (Berlin: Akademie, 1963).

Bibliographies:

Karl Heinrich Jördens, "Johann Jakob Bodmer," *Lexikon deutscher Dichter und Prosaisten,* volume 1 (Leipzig: Weidmann, 1806; reprint-

ed, Hildesheim & New York: Olms, 1970), pp. 119-160;

Martin Bircher and Heinrich Straumann, *Shakespeare und die deutsche Schweiz bis zum Beginn des 19. Jahrhunderts: Eine Bibliographie raisonnée* (Bern & Munich: Francke, 1971), pp. 46-66.

References:

Friedmar Apel, "Von der Nachahmung zur Imagination–Wandlungen der Poetik und der Literaturkritik," in *Aufklärung und Romantik 1700-1830,* edited by Klaus Siebenhaar and Christine Caemmerer, volume 4 of *Propyläen Geschichte der Literatur: Literatur und Gesellschaft der westlichen Welt,* edited by Erilea Wischer (Berlin: Propyläen, 1983), pp. 75-100;

Wolfgang Bender, Afterword to *Johann Jakob Breitinger: Critische Dichtkunst* (Stuttgart: Metzler, 1966);

Bender, *J. J. Bodmer und J. J. Breitinger* (Stuttgart: Metzler, 1973);

Eric A. Blackall, "The Revival of Metaphor," in his *The Emergence of German as a Literary Language 1700-1775,* second edition (Ithaca & London: Cornell University Press, 1978), pp. 276-313;

Helga Brandes, *Die "Gesellschaft der Maler" und ihr literarischer Beitrag zur Aufklärung: Eine Untersuchung zur Publizistik des 18. Jahrhunderts* (Bremen: Schünemann Universitätsverlag, 1974);

F. Andrew Brown, "Locke's 'Essay' and Bodmer and Breitinger," *Modern Language Quarterly,* 10 (March 1949): 16-32;

Jan Bruck, Eckart Feldmeier, Hans Hiebel, and Karl Heinz Stahl, "Der Mimesisbegriff Gottscheds und der Schweizer: Kritische Überlegungen zu Hans Peter Herrmann, *Naturnachahmung und Einbildungskraft,*" *Zeitschrift für deutsche Philologie,* 90 (December 1971): 563-578;

Fritz Budde, *Wieland und Bodmer* (Berlin: Mayer & Müller, 1910; New York: Johnson Reprint, 1967);

Daniel O. Dahlstrom, "The Taste for Tragedy: The *Briefwechsel* of Bodmer and Calepio," *Deutsche Vierteljahrsschrift für Literatur und Geistesgeschichte,* 59 (June 1985): 206-223;

Burghard Dedner, "Vom Schäferleben zur Agrarwirtschaft: Poesie und Ideologie des 'Landlebens' in der deutschen Literatur des 18. Jahrhunderts," *Jahrbuch der Jean-Paul Gesellschaft*, 7 (1972): 40-83;

Peter Faessler, "Die Zürcher in Arkadien: Der Kreis um J. J. Bodmer und der Appenzeller Laurenz Zellweger," *Appenzeller Jahrbücher*, 107 (1979): 3-49;

Manfred Gradinger, "Die Minnesang- und Waltherforschung von Bodmer bis Uhland," Ph.D. dissertation, University of Munich, 1970;

E. K. Grotegut, "Bodmer Contra Gellert," *Modern Language Quarterly*, 23 (December 1962): 383-396;

Karl S. Guthke, "Der junge Lessing als Kritiker Gottscheds und Bodmers," "Hallers 'Anteil' am Literaturstreit: Legende und Wahrheit," and "Hagedorn: das Dilemma des 'Friedfertigen' in den 'Gelehrten Kriegen,' " in his *Literarisches Leben im achtzehnten Jahrhundert in Deutschland und in der Schweiz* (Bern & Munich: Francke, 1975), pp. 24-117;

Helmut Henne, "Eine frühe kritische Edition neuerer Literatur: Zur Opitz-Ausgabe Bodmers und Breitingers von 1745," *Zeitschrift für deutsche Philologie*, 87 (May 1968): 180-196;

Hans Peter Herrmann, "Die Dichtungstheorien Bodmers und Breitingers," in his *Naturnachahmung und Einbildungskraft: Zur Entwicklung der deutschen Poetik von 1670 bis 1740* (Bad Homburg, Berlin & Zurich: Gehlen, 1970), pp. 163-275;

Hermann Hettner, "Die Dichtung: Gottsched und sein Kampf mit Bodmer und Breitinger," in his *Geschichte der deutschen Literatur im achtzehnten Jahrhundert*, volume 1, part 2 (Leipzig: List, 1929), pp. 210-229;

Christoph Hubig, " 'Genie'-Typus oder Original? Vom Paradigma der Kreativität zum Kult des Individuums," in *Aufklärung und Romantik 1700-1830*, edited by Siebenhaar and Caemmerer, volume 4 of *Propyläen Geschichte der Literatur: Literatur und Gesellschaft der westlichen Welt*, edited by Wischer (Berlin: Propyläen, 1983), pp. 187-210;

Barbara Kaltz, "Johann Jakob Bodmer als Grammatiker: Die 'Grundsätze der deutschen Sprache,' " in *Etudes allemandes: Recueil dédié à Jean-Jacques Anstett*, edited by Georges Brunet (Lyon: Presses universitaires de Lyon, 1979), pp. 27-46;

Dieter Kimpel, "Aufklärung, Bürgertum und Literatur in Deutschland," in *Aufklärung und Romantik 1700-1830*, edited by Siebenhaar and Caemmerer, volume 4 of *Propyläen Geschichte der Literatur: Literatur und Gesellschaft der westlichen Welt*, edited by Wischer (Berlin: Propyläen, 1983), pp. 52-74;

Christian Ewald von Kleist, *Werke*, edited by August Sauer, volume 2 (Berlin: Hempel, 1881), p. 212;

Hans-Dieter Kreuder, "Noch einmal frühe deutsche Milton-Übersetzungen," *Archiv für das Studium der neueren Sprachen und Literaturen*, 214 (1977): 80-82;

Erwin Leibfried, "Philosophisches Lehrgedicht und Fabel," in *Europäische Aufklärung*, volume 11 of *Neues Handbuch der Literaturwissenschaft*, edited by Walter Hinck (Frankfurt am Main: Athenäum, 1974), pp. 75-90;

Gisbert Lepper, Jörg Steitz, and Wolfgang Brenn, "Poetische Säkularisierung der Erbauungsschriften: Gegner Gottscheds–Bodmer, Breitinger, Klopstock," in their *Unter dem Absolutismus*, volume 1 of their *Einführung in die deutsche Literatur des 18. Jahrhunderts* (Opladen: Westdeutscher Verlag, 1983), pp. 92-107;

Bruno Markwardt, "Abwandlung und Auflockerung der 'kritischen' Poetik," in *Aufklärung, Rokoko, Sturm und Drang*, volume 2 of *Geschichte der deutschen Poetik*, edited by Markwardt (Berlin: De Gruyter, 1956), pp. 76-130;

Steven D. Martinson, "Concerning the Imagination" and "On Taste, Beauty and the Sublime," in his *On Imitation, Imagination and Beauty: A Critical Reassessment of the Concept of the Literary Artist During the Early German "Aufklärung"* (Bonn: Bouvier, 1977), pp. 56-144;

Reinhart Meyer, "Restaurative Innovation: Theologische Tradition und poetische Freiheit in der Poetik Bodmers und Breitingers," in *Aufklärung und literarische Öffentlichkeit*, edited by Christa Bürger, Peter Bürger, and Jochen Schulte-Sasse (Frankfurt am Main: Suhrkamp, 1980), pp. 39-82;

Jan-Dirk Müller, "J. J. Bodmers Poetik und die Wiederentdeckung mittelhochdeutscher Epen," *Euphorion*, 71, no. 4 (1977): 336-352;

Friedhelm Radandt, "The Challenge from Switzerland: Bodmer and Breitinger," in his *From Baroque to Storm and Stress* (London: Croom Helm / New York: Barnes & Noble, 1977), pp. 50-54;

Horst Dieter Schlosser, "Sprachnorm und regionale Differenz im Rahmen der Kontroverse zwischen Gottsched und Bodmer / Breitinger," in *Mehrsprachigkeit in der deutschen Aufklärung*, edited by Dieter Kimpel (Hamburg: Meiner, 1985), pp. 52-68;

Horst-Michael Schmidt, "Die Konzeption der Poetik Bodmers und Breitingers," in his *Sinnlichkeit und Verstand. Zur philosophischen und poetologischen Begründung von Erfahrung und Urteil in der deutschen Aufklärung (Leibniz, Wolff, Gottsched, Bodmer und Breitinger)* (Munich: Fink, 1982), pp. 124-176;

Jochen Schmidt, "Bodmer und Breitinger: Das Wunderbare und Erhabene als Medium zur Befreiung der 'Einbildungskraft' und zur Intensivierung der Affekte," in his *Von der Aufklärung bis zum Idealismus*, volume 1 of his *Die Geschichte des Genie-Gedankens 1750-1945* (Darmstadt: Wissenschaftliche Buchgesellschaft, 1985), pp. 47-65;

Herbert Schöffler, "Die Autoren" and "Ideen und Form," in his *Das literarische Zürich 1700-1750* (Frauenfeld & Leipzig: Huber, 1925): pp. 25-96; republished as "Anruf der Schweizer," in *Deutscher Geist im 18. Jahrhundert: Essays zur Geistes- und Religionsgeschichte*, edited by Götz von Selle, second edition (Göttingen: Vanderhoeck & Ruprecht, 1967), pp. 7-60;

Hans Skommodau, *Pygmalion bei Franzosen und Deutschen im 18. Jahrhundert* (Wiesbaden: Steiner, 1970);

Karl-Heinz Stahl, "Die psychologische Analyse und Bestimmung des Wunderbaren," in his *Das Wunderbare als Problem und Gegenstand der deutschen Poetik des 17. und 18. Jahrhunderts* (Frankfurt am Main: Athenaion, 1975), pp. 123-182;

Enrico Straub, *Der Brief-Wechsel Calepio-Bodmer: Ein Beitrag zur Erhellung der Beziehungen zwischen italienischer und deutscher Literatur im 18. Jahrhundert* (Berlin: Reuter, 1965);

Straub, "Marginalien zu Neudrucken der Werke Bodmers und Breitingers," *Arcadia: Zeitschrift für vergleichende Literaturwissenschaft*, 3, no. 3 (1968): 307-314;

J. H. Tisch, " 'Poetic Theology': *Paradise Lost* between Aesthetics and Religion in 18th Century Switzerland," *Revue de Littérature Comparée*, 49 (April-June 1975): 270-283;

Marilyn Torbruegge, "Bodmer und Longinus," *Monatshefte*, 63 (Winter 1971): 341-357;

Torbruegge, "Johann Heinrich Füßli und 'Bodmer-Longinus': Das Wunderbare und das Erhabene," *Deutsche Vierteljahrsschrift für Literaturwissenschaft und Geistesgeschichte*, 46 (January 1972): 161-185;

Hans Trümpy, *Schweizerdeutsche Sprache und Literatur im 17. und 18. Jahrhundert* (Basel: Krebs, 1955);

Theodor Vetter, Hans Bodmer, and Hermann Bodmer, eds., *Johann Jakob Bodmer: Denkschrift zum CC. Geburtstag* (Zurich: Müller, 1900);

Silvio Vietta, "Poetik und Ästhetik der deutschen Aufklärung," in his *Literarische Phantasie: Theorie und Geschichte. Barock und Aufklärung* (Stuttgart: Metzler, 1986), pp. 110-134;

Max Wehrli, Introduction to *Das geistige Zürich im 18. Jahrhundert*, edited by Wehrli (Zurich: Atlantis, 1943);

Wehrli, *Johann Jakob Bodmer und die Geschichte der Literatur* (Frauenfeld & Leipzig: Huber, 1936);

Angelika Wetterer, "Die sinnlichen Bedürfnisse des Publikums und die vernünftigen Maßstäbe der 'critischen' Poetik: Aspekte der Nachahmungsgrundsatzes bei den Schweizern," in *Publikumsbezug und Wahrheitsanspruch: Der Widerspruch zwischen rhetorischem Ansatz und philosophischem Anspruch bei Gottsched und den Schweizern*, edited by Wetterer (Tübingen: Niemeyer, 1981), pp. 161-228;

Jürgen Wilke, "Der deutsch-schweizerische Literaturstreit," in *Kontroversen, alte und neue: Akten des VII. internationalen Germanisten-Kongresses Göttingen 1985*, edited by Albrecht Schöne, volume 2 (Tübingen: Niemeyer, 1986), pp. 140-151;

Hans Wysling, "Die Literatur," in *Zürich im 18. Jahrhundert: Zum 150. Jahrestag der Universität Zürich*, edited by Wysling (Zurich: Gerichtshaus, 1983), pp. 131-188;

Carsten Zelle, "Zur Erinnerung an den 200. Todestag von Johann Jakob Bodmer," *Das achtzehnte Jahrhundert*, 7 (1983): 17-18.

Papers:

Johann Jakob Bodmer's papers are in the Zentralbibliothek Zürich.

Johann Jakob Breitinger

(March 1701 - December 1776)

Arthur D. Mosher
University of South Carolina

BOOKS: *In versus obscurissimos a Persio Sat. I. cita-
tos diatribe historico-litteraria* (Zurich: Bodmer,
1723);

Nachrichten aus der gelehrten Welt (N.p., 1723);

*Trost-Schrifft an das über dem frühezeitigen Ableben Jo-
hann Caspar Eschers, in Traur gesetzte woladeli-
che Eschersche Hauß zum Kindlein* (Zurich,
1726);

*Von dem Einfluß und Gebrauche der Einbildungs-
Krafft: Zur Ausbesserung des Geschmackes; oder,
Genaue Untersuchung aller Arten Beschreibungen worinne die außerlesenste Stellen der berühmtesten Poeten dieser Zeit mit gründtlicher Freyheit
beurtheilt werden*, anonymous, by Breitinger
and Bodmer (Frankfurt am Main & Leipzig
[actually Zurich], 1727);

*De linqua Deo familiari et quasi vernacula praeci puis-
que ejus virtutibus* (Zurich, 1731);

*Oratio Apologetica, qua demonstratur, religionem erudi-
tioni non esse inimicam, sed contra maximum in li-
teris verae religioni positum esse praesidium etc.*
(Zurich, 1735);

*Artis cogitandi principia, ad mentem recentiorum philo-
sophorum compendio exhibita atque in usum priva-
tae institutionis concinnata* (Zurich: Orell,
1736);

*Brevis de idiotismis sermonis hebraei commentarius: qui
linquae sanctae genium, indolem ac proprietatem
clare exponit* (Zurich: Heidegger, 1737);

*Critische Abhandlung von der Natur, den Absichten
und dem Gebrauche der Gleichnisse: Mit Beyspielen aus den Schriften der berühmtesten alten und
neuen Scribenten erläutert*, edited by Bodmer
(Zurich: Orell, 1740; reprinted, Stuttgart:
Metzler, 1967);

Critische Dichtkunst, 2 volumes, edited by Bodmer
(Zurich: Orell, 1740; reprinted, with afterword by Wolfgang Bender, Stuttgart: Metzler, 1966)—comprises volume 1, *Worinnen die
Poetische Mahlerey in Absicht auf die Erfindung
im Grunde untersuchet und mit Beyspielen aus
den berühmtesten Alten und Neuern erläutert
wird*; volume 2, *Worinnen die poetische Mahle-*

Johann Jakob Breitinger

*rey in Absicht auf den Ausdruck und die Farben ab-
gehandelt*;

*De principiis in examinanda et definienda religionis es-
sentia ex mente nuperi scriptoris galli adhibendis
amica disputatio* (Zurich: Orell, 1741);

*Zuverlässige Nachricht und Untersuchung von dem Al-
terthum der Stadt Zürich und von einer neuen Ent-
deckung merkwürdiger Antiquitäten einer bisher
unbekannten Stadt in der Herrschafft Knonau*
(Zurich: Heidegger, 1741);

*Vertheidigung der Schweitzerischen Muse, Herrn D. Al-
brecht Hallers*, anonymous (Zurich: Heidegger, 1744);

*Beurtheilung der Panthea, eines sogenannten Trauer-
spiels; Nebst einer Vorlesung für die Nachkommen und einer Ode auf den Nahmen Gottsched*,
by Breitinger and Bodmer (Zurich, 1746);

Critische Briefe, by Breitinger and Bodmer (Zurich: Heidegger, 1746; reprinted, Hildesheim: Olms, 1969);

Die Mütze: Eine französische Erzählung aus dem Lande der Freien, anonymous (N.p., 1746);

Der Mahler der Sitten: Von neuem überschen und starck vermehret, 2 volumes, by Breitinger and Bodmer (Zurich: Orell, 1746; reprinted, Hildesheim & New York: Olms, 1972);

Der gemißhandelte Opiz in der Trillerischen Ausfertigung seiner Gedichte, by Breitinger and Bodmer (Zurich, 1747);

Dissertatione logica VI argumenti quod a consensu multitudinis duci solet (Zurich, 1748);

De antiquissimo Turicensis Bibliothecae graeco psalmorum libro in membrana purpurae titulis aureis ac litteris argenteis exarato, Epistola (Zurich: Orell, Füßli, 1748);

Eclogae ex optimis Graecis Scriptoribus ad vitam studiosae juventutis informandam (Zurich, 1749);

Lessingische unäsopische Fabeln: Enthaltend die sinnreichen Einfälle und weisen Sprüche der Thiere. Nebst damit einschlagender Untersuchung der Abhandlung Herrn Lessings von der Kunst Fabeln zu verfertigen, anonymous, by Breitinger and Bodmer (Zurich: Orell, 1760);

Kurze Anweisung zur griechischen Sprache für Anfänger nebst einem bequemen Text zur Übersetzung (N.p., 1772);

Drey Reden bey Anlaß der feyerlichen Ankündigung und Einführung des mit Hoch-Oberlichkeitlichem Ansehen bevestigten Erziehungsplans in unsere öffentliche Schule, als Zugabe zu den Nachrichten von den neuen Schulanstalten in Zürich (Zurich, 1773);

Joh. Christoph Gottsched und die Schweizer J. J. Bodmer und J. J. Breitinger, edited by Johannes Crüger (Berlin & Stuttgart: Spemann, 1884; reprinted, Darmstadt: Wissenschaftliche Buchgesellschaft, 1965);

Chronick der Gesellschaft der Mahler: 1721-22, by Breitinger and Heinrich Meister, edited by Theodor Vetter (Frauenfeld: Huber, 1887);

Schriften zur Literatur, by Breitinger and Bodmer, edited by Volker Meid (Stuttgart: Reclam, 1980).

OTHER: *Die Discourse der Mahlern,* 4 volumes, edited by Breitinger and Johann Jakob Bodmer (volumes 1-3, Zurich: Lindinner, 1721-1722; volume 4, Zurich: Bodmer, 1723) —volume 4 published as *Die Mahler. Oder: Discourse von den Sitten der Menschen;*

Neue Zeitungen aus der gelehrten Welt: Zur Beleuchtung der Historie der Gelehrsamkeit, revised by Breitinger as Bibliophilo (Zurich, 1725);

Johann Caspar Suicer, *Thesaurus ecclesiasticus e patribus Graecis,* second edition, edited by Breitinger (Amsterdam: Wettstein, 1728);

Vetus Testamentum ex versione Septuaginta Interpretum, olim ad fidem Codicis Alexandrini summo studio & incredibili diligentia expressum, 4 volumes, edited by Breitinger and Johann Ernst Grabe (Zurich: Heidegger, 1730-1732);

Publicae pietatis omnia et vota pro salute Viri magnificentissimi: Domini Johannis Hoffmeisteri, cum ob summa in rem publicam merita ab illustris reipublicae tigurinae augusto CC virorum senatu consul esset designatus die XIII cal. Jun. 1734, edited by Breitinger (Zurich: Orell, 1734);

Helvetische Bibliothek, bestehend In historischen, politischen und critischen Beyträgen zu den Geschichten Des Schweitzerlands, 6 volumes, edited by Breitinger and Bodmer (Zurich: Orell, 1735-1741);

"Prolegomena Thesauri scriptorum historiae Helvetiae," in *Thesaurus historiae Helveticae continens lectissimos scriptores,* by Johann Jakob Lauffer, edited by Bodmer (Zurich: Orell, 1735);

Tempe Helvetica: Dissertationes atque observationes theologicas, philologicas, criticas exhibens, 6 volumes, edited by Breitinger and Johann Georg Altmann (Zurich: Heidegger, 1736-1743);

Certa et definita ad Latinitatem via, probatissimorum auctorum fragmentis munita: superiorum auspiciis in pubis scholasticae commodum fideliter aperta, edited by Breitinger and J. C. Hagenbuch (1736);

Lauffer, *Historische und Critische Beyträge zu der Historie der Eidsgenossen,* 4 volumes, edited by Breitinger and Bodmer (Zurich: Orell, 1739);

"Vorrede," in *Critische Betrachtungen über die poetischen Gemählde der Dichter, mit einer Vorrede von Johann Jakob Breitinger,* by Bodmer (Zurich: Orell, 1741; reprinted, Frankfurt am Main: Athenäum, 1971);

Sammlung critischer, poetischer, und andrer geistvollen Schriften, zur Verbesserung des Urtheils und des Wizes in den Wercken der Wolredenheit und der Poesie, 5 volumes, edited by Breitinger and Bodmer (Zurich: Orell, 1741-1744); republished as *Sammlung der Zürcherischen Streitschriften zur Verbesserung des deutschen Geschmacks wider die Gottschedische Schule, von 1741 bis 1744: vollständig in XII Stüken. Neue*

Ausgabe, 2 volumes, edited by Christoph Martin Wieland (Zurich: Orell, 1753);

Freymüthige Nachrichten von neuen Büchern, und andern zur Gelehrtheit gehörigen Sachen, 20 volumes, edited by Breitinger and Bodmer (Zurich: Heidegger, 1744-1763);

Suicer, *Novi Testamenti Glossarium Graeco-Latinum*, edited by Breitinger and Hagenbuch (1744);

Martin Opitz, *Martin Opitzens von Boberfeld Gedichte: Von J. J. B. und J. J. B. besorget. Erster Theil*, edited by Breitinger and Bodmer (Zurich: Orell, 1745; republished with new preface, 1755);

Johann Adolf Schlegel, *Vom Natürlichen in Schäfergedichten, wider die Verfasser der Bremischen neuen Beyträge verfertigt von Nisus einem Schäfer in den Kohlgärten, einem Dorfe vor Leipzig, zwelte Auflage, besort und mit Anmerkungen vermehrt von Hans Görgen, gleichfalls einem Schäfer daselbst*, edited by Breitinger and Bodmer (Zurich: Heidegger, 1746);

Museum Helveticum, 7 volumes, edited by Breitinger and Jakob Zimmerman (Zurich: Orell, 1746-1753);

Proben der alten schwäbischen Poesie des dreyzehnten Jahrhunderts: Aus der Maneßischen Sammlung, edited by Breitinger and Bodmer (Zurich: Heidegger, 1748; reprinted, Hildesheim: Gerstenberg, 1973);

Ulrich Boner, *Fabeln aus den Zeiten der Minnesinger*, edited by Breitinger and Bodmer (Zurich: Orell, 1757; reprinted, Leipzig: Zentralantiquariat der Deutschen Demokratischen Republik, 1973);

Chriemhilden Rache, und die Klage: Zwey Heldengedichte aus dem schwaebischen Zeitpuncte. Samt Fragmenten aus dem Gedichte von den Nibelungen und aus dem Josaphat. Darzu koemmt ein Glossarium, edited by Breitinger and Bodmer (Zurich: Orell, 1757);

Sammlung von Minnesingern aus dem schwaebischen Zeitpuncte CXL Dichter enthaltend: durch Ruedger Manessen, weiland des Rathes der uralten Zyrich. Aus der Handschrift der Königlich-Französischen Bibliothek herausgegeben, 2 volumes, edited by Breitinger and Bodmer (Zurich: Orell, 1758-1759);

Catechesis doctrinae politicae veterum testimoniis confirmata (N.p., 1773);

Orationes IIII solennes, quibus ecclesize Christi natales concelebravit (Zurich: Orell, 1776);

"Gutachten zum Großmünster," in *Eine Erinnerung aus der Geschichte des Großmünsters in Zürich. Zum Gedächtnis J. J. Breitinger 14 Dezem-*

ber 1776, edited, with contributions, by Rudolf Rahn (Zurich, 1872).

PERIODICAL PUBLICATIONS: "Der gestäubte Leipziger Diogenes, oder critische Urtheile über die erste Speculation des Leipziger Spectateurs," by Breitinger and Johann Jakob Bodmer, *Historischer und politischer Mercurius* [Zurich: Lindinner] (February 1723);

"Luculenta commentatio in antique monumenta in agro Tigurino nuper eruta," *Amoenitates litterariae*, 7 (1727): 1-74;

"Supplementum ad Commentationem in antiqua monumenta in agro Tigurino eruta," *Amoenitates litterariae*, 9 (1728): 822-826;

"Exercitatio critica in vitam A. Persii Flacci," *Amoenitates litterariae*, 10 (1729): 1103-1146;

"De nonnullis lapidibus litteratis, Romanae pietatis monumentis, amica disputatio," *Amoenitates litterariae*, 10 (1729): 1209-1235;

"Nothwendiges Ergäntzungs-Stücke zu der Schutz-Vorrede Hrn. Tr*ll*rs vor seinem neuen Aesopischen Fabelwercke," *Sammlung critischer, poetischer, und andrer geistvollen Schriften, Zur Verbesserung des Urtheils und des Wizes in den Wercken der Wolredenheit*, 2 (1741): 1-55;

"Echo des deutschen Witzes," *Sammlung critischer, poetischer, und andrer geistvollen Schriften, zur Verbesserung des Urtheils und des Wizes in den Wercken der Wolredenheit*, 4 (1742): 19-84;

"Fortsetzung der [sic] Echo des deutschen Witzes," *Sammlung critischer, poetischer, und andrer geistvollen Schriften, zur Verbesserung des Urtheils und des Wizes in den Wercken der Wolredenheit*, 6 (1742): 3-90;

"Herren Johann Christoph Gottscheds seltsame Vorrede zu seinem eigenen drey mahl wiederholten Versuche einer critischen Dichtkunst für die Deutschen ... von Wolfgang Erlenbach, Correct.," *Sammlung critischer, poetischer, und andrer geistvollen Schriften, zur Verbesserung des Urtheils und des Wizes in den Werken der Wolredenheit*, 6 (1742): 91-137;

"Von dem wichtigen Antheil, den das Glück beytragen muß, einen epischen Poeten zu formiren: Nach den Grundsätzen der Inquiry into the life and the Writings of Homer," *Sammlung critischer, poetischer, und andrer geistvollen Schriften, zur Verbesserung des Urtheils und des Wizes in den Wercken der Wolredenheit*, 17 (1743): 3-24;

"Abentheuer, das sich mit der Aeneis Hrn. Joh. Christoph Schwartzen in Conrector Erlenbachs Schule zugetragen," *Sammlung criti-*

scher, poetischer, und andrer geistvollen Schriften, zur Verbesserung des Urtheils und des Wizes in den Wercken der Wolredenheit, 7 (1743): 81-90;

"Wohlgemeinter Vorschlag, wie Schwartzen deutsche Aeneis von dem Gerichte der Makulatur noch zu erretten wäre," *Sammlung critischer, poetischer, und andrer geistvollen Schriften, zur Verbesserung des Urtheils und des Wizes in den Wercken der Wolredenheit,* 8 (1744): 33-53;

"Genaue Prüfung der Gottschedischen Uebersetzung Horazens von der Dichtkunst," *Sammlung critischer, poetischer, und andrer geistvollen Schriften, zur Verbesserung des Urtheils und des Wizes in den Wercken der Wolredenheit,* 9 (1744): 75-105;

"Critische Untersuchung, wie weit sich ein Poet des gemeinen Wahnes und der Sage bedienen könne," *Sammlung critischer, poetischer, und andrer geistvollen Schriften, zur Verbesserung des Urtheils und des Wizes in den Wercken der Wolredenheit,* 12 (1744): 1-32.

The unprecedented influence that Zurich-learned circles had on German literary theory in the first half of the eighteenth century can be directly traced to Johann Jakob Breitinger and his lifelong working companion, Johann Jakob Bodmer. Breitinger developed ideas and concepts suggested by Bodmer and others into theoretical constructs and attempted to systematize an approach to literary theory that departed from the authoritarian Gottschedian school. Johann Christoph Gottsched represented reaction against the Baroque adornment and ponderous rhetoric of Daniel Casper von Lohenstein and others. He attempted to codify a mechanical approach to the writing of verse; Breitinger argued against Gottsched that poetic fantasy required the freedom to imitate nature selectively and to use probable yet nonexistent worlds as points of departure.

Breitinger's birthdate is disputed. Sources mention 1 March, 5 March, and 15 March 1701 as likely dates. His baptism took place on 17 March in St. Peter's Church in Zurich. His parents were Franz Caspar Breitinger, a confectioner and former private secretary to Duke George of Württemberg, and Verena Schobinger Breitinger. The family had been citizens of Zurich since the late fourteenth century, and most had been tanners.

Breitinger's half brother Johann Heinrich, pastor in Märstetten and Uster, tutored Breitinger and introduced him to the study of ancient languages. At the age of ten Breitinger was able to enter the highest level class at the Latin Grammar School in Zurich, skipping four levels. He studied at the Collegium Humanitatis from 1713 until 1715, when he enrolled in the Collegium Carolinum, the professional school for candidates for the ministry and the only institution of higher education in early-eighteenth-century Zurich. At the Carolinum he developed lifelong friendships with Bodmer; Johann Caspar Hagenbuch, later professor of eloquence at the Carolinum; and Heinrich Meister. While at the Carolinum he became involved in a scientific dispute over the reporting and evaluation of data from an archeological expedition in the Canton of Aarau; the dispute led him to attempt to establish an independent journal of unbiased criticism, but school officials blocked the venture. Breitinger graduated from the Carolinum in 1720 and was ordained a minister in the Zurich Protestant Church.

Breitinger's second attempt at an independent critical journal met with greater, although still limited, success. With Bodmer, Meister, and several others Breitinger helped found the Gesellschaft der Mahlern (Society of Painters) in 1720. The society sought to critique customs, fashions, and literature in order to raise the general level of taste in Switzerland. The organ of the society, *Die Discourse der Mahlern* (The Discourse of the Painters, 1721-1723), was modeled after the English moral weeklies, most prominently Joseph Addison and Richard Steele's *Spectator,* French translations of which Bodmer had secured on a trip to Geneva and France. Breitinger wrote twenty-seven of the ninety-four articles in the *Discourse* and dealt mainly with moral and philosophical topics. In his "Die Kunst des Denkens" (The Art of Thinking), published in volume 1, number 9, John Locke's theories on the origin of ideas provide a general source for Breitinger's demand that ideas need to be traced to basic premises. Incorrect thinking results from haste, from too high a regard for authorities, or from inaccurate sense perceptions. His preference for the fable over other literary forms finds early expression in other articles, where he emphasizes the didactic nature of literature. The imagination is not free to create images out of whole cloth; its task is to recall and recombine what has been observed in nature and is thus bound to nature and observation. Behind these thoughts one can see an orthodox theologian who is skeptical about what comes out of the human heart and feels the necessity to prepare the mind for the truth revealed in God's creation. He coauthored thirteen additional articles with Bodmer. Breitinger is more critical than Bodmer in his contributions, but his writing was criticized by some as too academic for a weekly journal. In yet another article, Breitinger provided an edition of the diary of his ancestor, Johann Jakob Breitinger, the seventeenth-century senior pastor at the Grossmünster Cathedral in Zurich.

After the *Discourse* ceased publication Breitinger turned his attention more and more to ancient authors. In 1723 he published a prolegomena to a proposed new edition of Persius, in which he suggested several ingenious interpretations of difficult passages; this article was followed by a biographical essay on Persius (1729). In 1725 he became editor of the *Neue Zeitungen aus der gelehrten Welt: Zur Beleuchtung der Historie der Gelehrsamkeit* (New Periodical from the Learned World for the Illumination of Intellectual History), which ran for fifty-one issues. He then found employment as a tutor, first in the home of J. J. Leu and later to the children of the former Zurich mayor Johann Caspar Escher, upon the death of whose son he wrote an elegy (1726).

His friendship with Bodmer survived the failure of the *Discourse*. The two men visited each other almost daily and discussed literature and customs. Breitinger critiqued, developed, and systematized Bodmer's ideas in ways Bodmer himself never could have done. Breitinger was also the more jovial of the two; the ascetic Bodmer could never quite comprehend this side of his companion. This fruitful relationship resulted in the 1727 publication of the coauthored work *Von dem Einfluß und Gebrauche der Einbildungs-Krafft: Zur Ausbesserung des Geschmackes* (Concerning the Influence and Use of the Imagination for the Improvement of Taste), which was planned as the first volume of a comprehensive theory of the fine arts. Breitinger and Bodmer sought a philosophical basis for poetry and rhetoric in the philosophy of Christian Wolff, the leading disciple of Gottfried Wilhelm von Leibniz. In the Wolffian/ Enlightenment tradition, the authors sought to establish rules for the critique of poetic works. The imagination is seen as a receptive and productive faculty which recollects and recombines observed entities and events into new images. Through the operation of the imagination these images achieve greater clarity than that of the original im-

pressions from reality itself. They are then recorded in poetic form, which gives them the same or greater power than the original impression had. The basis of poetic delight thus lies in the comparison of the image with its original and the determination of the similarity or identity between the two. Hence, Breitinger aligns himself with the concept of poetry as the imitation of nature, almost in an Aristotelian sense. The poet has a distinct advantage over other artists because he can portray feelings and emotions, which in the graphic arts is only possible through gestures. The true poet is so overtaken by his passion that his recalled images become for him indistinguishable from his original observations of nature. The poet then makes the reader believe that those images are immediate to him as well.

In 1727 Breitinger helped found the Helvetische Gesellschaft (Swiss Society), and together with Bodmer and others edited and published several original documents and essays interpreting Swiss history. He compiled a list of manuscripts in the Zurich City Library concerning the Swiss Confederation, titled "Bibliotheca Scriptorum Historiae Helveticae universalis." This unpublished work formed the basis for G. E. Haller's *Bibliothek der Schweizergeschichte* (Library of Swiss History, 1763). His multivolume critical edition of the Septuagint, edited with Johann Ernst Grabe, appeared from 1730 to 1732. Combining his philological and theological interests, he advocated preaching founded on close study of biblical texts rather than on an uninspired recital of traditional Zurich orthodoxy.

In 1731 Breitinger was appointed professor of Hebrew language at the Carolinum humanitatis in Zurich. Three months later, he was invited to become acting professor at the Collegium Carolinum, where his friend Bodmer had been lecturing since 1725. In 1740 the position was made permanent, and Breitinger took on lecturing responsibilities for logic and rhetoric as well. His contemporaries viewed his contributions to education as at least as important as his literary work. He opposed narrow Protestant scholasticism in theology and wrote several textbooks, including a work on Hebrew idioms (1737), and a logic text (1736). On 25 October 1735 he married Esther Schinz; the couple had two daughters, both of whom grew up to marry clergymen.

Breitinger's major literary contributions appeared in 1740: *Critische Abhandlung von der Natur, den Absichten und dem Gebrauche der Gleichnisse: Mit Beyspielen aus den Schriften der*

Title page for the first volume of Breitinger's critical poetics

Critische Dichtkunst is divided into two volumes; the first seeks to establish the nature of poetry on a philosophical basis, while the second discusses poetic language. The book is a systematic summary of Bodmer and Breitinger's previously unpublished critical work on John Milton's *Paradise Lost* and other seventeenth- and early-eighteenth-century literature. Bodmer had published a German translation of *Paradise Lost* in 1732. Works of art are seen as logically possible worlds in a Leibnizian/Wolffian sense. A poem is, then, a story from another possible world and has a didactic function. Painting and sculpture share principles of imitation with poetry, but poetry is higher than the other arts because it produces a clearer image, one that is sometimes clearer than nature itself. The poet can select the essential characteristics of a subject, disregarding the unessential or accidental, and recombine them in new and stimulating but not impossible ways to capture the attention of readers. The poetic imagination is seen as a product of the poet's own subjectivity, which makes the writing of poetry essentially unlearnable. Things can be portrayed in their highest degree of perfection and thus produce a sense of wonder in the reader. Poetic imagination is limited only by the requirement that its source be a logically possible world and that it not range so far as to sacrifice probability. Probability can, however, be pushed to the extreme in the creation of the sense of wonder; "das Wunderbare" (the wonderful) then becomes so far removed from perceived reality that it seems improbable and can take on the appearance of falsehood. But the wonderful is founded on a real or probable truth, which it fleshes out in a deceptive form. The discovery of the deception by the reader results in "Ergötzen" (delight) and a sense of beauty. The beautiful will of necessity vary according to time and place–what moves the heart in one generation may have no effect in the next–but the fulfillment of didactic purposes remains constant. Under the influence of Jean Baptiste Dubo's *Réflexions critiques sur la poésie, la peinture et la musique* (1719), Breitinger thus places poetry and rhetoric in close relationship to one another through their common goals of persuasion and instruction.

In the second volume to which Bodmer probably contributed several chapters, Breitinger argues for the use of powerful words borrowed from dialects to express the sense of wonder. Writers should adopt a pathetic style to capture the imagination of the reader. Not much understand-

berühmtesten alten und neuen Scribenten erläutert (Critical Treatment of the Nature, the Goals, and the Use of Parables, Illustrated with Examples from the Writings of the Famous Ancient and Modern Writers) and *Critische Dichtkunst* (Critical Poetics). In the former work Breitinger contrasted the logic of understanding, which is based on concepts, with the logic of fantasy, which is expressed in images. Since images work more directly on average people than concepts do, Breitinger argues that didactic literary works must shroud general philosophical truths in pictures. Parables can fulfill illuminating and decorative purposes, but they find their highest purpose in the instruction of unlearned minds through the stimulation of the fantasy and the emotions.

IOANNES IACOBVS
BREITINGERVS.
*V. D. M. Prof. Græc. L. in Gymnasio Turicensi
Canonicus Templi majoris et
Collegii Carolini.
nat. d. 15 Mart. MDCCI*

Mezzotint by J. Jacob Haid, after a drawing by J. C. Füeßli

ing for the mechanics of verse is demonstrated, although German verse structure is recognized as dependent on word stress rather than on syllable length.

The programmatic works of 1740 and 1741 signaled the break between Bodmer and Breitinger on one side and Gottsched and his followers on the other. In the following years many essays were published in which much satire and ridicule but few rational arguments were used to defend each side's position and destroy the opponent's. Breitinger's *Vertheidigung der Schweitzerischen Muse, Herrn D. Albrecht Hallers* (Defense of the Swiss Muse, of Dr. Albrecht Haller, 1744) sought to defend Albrecht von Haller's use of imagination from the attacks of the Gottsched school.

After 1741, however, Breitinger's main ef-

forts returned to textual criticism. Together with Bodmer he published the first critical edition of a more German poet, *Martin Opitzens von Boberfeld Gedichte* (Poems of Martin Opitz of Boberfeld, 1745), and assisted Bodmer in the preparation of many editions of medieval German poetry and prose. The critical apparatus in the Opitz edition attempted to follow the genesis of the text and included all variants, along with comments on sound changes, syntax, morphology, and lexicon. Breitinger was responsible for the preparation of a copy of the Minnesinger Codex from the Royal Library in Paris (1758-1759); he had previously also published a description of a Greek Psalter found in the Zurich City Library (1748).

In 1745 Breitinger was appointed canon at the seminary at Grossmünster and innovated

Excerpt from a letter by Breitinger (Stadtbibliothek, Zurich)

changes in the homiletic training of new pastors which required students to preach two sermons each week to the assembly of pastors for critique. In 1768 he helped found the Ascetische Gesellschaft junger Geistlicher (Ascetic Society of Young Clergymen) to provide a forum for the discussion of questions of conscience and other pastoral problems.

When a fire destroyed the towers of the Grossmünster cathedral and an attempt was made to tear down the building, Breitinger wrote an essay (1763) on the significance of medieval architecture. As a result, the damaged towers were rebuilt in a neo-Gothic style. From 1772 until 1775 he was rector of the Zurich secondary school. As with his date of birth, there is uncertainty about his date of death: 13, 14, and 15 December 1776 are variously given in the literature. Goethe gave his impression of Breitinger in *Dichtung und Wahrheit* (Poetry and Truth, 1811-1833): "Breitinger war ein tüchtiger, gelehrter, einsichtsvoller Mann, dem, als er sich recht umsah, die sämtlichen Erfordernisse einer Dichtung nicht entgingen" (Breitinger was a diligent, learned, insightful man, who, when he carefully looked around, was conscious of all the requirements of poetry).

Letters:

Harold Thomas Betteridge, "Klopstock's Correspondence with Bodmer and Breitinger," *Modern Language Review*, 57 (July 1962): 357-372;

Walther Gose, "Ein theologischer Brief Breitingers," *Jahrbuch der Deutschen Schillergesellschaft*, 13 (1969): 1-12;

Imre Lengyel, "Breitinger und Debrecen," *Arbeiten zur deutschen Philologie*, 6 (1972): 55-76.

Biography:

Hermann Bodmer, *Johann Jakob Breitinger, 1701-1776: Sein Leben und seine litterarische Bedeutung* (Zurich: Zürcher & Furrer, 1897).

References:

Friedmar Apel, "Von der Nachahmung zur Imagination—Wandlungen der Poetik und der Literaturkritik," in *Aufklärung und Romantik 1700-1830*, edited by Klaus Siebenhaar and Christine Caemmerer, volume 4 of *Propyläen Geschichte der Literatur: Literatur und Gesellschaft der westlichen Welt*, edited by Erika Wischer (Berlin: Propyläen, 1983), pp. 75-100;

Jakob Baechtold, *Geschichte der deutschen-Literatur in der Schweiz* (Frauenfeld: Huber, 1919);

Wolfgang Bender, *J. J. Bodmer und J. J. Breitinger* (Stuttgart: Metzler, 1973);

Bender, "Rhetorische Tradition und Ästhetik im 18. Jahrhundert: Baumgarten, Meier und Breitinger," *Zeitschrift für deutsche Philologie*, 99 (1980): 481-506;

Eric A. Blackall, "The Revival of Metaphor," in his *The Emergence of German as a Literary Language 1700-1775*, second edition (Ithaca, N.Y. & London: Cornell University Press, 1978), pp. 276-313;

Helga Brandes, *Die "Gesellschaft der Maler" und ihr literarischer Beitrag zur Aufklärung: Eine Untersuchung zur Publizistik des 18. Jahrhunderts* (Bremen: Schünemann Universitätsverlag, 1974);

F. Andrew Brown, "Locke's 'Essay' and Bodmer and Breitinger," *Modern Language Quarterly*, 10 (March 1949): 16-32;

Jan Bruck, Eckart Feldmeier, Hans Hiebel, and Karl Heinz Stahl, "Der Mimesisbegriff Gottscheds und der Schweizer: Kritische Überlegungen zu Hans Peter Herrmann, *Naturnachahmung und Einbildungskraft*," *Zeitschrift für deutsche Philologie*, 90 (December 1971): 563-578;

Peter Faessler, "Die Zürcher in Arkadien: Der Kreis um J. J. Bodmer und der Appenzeller Laurenz Zellweger," *Appenzeller Jahrbücher*, 107 (1979): 3-49;

Manfred Gradinger, "Die Minnesang- und Waltherforschung von Bodmer bis Uhland," Ph.D. dissertation, University of Munich, 1970;

Karl S. Guthke, "Der junge Lessing als Kritiker Gottscheds und Bodmers," "Hallers 'Anteil' am Literaturstreit: Legende und Wahrheit," and "Hagedorn: das Dilemma des 'Friedfertigen' in den 'Gelehrten Kriegen,'" in his *Literarisches Leben im achtzehnten Jahrhundert in Deutschland und in der Schweiz* (Bern & Munich: Francke, 1975), pp. 24-117;

Helmut Henne, "Eine frühe kritische Edition neuerer Literatur: Zur Opitz-Ausgabe Bodmers und Breitingers von 1745," *Zeitschrift für deutsche Philologie*, 87 (May 1968): 180-196;

Hans Peter Herrmann, "Die Dichtungstheorien Bodmers und Breitingers," in his *Naturnachahmung und Einbildungskraft: Zur Entwicklung der deutschen Poetik von 1670 bis 1740* (Bad Homburg, Berlin & Zurich: Gehlen, 1970), pp. 163-275;

Hermann Hettner, "Die Dichtung: Gottsched und sein Kampf mit Bodmer und Breitinger," in his *Geschichte der deutschen Literatur im achtzehnten Jahrhundert*, volume 1, part 2 (Leipzig: List, 1929), pp. 210-229;

Christoph Hubig, " 'Genie'–Typus oder Original? Vom Paradigma der Kreativität zum Kult des Individuums," in *Aufklärung und Romantik 1700-1830*, edited by Siebenhaar and Caemmerer, volume 4 of *Propyläen Geschichte der Literatur: Literatur und Gesellschaft der westlichen Welt*, edited by Wischer (Berlin: Propyläen, 1983), pp. 187-210;

Dieter Kimpel, "Aufklärung, Bürgertum und Literatur in Deutschland," in *Aufklärung und Romantik 1700-1830*, edited by Siebenhaar and Caemmerer, volume 4 of *Propyläen Geschichte der Literatur: Literatur und Gesellschaft der westlichen Welt*, edited by Wischer (Berlin: Propyläen, 1983), pp. 52-74;

Clayton Koelb, "The *Schein der Falschheit* in Breitinger's Poetics," *Michigan German Studies*, 9 (1983): 129-140;

Erwin Leibfried, "Philosophisches Lehrgedicht und Fabel," in *Europäische Aufklärung*, volume 11 of *Neues Handbuch der Literaturwissenschaft*, edited by Walter Hinck (Frankfurt am Main: Athenäum, 1974), pp. 75-90;

Gisbert Lepper, Jörg Steitz, and Wolfgang Brenn, "Poetische Säkularisierung der Erbauungsschriften: Gegner Gottscheds–Bodmer, Breitinger, Klopstock," in their *Unter dem Absolutismus*, volume 1 of their *Einführung in die deutsche Literatur des 18. Jahrhunderts* (Opladen: Westdeutscher Verlag, 1983), pp. 92-107;

Bruno Markwardt, "Abwandlung und Auflockerung der 'kritischen' Poetik," in *Aufklärung, Rokoko, Sturm und Drang*, volume 2 of *Geschichte der deutschen Poetik*, edited by Markwardt (Berlin: De Gruyter, 1956), pp. 76-130;

Steven D. Martinson, "Concerning the Imagination" and "On Taste, Beauty and the Sublime," in his *On Imitation, Imagination and Beauty: A Critical Reassessment of the Concept of the Literary Artist During the Early German "Aufklärung"* (Bonn: Bouvier, 1977), pp. 56-144;

Reinhart Meyer, "Restaurative Innovation: Theologische Tradition und poetische Freiheit in der Poetik Bodmers und Breitingers," in *Aufklärung und literarische Öffentlichkeit*, edited by Christa Bürger, Peter Bürger, and Jochen Schulte-Sasse (Frankfurt am Main: Suhrkamp, 1980), pp. 39-82;

Uwe Möller, "Der Einfluß der Rhetorik auf das Poesieverständnis in Breitingers 'Critischer Dichtkunst,'" in his *Rhetorische Überlieferung und Dichtungstheorie im frühen 18. Jahrhundert: Studien zu Gottsched, Breitinger und G. Fr. Meyer* (Munich: Fink, 1983), pp. 44-70;

Friedhelm Radandt, "The Challenge from Switzerland: Bodmer and Breitinger," in his *From Baroque to Storm and Stress* (London: Croom Helm / New York: Barnes & Noble, 1977), pp. 50-54;

Horst Dieter Schlosser, "Sprachnorm und regionale Differenz im Rahmen der Kontroverse zwischen Gottsched und Bodmer/Breitinger," in *Mehrsprachigkeit in der deutschen Aufklärung*, edited by Dieter Kimpel (Hamburg: Meiner, 1985), pp. 52-68;

Horst-Michael Schmidt, "Die Konzeption der Poetik Bodmers und Breitingers," in his *Sinnlichkeit und Verstand: Zur philosophischen und poetologischen Begründung von Erfahrung und Urteil in der deutschen Aufklärung (Leibniz, Wolff, Gottsched, Bodmer und Breitinger)* (Munich: Fink, 1982), pp. 124-176;

Jochen Schmidt, "Bodmer und Breitinger: Das Wunderbare und Erhabene als Medium zur Befreiung der 'Einbildungskraft' und zur Intensivierung der Affekte," in his *Von der Aufklärung bis zum Idealismus*, volume 1 of his *Die Geschichte des Genie-Gedankens 1750-1945* (Darmstadt: Wissenschaftliche Buchgesellschaft, 1985), pp. 47-65;

Herbert Schöffler, "Die Autoren" and "Ideen und Form," in his *Das literarische Zürich 1700-1750* (Frauenfeld & Leipzig: Huber, 1925), pp. 25-96; republished as "Anruf der Schweizer," in *Deutscher Geist im 18. Jahrhundert: Essays zur Geistes- und Religionsgeschichte*, edited by Götz von Selle, second edition (Göttingen: Vandenhoeck & Ruprecht, 1967), pp. 7-60;

Karl-Heinz Stahl, "Die psychologische Analyse und Bestimmung des Wunderbaren," in his *Das Wunderbare als Problem und Gegenstand der deutschen Poetik des 17. und 18. Jahrhun-*

derts (Frankfurt am Main: Athenaion, 1975), pp. 123-182;

Enrico Straub, *Der Brief-Wechsel Calepio-Bodmer: Ein Beitrag zur Erhellung der Beziehungen zwischen italienischer und deutscher Literatur im 18. Jahrhundert* (Berlin: Reuter, 1965);

Straub, "Marginalien zu Neudrucken der Werke Bodmers und Breitingers," *Arcadia: Zeitschrift für vergleichende Literaturwissenschaft*, 3, no. 3 (1968): 307-314;

J. H. Tisch, "'Poetic Theology': *Paradise Lost* Between Aesthetics and Religion in 18th Century Switzerland," *Revue de Littérature Comparée*, 49 (April-June 1975): 270-283;

Hans Trümpy, *Schweizerdeutsche Sprache und Literatur im 17. und 18. Jahrhundert* (Basel: Krebs, 1955);

Silvio Vietta, "Poetik und Ästhetik der deutschen Aufklärung," in his *Literarische Phantasie: Theorie und Geschichte. Barock und Aufklärung* (Stuttgart: Metzler, 1986), pp. 110-134;

Max Wehrli, Introduction to *Das geistige Zürich im 18. Jahrhundert*, edited by Wehrli (Zurich: Atlantis, 1943);

Angelika Wetterer, "Die sinnlichen Bedürfnisse des Publikums und die vernünftigen Maßstäbe der 'critischen' Poetik: Aspekte des Nachahmungsgrundsatzes bei den Schweizern," in *Publikumsbezug und Wahrheitsanspruch: Der Widerspruch zwischen rhetorischem Ansatz und philosophischem Anspruch bei Gottsched und den Schweizern*, edited by Wetterer (Tübingen: Niemeyer, 1981), pp. 161-228;

Jürgen Wilke, "Der deutsch-schweizerische Literaturstreit," in *Kontroversen, alte und neue: Akten des VII. internationalen Germanisten-Kongresses Göttingen 1985*, edited by Albrecht Schöne, volume 2 (Tübingen: Niemeyer, 1986), pp. 140-151;

Hans Wysling, "Die Literatur," in *Zürich im 18. Jahrhundert: Zum 150. Jahrestag der Universität Zürich*, edited by Wysling (Zurich: Gerichtshaus, 1983), pp. 131-188.

Papers:
Johann Jakob Breitinger's papers are in the Zentzlbibliothek Zürich.

Matthias Claudius
(15 August 1740 - 21 January 1815)

Herbert Rowland
Purdue University

BOOKS: *Ob und wie weit Gott den Tod der Menschen bestimme, bey der Gruft seines geliebtesten Bruders Herrn Josias Claudius* (Jena: Marggraf, 1760);

Tändeleyen und Erzählungen, anonymous (Jena: Marggraf, 1763);

Eine Disputation zwischen den Herren W. und X. und einem Fremden über Herrn Pastor Alberti "Anleitung zum Gespräch über die Religion" und über Herrn Pastor Goeze "Text am 5ten Sonntage nach Epiphanias" unter Vorsitz des Herrn Lars Hochedeln, anonymous (Hamburg, 1772);

Asmus omnia sua secum portans oder Sämmtliche Werke des Wandsbecker Bothen, 7 volumes (volumes 1 and 2, Hamburg: Bode, 1775; volume 3, Breslau: Löwe, 1778; volume 4, Breslau: Löwe, 1783; volume 5, Hamburg: Bohn, 1790; volume 6, Hamburg: Perthes, 1798; volume 7, Hamburg: Perthes, 1803);

Ein Lied, nach dem Frieden Anno 1779, anonymous (Wandsbeck: Wörmer, 1779);

Ein Lied vom Reiffen d.d. den 7. December 1780, anonymous (Wandsbeck: Wörmer, 1780);

Weyhnachts-Cantilene, music by Johann Friedrich Reichardt (Copenhagen: Thiele, 1784);

Zwey Recensionen etc. in Sachen der Herren Leßing, M. Mendelssohn und Jacobi, as Asmus (Hamburg: Bohn, 1786);

Der Küster Christen Ahrendt, in der Gegend von Husum an seinen Pastor, betreffend die Einführung der Speciesmünze in den Herzogthümern Schleswig und Holstein, anonymous (Husum: Küster, 1788);

Politische Correspondenz zwischen dem Küster Ahrendt und dem Verwalter Olufsen insonderheit die Kriegssteuer betreffend, anonymous (Copenhagen: Prof, 1789);

Auch ein Beytrag über die Neue Politick, as Asmus (Hamburg, 1794);

Von und Mit dem ungenannten Verfasser der "Bemerkungen" über des H.O.C.R. und G. S. Callisen Versuch den Werth der Aufklährung unsrer Zeit betreffend (Hamburg: Wörmer, 1796);

Portrait by Friederike Leisching (Collection of the Agricola family, Hamburg)

Urians Nachricht von der neuen Aufklärung, nebst einigen andern Kleinigkeiten, as the Wandsbecker Bothe (Hamburg: Perthes, 1797);

An Frau Rebekka; bey der silbernen Hochzeit, den 15. März 1797 (Hamburg: Meyn, 1797);

Nachricht von der Neuen Aufklärung. Zweite Pause, die Philosophie betreffend, anonymous (Hamburg: Perthes, 1799);

An meinen Sohn H–, anonymous (Hamburg: Perthes, 1799);

Einfältiger Hausvater-Bericht über die christliche Religion an seine Kinder Caroline, Anne, Auguste, Trinette, Johannes, Rebekke, Fritz, Ernst und Franz. Nach der Heiligen Schrift (Hamburg: Perthes, 1804);

An den Naber mith Radt: "Sendschreiben an Sr. Hochgräflichen Excellenz den Herrn Grafen Friedrich von Reventlau, Ritter vom Dannebrog, Geheimen-Rath und Kurator der Universität Kiel." Van enen Holstener, anonymous (Hamburg: Perthes, 1805);

Schreiben eines Dänen an seinen Freund (Altona, 1807);

Das heilige Abendmahl (Hamburg: Perthes, 1809);

Zugabe zu den Sämmtlichen Werken des Wandsbecker Bothen; oder VIII. Theil, as Asmus (Hamburg: Perthes & Besser, 1812);

Predigt eines Laienbruders zu Neujahr 1814 (Lübeck: Michelsen, 1814);

Werke, 4 volumes (Hamburg: Perthes, 1819).

Editions in English: *Claudius; or The Messenger of Wandsbeck, and His Message*, translated anonymously (London: Ward, 1859);

All Good Gifts around Us, translated by Jane M. Campbell (Oxford: Mowbrays, 1977).

OTHER: *Hamburgische Adreß-Comtoir-Nachrichten*, edited by Claudius (1768-1770);

Der Wandsbecker Bothe (title changed in 1773 to *Der Deutsche, sonst Wandsbecker Bothe*), edited by Claudius (Hamburg: Bode, 1771-1775); reprinted, 5 volumes, edited by Karl Heinrich Rengstorf and Hans-Albrecht Koch (Hildesheim & New York: Olms, 1978);

Richard Twist, *Twiß's Reise durch Spanien und Portugal*, translated by Claudius (Leipzig, 1776);

Hessen-Darmstädtische privilegirte Land-Zeitung, edited by Claudius (Darmstadt: Invaliden-Anstalt, 1777); reprinted, edited by Jörg-Ulrich Fechner (Darmstadt: Roether, 1978);

Jean Terrasson, *Geschichte des egyptischen Königs Sethos*, 2 volumes, translated by Claudius (Breslau: Löwe, 1777-1778);

Andrew Michael Ramsay, *Die Reisen des Cyrus, eine moralische Geschichte: Nebst einer Abhandlung über die Mythologie und alte Theologie*, translated by Claudius (Breslau: Löwe, 1780);

Louis Claude de Saint-Martin, *Irrthümer und Wahrheit, oder Rückweiß für die Menschen auf das allgemeine Principium aller Erkenntniß*, translated by Claudius (Breslau: Löwe, 1782);

François Fénelon, *Fénelon's Werke religiösen Inhalts*, 3 volumes, translated by Claudius (Hamburg: Perthes, 1800-1811).

Matthias Claudius was one of the luminaries of the literary revival in Germany during the last third of the eighteenth century. He still occupies a permanent place in German literature as one of its most beloved poets; his position, however, rests on a mere handful of repeatedly anthologized pieces. Those pieces and the resultant stereotype of the author as a gentle singer of universal values such as family, nature, and religion are virtually all that survives the intellectual and sociopolitical upheavals at the end of the eighteenth century and the development of a Romantic, nationalistic literary canon in the nineteenth. While the real Claudius is only now returning to view, it is already clear that his thematic and formal range, his involvement with the issues of the times, and his debt to the Enlightenment were all greater than commonly acknowledged.

Claudius was born on 15 August 1740 in Reinfeld, near Lübeck in present-day Schleswig-Holstein, to Matthias Claudius, a Protestant pastor with pietistic leanings, and Marie Lorck Claudius. He grew up in a large, nurturing family. Upon completion of his classical schooling in 1759 he entered the University of Jena to study theology; but he soon turned to law and public administration, perhaps because of the uncongenial Lutheran orthodoxy and Wolffian rationalism prevalent at the time. The death of his beloved older brother Josias in 1760 led to his first publication, *Ob und wie weit Gott den Tod der Menschen bestimme* (Whether and to What Extent God Determines the Death of Men, 1760), a kind of unsuccessful theodicy in which rationalistic argument ultimately yields to a deeply personal lament and a desperate expression of faith. Possessing little literary merit, the piece nonetheless reflects the conflict between the rational and irrational that became his major concern and literary theme.

As a member of the German Society at the university, Claudius was introduced to modern German letters in the spirit of Johann Jakob Bodmer, Johann Jakob Breitinger, and Friedrich Gottlieb Klopstock. Christian Fürchtegott Gellert and Heinrich Wilhelm von Gerstenberg served as models for his poetic effort, *Tändeleyen und Erzählungen* (Trifles and Tales, 1763), a collection of anacreontic poems and sentimental moral verse narratives. The work was an artistic failure and met with devastating criticism.

Excerpt from a 1773 letter from Claudius to Johann Gottfried Herder (Sammlung Kippenberg, Leipzig)

Little is known of Claudius's activities during the six years that followed the completion of his studies in 1762. Five of them he spent in his parents' home, one (1764-1765) in Copenhagen as secretary to a government official. Although the period produced little more than frustrated efforts to find a congenial position, the year in Copenhagen acquainted him with members of Germany's literary elite, including Gerstenberg and Klopstock, as well as with the ideals of the nascent so-called Germanic Renaissance.

In 1768 Claudius became editor of the *Hamburgische Adreß-Comtoir-Nachrichten* (Hamburg Registry Office News). He channeled his creative energies into the feuilleton, writing fictional letters, short essays, and poems on a wide variety of subjects and in tones ranging from the whimsical to the highly serious. His review of Gotthold Ephraim Lessing's *Minna von Barnhelm* (1767), titled "Korrespondenz zwischen Fritz, seinem Vater und seiner Tante" (Correspondence between Fritz, His Father, and His Aunt), reveals not only his critical insight but also his formal innovativeness and perspectivistic epistemology. He casts his response to the play in a series of

five letters and a fictional introduction that illuminate the work from various complementary points of view. This and other pieces were harbingers of what became a pioneering achievement in German journalism. It was in the *Adreß-Comtoir-Nachrichten*, too, that "Ein Wiegenlied bei Mondschein zu singen" (A Lullaby to Be Sung by Moonlight), one of Claudius's most beloved poems, first appeared. Here motherly love attains the dimensions of a quasi-mythical power that transcends individual, time, and place.

Claudius resigned his position late in 1770 and shortly thereafter moved to the nearby town of Wandsbeck to assume the editorship of *Der Wandsbecker Bothe* (The Wandsbeck Messenger). Between 1771 and 1775 (in 1773 the name was changed to *Der Deutsche, sonst Wandsbecker Bothe* [The German, Formerly Wandsbeck Messenger]) he developed it into one of the most widely respected newspapers in Germany, soliciting pieces for its feuilleton from many of the most prominent writers of the time, including his friends Lessing and Johann Gottfried Herder. The paper became so identified with Claudius that he is still often referred to by its name. His own contributions are even more varied than those in the *Adreß-Comtoir-Nachrichten.*

Soon after moving to Wandsbeck, Claudius had fallen in love with the sixteen-year-old Rebekka Behn. One night in 1772 he invited the local pastor, Klopstock, and others to his home, where he and Rebekka were to entertain them. During the evening he began talking in a light-hearted way about getting married, then suddenly pulled a marriage license and marriage guide from a bag and had the ceremony performed on the spot. In this characteristically waggish fashion began one of the most celebrated marriages and family lives of the day, the deepest source of happiness for Claudius and the inspiration for several of his most intimate works. Claudius's work on the paper and his growing fame led to friendships, notably with Johann Heinrich Voß, and professional contact with most of the leading literary figures of the time. The critical success of the paper did not translate into profit, however; with his prospects growing increasingly dim, Claudius gradually lost interest in his work and finally his position as well.

In an attempt to alleviate his financial plight Claudius in 1775 published *Asmus omnia sua secum portans oder Sämmtliche Werke des Wandsbecker Bothen, I. und II. Theil* (Asmus Carrying All His Things; or, Collected Works of the Wandsbeck Messenger, Parts I and II). Assembled in one volume, Claudius's contributions create an even more variegated impression than they did in the newspapers. Greater, too, on the other hand, is the unity provided by the fictitious circle of friends and acquaintances in which they are framed. Dominated by the perceptive but whimsical and often ingenuous Asmus, his better-informed and more disciplined (unnamed) cousin, and their naive but soulful friend Andres, this device allows for a perspectivistic treatment of many issues. The most important of the lyrics center around the themes of motherly love and death. In "Der Tod und das Mädchen" (Death and the Maiden) a friendly grim reaper figure, Freund Hein–a name for death that Claudius contributed to the German language–embodies the stark terror as well as the eternal peace and possible salvation Claudius associated with death. The narrative "Eine Chria" (A Treatise) satirizes the attempt of school philosophy to rationalize all existence, asserting the intuitive nature of religious experience, while "Über das Genie" (On Genius) fancifully discloses an equally intuitive, pre-Romantic view of artistic cre-

ativity. In "Eine Disputation zwischen den Herren W. und X. und einem Fremden über Herrn Pastor Alberti 'Anleitung zum Gespräch über die Religion' und über Herrn Pastor Goeze 'Text am 5ten Sonntage nach Epiphanias' unter Vorsitz des Herrn Lars Hochedeln" (A Disputation between Mr. W. and Mr. X. and a Stranger on Pastor Alberti's "Introduction to Dialogue on Religion" and on Pastor Goeze's "Text for the Fifth Sunday after Epiphany"), which also was published separately in 1772, Claudius responds to a contemporary quarrel between conservative and liberal religious parties in Hamburg with a seriocomic plea for tolerance.

In 1776 Claudius moved to Darmstadt to assume a well-paid government position on a commission to raise the standard of rural life and the editorship of another newspaper, the *Hessen-Darmstädtische privilegirte Land-Zeitung* (Hesse-Darmstadt Privileged Country Newspaper). This attempt to gain financial security, however, proved futile. After he returned to Wandsbeck in 1777 Claudius's life became increasingly private. He nonetheless remained actively engaged with the world beyond in his collected works, the third part of which appeared in 1778. The most memorable of the poems in this volume include the convivial "Rheinweinlied" (Rhine-Wine Song) and the vibrant song of thanks "Täglich zu singen" (To Be Sung Daily). Claudius criticizes abuse of power and alludes to the subjectivity of language in "Wächter und Bürgermeister" (The Watchman and the Burgomaster), one of many pieces in which he regenerates the verse narrative and fable for purposes of topical commentary. His skeptical but conciliatory assessment of Johann Caspar Lavater's *Physiognomische Fragmente zur Beförderung der Menschenkenntnis und Menschenliebe* (Physiognomic Fragments toward the Advancement of Knowledge of Human Nature and Love of Mankind, 1775-1778) was a unique treatment of the review. The centerpiece of the volume and an equally unique variation on the travel book is "Nachricht von meiner Audienz beim Kaiser von Japan" (Report on My Audience with the Emperor of Japan). Utilizing a nonsensical Japanese complete with translation, Claudius reflects with whimsical earnestness on the intuitive and inspired nature of poesy, the superiority of revealed religion over its enlightened counterpart, and divine-right patriarchy as a sociopolitical ideal.

For the next few years Claudius sought to augment his income through tutoring and transla-

Engraving by Daniel Chodowiecki illustrating the collected works of "Asmus"

tally and physically ill to symbolize the literal godforsakenness of the human condition. The focal point of the volume is the narrative "Paul Erdmanns Fest" (Paul Erdmann's Jubilee), Claudius's definitive belletristic statement on society and politics, in which a farmer's celebration of his tenancy serves as the framework for a utopian affirmation of divine-right paternalism and its contemporary equivalent, enlightened despotism.

During the 1780s friends and benefactors continually assisted Claudius with gifts of money. The financial worries of the then ten-member family ended only in 1788, when Crown Prince Frederick of Denmark mediated Claudius's appointment as a bank official, a virtual sinecure. Throughout the 1780s and 1790s Claudius's relations with the increasingly rationalistic Herder and Voß gradually deteriorated, while those with Friedrich Heinrich Jacobi, Friedrich Leopold zu Stolberg, and conservative circles in Holstein and Westphalia became ever warmer. These developments are often said to reflect growing narrowness in Claudius's character and outlook. In actuality, they signify no fundamental change of view on his part but attest to the radicalization of the Enlightenment, the aestheticism of Weimar classicism (which formed a stark contrast to Claudius's functional concept of literature), and the outbreak and consequences of the French Revolution. Such phenomena seemed to call for more explicit formulations and more emphatic assertion of long-held convictions.

If Claudius's beliefs did not change, his collected works did. With Part Five (1790) one notices an increasing preponderance of prose; a preoccupation with religion, politics, and poetics; and a greater seriousness of tone and argumentativeness of style. One of the major pieces is "Zwey Recensionen etc. in Sachen der Herren Leßing, M. Mendelssohn und Jacobi" (Two Reviews, Etc., in the Matter of Messers Lessing, M. Mendelssohn, and Jacobi), which had been published separately in 1786, in which Claudius responds to the current controversy surrounding Lessing's alleged Spinozism by seeking to reconcile the principals and their views. In the other piece, *Von und Mit dem ungenannten Verfasser der "Bemerkungen" über des H.O.C.R. und G.S. Callisen Versuch den Werth der Aufklährung unsrer Zeit betreffend* (By and with the Unnamed Author of the "Remarks" on the Inquiry of H.O.C.R. and G. S. Callisen Concerning the Value of the Enlightenment of Our Time), published as a supple-

tion. His situation was still precarious in 1783, when Part Four of the collected works appeared. This volume is particularly rich in poetry. The ever-popular "Ein Lied hinterm Ofen zu singen" (A Song to Be Sung behind the Stove) neutralizes nature's power over man through a comic-ironic diminution of a personification of winter, while "Kriegslied" (Song of War) indicts the principals in the War of the Bavarian Succession. In "Abendlied" (Evening Song), his most famous poem, Claudius suggests faith and contemplation of nature as means of overcoming isolation from God. In "Der Mensch" (Man), on the other hand, he portrays the contradictoriness and senselessness of existence in isolation from God. And in the tale "Der Besuch im St. Hiob zu **" (The Visit to St. Job in **) he uses a hospital for the men-

ment to Part Five in 1796, he supports a beleaguered church official with a defense of revealed religion against the absolutism of reason. Part Six (1798) continued in much the same topical vein. "Auch ein Beytrag über die Neue Politick" (Another Contribution on the New Political System), also published separately in 1794, represents Claudius's lengthiest and most detailed critique of democracy and apology for patriarchy. "Eine Fabel" calls for abolishment of the much-abused freedom of the press, while "Urians Nachricht von der neuen Aufklärung" (Urian's Report on the New Enlightenment), published separately in 1797, parodies rationalism in politics and religion. At the same time the volume includes two of Claudius's best and most moving poems, "Christiane" and "Der Tod" (Death), written following the death of his second daughter, Christiane.

Part Seven of the collected works (1803) opens with "Eine asiatische Vorlesung" (A Lecture on Asia), a lengthy essay on the fundamental similarity and truth of all religions. Translations from the religious writings of Francis Bacon and Sir Isaac Newton are designed to lend the weight of philosophy and science to the cause of religion. In "Till, der Holzhacker" (Till, the Woodcutter) Claudius presents a highly imaginative travesty of rationalist philosophical method. And in "Einfältiger Hausvater-Bericht über die christliche Religion" (Simple Report of a Paterfamilias on the Christian Religion), published separately in 1804, he bequeaths a moral and religious legacy to his children and readers. This volume, too, shows the lyric poet at his best: "Die Sternseherin Lise" (The Stargazer Lisa) expresses the power of nature to bring man closer to God by strengthening his faith.

Although Part Seven was intended to be the last, Claudius published an eighth part in 1812 under the title *Zugabe zu den Sämmtlichen Werken des Wandsbecker Bothen* (Supplement to the Collected Works of the Wandsbeck Messenger). It contains primarily treatments of various aspects of Christianity such as the Eucharist and conscience, some in essay or sermon form, others in the more informal, pastoral "Briefe an Andres" (Letters to Andres). During his later years Claudius published many pieces that never found their way into the collected works: on a war tax in 1789, on Goethe and Schiller in the 1790s ("Kleinigkeiten," included in "Urians Nachricht von der neuen Aufklärung"), and on the English invasion of Denmark in 1807 (*Schreiben eines*

Claudius in 1804; oil painting by an unknown artist (Museum für Hamburgische Geschichte, Hamburg)

Dänen an seinen Freund [Letter of a Dane to His Friend]). "Bei ihrem Grabe" (At Her Grave), also written on the death of his daughter Christiane, is the best of the poems.

While exponents of the Enlightenment and Classicism roundly criticized Claudius, the Romantics hailed him as a spiritual father. Indeed, he had always appealed to a broad spectrum of readers, his home eventually becoming a place of pilgrimage. Some of his visitors were bothersome sightseers; he once led such an individual in silence to the cow behind his house and, brandishing his cap symbolically, wreaked havoc among the flies on its hide to suggest to the visitor that he was a pest. Always something of a rogue, Claudius nonetheless withdrew intellectually from the deeply disturbing march of events and ideas beyond Wandsbeck. And in 1813 he literally withdrew before the armies of the Napoleonic Wars, wandering for almost a year from friend to relative. He never recovered from the physical and spiritual rigors of the journey and died in Hamburg within a year of his return home, on 21 January 1815, at the age of seventy-four.

Letters:

Matthias Claudius: Briefe an Freunde, edited by Hans Jessen (Berlin: Eckart, 1938); revised as *Botengänge: Briefe an Freunde* (Witten & Berlin: Eckart, 1965);

Matthias Claudius und die Seinen: Briefe, edited by Jessen and Ernst Schröder (Berlin: Eckart, 1940);

Matthias Claudius schreibt an die Seinen: Familienbriefe, edited by Hans Jürgen Schultz (Witten & Berlin: Eckart, 1955).

Bibliographies:

Carl Christian Redlich, *Die poetischen Beiträge zum Wandsbecker Bothen, gesammelt und ihren Verfassern zugewiesen* (Hamburg: Meissner, 1871);

Karl Goedeke, *Grundriß zur Geschichte der deutschen Dichtung aus den Quellen*, third edition (Dresden: Ehlermann, 1916), volume 4, part 1, pp. 973-983;

Christel Matthias Schröder, "Alte und neue Matthias-Claudius-Literatur," *Protestantenblatt*, 74 (1941): 153-156.

Biographies:

Wilhelm Herbst, *Matthias Claudius der Wandsbecker Bote: Ein deutsches Stillleben*, third edition (Gotha: Perthes, 1863); fourth edition (Gotha: Perthes, 1878);

Urban Roedl, *Matthias Claudius: Sein Weg und seine Welt*, third edition (Hamburg: Wittig, 1969).

References:

Peter Berglar, *Matthias Claudius in Selbstzeugnissen und Bilddokumenten* (Reinbek bei Hamburg: Rowohlt, 1972);

Jörg-Ulrich Fechner, "Literatur als praktische Ethik: Das Beispiel des 'Wandsbecker Bothen' von Matthias Claudius," *Aufklärung und Pietismus im dänischen Gesamtstaat 1770-1820*, edited by Hartmut Lehmann and Dieter Lohmeier (Neumünster: Wachholtz, 1983) 217-230;

Fechner, "Matthias Claudius' 'Neujahrswunsch'– 'Des alten lahmen Invaliden sein Neujahrswunsch': Literarischer Text und mediale Vermittlung," in *Festgabe für Paul Gerhard Klussmann zum 25. Februar 1983*, edited by Jutta Kolkenbrock-Netz and others (Bochum: Ruhr Universität, 1983), pp. 97-113;

Fechner, "Matthias Claudius und die Literatursoziologie?: Überlegungen und unvollständige Anmerkungen zum Abschiedsbrief des Adreßcomptoir-nachrichtenschreibers," in *Geist und Zeichen: Festschrift für Arthur Henkel, edited by Herbert Anton, Bernhard Gajek, and Peter Pfaff (Heidelberg: Winter, 1977), pp. 57-74;

Fechner, "Nachwort," in *Hessen-Darmstädtische priviligirte Land-Zeitung 1777: Faksimileausgabe des von Matthias Claudius redigierten Teils und Nachlesse aus dem ersten Jahrgang 1777* (Darmstadt: Roether, 1978), pp. 217-282;

Reinhard Görisch, "Das 'Abendlied' von Matthias Claudius im Kirchengesangbuch: Skizze einer zwiespältigen Karriere," *Jahrbuch der Deutschen Schillergesellschaft*, 26 (1982): 125-143;

Görisch, *Matthias Claudius und der Sturm und Drang: Ein Abgrenzungsversuch. Vergleiche mit Goethe, Herder, Lenz, Schubart und anderen am Beispiel eschatologischer Vorstellungen im Kontext des Epochenbewußtseins* (Frankfurt am Main: Lang, 1981);

G. L. Jones, "The Worldly Christian: Matthias Claudius as a Critic of His Time," *Modern Language Review*, 71 (October 1976): 827-837;

Hans-Albrecht Koch, "Matthias Claudius und die Kinder: Mit einem Anhang: Unbekannte Briefe von Matthias Claudius," *Wolfenbüttler Studien zur Aufklärung*, 3 (1976): 227-257;

Koch, "Matthias Claudius und Hamburg: Eine Skizze. Mit unveröffentlichten Quellen," *Zeitschrift des Vereins für Hamburgische Geschichte*, 63 (1977): 181-204;

Koch and Rolf Siebke, "Unbekannte Briefe und Texte von Matthias Claudius nebst einigen Bemerkungen zur Claudius-Forschung," *Jahrbuch des Freien Deutschen Hochstifts* (1972): 1-35;

Burghard König, *Matthias Claudius: Die literarischen Beziehungen im Leben und Werk* (Bonn: Bouvier, 1976);

Annelen Kranefuss, *Die Gedichte des Wandsbeker Boten* (Göttingen: Vandenhoeck & Ruprecht, 1973);

Friedrich Loofs, *Matthias Claudius in kirchengeschichtlicher Beleuchtung: Eine Untersuchung über Claudius' religiöse Stellung und Altersentwicklung* (Gotha: Perthes, 1915);

Johannes Pfeiffer, *Matthias Claudius der Wandsbekker Bote: Eine Einführung in den Sinn seines Schaffens* (Dessau & Leipzig: Rauch, 1940);

Karl Heinrich Rengstorf, "Der Wandsbecker Bote: Matthias Claudius als Anwalt der Humanität," *Wolfenbüttler Studien zur Aufklärung*, 3 (1976): 195-226;

Herbert Rowland, "Eichendorff's Critical View of Matthias Claudius in *Der deutsche Roman des 18. Jahrhunderts*," *Michigan Germanic Studies*, 11 (1985): 50-61;

Rowland, *Matthias Claudius* (Boston: Twayne, 1983);

Rowland, "Matthias Claudius and C. M. Wieland," *Christoph Martin Wieland: North American Scholarly Contributions on the Occasion of the 250th Anniversary of His Birth*, edited by Hansjörg Schelle (Tübingen: Niemeyer, 1984), pp. 181-194;

Rowland, "Matthias Claudius's 'Paul Erdmanns Fest' and the Utopian Tradition," *Seminar*, 18 (February 1982): 15-26;

Rowland, "Topical Conservatism and Formal Radicality: The Fables and Verse Narratives of Matthias Claudius," *Lessing Yearbook*, 18 (1986): 151-177;

Georg-Michael Schulz, "Matthias Claudius' 'Abendlied': Kreatürlichkeit und Aufklärungskritik," *Deutsche Vierteljahrsschrift für Literaturwissenschaft und Geistesgeschichte*, 53 (June 1979): 233-250;

Rolf Siebke, "Arthur Schopenhauer und Matthias Claudius," *Schopenhauer-Jahrbuch*, 51 (1970): 22-31;

Siebke, "Nachwort," in Claudius's *Sämtliche Werke*, sixth edition (Munich: Winkler, 1987), pp. 973-989;

Wolfgang Stammler, *Matthias Claudius der Wandsbecker Bothe: Ein Beitrag zur deutschen Literatur- und Geistesgeschichte* (Halle: Waisenhaus, 1915).

Papers:

Matthias Claudius destroyed all of his manuscripts and requested that his letters either be burned or returned for burning. Much of what remained was destroyed during World War II. While the extant letters are scattered throughout Germany and beyond, the Staats- und Universitätsbibliothek Hamburg and the Schleswig-Holsteinische Landesbibliothek Kiel, hold the largest individual collections, including letters from and to Claudius and a few members of his family.

Johann Joachim Eschenburg

(7 December 1743 - 29 February 1820)

Mark R. McCulloh
Davidson College

BOOKS: *Zwey Oden an Herrn Johann Henrich Herold* (Hamburg: Piscator, 1762);

Theodorus an seinen Vater Clemens: Eine Heroide (Leipzig: Böger, 1765);

Comala: Ein dramatisches Gedicht (N.p., 1769);

An die kleine musikalische Familie des Herrn Schroeter (Brunswick, 1771);

Die Wahl des Herkules: Ein dramatisches Gedicht (Brunswick, 1773);

Am Sarge meiner früh vollendeten Tochter Johanna Elisabeth: Geboren den 16. Januar 1780, Gestorben den 1. Oktober 1781 (N.p., 1781);

Grundzüge der griechischen und römischen Fabelgeschichte zum Gebrauch bey Vorlesungen (Berlin & Stettin: Nicolai, 1783; revised, 1787);

Handbuch der klassischen Litteratur, Alterthumskunde und Mythologie (Berlin & Stettin: Nicolai, 1783); revised and enlarged as *Handbuch der klassischen Literatur, enthaltend: I. Archäologie; II. Notiz der Klassiker; III. Mythologie; IV. Griech. Alterthümer; V. Römische Alterthümer* (Berlin & Stettin: Nicolai, 1792); revised and enlarged as *Handbuch der klassischen Literatur, enthaltend I. Archäologie; II. Kunde der Klassiker; III. Mythologie; IV. Griech. Alterthümer; V. Römische Alterthümer* (Berlin & Stettin: Nicolai, 1801; revised and enlarged, 1808); translated by Nathan Welby Fiske as *Manual of Classical Literature: From the German of J. J. Eschenburg, with Additions* (Philadelphia: Key & Biddle, 1836);

Entwurf einer Theorie und Litteratur der schönen Wissenschaften: Zur Grundlage bey Vorlesungen (Berlin & Stettin: Nicolai, 1783; revised, 1789); revised and enlarged as *Entwurf einer Theorie und Litteratur der schönen Redekünste: Zur Grundlage bey Vorlesungen* (Berlin & Stettin: Nicolai, 1805; revised and enlarged, 1817); first edition reprinted (Hildesheim & New York: Olms, 1976);

An den Herrn Hofrath von Blum beim Tode seiner verlobten Braut, der Demoiselle Katharine Friederici im November 1784 (N.p., 1784);

Johann Joachim Eschenburg (oil painting by Friedrich Georg Weitsch, 1801; Städtisches Museum, Brunswick)

Motetten zur Begräbnissfeyer des Höchstseligen Durchlauchtigsten Herzogs Friedrich von Mecklenburg-Schwerin (Schwerin: Bärensprung, 1785);

Hygiea: Seiner hochfürstlichen Durchlaucht dem Herzog Ferdinand zu Braunschweig und Lüneburg den XII. Januar MDCCLXXXVII unterthänigst überreicht (N.p., 1787);

Ueber William Shakespeare (Zurich: Orell, Geßner, Füßli, 1787);

Ueber Johann Friedrich Wilhelm Jerusalem (Berlin: Vieweg, 1791);

Lehrbuch der Wissenschaftskunde: Ein Grundriß encyklopädischer Vorlesungen (Berlin & Stettin: Nicolai, 1792; revised and enlarged, 1800; revised and enlarged, 1809);

Der achtzigsten Geburtstagsfeier Ihrer Königlichen Hoheit der Frau Herzogin Mutter zu Braunschweig und Lüneburg: Den 13. März 1796 (Brunswick: Meyer, 1796);

Ueber den vorgeblichen Fund Shakespearischer Handschriften (Leipzig: Sommer, 1797);

Entwurf einer Geschichte des Collegii Carolini in Braunschweig (Berlin & Stettin: Nicolai, 1812; reprinted, 2 volumes, edited by Ernst-Eberhard Wilberg, Brunswick: Braunschweigischer Hochschulbund, 1974).

OTHER: *Der Primaner,* edited by Eschenburg (Hamburg: Bock, 1761);

Marie Leprince de Beaumont, *Briefe der Emerentia an Lucien von der Frau von Beaumont,* 2 volumes, translated by Eschenburg (Leipzig: Weidmann, 1766);

Unterhaltungen, 4 volumes, edited by Eschenburg (Hamburg: Bock, 1766-1767);

Marie Justine Benoîte Duronceray Favart, *Lucas und Hannchen: Eine Operette,* translated by Eschenburg (Brunswick: Waisenhaus, 1768);

John Brown, *Betrachtungen über die Poesie und Musik, nach ihrem Ursprunge, ihrer Vereinigung, Gewalt, Wachsthum, Trennung und Verderbniß: Aus dem Englischen. Mit Anmerkungen und zween Anhängen begleitet,* translated with annotations by Eschenburg (Leipzig: Weidmann & Reich, 1769);

Pierre-Alexandre Monsigny, *Der Deserteur: Eine Operette. Aus dem Französischen des M. J. Sedaine,* translated by Eschenburg (Mannheim: Schwan, 1771);

Elizabeth Montagu, *Versuch über Shakespears Genie und Schriften in Vergleichung mit den dramatischen Dichtern der Griechen und Franzosen: Aus dem Englischen übersetzt und mit einem doppelten Anhange begleitet,* translated with appendixes by Eschenburg (Leipzig: Schwickert, 1771);

Daniel Webb, *Betrachtungen über die Verwandtschaft der Poesie und Musik, nebst einem Auszuge aus den Anmerkungen über die Schönheiten der Poesie: Aus dem Englischen,* translated by Eschenburg (Leipzig: Schwickert, 1771);

George Frideric Handel, *Judas Makkabäus: Ein musikalisches Gedicht,* translated by Eschenburg (Brunswick: Waisenhaus, 1772);

Richard Hurd, *Horazens Episteln an die Pisonen und an den Augustus: Aus dem Englischen übersetzt und mit eigenen Anmerkungen begleitet,* 2 volumes, translated with annotations by Eschenburg (Leipzig: Schwickert, 1772);

François André Danican Philidor, *Der Holzhauer oder Die Drey Wünsche: Eine komische Oper in einem Aufzuge,* translated by Eschenburg (Berlin: Himburg, 1772);

Daniel Schiebeler, *Auserlesene Gedichte,* edited by Eschenburg (Hamburg: Bode, 1773);

Norberto Caimo, *Briefe eines Italiäners über eine im Jahre 1755 angestellte Reise nach Spanien: Aus der französischen Übersetzung des P. Livoy,* translated by Eschenburg (Leipzig: Schwickert, 1774);

Charles Avison, *Versuch über den musikalischen Ausdruck,* translated by Eschenburg (Leipzig: Schwickert, 1775);

William Shakespeare, *Schauspiele,* 13 volumes, translated and edited by Eschenburg (Zurich: Orell, Geßner, Füßli, 1775-1782; revised, 1798-1806);

Pietro Alessandro Guglielmi, *Robert und Kalliste oder Triumph der Treue: Eine Operette in drei Aufzügen,* translated by Eschenburg (Breslau & Leipzig, 1776);

Voltaire, *Zaïre: Trauerspiel. Neue Übersetzung in Iamben,* translated by Eschenburg (Leipzig: Schwickert, 1776);

Balladen und Lieder altenglischer und altschottischer Dichtart, translated by Eschenburg and others as August Friedrich Ursinus (Berlin: Himburg, 1777);

André Ernest Modeste Grétry, *Erast und Lucinde: Eine Operette in einem Aufzuge. Nach dem Silvain des Herrn Marmontel,* revised by Eschenburg (Münster: Perron, 1777);

Brittisches Museum für die Deutschen, 6 volumes, edited by Eschenburg (Leipzig: Weygand, 1777-1780);

Burkard Waldis, *Auswahl einiger Fabeln und Erzählungen: Mit kurzen Spracherklärungen,* edited by Eschenburg (Brunswick: Waisenhaus, 1777);

Niccolò Piccini, *Das gute Mädchen: Operette in drei Aufzügen. Nach dem Italienischen,* translated by Eschenburg (Leipzig: Schneider, 1778);

Friedrich Wilhelm Zachariä, *Fabeln und Erzählungen in Burkard Waldis Manier: Neue Ausgabe mit einem Anhang von ausgewählten Original-Fabeln des Waldis, und dazu nöthigen Spracherklärungen begleitet,* edited by Eschenburg (Reutlingen: Fleischauer, 1778);

Auserlesene Stücke der besten deutschen Dichter: von Martin Opitz bis auf gegenwärtige Zeiten, edited by Eschenburg and Zachariä (Brunswick: Waisenhaus, 1778):

Joseph Priestley, *Vorlesungen über Redekunst und Kritik*, translated by Eschenburg (Leipzig: Schwickert, 1779);

Charles Burney, *Abhandlung über die Musik der Alten*, translated by Eschenburg (Leipzig: Schwickert, 1781);

Annalen der Brittischen Litteratur vom Jahr 1780, edited by Eschenburg (Leipzig: Weygand, 1781);

Zachariä, *Hinterlassene Schriften*, edited by Eschenburg (Brunswick: Waisenhaus, 1781);

William Hay, *Religion des Philosophen oder Erläuterung der Grundsätze der Sittenlehre und des Christenthums aus Betrachtung der Welt, und der Lage des Menschen in derselben*, translated by Eschenburg (Brunswick: Waisenhaus, 1782);

Burney, *Nachricht von Georg Friedrich Händel's Lebensumständen und der ihm zu London im Mai und Juni 1784 angestellten Gedächtnissfeyer*, translated by Eschenburg (Berlin & Stettin: Nicolai, 1785);

Beispielsammlung zur Theorie und Literatur der schönen Wissenschaften, 9 volumes, edited by Eschenburg (Berlin & Stettin: Nicolai, 1788-1795);

Braunschweigisches Magazin, bestehend aus wöchentlichen gemeinnützigen Beilagen zu ... Braunschweigischen Anzeigen ..., 33 volumes, edited by Eschenburg (Brunswick: Fürstl. Intelligenzkomtoir, 1788-1820);

Gotthold Ephraim Lessing, *Kollektaneen zur Literatur*, 2 volumes, edited by Eschenburg (Berlin: Voß, 1790);

Lessing, *Leben des Sophokles*, edited by Eschenburg (Berlin: Voß, 1790);

Pasquale Anfossi, *Die Eifersucht auf der Probe*, translated by Eschenburg (Gera: Rothe, 1791);

Lessing, *Sämmtliche Schriften: Teile 5-30*, 26 volumes, edited by Eschenburg, Karl Gotthelf Lessing, and Friedrich Nicolai (Berlin: Voß, 1791-1794);

Friedrich Rambach, *Theseus auf Kreta: Ein lyrisches Drama*, foreword by Eschenburg (Leipzig: Barth, 1791);

Edward Gibbon, *Versuch über das Studium der Litteratur*, translated by Eschenburg (Hamburg: Herold, 1792);

Dramatische Bibliothek: Eine charakteristische und mit Proben ihrer Schauspiele begleitete Anzeige der vorzüglichsten dramatischen Dichter älterer und neuerer Zeit, edited by Eschenburg (Berlin & Stettin: Nicolai, 1793);

Johann Arnold Ebert, *Episteln und vermischte Gedichte: 2. Theil. Mit einem Grundrisse seines Le-*

bens und Charakters, edited by Eschenburg (Hamburg: Bohn, 1795);

Gabriel Sénac de Meilhan, *Vermischte Werke: Aus dem Französischen*, 2 volumes, translated by Eschenburg (Hamburg: Hoffmann, 1795);

Freiherr Kaspar van Voght, *Über Hamburgs Armenwesen*, translated by Eschenburg (Brunswick & Hamburg: Herold, 1796);

Gottfried August Bürger, *Lenore: Ballade. In drei englischen Übersetzungen*, edited by Eschenburg (Göttingen: Dieterich, 1797);

Shakespeare (attributed), *Leben und Tod Thomas Cromwell's*, translated by Eschenburg (Zurich: Orell, Füßli, 1798);

Shakespeare (attributed), *Der Londoner Verschwender*, translated by Eschenburg (Zurich: Orell, Füßli, 1798);

Shakespeare (attributed), *Ein Trauerspiel in Yorkshire*, translated by Eschenburg (Zurich: Orell, Füßli, 1798);

Denkmäler altdeutscher Dichtkunst, edited by Eschenburg (Bremen: Wilmans, 1799);

Alexander Pope, *Eloisa an Abelard: Frey übersetzt*, translated by Eschenburg and Bürger (Vienna: Sammer, 1799);

Friedrich Reinhard Ricklefs, *Neues vollständiges Taschenwörterbuch der englischen und deutschen Sprache enthaltend alle Gebräuchlichen Worte und Termen der Künste und Wissenschaften aus den besten englischen und deutschen Wörterbüchern zusammengetragen*, 2 volumes, foreword by Eschenburg (Bremen: Wilmans, 1799-1800);

Friedrich von Hagedorn, *Poetische Werke*, 5 volumes, edited by Eschenburg (Hamburg: Bohn, 1800);

Pope, *Versuch über die Kritik: Aus dem Englischen metrisch verdeutscht*, translated by Eschenburg (Vienna: Sauner, 1801);

Henry Fuseli, *Vorlesungen über die Malerei*, translated by Eschenburg (Brunswick: Vieweg, 1803);

Karl Philipp Moritz, *Vorlesungen über den Styl oder Praktische Anweisung zu einer guten Schreibart mit Beispielen aus den vorzüglichsten Schriftstellern: Neue Ausgabe*, edited by Eschenburg (Brunswick: Vieweg, 1808);

Ulrich Boner, *Edelstein in hundert Fabeln*, edited by Eschenburg (Berlin: Unger, 1810).

Johann Joachim Eschenburg was one of the foremost literary historians and aestheticians of the Age of Goethe. Although many of the issues ardently debated by Eschenburg and his contemporaries are no longer seriously discussed in aesthetics, his influence has been lasting in the elevation of Shakespeare to a prominent position in German dramaturgy. Eschenburg's sympathetic analysis of Shakespeare's appeal as a dramatist, promulgated in the 1780s, continued the critical work begun by Gotthold Ephraim Lessing in 1759 and helped establish a permanent and indispensable place for Shakespeare on the German stage. Aside from his esteemed classical scholarship and his ground-breaking work as a collector of German and world literature, Eschenburg's most notable achievement is the first complete German translation of Shakespeare (1775-1782), a thirteen-volume edition that was influential for years after its publication. The better-known translation by August Wilhelm Schlegel, Dorothea Tieck, and Wolf Heinrich von Baudissin (the "Schlegel-Tieck translation," 1797-1833) owes much to Eschenburg's work.

Eschenburg was born in Hamburg on 7 December 1743, the third child and first son of Aletta Elisabeth Prehn and Nikolaus Jakob Eschenburg. He received his early preparatory education at Hamburg's Johanneum from 1753 to 1762, transferred to the Academic Gymnasium, and entered the University of Leipzig in 1764. At Leipzig Eschenburg studied under the philologist Johann August Ernesti and the scholar and writer Christian Fürchtegott Gellert; he met Goethe, a fellow student, in 1765. He also made the acquaintance of Christian Felix Weisse, editor of the popular journal *Bibliothek der schönen Wissenschaften und Künste*. In 1767 Eschenburg moved to the University of Göttingen, where he attended the lectures of the well-known philologist Christian Gottlob Heyne and the prominent theologian Johann David Michaelis. Eschenburg's studies were, however, on a precarious financial footing. His father, a linen merchant, had declared bankruptcy in 1765 because of the privations of the Seven Years' War. When Eschenburg's funds were exhausted the young scholar was left to his own resources. Eager to avoid taking a nonacademic job, Eschenburg struggled to finish his studies and complete his examinations at Göttingen. His friend Karl Wilhelm Jerusalem, whom he had met at Leipzig, arranged a teaching position for him at the Collegium Carolinum in Brunswick, and Eschenburg soon began lecturing in classical philology, art history, and aesthetic theory. In addition to his pedagogical duties he worked on the editorial staff of the *Braunschweiger Anzeigen*. At the Carolinum he developed impor-

tant associations with sons of well-to-do families, including many young Englishmen whom he tutored in German. By 1772 he had published several translations from the English, among them Elizabeth Montagu's 1769 essay on Shakespeare, translated as *Versuch über Shakespears Genie und Schriften* (1771), and Daniel Webb's *Observations on the Correspondence between Poetry and Music* (1769, translated 1771). He was in the midst of preparing his first translations of Shakespeare's plays, beginning with *The Tempest*.

In 1773 Eschenburg was given the title of professor at the Carolinum, and his career seemed assured. In 1777 he was named full professor, succeeding the deceased Friedrich Wilhelm Zachariä in the chair of literature and philosophy. On 19 October of that year he married Maria Dorothea Schmid, the daughter of his colleague, the philologist Konrad Arnold Schmid.

Eschenburg's own artistic efforts, mainly operetta librettos and dramatic poems, had little success. His translations from the French, notably Michel Jean Sedaine's libretto of Pierre-Alexandre Monsigny's comic opera *Der Deserteur* (The Deserter, 1771) and Voltaire's tragedy *Zaïre* (1776), were, likewise, little noted. More important was the ambitious translation and critical writing Eschenburg began when he decided to revise Christoph Martin Wieland's incomplete translation of Shakespeare and to complete the whole dramatic corpus. In time he revised the ten plays Wieland had already translated and added twelve more, all of which, save *Richard III*, were in prose rather than verse. The first edition appeared in thirteen volumes between 1775 and 1782. Its popularity led to the unauthorized "Mannheim edition," published in 1782, and to an official second edition of twelve volumes (1798-1806). The eight-volume Schlegel-Tieck Shakespeare began appearing in 1797, however, and quickly surpassed the Eschenburg translation: it resolved virtually all questions of accuracy, consistently maintained iambic pentameter, and conveyed Shakespeare's genius more faithfully. Eschenburg's industriousness was not matched by his genius. Still, Eschenburg's work exerted considerable influence on the Schlegel-Tieck translation. Moreover, Eschenburg's treatise on the strengths and flaws of the great English dramatist, *Ueber William Shakespeare* (1787), was highly regarded in its time and is still considered insightful criticism.

Eschenburg's first significant original scholarly works were the product of years of research in connection with his teaching at the Collegium.

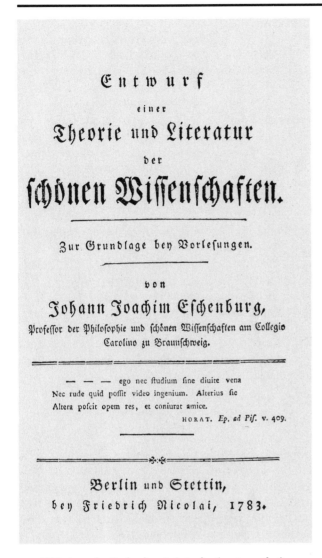

Title page for Eschenburg's introduction to aesthetics

In 1783 he published the internationally respected *Handbuch der klassischen Litteratur, Alterthumskunde und Mythologie* (Manual of Classical Literature, Ancient Science, and Mythology; translated as *Manual of Classical Literature*, 1836). Also in 1783 appeared his *Entwurf einer Theorie und Litteratur der schönen Wissenschaften* (Outline of a Theory and Bibliography of Literature), a guide to belles lettres that was renamed *Entwurf einer Theorie und Litteratur der schönen Redekünste* (Outline of a Theory and Bibliography of the Rhetorical Arts) with the 1805 edition. The book won general approval as a well-written introduction to aesthetics, received the praise of Johann Gottfried Herder, and was republished in five editions as well as in French and Dutch translations. While Lessing's stamp is to be found on many of Eschenburg's ideas, his aesthetic principles, as

Bruno Markwardt has pointed out, owe much to Johann Georg Sulzer, whose ambitious system of aesthetics, *Allgemeine Theorie der schönen Künste und Wissenschaften* (General Theory of the Fine Arts and Sciences, 1771-1774), was a dominant influence during the 1770s. Eschenburg saw the essential aim of art as "die Bewegung und Lenkung des Herzens" (the moving and guiding of the heart). Such beneficial effects of art were considered to be as important for the artist as for the beholder, if not more so. Eschenburg embraced the related idea, propounded by Germany's first modern aesthetician, Alexander Gottlieb Baumgarten, that poetry's purpose is to touch and delight the senses and fantasy so as to lead one to the highest degree of purposeful sensual power. Such a view of the moral impact of aesthetic experience is clearly akin to what Lessing had in mind for the German stage; indeed, Eschenburg considered Lessing the finest modern German writer. In the nine-volume *Beispielsammlung zur Theorie und Literatur der schönen Wissenschaften* (Collection of Examples for the Theory and Bibliography of Literature, 1788-1795), in which Eschenburg provided selections of the greatest literature of the ages according to his criteria, Lessing and some now-forgotten writers are quoted at length, while Goethe and Friedrich Schiller warrant barely thirty pages. Nonetheless, the anthology, like so many of Eschenburg's collections—for example, his *Dramatische Bibliothek* (Library of Drama, 1793)—was destined to become a standard work in German-speaking Europe; it was even translated into French in 1813. All the while Eschenburg continued to familiarize the German reading public with British literature by publishing translations such as the 1777 anthology *Balladen und Lieder altenglischer und altschottischer Dichtart* (Old English and Old Scottish Ballads and Songs) and the periodical *Brittisches Museum für die Deutschen* (British Museum for the Germans, 1777-1780).

Eschenburg was an untiring editor who produced contemporary collections as well as some of the first modern editions of older German literature. Among the former were editions of the works of his friends Zachariä (1781) and Johann Arnold Ebert (1795); Lessing's literary remains (1790); and part of an excellent edition of Lessing's collected works in twenty-six volumes (1791-1794), which he coedited with Lessing's brother, Karl, and Friedrich Nicolai. The latter category, which distinguishes Eschenburg as one of the founders of the field of Germanic studies, includes *Denkmäler altdeutscher Dichtkunst* (Monuments of Old German Poetry, 1799), Friedrich von Hagedorn's *Poetische Werke* (1800), and Ulrich Boner's 1461 collection of vernacular fables based on Aesop, *Edelstein in hundert Fabeln* (1810). Among literary magazines under Eschenburg's editorship were *Der Primaner* (1761), *Annalen der Brittischen Litteratur* (1780-1781), and the highly successful *Braunschweigisches Magazin* (1788-1820). In addition, Eschenburg was an active contributor of critical reviews to Nicolai's influential *Allgemeine Deutsche Bibliothek*. For his expertise and devotion to scholarship and general culture, Eschenburg received honorary doctoral degrees from Göttingen and Marburg and was knighted by King George IV of Great Britain, Elector of Hannover.

In his last years Eschenburg's productivity diminished only slightly. With the publication in 1792 of the encyclopedic *Lehrbuch der Wissenschaftskunde* (Manual for a Science of the Sciences) Eschenburg opened the way for the critical or scientific study of the sciences themselves, that is, for a "theory of science." The book, which attempted to define all salient concepts in every field from aesthetics to physics, went through seven editions by 1825. In 1812, nearing the age of seventy, he completed a history of the Collegium Carolinum. Throughout his life he maintained an abiding interest in music and wrote many hymns, some of which are still known today. On 29 February 1820 he died in Brunswick after a brief illness.

Biography:
Fritz Meyen, *Johann Joachim Eschenburg. Kurzer Abriß seines Lebens nebst Bibliographie* (Brunswick: Waisenhaus, 1957).

References:
Marion Candler Lazenby, *The Influence of Wieland and Eschenburg on Schlegel's Shakespeare Translations* (Baltimore: Privately printed, 1942);

Bruno Markwardt, *Geschichte der deutschen Poesie*, volume 2 (Berlin: De Gruyter, 1956), pp. 556-558;

M. Pirscher, "Johann Joachim Eschenburg: Ein Beitrag zur Literatur- und Wissenschaftsgeschichte des 18. Jahrhunderts," Ph.D. dissertation, University of Münster, 1960;

Hans Schrader, *Eschenburg und Shakespeare* (Marburg: Carstens, 1911);

H. Uhde-Bernays, *Der Mannheimer Shakespeare: Ein Beitrag zur Geschichte der ersten deutschen Shakespeare-Übersetzungen* (Berlin: Felber, 1902).

Papers:
The largest part of Johann Joachim Eschenburg's papers (more than thirty volumes of manuscripts, letters, and other papers) is in the Herzog August Bibliothek, Wolfenbüttel. Other manuscripts and letters (more than five volumes) are in the Staatsbibliothek Preußischer Kulturbesitz in West Berlin. A modest collection of letters, poems, and other manuscripts is preserved in the Niedersächsisches Staatsarchiv Wolfenbüttel.

Christian Fürchtegott Gellert

(4 July 1715 - 13 December 1769)

Robert Spaethling
University of Massachusetts, Boston

BOOKS: *Ode auf den heutigen Flor von Rußland* (Leipzig: Breitkopf, 1739);

Lieder, anonymous (Leipzig: Privately printed, 1743);

Das Band: Ein Schäferspiel in einem Aufzuge (Leipzig, 1744);

De poesi apologorum eorumque scriptoribus (Leipzig: Breitkopf, 1744);

Die Betschwester: Ein Lustspiel in drei Aufzügen (Leipzig & Bremen, 1745; reprinted, Stuttgart: Metzler 1966); translated and edited by Johanna Setzer and Elaine Gottesman as *Christian Fuerchtegott Gellert's The Prayer Sister: An 18th Century, 3 Act Comedy* (Flushing, N.Y.: International Council on the Arts, 1980);

Sylvia, ein Schäferspiel (Leipzig: Breitkopf, 1745);

Fabeln und Erzählungen, 2 volumes (Leipzig: Wendler, 1746-1748); selections translated by Joseph A. Nuske in *Fables: A Free Translation from the German of Gellert and Other Poets* (London: Whittaker, 1850);

Leben der schwedischen Gräfin von G***, anonymous, 2 volumes (Leipzig: Hahn 1746-1748); translated anonymously as *History of the Swedish Countess of Guildenstern* (London: Dodsley, 1752);

Das Loos in der Lotterie: Ein Lustspiel in fünf Aufzügen (Leipzig & Bremen, 1746);

Lustspiele (Leipzig: Wendler, 1747; reprinted, Stuttgart: Metzler, 1966)—includes *Die zärtlichen Schwestern, ein Lustspiel in drei Aufzügen*, translated by Thomas Holcroft as *The Tender Sisters: A Comedy, in Three Acts*, in *The Theatrical Recorder*, edited by Holcroft, volume 1 (London: Symonds, 1805), pp. 1-50;

Von den Trostgründen wider ein sieches Leben (Leipzig: Wendler, 1747);

Briefe, nebst einer Praktischen Abhandlung von dem guten Geschmacke in Briefen (Leipzig: Wendler, 1751; reprinted, Stuttgart: Metzler, 1971);

Pro comoedia commovente (Leipzig: Langenheim, 1751); translated by Gotthold Ephraim Lessing as *Abhandlung für das rührende Lustspiel*,

Christian Fürchtegott Gellert; painting by Anton Graff, 1769 (Freies Deutsches Hochstift, Frankfurter Goethe-Museum)

in Gellert's *Die zärtlichen Schwestern*, edited by Horst Steinmetz (Stuttgart: Reclam, 1965);

Lehrgedichte und Erzählungen (Leipzig: Wendler, 1754);

Sammlung vermischter Schriften, 2 volumes (Leipzig: Weidmann, 1756);

Geistliche Oden und Lieder, (Leipzig: Weidmann, 1757);

Anhang zu der Sammlung vermischter Schriften (Leipzig: Weidmann & Reich, 1759);

Betrachtungen über Religion (Leipzig, 1760);

Zwey Briefe, der I. von C. F. Gellert, der II. von G.W. Rabner [sic], by Gellert and Gottlieb Wilhelm Rabener (Leipzig & Dresden, 1761);

Vier Briefe, by Gellert and Rabener (Frankfurt am Main & Leipzig, 1761);

Fünfter und sechster Brief, by Gellert and Rabener (Leipzig & Dresden, 1761);

Von der Beschaffenheit, dem Umfange und dem Nutzen der Moral: Eine Vorlesung, auf Befehl und in hoher Gegenwart Sr. Churfürstl. Durchlauchtigkeit zu Sachsen, Friedrich Augusts, den 29sten April, 1765, auf der Universitäts-Bibliothek zu Leipzig gehalten (Leipzig: Weidmann & Reich, 1766);

Sämmtliche Schriften, 10 volumes, volumes 1-5 edited by Gellert, volumes 6-10 edited by Johann Adolf Schlegel, Gottlieb Leberecht Heyer, and Johann Andreas Cramer (Leipzig: Weidmann & Reich & Fritsch, 1769-1774; revised, 1775; reprinted, Hildesheim: Olms, 1968);

Vermischte Gedichte (Leipzig: Fritsch, 1770);

Moralische Vorlesungen, edited by Schlegel and Heyer (Leipzig: Weidmann, 1770); translated by Mrs. M. Douglas in *The Life of Professor Gellert by J. A. Cramer: With a Course of Moral Lessons, Delivered by Him in the University of Leipsick; Taken from a French Translation of the Original German,* 3 volumes (Kelso: Printed by A. Ballantyne for J. Hatchard, 1805); excerpt translated anonymously as *Instructions from a Father to His Son on Entering College: Translated from the German of C. F. Gellert* (Boston: Phelps & Farnham, 1823);

Siebenter bis achtzehnter Brief, by Gellert and Rabener (Berlin: Lange, 1770);

Letzte Vorlesungen: Herausgegeben und mit einer Vorrede begleitet von einem seiner Zuhörer (Leipzig: Büschel, 1770);

Nachtrag zu C. F. Gellerts Freundschaftlichen Briefen, 2 volumes, edited by Johann Peter Bamberger (Berlin: Stahlbaum, 1780-1781);

Sämmtliche Schriften, 10 volumes, edited by Julius Ludwig Klee (Leipzig: Weidmann & Hahn, 1839);

Chr. F. Gellert's Tagebuch aus dem Jahre 1761 (Leipzig: Weigel, 1862).

Modern Editions: *Die Betschwester: Lustspiel in drei Aufzügen,* edited by Wolfgang Martens (Berlin: De Gruyter, 1962);

Fabeln und Erzählungen: Historisch-kritische Ausgabe, edited by Siegfried Scheibe (Tübingen: Niemeyer, 1966);

Schriften zur Theorie und Geschichte der Fabel: Historisch-kritische Ausgabe, edited by Scheibe (Tübingen: Niemeyer, 1966);

Die Fahrt auf der Landkutsche; Dichtungen; Schriften; Lebenszeugnisse, edited by Karl Wolfgang Bekker (Berlin: Der Morgen, 1985);

Fabeln und Erzählungen: Historisch-kritische Ausgabe, edited by Karl-Heinz Fallbacher (Stuttgart: Reclam, 1986);

Gesammelte Schriften: Kritische Ausgabe, 6 volumes, edited by Bernd Witte, John Reynolds, Werner Jung, and Sibylle Späth (Berlin: De Gruyter, 1987-1989).

OTHER: Jacob Saurin, *Kurzer Begriff der christlichen Glaubens- und Sittenlehre, in Form eines Katechismus: Aus dem Französischen,* translated by Gellert (Chemnitz: Stössel, 1763).

PERIODICAL PUBLICATION: "C. F. Gellerts 'Un vollständige Nachrichten aus meinem Leben,' edited by Werner Jung and John F. Reynolds, *Jahrbuch des Freien Deutschen Hochstifts* (1988): 1-34.

The Reverend Friedrich August Wendeborn, minister of the German Chapel in London, published a German grammar in 1770, in the preface of which he took note of the growing popularity of the German language in Europe. Particularly in France and England, Wendeborn observed, interest in German literature was on the rise: "If we compare a German writer of the beginning of this century, with others who have written within these thirty years, we should hardly be able to persuade ourselves that they lived in the same age. . . . The French, who, in general, are thought to be rather partial to their own productions, have lately begun to study the German language, and to think favourably of German literature; against which they formerly entertained great prejudices. Among the English the German has been hitherto very little known; but there is reason to expect, that within a few years, even this country, so famous for the improvement and patronage of the arts and sciences, the language and literature of the Germans will no more be looked upon with indifference. Some translations made here lately, have already paved the way for this." Among the German works Wendeborn could have cited in this connection was Christian Fürchtegott Gellert's *Leben der schwedischen Gräfin von G**** (1746-1748, translated as *History of the Swedish Countess of Guildenstern,* 1752), a novel that was translated into English four times between 1752 and 1776. Even though the first announcement of the translation in the *Monthly Review* was somewhat restrained in its applause, later reviewers praised the novel as "beautiful" and "elegant," exhibiting "fine pictures of human nature."

The generous reception accorded Gellert in England is typical of his acceptance throughout Europe. After Boulenger de Rivery translated Gellert's fables into French as *Fables et Contes* (1754), Gellert's name became well known in literary circles in Paris. And when the Russian poet Nicolai Mikhailovich Karamzin visited Gellert's grave in Leipzig, he recalled with deep emotion how the tales and fables of the German writer had been part of his childhood in Russia. Even King Friedrich II of Prussia, generally disdainful of German art and literature, summoned Gellert to an interview in Leipzig on 18 December 1760. The poet, mild and meek but unabashed, won the king's favor as a skillful conversationalist and delighted the monarch by reciting one of his fables. Twenty years later, when Friedrich wrote his controversial *De la littérature allemande* (On German Literature, 1760), Gellert was one of the few German authors the royal critic deemed worthy of his praise.

Gellert's popularity continued well into the nineteenth century. When Julius Klee brought out a new edition of Gellert's works in 1839, it sold out within months. Gellert's fables had appeared by then in French, English, Russian, Italian, Danish, Dutch, Polish, Hebrew, and Latin. They were the most popular literary product to come out of Germany prior to Johann Wolfgang Goethe's *Die Leiden des jungen Werthers* (The Sorrows of Young Werther, 1774). Gellert became an international celebrity and a leading authority in matters of morals; many looked to him as the "Praeceptor Germaniae," the teacher and conscience of his nation.

Gellert was born in Hainichen, a small town in Saxony, on 4 July 1715 to Christian Gellert, a Lutheran minister, and Johanna Salome Schütz Gellert; he was the fifth in a family of thirteen children. At age thirteen he was accepted into the Fürstenschule (Prince's School) St. Afra in Meissen, where he studied Cicero and Horace and read contemporary German poets such as Benjamin Neukirch and Johann Christian Günther. In 1729 he went to Leipzig to study philosophy and theology; but before he could complete his degree, he ran out of money and was forced to return to Hainichen. There he assisted his father in his pastoral duties, earned money as a tutor, and in 1741 was ready to return to Leipzig. He resumed his studies in philosophy, taught himself French and English, and was soon drawn into

the circle around Johann Christoph Gottsched, the dominant literary figure of Leipzig, if not of Germany. Gellert assisted Gottsched with his translation (1741-1744) of Pierre Bayle's *Dictionnaire historique et critique* (1697-1706). In 1743 he acquired a master's degree in philosophy; a year later, after submitting a thesis on the history and theory of fable literature, *De poesi apologorum eorumque scriptoribus,* he was awarded the *venia legendi,* the right to teach at the university.

Gellert remained at the University of Leipzig throughout his life. He became one of the most popular teachers, and students flocked to him by the hundreds to hear him lecture on rhetoric, pedagogy, and practical morality; among them was Goethe, a teenage freshman from Frankfurt. In his autobiography, Goethe recalled with amusement that Gellert used to warn his students against the writing of poetry as one warns adolescents against an immoderate life-style. Indeed, Goethe's own poetic efforts were returned by the scrupulous teacher with a fair amount of red ink and neatly written admonitions. Still, Goethe remembered his teacher fondly: "Die Verehrung und Liebe, welche Gellert von allen jungen Leuten genoß, war außerordentlich. Ich hatte ihn schon besucht und war freundlich von ihm aufgenommen worden. Nicht groß von Gestalt, zierlich aber nicht hager, sanfte, eher traurige Augen, eine sehr schöne Stirn, eine nicht übertriebene Habichtsnase, ein feiner Mund, ein gefälliges Oval des Gesichts: alles machte seine Gegenwart angenehm und wünschenswert" (The veneration and love which Gellert enjoyed among all the young people was indeed extraordinary. I, too, had visited him and had been received with kindness. He was not a large man, delicate rather than thin, he had gentle, somewhat melancholic eyes, a beautiful forehead, a slightly curved nose, a delicate mouth, and a graceful oval face: everything made his presence pleasant and desirable).

In 1764, the year before Goethe arrived in Leipzig, Gellert had hosted another visitor. James Boswell, on a grand tour of Europe, had stopped in Leipzig to visit the two literary luminaries there: Gottsched and Gellert. He recorded his impressions of the latter: "At three I went to Gellert. They call him the [John] Gay of Germany. He has written fables and little dramatic pieces. I found him to be a poor, sickly creature. He said he had been twenty years hypochondriac. He said that during a part of his life, every night he thought to die, and every morning he wrote a fable. He said: 'My poetry is at an end. I no longer have the power of mind.' He spoke bad Latin and worse French: so I did my best with him in German. I found him a poor mind, with hardly any science. His conversation was like that of an old lady. You saw nothing of the ruins of a man–ruins have always something which mark the original building. He has just had a tolerable fancy and a knack of versifying, which has pleased the German ladies and got him a mushroom reputation. Poor man, he was very lean and very feeble, but he seemed a good creature."

It is tempting to dismiss Goethe's portrayal of Gellert as a romanticized memorial of his youth and accept Boswell's account as the realistic observations of a sober-minded Scotsman. Yet, to a degree, both observers are right. What Goethe remembered was Gellert's composure, the studied facade of a man who had become a German national treasure and tried to act the part. Boswell concentrated on the inner anguish brought on by Gellert's awareness that his fame had far outgrown his talent. Goethe remembered the mask; Boswell focused on what lay behind it.

Gellert died in Leipzig on 13 December 1769. He was 54 years old, had never married, and always suffered from poor health. But he had become the most widely read German poet and moralist of his generation, and his death was mourned throughout German-speaking Europe.

Gellert began his writing career as a poet and playwright. His early efforts in both genres are essentially undistinguished, but their simple, sincere, moralistic tone appealed to a spectrum of readers and theatergoers. His plays in particular–two pastorals, three sentimental comedies, several one-act farces–reflect the taste and ideals of the eighteenth-century German middle class.

Gellert's best play, *Die Betschwester* (1745; translated as *Christian Fuerchtegott Gellert's The Prayer Sister,* 1980) is Enlightenment theater, pure and simple. The play is designed around a strong central character, Frau Richardinn, whose life consists of nothing but praying–"Ihr Leben ist ein ständiges Gebet" (Her life is a permanent prayer). But in the end she is unmasked, like her literary cousin Tartuffe, as a penny-pinching hypocrite. Heartfelt rationalism and true generosity as demonstrated by the younger generation triumph over greed and deception. Frau Richardinn became one of the most desirable female acting roles in German theater prior to the

plays of Gotthold Ephraim Lessing; even today the play comes across as good didactic theater.

The subsequent plays, *Das Loos in der Lotterie* (The Lottery Ticket, 1746) and *Die zärtlichen Schwestern* (1747; translated as *The Tender Sisters,* 1805) continue to deliver Gellert's moralistic message: cultivate your mind and heart; beware of greediness. The plays were moderately successful on stage, but they are not great theater: they lack momentum, cohesion, and impact. By moving from the comedy of types to the sentimental comedy (*comédie larmoyante*), Gellert weakened his didactic thrust. He gained in psychological differentiation of his characters, but he diffused the action to the point of nervous, overwrought stage activity without salient dramatic effects. These works became the forerunners of the German soap opera.

Many elements contributed to the popular success of Gellert's only novel, *Leben der schwedischen Gräfin von G****: it is short and engaging, the reader is carried swiftly from one bloodcurdling event to another (murder, incest, suicide, and torture are standard fare), and it is narrated by a fictitious countess whose "mémoires" appealed to women, probably the fastest growing readership in the eighteenth century.

The first part of the novel relates the happy early years of the narrator's marriage to Count G***, a Swedish nobleman. But the couple's tranquility and marital bliss are transformed into a nightmare through the machinations of a prince. Count G*** is sent into battle–the novel is set against the background of a Russian-Swedish war, possibly the war of 1741-1743–and is reported killed in action. The countess flees to Holland, where she confronts one disaster after another and finally marries Mr. R., her husband's best friend. When the "dead" count returns from Russia, the problem is quickly and rationally resolved: the count and countess are reunited, and Mr. R. becomes once more a devoted friend of the family. The second part consists mainly of two lengthy epistolary reports by the count about his life in Siberia, his friendship with an English coprisoner, and his miraculous liberation with the aid of a noble Polish Jew. The narrative concludes with the couple's restored life in Holland and England. When Count G*** dies the unflappable countess and Mr. R. calmly resume their former union, living to the end a life of complete emotional control.

The novel is not original; Prevost's *Manon Lescaut* (1731), Marivaux's *La Vie de Marianne*

Title page for the first volume of Gellert's fables

tional literature, and Gellert's own poetic efforts in this direction would soon be mentioned together with the great masters of the genre: Aesop, Jean La Fontaine, John Gay, and Lessing. In fact, Gellert's two volumes of fables of 1746 and 1748 (translated, 1850) formed the pinnacle of his fame as a writer and moralist.

The genre comprises two major traditions: the animal fable derived from ancient allegories and folklore, with Aesop as its paragon; and "le conte" or "Erzählung," a witty, moralizing anecdote set in the human sphere. Both traditions seek to expose human foibles through wit and graceful artistry, to educate while entertaining. The poem "Der Maler" (The Painter) represents Gellert's favorite fable style: a versified narrative followed by a witty moral and a touch of self-irony (the translation is by John Quincy Adams, who translated thirteen of Gellert's fables while serving as minister plenipotentiary at the Court of Berlin):

> Ein kluger Maler in Athen,
> Der minder, weil man ihn bezahlte,
>
> Als weil er Ehre suchte, malte,
> Ließ einen Kenner einst den Mars im
>   Bilde sehn
> Und bat sich seine Meinung aus.
>
> Der Kenner sagt ihm frei heraus,
> Daß ihm das Bild nicht ganz
>   gefallen wollte,
> Und daß es, um recht schön zu seyn,
>
> Weit minder Kunst verrathen sollte.
> Der Maler wandte vieles ein:
>
> Der Kenner stritt mit ihm aus
>   Gründen
> Und konnt' ihn doch nicht
>   überwinden.
>
>
> Gleich trat ein junger Geck herein
> Und nahm das Bild in Augenschein.
> O! rief er bey dem ersten Blicke:
>
> Ihr Götter, welch ein Meisterstücke!
>
> Ach welcher Fuß! O, wie geschickt
>
> Sind nicht die Nägel ausgedrückt!
> Mars lebt durchaus in diesem Bilde.
>
> Wie viele Kunst, wie viele Pracht,
> Ist in dem Helm und in dem Schilde

(1731-1741), and Samuel Richardson's *Pamela* (1740) have long been recognized as literary models. Recent scholarship emphasizes Gellert's use of baroque narrative technique: the novel is structured as a series of episodes permeated with the author's Enlightenment message that reason and composure help us shape our destinies. The novel, then, is a document of eighteenth-century middle-class morality in which lessons in virtue and self-control are interwoven with adventure stories and the ever-popular travelogue. The work constitutes an important phase in the evolution of the German psychological novel and, therefore, has continued to hold the attention of literary historians and critics. Today Gellert's humanism revealed in this work–the plight of the persecuted woman and unjust prejudices against the Jews–can be appreciated as never before.

"Le petit genre des fables" had emerged by Gellert's time as the most popular form of educa-

Title page for Gellert's collection of religious odes and songs

Und in der Rüstung angebracht!

Der Maler ward beschämt gerühret

Und sah den Kenner kläglich an.
Nun, sprach er, bin ich überführet!

Ihr habt mir nicht zuviel gethan.
Der junge Geck war kaum hinaus,
So strich er seinen Kriegsgott aus.

Wenn deine Schrift dem Kenner
        nicht gefällt,
So ist es schon ein böses Zeichen;
Doch, wenn sie gar des Narren Lob
        erhält,
So ist es Zeit, sie auszustreichen.

(A painter of ingenuous heart,
Who rather work'd for fame than
        gold,

At Athens once, in days of old,
Shew'd to a critic in his art,
A Mars, that he had just design'd,
Of which he begg'd him speak his
        mind.
The critic candidly confess'd
He thought it not from failings free;
In too much art, the god was dress'd,
Not fierce and rough as Mars should
        be;
While each objection that he made
On specious principles was
        grounded,
The artist equal skill display'd,
To prove the censure not well
        founded;
And after having argued long,
Still could not think his labour
        wrong.

A foolish coxcomb now came in,
Upon the picture cast his eyes,
And gazing, with sagacious grin—

"Gods! what a master-piece!" he
        cries.
"Behold this foot! what nails are
        here!
You see the god himself appear;
How rich his garb! his arms, how
        fine!
Look; how the shield and helmet
        shine!"

The painter now, o'erwhelm'd with
        shame,
Turn'd to his friend, with visage sad;
"You're right," quoth he, "and I to
        blame,
I now confess my picture bad—"
Then, ere the coxcomb could retire,
He threw his war-god in the fire.

When critics disapprove your lays,

'Tis a bad omen for your lyre;
But when the fools begin to praise,

Throw, throw your verses in the
        fire!)

Karl Goedeke, the eminent nineteenth-century Germanist and bibliographer, remarked that Gellert's fables belong to the best literature produced by the German Enlightenment. Goedeke's assessment still holds true. Yet the fables are not Gellert's only literary achievement that endured beyond his time: his letters and religious songs belong in this category as well. Gellert's letters, especially those published as models in his famous "guide for letter writers," served a most important educational function: they taught his countrymen how to write. In his review of Gellert's *Briefe, nebst einer Praktischen Abhandlung von dem guten Geschmacke in Briefen* (Letters, with a Practical Discussion of Good Taste in Letters, 1751) Lessing wrote: "Die Briefe des Herrn Gellerts sind durchgängig Meisterstücke, die man eben so wenig als seine Fabeln zu lesen aufhören wird" (The letters of Mr. Gellert are masterpieces throughout, which, like his fables, will always find a reader).

The same is true of Gellert's *Geistliche Oden und Lieder* (Religious Odes and Songs, 1757). This work was published at a time when he was filled with debilitating anxieties about his health and creativity. In 1754 he had confided to a friend: "So viel merke ich, daß meine Gabe zu dichten u. zu schreiben sehr, wo nicht ganz, verloschen ist. Alles wird mir sauer, blutsauer" (This much I know, my gift for writing is nearly, if not completely, gone. Everything is tiring, extremely tiring). Indeed, his later didactic poetry had lost much of the spark, wit, and elegance of his earlier writings, and his themes had become increasingly religious. But even in the restless pietism of his final years Gellert remained, in his own manner, successful. Several of his spiritual songs became a permanent part of the Protestant hymnbooks and some of his odes were set to music by eminent composers, including C. P. E. Bach, Haydn, and Beethoven. Perhaps the best known of these compositions is Beethoven's setting for Gellert's version of Psalm 19: "Die Himmel rühmen des Ewigen Ehre" (The Heavens Resound with the Glory of God). In this grand majestic hymn, Beethoven helped preserve the memory of Christian Fürchtegott Gellert, an amiable moralist and teacher, a poet and Enlightener, who built some of the first bridges from eighteenth-century Germany to the literatures of the world.

Letters:

Christian Fürchtegott Gellerts Briefe, nebst einigen damit verwandten Briefen seiner Freunde: nach seinem Tode herausgegeben, 2 volumes, edited by Johann Adolf Schlegel and Gottlieb Leberecht Heyer (Leipzig: Weidmann & Reich, 1774);

Aufgefundene Familienbriefe mit einem Anhange, edited by August Theodor Leuchte (Freiberg: Cratz & Gerlach, 1819);

Briefwechsel Christian Fürchtegott Gellert's mit Demoiselle Lucius: Nebst einem Anhange, edited by Friedrich Adolf Ebert (Leipzig: Brockhaus, 1823);

C. F. Gellerts Briefwechsel, 2 volumes to date, edited by John F. Reynolds (Berlin & New York: De Gruyter, 1983-1987).

Bibliography:

Karl Goedeke, *Grundriß zur Geschichte der deutschen Dichtung,* volume 4, part 1 (Dresden: Ehlermann, 1904), pp. 74-78.

Biographies:

Johann Andreas Cramer, *Christian Fürchtegott Gellerts Leben,* volume 10 of Gellert's *Sämmtliche Schriften,* 10 volumes, edited by Gellert, Cramer, Johann Adolf Schlegel, and Gottlieb Leberecht Heyer (Leipzig: Weidmann & Reich & Fritsch, 1769-1774; revised, 1775); translated by Mrs. M. Douglas as *The Life of Professor Gellert by J. A. Cramer: With a Course of Moral Lessons, Delivered by Him in the University of Leipsick; Taken from a French Translation of the Original German,* 3 volumes (Kelso: Printed by A. Ballantyne for J. Hatchard, 1805); German version reprinted (Hildesheim: Olms, 1968);

Heinrich Döring, *Gellerts Leben,* 2 volumes (Greiz, 1833).

References:

James Boswell, *Boswell on the Grand Tour: Germany and Switzerland, 1764,* edited by Frederick A. Pottle (New York: McGraw-Hill, 1953), p. 127;

Diethelm Brüggemann, "Gellert, der gute Geschmack und die üblen Briefsteller," *Deutsche Vierteljahrsschrift für Literaturwissenschaft und Geistesgeschichte,* 45 (March 1971): 117-149;

Fritz Brüggemann, *Gellerts Schwedische Gräfin* (Aachen: Aachener Verlags- und Druckereigesellschaft, 1925);

John van Cleve, "A Countess in Name Only: Gellert's *Schwedische Gräfin,*" *Germanic Review,* 55 (Fall 1980): 152-155;

Cleve, "Tolerance at a Price: The Jew in Gellert's *Schwedische Gräfin,*" *Seminar,* 18 (February 1982): 1-13;

Johannes Coym, *Gellerts Lustspiele* (Berlin: Mayer & Müller, 1899; reprinted, New York: Johnson Reprint, 1967);

Walter Eiermann, *Gellerts Briefstil* (Leipzig: Avenarius, 1912);

Johann Wolfgang von Goethe, *Aus meinem Leben. Dichtung und Wahrheit,* in *Goethes Werke,* edited by Erich Trunz, volume 9 (Hamburg: Wegener, 1955), pp. 247ff;

Eugene K. Grotegut, "Gellert: Wit or Sentimentalist?," *Monatshefte,* 54 (January 1962): 117-122;

Daniel V. B. Hegemann, "Boswell's Interview with Gottsched and Gellert," *Journal of English and Germanic Philology,* 46 (1947): 260-263;

Fritz Helber, *Der Stil Gellerts in den Fabeln und Gedichten* (Würzburg: Triltsch, 1937);

David Hill, "Die schwedische Gräfin: Notes on Early Bourgeois Realism," *Neophilologus,* 65 (1981): 574-588;

Albert Leitzmann, "Goethe und Gellert," *Goethe: Viermonatschrift der Goethegesellschaft,* 8 (1943): 115-125;

Gotthold Ephraim Lessing, "Briefe . . . von C. F. Gellert," in *Gotthold Ephraim Lessings sämtliche Schriften,* edited by Karl Lachmann and Franz Muncker, volume 4 (Stuttgart: Göschen, 1889), p. 315;

Wolfgang Martens, "Lektüre bei Gellert," in *Festschrift für Richard Alewyn,* edited by Herbert Singer and Benno von Wiese (Cologne: Böhlau, 1967), pp. 123-150;

Martens, "Über Weltbild und Gattungstradition bei Gellert," in *Festschrift für Detlev W. Schumann,* edited by Albert Schmitt (Munich: Delp, 1970), pp. 74-82;

Kurt May, *Das Weltbild in Gellerts Dichtung* (Frankfurt am Main: Diesterweg, 1928);

Gottfried F. Merkel, "Gellerts Stellung in der deutschen Sprachgeschichte," in *Beiträge zur Geschichte der deutschen Sprache und Literatur,* edited by Gertaud Müller and Rudolf Grosse (Halle: Niemeyer, 1961), pp. 395-412;

Eckhardt Meyer-Krentler, *Der andere Roman: Gellerts Schwedische Gräfin* (Göppingen: Kümmerle, 1974);

Walter J. Morris, "J. Q. Adams' Verse Translations of C. F. Gellert's Fables," in *Helen Adolf Festschrift,* edited by Shema Z. Buehne, James L. Hodge, and Lucille B. Pinto (New York: Ungar, 1968), pp. 138-165;

Allessandro Pellegrini, "La crisi dell' 'Aufklärung': L'opera poetica di C. F. Gellert et la società del suo tempo," in *Dalla "Sensibilità" al Nichilismo* (Milan: Feltrinelli, 1962), pp. 11-77;

Katharine Russell, "Das Leben der schwedischen Gräfin von G . . . : A Critical Discussion," *Monatshefte,* 40 (October 1948): 328-336;

Carsten Schlingmann, *Gellert: Eine literarhistorische Revision* (Bad Homburg: Gehlen, 1967);

Matthaeus Schneiderwirth, *Das katholische deutsche Kirchenlied unter dem Einflusse Gellerts und Klopstocks* (Münster: Aschendorff, 1908);

Robert H. Spaethling, "Die Schranken der Vernunft in Gellerts Leben der schwedischen Gräfin," *Publications of the Modern Language Association of America,* 81 (June 1966): 224-235;

Israel Stamm, "Gellert: Religion and Rationalism," *Germanic Review,* 28 (October 1953): 195-203;

Alfred Stucki, *Christian Fürchtegott Gellert, der evangelische Sänger* (Basel: Majer, 1954);

Gebhardt Friedrich August Wendeborn, *An Introduction to German Grammar,* (London: Printed for G. G. J. and J. Robinson, 1790);

Emil Werth, *Untersuchungen zu Chr. F. Gellerts Geistlichen Oden und Liedern* (Breslau: Plischke, 1936);

Bernd Witte, "Die Individualität des Autors: Gellerts Briefsteller als Roman eines Schreibenden," *German Quarterly* 62 (Winter 1989): 5-14;

Witte, "Der Roman als moralische Anstalt. Gellerts 'Leben der schwedischen Gräfin von G . . .' und die Literatur des achtzehnten Jahrhunderts," *Germanisch-Romanische Monatsschrift,* new series, 30 (1980): 150-168.

Papers:

Christian Fürchtegott Gellert's papers are at the Sächsische Landesbibliothek, Dresden; the Universitätsbibliothek Leipzig; and the Deutsche Staatsbibliothek, Berlin.

Heinrich Wilhelm von Gerstenberg

(3 January 1737 - 1 November 1823)

Meredith Lee

University of California, Irvine

BOOKS: *Tändeleyen,* anonymous (Leipzig: Dyck, 1759; enlarged, 1765); excerpts translated anonymously as "The Kiss: A Tale. From the German of Mr. Gerstenberg," "The Nymph of Diana: From the German," *Oxford Magazine, or University Museum,* 1 (1768): 26, 50; German version reprinted, with afterword by Alfred Anger (Stuttgart: Metzler, 1966);

Prosaische Gedichte, anonymous (Altona: Iversen, 1759);

Kriegslieder eines Königlich Dänischen Grenadiers bey Eröffnung des Feldzuges, anonymous (Altona, 1762);

Handbuch für einen Reuter, as Ohle Madsen, Reuter (Altona: Iversen, 1763);

Gedicht eines Skalden, anonymous (Copenhagen, Odensee, & Leipzig: Roth & Proft, 1766);

Briefe über Merkwürdigkeiten der Litteratur, 3 volumes, anonymous, by Gerstenberg and others (Schleswig & Leipzig: Hansen, 1766-1767);

Ugolino: Eine Tragödie, in fünf Aufzügen, anonymous (Hamburg & Bremen: Cramer, 1768);

Über Merkwürdigkeiten der Litteratur: Der Fortsetzung 1. Stück (Hamburg & Bremen: Cramer, 1770);

Minona oder Die Angelsachsen: Ein tragisches Melodrama in vier Akten, music by Johann Abraham Peter Schulz (Hamburg: Hoffmann, 1785);

Die Theorie der Kategorien, entwickelt und erläutert, anonymous (Altona: Hammerich, 1795);

Gerstenbergs Vermischte Schriften von ihm selbst gesammelt und mit Verbesserungen und Zusätzen herausgegeben in drei Bänden, 3 volumes (Altona: Hammerich, 1815-1816; reprinted, Frankfurt am Main: Athenäum, 1971);

H. W. v. Gerstenbergs Rezensionen in der Hamburgischen Neuen Zeitung 1767-1771, edited by Ottokar Fischer (Berlin: Behr, 1904; reprinted, Nendeln, Liechtenstein: Kraus, 1968);

Ugolino: Eine Tragödie in fünf Aufzügen. Mit einem Anhang und einer Auswahl aus den theoretischen

Heinrich Wilhelm von Gerstenberg; engraving by J. F. M. Schreyer, 1777

und kritischen Schriften, edited by Christoph Siegrist (Stuttgart: Reclam, 1966);

Briefe über Merkwürdigkeiten der Litteratur (Hildesheim & New York: Olms, 1971)—includes *Briefe über Merkwürdigkeiten der Litteratur* and *Über Merkwürdigkeiten der Litteratur: Der Fortsetzung 1. Stück.*

OTHER: Jean-Baptiste-Joseph Damarzit de Sahuguet, Baron d'Espagnac, *Versuch über den großen Krieg,* 2 volumes, translated by Gerstenberg (Copenhagen & Leipzig: Ackermann, 1763);

Francis Beaumont and John Fletcher, *Die Braut: Eine Tragödie von Beaumont und Fletcher. Nebst kritischen und biographischen Abhandlungen über die vier größten Dichter des älteren brittischen Theaters und einem Schreiben an Weiße*, translated by Gerstenberg (Copenhagen & Leipzig: Roth & Proft, 1765);

Ariadne auf Naxos, in *Tragische Kantaten für eine oder zwo Singestimmen und das Clavier. Nemlich: des Herrn von Gerstenbergs Ariadne auf Naxos, und Johann Elias Schlegels Prokris und Cephalus. In die Musik gesezt, und nebst einem Sendschreiben, worinnen vom Recitativ überhaupt und von diesen Kantaten insonderheit geredet wird,* herausgegeben von Joh. Adolph Scheiben, Königl. Dän. Kapellmeister (Copenhagen, Flensburg & Leipzig: Momm, 1765); translated by William Taylor as *Ariadne on Naxos*, in his *Historical Survey of German Poetry*, volume 3 (London: Treuttel, 1830);

Der Hypochondrist: Eine holsteinische Wochenschrift von Herrn Zacharias Jernstrup, edited by Gerstenberg (Bremen & Schleswig: Cramer & Hansen, 1771).

Poet, dramatist, and literary critic, Heinrich Wilhelm von Gerstenberg was best known to his contemporaries as the author of the polished and popular collection of anacreontic verse titled *Tändeleyen* (Flirtations, 1759) and of the drama *Ugolino* (1768), a gruesome tragedy of imprisonment and starvation. His innovative *Gedicht eines Skalden* (A Skald's Poem, 1766) is credited with initiating the craze for bardic poetry in the late 1760s. His greatest and most lasting accomplishments, however, were his various contributions to the theoretical positions of the Sturm und Drang movement. In the single decade of his creative productivity between 1759 and 1771 he formulated, together with Johann Georg Hamann and Johann Gottfried Herder, the major premises of the new literary aesthetics. An enthusiastic advocate of Shakespearean drama and promoter of lyric poetry, Gerstenberg used his reviews and critical letters to champion original genius and to reject the norms of rationalist poetics. After 1771 Gerstenberg's productivity flagged and his reputation declined.

Born in Tondern, Schleswig, on 3 January 1737 to German-speaking parents–Heinrich Wilhelm and Elsabe Schröling von Gerstenberg–Gerstenberg was a Danish subject. After his school years in Husum and Altona he studied

law at the University of Jena from 1757 to 1759; during this time he was never free of financial worries. While still a law student he published two well-received collections of poetry and poetic prose pieces, *Tändeleyen* and *Prosaische Gedichte* (Prosaic Poems, 1759). In these early collections he revealed a keen ability to appropriate and refine established lyric conventions and to combine sentiment with playful wit. Tales of love set in classical landscapes are intertwined with mythological narratives. *Tändeleyen* in particular enjoyed extraordinary success; the volume was revised, reprinted, pirated, and imitated. It was highly praised not only by Johann Wilhelm Ludwig Gleim, Johann Peter Uz, Johann Georg Jacobi, and Friedrich Wilhelm Gotter, themselves poets in the anacreontic vein, but also by Gotthold Ephraim Lessing, the most feared of the German critics, who proclaimed its anonymous author a creative genius. Today scholars rank it among the best of German anacreontic poetry.

After leaving the university Gerstenberg followed in his father's footsteps and became an officer in the Danish army. From 1760 to 1768 he enjoyed steady advancement in both his military career and his literary reputation. Since 1759 he had been writing reviews for the prestigious journal *Bibliothek der schönen Wissenschaften*, edited by Christian Felix Weiße. He also became a regular contributor to *Der Hypochondrist*, a moral weekly that appeared for one year in 1762. Edited by a friend from Gerstenberg's university days, Jacob Friedrich Schmidt, *Der Hypochondrist* was modeled on the English *Tatler*. Gerstenberg's offerings, which made up more than a quarter of the journal's pages, include literary satires and parodies; essays on drama, aesthetics, and religious poetry; and an appreciation of the first two volumes of Friedrich Gottlieb Klopstock's epic *Der Messias* (The Messiah, 1748-1773). (In 1771 Gerstenberg republished the journal, editing it himself and writing additional pieces for it.) A brief mobilization against Russian troops in 1762 that involved no active hostilities occasioned a small collection of poetry, *Kriegslieder eines Königlich Dänischen Grenadiers* (Songs of War by a Royal Danish Grenadier, 1762), dedicated to Gleim and modeled on his popular narrative songs of 1758, *Preußische Kriegslieder in den Feldzügen 1756 und 1757 von einem Grenadier* (Prussian Songs of War in the Campaigns of 1756 and 1757 by a Grenadier). In his dual career as writer and officer he wrote a military handbook under the pseudonym Ohle Madsen (1763) and translated a treatise by

Tändeleyen

Dritte und vermehrte Auflage.

Leipzig, 1765.

in der Dyckischen Buchhandlung.

*Title page for Gerstenberg's first book, a collection of
Anacreontic poems*

d'Espagnac (1763). He also translated *The Maides
Tragedy* (1619) by Francis Beaumont and John
Fletcher and six essays on English drama (dealing
with Beaumont and Fletcher, Ben Jonson, and
Shakespeare). He published the play and the essays in a single volume in 1765, adding his own
prefatory remarks and notes.

In 1765 Gerstenberg married Margrethe
Sophia Trochmann and settled in Copenhagen,
becoming both a close friend of Klopstock and
an active participant in the influential circle of German writers gathered in the Danish capital. In
these happy and productive years he completed
his major critical works, establishing himself as a
new and challenging voice in the expanding

world of German literary essayists. Between 1767
and 1771 he wrote more than one hundred book
reviews for the *Hamburgische Neue Zeitung*, focusing primarily on recent German literature; his enthusiasm for the works of Klopstock is particularly evident. In 1766-1767 he published his
major critical work, *Briefe über Merkwürdigkeiten
der Litteratur* (Letters on Noteworthy Aspects of
Literature). Organized as a literary correspondence, the Schleswig Letters, as they are also
known, are modeled on the highly regarded
Briefe, die neueste Litteratur betreffend (Letters Concerning the Most Recent Literature, 1759-1765),
initially edited by Lessing. In this collection of epistolary essays, most of which Gerstenberg wrote
himself, he energetically promotes a reorienta-
tion and expansion of German literary taste. He
discusses a diverse selection of works from world
literature, including the writings of Homer,
Edmund Spenser, Ludovico Ariosto, and Miguel
de Cervantes as well as older Scandinavian literature. Celebrated above all others, however, is
Shakespeare. In letters 14-18, which open and conclude with an explicit attack on Christoph Martin
Wieland's Shakespeare translation, Gerstenberg
proves himself to be far ahead of his contemporaries in his appreciation of Shakespeare's dramatic
genius, powerful probing of human nature, and
nuanced revelation of character, and of the dramatic unity of Shakespeare's plays. He defends,
in particular, Shakespeare's frequent recourse to
wordplay and puns and admires his linguistic sub-
tlety in portraying differences in class, age, and
character. Equally innovative are Gerstenberg's
comments in letter 20 on original genius and
lyric poetry. Both are part of a larger interest in
promoting what he calls "wahre Poesie" (true poetry). In both the letters and the reviews
Gerstenberg identifies Homer, Sophocles, Shakespeare, John Milton, and Klopstock as the creators of true poetry. Unlike works of "bel esprit,"
that is, well-crafted works of intellect and wit,
true poetry is of the heart. Imagination, passion,
enthusiasm, inspiration, and creativity are among
the key qualities of such works. Lyric poetry, something of a stepchild within eighteenth-century
genre theory, acquires new status within the hierarchy of genres on the basis of the criterion of
"wahre Poesie" (with its attendant appeal to emotion). The so-called higher ode, in particular,
emerges as the leading form of literary expression. Despite his lack of interest in systematic poetics and despite the occasional nature of these reviews and essays, Gerstenberg provides a

*Title page for the first volume of Gerstenberg's major
critical work*

poem. A work in five parts, it begins as a skald named Thorlaug awakens from his grave in contemporary Denmark. He recounts the story of his great friendship for his comrade Halvard and of their deaths, employing abundant allusions to Scandinavian mythology. The widely read poem, with its stylized appeal to a Nordic past, sparked considerable interest and was followed by a brief boom in so-called bardic poetry, works written by self-proclaimed heirs to the Germanic poets of old.

As a dramatist Gerstenberg proved himself equally inventive but also aroused considerable controversy. His five-act tragedy *Ugolino* shocked his contemporaries. Adapting the account of the tormented Count Ugolino della Gheradesca from Dante's *Inferno*, canto 33, Gerstenberg focuses on the final hours in Ugolino's life as he and his three sons, imprisoned in a tower, face death by starvation. Agony, horror, hate, remorse, love, sympathy, hope, tenderness, pain, doubt, and despair succeed one another in the rhythmic prose. In the concluding scene, as music is introduced to augment the emotional intensity of the action, Ugolino faces his death with anguished cries to his Creator that yield in the end to affirmation and faith. Despite the final apotheosis, the lingering atmosphere is one of desperation and defeat. In a revised version published in 1815 in Gerstenberg's *Vermischte Schriften* (Miscellaneous Writings, 1815-1816) Ugolino commits suicide. Although it was performed in Berlin in 1769, the play reached its audiences primarily as a written text.

Among the reviews of the play, Herder's comments in the *Allgemeine Deutsche Bibliothek* stand out. Summing up his assessment of Gerstenberg's promise as a writer, he asserts "daß bei allen seinen Fehlern und übertriebenen Stellen ein Dichter der ersten Größe, von wilder und weicher Imagination, von tiefer Menschlicher Empfindung, und einem innern unnennbaren Sinne spreche, der unsrer Nation in der Folge was Ausserordentliches zusagt" (that despite all its flaws and extreme passages, a first-rank poet is speaking, one of wild and supple imagination, of deep human feeling and an ineffable inner understanding, one who holds extraordinary future promise for our nation). Herder's expectations were to be severely disappointed.

The death of the Danish king Frederik V in 1766 marked the beginning of a reversal in Gerstenberg's fortunes, although the consequences of the king's death and the attendant

coherent set of literary principles that are a fundamental departure from neoclassical literary norms.

During the Copenhagen years Gerstenberg was also productive as a poet and dramatist in his own right. Between 1765 and 1768 he published *Gedicht eines Skalden*, *Ugolino*, and the tragic cantata *Ariadne auf Naxos* (1765; translated as *Ariadne on Naxos*, 1830). (Although he did not himself set the cantata to music, he was a pianist and was musically gifted.) In 1775 *Ariadne auf Naxos* enjoyed immediate success when it was performed in Gotha by the Seyler troupe in an adaptation by Johann Christian Brandes set to music by Georg Benda. *Gedicht eines Skalden*, however, was Gerstenberg's most inventive and influential

Ugolino.

Eine Tragödie,

in fünf Aufzügen.

Hamburg und Bremen.
Bey Johann Hinrich Cramer. 1768.

Title page for Gerstenberg's tragedy about the death by starvation of Count Ugolino and his three sons

shifts in power and in the administration of the military were not immediately apparent. Promoted to Rittmeister (captain) in 1767, Gerstenberg had good reason to hope that secure employment within the military bureaucracy would accompany his growing fame as a writer and critic. But after the forced retirement of his patron, Field Marshal Count St.-Germain, in 1768, he was without assignment. His annual income precipitously reduced from 700 to 150 talers and with mounting debts, Gerstenberg retired from the military in 1771 and took a position in the German chancellery of the Danish civil service. He was never to recover financially or to regain creative momentum as a poet, dramatist, or critic.

The reasons for Gerstenberg's subsequent failures are not completely clear. His biographer, Albert Malte Wagner, suggests that he was plagued by indecisiveness and self-doubt and faults him for sentimentality and lethargy, explanations that seem inadequate at best. Others have identified his loss of creative energy as a more generalized phenomenon of artistic crisis, one that disproportionately threatens creative geniuses who reveal unusual promise at an early age. It is clear that Gerstenberg's financial woes–he had a wife and eight children to support–intensified his plight. He was unable to escape from them even after 1775, when he was appointed Danish resident (consul) in Lübeck. In 1783 he sought permission to sell his position to obtain funds to pay his creditors. This unusual request was granted, and he moved to nearby Eutin. His wife died in 1785. In Eutin he completed the ambitious but unsuccessful play *Minona oder Die Angelsachsen* (Minona; or, The Anglo-Saxons, 1785) in an apparent attempt to revive his literary talent and reclaim his reputation. In 1786 he moved to Altona, where he lived until his death. In 1789 the influence of friends won him a modest position in the directorate of the lotto commission in Altona, a political sinecure he held until his retirement in 1812. After eleven years as a widower Gerstenberg married Sophie Ophelia Stemann in 1796. Philosophical and theological studies occupied him in his later years. Although the three-volume edition of selected works that he published in 1815 at the urging of friends included a subscription list headed by King Frederik VI of Denmark, the volumes received little attention. Gerstenberg's considerable literary and critical achievements were long forgotten when he died on 1 November 1823 at the age of eighty-six.

Because he completed his most significant works during the 1760s, Gerstenberg has frequently been characterized as a transitional figure between the Enlightenment and the Sturm und Drang. The image is somewhat misleading and has hindered an appreciation of his role as a formative theorist and critic within the newly emerging literary culture. As an opponent of normative criticism, asserting in its place the primacy of the individual literary work over abstract rules of art, Gerstenberg never systematized his theoretical reflections in a single treatise. The book reviews and essays that he wrote between 1759 and 1771 are his principal critical legacy. Almost all modern appreciations of Gerstenberg are indebted to Klaus Gerth's 1960 monograph, which demonstrates that Gerstenberg is not merely a transitional figure but a cofounder of Sturm und Drang poetics. This accomplishment is

Gerstenberg's most significant contribution to German literary history.

Letters:

R. M. Werner, "Gerstenbergs Briefe an Nicolai nebst einer Antwort Nicolais," *Zeitschrift für deutsche Philologie*, 23 (1891): 43-67;

Albert Malte Wagner, "Ungedruckte Dichtungen und Briefe aus dem Nachlaß Heinrich Wilhelm von Gerstenbergs," *Archiv für das Studium der neueren Sprachen und Literaturen*, 134 (1916): 3-16; 135 (1916): 11-28; 136 (1917): 24-34, 209-228; 140 (1920): 1-24; 141 (1921): 1-23, 169-175.

Bibliography:

Karl Goedeke, *Grundriß zur Geschichte der deutschen Dichtung aus den Quellen*, third edition, volume 4, part 1 (Dresden: Ehlermann, 1916; reprinted, Nendeln, Liechtenstein: Kraus, 1975), pp. 188-190, 1116;

Klaus Gerth, "Bibliographie I," in *Studien zu Gerstenbergs Poetik: Ein Beitrag zur Umschichtung der ästhetischen und poetischen Grundbegriffe im 18. Jahrhundert* (Göttingen: Vandenhoeck & Ruprecht, 1960), pp. 222-226.

Biography:

Albert Malte Wagner, *Heinrich Wilhelm von Gerstenberg und der Sturm und Drang*, 2 volumes (Heidelberg: Winter, 1920-1924).

References:

Bruce Duncan, " 'Ich platze!': Gerstenberg's *Ugolino* and the Mid-life Crisis," *Germanic Review*, 53 (Winter 1978): 13-19;

John Wallace Eaton, "Gerstenberg and Danish Literature," in his *The German Influence in Danish Literature in the Eighteenth Century: The German Circle in Copenhagen 1750-1770* (Cambridge: Cambridge University Press, 1929), pp. 89-117;

Gloria Flaherty, *Opera in the Development of German Critical Thought* (Princeton: Princeton University Press, 1978);

Klaus Gerth, "Heinrich Wilhelm von Gerstenberg" in *Deutsche Dichter des 18. Jahrhunderts. Ihr Leben und Werk*, edited by Benno von Wiese (Berlin: Schmidt, 1977), pp. 393-411;

Gerth, *Studien zu Gerstenbergs Poetik: Ein Beitrag zur Umschichtung der ästhetischen und poetischen Grundbegriffe im 18. Jahrhundert* (Göttingen: Vandenhoeck & Ruprecht, 1960);

Karl S. Guthke, "Gerstenberg und die Shakespearedeutung der deutschen Klassik und Romantik," *Journal of English and Germanic Philology*, 58 (1959): 91-108;

Richard Hamel, "H. W. v. Gerstenberg," in Friedrich Gottlieb Klopstock's *Klopstocks Werke*, part 4: *Klopstocks "Hermanns Schlacht" und das Bardenwesen des 18. Jahrhunderts*, Deutsche National-Litteratur, 48, edited by Hamel (Berlin & Stuttgart: Spemann, 1883), pp. 193-204;

Ulrich Karthaus, "Heinrich Wilhelm von Gerstenberg," in *Deutsche Dichter*, volume 4: *Sturm und Drang, Klassik*, edited by Gunter E. Grimm and Frank Rainer Max (Stuttgart: Reclam, 1989), pp. 20-28;

Henry J. Schmidt, "The Language of Confinement: Gerstenberg's *Ugolino* and Klinger's *Sturm und Drang*," *Lessing Yearbook*, 11 (1979): 165-197;

Alexander von Weilen, introduction to Gerstenberg's *Briefe über Merkwürdigkeiten der Litteratur*, Deutsche Litteraturdenkmale, 29/30 (Stuttgart: Göschen, 1890).

Papers:

Heinrich Wilhelm von Gerstenberg's collected papers and unpublished manuscript materials, including a journal of more than four hundred pages that Gerstenberg kept from 1751 to 1757, in which he recorded his poems, are in the Bayerische Staatsbibliothek, Munich; a second large collection of manuscripts and letters is in the Landesbibliothek, Kiel.

Salomon Geßner
(1 April 1730 - 2 March 1788)

John L. Hibberd
University of Bristol

BOOKS: *Die Nacht,* anonymous (Zurich, 1753);

Daphnis, anonymous (Zurich: Geßner, 1754); translated anonymously as *Daphnis: A Poetical, Pastoral Novel. Translated from the German of Mr. Gessner, the Celebrated Author of The Death of Abel. By An English Gentleman, Who Resided Several Years at Hamburgh. To Which Is Prefixed, a Prefatory Discourse on the Origin and Use of Pastoral Poetry* (London: Sold by J. Dodsley, T. Cadell, W. Owen, G. Kearsley, J. Wilkie, W. Nicoll & W. Davenhill, 1768);

Idyllen von dem Verfasser des Daphnis, anonymous (Zurich: Geßner, 1756); translated anonymously as *Rural Poems* (London: Printed for T. Becket & P. A. De Hondt, 1762);

Inkel und Yariko: Zweiter Theil, anonymous (Zurich: Orell Füßli, 1756);

Der Tod Abels, in fünf Gesängen, anonymous (Zurich: Geßner, 1758); translated by Mary Collyer as *The Death of Abel, in Five Books: Attempted from the German of Mr. Gessner* (London: Printed for R. & J. Dodsley, D. Wilson, T. Durham & M. Collyer, 1761; Boston: Fowle & Draper, 1762);

Gedichte (Zurich: Orell, Geßner, 1762);

Schriften, 4 volumes (Zurich: Orell, Geßner, 1762); selections translated by Frederic Shoberl as *The Idylls of Solomon* [sic] *Gessner, Together with Dramatic and Miscellaneous Pieces* (London: Albion Press, 1815);

Moralische Erzählungen und Idyllen, by Geßner and Denis Diderot (Zurich: Orell, Geßner & Füßli, 1772);

Paysages dessinés et gravés par Gessner (Zurich: Orell & Geßner, 1772);

Neue Idyllen (Zurich: Orell Füßli, 1772); translated by William Hooper as *New Idylles* (London: S. Hooper, 1776; Philadelphia: Printed for William Duane, 1802);

Idyllen, 5 volumes (Zurich: Orell Füßli, 1772);

Schriften, 2 volumes (Zurich: Orell Füßli, 1777-1778);

Werke, edited by Adolf Frey (Berlin: Spemann, 1884; reprinted, Hildesheim: Olms, 1973);

Painting by Anton Graff, 1766; by permission of Schweizerisches Landesmuseum, Zurich, and Gottfried-Keller-Stiftung

Salomon Geßners Dichtungen, edited with an introduction by Hermann Hesse (Frauenfeld: Huber, 1922);

Sämtliche Schriften, 3 volumes, edited by Martin Bircher (Zurich: Orell Füßli, 1972-1974);

Idyllen: Kritische Ausgabe, edited by E. Theodor Voss (Stuttgart: Reclam, 1973).

Editions in English: *The Works of Solomon* [sic] *Gessner, Translated from the German. With Some Account of His Life and Writings,* translated anonymously (Liverpool: Printed by J. M'Creery for T. Cadell, Jr. & W. Davies, 1802);

Select Idylls; or, Pastoral Poems: Translated from the German of Salomon Gessner, translated by George Baker (London: Printed for Longman, Hurst, Rees & Orme by W. Savage, 1809).

OTHER: Johann Friedrich von Cronegk, *Einsamkeiten: Ein Gedicht in zween Gesängen*, edited by Geßner (Zurich: Geßner, 1758);

Sophocles, *Electra*, translated by J. J. Steinbrüchel, foreword by Geßner, 4 volumes (Zurich: Geßner, 1759-1760);

"Antwort auf die letzten Wünsche eines Helvetischen Patrioten," in *Verhandlungen der helvetischen Gesellschaft in Schinznach, im Jahr 1763* (Zurich, 1763);

Johann Wilhelm Ludwig Gleim, *Der blöde Schäfer*, foreword by Geßner (Zurich: Orell & Geßner, 1767);

"Brief über die Landschaftsmahlerey," *Geschichte der besten Künstler in der Schweiz*, by Johann Caspar Füssli, volume 3 (Zurich: Orell & Geßner, 1770), pp. xxxvi-Lxiv;

Franz Xaver Bronner, *Fischergedichte und Erzählungen*, 2 volumes, foreword by Geßner (Zurich: Orell, Geßner, Füßli, 1787).

Salomon Geßner was the first writer of German fiction to achieve international popularity and fame in his own time. His idylls (two collections, 1756 and 1772) and his prose epic *Der Tod Abels* (1758; translated as *The Death of Abel*, 1761) were immensely successful in the later eighteenth century and influential throughout Europe well into the nineteenth. Published in many editions and translated (often, as in the English translations, quite freely) into many languages, his works moved and delighted countless readers. His admirers included Johann Joachim Winckelmann, Jean-Jacques Rousseau, Maximilien Robespierre, Samuel Taylor Coleridge, and Benjamin Franklin. His works are central documents of pre-Romantic sensibility that did much to form a taste for the beauty and freedom of nature, peaceful rural life, domestic felicity, moral sentiment, and simple language. They encouraged the conviction that natural innocence and true civilized values existed in the countryside, and particularly in Geßner's native Switzerland. Geßner occupies a place of undisputed preeminence in the history of the idyll in modern times, even though subsequent developments (Johann Wolfgang von Goe-

Title page for Geßner's third book, a collection of idylls set in a vaguely classical Greece

the's idyllic epic *Hermann und Dorothea* ([1797], for example) were as much a reaction against as a continuation of his work. At a time when German was held by many European intellectuals to be a barbaric tongue, his musical prose persuaded Germans and foreigners alike that the language was capable of delicacy and beauty and could give poetic expression to tender and sublime feelings. His reputation has, however, not stood the test of time. Despite the praise of Hermann Hesse and others, he is now scarcely read, though he is still regarded as a historically significant figure. He was also an important publisher and an artist of some distinction.

Born on 1 April 1730 in Zurich to Hans Conrad Geßner and Esther Geßner, née Hirzel, Geßner spent almost all his life in that city and its immediate environs. An imaginative boy who did not thrive at school, he was placed in 1745 under a private tutor in the congenial setting of rural Switzerland. There he began to write verses celebrating nature, wine, women, and song. His

Etching by Geßner to illustrate his poem "Der erste Schiffer," from the first volume of the 1777-1778 collection of his writings

models were the nature poet Barthold Heinrich Brockes and the poetry of wit and charm and joy in life of Friedrich von Hagedorn and Johann Wilhelm Friedrich Gleim. In 1748 he entered his father's printing, publishing, and bookselling business. Soon he was sent to Berlin to gain experience in the book trade, but his position there proved far from his liking and he decided to become a painter. Yet in 1750 Geßner dutifully returned to his father's firm. He took work lightly and mixed with like-minded young men who sought the beauty of the countryside and read and wrote poetry, wineglass in hand. Abandoning verse for prose, he wrote *Die Nacht* (The Night, 1753), *Daphnis* (1754; translated, 1768), *Idyllen* (1756; translated as *Rural Poems*, 1762), and *Der Tod Abels. Die Nacht*, a short piece in the poetic prose that was to be his characteristic medium, took up the themes of his early verses. Its flippancy did not please his elders in Zurich. But with *Daphnis*, a story of young love inspired by Longus's *Daphnis and Chloe*, he turned to the pastoral scene and linked feeling for nature with virtue.

The idylls, too, followed the classical tradition and were set in a vaguely classical Greece. In these short scenes Geßner found his happiest form, marrying charm, wit, and lightness of touch (the rococo tradition) to serious moral sentiment. In the foreword he declared, as only a few had done before him, that Theocritus's idylls were preferable to the eclogues of Virgil–and above all superior to French pastoral poetry, which exhibited the alleged overrefinement of that nation. His etched illustrations expressed an admiration for the art of classical Greece. Geßner painted a Golden Age which he claimed once existed, and he insisted that innocence could still be found where countryfolk had escaped exploitation by townsmen and princes. In the idylls this innocence takes the form of joy in nature, kindness, spontaneous invention of song, the creation of simple artifacts, gratitude for divine benevolence, compassion for the unfortunate and for animals, family affection, and love that is inspired by physical beauty combined with moral goodness. Virtue is contrasted with discontent and envy and the pursuit of power. Geßner's carefully orchestrated prose is often free verse in disguise. His inspiration was probably prose translations of verse originals, such as Johann Jakob Bodmer's rendering of John Milton's *Paradise Lost* (1732). His is a musical language in which sound and rhythm are all important. By simplicity of expression and of construction and by avoiding regular metrical patterns, Geßner, who repeatedly observed that nature eschews formal regularity, achieves an impression of artlessness. In content as well as form, the idylls combine tradition with novelty: the realism in the nature descriptions and the emphasis on moral values were new. Geßner never suggests that sensuality is inherently sinful, and he has virtue rewarded on earth, not in heaven.

The critic Bodmer, who ruled the literary scene in Zurich and whose influence was felt throughout Germany, had not been pleased with Geßner's earlier writings but gave his full approval to the idylls. Bodmer's influence is noticeable in the five cantos of *Der Tod Abels*, where Geßner uses a rather more heightened style with clear echoes of the epic tradition. He departs from his biblical source by providing Cain and Abel with wives and children so as to increase the pathos. There is greater stress than in the idylls on the precariousness of the idyllic world, a world that depends on a certain attitude.

In 1760 Geßner started the Zurich newspaper, *Zürcher Zeitung*, which has since become, as the *Neue Zürcher Zeitung*, one of the world's lead-

*Geßner in 1781; painting by Anton Graff
(Kunsthaus, Zurich)*

new idylls, published in 1772 together with stories by Denis Diderot, included a new theme, the joys of marriage and parenthood. He sat on the town council and was given responsible posts as administrator of a rural parish and magistrate of an urban district in 1768, and as administrator of a forest in 1781. Many readers were moved to write to him of their heartfelt adulation for his writings and his personality; distinguished visitors from afar, including Czar Paul I, the Mozart family, and Goethe, made pilgrimages to his home.

In 1796 Geßner's biographer Johann Jacob Hottinger created a portrait of him which appealed to the middle class's sense of their own moral worth and to the growing demand for sincerity in literature. It is of a modest and wise man enviably untouched by formal education and modern civilization, who in his last years bore illness and a heart attack cheerfully, and who died on 2 March 1788 with a smile of contentment on his lips. It was such a person that Geßner's visitors sought in the forester's house he used as his summer residence. Recently, however, it has been discovered that Geßner's life was not all happiness and success. He was a disappointment to his father and to his practical wife, who expected more of him as a writer and artist once she had accepted that he was no businessman. Two of his five children died in infancy. After 1769 he was plagued with illness and feared that he would lose his sight. This reevaluation of his life has gone side by side with a reevaluation of the political implications of his work: in contrasting town and country he was not simply repeating a literary cliché but reacting to a Zurich ruled by self-interest and restrictive moral and religious precepts. He sympathized with liberal Enlightenment ideas, although to have voiced them too openly would have meant banishment from his homeland. In his writing he set down not his experience but his dreams of happiness in fictionalized and disguised form.

Each of these images of Geßner allows for a sensitive and imaginative man with both a keen sense of moral responsibility and a sense of fun. Each can accommodate, too, his self-assessment as "kein streitbarer Held" (no hero seeking confrontation). As a youngster he showed a harmlessly boisterous disregard for strict propriety. The years brought more dignity, but he was the life of many a social gathering. He disliked the Swiss Protestant church's killjoy emphasis on human sinfulness and was suspected of freethink-

ing dailies. In 1761 he married Judith Heidegger and joined in partnership with his brother-in-law, Johann Heinrich Heidegger, in the printing and publishing house Orell, Geßner and Company. (In 1770 the name was changed to Orell, Geßner & Füßli; in 1925 it became Orell Füßli.) The firm became a leader in its field, setting high standards of production and publishing many important works, often with title pages, illustrations, and vignettes etched by Geßner himself. Between 1762 and his death he published nine editions of his collected works. His name was largely made in Paris, where he was enthusiastically greeted as a natural poet who had transformed poetic tradition and whose works were morally and religiously edifying. French translations of his work spread his fame to the rest of Europe. His wife, who came from one of the most influential Zurich families, took over many business chores so that he could write, draw, and paint. During the 1760s, he devoted himself to art with considerable success. He was the model father of three children—Anna Dorothea, born in 1763; Konrad, born in 1764; and Heinrich, born in 1768—and when the poetic muse revisited him in 1770 his

Painting by Geßner of an Alpine stream (Kupferstichkabinett, West Berlin, Staatliche Museen Preußischer Kulturbesitz)

ing. Critical of stuffiness, he yet assumed a benevolently moralistic stance as a parent and was not enamored of the literary excesses of the Sturm und Drang. He was no revolutionary, but he had a pronounced sense of justice: he defended a friend who was banished from Zurich for freethinking, fought for the dismissal of a tyrannical administrator, and improved the lot of the forestry workers. His faith in divine providence was undoubtedly real; he believed that he saw it at work in 1771 when a South German priest helped a penniless boy reach relatives in Zurich after his parents and six brothers and sisters had perished. Genuine, too, were his love of art and his patriotism. He was a founding member of the Helvetische Gesellschaft (Helvetian Society), whose aims were to promote individual freedom, to call on the moral sense of all, and thus to counter the division of the nation into rulers (the town patricians) and the ruled (above all, the rural population).

Even in Geßner's lifetime dissenting voices were heard amid the general enthusiasm for his works, particularly in Germany. In 1767 Johann Gottfried Herder declared that while Theocritus had transformed reality into poetry, Geßner portrayed an imaginary and unconvincing ideal. In 1772 Goethe observed that Geßner's work lacked variety and interest. Herder had allowed that Geßner was a distinguished stylist and a source of moral inspiration, but in 1795 Friedrich Schiller, in his *Über naive und sentimentalische Dichtung* (On Naive and Sentimental Poetry), denied both claims. After 1800 such criticisms multiplied and foreshadowed the demise of Geßner's popularity. Increasingly his writing was judged to be artificial, his sentiments sentimental, and his simplicity dismissed as childishness. But this simplicity is deceptive; as Herder said in 1796, Geßner's method was to conceal his art. A vision of happiness that has evoked contradictory responses may not be as unambiguous as has often been assumed. Geßner's idyllic world is part escapism, part veiled social criticism, part proclamation of conventional morality, part rejection of illiberal Christian orthodoxy, part affirmation of existence on earth, and part longing for a better world.

Letters:

Salomon Gessners Briefwechsel mit seinem Sohne während dem Aufenthalte des Letztern in Dresden und Rom, in den Jahren 1784-85 und 1787-88 (Bern & Zurich: Geßner, 1801); translated as *The Letters of Gessner and His Family* (London: Vernor & Hood, 1804).

Biographies:

Johann Jacob Hottinger, *Salomon Gessner* (Zurich: Geßner, 1796);

Fritz Bergemann, *Salomon Gessner: Eine literaturhistorisch-biographische Einleitung* (Munich: Müller & Rentsch, 1913);

Paul Leeman-van Elck, *Salomon Gessner: Sein Lebensbild. Mit beschreibenden Verzeichnissen seiner literarischen und künstlerischen Werke* (Zurich: Orell Füssli, 1930).

References:

Gustav Albert Andreen, *Studies in the Idyl in German Literature* (Rock Island, Ill.: Augustan College, 1902);

Alfred Anger, "Landschaftsstil des Rokoko," *Euphorion*, 51, no. 2 (1957): 151-191;

Martin Bircher, Franz Hafner, and Richard Zürcher, *Geist und Schönheit im Zürich des 18. Jahrhunderts* (Zurich: Orell Füssli, 1968);

Eric Blackall, *The Emergence of German as a Literary Language* (Cambridge, University Press, 1959), pp. 377-386;

Renate Böschenstein-Schäfer, *Idylle* (Stuttgart: Metzler, 1967);

Berthold Burk, *Elemente idyllischen Lebens: Studien zu Salomon Gessner und Jean-Jacques Rousseau* (Frankfurt am Main & Bern: Lang, 1981);

Ulrich Fülleborn, *Das deutsche Prosagedicht* (Munich: Fink, 1970);

Johann Wolfgang von Goethe, *Gedenkausgabe der Werke, Briefe und Gespräche*, 24 volumes, edited by Ernst Barker (Zurich: Artemis, 1948-1954), XIV: 154-157;

Johann Gottfried Herder, *Sämtliche Werke*, 33 volumes, edited by Bernhard Suphan (Berlin: Weidmann, 1877-1913): I: 337-350; XVIII: 120;

John L. Hibberd, *Salomon Gessner: His Creative Achievement and Influence* (Cambridge: Cambridge University Press, 1976);

Gerhard Kaiser, *Wandrer und Idylle: Goethe und die Phänomenologie der Natur von Geßner bis Gottfried Keller* (Göttingen: Vandenhoeck & Ruprecht, 1977);

Maler und Dichter der Idylle: Salomon Gessner (Wolfenbüttel: Herzog August Bibliothek, 1980);

Lawrence Marsden Price, *Inkle and Jariko Album* (Berkeley: University of California Press, 1937);

Salomon Gessner: 1730-1930. Gedenkbuch zum 200. Geburtstag (Zurich: Lesezirkel Hottingen, 1930);

Frank Woodyer Stokoe, *German Influence in the English Romantic Period 1788-1818* (Cambridge: Cambridge University Press, 1926);

Paul van Tieghem, "Les idylles de Gessner et le rêve pastoral dans le préromantisme européen," in his *Le Préromantisme*, volume 2 (Paris: Rieder, 1930), pp. 204-311;

Heinrich Wölfflin, *Salomon Gessner* (Frauenfeld: Huber, 1889).

Papers:

Salomon Geßner's papers are in the Zentralbibliothek, Zurich.

Johann Wilhelm Ludwig Gleim

(2 April 1719 - 18 February 1803)

Meredith Lee
University of California, Irvine

BOOKS: *Versuch in Scherzhaften Liedern,* anonymous, 2 volumes (Berlin: Schütz, 1744-1745);

Gedicht über den Tod des Heldenmüthigen Fürsten, Herrn Friedrich Wilhelm, Prinzen in Preußen und Marggrafen von Brandenburg (Berlin, 1744);

Der Blöde Schäfer: Ein Lustspiel, anonymous (Berlin: Schütz, 1745);

Freundschaftliche Briefe, anonymous (Berlin: Schütz, 1746);

Der Alte Freyer: Eine Erzehlung, anonymous (Cologne, 1747);

Der Ursprung des Berlinischen Labyrinths, anonymous (Berlin, 1747);

Gebet bei Erblickung Sr. Königl. Hoheit, des jungen Prinzen Friedrichs von Preußen (Berlin, 1748);

Lieder, anonymous (Amsterdam [actually Halberstadt]: Friderich, 1749);

Lieder (Zurich [actually Halberstadt]: Friderich, 1749); excerpt translated as "Belinde, ein Sonnet von Herr Gleim," *Annual Register or a View of the History, Politics and Literature of the Year,* 31 (1789): 166;

Ode Als der Hochwohlgebohrne Herr, Herr Christoph Ludwig von Stille Generalmajor des Königs, Den 18ten October 1752 in die Ewigkeit gegangen war (Halberstadt: Friderich, 1752);

Fabeln, anonymous, 2 volumes (Berlin, 1756-1757);

Romanzen, anonymous (Berlin & Leipzig, 1756);

Sieges-Lied der Preußen, nach der Schlacht bei Roßbach, anonymous (Berlin, 1757);

Preußische Kriegslieder in den Feldzügen 1756 und 1757 von einem Grenadier: Mit Melodien, anonymous (Berlin: Voß, 1758);

Kriegs- und Siegeslieder der Preußen von einem Preußischen Grenadier: Nebst einem Anhang einiger an des Königs von Preußen Majestät gerichteter Gedichte, anonymous (Berlin, 1758);

Fortsetzung der Kriegs- und Sieges-Lieder der Preußen über die Siege bei Lowositz und Lissa, anonymous (Berlin, 1758);

Painting by G. Hempel, 1750 (Gleimhaus, Halberstadt)

Sieges-Lied der Preußen nach der Schlacht bei Lissa, den 5. December 1757, anonymous (Berlin, 1758);

Der Grenadier an die Kriegsmuse nach dem Siege bei Zorndorf, den 25. August 1758, anonymous (N.p., 1759);

Sechzig freundschaftliche Briefe von dem Verfasser des Versuchs in scherzhaften Liedern, anonymous (Berlin: Lange, 1760);

Klagen, anonymous (Berlin: Wever, 1762);

Gespräche mit der deutschen Muse, anonymous (Berlin, 1764);

Petrarchische Gedichte, anonymous (Berlin: Privately printed, 1764);

Sieben kleine Gedichte: Nach Anacreons Manier, anonymous (Berlin, 1764);

Lob des Landlebens, anonymous (Berlin, 1765);

Lieder nach dem Anakreon, von dem Verfasser des Versuchs in scherzhaften Liedern, anonymous (Berlin & Brunswick: Waysenhaus, 1766);

Neue Lieder: Von dem Verfasser der Lieder nach dem Anakreon, anonymous (Berlin: Typographische Gesellschaft, 1767);

Briefe von den Herren Gleim und Jacobi, by Gleim and Johann Georg Jacobi (Berlin, 1768);

Oden nach dem Horatz, anonymous (Berlin: 1769);

Zwey Lieder (Halberstadt, 1769);

Dem Oberbürgermeister Schulze zu Neu-Hallensleben: Den 21ten September 1769, anonymous (N.p., 1769);

An den Herrn Canonicus Jacobi, als ein Criticus wünschte, daß er aus seinen Gedichten den Amor herauslassen möchte (Berlin, 1769);

Sinngedichte: Als Manuscript für Freunde, anonymous (Berlin, 1769);

Der Apfeldieb: Ein dramatisches Sinngedicht, anonymous (Berlin, 1770);

Alexis und Elise, as Amint (Halberstadt, 1771); enlarged as *Alexis und Elise: Drey Gesänge,* anonymous (Berlin, 1771);

Der reiche Mann und Lazarus: Eine Erzählung (Halberstadt, 1771);

An die Musen (N.p., 1771);

Zwei Lieder eines armen Arbeitsmannes, zum Neujahrsgeschenk 1772 (Halberstadt: Groß, 1772);

Lobschrift auf Herrn Noël, nach dem Französischen des Kaisers von China (Berlin: Lange, 1772);

Die beste Welt, by Gleim and Jacobi (Halberstadt: Groß, 1772);

Lieder für das Volk (Halberstadt: Strodtmann, 1772);

Gedichte nach den Minnesingern (Berlin, 1773);

Halladat oder Das rothe Buch (Zum Vorlesen in den Schulen) (Hamburg: Bode, 1774);

Max, eine Romanze: Als eine Handschrift für Freunde, anonymous (Weimar, 1774);

Der gute Mann: Als dem Vater des Vaterlandes wegen eines Geschenks von dreyßig tausend Thaler ein Fest gefeyret wurde. Zum Besten der Armen (Halberstadt, 1775);

Das schöne weibchen: Zwanzig Exemplare für Freunde, anonymous (N.p., 1776);

Sinngedichte: Dreißig Exemplare für Freunde, anonymous (Berlin, 1776);

Romanzen, anonymous (N.p., 1777);

Preußische Kriegeslieder im März und April 1778: Von einem Grenadier, anonymous (Leipzig: Weygand, 1778);

Kriegeslieder im May, Junius, und Julius 1778: Von einem Grenadier, anonymous (Berlin, 1778);

Kriegeslieder im August 1778: Von einem Grenadier, anonymous (Berlin, 1778);

Lieder der Liebe, anonymous (N.p., 1778);

Der Rosenraub, anonymous (Berlin, 1778);

Friedensgesang: Am Friedensfest, zu Halberstadt, den 23. May 1779, anonymous (Halberstadt, 1779);

Gedichte nach Walter von der Vogelweide, anonymous (N.p., 1779);

Kriegeslieder im September 1778 bis in den April 1779: von einem Grenadier, anonymous (Berlin, 1779);

Salomo der Prediger: An den Fürsten von Dessau, anonymous (Berlin: Decker, 1780);

Lied, zu singen auf den Spiegel-Bergen, bey dem Grüningischen Weinfasse, anonymous (N.p., 1781);

An den Herrn Geheimden Rath Freyherrn Spiegel von und zu Pikkelsheim im Oktober 1781 (N.p., 1781);

An Ihro Hochwürden Gnaden den Herrn Dohmdechant Freyherrn Spiegel zum Diesenberg, by Gleim and Heinrich Benedictus Oppermann (N.p., 1781);

Episteln (Leipzig: Breitkopf, 1783);

Erzaehlungen (Halberstadt: Delius, 1783);

Trostgesang am Grabe seines Bruders (Halberstadt: Mevius, 1783);

Reisegespräch des Königs im Jahr 1779: Zum Besten armer Soldatenkinder in Druck gegeben vom Verfasser der preußischen Kriegeslieder, am Geburtstage des Landesvaters im Jahr 1784, anonymous (Halberstadt: Groß & Hartmann, 1784);

Blumen auf unsers Spiegels Grab, anonymous (Halberstadt, 1785);

Noch Blumen auf das Grab des Menschenfreundes, anonymous (Halberstadt: Privately printed, 1785);

Epoden, anonymous (N.p., 1785);

Als mein geliebtester Bruder Daniel Conrad Vollrad Gleim zur Erde bestattet wurde (Magdeburg, 1785);

Der König und Ziethen: Gesungen zu Halberstadt, anonymous (Halberstadt: Privately printed, 1785);

Blumen auf Leopolds Grab, anonymous (N.p., 1785);

Lied gesungen am Geburtstage des Königs zu Halberstadt den 24ten Januar 1785, anonymous (N.p., 1785);

Blumen auf Spiegels Grab, anonymous (Berlin: Maurer, 1786);

An unsre Dichter am Grabe Friedrichs des Einzigen (Berlin: Maurer, 1786);

Fabeln von Gleim (Berlin: Maurer, 1786);

Freudenlied: Gesungen im Lande der Preußen, den 24. Jenner 1786, vom Verfasser der Kriegslieder, anonymous (Berlin: Maurer, 1786);

Friedrich der Zweyte nach Seinem irdischen Leben: Gesungen vom Verfasser der Kriegslieder, anonymous (Berlin: Maurer, 1786);

Gesang der Musen und der Landleuthe, anonymous (Halberstadt: Mevius, 1786);

Grabgesang als Ziethen zur Ruhe gieng: Berlin, den 27. Jenner 1786, anonymous (Berlin: Maurer, 1786);

Grabgesang Friedrichs II., anonymous (Berlin: Maurer, 1786);

Lied gesungen in der Mitternacht vom Jahr 1785 zum Jahr 1786 (Halberstadt: Privately printed, 1786);

Ernst Möring (Halberstadt, 1786);

Oden (Berlin: Maurer, 1787);

Der beste König: Halberstadt, den 4ten Juny 1788 (Berlin: Königiche Preußische Akademische Kunst- und Buchhandlung, 1788);

Einige Gedichte für einige Leser auf dem Congreß zu Reichenbach und auf der Kaiserwahl zu Frankfurt am Main (Berlin: Matzdorff, 1790);

Preußische Marschlieder im May 1790, anonymous (Halberstadt: Kämpfer, 1790);

Preußische Soldatenlieder in den Jahren 1778 bis 1790, anonymous (Berlin: Unger, 1790);

Lieder, gesungen im Jahr 1792, anonymous (N.p., 1792);

Kriegslieder: Bey dem Ausmarsch des Halberstädtischen Regiments, anonymous (Halberstadt: Privately printed, 1792);

Zeitgedichte vom alten Gleim: Als Handschrift für Freunde (N.p., 1792);

Sinngedichte von Gleim: Als Handschrift für Freunde (N.p., 1792);

Zeitgedichte vor und nach dem Tode des heiligen Ludwigs XVI, anonymous (Leipzig: Dyck, 1793);

Siegeslied als Mainz überwunden war (Berlin: Privately printed, 1793);

Kriegslieder im Jahre 1793, anonymous (N.p., 1794);

Das Hüttchen, anonymous (Halberstadt: Dölle, 1794); excerpt translated by Benjamin Beresford as "The Invitation: From the German

of Gleim," *Poetic Register, and Repository of Fugitive Poetry*, 5 (1805): 462;

Forstenburg beklagt von Gleim (Halberstadt: Privately printed, 1794);

Fabeln für das Jahr 1795, anonymous (N.p., 1795);

Satirische Gedichte, anonymous (Halberstadt, 1795);

Nesseln auf Gräber, anonymous (N.p., 1795);

Amor und Psyche: 68 anakreontische Lieder, anonymous (N.p., 1796);

An Dohm: Am Gedächtnißtage seiner Ankunft zu Halberstadt, anonymous (Halberstadt: Delius & Matthias, 1796);

Kraft und Schnelle des alten Peleus: Im Jahr 1797, anonymous (N.p., 1797);

Schweizerische Kriegslieder, anonymous (N.p., 1798);

Zeitgedichte vom alten Gleim: Seinen Freunden zum Geschenke (Halberstadt, 1799);

An Deutschlands Fürsten im Jahr 1800 vom alten Gleim (Halberstadt: Privately printed, 1800);

Todtenopfer, als Herr Rektor Gottlob Nathanael Fischer . . . zur Erde bestattet wurde (Halberstadt: Dölle, 1800);

Preußische Volkslieder in den Jahren 1772 bis 1800 (Halberstadt, 1800); excerpt translated as "My Native Country, from Gleim," in *Literary Gazette, and Journal of Belles-Lettres, Sciences, etc.*, 12 (1828): 572;

Dramatische Gedichte, anonymous (Berlin, 1800);

Zeitgedichte für wenige Leser: Im Jänner 1801, anonymous (N.p., 1801);

Lieder zu einem Roman, anonymous (Halberstadt, 1801);

Zeitgedichte von einem alten Deutschen: Deutschland 1801, anonymous (Halberstadt, 1801);

Ein kleines Gedicht auf die Vermählung des Herrn Grafen Ferdinand Stolberg mit der lieblichen Gräfin Marie Agnes Stolberg, anonymous (Wernigerode: Privately printed, 1802);

Lied am Spiegelsfeste zu singen (Halberstadt: Privately printed, 1802);

Nachtgedichte vom alten Gleim, 2 volumes (N.p., 1802);

Sämmtliche Werke: Erste Originalausgabe aus des Dichters Handschriften, 8 volumes, edited by Wilhelm Körte (volumes 1-7, Halberstadt: Büreau für Literatur und Kunst, 1811-1813; volume 8, Leipzig: Brockhaus, 1841; reprinted, Hildesheim & New York: Olms, 1971);

Preußische Kriegslieder von einem Grenadier, edited by August Sauer (Heilbronn: Henninger,

1882; reprinted, Nendeln, Liechtenstein: Kraus, 1968);

Versuch in scherzhaften Liedern und Lieder: Nach den Erstausgaben von 1744/45 und 1749 mit den Körteschen Fassungen im Anhang kritisch herausgegeben, edited by Alfred Anger (Tübingen: Niemeyer, 1964);

Gedichte, edited by Jürgen Stenzel (Stuttgart: Reclam, 1969).

OTHER: Gotthold Ephraim Lessing, *Philotas: Ein Trauerspiel. Von dem Verfasser der preußischen Kriegslieder versificirt,* revised anonymously by Gleim (Berlin: Voß, 1760);

Friedrich Gottlieb Klopstock, *Der Tod Adam's: Ein Trauerspiel. In Verse gesetzt von dem Verfasser der preußischen Kriegslieder,* revised anonymously by Gleim (Berlin, 1766);

Ranchin and François-Augustin Paradis de Moncrif, *Der Vater, Nebenbuhler seines Sohns, und Magdalis, die eine Stifts-Dame ward: Zwey Gedichte. Nach dem Französischen,* translated anonymously by Gleim (N.p., 1769);

Pythagoras, *Die goldnen Sprüche des Pythagoras (Zum Vorlesen in den Schulen),* translated by Gleim (Halberstadt, 1775); enlarged as *Die goldnen Sprüche des Pythagoras: Aus dem Griechischen. Nebst einem Anhang von Gleim* (Halberstadt, 1786);

Frederick I, *Friedrichs des Einzigen Epistel an seinen Geist: Aus dem Französischen,* translated by Gleim (N.p., 1798).

Most successful and best loved of the anacreontic poets, popular promoter of Frederick II, friend and mentor to two generations of younger writers, and indefatigable correspondent, Johann Wilhelm Ludwig Gleim spent the bulk of his long years in the city of Halberstadt just northeast of the Harz Mountains. Acquainted with virtually every noted writer of his age, Gleim tended and nourished his friendships with care and not a little jealousy, and in his later years earned the affectionate title "Vater" (Father) Gleim for his generous and continuing support of younger poets. Poetry and letters–documents of an age of sentiment, quickening patriotism, and energetic literary activity–are his legacy. In addition to the anacreontic verses that dominate his immense production, he published popular collections of verse fables, romances, patriotic songs, adaptations from the Minnesang (medieval German love poetry), didactic pieces, and epigrammatic poetry. Many of his poems were set to music. Hon-

ored in his old age even when his poetry had long ceased to have any literary interest, he was buried with great fanfare when he died at the age of eighty-three.

One of twelve children of Laurentius Gleim, a Prussian tax collector, and Anna Gertraud Gleim, née Peill, Gleim was born in Ermsleben, near Halberstadt, on 2 April 1719. A neighboring pastor tutored the linguistically gifted boy in the classical languages. From 1734 to 1738 Gleim attended the Oberpfarrschule in Wernigerode. When he was orphaned at sixteen, local patrons provided assistance that allowed him to finish school and to begin law studies at the university in Halle in December 1738. There he was attracted to lectures on philosophical aesthetics. He also made the first in a long series of friendships based on poetry and sentiment with Johann Peter Uz and Johann Nikolaus Götz. Uz, Götz, and Gleim were to become the major figures in the development of German anacreontic poetry, the light, playful, and worldly verse whose name derives from a Renaissance collection of some sixty short lyrical poems on wine, love, and song mistakenly attributed to Anacreon of Teos, a poet of the sixth century B.C.

Gleim left the university in August 1741 and spent the next six years in a series of temporary positions in and near Berlin. A promising opportunity in Copenhagen failed to materialize after the untimely death of his patron, Adolph Ludewig von Reinhart. After an extended stay at the home of his sister, Gleim became a tutor in Potsdam in 1743. During the second Silesian War he served as secretary to Prince Wilhelm of Brandenburg-Schwedt, who died on the battlefield outside Prague in September 1744. Gleim accompanied the body back to Berlin and then worked as staff secretary to Leopold I, Prince of Anhalt-Dessau, from May to November 1745. No permanent position in Berlin materialized.

During the uncertain years in Berlin, Gleim actively extended his literary friendships. Closest among the new companions was the Prussian officer and poet Ewald Christian von Kleist, whom Gleim eagerly encouraged in his earliest literary efforts. His circle of intimates also included the poet and teacher Jakob Immanuel Pyra; Johann Georg Sulzer, in later years renowned as an aesthetic theorist; and Karl Wilhelm Ramler, who was to gain prominence as a poet and translator in the 1760s and 1770s. Gleim's extensive correspondence included the Swiss literary theorist and patron Johann Jakob Bodmer.

66

The Gleimhaus in Halberstadt, Gleim's residence from 1747 until his death in 1803. Today it is a museum.

Gleim's first collection of poems, *Versuch in Scherzhaften Liedern* (Sampling of Playful Songs), is the most important product of the Berlin years. Published anonymously in two volumes in 1744-1745, the work proved a popular and critical triumph and established Gleim's abiding reputation as the German Anacreon, the singer of worldly joys and playful pleasures. The collection of mostly rhymeless verse opens with an explicit tribute to "Anakreon, mein Lehrer" (Anacreon, my teacher), who "singt nur von Wein und Liebe" (sings only of wine and love). Less overtly learned than the poems of his well-known precursor Friedrich von Hagedorn and with a sustained air of naïveté and naturalness despite the technically skillful construction of many of the poems, the collection evokes a fictional world of intimate merriment, pleasurable flirtation, and charm. The poems have a garden setting with erotic overtones and occasional mythological references, far removed from the realities of either Berlin or the battlefield. Gleim uses his preface to heighten the reader's engagement in this world of anacreontic

sensibility. Ostensibly written by a young man to his beloved Doris, the preface introduces the poems as genuine products of the young man's affection. The collection went through multiple reprintings and was widely imitated, and many of the poems were set to music. Gleim returned repeatedly in later years to the flirtations and the seemingly artless tones of the anacreontic poetry that he did so much to establish, even long after he had exhausted his ability to adapt its narrow range of themes in new and interesting ways.

Gleim's pattern of sporadic employment was finally broken in October 1747 when, through the favor of a patron, he was appointed secretary of the cathedral chapter in Halberstadt. This lucrative sinecure was enhanced in 1756 by an additional appointment as canon of the Stift (endowment) Walbeck, allowing him to live his remaining years in complete financial security. In March 1753 Gleim became engaged to Sophie Mayer, but just before the planned May wedding Sophie broke off the relationship, a move Gleim ascribed to the jealousy of her father. Gleim never married; his household was directed from 1753 until his death by his niece Sophie Dorothea Gleim.

The transition to Halberstadt in no way diminished Gleim's cultivation of both old and new friends. Principal among the new was the poet Friedrich Gottlieb Klopstock, who had recently created a stir with the publication of the opening cantos of his epic poem *Der Messias* (The Messiah, 1748-1773), and Gotthold Ephraim Lessing, whom he met during a 1754-1755 winter visit to Berlin.

August 1756 brought the outbreak of the Seven Years' War. Gleim experienced the war directly in the marauding in Halberstadt and its environs by the French army in the fall and winter of 1757-1758, indirectly and even more forcefully in correspondence with Kleist. Although the war was to take the life of his friend, who was mortally wounded in the battle of Kunersdorf in August 1759, initially it provided Gleim with an opportunity for renewed literary prominence. Since his move from Berlin he had concentrated on writing additional poems in the anacreontic mode, two collections of fables, and romances in a popular ballad style adapted from the French writer François-Augustin Paradis de Moncrif. The events of the war, however, coupled with a strong allegiance to Frederick II, suggested a new poetic tack. The result was his exceptionally popular *Preußische Kriegslieder in den Feldzügen 1756 und 1757 von einem Grenadier* (Prussian Songs of War in the Campaign of 1756 and 1757 by a Grenadier), published anonymously in 1758 with an enthusiastic preface by Lessing and accompanying musical settings. The poems, written in a rhymed adaptation of an English ballad stanza popularly referred to in Germany as the Chevy-Chase stanza (after "The Ballad of Chevy Chase"), sustain the fiction that they are being written on the spot by a simple foot soldier. Naive in tone, exuberant in their patriotic energy, and totally admiring of the Prussian king, the eleven poems link king and foot soldier in a single righteous cause. The poems were widely read and imitated and were critically acclaimed; they fanned the fire of Prussian patriotism for many decades to follow. In later years Gleim wrote several additional collections of poems that drew on the same formula of earnest enthusiasm for the cause of king and country, expressed in a simple, direct voice in a stanza structure evocative of folk poetry. The 1772 collection *Lieder für das Volk* (Songs for the Common People), in particular, and the various collections of "Soldatenlieder" (Soldiers'

Title page for the first collection of Gleim's Prussian war songs, inspired by the Seven Years' War

Songs) and "Kriegeslieder" (Songs of War) of the 1790s celebrate the God-given rule of Prussian right and might and the virtues of loyalty, bravery, and contentment with the existing social order. Needless to say, Gleim had little sympathy for the French Revolution, against which he polemicized in letters and verse.

At the height of his fame, Gleim continued his production of anacreontic poetry and extended his circle of correspondents. Among the newest was the self-taught poet Anna Luise Karsch, who had attracted patronage in Berlin and was being feted by the social elite and praised by the critical elite, including Ramler, Lessing, and Moses Mendelssohn. Gleim did not return her romantic interest, which was evident during his 1761 visit to Berlin and her visit to Halberstadt later the same year, but he assisted in the publication of her poems in 1763 and continued an active correspondence with her until her death. He dubbed her the German Sappho, a name that gained wide currency.

Not all of the old friendships survived. As literary and personal differences mounted, Gleim broke relations with Ramler in 1765 and with an old Berlin friend, Johann Joachim Spalding, in 1771. But new and younger writers took their place. Gleim entertained thoughts of establishing an academy in Halberstadt to assure that his friends would be close at hand. With his assistance several younger men with shared literary interests secured positions in Halberstadt, although some only for a short time; their departures frequently gave rise to feelings of enormous loss, betrayal, and even bitterness on Gleim's part. Among these younger men was Johann Georg Jacobi, whose sentimentally stylized correspondence with Gleim was published in 1768. Some twenty years earlier Gleim and his Berlin friends had published the relatively well-received collection *Freundschaftliche Briefe* (Friendly Letters, 1746) in which the anacreontic sentiment popularized by Gleim's poetry had been adapted to an epistolary mode. Gleim's newest public display of literary affection, however, proved embarrassing to most readers and elicited widespread criticism.

Although he never again wrote a work that markedly influenced the development of German poetry, Gleim continued to produce volume after volume, most of them published at his own expense and distributed to friends. Many of his works proved repetitious, but within his narrow range and anacreontic preferences he also explored new poetic possibilities, including adaptations from Minnesang and didactic poems in an orientalized style loosely derived from German translations of the *Koran*. The latter he published in 1774 as *Halladat oder Das rothe Buch* (Halladat; or, The Red Book), a work he subtitled *Zum Vorlesen in den Schulen* (For Reading Aloud in the Schools) and optimistically distributed for classroom use.

Gleim continued to expand his network of friends and acquaintances for three more decades, cultivating sentimental bonds and fretting at the imagined or real flagging of reciprocal affection. His correspondence suggests that he was little interested in pursuing serious discussion of contemporary literary matters. But he remained well informed and politically engaged and for a time was involved in attempts to improve the writer's lot through the development of alternative, more remunerative publishing ventures. He also contin-

ued to support those in need, particularly younger poets such as Wilhelm Heinse and Johann Paul Friedrich Richter (Jean Paul). His hospitality was well known, and he greeted many writers in his Halberstadt home. Among them was Johann Gottfried Herder. Although Gleim and Herder had corresponded since the mid 1760s, the two men did not meet until 1775. Gleim's allegiance to both king and friends intensified in later years. After Frederick II's death in August 1786, Gleim gathered memorabilia such as the hat that the king had worn at Gleim's audience with him in December of the previous year and the sword Frederick had carried in the Seven Years' War. Friends were memorialized by an extensive portrait collection in a room that Gleim referred to as his "Musen- und Freundschaftstempel" (temple to the Muses and to friendship). Today this collection is housed in the Gleim Archive in the Gleimhaus in Halberstadt.

After fifty years of service, Gleim retired from his posts in 1797. Blind for the final two years of his life, he died at eighty-three on 18 February 1803 and was buried in his garden, surrounded by urns commemorating his deceased friends. Within a decade his grandnephew Wilhelm Körte published a biography of Gleim, seven volumes of his collected works, and three volumes of his correspondence; Gleim's protégé Klamer Schmidt edited two volumes of letters from the extensive correspondence with Klopstock and his family. By modern scholarly standards incomplete and unreliable, these editions underscore the need for a critical edition of both the works and the letters.

Letters:

Briefe der Schweizer Bodmer, Sulzer, Geßner: Aus Gleims litterarischem Nachlasse, edited by Wilhelm Körte (Zurich: Geßner, 1804);

Briefe zwischen Gleim, Wilhelm Heinse und Johann von Müller: Aus Gleims litterarischem Nachlasse, 2 volumes, edited by Körte (Zurich: Geßner, 1806);

Klopstock und seine Freunde: Briefwechsel der Familie Klopstock unter sich, und zwischen dieser Familie, Gleim, Schmidt, Fanny, Meta und andern Freunden. Aus Gleims brieflichem Nachlasse, 2 volumes, edited by Klamer Schmidt (Halberstadt, 1810); translated by Elizabeth Ogilvey Benger as *Klopstock and His Friends: A Series of Familiar Letters . . . 1750-1803* (London: Colburn, 1814);

Manuscript for four verses of a war song by Gleim, written in 1778 (from Gustav Könnecke, Bilderatlas
zur Geschichte der Deutschen Nationallitteratur, *1895)*

Briefwechsel zwischen Gleim und Heinse, 2 volumes, edited by Karl Schüddekopf (Weimar: Felber, 1894-1895);

Briefwechsel zwischen Gleim und Uz, edited by Schüddekopf (Tübingen: Litterarischer Verein in Stuttgart, 1899);

Briefwechsel zwischen Gleim und Ramler, 2 volumes, edited by Schüddekopf (Tübingen: Litterarischer Verein in Stuttgart, 1906-1907).

Bibliographies:

Max Friedländer, *Das deutsche Lied im 18. Jahrhundert; Quellen und Studien,* volume 2 (Stuttgart & Berlin: Cotta, 1902), pp. 57-68;

Karl Goedeke, *Grundriß zur Geschichte der deutschen Dichtung aus den Quellen,* third edition (Dresden: Ehlermann, 1916; reprinted, Nen-

deln, Liechtenstein: Kraus, 1975), volume 4, part 1, pp. 83-89.

Biography:

Wilhelm Körte, *Johann Wilhelm Ludwig Gleims Leben: Aus seinen Briefen und Schriften* (Halberstadt: Büreau für Literatur und Kunst, 1811).

References:

Klaus Bohnen, "Der 'Blumengarten' als 'Quell von unserm Wissen': Johann Wilhelm Ludwig Gleims Gedicht 'Anakreon,'" in *Gedichte und Interpretationen,* volume 2: *Aufklärung und Sturm und Drang,* edited by Karl Richter (Stuttgart: Reclam, 1983), pp. 113-123;

Gleim in 1790; painting by J. H. Ramberg
(Gleimhaus, Halberstadt)

Robert M. Browning, *German Poetry in the Age of the Enlightenment. From Brockes to Klopstock* (University Park: Pennsylvania State University Press, 1978), pp. 68-134;

Uwe-K. Ketelsen, "Ein Ossian der Hohenzollern: Gleims *Preußische Kriegslieder von einem Grenadier* zwischen Nationalismus und Absolutismus," in *Exile and Enlightenment: Studies in German and Comparative Literature in Honor of Guy Stern,* edited by Uwe Faulhaber and others (Detroit: Wayne State University Press, 1987), pp. 39-46;

Franz Muncker, "Johann Wilhelm Ludwig Gleim," in *Anakreontiker und preußisch-patriotische Lyriker* (Stuttgart: Union Deutsche Verlagsgesellschaft, 1892), pp. 179-204;

Christoph Perels, *Studien zur Aufnahme und Kritik der Rokokolyrik zwischen 1740 und 1760* (Göttingen: Vandenhoeck & Ruprecht, 1974), pp. 73-113;

Volker Riedel, "Gleim-Kolloquium in Halberstadt," *Weimarer Beiträge,* 31, no. 8 (1985): 1390-1392;

Riedel, ed., *Der Aufklärer Gleim heute* (Stendel: Winckelmann-Gesellschaft, 1987);

Horst Scholke and Gerlinde Wappler, *Briefe und Porträts,* volume 1 of *Die Sammlungen des Gleimhauses,* second edition (Halberstadt: Gleimhaus, 1986);

Jörg Schönert, "Schlachtgesänge vom Kanapee. Oder: 'Gott donnerte bei Lowositz': Zu den 'Preußischen Kriegsliedern in den Feldzügen 1756 und 1757' des Kanonikus Gleim," in *Gedichte und Interpretationen,* volume 2: *Aufklärung und Sturm und Drang,* edited by Karl Richter (Stuttgart: Reclam, 1983), pp. 124-139;

Karl-Otto Schulz and Scholke, *Bücher und Grafiken,* volume 2 of their *Die Sammlungen des Gleimhauses* (Halberstadt: Gleimhaus, 1980);

Jürgen Stenzel, "Johann Wilhelm Ludwig Gleim," in *Aufklärung und Empfindsamkeit,* volume 3 of *Deutsche Dichter,* edited by Gunter E. Grimm and Frank Rainer Max (Stuttgart: Reclam, 1988), pp. 135-140;

Gerlinde Wappler, ed., *Festschrift zur 250. Wiederkehr der Geburtstage von Johann Wilhelm Ludwig Gleim und Magnus Gottfried Lichtwer* (Halberstadt: Gleimhaus, 1969);

Jürgen Wilke, *Das "Zeitgedicht": Seine Herkunft und frühe Ausbildung* (Meisenhaim am Glan: Hain, 1974);

Herbert Zeman, *Die deutsche anakreontische Dichtung: Ein Versuch zur Erfassung ihrer ästhetischen und literarhistorischen Erscheinungsformen im 18. Jahrhundert* (Stuttgart: Metzler, 1972);

Zeman, "Friedrich von Hagedorn, Johann Wilhelm Ludwig Gleim, Johann Peter Uz, Johann Nikolaus Götz," in *Deutsche Dichter des 18. Jahrhunderts: ihr Leben und Werk,* edited by Benno von Wiese (Berlin: Schmidt, 1977), pp. 135-161.

Papers:

Johann Wilhelm Ludwig Gleim's literary remains, including more than ten thousand letters to and from four hundred correspondents, and a library of ten thousand books, are in the Gleim Archive at the Gleimhaus in Halberstadt.

Johann Christoph Gottsched

(2 February 1700 - 12 December 1766)

P. M. Mitchell
Cornell University

BOOKS: *Explicatio Leibnitiana mutatonis barometri in tempestatibus pluviis contra dubitationes* (Königsberg, 1719);

Schediasma historicum de Linda Mariana, Rastenburgum inter et Resselium sita, cum amputatis miseræ superstitionis romansium ramis, præmissamque in præsentiarum commentationem præliminarem, de idololatria gentilium sylvestro; et lucis religiosis, ex autoritate amplissimi philosophorum ordinis, pro receptione in eundem (Königsberg, 1720);

Dubia circa monades Leibnitianas quaternus: Ipsæ pro elementis corporum venditantur (Königsberg, 1721);

Genuinam omnipræsentiæ divinæ notionem distincte explicatam et observationibus defendent prorecep-tione (Königsberg, 1723);

Hamartigenia sive de fonte vitiorum humanorum quæstio philosophice soluta irriumque quibus Lipsiensis artium magistri gaudent obtinendorum ergo publico eruditorum examini submissa (Leipzig, 1724);

Des deutschen Persius satirischer Gedanken (N.p., 1724);

Ode, welche bey der öffentlichen Lob- und Trauer-Rede, so der weyland Allerdurchlauchtigsten Königin und Frauen, Frn. Christianen Eberhardinen Königin in Polen und Churfürstin zu Sachsen &c, &c, &c, im Jahr 1727 den 17. Oct. in der Academischen Kirche zu Leipzig gehalten wurde (Leipzig, 1727);

Vindiciarum systematis influxus physici, 3 volumes (Leipzig: Breitkopf, 1727-1729);

Vindiciarum systematis influxus physici sectio prior historica (Leipzig, 1728);

Grundriß zu einer vernunfftmäßigen Redekunst, mehrentheils nach Anleitung der alten Griechen und Römer entworfen und zum Gebrauch seiner Zuhörer ans Licht gestellet (Hannover: Förster, 1729);

Versuch einer critischen Dichtkunst vor die Deutschen: Darinnen erstlich die allgemeinen Regeln der Poesie, hernach alle besondere Gattungen der Gedichte, abgehandelt und mit Exempeln erläutert

Johann Christoph Gottsched; painting by L. Schorer, 1744 (Leipzig, Universitätsbibliothek)

werden, überall aber gezeiget wird daß das innere Wesen der Poesie in einer Nachahmung der Natur bestehe. Anstatt einer Einleitung ist Horatii Dichtkunst in deutsche Verse übersetzt, und mit Anmerckungen erläutert (Leipzig: Breitkopf, 1729 [dated 1730]; revised, 1737; enlarged, 1742; revised, 1751; reprinted, Darmstadt: Wissenschaftliche Buchgesellschaft, 1977);

Oratio inauguralis de poetas sistens philosophos, reipublicae generique humano utilissimos (Leipzig, 1730);

Sterbender Cato: Ein Trauerspiel, nebst einer Critischen Vorrede, darinnen von der Einrichtung desselben Rechenschaft gegeben wird (Leipzig: Teubner, 1732);

Dissertatio philosophica de regni, ex quo literae exulant, infelicitate quam amplissimi sophorum ordinis consensu (Leipzig: Zeidler, 1732);

Erste Gründe Der gesamten Weltweisheit, darinn alle philosophische Wissenschaften in ihrer natürlichen Verknüpfung abgehandelt werden, zum Gebrauch Academischer Lectionen entworfen, 2 volumes (Leipzig: Breitkopf, 1733-1734; revised and enlarged, 1735-1736; revised and enlarged, 1739; revised and enlarged, 1748-1749; revised and enlarged, 1756; revised and enlarged, 1762; reprinted, 1 volume, Hildesheim & New York: Olms, 1983);

De iniquitate exterorum in ferendo de eruditis nostratibus judicio J. Lockii et W. Molynaei exemplis confirmatam sistit (Leipzig, 1734);

Oratio pro utilitate et necessitate metaphysicae in contemtores eius quum publicum eam logicamque docendi munus in Academia Lipsiensi (Leipzig, 1734);

Gedichte, edited by Johann Joachim Schwabe (Leipzig: Breitkopf, 1736; enlarged, 2 volumes, 1751);

Ausführliche Redekunst, Nach Anleitung der alten Griechen und Römer, wie auch der neueren Ausländer: Geistlichen und weltlichen Rednern zu gut, in zweenen Theilen verfasset, und mit Exempeln erläutert (Leipzig: Breitkopf, 1736; reprinted, Hildesheim & New York: Olms, 1973);

Generosissimos atque nobilissimos commilitones ad praelectiones suas hiemales a. 1737 humanissime invitat (Leipzig: Breitkopf, 1737);

De Rationes humanæ praestentia contra Balbum L. III de Natura Deorum (Leipzig, 1737);

Voluntatis ab intellectu dependentiam amplissimi philosophorum ordinis consensu (Leipzig, 1737);

Ad audiendam orationem memoriae Riedelianae renovandae ergo . . . habendam invitat et amovenda a philosophia recentiori, foeda spizozismi macula pergit (Leipzig, 1738);

Ad memoriam viri dum viveret nobilissimi et consultissima Daniel Aegedii Henrici (Leipzig, 1738);

Ad solennem baccalaureorum philosophiae et L. L. A. A. Prometionem . . . instituendam invitat paucaque de dignitate baccalaureatus lipsiensis ex antiquitate academica (Leipzig, 1738);

Lob- und Gedächtnißrede auf den Vater der deutschen Dichtkunst, Martin Opitzen von Boberfeld nachdem selbiger vor hundert Jahren in Danzig Todes verblichen, zur Erneuerung Seines Andenkens im Jahre 1739 den 20 August auf der philosophischen Cather zu Leipzig gehalten (Leipzig: Breitkopf, 1739);

Grund-Riß einer Lehr-Arth ordentlich und erbaulich zu predigen nach dem Innhalt der Königlichen Preußischen allergnädigsten Cabinets-Ordre (Berlin: Haude, 1740);

Atalanta oder Die bezwungene Sprödigkeit: Ein Schauspiel in fünf Aufzügen (Hamburg: Nottebohm, 1742);

Gedächtnißrede auf den unsterblich verdienten Domherrn in Frauenberg, Nicolaus Copernicus, als den Erfinder des wahren Weltbaues, welche in hoher Gegenwart Zweyer Durchlaucht Königl., Pohln. und Churfürstel. Sächßisches Prinzen auf der Universitätsbibliothek zu Leipzig, im Maymonate des 1743 Jahres, und also zweyhundert Jahre nach seinem Tode, gehalten worden (Leipzig: Breitkopf, 1743);

Ode zum Andenken des 1646. den 23. Jun. und also fast vor hundert Jahren hier in Leipzig gebohrnen Gottfried Wilhelms von Leibnitz (Leipzig: Breitkopf, 1746);

Abhandlung von dem Flore der deutschen Poesie, zu Kaiser Friedrichs des ersten Zeiten, In Gegenwart Ihrer Königlichen Hoheiten . . . (Leipzig: Breitkopf, 1746);

Ad audiendas orationes tres quibus memoriam Henricianam Seyfertianam atque Riedelianam (Leipzig, 1746);

Ad renunciationem baccalaureorum solemnens . . . antiquo more instituendam invitat et de quibusdam philosophiae moralis apud germanos antiquiores speciminibus (Leipzig, 1746);

Zwey Lobschriften auf zweene in Gott ruhende Durchlauchtigste Sächsische Landes-Herren, weiland Churfürsten Friedrichen den Streitbaren, und Churfürsten August den Gütigen (Leipzig: Breitkopf, 1746);

Abhandlung von dem hohen Werthe und Vorzuge der auf der Könige, und Churfürstl. Biblioth. zu Dresden vorhandenen alten Abschrifft eines uralten Helden Gedichts auf Kaysers Carl des Großen Spanischen Feldzug (Leipzig: Breitkopf, 1747);

Rede, womit Sr. Königlichen Hoheit Dem Durchlauchtigsten Fürsten und Herrn, HERRN Friedrich Christian, Königlichen Prinzen in Pohlen, Churprinzen und Herzoge zu Sachsen &c. &c. Bey Gelegenheit Dero mit der Durchlauchtigsten Fürstinn und Frauen, FRAUEN Maria Antonia gebohrnen Kaiserlichen und Churfürstlichen Prinzessin zu Bayern, Ober- und Niederfalz &c. &c. unlängst vollzogenen Vermählung bey hoher Gegenwart Beyder Königlichen Hoheiten, den 10 October 1747 in der Paulinerkirche zu Leipzig, in Namen und auf Verordnung der Universität da-

selbt, Glück gewünschet worden unlängst vollzogenen Vermählung (Leipzig, 1747);

Grundlegung einer Deutschen Sprachkunst: Nach den Mustern der besten Schriftsteller des vorigen und jetzigen Jahrhunderts (Leipzig: Breitkopf, 1748; revised and enlarged, 1749; revised and enlarged, 1752);

Die Kaiserin am Theresien-Feste 1749. Allerunterthänigst besungen (Regensburg: Zunkel, 1749);

Neueste Gedichte auf verschiedene Vorfälle (Regensburg: Zunkel, 1749);

Gesaͤmlete Reden in Dreyen Abtheilungen, nochmals von ihm selbst übersehen und verbessert (Leipzig: Breitkopf, 1749);

Klag-Lied des Herrn Professor Gottsched über das rauhe Pfälzer-Land in einer Abschieds-Ode (N.p., 1750);

Das erhöhte Preußen, oder, Friedrich der Weise: Ein Gedicht Seinem werthen Vaterlande, zu dem den 18ten Jenner 1751 bevorstehenden fünfzigjährigen Andenken seiner Erhebung zur königlichen Würde gewidmet (Leipzig: Breitkopf, 1750);

Gesammlete Neueste Gedichte, herausgegeben von der Königlichen deutschen Gesellschaft (Königsberg: Königliche Hof- und Academischen Buchdruckerey, 1750);

Ad sollemnia anniversaria quibus primam philosphiae et L. L. A. A. Lauream decem optimae spei candidatis proxima de antiqua versione theotisca Magistri Tancredi (Leipzig: Breitkopf, 1750);

Zwey Gedichte womit gegen das Ende des 1749sten Jahres Beyderseits Römisch-Kaiserliche auch zu Hungarn und Böheim Königliche Majestäten allerunterthänigst verehret worden (Cassel: Cramer, 1750);

Singularia Vindobonensia Nuper a. MDCCL. d. XII mens. februar. oratione solemni in avditorio philosophor. Lipsiensi celebrata ab ord. philos. tum procancellario . . . praemittur prolusio academica dom. I. adv. a MDCCXLIX publici iuris facta aliquam nuperi itineris litteratii rationem reddens (Leipzig: Breitkopf, 1750);

Akademische Vorlesung, in hoher Gegenwart Sr. Königl. Hoheit des Durchl. Churprinzen zu Sachsen, und der Durchl. Churprinzessin Königl. Hoheit über die Frage: Ob man in theatralischen Gedichten allezeit die Tugend als belohnt, und das Laster als bestrafet vorstellen müsse? (Leipzig: Breitkopf, 1751);

Der Lorbeerkranz, welchen der Hoch- und Wohlgebohrne Herr, HERR Christoph Otto, des. H. R. R. Freyherr von Schönaich von E. löbl. philosophischen Facultät zu Leipzig feyerlichst erhalten hat. (Leipzig: Breitkopf, 1752);

Ad solennia anniversaria quibus primae Laureae philosophicae honores strenuis aliquot litterarum elegantiorum cultoribus . . . conferentur nomine apliss. ord. philos. lips. humanissime invitat et de temporibus teutonicorum vatum mythicis (Leipzig: Breitkopf, 1752);

Herrn Professor Gottscheds Gedicht, so Derselbe am 1ten des Augustmonates 1753, in der Königl. Deutschen Gesellschaft zu Göttingen abgelesen (Göttingen: Boßiegel, 1753);

Agis, König zu Sparta: Ein Trauerspiel (Vienna: Kraus, 1753);

Kern der Deutschen Sprachkunst, aus der ausführlichen Sprachkunst Herrn Professor Gottscheds, zum Gebrauche der Jugend, von ihm selbst ins Kurze gezogen (Leipzig: Breitkopf, 1753; revised, 1754);

Vorübungen der Beredsamkeit, zum Gebrauche der Gymnasien und größern Schulen, aufgesetzt (Leipzig: Breitkopf, 1754; revised, 1756; revised, 1764);

Historische Lobschrift des weiland hoch- und wohlgebohrnen Herrn HERRN Historische Christians, des H. R. R. Freyherrn von Wolf Erb- Lehn- und Gerichtsherrn auf Klein-Dölzing Sr. Königl. Maj. in Preußen geheimen Raths, der Universität zu Halle Kanzlers und Seniors, wie auch des Natur- und Völkerrechts, und der Mathematik Professors daselbst, Der kaiserl. Akademie zu Petersburg Prof. honor. der königl. Akad. der Wissenschaften zu London, Paris, Berlin und der zu Bologna Mitglied (Halle: Renger, 1755; reprinted, Hildesheim & New York: Olms, 1980);

Vorübungen der lateinischen und deutschen Dichtkunst, zum Gebrauche der Schulen entworfen (Leipzig: Breitkopf, 1756; revised, 1760);

Nöthiger Vorrath zur Geschichte der deutschen Dramatischen Dichtkunst oder Verzeichniß aller Deutschen Trauer- Lust- und Sing- Spiele, die im Druck erschienen, von 1450 bis zur Hälfte des jetzigen Jahrhunderts gesammlet und ans Licht gestellet, 2 volumes (Leipzig: Teubner, 1757-1765; reprinted, 1 volume, Hildesheim & New York: Olms, 1970);

Beobachtungen über den Gebrauch und Misbrauch vieler deutscher Wörter und Redensarten (Strasbourg & Leipzig: König, 1758; edited by Johannes Hubertus Slangen, Heerlen: Winant, 1955);

Akademische Redekunst, zum Gebrauch der Vorlesungen auf hohen Schulen als ein bequemes Handbuch eingerichtet und mit den schönsten Zeugnis-

sen der Alten erläutert (Leipzig: Breitkopf, 1759);

Handlexicon oder Kurzgefaßtes Wörterbuch der schönen Wissenschaften und freyen Künste: Zum Gebrauche der Liebhaber derselben herausgegeben (Leipzig: Fritsch, 1760; reprinted, Hildesheim & New York: Olms, 1970);

Friedrich Christian, der unvergeßliche Churfürst zu Sachsen, in der Gesellschaft der freyen Künste bey feierlichen Versammlung, durch drei pindarischen Oden den 8ten des Hornungs 1764 besungen: Welchem beygefüget ist die historische Lobschrift auf weiland Herrn Christian Gottlieb Kölnern Prof. der schön. Wissens zu Moskau (Leipzig: Jacobäer, 1764);

Erste Gründe der Vernunftlehre, aus den ersten Gründen der ganzen Weltweisheit, zum Gebrauche der Gymnasien und größern Schulen auf Begehren, nochmals übersehen und besonders ans Licht gestellt (Leipzig: Breitkopf, 1766);

Joh. Christoph Gottsched und die Schweizer J. J. Bodmer und J. J. Breitinger, edited by Johannes Crüger (Berlin & Stuttgart: Spemann, 1884);

Gesammelte Schriften: Ausgabe der Gottsched-Gesellschaft, 6 volumes (Berlin: Gottsched-Verlag, 1903-1906);

Sterbender Cato. Im Anhang: Auszüge aus der zeitgenössischen Diskussion über Gottscheds Drama, edited by Horst Steinmetz (Stuttgart: Reclam, 1964);

Ausgewählte Werke, 12 volumes to date, edited by Joachim Birke and P. M. Mitchell (Berlin & New York: De Gruyter, 1968-);

Schriften zur Theorie und Praxis aufklärender Literatur, edited by Uwe-Karsten Ketelsen (Reinbek: Rowohlt, 1970);

Schriften zur Literatur, edited by Horst Steinmetz (Stuttgart: Reclam, 1972).

OTHER: Johann Valentin Pietsch, *Gesamlete Poetische Schriften Bestehend aus Staats- Trauer- und Hochzeit-Gedichten, Mit einer Vorrede, Herrn le Clerc übersetzten Gedancken von der Poesie und Zugabe einiger Gedichte*, edited by Gottsched (Leipzig: Groß, 1725);

Die Vernünftigen Tadlerinnen, 2 volumes, edited by Gottsched (Halle: Spörl, 1725-1726);

Bernard le Bovier de Fontenelle, *Gespräche von Mehr als einer Welt zwischen einem Frauenzimmer und einem Gelehrten: Nach der neuesten Frantzösischen Auflage übersetzt auch mit Figuren und Anmerckungen erläutert. Am Ende findet man noch ein Pastoral, genannt Endimion,*

translated and edited by Gottsched (Leipzig: Breitkopf, 1726);

Nachricht von der erneuerten Deutschen Gesellschafft in Leipzig und ihrer jetzigen Verfassung, edited by Gottsched (Leipzig: Breitkopf, 1727);

Fontenelle, *Gespräche der Todten und Plutons Urtheil über dieselben zum erstenmahl ins Teutsche übersetzt und mit einer Vorrede, von Gesprächen überhaupt*, translated by Gottsched (Leipzig: Breitkopf, 1727);

Oden Der Deutschen Gesellschaft in Leipzig In vier Bücher abgetheilet An statt einer Einleitung ist des Herrn de la Motte Abhandlung von der Poesie überhaupt, und der Ode ins besondre vorgesetzet, edited by Gottsched (Leipzig: Gleditsch, 1728);

Der Biedermann, 2 volumes, edited by Gottsched (Leipzig: Deer, 1728-1729; reprinted, 1 volume, edited by Wolfgang Martens, Stuttgart: Metzler, 1975);

Der Deutschen Gesellschaft in Leipzig Eigene Schriften und Übersetzungen in gebundener und ungebundener Schreibart ans Licht gestellet und mit einer Vorrede versehen, edited by Gottsched (Leipzig: Breitkopf, 1730);

Fontenelle, *Historie Der Heydnischen Orackel . . . übersetzt, und mit einem Anhange Darinn aus dem Lateinischen Wercke Des berühmten van Dalen ein kurtzer Auszug enthalten ist: Aus dem Französichen übersetzt, und mit einem Anhange, darinn auf die Einwürfe eines Straßburgischen Jesuiten geantwortet wird, vermehret*, translated by Gottsched (Leipzig: Breitkopf, 1730);

Nachricht von der Deutschen Gesellschaft zu Leipzig Bis auf das Jahr 1731 fortgesetzt: Nebst einem Anhang, von ihrer Deutschen Rechtschreibung, edited by Gottsched (Leipzig: Breitkopf, 1731);

Der Deutschen Gesellschaft in Leipzig Gesammlete Reden und Gedichte, Welche bey dem Eintritte und Abschiede ihrer Mitglieder pflegen abgelesen zu werden: Nebst einer vorhergesetzten ausführlichen Erläuterung ihrer Absichten, Anstalten und der davon zu erwartenden Vortheile ans Licht gestellet, edited by Gottsched (Leipzig: Breitkopf, 1732);

Beyträge Zur Critischen Historie Der Deutschen Sprache, Poesie und Beredsamkeit, herausgegeben von Einigen Mitgliedern der Deutschen Gesellschaft in Leipzig, 8 volumes, edited by Gottsched (Leipzig: Breitkopf, 1732-1744);

Anti-Longin, Oder die Kunst in der Poesie zu kriechen, anfänglich von dem Herrn D. Swift Den Engelländern zum besten geschrieben itzo zur Verbesserung des Geschmacks bey uns Deutschen übersetzt und mit Exempeln aus Englischen, voremlich aber aus unsern Deutschen Dichtern durchgehends erläutert Diesem ist Beygefüget eben desselben Staatslügenkunst nebst einer Abhandlung ... Johann Christoph Gottscheds ... von dem Bathos in den Opern (Leipzig: Löwe, 1734);

Der Deutschen Gesellschaft in Leipzig Eigene Schriften und Übersetzungen in gebundener und ungebundener Schreibart: Der Andere Theil, edited by Gottsched (Leipzig: Breitkopf, 1734; enlarged, 2 volumes, 1735);

Jean Racine, *Trauerspiel Iphigenia vor einigen Jahren ins deutsche übersetzt, nunmehro aber mit einer Vorrede und einem Auszuge aus der griechischen Iphigenia des Euripides ans Licht gestellet*, translated by Gottsched (Leipzig: Breitkopf, 1734);

Der Deutschen Gesellschaft in Leipzig Oden und Cantaten in vier Büchern: Nebst einer Vorrede über die Frage Ob man auch in ungebundener Rede Oden machen könne?, edited by Gottsched (Leipzig: Breitkopf, 1738);

Friedrich Wilhelm von Eisenberg, *Cypressen-Zweige auf Fürstliche und Adel, Grufften gestreuet; Oder Reden bey dergleichen solennen Leichen-Begängnissen gehalten samt einer Vorrede*, edited by Gottsched (Altenburg: Richter, 1738);

Der Zuschauer: Aus dem Englischen übersetzt, 9 volumes, translated by Gottsched and Luise Gottsched (Leipzig: Breitkopf, 1739-1751);

Die Deutsche Schaubühne nach den Regeln und Exempeln der alten Griechen und Römer eingerichtet, und mit einer Vorrede herausgegeben, 6 volumes, edited, with contributions, by Gottsched (Leipzig: Breitkopf, 1741-1745; reprinted, Stuttgart: Metzler, 1972)–volume 6 includes *Die Bluthochzeit* and *Agis, König zu Sparta*, by Gottsched;

Pierre Bayle, *Gedanken bey Gelegenheit des Cometen, der im Christmonate 1880 erschienen, an einen Doctor der Sorbonne gesichtet: Aus dem Französischen übersetzt* (Hamburg: Felginer & Bohn, 1741);

Bayle, *Historisches und Critisches Wörterbuch nach der neuesten Auflage von 1740 ins Deutsche übersetzt mit einer Vorrede und verschiedenen Anmerkungen sonderlich bey anstößigen Stellen versehen*, 4 volumes, edited by Gottsched and Luise Adelgunde Victoria Gottsched (Leipzig: Breitkopf, 1741-1744; reprinted, Hildesheim & New York: Olms, 1974-1978);

Marcus Tullius Cicero, *Drey Bücher von der Menschlichen Pflicht, aus dem Lateinischen übersetzt und mit Anmerkungen wie auch mit des Cicero Leben erläutert*, translated by Johann Adolph Hofmann, foreword by Gottsched (Hamburg: Felginer & Bohn, 1742);

Johann Heyn, *Versuch Einer Betrachtung über die Cometen, die Sündflut und das Vorspiel des jüngsten Gerichts: Nach astronomischen Gründen und der heiligen Schrift angestellet*, foreword by Gottsched (Berlin & Leipzig: Haude, 1742);

Virgil, *Aeneis: Ein Heldengedicht in eben so viele Deutsche Verse übersetzet*, 2 volumes, edited by Johann Christoph Schwarz, foreword by Gottsched (Regensburg: Zunkel, 1742-1744);

Gottfried Wilhelm von Leibniz, *Theodicee, das ist, Versuch von der Güte Gottes, Freyheit des Menschen, und vom Ursprunge des Bösen; bei dieser vierten Ausgabe, durchgehend verbessert, auch mit verschiedenen Zusätzen und Anmerkungen vermehrt*, edited by Gottsched (Hannover & Leipzig: Förster, 1744);

Benjamin Neukirch, *Auserlesene Gedichte aus verschiedenen poetischen Schriften gesammlet und mit einer Vorrede von dem Leben des Dichters begleitet*, edited by Gottsched (Regensburg: Zunkel, 1744);

Lucian of Samasota, *Auserlesene Schriften von moralischem, satirischem und critischem Inhalte durch verschieden Federn verdeutscht: Und mit einer Vorrede, von Werthe und Nutzen der Uebersetzungen, ans Licht gestellt*, edited by Gottsched (Leipzig: Breitkopf, 1745);

Neuer Büchersaal der schönen Wissenschaften und freyen Künste, 10 volumes, edited by Gottsched (Leipzig: Breitkopf, 1745-1750);

Christian August Hausen, *Post obitum auctoris praematuro fato nuper extincti, ex msto eius editi accessit V. C. Henrici de Sanden dissertatio de succino electricorum principe, quam edidit et de vita B. Hausenii praefatus est*, edited by Gottsched (Quedlinburg: Schwan, 1746);

Peter von Muschenbroek, *Grundlehren der Naturwissenschaft: Nach der zweyten lateinischen Ausgabe, nebst einigen neuen Zusätzen des Verfassers, ins Deutsche übersetzt mit einer Vorrede ans Licht gestellt*, edited by Gottsched (Leipzig: Kiesewetter, 1747);

Melchior Polignac, *Anti-Lucretius, sive de deo et natura libri novem ... opus posthumum illustrissimi abbatis Caroli d'Orleans de Rothelin cura et studio editioni mandatum ad exemplar parisinum recensuit et de poetis philosophis, antiquis aeque ac recentioribus praefatus,* edited by Gottsched (Leipzig, 1748);

Ehrenmaal welches Dem weiland erlauchten und hochgebohrnen Reichsgrafen und Herrn, HERRN Ernst Christian des Heil. Röm. Reichs Grafen von Manteufel, Welchem Sein blosser Namen statt aller Titel ist, Nach seinem ruhmvollen Ableben aus wahrer Hochachtung von verschiedenen seiner Freunde und Diener wehmütig aufgerichtet worden, edited by Gottsched (Leipzig: Büschel, 1749);

Die Begebenheiten Neoptolems, eines Sohns des Achilles, aus dem Französischen des Herrn Chansierces in deutsche Verse übersetzt und durch mythologische Anmerkungen erläutert, nebst einer Vorrede . . . dem Drucke überlassen von M. Adam Bernhard Pantken, Pfarrern zu Kleinkniegnitz und Schwentnig, der königlichen deutschen Gesellschaft zu Königsberg, und der deutschen Gesellschaft zu Leipzig, Mitgliede, translated by Gottsched (Breslau, 1749);

Esprit Flechier, *Lob u. Trauerreden Nebst dem Leben desselben von einigen Mitgliedern der königl. deutschen Gesellschaft zu Königsberg übersetzt und mit einer Vorrede Hrn. Prof. Gottscheds ans Licht gestellt von Christian Cölestin Flottwellen, P. P. O. wie auch Directorn der Kön. Deutschen Gesellschaft zu Königsberg, Erster Theil,* foreword by Gottsched (Leipzig & Liegnitz, 1749);

Geschichte der königlichen Akademie der schönen Wissenschaften zu Paris: Erster Theil. Mit einer Vorrede ans Licht gestellet, edited by Gottsched (Leipzig: Krauß, 1749);

Virgil, *Hirtengedichte . . . in Deutschen Versen herausgegeben,* translated by Johann Daniel Overbeck, foreword by Gottsched (Helmstaedt: Weygand, 1750);

Fontenelle, *Auserlesene Schriften nämlich von mehr als einer Welt, Gespräche der Todten, und die Historie der heydnischen Orakel; vormals einzelnen herausgegeben, nun aber mit verschiedenen Zugaben und schönen Kupfern vermehrter ans Licht gestellet,* edited by Gottsched (Leipzig: Breitkopf, 1751);

Christoph Otto, Freiherr von Schönaich, *Hermann, oder Das befreyte Deutschland ein Heldengedicht: Mit einer Vorrede ans Licht gestellet,* foreword by Gottsched (Leipzig: Breitkopf, 1751); translated anonymously as *Arminius; or Germania Freed* (London: Printed for T. Becket & P. A. DeHondt, 1764);

Das Neueste aus der anmuthigen Gelehrsamkeit, 12 volumes, edited by Gottsched (Leipzig: Breitkopf, 1751-1762);

Heinrich von Alkmar, *Reineke der Fuchs mit schönen Kupfern; Nach der Ausgabe von 1498 ins Hochdeutsche übersetzet, und mit einer Abhandlung von dem Urhaber, wahren Alter und großen Werthe dieses Gedichtes versehen,* translated by Gottsched (Leipzig & Amsterdam: Schenk, 1752);

Sammlung einiger ausgesuchten Stücke, der Gesellschaft der freyen Künste zu Leipzig, 3 volumes, edited by Gottsched (Leipzig: Breitkopf, 1754-1756);

Auszug aus des Herrn Batteux, öffentlichen Lehrens der Redekunst zu Paris Schönen Künsten aus dem einzigen Grundsatze der Nachahmung hergeleitet: Zum Gebrauche seiner Vorlesungen mit verschiedenen Zusätzen und Anmerkungen erläutert, translated by Gottsched (Leipzig: Breitkopf, 1754);

Ermelinda Thalea [pseudonym of Maria Antonia, Electress of Saxony], *Der Triumph der Treue: Ein Schäferspiel, Aus dem von der Meisterhand der Durchlauchtigsten Ermelinda Thalea, einer arkadischen Schäferinn, verfertigten wälschen Singspiele, Il Triumfo della Fedeltà, seines Vortrefflichkeit wegen, verdeutschet,* translated by Gottsched (Leipzig: Breitkopf, 1754);

Muster der Beredsamkeit: Aus den besten geistlichen und weltlichen Rednern der Deutschen gesammlet und mit einigen Anmerkungen über die Beredsamkeit und mit einer Vorrede, edited by Johann Traugott Schulz, foreword by Gottsched (Leipzig: König, 1755);

Des Abtes Terrassons Philosophie, nach ihrem allgemeinen Einfluße, auf alle Gegenstände des Geistes und der Sitten: Aus dem Französischen verdeutschet, foreword by Gottsched (Leipzig: Breitkopf, 1756);

Claude-Adrien Helvétius, *Discurs über den Geist des Menschen,* foreword by Gottsched (Leipzig & Liegnitz: Siegert, 1760);

Freyherr von Bielefeld, *Lehrbegriff der Staatskunst,* 2 volumes, translated by Gottsched and Johann Joachim Schwabe (Breslau & Leipzig: Korn, 1761);

Luise Adelgunde Victoria Gottschedinn, *Sämmtliche Kleinere Gedichte, nebst dem, von vielen vornehmen Standespersonen Gönnern und Freunden beyderley Geschlechtes Ihr gestifteten Ehrenmaale, und Ihrem Leben herausgegeben von Ihrem hinterbliebenen Ehegatten,* edited by Gottsched (Leipzig: Breitkopf, 1763);

Thalea, *La Conversione di Sant' Agostino,* translated by Gottsched (Leipzig: Breitkopf, 1764);

Johann Andree Schachtner, *Poetischer Versuch in verschiedenen Arten von Gedichten*, foreword by Gottsched (Augsburg & Innsbruck: Wolff, 1765);

Thalea, *Thalestris Königinn der Amazonen: Aus dem vortrefflichen italienischen Singepiele Ihrer Königlichen Hoheit der unvergleichlichen Ermelinde Thalea in ein Deutsches Trauerspiel verwandelt*, translated by Gottsched (Zwickau: Stieler, 1767).

If one should ask who was the most widely read German philosopher of the first half of the eighteenth century, who the leading critic, who the major promoter of a German theater, who the compiler of the most widely used German grammar, who the foremost teacher of rhetoric, and who the academic champion of woman's rights, in each case the answer would be Johann Christoph Gottsched. Gottsched was also one of the principal editors of the time, the author of one of the most influential moral weeklies, a prominent teacher at the University of Leipzig, and a thoroughgoing German patriot. Nevertheless, today the average student of German literature and culture knows little more than Gottsched's name and probably dismisses him as a slightly ridiculous figure, without having read a line from his many works.

The reasons are, first, that Gottsched was pushed aside by a younger generation of brilliant critics led by Gotthold Ephraim Lessing and Friedrich Nicolai and, second, that Gottsched was so egotistical, self-satisfied, and inflexible that he did not evoke continuing admiration from the very persons who might have laid the basis for a more flattering—and more just—evaluation of his contributions. From a distance of two centuries it is possible to bring Gottsched into proper perspective as the central figure of the German literary scene between 1725 and about 1760.

Born on 2 February 1700 to Christoph Gottsched, a clergyman, and Regina Gottsched, née Biemann, in Juditten, a village outside Königsberg in northeast Prussia, Gottsched received his early education from his father. In 1714 he entered the University of Königsberg, where he studied theology, philosophy, and poetry. Even at this time he gave evidence of a poetic vein, for he wrote occasional verse that began to be published when he was eighteen years old. In 1721 he presented a magisterial thesis that questioned Gottfried Wilhelm von Leibniz's theory of monads. Two years later he ob-

tained the right to teach on the university level by defending a dissertation on the omnipresence of the divine. At this juncture Gottsched learned, apparently through some betrayal of military confidence, that he was in imminent danger of being conscripted into the army of Friedrich Wilhelm II. The only way to avoid conscription was to flee Prussia. Gottsched and his brother Johann Heinrich went to the cultural center of the German states of the time, Leipzig, which lay safely within the Electorate of Saxony. Quickly recognized as talented and promising, Gottsched was engaged by Professor Johann Burkhard Mencke to assist with Mencke's enormous private library. The association with Mencke gave Gottsched access to academic circles in Leipzig. In November 1724 Gottsched and his brother presented a new thesis at the University of Leipzig on the origin of human imperfection, an essay that took its orientation from Leibniz's teleological argument in the *Théodicée* (1710).

In 1725 appeared Gottsched's first publication in book form, an unauthorized edition of the poems of his erstwhile Königsberg teacher Johann Valentin Pietsch. The collection was augmented by four of Gottsched's own occasional poems, including one to his new mentor, Mencke. That same year he started a moral weekly, *Die Vernünftigen Tadlerinnen* (The Intelligent Women Critics, 1725-1726). Although nominally the work of several pseudonymous learned ladies, the weekly was written almost entirely by Gottsched. Of the hundreds of German moral weeklies in eighteenth-century Germany that sprang up in the wake of the successful English *Spectator*, *Die Vernünftigen Tadlerinnen* was among the most widely read and admired.

In 1726 Gottsched published a new translation of Bernard le Bouvier de Fontenelle's *Entretien sur la Pluralité des Mondes* (1686) that was well received. The translation marked the beginning of Gottsched's relationship with Bernhard Christoph Breitkopf. Apparently the translation was such a financial success that it helped establish the young and ambitious Breitkopf as a publisher. Breitkopf published most of Gottsched's later books.

The wit and wisdom exuded by *Die Vernünftigen Tadlerinnen*, coupled with its economic success, led a different publisher to engage Gottsched to undertake a second such journal. Gottsched responded with *Der Biedermann* (The Man of Honor), which appeared between June 1727 and April 1728 and was collected and

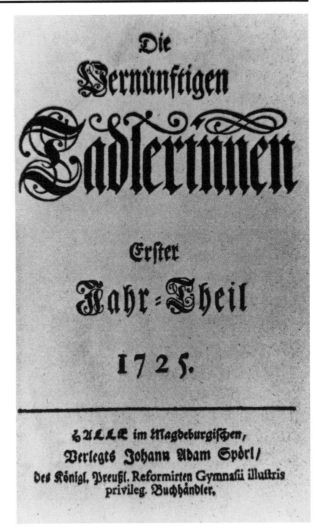

Frontispiece and title page for the first volume of the collected edition of Gottsched's first moral weekly

republished in 1728 and 1729, without, however, enjoying the same renown as the earlier journal.

While Gottsched was publishing his moral weeklies, he was also teaching poetic theory at the University of Leipzig. There is a demonstrable connection between some of the ideas that inform *Die Vernünftigen Tadlerinnen* and those in Gottsched's major contribution to literary theory and criticism, *Versuch einer critischen Dichtkunst vor die Deutschen* (Attempt at a Critical Poetics for the Germans, 1729), generally known as the *Critische Dichtkunst*. The poetics tends to be the only work by Gottsched that is regularly mentioned. It was, however, neither his first book-length scholarly publication nor his most successful in terms of sales. The first version of Gottsched's rhetoric, *Grundriß zu einer vernunfftmäßigen Redekunst* (Outline of a Reasonable Rhetoric), had appeared in Hannover earlier in 1729; it was supplanted by

his *Ausführliche Redekunst* (Complete Rhetoric) in 1736. Gottsched's continuing concern with rhetoric is indicated by an edition of his own addresses, *Gesamlete Reden in Dreyen Abtheilungen* (Collected Speeches in Three Divisions), in 1749 and *Akademische Redekunst* (Academic Rhetoric) a decade later.

The poetics bore a telling full title in the first edition: *Versuch einer critischen Dichtkunst vor die Deutschen: Darinnen erstlich die allgemeinen Regeln der Poesie, hernach alle besondere Gattungen der Gedichte, abgehandelt und mit Exempeln erläutert werden, überall aber gezeiget wird daß das innere Wesen der Poesie in einer Nachahmung der Natur bestehe. Anstatt einer Einleitung ist Horatii Dichtkunst in deutsche Verse übersetzt, und mit Anmerckungen erläutert* (Attempt at a Critical Poetics for the Germans: In Which First the General Rules for Poetry, Thereafter all the Particular Kinds of Poetry Are Treated and Illustrated by Examples, Everywhere, However, Is Shown that the Inner Nature of Poetry Is the Imitation of Nature. Instead of an Introduction Horace's Poetics Is Translated into German Verse and Explained in Notes). The book immediately established Gottsched as Germany's leader in the field of poetic theory and was warmly received by the many journals that reviewed it into the 1750s. Each of the three later editions differs from the first and from one another, but the fourth and final edition of 1751 is marred by the bias resulting from a literary feud with the Swiss critics Johann Jakob Bodmer and Johann Jakob Breitinger that was carried on in the 1740s and that has damaged Gottsched's reputation because of Gottsched's negative and the Swiss critics' positive assessments of Shakespeare and John Milton. As a consequence, the third edition of 1742 must be viewed as the canonical text.

As can be deduced from the subtitle of his poetics, Gottsched was steeped in the classical poetics of Aristotle and Horace; he also cites many other classical authors. He is, however, trying to further the tradition of Renaissance poetic theory, primarily that of Julius Caesar Scaliger. While Gottsched avers that he is not original and is carrying on from where Martin Opitz left off a century before, he is actually creating his own synthesis. What is of greatest importance, and what links Opitz and Gottsched, was the willingness of both men to write in German and their faith in German as a poetic and scholarly language; the language of West European learning of the time was overwhelmingly Latin, and even much poetry was written in that tongue.

In the poetics Gottsched methodically discusses the various aspects of imaginative writing and draws constantly on important writers from the distant and recent past, always employing the principle of reason as the norm in his arguments. After a historical sketch, Gottsched defines the character of the successful poet and addresses the difficult question of what constitutes good taste. The rest of part one deals with the supernatural, the probable, the use of poetic diction and figures of speech, and questions of style and euphony. Part two takes up the various genres and provides examples (in the first edition many of these derive from Gottsched himself). Of note is Gottsched's skepticism about the validity of opera, especially Italian opera, which he felt to be artificial and not the imitation of nature that should be the basis of all art.

Title page for Gottsched's major work on poetic theory, which actually appeared in 1729 although it is dated 1730

The classical writers upon whom Gottsched draws most frequently besides Aristotle and Horace are Aristophanes, Cicero, Homer, Lucan, Ovid, Plato, Plautus, Seneca, Terence, and Virgil. The German writers are not all equally well known today: Christian Henrich Amthor, Johann von Besser, Friedrich von Canitz, Simon Dach, Paul Fleming, Andreas Gryphius, Johann Christian Günther, Carl Gustave Hermäus, Johann Ulrich König, Daniel Casper von Lohenstein, Christian Friedrich Hunold ("Menantes"), Benjamin Neukirch, Magnus Daniel Omeis, Opitz, Pietsch, Joachim Rachel, Andreas Tscherning, and Heinrich Anselm von Ziegler und Kliphausen. Gottsched intentionally avoided drawing examples from the works of his German contemporaries, although he did cite some contemporary foreign writers. The principal French writers cited are Pierre Bayle, Nicolas Boileau-Despréaux, Pierre Corneille, François Fénelon,

Fontenelle, Molière, Jean Racine, and Voltaire. The favored English writers are Richard Addison and Joseph Steele, Alexander Pope, and Shaftesbury, although there are frequent references to Milton. Several Italian authors are mentioned, such as Ludovico Ariosto, Giovanni Crescimbeni, and Torquato Tasso, but Spanish literature is represented only by Miguel de Cervantes and Scandinavian literature only by Ludvig Holberg.

Despite the rejection of Gottsched in certain quarters after the mid 1740s, the *Critische Dichtkunst* continued to be used as a standard work. Thus, as late as 1766, the year of Gottsched's death, the young Johann Wolfgang von Goethe, then a student at the University of Leipzig, was directed to the *Critische Dichtkunst*, and, according to his testimony in his autobiography, *Dichtung und Wahrheit* (Poetry and Truth, 1811-1833), found it useful and instructive–but a book that presumed not only historical knowledge but also natural genius if a poet were to attempt the genres that Gottsched discussed. Gottsched's stress on the essential need for a poetic gift, suggested by Goethe, contradicts the superficial judgment that Gottsched believed one need only follow certain rules in order to produce acceptable poetry.

Soon after his arrival in Leipzig, Gottsched had joined a local literary society. Four years later he had become the leading spirit of the group and had given it a new name–Deutsche Gesellschaft (German Society)–and new goals: to cultivate German as a means of literary expression, mutually to criticize the efforts of the members with an eye to publication of what they wrote, and (although this hope never was formulated in so many words) to create a German equivalent of the French Academy. While no German academy evolved from Gottsched's efforts, the concept of the Deutsche Gesellschaft resonated elsewhere; soon sixteen similar societies using the same name and patterned after the Leipzig group were founded. The two most vigorous outside of Leipzig were in Königsberg and Göttingen, and both looked to Gottsched for spiritual leadership. Noteworthy about these new literary associations that in name suggested the Sprachgesellschaften (language societies) of the previous century was that they, unlike the Sprachgesellschaften, were bourgeois undertakings, despite some gestures of deference to noble patrons.

The Leipzig society published several volumes of poetry and prose, edited by Gottsched be-

fore he broke with the society in 1738 because it had elected as a member a man of whom he did not approve. Without Gottsched the energy of the society rapidly diminished, although the society existed in name, albeit with different goals, until World War II.

Gottsched also established two public speaking societies for university students, the so-called Redegesellschaften (rhetorical societies). The societies met under Gottsched's guidance on two different days during the week.

Another effort made by the young Gottsched was to establish a German theater that would present not only mindless slapstick comedies adapted from the Italian but also comedies such as those by Molière and Holberg, as well as tragedies. The means to attempt this reformation of the theater were at hand in the form of a theatrical company headed by Caroline Neuber, a leading actress of the day. For a time she and Gottsched worked together to try to establish something other than a traveling theater. While they did not achieve their goals, and had a falling-out in 1741, theirs was a remarkable effort, a forerunner of the national theaters in Hamburg and Mannheim. Gottsched wrote a tragedy for Neuber's company, *Sterbender Cato* (Dying Cato), which was published in 1732. The most successful of Gottsched's plays, it was based on earlier tragedies by Joseph Addison and François Deschamps. It was performed on several stages in addition to Neuber's and was republished several times. *Atalanta*, a so-called Schäferspiel (pastoral), appeared in 1742, and two further tragedies were published in 1745: *Die Bluthochzeit* (The Bloodbath) a drama about Henri of Navarre and the Massacre of St. Bartholomew's Eve (based on Jacques Auguste de Thou's history), and *Agis, König zu Sparta* (Agis, King of Sparta). The plays are in iambic hexameter. At least three of the later editions of *Sterbender Cato*, two of *Agis*, and one of *Atalanta* were unauthorized reprints, an indication of at least a modicum of success in the book market. Gottsched also translated five plays; his German version (1734) of Racine's *Iphigénie* (1674) was the best received of these translations and went through seven editions.

In 1732 Gottsched began to edit the first of three critical journals, *Beyträge Zur Critischen Historie Der Deutschen Sprache, Poesie und Beredsamkeit* (Contributions to the Critical History of the German Language, Poetry, and Rhetoric). The *Critische Beyträge*, as it was generally known, was originally an organ of the Leipzig Deutsche

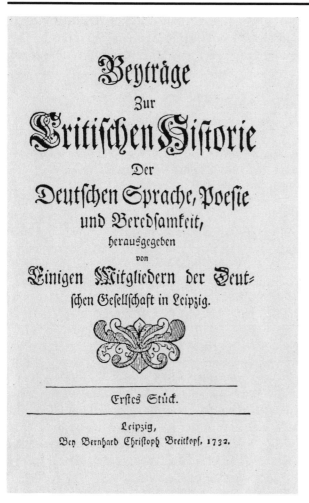

Title page for the first issue of the critical journal Gottsched edited until 1744

Gesellschaft; but after Gottsched withdrew from the society it continued under his editorship until 1744 as one of the leading critical periodicals of Protestant Germany. Just how much of the contents of the journal came from Gottsched's own pen and how much from other contributors is unknown, although an effort has been made to identify Gottsched's contributions in the bibliography that comprises volume 12 (1987) of Gottsched's *Ausgewählte Werke* (Selected Works, 1968-). It is rarely possible to identify the other contributors, for, with few exceptions, articles and reviews were printed anonymously, as was the wont of the time. The early issues echo the concerns of the Deutsche Gesellschaft. The initial number contains a statement signed by Gottsched on the advantages that would derive from a better knowledge of the etymologies of words. Other articles include a discussion of the word *Biedermann*, an answer to criticism that had been leveled against

Gottsched's *Sterbender Cato*, and reviews of books by such authors as Leibniz, Johann Christian Günther, and Bodmer. (Bodmer, with whom Gottsched was to have a lengthy feud, was an early contributor to the journal, suggesting a similarity in the aims of the later adversaries.) With regard to belles lettres, the *Critische Beyträge* was an extension of the ideas formulated in the *Critische Dichtkunst* and reflected Gottsched's interest in German language, poetry, and rhetoric. The two later journals were to spread a somewhat larger net and were more generally in the service of the Enlightenment. The classical orientation remained pronounced in Gottsched's writings, however. Gottsched transmuted his lectures on philosophical topics into book form as *Erste Gründe Der gesamten Weltweisheit* (Fundamentals of a Complete Philosophy, 1733-1734). Gottsched's philosophy is based on the writings of Christian Wolff, who in turn was the major disciple of Leibniz. Gottsched became the foremost interpreter of Wolff and thus the leading popular philosopher of the day. Although Gottsched's literary opinions and judgments came to be questioned, his philosophy book remained a standard work even after his death. No fewer than seven editions of the *Weltweisheit*, as it was known, appeared during his lifetime; in 1766 a shortened version was published for school use. A large part of the first volume of the *Weltweisheit* is devoted to sketching the philosophical principles identifiable with the peoples of the past—the Chinese, Phoenicians, Egyptians, and the "Africans." After outlining the philosophical thought of the Greeks and the Romans, Gottsched describes the "Vernunftlehre" (principle of reason), which is concerned with the niceties of language. There follow basic metaphysical ideas that are divided into the categories of ontology, the physical structure of the world, the kinds of material substances, and the structure of the universe. The planet earth is discussed in detail with reference to weather, bodies of water, and geology. Attention is then turned to plants, animals, and the human body. Virtues such as industry, thrift, generosity, friendship, justice, and honesty are examined. The work concludes pragmatically with remarks about problems of the household, including the disciplining of children (Gottsched had none), and about the duties of a ruler to ensure the common good. A modern analysis and assessment of Gottsched's philosophy, the dominant philosophy of the mid eighteenth century, is a scholarly desideratum.

Gottsched's elevation to a full professorship in 1734 gave him a regular income for the first time and enabled him to marry in 1735. His bride, who was thirteen years his junior, was also from Königsberg and had given evidence of high intelligence and poetic gifts. Luise Adelgunde Victoria Kulmus Gottsched, to whom Gottsched had been attracted since she was thirteen years old, is most frequently referred to in German as "die Gottschedin." She became a collaborator with her husband on various projects and was a minor playwright and an able translator in her own right. In addition to writing five plays of her own, she translated three plays from the French. She also translated several volumes of the transactions of the French Academy. Apparently more at home in English than her husband, she made a German translation of Pope's *Rape of the Lock* and provided most of the translations of the English *Spectator* as *Der Zuschauer* (1739-1751). She worked with Gottsched on the German translation of Pierre Bayle's biographical encyclopedia, *Dictionaire historique et critique* (1697-1706), which appeared from 1741 to 1744 in four folio volumes under the title *Historisches und Critisches Wörterbuch*. They based the text on the French edition of 1740, and Gottsched added many lengthy footnotes that give the German version added value. No other work of its time equaled Bayle's dictionary in impact. The storm of criticism that it had originally evoked because of its liberal theological bent was not revived through the appearance of the German translation, in part because, for most readers, Leibniz had successfully countered Bayle's suggested heresy with his *Théodicée* (the German translation of which Gottsched edited in 1744).

Gottsched's six-volume anthology of plays, *Die Deutsche Schaubühne nach den Regeln und Exempeln der alten Griechen und Römer* (The German Stage According to the Rules and Examples of the Ancient Greeks and Romans), appeared between 1741 and 1745. The title was meant to imply that the plays could be given on German stages but were not all German in origin. In volume two, the first volume to appear, there were plays by Racine, Saint-Évremond, Marie Anne Barbier, Addison, Voltaire, and Holberg. Later volumes contained plays by Corneille, Charles-Rivière Dufresny, Molière, Philippe Destouches, Gottsched himself, and no fewer than five by Gottsched's wife. There were also several plays by lesser-known German playwrights. It is apparent that Gottsched was, on the one hand, making available French and Danish models for aspiring German playwrights and, on the other, attempting to demonstrate that there were plays by German dramatists that were worthy of production. (It has been suggested that Gottsched borrowed the title of his collection from Holberg, whose plays had been published as *Den Danske Skueplads* [The Danish Stage, 1731-1754].)

Both the *Critische Beyträge* and its immediate successor, *Neuer Büchersaal der schönen Wissenschaften und freyen Künste* (New Library of Belles Lettres and Liberal Arts, 1745-1750) paid particular attention to the Greek and Latin classics and took pains to record translations of classical works into German. While the *Critische Beyträge* clearly had a humanistic bias, the *Neuer Büchersaal* embraced the natural sciences as well as French, English, and Italian literature in its reviews. There was notable emphasis on the work of Pope and Fontenelle, both important spirits of the European Enlightenment. On the whole, the second journal was more factual and a less critical work than its predecessor.

Although the cultivation of the German language had been a major concern for Gottsched from his first years in Leipzig, it was not until 1748 that his description of German grammar, syntax, style, and usage appeared as the *Grundlegung einer Deutschen Sprachkunst* (Basics of the German Language). He had expected to complete work on the book much earlier than was the case and had actually ventured announcements of forthcoming publication more than once. Although *Grundlegung einer Deutschen Sprachkunst* does not reflect much originality on Gottsched's part, it is a monument to his ability to analyze and to synthesize. Gottsched's motivation was to gain for the German language a position comparable to that of French in the European community. As Herbert Penzl has pointed out in his commentary on the work in volume 8 of the *Ausgewählte Werke*, Gottsched was actually describing his own usage—the form of German that he felt should be used as standard. *Grundlegung einer Deutschen Sprachkunst* is descriptive as well as prescriptive, broadly conceived, and readily comprehensible; it is significant because of its use of German rather than Latin terminology and its many illustrative examples. To classify it merely as a grammar is misleading, since it also addresses orthography, diction, usage, metrics, and figures of speech; in addition, it contains a list of proverbs. More than seven hundred pages long, it became Gottsched's most widely known and used book. There were five editions in his lifetime; by 1778 translations into French, Latin, Polish, Danish, Serbo-Croatian, English, Hungarian, Dutch, and Russian had been published. There were, in addition, reworkings of Gottsched's grammar in several languages; the last, in French, appeared seventy-six years after Gottsched's death. By that time some 125 new editions, translations, and reworkings had been published. As with the *Critische Dichtkunst*, there were also shortened versions for school use. The last edition of Gottsched's own schoolbook version, *Kern der deutschen Sprachkunst* (Essentials of German Grammar, 1753), appeared in 1784.

The twelve volumes of Gottsched's last critical journal, *Das Neueste aus der anmuthigen Gelehrsamkeit* (The Latest News of Genial Scholarship, 1751-1762) continued along the same lines as the *Neuer Büchersaal*, but the number of the editor's own contributions increased. Among the reviews in *Das Neueste* was Gottsched's 1753 evaluation of Samuel Johnson's *The Plan of a Dictionary of the English Language* (1747). (In 1764 James Boswell, Johnson's future biographer, called upon Gottsched and was cheerfully received. Boswell and Gottsched made unfulfilled promises about corresponding.) Two separate works from the 1750s warrant special notice. Gottsched's High German translation of the Low German epic of Reynard the Fox (1752) is memorable as the source that Goethe transformed into his *Reineke Fuchs* (1794). And in 1757 Gottsched published a lengthy bibliography of German plays under the title *Nöthiger Vorrath zur Geschichte der deutschen Dramatischen Dichtkunst* (Essential Source for the History of German Dramatic Art); a second part of the bibliography appeared in 1765.

Over the years Gottsched wrote many incidental pieces, including addresses, memorials, and academic papers in Latin; some of these publications were related to the rectorship of the University of Leipzig, a position to which he was elected five times. He edited or wrote the introductions to many books, such as translations of works by Virgil (1742 and 1750), Lucan (1745), Cicero (1758), and Claude-Adrien Helvétius (1760), as well as the translations of the French Academy proceedings that his wife had undertaken (1751). He edited a volume of Benjamin Neukirchs's works (1744) and, after his wife died in 1762, a volume of her poetry (1763). Among the many publications of Gottsched's later years was the first popular encyclopedia in German, the *Handlexicon oder Kurzgefaßtes Wörterbuch der*

schönen Wissenschaften und freyen Künste (Lexicon; or, Brief Dictionary of the Liberal Arts and Sciences, 1760). The work is evidence of Gottsched's continued commitment to the ideals of the Enlightenment. The Gottsched bibliography that constitutes volume 12 of the *Ausgewählte Werke* records more than 840 items published in Gottsched's lifetime.

The death of his wife meant the loss of Gottsched's constant helpmate. For two or three years a niece served as his housekeeper. In 1765, after she left to marry, Gottsched took a young bride–Ernestine Susanne Katharina Neunes, a woman who was not his intellectual equal and about whom next to nothing is known. Sixteen months later Gottsched died; the cause of death was given as edema. His reworking of the singspiele *Thalestris* by "Ermelinde Thalea"–that is, Maria Antonia Walpurgis, consort of the Elector of Saxony–was apparently not completed when he died, but in 1767 it was published under the supervision of his niece, who dated the work 12 December 1766, the day of Gottsched's death.

The feud between "the Swiss," that is, Bodmer and Breitinger, and "Leipzig," that is, Gottsched and his followers, resulted in the diminution of Gottsched's authority in the 1740s and 1750s on some fronts, but on others he retained his reputation and stature. Time and again he is referred to in writings of the period as "der berühmte Professor Gottsched" (the famous Professor Gottsched). In the 1750s severe criticism came from a new quarter: Friedrich Nicolai and his colleagues launched one attack after another on Gottsched and denied him any virtues whatsoever, even suggesting that a dog had more musical sense than Professor Gottsched. The earliest of Nicolai's criticisms was well founded: Gottsched had believed the claims that one William Lauder had put forward about Milton's lack of originality in *Paradise Lost* and had failed to retract his positive review of Lauder's book even after Lauder confessed that the charges were fraudulent. After that Nicolai had no good word for the Leipzig professor and ridiculed him in chapter after chapter of his *Briefe über den itzigen Zustand der schönen Wissenschaften in Deutschland* (Letters on the Present Condition of the Liberal Arts in Germany, 1754). Later, in the well-known "Siebzehnter Literaturbrief" (Seventeenth Letter on Literature, 1759), in Nicolai's *Briefe, die neueste Literatur betreffend* (Letters Pertaining to the Most Recent Literature), the young Gotthold Ephraim

Lessing denied outright—and unjustly—that Gottsched had made any contribution to the German theater. Lessing's clever and sarcastic argument had a lasting effect among German intellectuals, so that, despite the long life of the *Critische Dichtkunst*, the *Redekunst*, and the *Sprachkunst*, Gottsched lost his position on the pinnacle of Parnassus and, for two hundred years, was looked upon more as a comical than an influential figure in histories of German literature. It was not until 1968 that a critical edition of Gottsched's works began to appear under the editorship of Joachim Birke. Since then Gottsched may be said to have come into his own as the subject of a series of new appraisals of his contribution to the development of German theater, belles lettres, rhetoric, and philology.

Letters:

Gottsched und seine Zeit: Auszüge aus seinem Briefwechsel, edited by Theodor Wilhelm Danzel (Leipzig: Dyk, 1848);

Neues aus der Zopfzeit: Gottscheds Briefwechsel mit dem Nürnberger Naturforscher Martin Frobenius Ledermüller und dessen seltsame Lebensschicksale. Im Anhang: Gottscheds Briefe und ein Schreiben Gellerts an den Altdorfer Professor Georg Andreas Will, edited by Emil Reicke (Leipzig: Scholtze, 1923);

Ein Schreiben Gottscheds an Ludwig Ernst Borowski von 18. November 1764 (Leipzig: Günther, Kirstein & Wendler, 1927).

Bibliography:

Gottsched-Bibliographie, volume 12 of Gottsched's *Ausgewählte Werke*, edited by P. M. Mitchell (Berlin & New York: De Gruyter, 1987).

References:

G. Belouin, *De Gottsched à Lessing: étude sur les commencements du théâtre modern en Allemagne (1724-1760)* (Paris: Hachette, 1909);

Joachim W. Birke, *Christian Wolffs Metaphysik und die zeitgenössische Literatur- und Musiktheorie: Gottsched, Scheibe, Mizler* (Berlin: De Gruyter, 1966);

Birke, "Gottscheds Critische Dichtkunst: Voraussetzungen und Quellen," Ph.D. dissertation, University of Illinois, 1964;

Eric A. Blackall, *The Emergence of German as a Literary Language* (Cambridge: University Press, 1959);

Peter Borjans-Heuser, *Bürgerliche Produktivität und Dichtungstheorie: Strukturmerkmale der poeti-*

Luise Adelgunde Victoria Kulmus Gottsched, whom Gottsched married in 1735 and who collaborated with him on many of his projects; painting by Schorer (Leipzig, Universitätsbibliothek)

schen Rationalität im Werke von Johann Christoph Gottsched (Frankfurt am Main: Lang, 1981);

Dennis Robert Bormann, "Gottsched's Enlightened Rhetoric: The Influence of Christian Wolff's Philosophy on Johann Gottsched's Ausführliche Redekkunst," Ph.D. dissertation, University of Iowa, 1968;

Jan Bruck, "Der aristotelische Mimesesbegriff und die Nachahmungstheorie Gottscheds und die Schweizer," Ph.D. dissertation, University of Erlangen-Nürnberg, 1972;

David Connor, "Johann Christoph Gottsched and the Growth of German Literature," Ph.D. dissertation, Yale University, 1969;

Richard Daunicht, *Die Entstehung des bürgerlichen Trauerspiels in Deutschland* (Berlin: De Gruyter, 1963);

Hans Freier, *Kritische Poetik: Legitimation und Kritik der Poesie in Gottscheds Dichtkunst* (Stuttgart: Metzler, 1973);

Ekkehard Gühne, *Gottscheds Literaturkritik in den "Vernünftigen Tadlerinnen" (1725-26)* (Stuttgart: Heinz, 1978);

Hilde Haider-Pregler, *Des sittlichen Bürgers Abendschule: Bildungsanpruch und Bildungsauftrag des Berufstheaters im 18. Jahrhundert* (Vienna & Munich: Jugend und Volk, 1980);

Robert R. Heitner, *German Tragedy in the Age of Enlightenment: A Study in the Development of Original Tragedies, 1724-1768* (Berkeley & Los Angeles: University of California Press, 1963);

Hans Peter Herrmann, *Naturnachahmung und Einbildungskraft: Zur Entwicklung der deutschen Poetik von 1670 bis 1740* (Bad Homburg: Gehlen, 1970);

Hans Hiebel, *Individualität und Totalität: Zur Geschichte und Kritik des bürgerlichen Poesiebegriffs von Gottsched bis Hegel anhand der Theorien über Epos und Roman* (Bonn: Bouvier, 1974);

Peter Carl Johannson, "Two Aspects of Gottsched's Deutsche Sprachkunst: The Phonetic Norm and the Idea of the 'Best Writers,'" Ph.D. dissertation, University of California, Santa Barbara, 1977;

Ulf Lehmann, *Der Gottschedkreis und Rußland: Deutsch-russische Literaturbeziehungen im Zeitalter der Aufklärung* (Berlin: Akademie-Verlag, 1966);

Monica Lemmi, "La 'Deutsche Sprachkunst' di Johann Christoph Gottsched: Sfondo, fortuna, effetività," Ph.D. dissertation, University of Florence, 1983;

Wolfgang Martens, *Die Botschaft der Tugend: Die Aufklärung im Spiegel der deutschen moralischen Wochenschriften* (Stuttgart: Metzler, 1968);

Alberto Martino, *Geschichte der dramatischen Theorien in Deutschland im 18. Jahrhundert I: Die Dramaturgie der Aufklärung (1730-80)* (Tübingen: Niemeyer, 1972);

Uwe Möller, *Rhetorische Überlieferung und Dichtungstheorie im frühen 18. Jahrhundert: Studien zu Gottsched, Breitinger und G. F. Meier* (Munich: Fink, 1983);

Joachim Müller, *Shakespeare und ein deutscher Anfang: Die von Borcksche Übersetzung des "Julius Caesar" von 1741 im Streitfeld von Gottsched und Johann Elias Schlegel* (Berlin: Akademie-Verlag, 1977);

Alessandro Pellegrini, *Gottsched, Bodmer, Breitinger e la poetica dell' Aufklärung* (Universitá de Catania, 1952);

Thomas Rauter, "The Eighteenth-Century 'Deutsche Gesellschaft': A Literary Society of the German Middle Class," Ph.D. dissertation, University of Illinois, 1970;

Eugen Reichel, *Gottsched*, 2 volumes (Berlin: Gottsched-Verlag, 1908-1912);

Werner Rieck, *Johann Christoph Gottsched: Eine kritische Würdigung seines Werkes* (Berlin: Akademie-Verlag, 1972);

Dieter Romboy, "Gottsched: Myth and Fact," Ph.D. dissertation, University of Utah, 1974;

Isabella Rossmann, "Gottscheds Redelehre und ihre antiken Quellen," Ph.D. dissertation, University of Graz, 1971;

Hartmut Scheible, *Wahrheit und Subjekt: Ästhetik im bürgerlichen Zeitalter* (Bern & Munich: Francke, 1984);

Klaus R. Scherpe, *Gattungspoetik im 18. Jahrhundert: Historische Entwicklung von Gottsched bis Herder* (Stuttgart: Metzler, 1968);

Claus Schuppenhauer, *Der Kampf um den Reim in der deutschen Literatur des 18. Jahrhunderts* (Bonn: Bouvier, 1970);

Jakob Steigerwald, "Die Bremer Beiträge: Ihr Verhältnis zu Gottsched, und ihre Stellung in der Geschichte der deutschen Literatur," Ph.D. dissertation, University of Cincinnati, 1975;

Gustav Waniek, *Gottsched und die deutsche Literatur seiner Zeit* (Leipzig: Breitkopf & Härtel, 1897);

Marianne Wehr, "J. C. Gottscheds Briefwechsel: Ein Beitrag zur Geschichte der deutschen Frühaufklärung," Ph.D. dissertation, University of Leipzig, 1965;

Angelika Wetterer, *Publikumsbezug und Wahrheitsanspruch: Der Widerstand zwischen rhetorischem Ansatz und philosophischem Anspruch bei Gottsched und den Schweizern* (Tübingen: Niemeyer, 1981;

Marianne Winkler, "J. Ch. Gottsched im Spiegelbild seiner kritischen Journale: Eine Teiluntersuchung zum gesellscheftlichen und philosophischen Standort des Gottschedianismus," *Beiträge zur Universitätsgeschichte*, 1 (1959): 145-192;

Eugen Wolff, *Gottscheds Stellung im deutschen Bildungsleben*, 2 volumes (Kiel & Leipzig: Lipsius & Tischer, 1894-1897).

Johann Nikolaus Götz
(9 July 1721 - 4 November 1781)

Erich P. Hofacker, Jr.
University of Michigan

BOOKS: *Versuch eines Wormsers in Gedichten,* anonymous (N.p., 1745);

Über den Tod seines Bruders Cornelius Georg Götzens: Damon (N.p., 1747);

Die Mädchen-Insel: Eine Elegie, anonymous, edited by Karl Ludwig von Knebel (Potsdam, 1773);

Vermischte Gedichte, 3 volumes, edited by Karl Wilhelm Ramler (Mannheim: Schwan, 1785);

Vermehrte Gedichte, 3 volumes, edited by Ramler (Mannheim: Schwan, 1807);

Gedichte von Johann Nicolaus Götz aus den Jahren 1745-1765 in ursprünglicher Gestalt, edited by Carl Schüddekopf (Stuttgart: Göschen, 1893; reprinted, Nendeln, Liechtenstein: Kraus, 1968).

OTHER: Anacreon [attributed], *Die Oden Anakreons in reimlosen Versen: Nebst einigen andern Gedichten,* translated anonymously by Götz and Johann Peter Uz (Frankfurt am Main & Leipzig, 1746);

Jean Baptiste Louis Gresset, *Paperle: In vier Gesängen,* translated anonymously by Götz (Frankfurt am Main & Leipzig, 1750);

Montesquieu, *Der Tempel zu Gnidus: Aus dem Französischen des Gresset,* translated anonymously by Götz (Karlsruhe, 1759);

Anacreon [attributed] and Sappho, *Die Gedichte Anakreons und der Sappho Oden: Aus dem Griechischen übersetzt und mit Anmerkungen begleitet,* translated by Götz (Karlsruhe: Macklot, 1760; reprinted, with an afterword by Herbert Zeman, Stuttgart: Metzler, 1970).

Johann Nikolaus Götz was "ein unfehlbar den ersten Dichtern aller Völker und Zeiten gleichzustellender Liebling der Musen und Grazien" (most certainly a favorite of the muses and graces and equal in rank to the greatest poets of all nations and ages), said Christoph Martin Wieland in attempting to acquire Götz's literary remains for the library of Duke Karl August of Weimar. To Johann Gottfried Herder,

Johann Nikolaus Götz; engraving by H. Sintzenich after a painting by P. LeClerc

"Götzens Gedichte sind eine Dactyliothek, voll lieblicher Bilder, eben so bedeutungsreich als zierlich gefaßt und anmuthik-wechselnd" (Götz's poems are a library of dactyls, full of lovely images, with just as great a wealth of meaning as they are delicately composed and gracefully variable). Herder spoke of the allegories and garlands of poetic flowers in the work of the poet as a treasure to be found in no other language except the original Greek. Modern literary historians consider his translation of Greek poetry the source of a new flexibility in the German language.

Götz was born in Worms in the Rhineland-Palatinate on 9 July 1721 to Peter Götz and Anna Rosina Götz, née Roos. He was descended from nine generations of Lutheran pastors on his father's side. Upon completion of the orthodox Lutheran gymnasium in Worms he matriculated in 1739 at the University of Halle. The university had long been a stronghold of pietism, but a new rationalist philosophy had recently been introduced there by Christian Wolff. Thus at eighteen Götz found himself suddenly exposed to conflicting theological, philosophical, and literary currents. With two other students, Johann Wilhelm Ludwig Gleim and Johann Peter Uz, he studied the *Meditationes Philosophicae* (1735) of Alexander Gottlieb Baumgarten, a disciple of Wolff. He collaborated with Uz for two years in the translation of Greek anacreontic verse, a poetic form then becoming fashionable in Germany.

In 1554 the *Anacreontea,* a collection of poems reputedly by the ancient Greek poet Anacreon of Teos, had been published in Paris from a tenth-century text appended to the *Heidelberg Codex Palatinus*; their authenticity was already in question when Götz was writing. In the seventeenth and eighteenth centuries, French and Latin imitations of the poems proliferated. The designation *anacreontic* came to be applied to poetry with pastoral motifs devoted to wine, women (or boys), and song. The efforts to achieve perfection in the translation and adaptation of the *Anacreontea* resulted in one of the most productive periods in the development of German lyric poetry, and Götz became Germany's most successful translator of anacreontic verse. He had learned delicacy of word and phrase from the works of Friedrich von Hagedorn, whose poetry benefited from French and English as well as ancient Greek models and was filled with lightheartedness, wit, and good-natured worldly wisdom. Building on the skills of Hagedorn, Germany's first anacreontic poet, Götz learned to write in a simple and natural style.

Götz and Uz borrowed their poetic form from Johann Christoph Gottsched's 1733 renderings of the first three poems of the *Anacreontea* into unrhymed German trochaic dimeter. After Uz made literal translations, Götz captured the grace and charm of the Greek originals, following the Greek of the *Anacreontea* in the number of lines and syllables used. Götz and Uz collaborated until 1741, after which a rift developed and their friendship cooled.

Götz ended university studies in 1742 to become a tutor and private pastor to the family of Baron von Kalkreuter in Emden on the North Sea coast in East Frisia. But he suffered in the cold and damp of the region and on the advice of a physician journeyed south to Worms. During a stopover in Holland he suffered from hemorrhaging which confined him to bed for three weeks. This episode marked the onset of the ill health that would plague him the rest of his life. In "Bey Erblickung seiner Vaterstadt" (At the Sight of His Hometown) he recounts his experiences on the difficult trip. The poem gives evidence of new beginnings in the subjectivism of its personal narrative but reverts to the baroque tradition of reflection, the entreaty of Providence, and the enumeration of the trials that faced the poet. The young clergyman remained in Worms only a few months before accepting a position in the spring of 1744 as a private pastor to an elderly lady of nobility. In 1746 he accompanied her grandsons to a school for young noblemen at Lunéville in northern France.

Götz published his first collection of poetry in 1745. *Versuch eines Wormsers in Gedichten* (Poetic Attempt of a Citizen of Worms) contains a tribute to a friendship of the poet's youth. "An seinen Freund Damon" (To His Friend Damon) is free of playful anacreontic motifs; instead, it reflects a strong desire for genuine expression of the soul and brings Götz closer than any other anacreontic poet to the pietists I. Jakob Pyra and Samuel Gotthold Lange, publishers of *Thirsis und Damons freundschaftliche Lieder* (The Songs of Friendship of Thirsis and Damon, 1745). Götz's poem begins, "Geliebter, glaube mir, ein Mensch ist glücklich dran, / Der in dem treuen Schoos von Freunden ruhen kann" (My dear friend, believe me, that person is fortunate, / Who can rest on the faithful bosom of friends). In this early example of Götz's artistic development, the use of the Alexandrine line and of rhyme suggests borrowing from an obsolete poetic tradition. The forty-two-line poem shows a tendency toward sentimental lyric and first-person expression. In a 1747 letter to Gleim, Götz included a poem subtitled "Damon," eulogizing his deceased brother Cornelius Georg. A comparison of the two "Damon" poems exemplifies the change in aesthetic concept announced in the motto accompanying the 1747 poem: "Kein Reim entweih dies dir geweihte Lied" (Let no rhyme desecrate this poem dedicated to you).

To Götz's surprise, his and Uz's translation of the *Anacreontea* appeared in 1746 as *Die Oden Anakreons in reimlosen Versen: Nebst einigen andern Gedichten* (The Odes of Anacreon in Unrhymed Verses: In Addition to Some Other Poems). The volume had been published by Gleim, who had served as an adviser during the translation. The first ode, "Auf seine Leyer" (To His Lyre), sets the tone of the collection, which rejects the "Hochstil" (elevated style in praise of heroes). Götz preferred to pay tribute to a world in which love rather than heroic deeds held sway.

> Ich möchte die Atriden,
> Ich möcht' auch Kadmus preisen;
> Doch meiner Leyer Saiten
> Erthönen bloß von Liebe....

> (I would like to praise the Atrides,
> I would also like to praise Cadmus;
> But the strings of my lyre
> Resound merely of love....)

The book was a cheerful, playful affirmation of life; but it was poorly printed, causing Götz "recht hertzfressende Ärgernisse" (vexation that ate away at [his] heart). The typesetting contained many errors and whole stanzas were omitted or misplaced. Despite his "weltliche Poesie" (worldly poetry), Götz was a poor judge of human nature and too trusting of Gleim. In 1747 he mailed Gleim his complete revised manuscript of anacreontic translations with the request that Gleim comment and supply some notes. Gleim did not respond to the request and did not return the manuscript for eight years, apparently wishing to prevent its publication until he could prepare and publish his own version.

Retiring by nature, Götz longed for a retreat into his own private world and the opportunity to devote himself more completely to his literary endeavors. But he reluctantly left France in 1750 and went to serve a parish in the small town of Hornbach in central Germany. *Paperle*, his translation of a work by the French poet Jean Baptiste Louis Gresset, was published that year. In 1752 he married Christina Hautt, the widow of his predecessor, who bore him a son, Gottlieb Christian, that same year. The following year Götz accepted a better position in Meisenheim, where his daughter, Henrietta Luise Christina, was born.

In 1755 Gleim finally "found" and returned the allegedly mislaid revision of the odes. Götz asked Gleim to keep him informed of literary de-

Title page for Götz's revised translation of ancient Greek poems

velopments in Germany, since Meisenheim was "halb in der Barbarey" (almost in the wilds). Gleim did not respond; but he sent some of Götz's revisions to Karl Wilhelm Ramler, who had included several of Götz's translations from the 1746 volume in his anthology *Oden mit Melodien* (Odes with Melodies, 1755). Ramler began an active correspondence with Götz. The two men never met, but Ramler became Götz's trusted adviser and editor.

Der Tempel zu Gnidus, Götz's translation of a work by Montesquieu, appeared in 1759. Based on the revisions returned by Gleim in 1755, a completely reworked and accurately printed edition of translated Greek poems was published in 1760: *Die Gedichte Anakreons und der Sappho Oden* (The Poems of Anacreon and the Odes of Sappho). Greatly improved over the 1746 edition in vocabulary, phrasing, and punctuation, the translation shows new vitality. The language is better suited to the meter, more modern, freer, and, in line with the goal of "Scherzhaftigkeit" (playful tone), the poems are wittier and more jocular. Abstractions are limited and erotic images are clearer: instead of Cupid, a young man awakens a girl and rather than merely urging her, he compels her "Mit Gewalt zu mehr, als Küssen" (By force, to more than kiss). Herbert Zeman, who has published a facsimile edition of this text (1970), considers it Götz's most important literary achievement and the linguistic high point of the Enlightenment. It served as an example for the diction of all contemporary anacreontic poetry and set the standard for later generations. Traces of its language are found in the lyric poetry of Gotthold Ephraim Lessing as well as in Johann Wolfgang Goethe's love poems in *West-östlicher Divan* (West-East Divan, 1819).

In 1761 Götz accepted a pastorate in Winterburg, a small town near Bad Kreuznach that he described as "fünfzig Stunden von der Zivilisation" (fifty hours from civilization). There his need for intellectual stimulation was met in part by his friendship with the merchant Gerhard Heinrich Schmerz, a man schooled in the arts who possessed an excellent library. Nevertheless, Götz looked to Berlin as the center of intellectual life and for the fulfillment of his literary aspirations; he longed to move there, to go "von Arkadien nach Athen, von der Barbarei in die Zivilisation" (from Arcadia to Athens, from the wilds to civilization), but he never did. Götz could achieve fame only as "Ramlers Anonymus" (Ramler's anonymous poet), for his religious calling, in which he found ever less pleasure, denied him an identity in the world of poetry. To preserve a little time for his poetry, he long resisted promotion to an administrative position. Götz's elegy *Die Mädchen-Insel* (The Isle of Maidens, 1773) was the only piece of German literature praised by the Francophile Prussian king Frederick II in his *De la littérature allemande* (Concerning German Literature, 1780).

In 1774 Ramler wrote to Götz that his anacreontic verse was beginning to lose favor in a changing world. A reworking had been in progress for some time, but age and failing health were taking their toll. Weighed down by professional duties, he wrote in 1778 that he was too "kalt" (cold) to continue, that he had lost his inspiration and joy in writing. On his way to church on Easter Mon-day 1781, Götz suffered a stroke. He died on 4 November and is buried in Winterburg.

Herder wrote of Götz in 1803: "Ja, soll er noch vergessen seyn, der in seinem Leben verborgne Dichter, der aus seiner Winterburg wie eine Nachtigall hinter dichten Zweigen sang, in seiner Sprache die zierlichsten Kränze flocht und sich in Reimen und ohne Reim in jedem angenehmen Sylbenmasse versuchte?" (Shall he be forgotten, this poet who concealed himself behind the circumstances of his external life, who sang like a nightingale out of his Winterburg from behind heavy brush, sang in a language which wove the most delicate wreaths and showed his skill with rhyme and without it in every pleasing meter?). Götz consequently became known to posterity as the "Nightingale of Winterburg," a romantic trivialization which does not do justice to the deeper content of much of his poetry.

Letters:
Briefe von und an Johann Nikolaus Götz: Nach den Originalen herausgegeben, edited by Carl Schüddekopf (Wolfenbüttel: Zwissler, 1893).

References:
Alfred Anger, "Und mein einzig Eigenthum," in *Gedichte und Interpretationen,* edited by Karl Richter, volume 2 (Stuttgart: Reclam, 1983), pp. 150-161;

Willy Mathern, *Johann Nikolaus Götz: Die Winterburger Nachtigall. Lebensbild eines deutschen Dichters* (Bad Kreuzbach, 1972);

Wolfgang Neuber, "Johann Nikolaus Götz zum 200. Todestag. Versuch zur Kenntlichmachung eines Paradigmas," *Blätter der Carl-Zuckmayer-Gesellschaft,* 7 (1981): 63-134;

J. M. Ritchie, "The Anacreontic Poets: Gleim, Uz, Götz," in *German Men of Letters,* volume 6, edited by Alex Natan and Brian Keith-Smith (London: Wolff, 1972), pp. 123-145;

Herbert Zeman, "Friedrich von Hagedorn, Johann Wilhelm Gleim, Peter Uz, Johann Nikolaus Götz," in *Deutsche Dichter des 18. Jahrhunderts. Ihr Leben und ihr Werk,* edited by Benno von Wiese (Berlin: Schmidt, 1977), pp. 135-161.

Papers:
Johann Nikolaus Götz's literary estate was passed on to his grandson and was eventually stored with the papers of Friedrich Müller, known as "Maler Müller" (Müller the Painter). When these papers were auctioned off in Leipzig in 1904, all

traces of the manuscripts left behind by Götz disappeared. A letter from Götz to Johann David Michaelis is in the library of Göttingen University.

Johann Georg Hamann
(27 August 1730 - 21 June 1788)

James C. O'Flaherty
Wake Forest University

BOOKS: *Glückwunsch eines Sohnes am Geburtstage seines Vaters*, anonymous (Königsberg, 1749);

Commentatio philosophica de somno et somniis: Quam D. S. A. consensu amplissimi philosophorum ordinis publice defendent praeses Ioannes Gotthelf Lindner, philos. et art. liberal. magister et respondens Ioannes Georgius Hamann, art. lib. cultor, contra amicum Ionannem Christophorum Wolson, by Hamann and Johann Gotthelf Lindner (Königsberg, 1751);

Freundschaftlicher Gesang auf die Heimkunft des Herrn S. G. H., anonymous (Königsberg, 1751);

Auf den Zwey und Zwanzigsten des Christmonats, anonymous (Königsberg, 1751);

Trauerschrift auf den Tod der Hochedlen Frau, Catharina Elisabeth Rentzen, gebornen Saturgus, anonymous (Königsberg: Hartung, 1752);

Denkmal, anonymous (Königsberg, 1756);

Beylage zu Dangeuil's Anmerkungen, anonymous (Mitau & Leipzig: Petersen, 1756);

Sokratische Denkwürdigkeiten für die lange Weile des Publicums zusammengetragen von einem Liebhaber der langen Weile: Mit einer doppelten Zuschrift an Niemand und an Zween, anonymous (Amsterdam [actually Königsberg]: Hartung, 1759; edited by Fritz Blanke, Gütersloh: Mohn, 1959); translated by James C. O'Flaherty as *Hamann's Socratic Memorabilia: A Translation and Commentary* (Baltimore: Johns Hopkins University Press, 1967);

Vermischte Anmerkungen über die Wortfügung in der französischen Sprache zusammengeworfen, mit patriotischer Freyheit, von einem hochwohlgelahrten Deutsch-Franzosen, anonymous (Königsberg: Kanter, 1760);

Painting by an unknown artist, circa 1755 (Historisches Bildarchiv Lolo Handke, Berneck)

Klaggedicht, in Gestalt eines Sendschreibens über die Kirchenmusik: An ein geistreiches Frauenzimmer außer Landes, anonymous (N.p., 1760);

Die Magi aus Morgenlande zu Bethlehem, anonymous (Königsberg: Kanter, 1760); translated by Ronald Gregor Smith as "The Wise Men from the East in Bethlehem," in his *J. G. Hamann, 1730-1788: A Study in Christian Existence* (New York: Harper, 1960), pp. 159-173;

Versuch über eine akademische Frage, as Aristobulus (Königsberg: Kanter, 1760);

Abaelardi Virbii Beylage zum zehnten Theile der Briefe die Neuste Literatur betreffend, anonymous (N.p., 1761);

Lettre néologique & provenciale sur l'Inoculation du bon sens, anonymous (N.p., 1761);

Französisches Project einer nützlichen, bewährten und neuen Einpropfung: Oder Beylage zum Magazin für alle. . . . Übersetzt nach verjüngtem Maßstab, anonymous (Thorn [actually Königsberg: Kanter], 1761);

Wolken: Ein Nachspiel Sokratischer Denkwürdigkeiten. Cum notis variorum in usum Delphini, anonymous (Altona [actually Königsberg: Kanter], 1761);

Chimärische Einfälle über den zehnten Theil der Briefe die neuesten Litteratur betreffend, anonymous (Königsberg: Kanter, 1761);

Schriftsteller und Kunstrichter: Geschildert in Lebensgröße, von einem Leser, der keine Lust hat, Kunstrichter und Schriftsteller zu werden. Nebst einigen andern Wahrheiten für den Herrn Verleger, der von nichts wußte, anonymous (Mitau, 1762);

Leser und Kunstrichter: Nach perspectivischem Unebenmaße. Im ersten Viertel des Brachscheins, anonymous (Mitau, 1762);

Kreuzzüge des Philologen, anonymous (Königsberg: Kanter, 1762);

Essais à la mosaique, anonymous (Mitau, 1762);

Fünf Hirtenbriefe das Schuldrama betreffend, anonymous (Königsberg, 1763);

Hamburgische Nachricht; Göttingische Anzeige; Berlinische Beurtheilung der Kreuzzüge des Philologen, anonymous (Mitau: Hartknoch, 1763);

Beylage zur Warnerschen Übersetzung von der Gicht aus der Königsbergischen gelehrten Zeitung, No. 64, den 10ten August 1770 (N.p., 1770);

Beylage zum Denkwürdigkeiten des seligen Sokrates: Von einem Geistlichen in Schwaben, anonymous (Halle, 1772);

Zwo Recensionen nebst einer Beylage, betreffend den Ursprung der Sprache, anonymous (N.p., 1772);

Des Ritters von Rosencreuz letzte Willensmeynung über den göttlichen und menschlichen Ursprung der Sprache: Aus einer Caricaturbilderurschrift eilfertig übersetzt vom Handlanger des Hierophanten, anonymous (Königsberg: Kanter, 1772);

Neue Apologie des Buchstaben h oder Außerordentliche Betrachtungen über die Orthographie des Deutschen, as H. S. Schullehrer (Pisa [actually Frankfurt am Main: Hinz], 1773); translated by Smith as "New Apology of the Letter h by Itself," in his *J. G. Hamann, 1730-1788: A Study in Christian Existence*, pp. 201-205;

An die Hexe zu Kadmonbor, anonymous (Berlin [actually Frankfurt am Main], 1773);

Lettre perdue d'un sauvage du Nord à un financier de Pe-Kim, anonymous (Riga, 1773);

Selbstgespräch eines Autors: Mit 45 Scholien, anonymous (Riga, 1773);

Le Kermes du Nord ou La Cochenille de Pologne, anonymous (Mitau: Hinz, 1774);

Mancherley, und Etwas zur Bolingbroke-Hervey-Hunterschen Uebersetzung von einem Recensenten trauriger Gestalt, anonymous (Mitau [actually Hamburg: Bode], 1774);

Christiani Zacchei Telonarchoe Prolegomena über die neueste Auslegung der ältesten Urkunde des menschlichen Geschlechts: In zweyen Antwortschreiben an Apollonium Philosophum, anonymous (N.p., 1774);

Briefe über Asmus' Werke (N.p., 1775);

Vetii Epagathi Regiomonticolae hierophantische Briefe, anonymous (N.p., 1775);

Freund Hain an alle "belesene und empfindsame Persohnen" in Ost- und West-Preußen, welche "Noch ein Dito beym Mondscheine zu singen" Lust und Gnüge finden (Königsberg: Kanter, 1775);

Versuch einer Sibylle über die Ehe, anonymous (Riga: Hartknoch, 1775);

Zweifel und Einfälle über eine vermischte Nachricht der Allgemeinen deutschen Bibliothek (Band XXIV, Stück I, S. 288-296) an Vetter Nabal, anonymous (Riga: Hartknoch, 1776);

Konxompax: Fragmentae einer apokryphischen Sibylle über apokalyptische Mysterien, anonymous (N.p., 1779);

Zwey Scherflein zur neusten Deutschen Litteratur, anonymous (Weimar, 1780);

Golgatha und Scheblimini! Von einem Prediger in der Wüsten, anonymous (Riga: Hartknoch, 1784; edited by Lothar Schreiner, Gütersloh: Bertelsmann, 1956); translated by Stephen N. Dunning in his *The Tongues of Men: Hegel and Hamann on Religious Language and History* (Missoula, Mont.: Scholars Press, 1979), pp. 210-226;

A-Ω! Entkleidung und Verklärung: Ein Fliegender Brief an Niemand den Kundbaren, anonymous (Mühlheim: Eyrich, 1785);

Betrachtungen über die Heilige Schrift, 2 volumes, edited by Friedrich von Roth (volume 1, Altdorf: Hessel, 1816; volume 2, Nuremberg: Lechner, 1816);

Sibyllinische Blätter des Magus im Norden: Nebst mehreren Beilagen, edited by Friedrich Cramer (Leipzig: Brockhaus, 1819);

Hamann's Schriften, 8 volumes, edited by Roth and G. A. Wiener (Berlin: Reimer, 1821-1843);

Christliche Bekenntnisse und Zeugnisse: Ein geordneter Auszug aus dessen gesamten Nachlaß mit genauer Hinweisung auf denselben nebst einem Anhang vermischter Fragmente, edited by A. W. Moller (Münster: Regensberg, 1826);

Sämtliche Werke: Historisch-kritische Ausgabe, 6 volumes, edited by Josef Nadler (Vienna: Herder, 1949-1957);

Heirophantische Briefe; Versuch einer Sibylle über die Ehe; Knoxompax; Schürze von Feigenblattern, edited by E. Jansen Schoonhoven and Martin Seils (Gütersloh: Mohn, 1962);

Entkleidung und Verklärung: Eine Auswahl aus Schriften und Briefen des "Magus im Norden," edited by Seils (Berlin: Union, 1963);

Zwo Recensionen nebst einer Beylage betreffend den Ursprung der Sprache; Des Ritters von Rosenkranz letzte Willensmeynung über den göttlichen und menschlichen Ursprung der Sprache; Philologische Einfälle und Zweifel; Au Salomon de Prusse, edited by Elfriede Büchsel (Gütersloh: Mohn, 1963);

Schriften zur Sprache, edited by Josef Simon (Frankfurt am Main: Suhrkamp, 1967);

Sokratische Denkwürdigkeiten; Aesthetica in nuce: Mit einem Kommentar, edited by Sven-Aage Jorgensen (Stuttgart: Reclam, 1968);

Philologia crucis: Zu Johann Georg Hamanns Auffassung von der Dichtkunst. Mit einem Kommentar zur Aesthetica in nuce, edited by Hans-Martin Lumpp (Tübingen: Niemeyer, 1970).

OTHER: Louis Joseph Plumard de Danguel, *Des Herrn von Dangueil Anmerkungen über die Vortheile und Nachtheile von Frankreich und Großbritannien in Ansehung des Handels und der übrigen Quellen von der Macht der Staaten: Auszug eines Werks über die Wiederherstellung der Manufacturen und des Handels in Spanien,* translated anonymously by Hamann (Mitau & Leipzig: Petersen, 1756);

Ferdinand Warners vollständige und deutliche Beschreibung der Gicht, aus dem Englischen übersetzt, mit einer Vorrede, translated by Hamann (Königsberg: Kanter, 1770);

Heinrich St. Johann Vitzgraf Bolingbroke und Jacob Hervey: Übersetzt, translated by Hamann (Mitau: Hinz, 1774);

"Metakritik über den Purismum der Vernunft," in *Mancherley zur Geschichte der metacritischen Invasion,* edited by F. T. Rinck (Königsberg: Nicolovius, 1800), pp. 120-134.

Johann Georg Hamann is a seminal figure in the development of modern German literature and philosophy. To many generations of cultural historians and students of German literature he has been known as the "father" of the Sturm und Drang and a principal forerunner of the Romantic movement. His influence on German Idealism was also considerable, even though much of it rested upon a misunderstanding of his true intentions. Through the mediation of Johann Gottfried Herder, Hamann became a major influence on the young Johann Wolfgang Goethe. That was to last, to varying degrees, throughout Goethe's long life. Other contemporaries who felt his impact as a religious thinker were Theodor Gottlieb Hippel, Johann Kaspar Lavater, Matthias Claudius, and, above, all, Friedrich Heinrich Jacobi. Even Immanuel Kant, Hamann's friendly adversary, owed much to him, since it was Hamann who called Kant's attention to the empiricist philosophy of David Hume and, in so doing, contributed to the awakening of the German philosopher from his "dogmatic slumber." Johann Paul Friedrich Richter (Jean Paul), Georg Wilhelm Friedrich Hegel, and Søren Kierkegaard in the nineteenth century and Ernst Jünger and Johannes Bobrowski in the twentieth are the most prominent among many important thinkers and writers who have responded creatively to the stimulus of his writings. But from the strictly epistemological standpoint, the true heirs of Hamann's thought are Goethe and Friedrich Nietzsche.

By no means, however, is Hamann's significance exhausted by tracing his widespread influence. His essays and letters are a mine of ideas that speak directly to vital twentieth-century concerns in theology, philosophy of language, philosophy of history, hermeneutics, and literary criticism. Hamann's writings deal with fundamental problems of present-day concern such as political freedom, freedom of expression, the relation of church and state, and the proper view of nature. Although he became a major source of the Sturm und Drang, or Counter-Enlightenment, especially with the publication of *Sokratische Denkwürdigkeiten* (1759; translated as *Hamann's Socratic Memorabilia*, 1967) and "Aesthetica in nuce" (Aesthetics in a Nutshell, 1762), Hamann was in many ways a child of the Enlightenment. This aspect of his thought is manifested not only in his critique, or, to use his own term, "Metakritik" (metacritique) of the underlying assumptions of the Enlightenment as a philosophical movement but also in his bitter attacks on the institutionalized Enlightenment in the Prussian state.

Earlier than in the other cultural centers of Germany in the eighteenth century, there converged in Königsberg two powerful streams of influence: Pietism, emanating from the University of Halle; and the Enlightenment, dominated by the dogmatic rationalism of Christian Wolff. It is surprising that such disparate movements did not erupt into open conflict and that they could, in some cases, be equally espoused by one and the same individual. It was into such a superficially peaceful but potentially explosive situation that Hamann was born. In the course of his relatively short lifetime he would emerge as head of a movement rooted in the religious heritage but no longer simply pietistic, while his compatriot Kant would emerge as head of a philosophical movement nurtured in dogmatic rationalism but no longer dogmatic. However philosophically antithetical the two movements were, without both of them the subsequent course of German intellectual and cultural history is unthinkable.

Hamann was born on 27 August 1730 in Königsberg (now Kaliningrad, U.S.S.R.) to Johann Christoph Hamann, a barber-surgeon who also supervised the public bathing establishment of the city, and Maria Magdalene Hamann, née Nuppenau. A paternal uncle, also named Johann Georg, was a notable literary figure who compiled a poetic lexicon and composed hymns as well as other pieces, some of which were set to music by Georg Philipp Telemann; he also wrote a sequel (1724) to the baroque novel *Die asiatische Banise* (The Asian Banise, 1689) by Heinrich Anselm von Ziegler und Kliphausen.

The home in which Hamann grew up was characterized by a genuine though not oppressive Pietism that in no way inhibited intellectual interests or dampened congeniality. The barber-surgeon father, who had aspired to more scientific training, was a popular figure in the city, and the small household was a sociable one. Hamann maintained a lifelong affection for his father and drew some of his most vivid and earthy metaphors from his father's profession. The darkest cloud to form over the family was the slow mental decline of Hamann's younger brother, Johann Christoph.

At first Hamann was tutored at home by university students; in this way he was exposed to bits of Greek, French, and Italian as well as instructed in music, dancing, and painting. Later he attended two inferior private schools; he lamented in his memoirs that only mechanical translation from Latin was required in one of the schools and that he received no instruction in history, geography, German composition, or poetry. He later attended the Kneiphof gymnasium, where the deficiency in basic subjects was remedied; in his last year he stood at the head of his class. The pietistic orientation of the gymnasium strengthened the religious influence of his home.

On 30 March 1746 the fifteen-year-old Hamann matriculated at the University of Königsberg as a student of theology; later he transferred to law and economics. At that time the university provided no opportunity for the study of literature or philology. Hamann was deeply influenced by two quite different professors. Martin Knutzen, who also greatly influenced Kant, lectured on mathematics, philosophy, and English. The most eminent member of the faculty, he strove to combine Wolffian rationalism with pietistic Christianity. Karl Heinrich Rappolt, on the other hand, who lectured on natural science, was outspokenly antipietistic; but his devotion to Latin humanism and his friendly nature appealed to Hamann, who spoke of him later as a "christlicher Weltweise" (Christian philosopher) for whom he had great affection. However important these two teachers were for Hamann, he apparently profited little otherwise from his university studies.

During his university years Hamann collaborated with friends on a periodical for women, titled *Daphne*, which was modeled somewhat after the English *Tatler* and *Spectator* but was also influenced by the writings of Friedrich von Hagedorn and Christian Fürchtegott Gellert. Hamann's pseudonymous contributions deal with the more serious religious and moral themes of the periodical. The concept of Empfindung (sensibility), later to become a basic concept in his philosophy, first emerges in these essays. He says that Zufriedenheit (contentment), the proper goal of life, is to be found in man's innate capacity to harmonize sensibility and reason; he later repudiated this view. The sensibility of women is finer than that of men, he maintained, hence the importance of their contribution to its cultivation. Of his later consuming concern with the problem of language there is no trace here, but it was beginning to emerge in his letters of the period.

While at the university Hamann made lasting friendships with Johann Christoph Berens and Samuel Gotthelf Hennings. Hamann always manifested an unusual capacity for friendship, and these early relationships foreshadow later ones that were to become important for the intellectual and cultural history of Germany–those with Herder, Hippel, Jacobi, Moses Mendelssohn, and Kant. In his autobiography, *Dichtung und Wahrheit* (Poetry and Truth, 1811-1833), Goethe wrote of Hamann: "Mir scheint er in Lebens- und Freundschaftsverhältnissen höchst klar gewesen zu sein und die Bezüge der Menschen untereinander und auf ihn sehr richtig gefühlt zu haben" (He seems to have been most clear about the relationships of life and between friends, and to have intuited the relations of individuals to one another and to himself with a great deal of acumen).

In 1752 Hamann left the university without a degree to become a tutor on estates of the minor nobility in the Baltic area. In his wideranging reading of this period he came under the influence of the Italian humanism of the Renaissance and its northern representatives Rudolphus Agricola, Francis Bacon, and Shaftesbury. This influence was important for his emerging philosophy of language and for his developing historical interests. In the summer of 1756 he was offered and accepted a post in Riga with the Berens family's firm, which was engaged in a thriving wholesale trade. Hamann devoted himself to the study of political economy and translated a treatise from the French of Louis Joseph Plumard de Dangeul dealing with foreign trade (1756). To this work he provided his own supplement, *Beylage zu Dangeuil's [sic] Anmerkungen* (Supplement to Dangeul's Remarks, 1756), in which he advocates "enlightened" bourgeois ideals and combines humanistic with mercantilistic ideas. Significantly, in the Prussia of Frederick II, he predicts that the merchant will replace the warrior as the nobleman of the future. After his religious conversion he repudiated the work as the embodiment of the ideals of the rationalistic Enlightenment.

Hamann gave up his tutorial post to join the Berens firm in Riga. His mother died in July 1756, and Hamann returned to Königsberg. He remained there until the beginning of October, when he went to London via Berlin, Lübeck, and Amsterdam. In Berlin, where he tarried for almost two months, he met old friends and made new ones; among the latter were Mendelssohn, Johann Georg Sulzer, and Karl Ramler. Christoph Berens had arranged Hamann's contacts with these men, all of whom represented the prevailing Enlightenment. In this way Hamann's patron and would-be mentor sought to orchestrate his charge's initiation into the career he had planned for him, an undertaking that was to fail dramatically. After spending much of the winter in Lübeck with maternal relatives, Hamann arrived in London on 18 April 1757.

When he delivered a message from the Berens firm to the Russian embassy, "Man erstaunte über die Wichtigkeit meiner Angelegenheit, noch mehr über die Art der Ausführung und vielleicht am meisten über die Wahl der Person, der man selbige anvertraut hatte" (There was astonishment at the importance of my affair, more astonishment at the way I carried it out, and perhaps most of all at the choice of the person to whom it was entrusted), and he was summarily dismissed. He wrote a memorandum to the Russian ambassador but was informed that his mission was hopeless.

"Ich war der Verzweiflung nahe, und suchte in lauter Zerstreuungen selbige aufzuhalten und zu unterdrücken" (I was near despair, and sought to hold it off and overcome it by outright dissipation), Hamann wrote later. As his funds ran out he began to think of earning money by playing the lute; in pursuing this plan he became involved with a young Englishman, who, he learned later, had a homosexual relationship with a rich friend. As a result of this episode, some scholars have maintained that Hamann himself had a homosexual experience. His health began to suffer from his irregular life-style.

In early February 1758 Hamann rented a room in the home of a respectable family. There he isolated himself and turned for consolation to the books he had purchased, above all the Bible. In the following weeks he read through the Old and New Testaments and came to the conclusion that God had asked for his heart. His response was unequivocal: "Da ist es mein Gott! . . . Reinige es, schaffe es neu, und laß es die Werkstatt deines guten Geistes seyn. . . . Es ist ein

Leviathan, den du allein zähmen kannst...."
(Here it is, Lord! . . . Cleanse it, create it anew,
and let it become the workshop of your good
Spirit....It is a Leviathan that you alone can
tame...). Though his beliefs after his conversion
manifested certain pietistic elements, his religion
was less subjective than Pietism: he did not simply turn inward to cultivate his own spiritual life;
his previous concern with the things of this world
was broadened and deepened, but seen in a new
light; further, he did not reject the sensual nature of man as essentially wicked. The mechanistic world order of Isaac Newton, which some Pietists could reconcile with their faith, Hamann
rejected completely; in its place he found a new
sense of order, biblically derived.

In the weeks following his conversion
Hamann's literary productivity was greater than
at any other comparable period in his life.
Within about two months he had produced
"Biblische Betrachtungen eines Christen" (Biblical Reflections of a Christian), a commentary on
the Bible published in *Hamann's Schriften*
(Hamann's Writings, 1821-1843). This work, plus
several short devotional writings, he referred to
collectively as "Tagebuch eines Christen" (Diary
of a Christian). It was also at this time that he
wrote "Gedanken über meinen Lebenslauf"
(Thoughts concerning My Life), published in
Hamann's Schriften.

Hamann left London at the end of June
1758 and arrived in Riga at the end of July. In
spite of the failure of his mission and the fruitless expenditure of the firm's money during his
long stay in London, he was well received by the
Berens family. The political climate by that time
was such that whatever commercial or diplomatic
plans the family had had would have been ne-
gated in any case. All went well until it became
clear that the fledgling merchant had undergone
a radical change; to say that Christoph Berens
was dismayed and disgusted is to put it mildly.

By January of the following year Hamann
had returned to his father's home in Königsberg.
For the next four years he was unemployed but
by no means idle. During that time he devoted
himself to intensive reading in theology–
especially the works of Martin Luther and Johann Albrecht Bengel–philosophy, the classics,
and contemporary literature. He also assiduously
studied Greek, Hebrew, and Arabic, mastering
the last to the extent of reading the Koran in the
original. But above all this was the highly productive first period of his "Autorschaft" (author-

ship), as he liked to call his writings intended for
publication. It is customary, if not entirely accurate, to divide his literary career into three periods: in the first, from 1759 to 1763, he treated
chiefly literary and aesthetic subjects; in the second, from 1772 to 1776, he dealt with language
and religious mysteries; and in the third, from
1778 to 1779, he was mainly concerned with philosophy and theology. His writings were occasional, written in response to specific challenges
posed by his religious or philosophical adversaries.

One of Hamann's most important works is
Sokratische Denkwürdigkeiten. This multidimen-
sional essay is an answer to the attempt of his
friends Berens and Kant to reconvert him from
evangelical Christianity to the tenets of the Enlightenment. The work proceeds on three levels:
it is an account of the life and teaching of Socrates, a typological interpretation of the Greek philosopher as a forerunner of Christ, and an attack
on the metaphysical, epistemological, aesthetic,
and sociological assumptions of the Enlightenment. In regard to epistemology Hamann seeks
to reinstate faith by appealing to the philosophy
of Hume; he also suggests the priority of dialectical over discursive logic by upholding the paradox as the proper mode of expressing truth. The
creative freedom of the genius is opposed to the
constraint of aesthetic rules: Homer and Shakespeare are cited as prime examples. The work concludes with a powerful indictment of the individual who acquiesces in the repressive conditions of
the ancien régime, and indicates that if one
would be "geschickt zum Dienst der Wahrheit"
(fit for the service of truth) he must be willing to
sacrifice his life. In this essay Hamann introduces
almost all the major themes of his oeuvre: faith
and reason, divine condescension, history, myth,
the philosophy of language, paradox, genius, and
pedagogy. He had not yet reached the apogee of
his style, but the work was powerful in its effect
on the intellectual climate of mid-eighteenth-
century Germany.

The beginning of Hamann's serious reflection on the relation of language and reason is
found in *Versuch über eine akademische Frage* (Essay
on an Academic Question, 1760). The essay was
occasioned by Johann David Michaelis's treatise
on the origin of language, which had been
awarded a prize by the Berlin Academy. The gist
of Michaelis's argument is that man invents language through reason. Hamann naturally rejects
this thesis, but he does not deal directly with it. In-

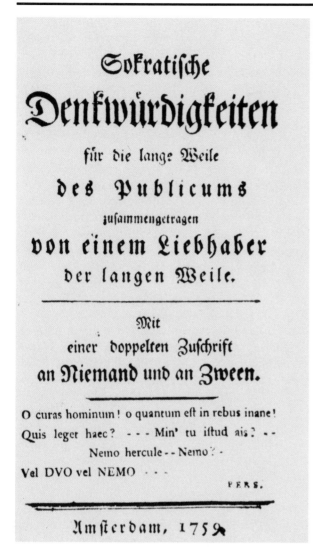

Sokratische

Denkwürdigkeiten

für die lange Weile

des Publicums

zusammengetragen

von einem Liebhaber

der langen Weile.

Mit
einer doppelten Zuschrift
an Niemand und an Zween.

O curas hominum! o quantum est in rebus inane!
Quis leget haec? --- Min' tu istud ais? --
Nemo hercule -- Nemo? -
Vel DVO vel NEMO ---
                                        PERS.

Amsterdam, 1759.

Title page for Hamann's defense of evangelical Christianity against rationalistic attacks

In *Wolken: Ein Nachspiel Sokratischer Denkwürdigkeiten* (Clouds: A Sequel to the Socratic Memorabilia, 1761) Hamann comes to terms with a reviewer who called him a "wahnwitziger Schwärmer" (mad dreamer). Hamann suspected that Berens and Kant were behind the review. *Wolken* is important for its relation of genius to putative madness and for its relation of sexuality to cognition by comparing rationalists to eunuchs.

"Aesthetica in nuce," first published in 1762 in the collection *Kreuzzüge des Philologen* (Crusades of the Philologist), is more characteristic of Hamann's style. It is an open and impassioned witness to the divine revelation in nature, history, and scripture. The underlying conception of the work is the condescension of God, who, for man's salvation, appears in the "Knechtsgestalt" (form of a servant), according to Philippians 2:7. He thus becomes the divine Author, who addresses man not in the abstract language of the philosophers but in the everyday idiom natural to human beings everywhere. God is not only the author of the "Bücher des Bundes" (Books of the Covenant) but also of the "Buch der Schöpfung" (Book of Creation) and the "Buch der Geschichte" (Book of History). Hamann's main concern in the work is the proper interpretation of scripture, on which the proper interpretation of nature and history depends. The biblical scholar Michaelis is the target of his attack. Michaelis's rationalistic hermeneutics ruled out all levels of meaning except the literal; according to Hamann, he ignored the spiritual aspect of the Bible because he discounted its poetry. God, the Creator, is "der Poet am Anfange der Tage" (the Poet at the beginning of days); he speaks to man in poetic language, and insofar as man answers God with his whole being, he too speaks poetically. Further, to the extent that one speaks to the deepest levels of his fellowman's being, he speaks in poetic form. For "Poesie ist die Muttersprache des Menschengeschlechts" (Poetry is the mother tongue of the human race).

Whereas the Socratic essay related Christianity to classical culture, "Aesthetica in nuce" demonstrates its deep roots in Oriental culture. The thought forms of that culture are, in Hamann's view, not only more natural than those derived from Graeco-Roman civilization but also speak more powerfully to the spirit of man. "Wodurch sollen wir aber die ausgestorbene Sprache der Natur von den Todten wieder aufwecken?– Durch Wallfahrten nach dem glücklichen Ara-

stead, he criticizes the Academy's formulation of the prize question: "Einfluß der Meinungen in die Sprache und der sprache in die Meinungen" (influence of opinions on language and of language on opinions), observing that the term *opinions* is ambiguous. Thus, he turns a main weapon of the Enlighteners–the demand for clarity of thought–against them. In the interest of clarity he even presents his own definition of language: "das Mittel unsere Gedanken mitzutheilen und anderer Gedanken zu verstehen" (the means of communicating our thoughts and of understanding the thoughts of others"). But there is no hint of the originality of his philosophy of language, which would emerge two decades later in his "metacritique" of Kant.

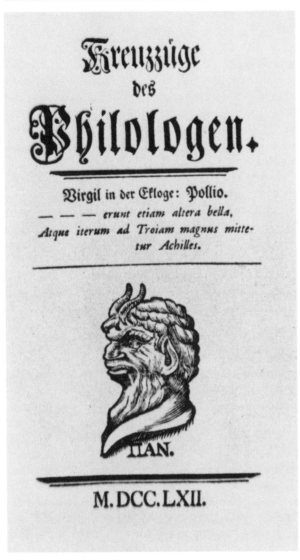

*Title page for the collection in which Hamann's essay
"Aesthetica in nuce" was first published*

Although primarily religious in intention, "Aesthetica in nuce," with the Socratic essay, clears the way for a new understanding of reason and its relation to faith. Adherents of the Sturm und Drang as well as the later Romantics were to embrace Hamann's view of the nature of reason but, with few exceptions, divorced it from religious faith and instead wedded it to the imagination alone.

Of the remaining essays in *Kreuzzüge des Philologen*, three are of particular importance. In "Chimärische Einfälle" (Chimerical Ideas), an expansion of an essay he had published separately in 1761, Hamann comes to the defense of Jean-Jacques Rousseau's *La nouvelle Heloïse*, which had been adversely criticized in the journal *Literaturbriefe*. In "Kleeblatt Hellenistischer Briefe" (Cloverleaf of Hellenistic Letters), the first letter is a defense of the Koine Greek of the New Testament against classical Greek on both rational and religious grounds. In the second letter Hamann argues for an eschatological view of history: it is the future, which can be divined only through prophecy, that makes possible an understanding of the present and past. In the third letter he advocates a hermeneutical approach to interpreting the Bible, pointing out that however useful a rigorous philological procedure may be—and Hamann certainly used such a procedure at times—it cannot replace faith in understanding scripture. "Die Magi aus Morgenlande zu Bethlehem" (translated as "The Wise Men from the East in Bethlehem," 1960), which was also published separately in 1760, is a tract on Matthew 2:1-12. Though quite brief, it presents some of his most characteristic ideas. Occidental thinkers, he says, tend to regard "der blosse Körper einer Handlung" (the mere body of an action), but for Oriental thinkers only the symbolic interpretation of nature, history, and man can yield "anschauende Erkäntniß" (intuitive knowledge) of the human soul.

In *Schriftsteller und Kunstrichter* (Writers and Critics, 1762) Hamann justifies the role of the literary critic insofar as he approaches a work with empathy and without preconceived critical norms. *Leser und Kunstrichter* (Readers and Critics), published in the same year, challenges the ideas of Christian Ludwig Hagedorn, who had espoused neoclassical, rococo artistic norms in a popular work, *Betrachtungen über die Malerei* (Reflections on Painting, 1762). Hamann's views on mimesis in all genres of literary art are made clear in *Fünf Hirtenbriefe das Schuldrama betreffend* (Five Pas-

bien, durch Kreuzzüge nach den Morgenländern, und durch die Wiederherstellung ihrer Magie. . . ." (But how shall we awaken the extinct language of nature again from the dead?– Through pilgrimages to fortunate Arabia, through crusades to the lands of the East, and through the restoration of their magic. . .). Hamann subtitled "Aesthetica in nuce" "Eine Rhapsodie in Kabbalistischer Prosa" (A Rhapsody in Cabalistic Prose), thus combining classical and Hebraic motifs. In spite of its rhapsodic and seemingly cabalistic nature, however, "Aesthetica in nuce" contains more penetrating insights into the nature of language than any other single work of Hamann's: the nature and importance of imagery, multivalence in language, and affect.

toral Letters on the School-Drama, 1763). In contrast to the classical conception that genres should not be mixed he defends the mixing of tragic and burlesque elements on the basis of man's essential nature as reflected in the biblical revelation. The dependence of great art on genius, not on aesthetic rules, is also stressed.

With the end of the Seven Years' War in 1763, East Prussia was released from the relatively lax Russian occupation and returned to the rigid despotism of the military state of Frederick II. For Hamann, who had left the university without preparing for a profession and who was further handicapped by a stammer, prospects for long-term employment in Königsberg lay only in the Prussian bureaucracy. In 1763 he became a copyist in the municipal administration of Königsberg, but transferred after three weeks to the Department of War and Crown Lands as chancery clerk and copyist. In January 1764 his father suffered a stroke, and Hamann gave up his job to aid in his care. During this year Hamann began a friendship with Herder that was to last for the rest of Hamann's life.

By the summer Hamann was seeking employment outside Prussia. The Hessian statesman and writer Karl von Moser had earlier offered him a post as tutor in a noble family. It was Moser who had first bestowed the epithet *Magus in Norden* (Magus of the North) on Hamann because Hamann had "seen the star" of Bethlehem. This was Moser's way of acknowledging and paying tribute to Hamann's Christian belief. Hamann journeyed to Frankfurt am Main with a view to obtaining the job; but Moser was not in the city, and Hamann returned to Königsberg. In the summer of the following year he became secretary to a lawyer, accompanying him to Mitau and Warsaw. In January 1766 he returned to Königsberg and obtained, through the mediation of Kant, a post as clerk and translator with the General Excise and Customs Administration under French tax collectors who had been imported by the king to exact larger revenues from the populace.

A few years earlier Hamann had entered into a liaison with a young peasant woman, Anna Regina Schumacher, who had been employed to help with the care of his father. This so-called Gewissensehe (marriage of conscience) was to last until his death. To the relationship with his "hamadryad," as he called her on account of her rustic origin, was born a son, Johann Michael, and three daughters: Elisabeth Regine, Magdalena Katharina, and Marianne Sophie. Though lack-

Hamann in 1765; painting by an unknown artist. The original was destroyed in 1944; this photograph is in the possession of Erich Trunz, Kiel.

ing the sanction of marriage, the liaison was quite bourgeois in character. The failure of an earlier proposal of marriage to Christoph Berens's sister Katharina, whom he had always considered his destined bride, may account for his decision not to legitimate the relationship. It is probable that his attempt to secure the tutorial post in Darmstadt was partly motivated by a desire to flee, at the outset, his involvement with Anna Regina as well as to escape the Prussia of Frederick II.

A unique aspect of Hamann's oeuvre is the group of essays written in French. Most of them were written in his second literary period, after he had had considerable experience in the Prussian bureaucracy, and combine broad criticism of the Prussian state with personal grievances in a way highly characteristic of Hamann. The most important among the essays are *Lettre néologique & provinciale sur l'inoculation du bon sens* (Neological and Provincial Letter on the Inoculation with Sound Reason, 1761), which he reprinted the following year with the essay "Glose Philippique" (Philippic Gloss) under the title *Essais à la mosaique* (A Mosaic of Essays), and "Au Salomon de Prusse" (To the Solomon of Prussia), written in 1772. Because of its explosive nature and possible lèse-majesté, the latter essay was not published during his lifetime–though he courageously, if foolishly, submitted it to the *Allgemeine Deutsche Bibliothek* in Berlin. It was published in *Hamann's Schriften* in 1842.

Hamann wrote in French in the hope of attracting the attention of the king, who despised his mother tongue and preferred to use French. The essays are noteworthy for their stinging criticism of the pervasive influence of French culture in Germany, including its economic policies, for their mixture of praise and criticism of Frederick, and for their advocacy of a Christian monarchy in Prussia. In addition, they offer excellent examples of the use of "metaschematism," a favorite literary device of Hamann's. To "metaschematize" means to substitute a set of objective relationships for an analogous set of subjective or personal relationships so as to throw light on their meaning. Hamann adopts the term from 1 Corinthians 4:6, where Paul uses the term μετεσχημάτισα, meaning "transferred in a figure." A striking example of its use is Hamann's adoption of the mask of Socrates to exemplify both his common ground and differences with the Enlightenment.

Herder's *Abhandlung über den Ursprung der Sprache* (Treatise on the Origin of Language, 1772) elicited from Hamann *Des Ritters von Rosencreuz letzte Willensmeynung über den göttlichen und menschlichen Ursprung der Sprache* (The Knight of the Rose-Cross's Last Will and Testament on the Divine and Human Origin of Language, 1772), and the posthumously published "Philologische Einfälle und Zweifel über eine akademische Preisschrift" (Philological Ideas and Doubts about an Academic Prize-Essay, published in *Hamann's Schriften* in 1822). In the former work Hamann rejects Herder's thesis, which had been awarded a prize by the Berlin Academy, that language had a purely human origin. Herder argues that man is able by means of "Besonnenheit" (reflection) to single out from "dem ganzen Ozean von Empfindungen" (the vast ocean of sensations) one wave, and give it a distinguishing mark, "Wort der Seele" (a word of the soul). Thus man "invents" language. But in Hamann's view, man did not invent language, for every phenomenon of nature was already a word spoken by God to man: "Mit diesem Worte im Mund und im Herzen war der Ursprung der Sprache so natürlich, so nahe und leicht, wie ein Kinderspiel" (With this word in his mouth and in his heart, the origin of language was as natural, as near, and as easy as child's play). Thus, language is a *given* in the human condition, an interplay of divine and human energy and ideas. In *Des Ritters von Rosenkreuz* Hamann seizes the opportunity to criticize the rationalistic assumptions underlying the question posed by the Berlin Academy. He lays the blame for its approach on the secular Kulturpolitik of Frederick II, whom he attacks in necessarily masked terms. In this way he tries to exculpate his friend Herder for his answer to the question posed by the Academy. In "Philologische Einfälle und Zweifel" Hamann continues the argument against Herder's theory of language, which he dubs "Platonic." By virtue of the gift of language man is, according to Hamann, characterized by "Kritische und obrigkeitliche Würde" (a critical and magisterial dignity). But Herder had condescended to argue in the mode of a century that fosters "Kritische und archontische Scbwäche"(critical and magisterial weakness). Both treatises are intended to be principally indictments of the Frederican state; in fact, Hamann had originally hoped to publish "Au Salomon de Prusse" and "Philologische Einfälle und Zweifel" together.

In *Vetii Epagathi Regiomonticolae hierophantische Briefe* (Hierophantic Letters, 1775) Hamann rejects the identification of New Testament Christianity with Deism by theologians such as Johann August Starck. *Versuch einer Sibylle über die Ehe* (Essay of a Sibyl on Marriage, 1775) deals frankly with the sexual basis of marriage but relates it to the equally important moral and spiritual aspects. Perhaps the most delightful example of sustained irony and humor in his writings is *Neue Apologie des Buchstaben h* (New Apology of the Letter h, 1773; translated as "New Apology of the Letter h by Itself," 1960), in which he criticizes the attempt of a rationalistic orthographer to expunge the silent letter "h" as unnecessary. The work expresses not only Hamann's view of language but also his deepest religious convictions. The metaphysical principle of the coincidence of opposites, which Hamann opposes to Kant's "Causalitätsstürmerei (blustering about causality), is nowhere better illustrated in his writings than here. Ironically, Kant was so pleased with the work that he expressed the hope that Hamann would continue to write in the same vein.

In Hamann's third period the especially difficult *Konxompax* (1779) compares deism to the ancient mystery religions and finds them all nihilistic. One of the most important writings of this period is "Metakritik über den Purismum der Vernunft" (Metacritique of the Purism of Reason, 1800), written in 1781 but not published until after his death. Hamann, who had originally turned Kant's attention to Hume and who had invoked Hume against Kant, was not slow to react to the *Kritik der reinen Vernunft* (Critique of Pure Reason, 1781), which he had read in proof. If Kant's great work may be considered an investigation of reason in the light of reason, Hamann's brief, highly condensed "Metakritik" may be considered a prolegomenon to an understanding of reason in the light of language. With this approach, Hamann anticipated the twentieth-century criticism of Kant's neglect of the role of language in cognition. Hamann sets Kant's effort to "purify" reason in a historical context. If the Enlightenment had sought to eliminate all tradition–that is, historical experience–from cognition, Kant attempted to eliminate all experience from the cognitive process. There remains only a third possible stage in the progress of purification: the elimination of language itself. But since this is impossible, the fundamental error in the whole process is revealed. "Nicht nur das ganze Vermögen zu denken beruht auf Sprache. . . , sondern Sprache ist auch der Mittelpunct des Misverstandes der Vernunft mit ihr selbst . . . " (Not only does the whole capacity to think depend on language. . . , but language is also the center of the misunderstanding of reason with itself. . .). In stressing man's dependence on experience, Hamann goes so far as to maintain that the concepts of space and time are empirically derived. In this way he contravenes the basic concept of the Kantian critical philosophy. As an act of deference to his friend, Hamann did not publish the "Metakritik" but shared it in manuscript form with Herder and Jacobi.

One of Hamann's last and most important works–Hegel considered it the most important–is *Golgatha und Scheblimini!* (1784; translated, 1979). The first word of the title signifies the crucifixion of Christ; the second is a transliteration of the Hebrew of Psalm 110:1 and signifies Christ's elevation to the right hand of God. It was written in response to Moses Mendelssohn's *Jerusalem oder Über religiöse Macht und Judentum* (Jerusalem; or, On Religious Power and Judaism, 1783). In that work Mendelssohn differentiates between Judaism, as natural law uniquely revealed to the Jews, and Christianity, which holds that certain dogmas and truths are necessary for salvation. Hamann rejects this distinction, arguing that the characteristic difference between Judaism and Christianity has to do with "Geschichtswahrheiten, die zu einer Zeit zugetragen haben und niemals wiederkommen" (historical truths, which occurred at one time and shall never return). Mendelssohn sought to solve the problem of the relationship of church and state by sharply delimiting their respective spheres: religion deals with man's relation to God, the state with his relation to his fellowman. "Convictions" were relegated to the sphere of the church, "actions" to the sphere of the state. Thus Mendelssohn, the gentle and humane philosopher, unintentionally aided and abetted, by virtue of his banishment of religious influence from the public arena, the soulless and crushing mechanism of the Prussian state. There is rare irony in the fact that Hamann, the devoted Christian, would defend traditional Judaism against its misinterpretation by Mendelssohn, whose conception of loyalty to his faith consisted in equating Jewish legalism with the moralism of the Enlightenment. In his polemic against Mendelssohn, Hamann refers to the Jew as "immer der eigentliche ursprüngliche *Edelmann* des ganzen menschlichen Geschlechts" (always the authentic original *nobleman* of the human race).

In the unfinished *A-Ω! Entkleidung und Verklärung: Ein Fliegender Brief an Niemand den Kundbaren* (A-Ω! Divestiture and Transfiguration: A Flying Letter to Nobody, the Notorious, 1785), Hamann recapitulates the main themes of his entire "Autorschaft" from the Socratic essay on. Finally, "Das letzte Blatt' (The Final Page), written a month before his death in Münster, is a unique compilation, mostly of biblical passages, representing a remarkably concentrated summary of his Pauline-Lutheran faith. In it he describes himself, partly in reference to II Thessalonians 2:16, as "metacriticus bonae spei" (metacritic of good hope). In addition to his original writings, Hamann translated several treatises. By far the most important was his translation of Hume's *Dialogues concerning Natural Religion* (1780), which won Kant's approbation but which Hamann did not publish. (It was first published in his *Sämtliche Werke* [Collected Works, 1951].)

Ten years after returning to Königsberg from Warsaw, Hamann became superintendent of the customs warehouse in that city. He remained in the position until 1787, when, upon petitioning the king for a leave, he was summarily dismissed with a small pension. The last year of his life was spent among admiring friends. Amalia, Princess von Gallitzin, a deeply religious person who had given up court life to devote herself to the practice of her faith and to intellectual inquiry, invited him to be her guest in Münster, Westphalia. There he could enjoy the company of the so-called Münster circle, among whom were Franz Friedrich von Fürstenberg and Franz Hemsterhuis. The journey, on which Hamann was accompanied by his son, was financed by Franz Kaspar Buchholtz, who had earlier provided for the education of Hamann's children. During this year Hamann was often the guest of Buchholtz and of Friedrich Heinrich Jacobi in Düsseldorf. After a brief illness, he died in Münster on 21 June 1788 and was interred there.

Hamann's formal writings are, for the most part, exceedingly difficult and almost always require a commentary for a proper understanding. The difficulty arises from his highly original and idiosyncratic use of the devices of classical rhetoric. His letters, however, are generally clear and straightforward. Only with the publication of the Ziesemer-Henkel edition of his letters the complete correspondence (1955-1979) has become available. Not only are the letters indispensable for an understanding of his life and thought; they also constitute an exceedingly important resource for an understanding of the intellectual ferment in eighteenth-century Germany.

Recent scholarship has tended to stress Hamann's identification with the Enlightenment rather than his opposition to it. In an important 1988 work, Oswald Bayer interprets Hamann as a "radikaler Aufklärer" (radical Enlightener) insofar as he prolongs the critical aspect of the Enlightenment with his "metacriticism." A model example of Hamann's procedure is his penetrating analysis of Kant's essay "Beantwortung der Frage: Was ist Aufklärung?" (Answer to the Question: What is Enlightenment?, 1784) in an 18 December 1784 letter to Christian Jacob Kraus in which he exposes Kant's hidden assumptions and indicates their practical consequences. Nevertheless, an important distinction must be made in this regard: the eighteenth-century Enlightenment was characterized by two distinct uses of reason, one critical, the other constructive; and Hamann shared only in its critical aspect. Thus, he may be considered part of the Enlightenment only insofar as he engaged in the critical use of rea-

Hamann in early July 1787, engraving based on a drawing, probably by Agathe Alberti (Königsberger Gelehrten-Gesellschaft)

son. But reason, in his view, could not have a decisive role in the matters of greatest human concern. For, in that case, the need for faith would be eliminated, and since "der *Glaube* zu *den natürlichen Bedingungen* unserer Erkenntniskräfte und zu den *Grundtrieben* unserer Seele gehört" (*faith* belongs to the *natural conditions* of our cognitive powers and to the *basic impulses* of our soul), Hamann could only reject the Enlightenment's position out of hand. In calling himself at the end of his life "metacriticus bonae spei" he combined the two strands of his life's work—the one characterized by radical criticism, hence negative, the other characterized by religious belief, hence positive—for the "bonae spei" or "good hope" is specifically that of New Testament Christianity.

Letters:

Johann Georg Hamann: Briefwechsel, 7 volumes, edited by Walther Ziesemer and Arthur Henkel (Wiesbaden & Frankfurt am Main: Insel, 1955-1979).

Biography:

Josef Nadler, *Johann Georg Hamann: Der Zeuge des Corpus Mysticum* (Salzburg: Müller, 1949).

References:

William M. Alexander, *Johann Georg Hamann: Philosophy and Faith* (The Hague: Nijhoff, 1966);

Max L. Baeumer, "Johann Georg Hamanns Mythologisierung von Sinnen und Leidenschaften," *Monatshefte*, 67 (Winter 1967): 370-386;

Georg Baudler, *Im Worte Sehen: Das Sprachdenken Johann Georg Hamanns* (Bonn: Bouvier, 1970);

Oswald Bayer, *Zeitgenosse im Widerspruch: Johann Georg Hamann als radikaler Aufklärer* (Munich & Zurich: Piper, 1988);

Bayer, Bernhard Gajek, and Josef Simon, eds., *Insel-Almanach auf das Jahr 1988* (Frankfurt am Main: Insel, 1987);

Elfriede Büchsel, *Biblisches Zeugnis und Sprachgestalt bei J. G. Hamann* (Gießen: Brunnen, 1988);

Büchsel, "Geschärfte Aufmerksamkeit: Hamannliteratur seit 1972," *Deutsche Vierteljahrsschrift*, 60 (September 1986): 375-425;

Stephen Dunning, *The Tongues of Men: Hegel and Hamann on Religious Language and History* (Missoula, Mont.: Scholars Press, 1979);

Bernhard Gajek, *Sprache beim jungen Hamann* (Bern: Lang, 1967);

Gajek, ed., *Acta des zweiten Hamann-Colloquiums im Herder-Institut zu Marburg/Lahn 1980* (Marburg: Elwert, 1983);

Gajek, ed., *Hamann-Kant-Herder: Acta des vierten Hamann-Colloquiums im Herder Institut zu Marburg/Lahn* (Frankfurt am Main: Lang, 1987);

Gajek, ed., *J. G. Hamann: Acta des internationalen Hamann-Colloquiums in Lüneburg 1976* (Frankfurt am Main: Klostermann, 1979);

Gajek, ed., *J. G. Hamann und Frankreich: Acta des dritten Internationalen Hamann-Colloquiums im Herder-Institut zu Marburg/Lahn 1982* (Marburg: Elwert, 1987);

Terence J. German, *Hamann on Language and Religion* (Oxford: Oxford University Press, 1981);

Karlfried Gründer, *Figur und Geschichte* (Freiburg & Munich: Alber, 1958);

G. W. F. Hegel, "Hamanns Schriften," in his *Sämtliche Werke*, edited by J. Hoffmeister, volume 11 (Hamburg: Meiner, 1956), pp. 221-294;

Arthur Henkel, "Goethe und Hamann: Ergänzende Bemerkungen zu einem denkwürdigen Geistergespräch," *Euphorion*, 77, no. 4 (1983): 453-469;

Volker Hoffmann, *Johann Georg Hamanns Philologie* (Stuttgart: Kohlhammer, 1972);

Sven-Aage Jørgensen, *J. G. Hamann: Fünf Hirtenbriefe, das Schuldrama betreffend. Einführung und Kommentar* (Copenhagen: Munksgaard, 1962);

Jørgensen, *J. G. Hamann, Sokratische Denkwürdigkeiten/Aesthetica in nuce: Mit einem Kommentar* (Stuttgart: Reclam, 1968);

Jørgensen, *Johann Georg Hamann* (Stuttgart: Metzler, 1976);

Jørgensen, "Zu Hamanns Stil," *Germanisch-Romanische Monatsschrift*, new series 16 (October 1966): 374-387;

Renate Knoll, *J. G. Hamann und Friedrich Heinrich Jacobi* (Heidelberg: Winter, 1963);

Hans-Martin Lumpp, *Philologia crucis: Zu J. G. Hamanns Auffassung von der Dichtkunst* (Tübingen: Niemeyer, 1970);

Ingemarie Manegold, *J. G. Hamanns Schrift "Konxompax"* (Heidelberg: Winter, 1963);

Philip Merlan, "From Hume to Hamann," *The Personalist*, 33 (1951): 11-18;

Erwin Metzke, *J. G. Hamanns Stellung in der Philosophie des 18. Jahrhunderts* (Halle, 1934);

Josef Nadler, *Die Hamannausgabe* (Halle: Niemeyer, 1930; reprinted, Bern, Frankfurt am Main & Las Vegas: Lang, 1978);

James C. O'Flaherty, *Hamann's Socratic Memorabilia: A Translation and Commentary* (Baltimore: Johns Hopkins University Press, 1967);

O'Flaherty, *Johann Georg Hamann* (Boston: Hall, 1979); revised and translated as *Johann Georg Hamann: Einführung in sein Leben und Werke* (Frankfurt am Main, Bern, New York & Paris: Lang, 1989);

O'Flaherty, *The Quarrel of Reason with Itself: Essays on Hamann, Michaelis, Lessing, Nietzsche* (Columbia, S.C.,: Camden House, 1988);

O'Flaherty, *Unity and Language: A Study in the Philosophy of Hamann* (Chapel Hill: University of North Carolina Press, 1952; reprinted, New York: AMS Press, 1966);

H. A. Salmony, *J. G. Hamanns metakritische Philosophie* (Zollikon: Evangelischer Verlag, 1958);

Martin Seils, *Theologische Aspekte zu gegenwärtigen Hamann-Deutungen* (Göttingen: Vandenhoeck & Ruprecht, 1957);

Harry Sievers, *J. G. Hamanns Bekehrung: Ein Versuch, sie zu verstehen* (Zurich: Zwingli, 1969);

Josef Simon, "Spuren Hamanns bei Kant?," in *Acta des vierten Internationalen Hamann-Kolloquiums im Herder-Institut zu Marburg/Lahn 1985*, edited by Bernhard Gajek (Frankfurt am Main: Lang, 1987), pp. 89-110;

Rudolf Unger, *Hamann und die Aufklärung*, 2 volumes (Jena: Diederichs, 1911);

Larry Vaughan, *Johann Georg Hamann: Metaphysics of Language and Vision of History* (New York, Bern, Frankfurt am Main & Paris: Lang, 1989);

Reiner Wild, "*Metacriticus bonae spei*": *J. G. Hamanns "Fliegender Brief": Einführung, Text und Kommentar* (Frankfurt am Main & Bern: Lang, 1975).

Papers:
Almost all of Johann Georg Hamann's literary remains were destroyed in World War II. But Josef Nadler had photocopied the papers, and in 1955 the photocopies were deposited in the library of the University of Münster, Westphalia.

Johann Gottfried Herder

(25 August 1744 - 18 December 1803)

Erdmann Waniek
Emory University

BOOKS: *An Ihro Hochfürstliche Durchlauchten, Den Herzog Ernst Johann, am Tage Höchst Dero Huldigung in Mitau, von J. J. Kanter, Buchhändler in Mitau* (Königsberg: Mitau, 1763);

Fragment zweener dunkeln Abendgespräche: An Herrn Kurella nach dem Tode seines Vaters (Königsberg: Kanter, 1763);

Bey dem Sarge der Hochedlen Jungfer Jungfer Maria Margaretha Kanter (Königsberg, 1763);

Über die Asche Königsbergs: Ein Trauergesang, anonymous (Mitau: Kiedke, 1765);

Haben wir noch jetzt das Publikum und Vaterland der Alten?: Eine Abhandlung, Zur Feier der Beziehung des neuen Gerichtshauses (Riga: Frölich, 1765);

Ode der Urne des Hochwohlgebohrnen Herrn Gustav Christian von Handtwig geweihet (Mitau: Liedtke, 1765);

Der Opferpriester: Ein Altarsgesang; der Abreise eines Freundes geheiligt, anonymous (Mitau: Hartknoch, 1765);

Als die ... Vermählung des ... Herrn Peter in Liefland zu Kurland und Sengallen Erbprinzen mit ... Frau Karoline Lowise gebohrnen Fürstinn zu Waldeck ... wurde Kurlandes freudenvolle Hoffnung ... in einer durch ... Veichtner in die Musick gesetzten Cantate besungen (Mitau, 1765);

Denkmal dem Andenken ... Christine Regine Zuckerbecker ... bei ihrem Grabe geweihet (Riga, 1766);

Kantate zur Einweihung der Katharinen Kirche auf Bikkern (Riga: Frölich, 1766);

Nachricht von einem neuen Erläuterer der H. Dreieinigkeit, anonymous (N.p., 1766);

Über die neuere Deutsche Litteratur: Eine Beilage zu den Briefen, die neueste Litteratur betreffend, 3 volumes, anonymous (volumes 1-2, N.p., 1767; volume 3, Riga: Hartknoch, 1767);

*Johann Gottfried Herder; engraving by C. H. Pfeiffer after a
painting by Friedrich August Tischbein*

Über die neuere Deutsche Litteratur: Fragmente, anonymous (Riga: Hartknoch, 1768);

*Über Thomas Abbts Schriften: Der Torso von einem
Denkmaal, an seinem Grabe errichtet. Erstes
Stück*, anonymous (N.p., 1768);

*Drey moralische Lieder dem moralischen Schwartz- und
Berensschen Brautpaar zum freundschaftlichen
Denkmahl verehret*, anonymous (Riga: Frölich,
1768);

*Kritische Wälder: Oder Betrachtungen, die Wissen-
schaft und Kunst des Schönen betreffend, nach
Maasgabe neuerer Schriften*, 3 volumes (volumes 1-2, N.p., 1769; volume 3, Riga: Hartknoch, 1769)—comprises as volume 1, *Erstes
Wäldchen: Herrn Lessings Laokoon gewidmet*; as
volume 2, *Zweites Wäldchen: Über einige Klotzische Schriften*; as volume 3, *Drittes Wäldchen:
Noch über einige Klotzische Schriften*;

*Abhandlung über den Ursprung der Sprache, welche
den von der Königl. Academie der Wissenschaften für das Jahr 1770 gesetzten Preis erhalten
hat* (Berlin: Voß, 1772); translated anonymously as *Treatise upon the Origin of Language* (London: Longman, Rees, Orme,
Brown & Green, 1827); German version republished as *Abhandlung über den Ursprung*

der Sprache: Text, Materialien, Kommentar, edited by Wolfgang Pross (Munich: Hanser,
1978);

*Auszug aus einem Briefwechsel über Ossian und die Lie-
der alter Völker*, anonymous (Hamburg:
Bode, 1773);

Wie die Alten den Tod gebildet, anonymous (Hannover: Schlüter, 1774);

*Brutus: Ein Drama zur Musik. In Musik gesetzt von
dem Concertmeister Bach zu Bückeburg*, anonymous (N.p., 1774);

An Prediger: Funfzehn Provinzialblätter, anonymous
(Riga: Hartknoch, 1774);

*Auch eine Philosophie der Geschichte zur Bildung der
Menschheit: Beytrag zu vielen Beyträgen des Jahrhunderts*, anonymous (Riga, 1774); translated
by Eva Herzfeld as "Johann Gottfried von
Herder's 'Yet Another Philosophy of History for the Education of Humanity': A
Translation with a Critical Introduction and
Notes," Ph.D. dissertation, Columbia University, 1968;

Älteste Urkunde des Menschengeschlechts, 2 volumes
(Riga: Hartknoch, 1774-1776);

*Briefe zweener Brüder Jesu in unserm Kanon: Nebst
einer Probe nichtiger Conjekturen übers N. T.
zum Anhange* (Lemgo: Meyer, 1775);

*Erläuterungen zum Neuen Testament, aus einer neuer-
öffneten Morgenländischen Quelle*, anonymous
(Riga: Hartknoch, 1775);

*Ursachen des gesunknen Geschmacks bei den verschied-
nen Völkern, da er geblühet: Eine Abhandlung,
welche den von der Königl. Academie der Wissenschaften für das Jahr 1773 gesetzten Preis erhalten hat. Auf Befehl der Academie hrsg.* (Berlin:
Voß, 1775);

*Gebet am Grabmaale Ihro Erlauchten der weil. regieren-
den Gräfin von Schaumburg-Lippe &c. Maria
Barbara Eleonora gebohrnen Gräfin und edlen
Frauen zur Lippe und Sternberg &c. gehalten
den 7ten September 1776 zum Baum* (Stadtha-
gen: Althaus, 1776);

*Lieder der Liebe: Die ältesten und schönsten aus Morgen-
lande. Nebst vier und vierzig alten Minneliedern*
(Leipzig: Weygand, 1778);

*Plastik: Einige Wahrnehmungen über Form und Ge-
stalt aus Pygmalions bildendem Traume*, anonymous (Riga: Hartknoch, 1778; edited by Siegfried Heinz Begenau, Dresden: Verlag der
Kunst, 1955; edited by Lambert A. Schneider, Cologne: Hegner, 1969);

*Vom Erkennen und Empfinden der menschlichen Seele:
Bemerkungen und Träume*, anonymous (Riga:
Hartknoch, 1778);

Kantate beim Kirchgange der regierenden Herzogin Hochfürstl. Durchlaucht . . ., anonymous (Weimar: Hoffmann, 1779);

Maran atha: Das Buch von der Zukunft des Herrn, des Neuen Testaments Siegel, anonymous (Riga: Hartknoch, 1779);

Dissertation sur l'influence des Sciences sur le Gouvernement et du Gouvernement sur les Sciences, qui a remporté le prix proposé par l'Academie Royale des Sciences et Belles-Lettres pour l'année MDCCLXXIX (Berlin: Decker, 1780); republished as *Vom Einfluß der Regierung auf die Wissenschaften, und der Wissenschaften auf die Regierung* (Berlin: Decker, 1781);

Briefe, das Studium der Theologie betreffend, 4 volumes, anonymous (Weimar: Hoffmann, 1780-1781);

Händel's Meßias, anonymous (N.p., 1780);

Zwo heilige Reden bey einer besondern wichtigen Veranlassung gehalten, anonymous (N.p., 1780);

Osterkantate (Weimar: Hoffmann, 1781);

Über den Einfluß der schönen in die höhern Wissenschaften (Munich, 1781);

Über die Wirkung der Dichtkunst auf die Sitten der Völker in alten und neuen Zeiten (Munich, 1781);

Vom Geist der ebräischen Poesie: Eine Anleitung für die Liebhaber derselben, und der ältesten Geschichte des menschlichen Geistes, 2 volumes (Dessau: Buchhandlung der Gelehrten, 1782-1783); translated by James Marsh as *The Spirit of Hebrew Poetry*, 2 volumes (Burlington, Vt.: Smith, 1833; reprinted, Naperville, Ill.: Aleph Press, 1971);

Kantate bei dem Kirchgange der regierenden Herzogin von Sachsen-Weimar und Eisenach Hochfürstl. Durchlaucht, nach der Geburt des Erbprinzen: In Musik gesetzt und . . . aufgeführt von E. W. Wolf (Weimar: Hoffmann, 1783);

Zwo Predigten bei Gelegenheit der Geburt des Erbprinzen Karl Friedrich von Sachsen-Weimar und Eisenach (Weimar: Hoffmann, 1783);

Rede bei der Taufe des Durchlauchtigsten Erbprinzen Carl Friedrich, Herzogs zu Sachsen-Weimar und Eisenach (Weimar: Glüsing, 1783);

Ideen zur Philosophie der Geschichte der Menschheit, 4 volumes (Riga & Leipzig: Hartknoch, 1784-1791); translated by T. Churchill as *Outlines of a Philosophy of the History of Man* (London: Printed for J. Johnson by L. Hansard, 1800; reprinted, Atlantic Highlands, N.J.: Humanities Press, 1977); German version republished, 2 volumes (Berlin: Aufbau, 1965);

The house in Mohrungen where Herder was born

Zerstreute Blätter, 6 volumes (Gotha: Ettinger, 1785-1797);

Buchstaben- und Lesebuch, anonymous (N.p., 1787);

Gott: Einige Gespräche (Gotha: Ettinger, 1787); revised as *Gott: Einige Gespräche über Spinoza's System; nebst Shaftsburi's Naturhymnus* (Gotha: Ettinger, 1800); translated by Frederick H. Burkhardt as *God: Some Conversations. A Translation, with a Critical Introduction and Notes* (Indianapolis: Bobbs-Merrill, 1940);

Persepolis: Eine Muthmassung (Gotha: Ettinger, 1787);

Briefe zu Beförderung der Humanität, 10 volumes (Riga: Hartknoch, 1793-1797);

Von der Gabe der Sprachen am ersten christlichen Pfingstfest (Riga: Hartknoch, 1793 [dated 1794]);

Von der Auferstehung, als Glauben, Geschichte und Lehre (Riga: Hartknoch, 1794);

Terpsichore, 3 volumes (Lübeck: Bohn, 1795-1796);

Vom Erlöser der Menschen: Nach unsern drei ersten Evangelien (Riga: Hartknoch, 1796);

Von Gottes Sohn, der Welt Heiland: Nach Johannes Evangelium. Nebst einer Regel der Zusammenstimmung unsrer Evangelien aus ihrer Entstehung und Ordnung (Riga: Hartknoch, 1797);

Vom Geist des Christenthums: Nebst einigen Abhandlungen verwandten Inhalts (Leipzig: Hartknoch, 1798);

Luthers Katechismus, mit einer katechetischen Erklärung zum Gebrauch der Schulen (Weimar: Glüsing / Halle: Ruff, 1798);

Confirmation Seiner Hochfürstl. Durchlaucht Carl Friedrich, Erbprinzen von Sachsen Weimar und Eisenach (Weimar, 1799);

Eine Metakritik zur Kritik der reinen Vernunft, 2 volumes (Frankfurt am Main & Leipzig: Hartknoch, 1799)–comprises volume 1, *Verstand und Erfahrung*; volume 2, *Vernunft und Sprache: Mit einer Zugabe, betreffend ein kritisches Tribunal aller Fakultäten, Regierungen und Geschäfte*; reprinted, 1 volume (Berlin: Aufbau, 1955; reprinted, 2 volumes, Brussels: Culture et civilisation, 1969);

Kalligone, 3 volumes (Leipzig: Hartknoch, 1800)–comprises as volume 1, *Vom Angenehmen und Schönen*; as volume 2, *Von Kunst und Kunstrichterei*; as volume 3, *Vom Erhabnen und vom Ideal*; 1 volume, edited by Heinz Begenau (Weimar: Böhlau, 1955);

Aeon und Aeonis: Eine Allegorie (N.p., 1802);

Johann Gottfried von Herder's sämmtliche Werke, 45 volumes, edited by Maria Caroline von Herder, Wilhelm Gottfried von Herder, Christian Gottlob Heyne, Johann Georg Müller, and Johann von Müller (Tübingen: Cotta, 1805-1820; revised, 60 volumes, 1827-1830);

Sophron: Gesammelte Schulreden, edited by Johann Georg Müller (Tübingen: Cotta, 1810);

Der deutsche Nationalruhm: Eine Epistel (Leipzig: Hartknoch, 1812);

Aus Herders Nachlaß, 3 volumes, edited by Heinrich Düntzer and Ferdinand Gottfried von Herder (Frankfurt am Main: Meidinger, 1856-1857);

Herders sämmtliche Werke, 33 volumes, edited by Bernhard Suphan, Carl Christian Redlich, Otto Hoffmann, and Reinhold Steig (Berlin: Weidmann, 1877-1913; reprinted, Hildesheim: Olms, 1967);

Herder's Werke: Nach den besten Quellen revidirte Ausgabe, 24 volumes, edited by Düntzer and

Anton Eduard Wollheim da Fonseca (Berlin: Hempel, 1879);

Denkmal Johann Winckelmann's: Eine ungekrönte Preisschrift aus dem Jahre 1778. Nach der Kasseler Handschrift zum ersten Male herausgegeben und mit literar-historischer Einleitung versehen, edited by A. Duncker (Cassel: Kay, 1882);

Luther, ein Lehrer der Deutschen Nation: 1792. Erster Druck, edited by Suphan (N.p., 1883);

Benjamin Franklin's Rules for a Club established in Philadelphia, übertragen und ausgelegt als Statut für eine Gesellschaft von Freunden der Humanität: 1792. Aus dem Nachlaß veröffentlicht, edited by Suphan (Berlin: Weidmann, 1883);

Werke, 15 volumes, edited by Ernst Naumann (Berlin: Bong, 1912);

Werke, 2 volumes, edited by Karl-Gustav Gerold (Munich: Hanser, 1953);

Werke, 5 volumes, edited by Wilhelm Dobbek (Weimar: Volksverlag, 1957);

Journal meiner Reise im Jahr 1769: Historisch-kritische Ausgabe, edited by Katharina Mommsen, Momme Mommsen, and Georg Wackerl (Stuttgart: Reclam, 1976);

Werke, 2 volumes to date, edited by Wolfgang Pross and Pierre Penisson (Munich: Hanser, 1984-);

Werke, 3 volumes to date, edited by Martin Bollacher and others (Frankfurt am Main: Deutscher Klassiker Verlag, 1985-).

Editions in English: *A Tribute to the Memory of Ulric of Hutten: Translated from the German of Goethe* [sic]. *With an Appendix Containing Extracts from Some of Hutten's Performances, a List of His Works, and Other Explanatory and Interesting Papers*, translated by Anthony Aufrere (London: Dodsley, 1789);

Oriental Dialogues: Containing the Conversations of Eugenius and Alciphron on the Spirit and Beauties of the Sacred Poetry of the Hebrews. Selected from the German Dialogues and Dissertations of the Celebrated Herder, translated anonymously (London: Printed by A. Strahan for T. Cadell jun. and W. Davies, 1801);

Leaves of Antiquity; or, The Poetry of Hebrew Tradition, translated by Caroline M. Sawyer (New Haven, Conn.: Printed by M. A. Moses, 1847);

"Journal of My Travels in the Year 1769," translated by John Francis Harrison, Ph.D. dissertation, Columbia University, 1952;

J. G. Herder on Social and Political Culture, translated and edited by Frederick M. Barnard

Kritische Wälder.

Ober

Betrachtungen,

die

Wissenschaft und Kunst

des Schönen

betreffend,

nach Maasgabe neuerer Schriften.

ΣΩΚΡΑΤΗΣ

Leser, wie gefall ich dir?
Leser, wie gefällst du mir?   Logau.

Erstes Wäldchen.
Herrn Leßings Laokoon gewidmet.

1 7 6 9.

Title page for the first volume of Herder's critical treatise, in which he attacks Gotthold Ephraim Lessing's aesthetic theory as expressed in Laokoon

(London: Cambridge University Press, 1969).

OTHER: *Gesang an den Cyrus: Aus dem Hebräischen übersetzt,* translated anonymously by Herder (St. Petersburg, 1762);

Von deutscher Art und Kunst: Einige fliegende Blätter, edited with contributions by Herder (Hamburg: Bode, 1773; edited by Edna Purdie, Oxford: Clarendon Press, 1964);

Alte Volkslieder, 2 volumes, edited by Herder (volume 1, Altenburg, 1774; volume 2, Riga: Hartknoch, 1774);

Volkslieder, 2 volumes, edited anonymously by Herder (Leipzig: Weygand, 1778-1779); republished as *Stimmen der Völker in Liedern,* 1 volume, edited by Johannes von Müller (Tübingen: Cotta, 1807; republished, edited by Christel Käschel, Leipzig: Reclam, 1968; republished, edited by Heinz Rölleke, Stuttgart: Reclam, 1975);

Jeremias Klagegesänge übersetzt und mit Anmerkungen, translated by J. G. Börmel, foreword by Herder (Weimar: Hoffmann, 1781);

James Burnett, *Des Lord Monboddo Werk von dem Ursprunge und Fortgange der Sprache,* translated by A. Schmid, foreword by Herder (Riga: Hartknoch, 1784);

Johann Valentin Andreä, *Dichtungen zur Beherzigung unsers Zeitalters,* foreword by Herder (Leipzig: Göschen, 1786);

Palmblätter: Erlesene morgenländische Erzählungen für die Jugend, foreword by Herder (Jena: Akademische Buchhandlung, 1786);

Alexander Pope, *The Dying Christian to His Soul: An Ode . . . Together with a German Translation Written by Mr. Herder,* translated by Herder (London: Corr & Dussek, 1787);

W. G. Günther, *Andachten bey der Communion,* foreword by Herder (Gotha: Ettinger, 1789);

Johann G. Müller, ed., *Bekenntnisse merkwürdiger Männer von sich selbst,* introduction by Herder (Winterthur: Steiner, 1791);

Weimarisches Gesangbuch. Nebst einem Anhang, enthaltend: Einige Gebete zur öffentlichen und häuslichen Andacht, foreword by Herder (Weimar: Hoffmann, 1795);

F. Majer, *Zur Kulturgeschichte der Völker: Historische Untersuchungen,* 2 volumes, foreword by Herder (Leipzig: Hartknoch, 1798);

Adrastea, 6 volumes, edited by Herder and Wilhelm Gottfried von Herder (Leipzig: Hartknoch, 1801-1803);

Kalidasa, *Sakontala oder Der entscheidende Ring: Ein indisches Schauspiel. Aus den Ursprachen Sanskrit und Prakrit ins Englische und aus diesem ins Deutsche übersetzt mit Erläuterungen,* translated and annotated by Georg Forster, edited by Herder (Frankfurt am Main: Hermann, 1803);

Der Cid: Nach spanischen Romanzen besungen, translated by Herder, edited by Johann von Müller (Tübingen: Cotta, 1805); translated anonymously as *The Cid* (London: Graves, 1828);

Griechische Anthologie für Schulen, edited by Herder (Gießen: Tasche & Müller, 1805);

Altenglische Balladen, translated by Herder (Munich: Hyperion, 1922).

PERIODICAL PUBLICATIONS: "Über den Fleiß in mehreren gelehrten Sprachen," *Gelehrte Beiträge zu den Rigaschen Anzeigen* (October 1764): 185-190;

"Warum wir noch keine Geschichte der Deut-
    schen haben?," *Neue Deutsche Monatsschrift*
    (1795): 326-330;
"Iduna, oder Der Apfel der Verjüngung," *Die
    Horen* (1796): 1-18.

In the judgment of Arthur Schopenhauer
and Friedrich Nietzsche, Johann Gottfried Herder was not a great original thinker. With some justification Nietzsche derided the "ehrgeizige
Priester, der so gerne der Geister-Papst seiner
Zeit gewesen wäre" (ambitious priest who would
have liked to be intellectual pope of his time).
Nowadays Herder leads a shadow existence,
eclipsed by others whom he influenced decisively,
such as Johann Wolfgang von Goethe, or who surpassed him by building on his achievements, such
as Wilhelm von Humboldt in linguistics and
G. W. F. Hegel in the philosophy of history.
Fresh appreciation of Herder's work is made difficult by his often breathless and rapturous style,
by his stupendous grasp and diversity, and by his
disregard for academic boundaries. The literary
historian, presumably eager to acknowledge the
critical role of Herder's theories in shaping a national German literature, is in the end more interested in the works of the Sturm und Drang and
the subsequent Romantic movement. And the historian of philosophy who considers Immanuel
Kant the dominant figure of this time is prone to
underrate Herder as quixotic, disorderly, and
much too poetic. Nonetheless, Herder is central
and uniquely seminal in eighteenth-century German thought. His reputation may benefit from recent developments in philosophy that favor un-
systematic thought such as Nietzsche's; In the
meantime Goethe's appraisal of 1825 remains
true. It is supreme compliment and final dismissal in one: Herder's notions, Goethe said, have
been so fully absorbed into German (one might
even say Western) culture that one does not need
to read his works in order to know them.

Herder was born in Mohrungen, East Prussia, on 25 August 1744. He was the third child of
Anna Elisabeth Herder, née Peltz, and Johann
Herder, a pious weaver turned churchwarden. In
1762 he was offered the chance to study medicine at the University of Königsberg but fainted
during his first visit to the *theatrum anatomicum*.
Herder decided to study theology instead, but
without limiting himself to that field. Kant's lectures on physical geography, in which he examined the effects of climatic and other geographi-
cal conditions on human development, made a

deep impression on Herder; Kant also introduced Herder to the thought of Jean-Jacques
Rousseau and the British empiricists. Johann
Georg Hamann's opposition to a dead cult of
knowledge first planted the seed for Herder's
eventual sharp rejection of Enlightenment rationalism. Hamann also fostered Herder's lifelong insistence on the unity and value of experience and
on the limits of reason.

In 1764 Herder secured a position at the
Domschule (cathedral school) in Riga. He was ordained and appointed minister at two Riga
churches in 1767. His first essays, "Über den
Fleiß in mehreren gelehrten Sprachen" (On Diligence in Several Learned Languages, 1764) and
*Haben wir noch jetzt das Publikum und Vaterland der
Alten?* (Do We Still Have the Public and Father-
land of the Ancients?, 1765), contain the core of
Herder's questions: What are the reasons for diversity in nature and in society; is there a unify-
ing principle; what is the connection between language and thought; what are the differences
between the ancients and our time; and how is
the public aspect of writing and speaking best
served in modern times? The essays provide an initial glimpse of his zest for public education and
of the biological imagery–here language as a
plant–that will permeate his thought. Perhaps
most remarkable is his already unlimited desire
to embrace cultural diversity: "Ich sammle den
Geist jedes Volkes in meiner Seele!" (I collect the
spirit of every people in my soul!).

Herder also pursued the problems of the origin of poetry in general and the lyric in particular during his years in Riga in the essays
"Abhandlung über die Ode" (Treatise on the
Ode), written in 1764, and "Versuch einer
Geschichte der lyrischen Dichtkunst" (Attempt at
a History of Lyric Poetics), written in 1766.
While he incorporated his findings in subsequent
works, these early drafts were published only posthumously. Herder's first important publication is
typical of his method; in *Über die neuere Deutsche
Litteratur* (On Recent German Literature, 1767)
he continues the discussion about the current
state of German letters and the possibilities for a
genuine national literature that Gotthold
Ephraim Lessing and several collaborators had
begun in their *Briefe, die Neueste Litteratur
betreffend* (Letters concerning Contemporary Literature, 1759-1765), usually referred to as the
Literaturbriefe.

Herder planned his work as a systematic commentary on the *Literaturbriefe* but soon followed

his own agenda. He weaves a vast net of observations proceeding from three premises: that language is sensuous and that all thinking is rooted in the senses; that the language of a people determines the kind of literature that is possible for that people ("Der Genius der Sprache ist also auch der Genius von der Litteratur einer Nation" [The genius of a language is thus also the genius of the literature of a nation]); and that human culture can be understood by using organic models with a circular movement in time rather than mechanistic ones suggesting linear progress. Observations on the characteristics of German are embedded in a general theory of organic linguistic development. In its childhood, language lacks concepts but is strong in emotional responses. In its youth, this emotional impetus is retained but channeled by the use of linguistic symbols, imagery, metaphors, and rhythmic expression; language has then reached the age of poetry. Manhood, the age of dry prose, grammar, and reason, follows. Poetry is still possible but is no longer a direct expression of nature. It is now an art, characterized by order. In the old age of a language, the period of philosophy, considerations of correctness dominate its use.

Herder places German at the stage of prose but suggests that a renewal is possible. He calls for a spirit of early poetry and expressiveness in the age of prose, and in Lessing's, Hamann's, and especially Friedrich Gottlieb Klopstock's use of German he finds examples of such expressiveness. Their language should not be measured against French or Latin practice; Herder argues against misguided dependence and emulation that disregard fundamental differences between cultures. German literature needs to be commensurate with the German language, religion, customs, and history if it is ever to perform the same function in German culture that Greek literature performed in Greek culture.

In Herder's view there are no grounds for any battle between the ancients and the moderns, since works of art and their reception are inevitably molded by historically different conditions. For works of other eras, the reader's and the critic's task is to reconstitute those conditions on the basis of "Einfühlung" (empathy or sympathetic identification–Herder's neologism); this task obviously becomes more difficult as the era recedes into the past. With this position Herder became the founder of a historical and genetic interpretation of literature and the arts. His admonition that the critic should aim to understand rather than judge found echoes in Goethe, Friedrich Schlegel, Adam Müller's notion of "vermittelnde Kritik" (mediating criticism), and Wilhelm Dilthey. Today the nascent "new historicism" is proof that views derived from Herder are still alive.

In the first volume of *Kritische Wälder* (Critical Forests, 1769) Herder criticizes Lessing's *Laokoon* (1766), which proposed several characteristics that separate poetry from the visual arts. Herder insists that the plastic arts appeal to the sense of touch and therefore should not be grouped with painting, which appeals to the visual sense. Poetry does not work on any one sense but energizes the imagination and the soul. In 1778 Herder expanded his observations on sculpture in *Plastik*, advocating greater expressiveness in art. "Gefühl" (touch; but the word also means emotion or feeling) rather than vision is the primary sense. The innocent life of the naked body in sculpture captures the dynamic physical truth. Great Greek statues approach an ideal of wholeness by fusing inner and outer life; not affected by artificial rules of art, they reveal "die *natürliche Sprache der Seele durch unsern ganzen Körper*" (the *natural language of our soul throughout our body*). Herder here checks his relativism by proclaiming that the ideal transcends time, place, or culture.

Growing dissatisfied with his narrow, dusty learnedness, Herder asked for a leave of absence. In May 1769 he departed on an outwardly uneventful but, with respect to his inner life, most adventurous and, as he understood it, deeply symbolic voyage to France. His *Journal meiner Reise im Jahr 1769* (published in *Lebensbild* ([Biographical Sketch], 1846; translated as "Journal of My Travels in the Year 1769," 1952) is a disturbing, grandiose document, revealing a restless character subject to severe swings of mood and consumed by ambition: "Ich gehe durch die Welt, was hab' ich in ihr, wenn ich mich nicht unsterblich mache?" (I am going through the world; what do I have in it, if I do not make myself immortal?). Instead of a chronological diary the journal is a summarizing judgment of Herder's past at Riga and, inspired by the vast horizons of the sea and by the tightly organized ship as a metaphor of human society, a vision of a life of boundless thought and action. He will draft a constitution for Russia; he will be a new Luther for the Baltic countries; he outlines a school system that would downplay Latin grammar and stress knowledge of the world and the unity of all learning. His book projects include a translation of the

Bible, a life of Jesus, and an anthology of European literature, all of them, like his studies of language and literature, building stones for an all-encompassing "Universalgeschichte der Bildung der Welt" (universal history of the shaping of the world).

France, in Herder's eyes, was a declining court culture. His experiences there increased his awareness that he was German and strengthened his conviction that the renewal of culture must grow from a popular base. During four months in Nantes he wrote *Journal meiner Reise im Jahr 1769* and absorbed current French thought; his stay in Paris, where casual acquaintance with some of the Encyclopedists did not shake his deep reservations about their views, was cut short when he accepted an invitation to become the tutor and companion of the crown prince of Holstein-Gottorp on his grand tour to Italy.

On the way to Eutin to join the prince, Herder spent some time in Holland and, at the end of February 1770, in Hamburg. There he met Lessing and Matthias Claudius. The tour with his princely charge began in July 1770 and with stops in Hannover, Cassel, and Darmstadt, was supposed to take three years, but Herder soon felt unappreciated. He resigned his post as the prince's tutor, having been invited to succeed Thomas Abbt as chief pastor at the court of Bückeburg. Before assuming his new duties Herder decided to seek a cure for an old eye ailment at the medical school of Strasbourg University. The operation failed; but during his stay he met Goethe, who was studying law there. Herder, five years Goethe's senior, found in the younger man a receptive mind for his ideas of a revival of poetry inspired by Volksdichtung (folk poetry) and Shakespeare. Goethe was the genius ready to realize some of these ideas in a personal poetry of sense-mediated inner experience using a simple, strong language.

In his prizewinning *Abhandlung über den Ursprung der Sprache* (1772; translated as *Treatise upon the Origin of Language*, 1827), a work that philosopher Ernst Cassirer has described as "the first psychological and philosophical beginning of a theory of language," Herder dismisses as "Unsinn" (nonsense) the theory of a divine creation of language. He also refutes the speculation that language is a human invention that originated in a deliberate agreement and Etienne Bonnot de Condillac's sensualistic theory, which derived language from natural sounds. Instead, Herder claims to present *"veste Data aus der*

Caroline Flachsland, whom Herder married in 1773 (from Hans Register, Johann Gottfried Herder, *1942)*

Menschlichen Seele, der Menschlichen Organisation, dem Bau aller alten und wilden Sprachen und *der ganzen Haushaltung des Menschlichen Geschlechts"* (*solid facts of the human soul, the human organization, the structure of all old and barbaric languages* and *the economics of the human race*). Man is the only being that does not live in a specific "Sphäre" (sphere) in which, as for animals, needs and means are matched. To appropriate the world man must make up for his lack of instinct, strength, and adaptability. Human beings are endowed with "Besonnenheit" (presence of mind), Herder's term for the interaction of discernment, memory, and reflection that expresses itself in language. To be human is to have language: *"Der Mensch ist zum Sprachgeschöpfe gebildet"* (*The human being is formed to be a speaking creature*). There is another difference between animals and human beings: an animal is always fully what it is meant to be; the human being is "gleichsam nie der *ganze* Mensch: Immer in Entwicklung, im Fortgange, in Vervollkommnung" (never, as it were, the *complete* human being: Always in development, in progress, in the process of perfection). Here is

Herder in 1775; painting by J. L. Strecker (Darmstadt, Hessisches Landesmuseum)

the bridge between history and a language-based anthropology: history is the path to becoming fully human. Human beings are masters of their world and fate: "Nicht mehr eine unfehlbare Maschiene in den Händen der Natur, wird er sich selbst Zweck und Ziel der Bearbeitung" (no longer an infallible machine in the hands of nature, the human being becomes the purpose and goal of his activities).

In May 1771 Herder arrived in Bückeburg to work for the count of Schaumburg-Lippe, first as pastor and councillor, then as superintendent. Shortly after his arrival old concerns, stirred up again in the Strasbourg exchange with Goethe, came to fruition in essays on Ossian and Shakespeare. Herder published them in 1773 in *Von deutscher Art und Kunst* (Of German Kind and Art), a collection that also includes an essay by Goethe on the Strasbourg Cathedral; one by Justus Möser, author of *Osnabrückische Geschichte* (Osnabrückian History, 1768); and a translation of an essay by Paolo Frisi hostile to Gothic art. In retrospect, this somewhat haphazard collection ap-

pears as a purposeful manifesto declaring the North's artistic expressions to be as valid as those of Greek antiquity. For Herder, Ossian's songs remain, despite doubts about their authenticity, "*Lieder, Lieder des Volks*, Lieder eines ungebildeten sinnlichen Volks" (*songs, songs of the people*, songs of an uneducated, sensuous people). Comparing misleading German translations of Ossian with the true "Geist des Werks" (spirit of the work), Herder refines his concept of early poetry as "Naturpoesie" (natural poetry) characterized by a sensuous language, clear images, and a lively simplicity without rhetorical flourishes. In 1774 he put together a collection of English and German songs but withdrew it from publication. A decade later, in *Vom Geist der ebräischen Poesie* (1782-1783; translated as *The Spirit of Hebrew Poetry*, 1833), Herder would analyze what he considered the prime example of early poetry as an expression of a people's identity.

In his appraisal of Shakespeare, Herder again emphasizes the need to understand the poet in his time. Though worlds apart, Shakespeare and Sophocles are brothers: each writes in harmony with his own historical conditions. The much-belabored unities of time, place, and action are not legislated rules of art but an expression of Greek "natural" conditions that no longer exist— just as Shakespeare's different dramatic form is of his time, also quickly receding. Shakespeare's historical dramas are a small-scale analogy for conceiving history and God's role in it. The essay, ending with the announcement of Goethe's *Götz von Berlichingen* (1773), marks a transition in emphasis from language and literature to history; and Shakespeare, this "große Schöpfer von Geschichte und Weltseele" (great creator of history and universal soul), is the link.

At Bückeburg Herder was soon unhappy with his circumstances. A religious crisis was eased by a renewal of faith that was helped along by his reading of the writings of Blaise Pascal, a second Hamann for him. Herder's self-doubts were resolved to some extent when in May 1773 he married Caroline Flachsland, to whom he had become engaged in Darmstadt in the summer of 1770. He was able to write again, and works on theology, history, and aesthetics appeared in quick succession.

Two works stand out. In *Älteste Urkunde des Menschengeschlechts* (Oldest Document of the Human Race, 1774-1776) he tries to demonstrate both the sacred character and the historical conditions of the first book of Genesis. He provides a

Volkslieder.

— Sind Veilchen in des Jahres Jugend, sind
Erstlinge der Natur, früh und nicht daurend,
Süß, aber bald dahin: der Duft, die Blüthe
Von wenigen Minuten —

Shakespear's Hamlet.

Erster Theil.

Leipzig,
in der Weygandschen Buchhandlung
1778

*Title page for the first volume of Herder's collection of folk
songs from various cultures*

far-flung commentary that draws on comparative religion and mythology, and he attempts a new translation in a remarkable German modeled after the Hebrew original. The work, dear to Herder because he hoped to initiate a new reformation with it, is his wildest and most cryptic one; it was not well received, though Goethe admired it as a "mystisch weitstrahlsinniges Ganze" (mystically far-radiating whole).

Decidedly more accessible is Herder's ironically titled *Auch eine Philosophie der Geschichte zur Bildung der Menschheit* (1774; translated as "Yet Another Philosophy of History for the Education of Humanity," 1968), his combative response to the linear models of history offered by orthodox Christianity, Voltaire, and Rousseau. Herder portrays history as a process of natural growth and decline, and traces the development of specific cultures and of mankind from childhood through maturity to weak old age. These terms can be used persuasively for presenting ancient history from the Orient through Egypt to Greece and Rome, but post-Roman history does not continue the pattern as neatly. A new cycle of life stages can be said to begin with Christianity, and the Middle Ages in Herder's view were a strong, spontaneous period; but his own age is not what it could be. The essay, which contributed to the Romantic revaluation of the "dark" Middle Ages, is written out of an intense dissatisfaction with prevailing social and political conditions, and in the second part Herder shifts to an openly severe critique. He especially denounces the pervasive mechanical spirit of the age, which regards the state as a machine and the individual as a cog in it. But individuals and societies are living organisms. Late eighteenth-century Europe, complacently arrogant and convinced of its superior progress, lacks warm, pulsating life. Herder deplores the dehumanizing separation of heart and hand and castigates the subjugation of other societies. The unconscionable exploitation of the colonies will haunt Europe; it is a crime that highlights the urgent need for drastic change. Herder was to welcome such change in the French Revolution a decade and a half later.

Aspects of Herder's attack on his age were varied and expanded by Goethe, Karl Philipp Moritz, Friedrich Schiller, and above all by Karl Marx. His model of cultural growth and decline, reminiscent of Giambattista Vico, of whom he may or may not have known at this time, anticipates those by Oswald Spengler and Arnold Toynbee. Another seminal breakthrough stems from Herder's claim (though he does not exercise the implied dispassionate neutrality when dealing with his own age): "jede Nation hat ihren *Mittelpunkt* der Glückseligkeit *in sich*, wie jede Kugel ihren Schwerpunkt" (every nation has its own *inner center* of happiness, as every sphere its own center of gravity). Herder advocated the attempt to recover and understand the concrete and unique individuality of cultures, a program that was to come fully into its own in nineteenth-century historicism. This sketch of 1774 has been called "the splendid charter of historicism," but Friedrich Meinecke finds still "too much transcendence" in Herder's outlook. Herder's guiding conviction is that history shows the "*Gang Gottes über die Nationen!*" (*God's course over the nations!*). If we cannot clearly see it, it is because our point of view is limited: we lack the divine "Allanblick" (omnivision).

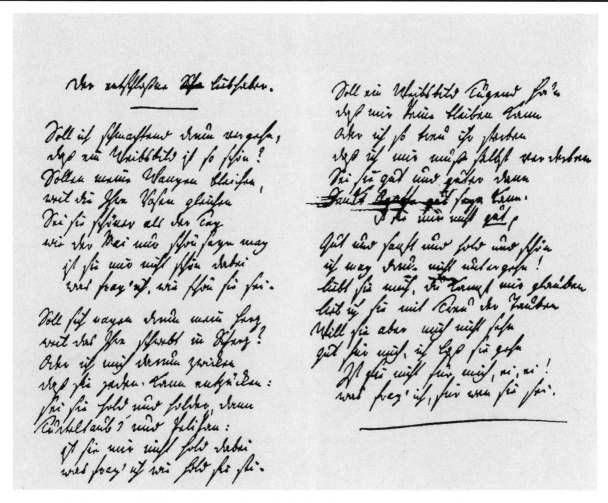

Manuscript for a Spanish folk song from Herder's Volkslieder *(from Gustav Könnecke,* Bilderatlas zur Geschichte der deutschen Nationallitteratur, *1895)*

In 1776 Herder's hopes for a position at Göttingen University were disappointed. With the help of Goethe, who had arrived at Weimar in 1775, however, he obtained the post of general superintendent there. But the friendship between Herder and Goethe could no longer be the one of mentor and disciple that it had been in Strasbourg. It took until 1783 for the two men to find a new basis of equality and common pursuits. During these years, Herder continued his appropriation and mediation of foreign cultures. Somewhat to his surprise, his two-volume collection *Volkslieder* (Folk Songs, 1778-1779), with samples from almost all European languages and from as far away as Peru and Greenland, was highly successful. The heterogeneous collection was meant to present poetry, whether anonymous folk songs or not, that captures an intense experience of lived reality in a simple form, fuses thought and expression, and is ideally, like the poems of Ossian, the expression of a people. Herder's enthusiasm for a "Sprache des Sturms der Wahrheit und Empfindung" (language of the storm of truth and feeling) in these volumes influenced the lyrical style of the Romantics. The collection also prepared Goethe's and the Romantics' approaches to Weltliteratur (world literature).

In *Auch eine Philosophie der Geschichte zur Bildung der Menschheit* Herder had lashed out against conditions that deform human beings. His 1778 essay *Vom Erkennen und Empfinden der menschlichen Seele* (On Cognition and Sensation in the Human Soul) summarizes his views on how a human being truly lives in the world. Hans Dietrich Irmscher sees Herder pursuing an ontology based on the double sense of *Gefühl* with the premise, stated in an early sketch for *Plastik:* "Ich fühle mich! Ich bin!" (*I feel myself! I am!*). We apprehend and understand the world only because, and to the extent to which, it is analogous to our-

Title page for the first volume of Herder's philosophical magnum opus

selves. Our perception of the world is not filtered through separate faculties of different rank; rather, cognition and sensation work interdependently in our experience of the world. In fact, all our faculties are only one, and each individual constitutes one indivisible process.

Opposed to the Cartesian split between body and mind and intent on showing the unity of living, Herder embarked on his four-volume magnum opus, *Ideen zur Philosophie der Geschichte der Menschheit* (1784-1791; translated as *Outlines of a Philosophy of the History of Man*, 1800). The work, the climax of what Isaiah Berlin calls Herder's "heroic effort to see the universe as a single process," is a synthesis of Herder's thought and reading that had absorbed the historical, scientific, and philosophical literature of his day. Written during a time of renewed, sometimes daily exchanges with Goethe, *Ideen zur Philosophie der Geschichte der Menschheit*, though less strident than *Auch eine Philosophie der Geschichte zur Bildung der Menschheit*, is not new in tenor or structure. After describing the place of the earth within the cosmos and life on earth, the first volume of *Ideen zur Philosophie der Geschichte der Menschheit* defines human distinctness. The second volume explains the general characteristics of human culture by col-

lating observations about people from around the world. Herder locates the beginnings of human culture in northern India, thus initiating the Romantic fascination with the subcontinent. The historical and anthropological survey in the third and fourth volumes stretches from the Far East to the late Middle Ages in Europe. The thirteenth book of volume 3 amplifies the description of Greece as the unique fulfillment of the human potential for perfection that Herder had offered in 1775 in the prizewinning essay *Ursachen des gesunknen Geschmacks bei den verschiedenen Völkern, da er geblühet* (Causes of the Degeneration of Taste of Various Peoples, in which it had blossomed). A fifth volume, never written, was to treat the modern period.

In amassing this vast amount of material Herder pursues two purposes. He wants first to situate the human being as a "Mittelgeschöpf" (middle creature) in the universe and in nature. Kant had stated in *Idee zu einer allgemeinen Geschichte in weltbürgerlicher Absicht* (Idea for a General History from a Cosmopolitan Viewpoint, 1784) that man is an animal that needs a master. Herder maintains on the contrary that the human being who needs a master is an animal. Animals are controlled by instinct, but man is not: "Der Mensch ist der erste *Freigelassene* der Schöpfung; er stehet aufrecht" (The human being is the first *freed creature* of creation; he stands upright). This freedom prepares and obliges us to practice "Selbstbestimmung" (self-determination), in a process toward individuality that is analogous for the single person and for a Volk. The life of the individual and that of the race as realized in different cultures throughout history are small steps toward the elusive goal of humanitarian culture. While Herder rejects the notion of providence as mechanistic, he propagates a vision of human perfectibility. Complete human perfection cannot, however, be realized in this world; only by passing through death will we shed our animal nature, and only in the other world may we reach a "*Gottähnliche Humanität*, die verschlossene Knospe der wahren Gestalt der Menschheit" (Godlike humanity, the closed bud of the true form of humankind).

Herder's second purpose, much more directly pursued here than in *Auch eine Philosophie der Geschichte zur Bildung der Menschheit*, is to elucidate the "harmonische göttliche Ordnung" (harmonious divine order) in the labyrinth of history. We are order-seeking creatures, and Voltaire's suggestion that history is irrational, indeed chaotic,

*Limestone bust of Herder by Martin Gottlieb Klaurer (from
Hans Register,* Johann Gottfried Herder, *1942)*

Goethe called *Ideen zur Philosophie der
Geschichte der Menschheit* "das liebenswerteste
Evangelium" (the most endearing gospel). The
work still exacts admiration for its reach and for
its vision of humanity. Perhaps most appealing
today are Herder's fertile notions of self-
determination and his penetrating awareness of
"Ganzheit" (totality) and "Verflechtung" (interre-
latedness). This early perception of an encompass-
ing, natural *and* social, historical "ecology" is, for
Herder, religiously motivated through the concept of plenitude, the notion that everything that
can exist does exist (he warns that dire consequences will result from the extinction of any
one species). The work's unresolved tensions also
stand out. Herder's basic teleological orientation
is at odds with his historical relativism—he focuses
on the motifs of duration and change, but by proclaiming that everything is always adequate to the
conditions of its existence he provokes the question of why there should be any historical change
at all; though he wants to present only empirical
data, his use of an extended organic metaphor
and his recourse to a unified organic force justify
Kant's charge of metaphysical flight. Perhaps
these tensions are inevitable in an account of the
world based on data yet aimed at proving God in
history.

In *Gott: Einige Gespräche* (1787; translated as
God: Some Conversations, 1940) Herder uses the debate between Moses Mendelssohn and Friedrich
Heinrich Jacobi over Spinoza and pantheism to re-
iterate some of his views. Jacobi claimed that Lessing had been persuaded by Spinoza's philosophy; Mendelssohn defended Lessing against such
an insinuation, which amounted to a charge of
atheism. Herder's book, consisting of five conversations, is intended as a correction of the public
perception that Spinoza equated God and nature. In fact, Herder identifies Spinoza's God
with his own notion of a "*Kraft,* d.i. die Urkraft
aller Kräfte, die Seele aller Seelen" (*force,* that is,
the primal force of all forces, the soul of all
souls), which reveals itself in infinite ways.

Between 1785 and 1797 Herder published
the didactic, six-volume *Zerstreute Blätter* (Scattered Leaves), a motley gathering of old, revised,
and new items: essays on the fable and on the history and theory of the epigram, translations from
the Greek, adaptations, and his own poetry. Noteworthy are his "Paramythien," an attempt to revive myth with features of allegory, fable, and
fairy tales, and his treatment in the second volume of nemesis as governing the course of his-

is deeply repugnant to Herder. If God's will is
present in the order of nature it must also reveal itself in history. Herder wants to be the Newton of
history, to discover its organic laws. He furthermore wants to persuade the reader that history reveals the workings of a benevolent divine spirit.
What does not serve the great purpose of
Humanität does not endure. The principle of
"nemesis," of measure and restraint, balances the
course of history. Herder thus recasts Hamann's
dictum that history is God becoming flesh. History is the unfolding of Humanität. "Es ist nur
Ein Bau, der fortgeführt werden soll . . ." (It is
only One edifice that is to be continued . . .). If
Herder's insistence on individuality shattered the
coherence of a static, mechanistic worldview, his
emphasis on one process seeks to establish a different coherence in time. Herder's view subsumes nature and history: "Unser Erdball ist ein großes Laboratorium zur Organisation wirkender
Kräfte" (Our planet earth is a great laboratory
for the organization of active forces), and God is
the ultimate force that is manifest not only in nature but also in the constantly changing creation
that makes up history.

tory. Also of interest is his essay about palingenesis in the sixth volume, where he says: "Alle sind wir von Einem Welt- und Lebensgeist auf kurze Zeit beseelt" (All of us are animated for a brief time by One World- and Life-Spirit).

In the fall of 1783 Herder was made director of the school system in Weimar, and in 1786 he presented his plans for its reorganization, emphasizing lively instruction and the goal of Humanität. From August 1788 to June 1789 he traveled in Italy. On his return he declined the offer of a professorship in Göttingen. The decade ended with Herder's growing isolation, partly owing to Goethe's new friendship with Schiller and partly to the disagreement in Weimar circles over the French Revolution and the role of the artist in society.

Before his Italian journey Herder had outlined a plan for a "patriotisches Institut für den Allgemeingeist Deutschlands" (Patriotic Institute for the Public Spirit in Germany). After his return he responded to the French Revolution and the prospect of imminent, radical change for Germany in *Briefe zu Beförderung der Humanität* (Letters for the Advancement of Humanity, 1793-1797). Herder does not abandon his historical perspective, but his sketch of a history of world literature is slanted toward the moral content of the works and the social obligations of the author. His educational purpose skews his review of contemporary German literature and partly accounts for his preference of Lessing to Goethe and of minor poets of the previous generation to Schiller, whose concept of aesthetic education Herder opposed.

Except for a late friendship with Johann Paul Friedrich Richter (Jean Paul), who suggested a journal to combat the influence of Kant, Goethe, and Weimar classicism, Herder, beset by illness and family problems, spent his declining years in lonely dissatisfaction. His energy was consumed by the fight against Kant's critical philosophy, which, he believed, dismembered the indivisible person and the unity of experience. Once more Herder argued, in *Eine Metakritik zur Kritik der reinen Vernunft* (A Metacritique of the Critique of Pure Reason, 1799), against "Fächer in unsrer Seele" (compartments in our soul) and for the wholeness of being, against abstract dissection and for the process of living. Kant's problems with the mediation between mind and reality are, for Herder, a case of linguistic confusion and trickery. Herder's belief in the God-given correspondence between subject and world renders any epis-

temological doubts superfluous. From such a position Kant's enterprise of analyzing the operations of the mind leads into "Nichts" (nothingness). Herder never wavered from his early conviction that philosophy must become anthropology if it is to be useful.

A similar perspective governs Herder's critique in *Kalligone* (1800) of Kant's aesthetics and its key notions of purposiveness without purpose and disinterested pleasure. Herder opposes this attempt at a logical definition of taste and beauty with an aesthetics grounded in empirical psychology and in the notion that all art is historical. Beauty demands the viewer's emotional participation, which the artist ought to facilitate. In general, the tendencies prevailing in literature at the turn of the century could hardly please Herder. In his eyes Weimar classicism was weakening the moral and social core of art by emphasizing formal concerns; and the Romantic movement, which owed so much to him, no longer subscribed to his view of art serving the grand goal of Humanität. Against the proclamations of an autonomous art Herder insisted on the usefulness and public function of art.

The weaknesses that mar *Briefe zu Beförderung der Humanität* and the writings against Kant—an obsession with detail that obscures the main points and Herder's blatantly partisan view of the present—are compounded in his last collection, *Adrastea* (1801-1803), intended as an assessment of the achievements of the eighteenth century. In this farewell welter of observations and insights, his outline of a future society is the most remarkable element. Liberty and equality can be enjoyed only as the result of an educational process structured and controlled through state supervision of the universities. Herder now favors restrictive measures, an understandable position after the Reign of Terror and the spectacle of a chaotic freedom but an ironic one in view of his earlier antistate ideals. Whether in aesthetics, literary judgment, or public policy, the aging Herder was left behind by a new age for which, as Richter said, "er selbst die Schranken geöffnet hatte" (he himself had opened the gates). Herder died in Weimar on 18 December 1803.

Herder was by no means always original. His debt to English and French authors such as Blackwell, David Hume, Lowth, Montesquieu, and Rousseau is often obvious. His fertile appropriations have been outlined by Rudolf Haym, Meinecke, Max Rouché, and Isaiah Berlin, and are documented in exhaustive detail in modern

Herder's house in Weimar; lithograph by E. Lobe

editions of his works. The diversity in Herder's sources is matched by the wide range of his direct or indirect influence and his anticipation of later developments: Goethe's view and practice of natural science; the Romantic infatuation with the Volkslied and the Middle Ages; Hippolyte Taine's and Wilhelm Scherer's aesthetic positivism; Sauer's and Nadler's efforts to write a "tribal" or regional history of German literature; Marxist thought on the function of literature and the arts; the Pan-Slavic movement; the vitalistic philosophies of Schopenhauer and Henri Bergson; the notion of Gestalt and Gestalt psychology; the concept of the unconscious and its expression in Surrealism; and the Romantic as well as the recent interest in myth.

This bewildering spectrum hints at a certain lack of consistency in thought. Two factors account for this lack of consistency: in his tireless quest for "das Ganze" (the totality) Herder kept discovering new points of view; and he was always responding to specific situations. His thought was itself historical; it changed with the challenges, was "immer in Entwicklung" (always in development). Yet at the same time Herder is almost always fully himself and is present in each sentence, almost each word. He writes with the full force of his personality; and while Buffon's bon mot—the style is the man—is apt, Herder's own dictum applies even better: "Überall aber würkt die ganze unabgetheilte Seele" (yet everywhere the whole, undivided soul is at work). In reading Herder one has to learn his language, which celebrates and practices an order of its own: diversity, irregularity, and individuality.

Beneath all contradictions and shifts a stable core emerges: Herder's effort—noble, heroic, and tragic—at a sustained monism of person and work, of action and world. He pursued his vision of Humanität at a time when the conditions for its realization, such as the small community and the unity of home and work, were deteriorating beyond recovery. The times, if they ever existed, were gone "da Ein Mensch mehr als Eins und jeder alles war, was Er seyn konnte" (when one person was more than One and everybody was all that he could be). Herder knew that he was witnessing the end of an age that had been formed by antiquity and Christianity. Despite his purposeful and optimistic orientation toward the future he engages in a historiography of Heimweh (homesickness). Against Nietzsche's verdict can be placed Richter's praise of Herder as one of the swans that during the cold season keep the waters open through their moving, or Cassirer's drier judgment of Herder as the "Copernicus of history." There are good reasons for extending the analogy and proclaiming Herder the Copernicus of man's self-interpretation. In this respect even Nietzsche stands deeply in his debt.

Labels such as pre-Romantic or anti-Enlightenment cannot encompass Herder, a complex writer of seemingly inexhaustible public optimism and increasing private doubts about the course of humankind. His legacy is vast, and it has been ambiguously seminal. Some of his ideas were isolated and used for purposes alien or even opposed to his intentions. He, perhaps more than anyone else, helped to formulate an ethics of individualism; but he balanced it with an unprecedented insistence on "Gebundenheit" (constraint)–populism, in Berlin's term. He also propagated the values of Volk and Nation but curbed their potential virulence by sharply separating them from the state and by emphasizing the bond of common humanity. Herder cannot be held responsible for subsequent distortions of his ideas: the groundless subjectivism of the German Romantics, nineteenth-century nationalism, or, worst, twentieth-century inhuman excesses in the name of Volk that violate, indeed eradicate, his notions of Humanität and Selbstbestimmung. These notions are among his lasting contributions to our self-interpretation, as are his explorations of the oneness of our nature and his insights into our potential and responsibility, both psychologically as individuals and historically as a people or a race: "Wir leben immer in einer Welt, die wir uns selbst bilden" (We live always in a world that we are forming ourselves).

Letters:

Lebensbild: Sein chronologisch-geordneter Briefwechsel, verbunden mit den hierhergehörigen Mittheilungen aus seinem ungedruckten Nachlasse, und mit den nöthigen Belegen aus seinen und seiner Zeitgenossen Schriften, 6 volumes, edited by Emil Gottfried von Herder (Erlangen: Bläsing, 1846; reprinted, Hildesheim & New York: Olms, 1977);

Aus Herders Nachlaß, 3 volumes, edited by Heinrich Düntzer and Ferdinand Gottfried von Herder (Frankfurt am Main: Meidinger, 1856-1857; reprinted, Hildesheim: Olms, 1976);

Reise nach Italien: Briefwechsel mit seiner Gattin, vom August 1788 bis Juli 1789, edited by Düntzer and Ferdinand Gottfried von Herder

(Gießen: Ricker, 1859; reprinted, Hildesheim & New York: Olms, 1977);

Von und an Herder: Ungedruckte Briefe aus Herders Nachlaß, 3 volumes, edited by Düntzer and Ferdinand Gottfried von Herder (Leipzig: Dyk, 1861-1862; reprinted, Hildesheim & New York: Olms, 1981);

Briefwechsel mit Nicolai: Im Originaltext, edited by Otto Hoffmann (Berlin: Nicolai, 1887);

Herders Briefe an Joh. Georg Hamann: Im Originaltext, edited by Hoffmann (Berlin: Gaertner, 1889; reprinted, Hildesheim & New York: Olms, 1975);

Herders Briefwechsel mit Caroline Flachsland, nach den Handschriften des Goethe- und Schiller-Archivs, 2 volumes, edited by Hans Schauer (Weimar: Verlag der Goethe-Gesellschaft, 1926-1928);

Herders Dresdener Reise: Zehn Briefe J. G. Herders aus dem Jahre 1803, edited by Schauer (Dresden: Jess, 1929);

Briefe, edited by Wilhelm Dobbek (Weimar: Volksverlag Weimar, 1959);

Herders Briefe in einem Band, edited by Regine Otto (Berlin: Aufbau, 1970);

Briefe: Gesamtausgabe, 1763-1803, 9 volumes, edited by Karl-Heinz Hahn, Wilhelm Dobbek, and Günter Arnold (Weimar: Böhlau, 1977-1988);

Bloß für Dich geschrieben: Briefe und Aufzeichnungen über eine Reise nach Italien 1788/89 (Berlin: Rütten & Loening, 1980).

Bibliography:

Gottfried Günther, Albina A. Volgina, and Siegfried Seifert, *Herder-Bibliographie* (Berlin: Aufbau, 1978).

Biographies:

Robert T. Clark, *Herder: His Life and Thought* (Berkeley: University of California Press, 1955);

Walter Dietze, *Johann Gottfried Herder: Abriß seines Lebens und Schaffens* (Berlin: Aufbau, 1980).

References:

Emil Adler, *Herder und die deutsche Aufklärung* (Vienna: Europa, 1968);

Frederick M. Barnard, *Herder's Social and Political Thought: From Enlightenment to Nationalism* (Oxford: Oxford University Press, 1965);

Heinz Begenau, *Grundzüge der Ästhetik Herders* (Weimar: Böhlau, 1956);

Isaiah Berlin, "Herder and the Enlightenment," in *Aspects of the Eighteenth Century*, edited by Earl R. Wasserman (Baltimore: Johns Hopkins University Press, 1965), pp. 47-104;

Berlin, *Vico and Herder: Two Studies in the History of Ideas* (London: Hogarth Press, 1976);

Eric A. Blackall, "The Imprint of Herder's Linguistic Theory on His Early Prose Style," *PMLA*, 76 (December 1961): 512-518;

Emile Callot, *Les trois moments de la philosophie théologique de l'histoire: Augustin, Vico, Herder. Situation actuelle* (Paris: La Pensée Universelle, 1974);

Ernst Cassirer, *Freiheit und Form* (Berlin: Cassirer, 1916);

Cassirer, *The Philosophy of Symbolic Forms* (New Haven: Yale University Press, 1953);

Cassirer, *The Philosophy of the Enlightenment* (Princeton: Princeton University Press, 1951);

Robert T. Clark, "Herder's Conception of 'Kraft,'" *PMLA*, 57 (7 September 1942): 737-752;

Walter Dietze, *"Ein würdiger Lehrer der Menschheit zu werden—": Über Johann Gottfried Herders schriftstellerische Anfänge* (Berlin: Akademie-Verlag, 1978);

Dietze, ed., *Herder-Kolloquium 1978: Referate und Diskussions Beiträge* (Weimar: Böhlau, 1980);

Wilhelm Dobbek, *Johann Gottfried Herder Weltbild: Versuch einer Deutung* (Cologne: Böhlau, 1969);

Ulrich Faust, *Mythologien und Religionen des Ostens bei Johann Gottfried Herder* (Münster: Aschendorff, 1977);

Wilhelm Ludwig Federlin, *Vom Nutzen des geistlichen Amtes: Ein Beitrag zur Interpretation und Rezeption Johann Gottfried Herders* (Göttingen: Vandenhoeck & Ruprecht, 1982);

Peter Frenz, *Studien zu traditionellen Elementen des Geschichtsdenkens und der Bildlichkeit im Werk Johann Gottfried Herders* (Frankfurt am Main: Lang, 1983);

Joseph Fugate, *The Psychological Basis of Herder's Aesthetics* (The Hague: Mouton, 1966);

Karl-Gustav Gerold, *Herder und Diderot: Ihr Einblick in die Kunst* (Hildesheim, 1974);

Gerold, *Johann Gottfried Herder: 1803/1978* (Bonn & Bad Godesberg: Inter Nationes, 1978);

Alexander Gillies, *Herder* (Oxford: Blackwell, 1945);

Gillies, "Herder und Faust," *Publications of the English Goethe Society*, new series 16 (1947): 90-111;

Rudolf Haym, *Herder: Nach seinem Leben und seinen Werken dargestellt*, 2 volumes (Berlin: 1880-1885; reprinted, Berlin: Aufbau, 1958);

Bertold Heizmann, *Ursprünglichkeit und Reflexion: Die poetische Ästhetik des jungen Herder im Zusammenhang der Geschichtsphilosophie und Anthropologie des 18. Jahrhunderts* (Frankfurt am Main: Lang, 1981);

Elisabeth Hoffart, *Herders "Gott"* (Walluf & Nendeln: Sändig, 1975);

Hans Dietrich Irmscher, "Die geschichtsphilosophische Kontroverse zwischen Kant und Herder," in *Hamann-Herder-Kant*, edited by Bernhard Gajek (Frankfurt am Main: Lang, 1987), pp. 111-192;

Irmscher, *Der handschriftliche Nachlaß Johann Gottfried Herders: Katalog* (Wiesbaden: Harrassowitz, 1979);

Irmscher, "Johann Gottfried Herder," in *Deutsche Dichter des 18. Jahrhunderts: Ihr Leben und Werk*, edited by Benno von Wiese (Berlin: Schmidt, 1977), pp. 524-550;

Irmscher, "Probleme der Herder Forschung: I. Teil. Zur Quellenlage," *Deutsche Vierteljahrsschrift*, 37 (1963): 266-317;

Friedrich Wilhelm Katzenbach, *Johann Gottfried Herder in Selbstzeugnissen und Bilddokumenten* (Reinbek: Rowohlt, 1970);

Wulf Koepke, *Johann Gottfried Herder* (Boston: Twayne, 1987);

Koepke and Samson B. Knoll, eds., *Johann Gottfried Herder: Innovator through the Ages* (Bonn: Bouvier, 1982);

Werner Kohlschmidt, *Herder-Studien: Untersuchungen zu Herders kritischem Stil und zu seinen literaturkritischen Grundeinsichten* (Berlin: Junker & Dünnhaupt, 1929);

Dieter Lohmeier, *Herder und Klopstock: Herders Auseinandersetzung mit der Persönlichkeit und dem Werk Klopstocks* (Bad Homburg: Gehlen, 1968);

Wilfried Malsch, "Hinfällig geoffenbartes Urbild: Griechenland in Herders typologischer Geschichtsphilosophie," *Jahrbuch der Deutschen Schillergesellschaft*, 30 (1986): 161-195;

Johann Gottfried Maltusch, ed., *Bückeburger Gespräche über Johann Gottfried Herder 1971* (Bückeburg: Grimme, 1975);

Maltusch, ed., *Bückeburger Gespräche über Johann Gottfried Herder 1975* (Bückeburg: Grimme, 1976);

Robert S. Mayo, *Herder and the Beginnings of Comparative Literature* (Chapel Hill: University of North Carolina Press, 1969);

Friedrich Meinecke, *Die Entstehung des Historismus* (Munich: Oldenbourg, 1936); translated by J. E. Anderson and H. D. Schmidt as *Historicism* (New York: Herder & Herder, 1972);

Hugh B. Nisbet, *Herder and the Philosophy and History of Science* (Cambridge: Modern Humanities Research Association, 1970);

Heidi Owren, *Herders Bildungsprogramm und seine Auswirkungen im 18. und 19. Jahrhundert* (Heidelberg: Winter, 1985);

Brigitte Poschmann, ed., *Bückeburger Gespräche über Johann Gottfried Herder 1983* (Rinteln: Bösendahl, 1984);

Alfons Reckermann, *Sprache und Metaphysik: Zur Kritik der sprachlichen Vernunft bei Herder und Humboldt* (Munich: Fink, 1979);

Hans Register, *Johann Gottfried Herder* (Berlin: 1942);

Lutz Richter, ed., *Johann Gottfried Herder im Spiegel seiner Zeitgenossen: Briefe und Selbstzeugnisse* (Göttingen: Vandenhoeck & Ruprecht, 1978);

Max Rouché, Introduction to Herder's *Une autre philosophie de l'histoire* (Paris: Editions Montaigne, 1943);

Edgar B. Schick, *Metaphorical Organicism in Herder's Early Works: A Study of the Relation of Herder's Literary Idiom to His World-View* (The Hague: Mouton, 1971);

Eva Schmidt, ed., *Herder im geistlichen Amt: Untersuchungen, Quellen, Dokumente* (Leipzig: Koehler & Amelang, 1956);

Albert R. Schmitt, *Herder und Amerika* (The Hague: Mouton, 1967);

Jochen Schütze, *Die Objektivität der Sprache: Einige systematische Perspektiven auf das Werk des jungen Herder* (Cologne: Pahl-Rugenstein, 1983);

Martin Schütze, "The Fundamental Ideas in Herder's Thought," *Modern Philology*, 18 (June 1920): 67-78; (October 1920): 289-302; 19 (November 1921): 113-130; (May 1922): 361-382; 21 (August 1923): 29-48; (November 1923): 113-132;

Wolfgang Stellmacher, *Herders Shakespeare-Bild: Shakespeare-Rezeption im Sturm und Drang. Dynamisches Weltbild und bürgerliches Nationaldrama* (Berlin: Rütten & Loening, 1978);

Claus Träger, *Die Herder-Legende des deutschen Historismus* (Berlin: Akademie-Verlag, 1979);

René Wellek, *A History of Modern Criticism: 1750-1950*, volume 1: *The Later Eighteenth Century* (New Haven: Yale University Press, 1955), pp. 176-200;

George Wells, *Herder and After: A Study in the Development of Sociology* (The Hague: Mouton, 1959);

Hayden White, *Metahistory: The Historical Imagination in Nineteenth-Century Europe* (Baltimore: Johns Hopkins University Press, 1973), pp. 69-80;

Walter Wiora, ed., *Herder-Studien* (Würzburg: Holzner, 1960);

Hans M. Wolff, "Der junge Herder und die Entwicklungsidee Rousseaus," *PMLA*, 57 (September 1942): 753-819.

Papers:

The majority of Johann Gottfried Herder's papers are in the Staatsbibliothek Preußischer Kulturbesitz in West Berlin. Smaller collections of manuscripts are in the Archiv der Deutschen Akademie der Wissenschaften in Berlin, the Deutsche Staatsbibliothek in East Berlin, the Landeshauptarchiv and the Goethe- und Schiller-Archiv in Weimar, the Frankfurt Goethe Museum (mostly letters), the Fürstliche Hausarchiv in Bückeburg, and the Stadtbibliothek in Schaffhausen.

Johann Timotheus Hermes

(31 May 1738 - 24 July 1821)

Erich P. Hofacker, Jr.
University of Michigan

BOOKS: *Versuch über die Ansprüche eines Christen auf die Güter des gegenwärtigen Lebens* (Berlin: Mylius, 1764);

Geschichte der Miss Fanny Wilkes, so gut als aus dem Englischen übersetzt, 2 volumes, anonymous (Leipzig: Junius, 1766; enlarged, 3 volumes, 1770; reprinted, Frankfurt am Main: Minerva, 1970);

Die beste Anwendung der Abendstunden des menschlichen Lebens (Leipzig: Junius, 1768);

Sophiens Reise von Memel nach Sachsen, 5 volumes, anonymous (Leipzig: Junius, 1769-1773; enlarged, 6 volumes, 1776; revised and enlarged, 6 volumes, 1778; first edition abridged, edited by Fritz Brüggemann, Leipzig: Reclam, 1941; reprinted, Darmstadt: Wissenschaftliche Buchgesellschaft, 1967);

Predigten an die Kunstrichter und Prediger, 2 volumes (Leipzig: Junius, 1771);

Vom Werth plötzlicher Bekehrung (Leipzig: Jacobäer, 1773);

Predigtentwürfe über Evangelia auf 1776. 77. 78. (Breslau: Korn, 1775);

Beitrag zu den Beweisen der Gottheit Jesu (Breslau, 1777);

Gelegenheitspredigten (Breslau, 1779);

Lieder und Arien aus Sophiens Reise, music by Johann Adam Hiller (Leipzig: Junius, 1779);

Andachtsbuch für die Feier der Leidenszeit Jesu, 2 volumes (Leipzig: Jacobäer, 1781-1782);

Predigten über die evangelischen Texte an den Sonn- und Festtagen des ganzen Jahres, 2 volumes (Berlin & Stettin: Nicolai, 1782);

Beyträge zur Verbesserung des öffentlichen Gottesdienstes (Leipzig, 1786);

Kommunionbuch (Berlin, 1787);

Für Töchter edler Herkunft: Eine Geschichte, 3 volumes, anonymous (Leipzig: Jacobäer, 1787);

Manch Hermäon im eigentlichen Sinn des Worts vom Verfasser von Sophiens Reise, 2 volumes, anonymous (Vienna: Hörling / Leipzig: Jacobäer, 1788);

Für Eltern und Ehelustige unter den Aufgeklärten im Mittelstande: Eine Geschichte vom Verfasser von

Johann Timotheus Hermes

Sophiens Reise, 5 volumes, anonymous (Carlsruhe: C. G. Schmieder, 1789-1790);

Zween literarische Märtyrer und deren Frauen, vom Verfasser von Sophiens Reise, 2 volumes, anonymous (Leipzig: Junius, 1789); republished as *Meine, Herrn Grundleger und unserer Frauen Geschichte*, 2 volumes, anonymous (Leipzig: Junius, 1798);

Predigten für alle Sonn- und Festtage (Berlin: Franke, 1792);

Neue Predigten (Breslau: Feind, 1793);

Anhang zu den Predigten für die Sonntage und neuen Predigten (Breslau & Leipzig, 1796);

Lieder für die besten bekannten Kirchenmelodien (Breslau: Barth, 1801);

Anna Winterfeld, oder Unsere Töchter eingewiesen in ihre gekränkten Rechte: Eine Geschichte in Briefen, as Heinrich Meister (Gotha, 1801);

Verheimlichung und Eil, oder Lottchens und ihrer Nachbarn Geschichte, 2 volumes, as T. S. Jemehr (Berlin: Braun, 1802);

Zweiter Anhang zu seinen Predigten und neuen Predigten (Breslau, 1807);

Mutter, Amme und Kind, in der Geschichte Herrn Leopold Kerkers, 2 volumes, anonymous (Berlin, 1808-1809);

Briefe und Erzählungen, 2 volumes (Vienna, 1808);

Predigten fürs Zeitbedürfnis, gehalten seit Glogaus Belagerung (Breslau, 1808);

Sammlung von Traureden (Breslau, 1808);

Dritter Anhang zu seinen Predigten, neun Predigten und Predigten fürs Zeitbedürfnis (Breslau, 1817).

Johann Timotheus Hermes, who also wrote under the anagrammatic pseudonyms Heinrich Meister and T. S. Jemehr, established his place in literary history with *Sophiens Reise von Memel nach Sachsen* (Sophie's Trip from Memel to Saxony, 1769-1773), the first novel of German family life as well as the first German psychological novel. Christoph Martin Wieland praised it as a work unique in its concern with problems of human happiness. Swollen to four thousand pages by its third edition in 1778, *Sophiens Reise von Memel nach Sachsen* was one of the most widely read novels of the eighteenth century and quickly became a "Hausbuch" (a work considered an essential addition to home libraries) among the German bourgeoisie. Its six volumes did not usher the reader into a world of fantasy and high adventure among aristocrats but accurately portrayed conditions in Germany of that day. No other novel by Hermes approached the significance of this work.

Hermes was born on 31 May 1738 to Georg Vivigenz Hermes, a clergyman, and Lukrezia Hermes, née Becker, in Petznick, near Stargard in the province of Pomerania. He received his first education at home from his father, who was a disciple of Christian Wolff, the rationalist philosopher at the University of Halle. A tutor prepared him for the gymnasium, where he acquired an excellent knowledge of French and cultivated a lifelong love of books. Between 1756 and 1764 Hermes studied theology at Königsberg and was employed there and in Danzig as a tutor in

French and as a book auctioneer. During these years he immersed himself in the novels of Samuel Richardson and Henry Fielding. While teaching at a Ritterakademie (school for young aristocrats) in Berlin between 1764 and 1766 Hermes wrote his first novel, *Geschichte der Miss Fanny Wilkes, so gut als aus dem Englischen übersetzt* (The History of Miss Fanny Wilkes, Practically Translated from English, 1766). Although it is not a translation of an English novel, close parallels in the epistolary and episodic form as well as its sentimental tone make it appear to be. Miss Fanny does not appear in the story; the name in the title was intended only to attract readers, which it did with great success in Germany, France, and Holland.

The heroine is Jinny, a delicate and melancholy young woman. The hero is the widower Handsom, a mature man of virtue and sensitivity who proves to be too timid to profess his platonic love to Jinny. Jinny is kidnapped and wakes up in a house of prostitution. When she beholds her intended colleagues in the oldest profession she can only gasp, "Welch ein Anblick!" (What a sight!), but she must fall silent in shame when she discovers that her captors have chosen even less modest attire for her than for the others. Handsom, in rapidly failing health, rescues Jinny; he finally declares his love, just before lapsing into unconsciousness. A miraculous cure follows; but, as the lovers anticipate a life of marital bliss, fate steals their happiness through the revelation of a close blood relationship. All is conveyed in letters to, from, and between the characters. The collision of strict virtue with bold depravity results in a heavy dose of trivial pathos.

Hermes became a field chaplain to a regiment in Lüben in 1766; three years later he was made chaplain at the royal court as well as superintendent and ranking Protestant pastor in the school system in Pless. Also in 1769 he married Christiane Caroline Bräuer and began to publish *Sophiens Reise von Memel nach Sachsen*. In 1772 he was called to Breslau to become pastor of the church of St. Mary Magdalene.

Most of the characters in *Sophiens Reise von Memel nach Sachsen* are average citizens rather than aristocrats. Sophie is an orphan who is taken in and treated kindly by a wealthy widow in Memel. The old lady has some important papers that she wants to send to her daughter in Dresden (Saxony); Sophie volunteers to carry them personally, despite the upheaval of the Seven Years' War, because she considers the jour-

Sophiens

Reife

von Memmel nach Sachsen.

Leipzig,
bey Johann Friedrich Junius. 1770.

Title page for Hermes' novel about the adventures of a young woman on a journey through Germany during the Seven Years' War

ney an opportunity to get to know the world and mankind. Her trip in a coach begins in safe and pleasant company, but conditions soon deteriorate. Sophie's many encounters range from sharing a hotel room "in allen Ehren" (in all honor) with the upright Mr. Less to falling into the hands of "eines liederlichen Studenten" (a disreputable student) and being spirited off to become the mistress of a Russian general. Though rescued time and again from her predicaments by "den ehrlichen Puff" (the honorable Mr. Puff), she rejects his offers of marriage because she has lost her heart to the unreciprocating Mr. Less. Egotistical behavior eventually causes Sophie to lose the support even of her old benefactress in Memel. In the end, however, she marries a schoolteacher, undergoes a radical personality change, and settles down as a model housewife.

An ideal heroine in the Age of Enlightenment would accept adversity as the will of God, as had the Swedish countess in a widely read novel by Christian Fürchtegott Gellert two decades earlier. But such an individual was becoming an improbable figure no longer quite in harmony with the postwar age. Hermes was the product of a transitional period, too young to identify with the rationalism of his father–that is, with Gotthold Ephraim Lessing and the true Age of Enlightenment–but too old to be gripped by the revolutionary fervor of the incipient Sturm und Drang movement. Sophie's problems are those of a new type of individual: she cannot adopt the rigid prescriptions of men twenty years her senior and accept the vicissitudes of fate with objectivity, but neither can she allow herself the freedom to reject the concept of a dominant fate and to encounter the world subjectively. She remains in the control of "eine reflektierende Redlichkeit" (an honesty contingent upon circumstances), which leads her to consider the relative material position of her conversational partner before giving an "honest" answer to a question. The objective, rationalistic spirit that pervades *Sophiens Reise von Memel nach Sachsen* is undermined when Hermes criticizes the "fromme Untätigkeit" (pious inactivity) of the Enlightenment. The author views favorably the more natural interpersonal behavior emerging in the last decades of the eighteenth century.

The clergyman Hermes had a didactic and moral purpose in writing. He believed, as did the writers of the flood of "moralische Wochenschriften" (moral weeklies) being published in England and Germany, that a virtuous life was indispensable to happiness. To this end he inserted in *Sophiens Reise von Memel nach Sachsen* and other novels countless moral observations on political, social, and religious topics: on marriage, education, the state of society, and the abuses of the day. Though stylistically superior to the tedious essays of the average moral weekly, his discourses nevertheless offer a surfeit of dry moralizing and theological rhetoric. The many lectures inserted into Sophie's letters in a tone of authority and superior knowledge suggest that Hermes himself was not free of vanity. The didacticism seems seriously out of place in an eighteen-year-old girl venturing out into the world for the first time. Everyone in the novel, regardless of age, speaks with the wisdom of long experience.

In the preface to the second edition of *Sophiens Reise von Memel nach Sachsen* (1776) Hermes complains of the difficulty in writing a "harmlosen" (innocent) and edifying novel which effectively communicates the moral truths he has discovered in his observation of humanity. In the twelfth letter of the first volume, Sophie's long epistle to the old lady in Memel outlines Hermes' approach to the novel: "Ich würde durch einen ganzen Roman das Interesse teilen, so daß man emsig lesen müßte, um zu erfahren, an wem das Herz am meisten Anteil nehmen soll; . . . ich würde die Geschichte der Personen dem Ansehen nach einschieben, aber hernach zeigen, daß ich vorherwusste, ich würde keiner dieser Erzählungen entbehren können; ich würde den Leser in der Meinung lassen, die als Hauptperson angegebne Person könne das nicht sein, wofür der Titel sie erklärt, und nur spät zeigen, daß eben sie die ganze Geschichte von Anfang an bis zu Ende wenden konnte; . . . ich würde auf die möglichst natürliche Art die Erwartung der Leser auf den entscheidenden Punkt führen–und sie dann schlechterdings täuschen und vielleicht nach einigen Jahren mich wieder mit ihnen auszusöhnen suchen, wenn etwa mein Herz sich . . . anders belehren ließe . . . " (For example, I would scatter the points of interest to the reader throughout a novel so that diligent reading would be required to select the character upon which the greatest affection should be bestowed; . . . I would appear to insert casually the life histories of certain individuals and later show that I knew beforehand that not one of these life stories could be dispensed with; I would allow the reader to believe that the character indicated as central in the title could not be such and then, only much later, show that he does indeed control the plot from beginning to end; . . . I would in the most natural way possible direct the expectations of the reader to a certain point, only to deceive him completely. After the passage of some years I would make it up to him, when my heart told me to do so. . .). The author's long list of tricks of the trade impresses one as the confessions of a trivial novelist. Nevertheless, such guidelines contributed to a successful formula, for publication figures indicate that the bourgeoisie much preferred *Sophiens Reise* to the great works of German literature contemporary with it. Hermes seemed little interested in aesthetic effect and chose the epistolary form for most of his novels because of his earlier success with it. There is no evidence of a preconceived plan of composition; instead, the letters are arranged almost arbitrarily, and the second does not necessarily respond to the first. Into his loose plot structure he inserted many episodes, usually with a didactic purpose. An example is the sudden introduction of the story of the seduction of a hitherto unmentioned housemaid, which appears to follow Richardson's account in *Pamela, or Virtue Rewarded* (1740).

Sophiens Reise von Memel nach Sachsen includes love songs and nature and religious poems; Johann Adam Hiller published a collection of these verses in 1779 which he had set to music, and one song, "Ich hab von ferne Herr deinen Thron erblickt" (From the Distance, Lord, I Have Seen your Throne) made its way into Protestant hymnals. A poem lampooning the aristocrats is clever and humorous: a servant girl ridiculed by her mistress finds revenge in writing and reciting a new story of the creation of man, with the emphasis on a fundamental distinction between noblemen and commoners. Prometheus, in Greek mythology the Titan who created human beings out of clay, now takes beer as his raw material. From the foam on top of his mug he creates the upper classes; he assumes that a second froth will appear, from which the lower social stratum can be formed. When none materializes and the aristocrats impatiently cry out "schaff Knechte!" (create servants!), Prometheus has to use the more substantial beer itself. Pronouncing the aristocrats "dumm" (stupid), this god of creation swears the working class to silence concerning its superior origin. Thus does Hermes explain the "verkehrte Welt" (topsy-turvy world), a perception that may have impressed itself upon him in his two positions as field chaplain to the common soldiers and as chaplain to the royal court.

The novels Hermes published after the third edition of *Sophiens Reise von Memel nach Sachsen* in 1778 did not approach the latter in popularity or significance. *Für Töchter edler Herkunft* (For Girls of Noble Origin, 1787), composed of letters and diary entries, is the tale of an impoverished young noblewoman who turns out to be the daughter of a secretly married priest. Maxims for proper behavior and the avoidance of moral pitfalls are the primary concern in the novel. *Manch Hermäon im eigentlichen Sinn des Worts* (Many a Hermes in the Actual Sense of the Word, 1788), influenced by the contemporary French author Jean-Jacques Rousseau, is a collection of stories about country girls who go to the city and fall into the hands of aristocrats whose "Lebensberuf " (life's calling) is the seduction of such innocents. Their fates occasion Hermes's moral observations. *Zween literarische Märtyrer und deren Frauen* (Two

Literary Martyrs and Their Wives, 1789) intimidated readers with the word *literarische*. The second edition with a new title sold better: *Meine, Herrn Grundleger, und unserer Frauen Geschichte* (My Story and the Story of Mr. Grundleger and Our Wives, 1798). Although it is not an epistolary novel, Hermes considered it his best work. The plot concerns two hardworking scholars: one progresses from schoolteacher to professor; the other, aided by influential friends, becomes a successful physician. Both are later beset by misfortune and descend to more modest levels. *Verheimlichung und Eil, oder Lottchens und ihrer Nachbarn Geschichte* (Concealment and Haste; or, The Story of Lottchen and her Neighbors, 1802) was published under the pseudonym T. S. Jemehr. Against the backdrop of the courtship of the chambermaid Lottchen and the pastor Ruhig, Hermes presents many episodes which point up the deplorable state of society. *Briefe und Erzählungen* (Letters and Narrations, 1808), Hermes' final work of fiction, contains three stories conveyed in letters. The principal theme is marriage between aristocrats and commoners.

Hermes was professor of dogmatics at the Gymnasium of St. Mary Magdalene and at St. Elisabeth's, as well as inspector of churches, from 1809 to 1814. He served as superintendent of schools from 1810 until 1817. Hermes received his doctorate in philosophy at the University of Breslau in 1803 and his doctorate in theology in 1816. His last years were spent in ill health; he died in Breslau on 24 July 1821.

References:

J. Buchholz, "Johann Timotheus Hermes' Beziehung zur englischen Literatur," Ph.D. dissertation, University of Marburg, 1912;

Johannes Carl Leo Cholevius, *Die Verkehrssprache in Sophiens Reise von Memel nach Sachsen* (Königsberg: Dalkowski, 1873);

Gisela Elisabeth Kapaun, "The Role of the Fictive Readers in the Epistolary Novel of the 18th Century," Ph.D. dissertation, University of California, Los Angeles, 1985;

Konstantin Muskalla, *Die Romane von Johann Timotheus Hermes* (Breslau: Hirt, 1912);

Christoph Perels, "Georg Vivigenz Hermes: Nachricht von der Familie Hermes," *Lessing Yearbook*, 12 (1980): 175-184;

A. van Rinsum, "Der Roman 'Sophiens Reise von Memel nach Sachsen' von Johann Timotheus Hermes als geistesgeschichtlicher und kulturhistorischer Ausdruck seiner Zeit," Ph.D. dissertation, University of Marburg, 1949;

Klaus Schaefer, "Prometheus bei J. T. Hermes," *Weimarer Beiträge*, 17, no. 12 (1971): 169-173;

G. Schulz, "Johann Timotheus Hermes," *Jahrbuch der Schlesischen Friedrich Wilhelm Universität zu Breslau*, 6 (1961);

E. T. Voss, "Erzählprobleme des Briefromans, dargestellt an vier Beispielen des 18. Jahrhunderts," Ph.D. dissertation, University of Bonn, 1958;

Papers:

Letters by Johann Timotheus Hermes are in the Stadtarchiv Altona; the Staatsbibliothek Berlin; the Stadtbibliothek Breslau; the Goethe-Museum, Frankfurt am Main; the Staats- und Universitätsbibliothek Hamburg; the Universitätsbibliothek Leipzig; the Staatsbibliothek Munich; and the Lutherhalle Wittenberg.

Theodor Gottlieb von Hippel

(31 January 1741 - 23 April 1796)

Timothy F. Sellner
Wake Forest University

BOOKS: *Rhapsodien,* anonymous (Königsberg, 1757);

Das christliche Ehepaar: Dem Hippel- und Böckert-schen Hochzeitstage gewidmet, anonymous (Königsberg: Driest, 1760);

Das schöne Herz J. F. N., anonymous (N.p., 1760);

Galimafreen nach dem heutigen geschmack, anonymous (Königsberg: Kanter, 1761);

Gedanken über die Unzufriedenheit von H**W: Nebst Zuschrift, Vorrede und Motto. Zuschrift an Hrn. **, anonymous (N.p., 1761);

Makulatur zum bewusten Gebrauch, anonymous (Königsberg, 1762);

Auf die Abreise des Feldpredigers Preyß nach Potsdam, anonymous (N.p., 1763);

Rhapsodie, anonymous (Königsberg: Kanter, 1763);

Der Funckschen Gruft im Namen einiger Freunde gewidmet (Königsberg: Kanter, 1764);

Zur Verbindung seines Freundes R. mit Marianen, anonymous (N.p., 1764);

Der Mann nach der Uhr, oder der ordentliche Mann: Ein Lustspiel in Einem Aufzuge, anonymous (N.p., 1765; edited by Erich Jenisch, Halle: Niemeyer, 1928);

Freymäurerreden, anonymous (Königsberg: Kanter, 1768);

Die ungewöhnlichen Nebenbuhler: Ein Lustspiel in drey Aufzügen, anonymous (Königsberg: Kanter, 1768);

Auf die Frage: Ist es rathsam, Missethäter durch Geistliche zum Tode vorbereiten, und zur Hinrichtung begleiten zu lassen?, anonymous (Königsberg: Kanter, 1769);

An Herrn Schefner, an meinem Geburtstage, 1770, anonymous (N.p., 1770);

Geistliche Lieder, anonymous (Berlin: Haude & Spener, 1772);

Lieder für Freymäurer, anonymous (Königsberg: Kanter, 1772);

Über die Ehe, anonymous (Berlin: Voß, 1774; revised, 1776; enlarged, 1792; enlarged, 1793; edited by Wolfgang Max Faust, Stuttgart:

Painting by Agathe von Rüdgisch, presumed lost during World War II

Deutsche Verlags-Anstalt, 1972; reprint of fourth edition, Selb: Notos, 1977);

Pflichten des Maurers bey dem Grabe eines Bruders: Eine Freymäurer-Rede in der Loge zu den dreyen Kronen in Königsberg, as B. E------(Danzig: Flörke, 1777);

Lebensläufe nach aufsteigender Linie nebst Beylagen A, B, C, 4 volumes, anonymous (Berlin: Voß, 1778-1781);

Bedencken über die historisch kritische Beleuchtung der Frage: Hat die Preußische Ritterschaft das Recht ein beständiges Corps zu formiren, ihre immerwäh-

rende Deputirte zu halten und durch solche über allgemeine Landessachen Berathschlagungen anzustellen, und worauf gründet sich dasselbe?, anonymous (N.p., 1787);

Handzeichnungen nach der Natur, anonymous (Berlin: Voß, 1790);

Zimmermann der I. und Friedrich der II., as Johann Heinrich Friedrich Quitenbaum, Bildschnitzer in Hannover, in ritterlicher Assistenz eines Leipziger Magisters (London: Gedruckt in der Einsamkeit [actually Berlin: Lagarde], 1790);

Das Königsbergische Stapelrecht: Eine Geschichts- und Rechtserzählung mit Urkunden (Berlin: Lagarde, 1791);

Über die Mittel gegen die Verletzung öffentlicher Anlagen und Zierrathen, anonymous (Berlin: Voß, 1792);

Nachricht, die von K---sche Untersuchung betreffend: Ein Beytrag über Verbrechen und Strafen, anonymous (Königsberg: Nicolovius, 1792);

Über die bürgerliche Verbesserung der Weiber, anonymous (Berlin: Voß, 1792; edited by Ralph-Rainer Wuthenow, Frankfurt am Main: Syndikat, 1977); translated and edited by Timothy F. Sellner as *On Improving the Status of Women* (Detroit: Wayne State University Press, 1979); German version republished, edited by Juliane Dittrich-Jacobi (Vaduz: Topos, 1981);

Kreuz- und Querzüge des Ritters A bis Z: Von dem Verfasser der Lebensläufe nach aufsteigender Linie, 2 volumes, anonymous (Berlin: Voß, 1793-1794);

Nachlaß über weibliche Bildung (Berlin: Voß, 1801);

Biographie des Königl. Preuß. Geheimen Kriegsraths zu Königsberg Theodor Gottlieb von Hippel, zum Theil von ihm selbst verfaßt: Aus Schlichtegrolls Nekrolog besonders abgedruckt (Gotha: Perthes, 1801; reprinted, with epilogue by Wuthenow, Hildesheim: Gerstenberg, 1977);

Über Gesetzgebung und Staatenwohl: Nachlaß (Berlin: Voß, 1804; reprinted, Königstein: Scriptor, 1978);

Th. G. v. Hippel's sämmtliche Werke, 14 volumes (Berlin: Reimer, 1828-1839; reprinted, Berlin: De Gruyter, 1978).

Described by Ferdinand Josef Schneider in his 1911 biography as "die rätselhafteste und widerspruchsvollste Persönlichkeit in der deutschen Literatur" (the most puzzling and self-contradictory personality in German literature), Theodor Gottlieb von Hippel was both the quint-essential man of the eighteenth century and a writer whose work speaks to readers today with astonishing, almost uncanny relevance. Paradox abounds in his life and work. Hippel was a rationalist who abandoned the principles of reason when he felt that they interfered with the search for truth, and a devout Christian who struggled his entire life with the fact of death. He once wrote that he considered liars detestable and a lie one of the most heinous crimes; yet he published his works in the strictest anonymity, and his almost pathological insistence on the preservation of that anonymity often forced him into outright denials when he was confronted by those who suspected his authorship. His most famous work was a treatise on marriage, and he recommended the institution to all who would listen; but he remained a bachelor all his life. He gleefully pilloried secret societies in his writing, all the while remaining an active member of a Masonic lodge. Although confident, almost dictatorial, in his manner, he often complained to his closest friend, Johann Georg Scheffner, of hypochondria, melancholy, and fits of weeping. He upbraided others for their greed, but when called upon to defend himself against even his friends' charges of stinginess he pleaded utter bewilderment as to how he had acquired such a large fortune.

Hippel was born on 31 January 1741 in the small East Prussian town of Gerdauen to Melchior and Eleonore Thime Hippel. His father was a school principal with noble antecedents, although his forebears had allowed the patent of nobility to expire, and the family no longer included the prefix "von" in their surname. Their pietistic upbringing and the deep spiritual convictions of their parents were responsible for the decision of Hippel and his only brother, Gotthard Friedrich, to enter the ministry. Hippel enrolled at the University of Königsberg in the autumn of 1756, shortly before his sixteenth birthday, to study theology. By 1760 he had taken all of his preparatory courses for the degree, but he never completed his studies. That year he received an invitation from an acquaintance, a Russian lieutenant named Von Keyser, to accompany him on a political mission to Russia. Keyser's father was a vice admiral who lived in some splendor in Kronstadt (Hungary), and it was Hippel's sojourn in this household, more than anything else in an exceedingly illuminating journey, that brought about a radical change in his life. There he first came to know the world of polite society and met men not only of learning but also of influence and reputation. He returned home the next February in a state of crisis. Unable or unwilling to apply himself to the study of theology, he accepted a position as a tutor for a wealthy family in Königsberg. Contact for a second time with the manners and life of the rich–this time on a more intimate basis–exacerbated Hippel's crisis. Moreover, he fell in love with the daughter of his employer. Because of the difference between their stations such a love affair could only end unhappily, and Hippel was forced to relinquish not only his love but his tutorial position as well. According to Friedrich Schlichtegroll, who completed Hippel's autobiography (1801) after his death, Hippel resolved to become her equal someday in wealth and social position. From this time on he pursued his career with relentless energy. Worldly success, wealth, and reputation seemed to be his only goals; and in 1762 he returned to the university–this time to study law, a more useful vehicle for the attainment of his ends.

For a year and a half Hippel tolerated severe poverty to finish his degree. To improve his already pleasant speaking voice he took lessons in declamation. In 1765 he obtained a position as a lawyer in the Königsberg court of justice. There was little to hold him back in his career as a bureaucrat: he was practiced in manners, a tireless worker, a natural orator who often overpowered his opponents with his keenness of understanding and the brilliance of his logic, and a man who seemed born to lead. He rose quickly in the government of Königsberg from counselor of criminal affairs to city counselor, to director of the criminal court, and then to director of police. In 1780 he was appointed a member of the commission to oversee the introduction of Prussian state law; that same year, at thirty-nine, he was appointed governing mayor of Königsberg, the largest and most important city in East Prussia.

Hippel's first published work of any consequence was *Rhapsodie* (1763), a poem giving vent to his sentiments after the unfortunate love affair with his employer's daughter the previous year. It was followed by two short comedies in the French manner (1765, 1768) and a series of discourses on Freemasonry (1768). In 1772 he published *Geistliche Lieder* (Spiritual Songs), a collection of Christian hymns of a strongly pietistic bent; some of them have become a permanent part of Protestant hymnody in Germany. In 1774, the year in which Johann Wolfgang Goethe's *Die Leiden des jungen Werthers* (The Sorrows of Young Werther) appeared, Hippel pub-

Title page for the third edition of Hippel's treatise on marriage, which advocated equality of the sexes

lished his treatise *Über die Ehe* (On Marriage), a work which in some respects was hardly less of a literary sensation than *Die Leiden des jungen Werthers*; four editions were published before 1794. While the first and second (1776) editions follow tradition in their advocacy of the supremacy of the male in the marriage relation and contain some censorious comments on the behavior of females, the third edition of 1792 and the fourth of 1793 completely reverse this position and advocate the emancipation of women and equality between the sexes in marriage. The misogyny and disregard for the marriage bond that characterized Frederick II exerted a strong influence on Hippel's thinking and played a part in setting the tone of the first edition. Hippel's letters from this period reveal that he was willing to acknowledge only a few women to be entirely free from frivolity and superficiality and to be capable of true friendship as the eighteenth century conceived of it. Hippel's change in attitude appears to have resulted from several factors. First, as a lawyer he daily witnessed the injustice and prejudice to which women were subjected by the legal system. Second, along with the proclamations of the rights of man which accompanied the American and French revolutions, a lively debate had ensued concerning the rights of women as well; Hippel's work indicates that he had read the writings of Voltaire, Rousseau, Helvétius, Montesquieu, D'Holbach, Condorcet, and Talleyrand on the subject. Finally, although the French Revolution had led many to hope that the liberty and equality advocated by the Enlightenment would at last attain universal legal sanction, the French Constitution of 1791 had failed to grant equal rights to women even though it spoke grandiloquently of "universal" suffrage. Hippel thus came to believe that marriage–the most basic "social contract" and, like humanity itself, capable of continual improvement through reason–could not be perfected until true equality between the sexes had been achieved.

Like his treatises, Hippel's novels are a rambling hodgepodge of facts, anecdotes, quotations, sermonettes, panegyrics, and philosophical musings, liberally seasoned with a humor gently chiding and bitterly sarcastic by turns. His first, best, and most popular novel, *Lebensläufe nach aufsteigender Linie* (Biographies on an Ascending Line), published in four volumes from 1778 to 1781, has earned Hippel a niche in literary history as the chief German imitator of Laurence Sterne and the predecessor of Johann Paul Friedrich Richter (Jean Paul). Though derivative, intimidating in length, and exhausting in its plot digressions, the novel is not without literary merit. In accordance with Hippel's notion that history should be taught backwards, the narrator announces his intention of relating three generations of his family chronicle, beginning with himself and working back to his grandfather. In each case the death of the person is to stand at the beginning of the biography, his birth at the end.This monumental task was never completed, however, and the narrator never moves beyond the events of his own generation. The novel, like Hippel's treatises on legal and social issues, reveals the influence of Rousseau and Montesquieu, and it caused some sensation by revealing the basic tenets of his friend Immanuel Kant's philosophical system before the latter had published

any of his major works. Although *Lebensläufe nach aufsteigender Linie* contains passages of considerable beauty, and its historical value as a depiction of the situation of the Courland Germans of the period is unquestioned, its importance today lies mainly in its treasure of aphoristic wisdom on life and human institutions.

In 1792 Hippel addressed the question of the rights of women outside the marriage bond in *Über die bürgerliche Verbesserung der Weiber* (translated as *On Improving the Status of Women*, 1979). His most modern work, it and Mary Wollstonecraft's complementary work of the same year, *A Vindication of the Rights of Woman*, can be regarded together as the first complete manifesto of feminism. Where Wollstonecraft addresses herself to women, Hippel calls upon men to change their ways. Where Wollstonecraft perceives equality for women as dependent on a social revolution abolishing all ranks and classes, Hippel believes that change can be brought about more quickly by the application of right reason to the act of governing rather than to the institutions of government. For Wollstonecraft the sexes are inherently equal in all abilities, the difference deriving from the greater freedom of the men; for Hippel the human race consists of two equal but in many respects different parts, and only when the differences between the sexes, and not the sexes themselves, are exploited will the race achieve its divinely ordained goal: the perfection of humanity.

Hippel's second novel, published in 1793-1794 at a time when he had long since abandoned belles lettres for the demands of life as a bureaucrat, was less successful than the first. As suggested by the title, *Kreuz- und Querzüge des Ritters A bis Z* (Crusadings of the Knight A to Z), the work is a satirical novel after the manner of *Don Quixote* (1605-1615) which takes as its target the lodges and secret societies of the day.

The death of Frederick II and the accession of his nephew, Frederick William II, in 1786 brought no change in the favorable light in which Hippel was viewed at the Prussian court in Berlin. During a short stay in Königsberg in 1786 Frederick William II personally decorated him for his services to the state; later that year he was promoted to the titular office of city president, which he held until his death. In 1790, by means of secret negotiations with the court of the Holy Roman Emperor, Joseph II, he received the right to renew the hereditary patent of nobility for himself and his relatives, a piece of snobbery

Engraving of Hippel by F. Bolt, 1802

for which he was roundly criticized by his middle-class friends. Three years later he was called to Danzig by his friend Baron von Schrötter, the highest civil servant in the province of Old Prussia, to supervise the incorporation of Danzig into the political organization of Prussia after the second partition of Poland. Although Hippel accomplished this task with distinction, the change in his strictly regulated way of life and the pressures of the assignment were disastrous to his health. His constitution became permanently weakened, and before he left Danzig in March 1794 he had developed an infection which caused him to lose an eye. When he died in Königsberg on 23 April 1796 of, according to the official reports, "dropsy of the chest," his estate, not including his mansion in Königsberg, amounted to 140,000 talers, a sum of staggering proportions for the time.

The greater part of Hippel's legal writings treats aspects of the local Prussian code; a much more comprehensive work on legislation and the rights of states, *Über Gesetzgebung und Staatenwohl* (On Legislation and the Commonweal), remained a fragment and was not published until 1804. Hippel's complete works were published from 1828 to 1839 in fourteen volumes; the first and only reprinting occurred in 1978 as a consequence of renewed interest in his writings on the emancipation of women. A thorough examination of the complete body of his writings, however, reveals Hippel as a novelist and poet of great wisdom and often touching sensibility; as a political thinker who accepted only those forms of government which guaranteed liberty, equality, fraternity, justice, peace, respect for the individual, and intellectual, moral, and material progress; and finally as an emancipator whose ideas still challenge the late twentieth century to rethink its deeply held notions about the relationship between the sexes.

Biographies:

Ferdinand Josef Schneider, *Theodor Gottlieb von Hippel in den Jahren 1741-1781 und die erste Epoche seiner literarischen Tätigkeit* (Prague: Taussig & Taussig, 1911);

Josef Kohnen, *Theodor Gottlieb von Hippel, 1741-1796: L'homme et l'oeuvre,* 2 volumes (Bern: Lang, 1983).

References:

Léon Abensour, *Histoire générale du féminisme, des origines à nos jours* (Paris: Librairie Delagrave, 1921), pp. 180-192;

Hamilton Beck, "Hippel and the Eighteenth-Century Novel," Ph.D. dissertation, Cornell University, 1980;

Beck, "Tristram Shandy and Hippel's *Lebensläufe nach aufsteigender Linie,*" *Studies in Eighteenth-Century Culture,* 10 (1981): 261-278;

Ruth Dawson, "The Feminist Manifesto of Theodor Gottlieb von Hippel (1741-96)," *Amsterdamer Beiträge zur neueren Germanistik,* 10 (1980): 13-32;

Franz Erdmann, *Theodor Gottlieb von Hippel: Über die Ehe. Eine literarhistorische und sprachliche Untersuchung* (Breslau: Hochschulverlag, 1924);

Robert Losno, *Theodor Gottlieb von Hippel, 1741-1796: Thèse d'État* (Paris, 1981);

Timothy F. Sellner, Introduction and Appendix to his translation of Hippel's *On Improving the Status of Women* (Detroit: Wayne State University Press, 1979), pp. 19-49, 219-221;

Helga Vormus, "Theodor Gottlieb von Hippel: *Lebensläufe nach aufsteigender Linie nebst Beilagen A, B, C.*: Eine Interpretation," *Etudes Germaniques,* 21 (January-March 1966), 1-16;

Fritz Werner, *Das Todesproblem in den Werken Theodor Gottlieb von Hippels* (Walluf: Sändig, 1973).

Papers:

Most of Theodor Gottlieb von Hippel's papers are believed to have been destroyed in World II.

Johann Georg Jacobi

(2 September 1740 - 4 January 1814)

John B. Rutledge
University of North Carolina at Chapel Hill

BOOKS: *Vindiciae Torquati Tassi* (Göttingen, 1763);

Der Tempel der Glückseligkeit (Mannheim, 1764);

Poetische Versuche, as J. G. J. (Düsseldorf: Stahl, 1764);

Leander und Seline, oder Der Paradeplatz, anonymous (Mannheim, 1765);

Programma de lectione poetarum recentiorum pictoribus commendanda (Halle, 1766);

Briefe von Herrn Johann Georg Jacobi (Berlin, 1768);

Briefe von den Herren Gleim und Jacobi, by Jacobi and Johann Wilhelm Ludwig Gleim (Berlin, 1768);

Zwey Gedichte (Halberstadt, 1768);

An den Herrn Canonicus Gleim (Halle, 1768);

An den Herrn Geheimenrath Klotz (Halle, 1768);

Abschied an den Amor (Halle, 1769);

An die Gräfinn von **** (Halberstadt, 1769);

Legende von dem Heiligen Hippolytus und dem Seliggesprochnen Gericus (Halberstadt: Groß, 1769);

Nachtgedanken (N.p., 1769);

Über den Apollo: An den Domherren von R (Halberstadt, 1769);

Die Winterreise (Düsseldorf, 1769);

Apollo unter den Hirten: Ein Vorspiel mit Arien. An dem Geburtsfeste Ihro Majestät des Königes von England den 4ten Junii 1770 aufgeführt (Halberstadt: Groß, 1770);

Zwei zu Düsseldorf gehaltene Predigten (Halberstadt: Groß, 1770);

Elysium: Ein Vorspiel mit Arien an dem Geburtsfeste Ihro Maiestät der Königinn aufgeführt von der Königlicher Schauspieler zu Hannover den 18ten Januar 1770 (Halberstadt: Groß, 1770);

An die Einwohner der Stadt Celle (Halberstadt, 1770);

Das Lied der Grazien: Dem Geburtstage des Herrn Canonicus Gleim gewidmet (Halberstadt, 1770);

Die Sommerreise (Halle: Hemmerde, 1770);

Sämmtliche Werke, 3 volumes (Halberstadt: Groß, 1770-1774; enlarged edition, 8 volumes, Zurich: Orell, 1807-1822);

Engraving after an 1807 portrait by Josef Zoll

Zween Briefe von Jacobi und Michaelis, Pastor Amors Absolution betreffend, by Jacobi and Johann David Michaelis (Halberstadt: Groß, 1771);

Die ersten Menschen (Halberstadt: Groß, 1771);

An Aglaia (Düsseldorf, 1771);

Von der Liebe gegen Gott (Düsseldorf, 1771);

Cantate, auf das Geburtsfest des Königs (Halberstadt: Groß, 1771);

An das Publikum (Halberstadt: Groß, 1771);

Schreiben eines Freydenkers an seine Brüder (Berlin, 1771);

133

Durch den Glauben gelangen wir zur Ruhe (Halberstadt, 1771);

Über die Wahrheit nebst einigen Liedern (Düsseldorf, 1771);

Warnung vor einem falschen Gottesdienst: Eine Predigt (Halberstadt, Groß, 1772);

Zween Briefe von Gleim und Jacobi. Des letzteren Oper: "Die Dichter" betreffend, by Jacobi and Gleim (Halberstadt: Groß, 1772);

Cantate am Charfreytage (Halberstadt: Groß, 1772);

Zwote Cantaten auf das Geburtsfest des Königs (Halberstadt: Groß, 1772);

Die Dichter, eine Ode (Halberstadt: Groß, 1772);

Die Dichter: Eine Oper, gespielt in der Unterwelt, gesehen von Jacobi (Halberstadt: Groß, 1772);

Über den Ernst (Halberstadt: Groß, 1772);

Über das von dem Herrn Professor Hausen entworfene Leben des Herrn Geheimenrath Klotz, anonymous (Halberstadt: Groß, 1772);

Der Schmetterling, nebst drey Liedern (Halberstadt: Groß, 1772);

Charmides und Theone, oder Die sittliche Grazie (Halberstadt: Groß, 1774);

Des Herrn Jacobi Allerley (Frankfurt am Main & Leipzig, 1777);

Lieder aus der Iris (Berlin, 1778);

Sämmtliche Werke, 3 volumes (Frankfurt am Main, 1779);

Johann Jacob Rousseau, Bürger von Genf: Eine karakteristische Anekdote des achtzehenden Jahrhunderts (Frankfurt am Main, 1779);

Nessir und Zulima: Eine Erzählung nach Raphael (Berlin & Leipzig: Decker, 1782);

Auserlesene Lieder, edited by Johann Georg Schlosser (Basel: Thurneysen, 1784);

Zwey Predigten zu Vaels bey Aachen gehalten (Breslau: Löwe, 1786);

Phädon und Naide, oder Der redende Baum: Ein Singspiel in zwey Aufzügen (Leipzig: Göschen, 1788);

Trauerrede auf Kaiser Joseph den Zweyten (Freiburg, 1790);

Theatralische Schriften: Nachtrag zu seinen sämtlichen Werken (Leipzig: Göschen, 1792)–includes *Die Wallfahrt nach Compostel: Lustspiel* and *Der Neujahrstag auf dem Lande: Vorspiel;*

Trauerrede auf Leopold II. (Freiburg: Satron, 1792).

OTHER: Luis de Góngora y Argote, *Romanzen: Aus dem Spanischen*, translated by Jacobi (Halle: Gebauer, 1767);

Iris: Vierteljahresschrift für Frauenzimmer, 8 volumes, edited by Jacobi (volumes 1-4, Düsseldorf, 1774-1775; volumes 5-8, Berlin: Haude & Spener, 1776-1777);

Taschenbuch von J. G. Jacobi und seinen Freunden, 4 volumes, edited by Jacobi and others (volumes 1-2, Königsberg: Nicolovius, 1795-1796; volumes 3-4, Basel, 1798-1799);

Beschreibung einiger der vornehmsten geschnittenen Steine mythologischen Inhalts aus dem Kabinette des Herzogs von Orleans, translated and annotated by Jacobi (Zurich, 1796);

Überflüssiges Taschenbuch für das Jahr 1800, edited by Jacobi (Hamburg: Perthes, 1800);

Taschenbuch für das Jahr 1802, edited by Jacobi (Hamburg: Perthes, 1802);

Iris, ein Taschenbuch, 11 volumes, edited by Jacobi (Zurich: Orell Füssli, 1803-1813).

PERIODICAL PUBLICATION: *Der Tod des Orpheus: Ein Singspiel in drey Aufzügen, Neues deutsches Museum*, (1790): 863ff.

Johann Georg Jacobi was an important figure of German belles lettres during the 1770s and 1780s. Although his poetry matured and developed beyond the anacreontic style in which he began, he has been unjustly seen as a frenchifying versifier in the style of Jean-Baptist-Louis Gresset and the Abbé de Chaulieu (Guillaume Amfrye). Although he experimented with several genres, Jacobi was most successful as a lyric poet whose self-description as a "little singer of small songs" seems quite accurate. His work falls into three phases: the youthful anacreontic phase; a more mature and serious phase beginning at about his thirty-fifth year, based on influence from Johann Wolfgang Goethe and a love affair with his cousin Caroline Jacobi; and the mature phase in Freiburg. While he wrote of ordinary things, his poems display smoothness and appropriateness of form; his language is polished, unforced, and euphonious. His strength is in putting into verse the gentler emotions and perceptions. Many of his poems have been set to music. He wrote several librettos for singspiels, a dramatic ancestor of the operetta. Acquainted with Enlightenment thought, Jacobi did not reject religion but preached a nondogmatic Christianity. The Sturm und Drang movement and, later, Romantics were alien to him. He knew personally many of the most important eighteenth-century figures of German literature, including Goethe and Christoph Martin Wieland. His literary almanacs *Iris* (1774-1777), the *Überflüssiges Taschenbuch* (Superfluous Almanac, 1800), and the second *Iris* (1803-1813) number among his major contributions to German literature.

Born into a well-to-do merchant family in Düsseldorf on 2 September 1740, Jacobi absorbed the atmosphere of Lutheran piety that filled his parents' home. His mother, Johanna Maria Fahlmer Jacobi, died when he was six years old. His father, Johann Konrad Jacobi, then married the twenty-year-old Maria Katharina Lausberg, a kind and selfless woman who was evidently loved and accepted by the children of the first marriage. Private tutors, usually theology students, were employed in the home, and Jacobi was sent to French schools; the household included a French governess as well. At fifteen Jacobi wrote a play in French. At eighteen he went to the University of Göttingen, where he studied theology before turning to the law. But the law was not to his taste, either. His friend and biographer J. A. von Ittner relates how Jacobi, finally receiving his father's permission to switch from law to humanities, threw his law textbook out the window. (It was caught by its next owner, who, by prearrangement, was waiting below.) Encouraged by the writer Christian Adolph Klotz, to the study of the classics and the modern languages. He wrote a Latin dissertation on Torquato Tasso (1763) and prepared for a career as a professor of literature.

In 1764 he published *Poetische Versuche* (Poetic Experiments), a small collection that included a translation from Dante. In 1766 he was called to Halle as a professor of philosophy and humanities. There he lectured on foreign literature and produced a translation of Luis de Góngora y Argote's romances (1767) which brought him his first critical attention and praise.

Jacobi was influenced by Laurence Sterne, whose simplicity and sensitivity he admired. Taking a cue from the episode in Sterne's *Sentimental Journey* (1768) in which Lorenzo and Yorick exchange snuffboxes as a sign of reconciliation and friendship, Jacobi bought a quantity of these boxes and distributed them to his friends. If the friends ever quarreled, one of them needed only to hold forth the snuffbox to remind the other of the duties of friendship. His enthusiasm for Sterne was so great that Jacobi was nicknamed "Toby."

Jacobi formed an important and lasting friendship with Johann Wilhelm Ludwig Gleim. A collection of their letters in mixed verse and prose, which was widely criticized for its expression of tenderness between men, was published

Jacobi in 1770; painting by Benjamin Calau (Gleimhaus, Halberstadt)

in 1768. In that same year Gleim procured a benefice for Jacobi in Halberstadt as a lay canon of a Protestant religious community. Jacobi used the required initiatory nighttime visit in the chapter commons to jot down his *Nachtgedanken* (Night Thoughts, 1769), which was not a parody of Edward Young's *Night Thoughts* (1742-1745) but rather a criticism of the German imitators of that work. In Halberstadt his literary acquaintances included Johann David Michaelis, Lorenz Benzler, Klamer Eberhard, Karl Schmidt, and Christoph Friedrich Sangershausen. The benefice gave him sufficient free time to write poetry. The excesses of his early period earned him criticism from Johann Jakob Bodmer, Heinrich Wilhelm von Gerstenberg, Georg Christoph Lichtenberg, and Friedrich Gottlieb Klopstock, who found his anacreontic love poetry too frivolous. The rationalist writer and critic Friedrich Nicolai thought Jacobi sufficiently ridiculous to skewer him as "Herr von Säugling" (Baron Suckling) in the novel *Das Leben und die Meinungen des Herrn Magister Sebaldus Nothanker* (The Life and Opinions of the Schoolmaster Sebaldus Nothanker, 1773-1776); Goethe also satirized him in two farces.

The poem *Abschied an den Amor* (Farewell to Love, 1769) marks a turning away from the decorative, frothy anacreontic poetry. His travelogues written in the manner of Sterne, *Die Sommerreise*

(The Summer Journey, 1770) and *Die Winterreise* (The Winter Journey, 1769), were widely reviewed by literary magazines. Both books are characterized by sentimentality which at this point replaces the anacreontic mode in his writing.

Jacobi's first dramatic attempt, *Elysium* (1770), a singspiel in the form of a poetic dialogue of the dead, was performed in Celle. His reputation grew with the publication of his collected works from 1770 to 1774. Through Sophie von La Roche he made the acquaintance of Wieland in 1771 and formed an important friendship: Wieland was one of the most enthusiastic defenders of the young Jacobi, although even he occasionally criticized his writing as trivial.

In 1774 Jacobi returned to Düsseldorf, where he came under the influence of more vital forces, particularly Goethe. With Wilhelm Heinse he edited *Iris*, a journal of cultural uplift for ladies, imparting lore of the Greek gods, current events, and the basic elements of literary theory. *Iris* also contained many of Jacobi's poems. The journal, a project designed to earn money, survived for eight volumes; after its demise, Jacobi contributed to Wieland's better-known *Der teutsche Merkur*. The Düsseldorf period produced his best poetry. His acquaintance with Goethe, whom he genuinely admired, and the love affair with his cousin Caroline Jacobi enabled his poetry to move from convention to confession and to feelings he had actually experienced.

Throughout his early career Jacobi struggled for financial success; he was engaged to Caroline Jacobi but did not marry her because of his precarious circumstances. His lot was enormously improved by a call to the University of Freiburg in 1784. The first Protestant professor at the university, he remained there for thirty years as a celebrated and popular professor of literature and philology. During this phase of Jacobi's life he was widely praised as lovable, kindhearted, and sociable; yet he also enjoyed the solitude of the forest and the garret. He stimulated his students by his explications of the Latin classics, which went beyond mere philological exegeses. He exercised his talents as a speaker by occasionally preaching in the nearby Protestant town of Emmendingen.

His home became an asylum for refugees from the French Revolution. He also found his French training useful during the Napoleonic occupation, when he represented his city to the French authorities. He represented the university at the funeral of the emperor Joseph II in 1790, delivering the funeral oration. Able at last to support a family, in 1791 he married Maria Ursula Müller, a country girl from the Black Forest who appears in his poetry as Naide. At the relatively late age of fifty-four he became the father of a son, whom he named for his younger brother, the philosopher Friedrich Heinrich Jacobi.

The Freiburg period, during which Jacobi was deprived of association with the most creative forces in German poetry, marked a less important phase in his literary career. The poetry of this period is one of reflection and taking stock; the role played by reason increases; the poet pays greater attention to the world outside the self.

Between 1795 and 1813 Jacobi edited other almanacs, including a revival of *Iris* and the *Überflüssiges Taschenbuch*, which offered contributions by Johann Paul Friedrich Richter (Jean Paul), Johann Heinrich Voß, Matthias Claudius, Gottlieb Konrad Pfeffel, Klopstock, Jens Immanuel Baggesen, and Johann Gottfried Herder. The poetry of his old age deals with friendship, love, nature, and God. During his later years, however, he was not an influential poet on the national scene.

The death of his son at age seventeen in 1811 broke Jacobi's spirit. Jacobi lived to see the victory of the German troops over Napoleon at the Battle of Leipzig in October 1813. His last poem, written on his deathbed, was a patriotic one.

Jacobi died on 4 January 1814. His funeral involved the entire university, with townsfolk participating as well. A girls' chorus led the procession, singing his somber poem "Am Aschermittwoch" (Ash Wednesday). His grave in the university cemetery was marked by a simple black cross.

Letters:

Ungedruckte Briefe von und an Johann Georg Jacobi mit einem Abrisse seines Lebens und seiner Dichtung, edited by Ernst Martin (Strasbourg: Trübner, 1874).

Biography:

J. A. von Ittner, *Leben Johann Georg Jacobi's: Von einem seiner Freunde* (Zurich: Orell, Füßli, 1822).

References:

Hermann Bräuning-Oktavio, "Johann Georg Jacobis 'Schreiben eines Freydenkers an seine

Chlor an Phyllis.

*Zwo Nachtigallen küßten sich;
Zwo Turteltauben hatten
Ihr zärtlich Spiel: da fandst du mich
In junger Myrthen Schatten.*

*Du fandst mich; u. ich war dir gut
Vor allen andern Hirten;
Du sangst; ich kränzte deinen Hut
Im Schatten junger Myrthen.*

*Zum Angedenken, wollen wir
Zween Myrthenbäume weihen:
Der großen Liebe diesen hier,
Und ihnen der getreuen.*

Manuscript for a poem by Jacobi, written on 22 December 1774 (from Gustav Könnecke, Bilderatlas zur Geschichte der deutschen Nationallitteratur, *1895)*

Brüder' (1771)," *Weimarer Beiträge*, 7 (1961): 694-738;

Walter Falk, "Die erste deutsche Begegnung mit Gongora [Gleim, Jacobi, Herder]," Germanisch-Romanische Monatsschrift, 17 (January 1967): 26-52;

Karl Goedeke, *Grundriss zur Geschichte der deutschen Dichtung* (Dresden: Ehlermann, 1910-1916), volume 4, part 1, pp. 667-671;

Carl Hammer, Jr., "Jacobi's Memorial to Rousseau," *Die neueren Sprachen*, new series 14 (1965): 280-283;

Robert Hassencamp, *Beiträge zur Geschichte der Brüder Jacobi: Die Beziehungen des Dichters J. G. Jacobi zu Sophie von La Roche* (Düsseldorf: Lintz, 1895);

Joseph Longo, *Laurence Sterne und Johann Georg Jacobi: Programmschrift* (Krems: Realschule, 1898);

Otto Manthey-Zorn, "Johann Georg Jacobis 'Iris,' " Ph.D. dissertation, University of Leipzig, 1905;

Ernst Martin and Wilhelm Scherer, "Über Johann Georg Jacobi," *Zeitschrift für deutsches Alterthum*, 20 (1876): 324-340;

Karl von Rotteck, *Gedächtnissrede auf Johann Georg Jacobi* (Freiburg, 1814);

Ursula Schober, *Johann Georg Jacobis dichterische Entwicklung* (Breslau: Maruschke & Berendt, 1938);

H. Soucek, "Johann Georg Jacobi: Lyrischer Stil und Vorbilder, " Ph.D. dissertation, University of Vienna, 1941;

H. A. Weisser, "Johann Georg Jacobis Singspiele," Ph.D. dissertation, University of Freiburg im Breisgau, 1922.

Papers:
Thirteen boxes of Johann Georg Jacobi's papers are held by the University Library of Freiburg.

Anna Louisa Karsch

(1 December 1722 - 12 October 1791)

Helene M. Kastinger Riley
Clemson University

BOOKS: *Freudige Empfindungen redlicher Herzen, die, wegen des verliehenen herrlichen Sieges dem höchsten Dank opferten, welchen Se. Königl. Majest. von Preußen den 5ten December 1757, bey Fröbelwitz, zwischen Neumarck und Lissa über die Österreichische große Armee erfochten haben: Beschrieben von Anna Louise Karschin, geb. Dürbachin, eines Schneiders Frau aus Glogau* (Glogau, 1757);

Zwei Oden auf den großen Brand in Glogau (Glogau: Günther, 1758);

Die gedemüthigten Russen (Glogau, 1758);

Siegesode Friedrich . . . (Glogau: Schweickhardt, 1758);

Friedrich der Beschützer und Liebenswürdige (N.p., 1759);

Den 3ten November 1760: Groß durch den Sieg des Königs bey Torgau, beschrieb Anna Louise Karschin, gebohrne Dürbachin (Glogau, 1760);

Die Spazier-Gaenge von Berlin (Berlin: Winter, 1761; reprinted, Berlin: Gesellschaft der Bibliophilen, 1921);

Der Einzug Friedrichs des Unüberwindlichen (Berlin: Winter, 1763);

Gesänge bey Gelegenheit der Feyerlichkeiten Berlins (Berlin: Winter, 1763);

Gesänge bey Gelegenheit der Feyerlichkeiten Berlins (Berlin, 1763)—contains different poems from the volume with the same title above;

An Gott . . ., anonymous (Berlin: Winter, 1763);

An den König (Berlin: Winter, 1763);

An Ihro Majestät die Königin . . ., anonymous (Berlin: Winter, 1763);

Ode bei dem jubelvollen Empfange der Königin, anonymous (Berlin: Winter, 1763);

Poetische Einfälle: Erste Sammlung (Berlin: Winter, 1764);

Auserlesene Gedichte, edited by Johann Georg Sulzer (Berlin: Winter, 1764; reprinted, Stuttgart: Metzler, 1966);

An Ihro Königliche Hoheit die Herzogin von Braunschweig in Charlottenburg (Berlin, 1764);

Moralische Neujahrswünsche (Berlin: Winter, 1764);

Einige Oden über verschiedene hohe Gegenstände (Berlin: Winter, 1764);

Kleinigkeiten (Berlin: Winter, 1765);

An . . . die . . . Fürstin von Anhalt-Dessau (N.p., 1767);

Dem Herrn Canonicus Gleim, anonymous (Berlin, 1767);

An die Prinzessin Friderica (Berlin: Decker, 1770);

Auf den Tod der jungen Elise (Berlin: Winter, 1770);

Lied der Clio (Berlin, 1771);

Auf Bielefelds Tod (Berlin, 1771);

Ein mütterlicher Traum (Berlin, 1771);

Auf die Geburtsfeier Ihro . . . Durchlaucht der Gemahlin des Prinzen Friedrich von Braunschweig-Wolfenbüttel (Berlin: Decker, 1772);

Gedichte auf die Huldigung in Neupreußen und auf die Anwesenheit der Königin von Schweden (Berlin, 1772);

Neue Gedichte (Mietau & Leipzig: Hinz, 1772);

Gesang auf die Eheverbindung des Kochischen Acteurs Herrn Henkens . . . mit Mademoiselle Schickin . . . den 12ten April 1772 (Berlin, 1772);

Versificiertes Allerley zum neuen Jahre (Berlin, 1773);

Dem fürstlichen Beylager des regierenden Landgrafen von Hessen-Kassel (Berlin: Decker, 1773);

An Ihro Majestät die Königin von Schweden bey der Geburtsfeyer des Prinzen Ferdinand Kgl. Hoheit, den 23. May 1773 (Berlin: Rellstab, 1773);

Lied an Prinz Heinrichs Königliche Hoheit in Rheinsberg (Berlin: Decker, 1776);

An die preußische Armee bey Eröffnung des Feldzuges 1778 (Berlin, 1778);

Lied an die Ankunft . . . Ferdinands (Berlin, 1779);

Beym heiligen Überreste des . . . Barez (Berlin, 1785);

Der . . . Ehegattin des . . . Chodowiecky (Berlin, 1785);

An die Helden des Alterthums, anonymous (Berlin, 1785);

Der Nachruhm, anonymous (Berlin: Decker, 1785);

Auf Leopolds Opfertod (Berlin: Decker, 1785);

Brief an den Herrn von Simmingsköld ueber den Tod Friederichs, regierenden Herzogs von Mecklenburg-Schwerin (Jena, 1785);
Allen Freunden Gleims, anonymous (Berlin, 1786);
Auf Friedrichs des Zweiten Tod (Berlin, 1786);
An die Sonne bey dem Leichenbegängnisse Friedrichs des Großen (Berlin: Decker, 1786);
Zur ersten Geburtsfeyer auf dem Thron, der regierenden Königin von Preußen gewidmet (Berlin, 1786);
Zuruf an den Fremdling beym Marmorsarge Friedrichs des Großen (Berlin: Decker, 1786);
Gedicht an die regierende Herzoginn von Würtemberg enthaltend die Bitte und den Wunsch vieler Tausenden (Frankfurt am Main, 1787);
Trostgesang für Neuruppin (Berlin, 1787);
Zuruf an Schubarts Liebhaber in der ganzen Welt (Frankfurt am Main, 1787);
Gedichte von Anna Louisa Karschin geb. Dürbach, nach der Dichterin Tode nebst ihrem Lebenslauff herausgegeben von ihrer Tochter, edited by Caroline Louise von Klenke (Berlin: Diterici, 1792);
Das Lied der Karschin: Die Gedichte der Anna Luise Karschin mit einem Bericht ihres Lebens, edited by Herybert Menzel (Hamburg: Hanseatische Verlagsanstalt, 1938);
Herzgedanken: Das Leben der "deutschen Sappho" von ihr selbst erzählt, edited by Barbara Beuys (Frankfurt am Main: Societäts-Verlag, 1981);
O, mir entwischt nicht, was die Menschen fühlen (Frankfurt am Main: Fischer, 1982).

OTHER: *Leipziger Musenalmanach aufs Jahr 1776,* contributions by Karsch (Leipzig: Schwicket, 1776), pp. 121-123, 148.

Anna Louisa Karsch, called "die Karschin" and "die deutsche Sappho" (the German Sappho) by her contemporaries, received international acclaim during her lifetime and was viewed as a social and intellectual phenomenon. Born near Schwiebus, Silesia, on 1 December 1722, the daughter of the peasant and pubkeeper Christian Dürbach, she received no formal education and lived in poverty first with her parents, then in two successive marriages. Her inquisitive mind, a quick and sometimes caustic wit, and the unusual gift of being able to create poems extemporaneously on virtually any subject proposed to her helped to make her so famous that in 1785 a marble monument was erected depicting her, in Greek attire and with lyre in hand, as "Die

Anna Louisa Karsch; painting by K. Christian Kehrer, 1791 (Gleimhaus, Halberstadt)

deutsche Sappho." At the height of her career she dined with nobles, kings, and princes as the first German woman to earn her livelihood as poet. Frederick II summoned her to Sans-Souci for an audience and a reading of her work, although he had her poems first translated into French because he disliked the German language.

Much of Karsch's poetry falls into the category of Gelegenheitsdichtung (occasional writing), poems in honor of special occasions such as weddings or births or to commemorate significant events and people. She delivered many of these poems orally on an impromptu basis, and her benefactors often delighted in attempting to find a subject that would render her speechless. Her fame attests that they were unsuccessful.

An excellent example of her acute perception and extraordinary linguistic skill is the poem "Das Harz-Moos" (The Harz Moss), prompted by Baron Spiegel zum Diesenberg, who showed her some moss he had collected during a trip to the Harz mountains and requested her lyrical comment. With its emphasis on the rational description of a common object and the attempt to imbue it with symbolic meaning, the poem is an early forerunner of the Ding-Gedicht (thing poem), a genre made famous much later by Conrad Ferdinand Meyer and Rainer Maria Rilke. Karsch begins by establishing the existence of a structural hierarchy in God's creation: some things in nature are great, impressive, and powerful; others are inconspicuous, plain, and homely. The moss belongs to the class of seemingly insignificant items. Karsch continues by examining the plant carefully: it has intricately detailed branches like the great cypress trees and is full of pink gemmae–little buds sprinkled through the moss like the blush arising on a maiden's cheeks when she meets the gaze of a young man. With this comparison the symbolic connection has been made between moss and maiden, two apparently insignificant and modest living things in a world of superlatives. Yet Karsch reserves for them the ultimate triumph: while other and more splendid flowers wither and die in the harshness of winter, the inferior moss survives even deep under the snow; similarly, though Karsch's art has had to serve in praise of those who hold her in contempt, she–unlike her socially superior patrons–has achieved immortality through her own efforts. The poem concludes:

Wie ähnlich ist es mir! tief lag ich unter Gram
Viel schwere Jahre lang, und als mein Winter kam,
Da stand ich unverwelkt und fieng erst an zu
    grünen.
Ich muste, wie das Moos, dem Glück zum weichen
    Tritt,
Dem Thoren zur Verachtung dienen.
Einst sterb ich! Doch mein Lied geht nicht zum
    Grabe mit!

(How it is so like me! I, too, lay under gloom
Of grief so many years, and when my winter came,
I stood unwithered yet and only rose to bloom.
I cushioned softly, just like moss, the step of luck
    and fame,
And served the scorn of fools for raw contempt.
Some day I'll die! But from the grave my song will
    be exempt!).

"Das Harz-Moos" reveals her gift of treating an uninspiring subject on command with poetic insight and prosodic skill. It also shows Karsch's social awareness and her pride in her own accomplishment.

The many years of deprivation to which she refers in the poem are described in several long letters she wrote in 1762 to Johann Georg Sulzer, professor of aesthetics in Berlin. She seems to have felt unwanted at home, especially after her father died and her mother remarried. The most significant years of her childhood, from 1728 to 1732, were spent in Poland with her great-uncle, a widower with no children of his own who spent considerable time with his niece and taught her to read and write. This time span proved to be the happiest of her childhood and provided her with the skills she later needed for survival. After her return home she was hired out as a maidservant and forced to perform duties beyond the physical abilities of a twelve-year-old. Rebelling against her treatment, she ran away and returned home, where she was unwelcome. In 1738 her mother arranged her marriage to a weaver named Hirsekorn, with whom she soon had two sons. The marriage was a disaster, no doubt in part because Louisa was not the submissive, patient woman an honest man had a right to expect in those days. Karsch later described the marriage in terms of a battle between a conquering soldier and a woman being raped: "Ohne Regung, die ich oft beschreibe, / Ohne Zärtlichkeit ward ich zum Weibe, / Ward zur Mutter! Wie im wilden Krieg, / Unverliebt ein Mädchen werden müßte, / Die ein Krieger halb gezwungen küßte, / Der die Mauer einer Stadt erstieg" (No oft-described emotion, no caress, / Made me a wife; / Nor even tenderness / A mother! But as in raging battle's thrall, / A maid is kissed, unyielding still, / To th' warrior's demand and will, / Who overran the city's wall, / So did I learn of woman's call). In 1748 Hirsekorn demanded a divorce, and Louisa was the first woman whose marriage was dissolved under the new divorce law instituted by Frederick II.

Pregnant with their third child and virtually penniless, she was put on the streets while Hirsekorn retained their sons and her dowry. Even so, she was jubilant; but her freedom was of short duration. At her mother's insistence she married a tailor named Karsch in 1749. Her new husband turned out to be an alcoholic who spurned work and squandered every penny. The destitute couple had four children, of whom the two youngest daughters soon died. The young mother was forced to cook water mixed with some flour for nourishment. "Nimmer soll es meine Seele vergessen, wie tief herunter ich gesunken und wie hoffnungslos mein Zustand war" (Never shall my soul forget how deep I had sunk and how hopeless my condition was), she wrote later. Her poem "Der Winter hauchet Frost" (Winter's Chill) describes the penury of those days.

Yet from this want her spirit arose stronger. She began to write verses to commemorate the festive occasions of more fortunate citizens and was rewarded with small gifts, books, and invitations to table. Soon she produced her songs on a daily basis, flattering the pride of her benefactors and astonishing guests with her ability to create "instant poetry." Her fame spread even farther when a grateful postmaster, whose wedding she had commemorated, had the poem printed. She wrote verses to proclaim Frederick's victories, and they, too, were published. On 13 May 1758 a fire devastated the town of Glogau. Karsch, moved by the experience, wrote "Der Tag des Schreckens in Glogau" (The Day of Terror in Glogau). The poem bears a certain resemblance to Friedrich Schiller's "Das Lied von der Glocke" (The Song of the Bell, 1800) in its descriptive phrases and gripping narrative. It was published by the bookseller Heinke and established her fame as a poet.

Increasingly, she enjoyed the patronage of nobility. Her husband being an embarrassment and a second divorce being impossible, the tailor was inducted into the army in 1760 with the help of Louisa's influential friends. She never saw him again. In 1761 her son was placed in foster care, and Karsch moved to Berlin with her daughter Caroline under the protection of Baron von Kottwitz (she gratefully immortalized him with one of her best-known laudatory poems). Karsch soon became the darling of high society. She was received by the rich and famous, counted the foremost poets of the time among her friends (Goethe visited her on 18 May 1778, during his only trip to Berlin), and married her daughter off to a nobleman. Frederick II granted her an audience on 11 August 1763. When her biting sarcasm and poignant wit targeted the foibles of the ruling class, she enjoyed the license of a court jester.

While the occasional poems established her renown and form the largest body of her work, Karsch possessed a truly innovative poetic gift that was free from the strict prosodic forms of her time. Relatively few studies, however, have explored the poems she wrote in dialect, a genre that gained critical recognition and popularity only in the twentieth century. In "Schlesisches

Etching of Karsch by G. F. Schmidt, 1763

Bauerngespräch" (Silesian Peasant Talk) the cares and fears as well as the simple pleasures of Silesian peasants are depicted in dialogue form. Far from emulating contemporary portrayals of the peasant as a ridiculous, ignorant, and unrefined figure, Karsch gives the lowest class the status that, in her view, it deserves. As provider of food and supplier of troops and horses, the peasant is vital to the nation's well-being and defense. She describes what no other writer of her time knew from such vivid personal experience: the daily life, character, and speech of the unappreciated populace.

The free verse and flowing rhythm of her poem "Die Abendmahlzeit auf dem Lande" (Dinnertime in the Country) also seem quite modern. She contrasts the natural simplicity of a country-style dinner with the affectation and pretense of a princely feast:

> Freund, nicht in fürstlichen Sälen
> Bei dem glattsteinigten Tisch,
> Bedeckt mit köstlicher Leinwand,
> Wohnt das Vergnügen allein.
> Auch im kleinräumichten Hause,
> Gebaut nach ländlicher Art,

Auf schlechtem, reinlichem Zwillich.
Mit *einer* Schüssel besetzt,
Schmeckt dem nicht wählenden Gaumen
Die ungekünstelte Kost . . .

(Friend, not in princely halls
At smooth-polished tables,
Covered with exquisite linen,
Reigns pleasure alone.
Also in the tiniest homestead,
Built in the country style,
On clean, homespun cotton.
Set with *one* dish,
The nondiscriminating palate delights
In the simplest of fares. . .).

The enjambment, free verse, and flowing speech rhythms–all uncharacteristic of the restrictive prosody of her time–give this poem an innovative tone. Like many of her poems it is contrastive in structure and seeks to dispel class prejudice.

Many contemporaries sought to imitate her "naturalness" by choosing countrified or commonplace subjects for their lyric production. In the aftermath of her success with lyrics on certain foods–coffee in "Der Winter hauchet Frost," fish in "Die Abendmahlzeit"–many wrote poems on mundane subjects such as steak, potatoes, fruit, and tea. Virtually none achieved the delicate balance of simplicity and poetic finesse that characterizes her "Lob der schwarzen Kirschen" (Praise of the Black Cherry). Karsch's poems do not degenerate into mere descriptions of common things; she abstracts from them a symbolic value common to specific human situations or experiences. Her letter to Karl Ludwig von Knebel shows, in her sensitive critique of an ode he had sent her for comment, that she was far more aware of the basic rules of prosody than has generally been assumed; and a letter to her friend Johann Wilhelm Ludwig Gleim contains, under the heading "Den 22. Juny 1761," one of the most tender and touching love poems ever written by a woman.

Despite her success she frequently encountered prejudice against her class and sex. Many of her poems contain scathingly sarcastic rebuttals to slights and insults from her social superiors. When the king reneged on his promise to build her a house and instead sent her two coins, she sent them back with the note: "Zwei Taler gibt kein großer König, / Und sie erhöhen nicht mein Glück. / Nein, sie erniedern mich ein wenig, / Drum send ich sie zurück!" (Two talers gives no king so great, / And they don't raise my

cheer. / No, they do rather denigrate, / So I'll return them here!). Amused by her pluck, in 1789 the king fulfilled his promise. A young man who showed excessive pride in his noble lineage received the following comment in his album:

Aus hocherhobenem Stamm entstehn,
Vornehm geboren sein, ist Zufall nur zu nennen;
Selbst seines Stammes Ruhm erhöhn,
Durch eigenes Verdienst sich Glanz verschaffen
    können,
Mit einem Herzen gut und schön,
Auf karg beblümten Fleißesbahnen,
Dies übertrifft den Glanz von sechzehn grauen
    Ahnen.

(To spring from lofty family tree,
Highborn, counts but as chance;
Yourself the splendor of family,
By merit to enhance,
On paths of sober industry,
With a kind heart that beauteous be,
Exceeds the gilded ancestry of sixteen graying
    grands.).

Karsch died in Berlin on 12 October 1791. Her daughter, Caroline von Klencke, and her granddaughter, Helmina von Chézy, also became poets.

All editions of Karsch's work emphasize her occasional and laudatory poems. Those poems assured her phenomenal rise in society, and the flattered recipients assured their publication; yet they show only a small aspect of Karsch's poetic skill, and frequently not the best. Johann Gottfried Herder praised her many original traits as the true contribution of her work. She was one of the first "Mundartdichter" (dialect poets), popularized free verse, and made the life and concerns of peasants an acceptable topic for serious poetry.

Letters:
Die Karschin: Friedrichs des Großen Volksdichterin. Ein Leben in Briefen, edited by Elisabeth Hausmann (Frankfurt am Main: Societäts-Verlag, 1933);
Reinhard M. G. Nickisch, "Die Frau als Briefschreiberin im Zeitalter der deutschen Aufklärung," in *Wolfenbütteler Studien zur Aufklärung*, edited by G. Schulz, volume 3 (Wolfenbüttel: Jacobi, 1976), pp. 49-51.

References:
Erna Arnhold, *Goethes Berliner Beziehungen* (Gotha: Klotz, 1925), pp. 7-10;

Ludwig Achim von Arnim, "Französisches Theater in Berlin," *Monatliche Beiträge zur Geschichte dramatischer Kunst und Literatur*, 1 (October-December 1827): 192-194;

Barbara Beuys, *Familienleben in Deutschland* (Reinbek: Rowohlt, 1980);

Gisela Brinker-Gabler, *Deutsche Dichterinnen vom 16. Jahrhundert bis zur Gegenwart: Gedichte und Lebensläufe* (Frankfurt am Main: Fischer, 1979), pp. 134-141, 416;

Helmina von Chézy, *Aurikeln: Eine Blumengabe von deutschen Händen*, volume 1 (Berlin: Dunker & Humblot, 1818), pp. 27-29;

Wilfred Franz, "Ein unbekannter Brief Goethes an Franz Graf von Waldersee: Mit biographischen Erläuterungen, zwei unveröffentlichten Gedichten der Karschin und zwei Portraits," *Jahrbuch des Freien Deutschen Hochstifts* (1976): 53-81;

Johann Wilhelm Ludwig Gleim, "Am Geburtstage der Anna Louise Karschin: Den 1. December," *Der Teutsche Merkur*, 3 (1798): 379;

Johann Gottfried Herder, "Gedichte von Anna Louisa Karschin, herausgegeben von C. L. v. Klenke, geb. Karschin. Berlin. 2. Auflage. 1797," in *Herders Sämmtliche Werke*, edited by Bernhard Suphan and others, volume 20 (Berlin: Weidmann, 1880), pp. 269-276;

Herder, "Sappho und Karschin," in *J. G. v. Herders sämmtliche Werke*, edited by I. F. Heyne, volume 18 (Carlsruhe: Bureau der deutschen Classiker, 1821), pp. 136-142;

Johann Kaspar Lavater, *Physiognomische Fragmente zur Beförderung der Menschenkenntniß und Menschenliebe*, volume 3 (Winterthur: Steiner, 1787), p. 312;

I. Molzahn, "Die Karschin: Eine 'Schlesische Nachtigall,'" *Schlesien*, 10 (1965): 76-80;

Franz Muncker, *Anakreontiker und preußisch-patriotische Lyriker: Hagedorn. Gleim. Uz. Kleist. Ramler. Karschin* (Stuttgart: Union Deutsche Verlagsgesellschaft, 1895);

Otto Pniower, *Goethe in Berlin und Potsdam* (Berlin: Mittler, 1925), pp. 1, 30, 32, 60-66;

Helene M. K. Riley, *Die weibliche Muse: Sechs Essays über künstlerisch schaffende Frauen der Goethezeit* (Columbia, S.C.: Camden House, 1986), pp. 1-25, 181-184, 215-218.

Heiner Schmidt, *Quellenlexikon der Interpretationen und Textanalysen*, volume 4 (Duisburg: Verlag für Pädagogische Dokumentation, 1985), p. 252;

Heidi Maria Singer, "Leben und Zeit der Dichterin A. L. Karschin," Ph.D. dissertation, City University of New York, 1983;

F. von Zobeltitz, *Liebes von der alten Karschin* (Langensalza, 1926).

Papers:

Manuscripts and letters by Anna Louisa Karsch are at the Gleimhaus in Halberstadt and the Stadtbibliothek Berlin.

Ewald von Kleist
(7? March 1715 - 24 August 1759)

Christoph E. Schweitzer
University of North Carolina at Chapel Hill

BOOKS: *Der Frühling: Ein Gedicht,* anonymous (Berlin: Voß, 1749); enlarged as *Der Frühling: Ein Gedicht. Nebst einem Anhang,* anonymous (Berlin: Voß, 1750); enlarged as *Der Frühling: Ein Gedicht. Nebst einem Anhang anderer Gedichte von demselben Verfasser,* anonymous (Zurich: Heidegger, 1751);

Gedichte von dem Verfasser des Frühlings, anonymous (Berlin: Voß, 1756)–includes revised version of "Der Frühling";

Ode an die Preußische Armee, anonymous (N.p., 1757);

Neue Gedichte vom Verfsser des Frühlings, anonymous (Berlin: Voß, 1758)–includes *Seneka ein Trauerspiel*;

Ciβides und Paches in drey Gesängen von dem Verfasser des Frühlings, anonymous (Berlin: Voß, 1759);

Sämtliche Werke, 2 volumes, edited by Karl Wilhelm Ramler (Berlin: Voß, 1760);

Sämmtliche Werke nebst des Dichters Leben aus seinen Briefen an Gleim, 2 volumes, edited by Wilhelm Körte (Berlin: Unger, 1803);

Ewald von Kleist's Werke, 3 volumes, edited by August Sauer (Berlin: Hempel, 1881-1882; reprinted, Bern: Lang, 1968);

Sämtliche Werke, edited by Jürgen Stenzel (Stuttgart: Reclam, 1971);

Ihn foltert Schwermut, weil er lebt: Sämtliche Werke und ausgewählte Briefe, edited by Gerhard Wolf (Berlin: Buchverlag der Morgen, 1982; Frankfurt am Main: Fischer, 1983).

Ewald von Kleist achieved fame on the basis of *Der Frühling* (The Spring, 1749), a long poem that praises the beauty of nature and the simple life of the countryside. His works show a mixture of sentimental yearning for tranquillity and the glorification of steadfast virtue and heroic patriotism.

Ewald Christian von Kleist was born around 7 March 1715 in Zeblin, Pomerania (now Poland), to Joachim Ewald von Kleist and Juliane von Kleist, née von Manteuffel; the famous play-

Ewald von Kleist; painting by W. Hempel
(Gleimhaus, Halberstadt)

wright Heinrich von Kleist, born some sixty years later, was a distant relative. Kleist studied law in Königsberg from 1731 to 1735; he was also well read in the classical literatures, which were to serve as a model for many aspects of his works. The family was relatively poor, making military service an appropriate career for Kleist. He joined the Danish army in 1736; after Frederick II's accession to the throne in 1740, he entered the Prussian army in 1741. Kleist could not afford to marry his beloved, Wilhelmine von der Goltz, ultimately losing her to another man. As an officer he spent most of his time drilling recruits in Potsdam, an assignment he did not enjoy. He participated in the Second Silesian War from 1744 to 1745, was promoted to captain in

1749, and was in Zurich as a recruiting officer from 1751 to 1752.

Kleist found compensation for the lost Wilhelmine and for the monotony of garrison life in his writings. His hypochondria is evident in such lines as "Ich bin der Quaal, ich bin des Unglücks Sohn: / Der Tod allein kann meinen Kummer lindern" (I am the child of torment, the child of misfortune: / Death alone can assuage my sorrow). The Rococo poet Johann Ludwig Gleim, whom he met in 1743, was the first to encourage Kleist in his poetic efforts; Kleist cultivated Gleim's friendship in rather emotional language, as their extensive correspondence shows. Kleist received from Gleim the support he needed; Gleim, in turn, profited from Kleist's military knowledge for his *Preußische Kriegslieder in den Feldzügen 1756 und 1757 von einem Grenadier* (Prussian Songs of Wars in the Campaigns of 1756 and 1757 by a Grenadier, 1758). Soon Kleist's circle of literary acquaintances widened to include Karl Wilhelm Ramler, Salomon Geßner, and Gotthold Ephraim Lessing. The latter had Kleist in mind when he addressed his literary weekly *Briefe, die Neueste Litteratur betreffend* (Letters on the Most Recent Literature, 1759-1760) to "Herrn von N**." Lessing might also have been thinking of Kleist when he created the character Tellheim in *Minna von Barnhelm* (1767).

Kleist experimented with a variety of genres; some of these, such as the epigram, were in the tradition of the preceding Baroque period. He wrote anacreontic poetry, but its lightness did not suit his temperament. The predominant theme of his poems is praise of the countryside, a theme that goes back to Virgil and Horace and one that found expression in the eighteenth century in Albrecht von Haller's *Die Alpen* (The Alps, 1729) and James Thomson's *The Seasons* (1726-1730; translated into German by Barthold Heinrich Brockes as *Die Jahreszeiten*, 1745). Peculiar to Kleist is his subjective, sentimental approach to nature, an approach that makes him mourn again and again the lost harmony of man with nature and criticize the evils of the court and the city. Enjoyment of the beauty of nature—the forest, the flowers, wild and domesticated animals, the shepherd, and the farmer and his family—often yields to melancholic longing for an idyllic pastoral life. The reader learns as much about the author's sentiments and his meditations as about the natural setting that releases his varying moods. Good examples are "Das Landleben" (Life in the Countryside), "Sehnsucht nach Ruhe" (Longing for Peace), and especially *Der Frühling*. (Kleist repeatedly revised the latter poem; when it first appeared it had 460 lines, but only 398 lines make up the last version published during the author's life [1756]. It is written in Homeric hexameter but with anacruses—that is, each line begins with an unstressed syllable.)

Lessing's *Nathan der Weise* (Nathan the Wise, 1779) made blank verse (unrhymed iambic pentameter) *the* verse for the so-called classical dramas of Johann Wolfgang von Goethe and Friedrich Schiller. Kleist, though, had already used blank verse in *Cißides und Paches* (1759), with all masculine lines. The poem celebrates the heroism of two Macedonian warriors who are defending Lamia against the vastly superior force of the Athenians and who die rather than surrender. *Ode an die Preußische Armee* (Ode to the Prussian Army, 1757), in which Kleist directly addresses Friedrich II, is in the same heroic-patriotic vein. Kleist also tried his hand at a dramatic dialogue, *Seneka ein Trauerspiel* (Seneca, a Tragedy, 1758), which tells of the death of the Stoic philosopher and his wife. It is patterned on Klopstock's *Der Tod Adams* (The Death of Adam, 1757).

During the Seven Years' War Kleist was stationed in Saxony; he was promoted to major in 1757. His wish to prove his patriotism and courage in battle was fulfilled when he led a charge at the battle of Kunersdorf on 12 August 1759 and was wounded. He died from his wounds in nearby Frankfurt an der Oder on 24 August. As Lessing was to comment: "Er hat sterben *wollen*" (He *wanted* to die).

While *Der Frühling* remained popular into the nineteenth century, especially as a text used in schools, critics perceived weaknesses in Kleist's works. In *Laokoon* (1766) Lessing says that Kleist was conscious that *Der Frühling* consisted of an accumulation of arbitrarily selected landscape pictures and intended to give the poem a more sequential structure. Such a change, however, would have produced a different poem, one that no longer would arouse emotions. Schiller, in the landmark aesthetic essay *Über naive und sentimentalische Dichtung* (On Naive and Sentimental Poetry, 1795-1796), places Kleist among the sentimental authors and characterizes him as one "who flees that which is in himself and searches for what is forever outside of him; never is he able to overcome the bad influence of his century."

Manuscript for the beginning of a poem by Kleist (Gustav Könnecke,
Bilderatlas zur Geschichte der deutschen
Nationallitteratur, *1895)*

Letters:

Bruno Hirzel, "Briefe von Christian Ewald von Kleist an Johann Kaspar Hirzel," *Euphorion*, 18 (1911): 658-679; 19 (1912): 91-107.

References:

Hugo Aust, "Ewald von Kleist," in *Deutsche Dichter des 18. Jahrhunderts: Ihr Leben und Werk*, edited by Benno von Wiese (Berlin: Schmidt, 1977), pp. 98-114;

Robert M. Browning, *German Poetry in the Age of the Enlightenment: From Brockes to Klopstock* (University Park & London: Pennsylvania State Press, 1978), pp. 44-52;

Hans Christoph Buch, "*Dulce et decorum est pro patria mori*: Über Ewald Christian von Kleist," in *Begegnungen–Konfrontationen: Berliner Auto-*

ren über historische Schriftsteller ihrer Stadt, edited by Ulrich Janetzki (Frankfurt am Main & Berlin: Ullstein, 1987), pp. 9-25;

Buch, *Ut pictura poesis: Die Beschreibungsliteratur und ihre Kritiker von Lessing bis Lukács* (Munich: Hanser, 1972), pp. 116-143;

Yves Carbonnel, "Les tourments d'un soldat poète: Ewald von Kleist (1715-1759)," *Cahiers d'études germaniques*, 3 (1979): 45-63;

Hans Guggenbühl, "Ewald von Kleist: Weltschmerz als Schicksal," Ph.D. dissertation, University of Zurich, 1948;

Johannes Haußleiter, "Ewald von Kleist und Seneca," *Euphorion*, 54 (1960): 442;

Erhard Hexelschneider, "Noch einmal: A. N. Radiščevs 'Žuravli' nach Ewald von Kleist. Zu einem Berührungspunkt zwischen Radiščev,

Kleist und Herder," *Zeitschrift für Slawistik*, 29, no. 4 (1984): 511-521;

Renate Körner, "Die russische Rezeption von Ewald von Kleists Fabel 'Der gelähmte Kranich,'" in *Festschrift Alfred Rammelmeyer*, edited by Hans-Bernd Harder (Munich: Fink, 1975), pp. 111-122;

Bodo Lecke, *Das Stimmungsbild: Musikmetaphorik und Naturgefühl in der dichterischen Prosaskizze 1721-1780* (Göttingen: Vandenhoeck & Ruprecht, 1967), pp. 49-58;

Andreas Müller, *Landschaftserlebnis und Landschaftsbild: Studien zur deutschen Dichtung des 18. Jahrhunderts und der Romantik* (Stuttgart: Kohlhammer, 1955), pp. 34-37;

Brigitte Peucker, "The Poem as Place: Three Modes of Scenic Rendering in the Lyric," *PMLA*, 96 (1981): 904-913;

Werner Rieck, "Ewald von Kleist–Versuch einer Positionsbestimmung," *Kwartalnik neofilologiczny*, 23 (1976): 383-392;

August Sauer, "Briefe über den Tod Ewald von Kleists," *Archiv für Litteraturgeschichte*, 11 (1882): 457-483.

Papers:

Most of Ewald von Kleist's papers are in the Gleimhaus, Halberstadt.

Friedrich Gottlieb Klopstock

(2 July 1724 - 14 March 1803)

Beth Bjorklund
University of Virginia

BOOKS: *Der Messias: Ein Heldengedicht*, anonymous (Halle: Hemmerde, 1749); enlarged as *Der Messias: Erster Band*, anonymous (Halle: Hemmerde, 1751; reprinted, edited by Eberhard Haufe, Berlin: Union, 1975); enlarged as *Der Messias*, 2 volumes, anonymous (Copenhagen: Lillie, 1755);

Oden (Zurich, 1750);

Ode an Gott (N.p., 1751);

Ode an Ihre Majestät Friedrich V. König in Dännemark und Norwegen (Copenhagen, 1751);

Ode an den König (Copenhagen, 1752);

Drey Gebete, eines Freygeistes, eines Christen und eines guten Königs, anonymous (Hamburg: Bohn, 1753);

Nachricht von des Messias neuer correcter Ausgabe, anonymous (Copenhagen, 1753);

Psalm, anonymous (Hamburg: Bohn, 1753);

Der Tod Adams: Ein Trauerspiel, anonymous (Copenhagen & Leipzig: Pelt, 1757); translated by Robert Lloyd as *The Death of Adam: A Tragedy. In Three Acts. From the German of Mr. Klopstock* (London: Printed by Dryden Leach for T. Becket and P. A. de Hondt, 1763); German version edited by Henning Boetius (Stuttgart: Reclam, 1973);

Geistliche Lieder, 2 volumes, anonymous (Copenhagen & Leipzig: Pelt, 1758-1769);

Fragmente aus dem zwanzigsten Gesang des Messias: Als Manuskript für Freunde, anonymous (N.p., 1764);

Salomo, ein Trauerspiel (Magdeburg: Hechtel, 1764); translated by Robert Huish as *Solomon: A Sacred Drama in Five Acts* (London: Hatchard, Sherwood, 1809);

Rothschilds Gräber, anonymous (Halle: Hemmerde, 1766);

Der Messias: Dritter Band, anonymous (Copenhagen: Lillie, 1768);

Hermanns Schlacht: Ein Bardiet für die Schaubühne (Hamburg & Bremen: Cramer, 1769);

Klopstocks Oden und Elegien: Vier und dreyssigmal gedrukt (Darmstadt: Wittich, 1771; reprinted, edited by Jörg-Ulrich Fechner, Stuttgart: Metzler, 1974);

Oden, anonymous (Hamburg: Bode, 1771; reprinted, Bern: Lang, 1971);

J. H. W. Tischbein, 1802, (private collection; from Deutsche Schriftsteller im Porträt, *1980)*

Kleine poetische und prosaische Werke, 2 volumes, edited by Christian Friedrich Daniel Schubart (Frankfurt am Main & Leipzig: Verlag der Neuen Buchhändler Gesellschaft, 1771);

David, ein Trauerspiel (Hamburg: Bode, 1772);

Der Messias: Vierter Band, anonymous (Halle: Hemmerde, 1773);

Die deutsche Gelehrtenrepublik: Ihre Einrichtung. Ihre Gesetze. Geschichte des letzten Landtags. Auf Befehl der Aldermänner durch Salogast und Wlemar. Herausgegeben von Klopstock. Erster Theil (Hamburg: Bode, 1774);

Oden und Lieder beym Clavier zu Singen: In Musik gesetzt von Herrn Ritter Gluck (Vienna: Artaria, 1776);

Über die deutsche Rechtschreibung (Leipzig: Weygand, 1778);

Ueber Sprache und Dichtkunst: Fragmente, 3 volumes (Hamburg: Herold, 1779-1780);

Der Messias: Ausgabe der letzten Hand, 2 volumes (Altona: Eckhardt, 1780);

Ihr Tod (Vienna: Kurzbeck, 1780);

Ode an den Kaiser (Greifswald, 1782);

Hermann und die Fürsten: Ein Bardiet für die Schaubühne, anonymous (Hamburg: Herold, 1784);

Klopstocks Werke, 8 volumes (Troppau: Trassler, 1784-1786);

Die Lehrstunde: Oden. In Musik gesetzt von Naumann (Dresden, 1785);

Hermanns Tod: Ein Bardiet für die Schaubühne, anonymous (Hamburg: Hoffmann, 1787);

Das Vaterunser, ein Psalm (Leipzig, 1790);

Grammatische Gespräche (Altona: Kaven, 1794);

Klopstock's Werke, 12 volumes (Leipzig: Göschen, 1798-1817);

Eine Reliquie (Zurich: Orell, 1810);

Klopstock's Nachlaß, 2 volumes, edited by C. A. H. Clodius (Leipzig: Brockhaus, 1821);

Sämmtliche Werke, 19 volumes, edited by August Leberecht Back, A. R. C. Spindler, and Heinrich Döring (volumes 1-12, Leipzig: Göschen, 1823; supplemental volume, Weimar: Hoffmann, 1825; volumes 13-18, Leipzig: Fleischer, 1830);

F. G. Klopstocks sämmtliche Werke, ergänzt in drei Bänden durch seinen Briefwechsel, lebensgeschichtliche und andere interessante Beiträge, 3 volumes, edited by Hermann Schmidlin (Stuttgart: Scheible, 1839);

Sämmtliche Werke: Erste vollständige Ausgabe, 10 volumes (Leipzig: Göschen, 1844-1845);

Sämtliche Werke, 10 volumes (Leipzig: Cotta, 1854-1855);

Klopstock's Werke: Nach den besten Quellen revidirte Ausgabe, 6 volumes, edited by Robert Boxberger (Berlin: Hempel, 1879);

Klopstocks Werke, 4 volumes, edited by Richard Hamel (Berlin & Stuttgart: Spemann, 1884-1890);

Klopstocks gesammelte Werke, 4 volumes, edited by Franz Muncker (Stuttgart: Cotta, 1887);

Werke und Briefe: Historisch-kritische Ausgabe, 18 volumes to date, edited by Horst Gronemeyer and others (Berlin & New York: De Gruyter, 1974-　).

Editions in English: *The Messiah: Attempted from the German of Mr. Klopstock. To Which Is Prefix'd His Introduction on Divine Poetry*, translated by Mary Collyer and Joseph Collyer (2 volumes, London: Printed for R. and J. Dodsley, T. Durham, T. Field & J. Collyer, 1763; 1 volume, New York: Printed by F. Forman for E. Duyckinck & Co., 1795);

*Memoirs of Frederick and Margaret Klopstock: Trans-
lated from the German*, compiled and translated by Elizabeth Smith (Bath, U.K.: Printed
by R. Cruttwell, 1808; Philadelphia: Printed
by Fry & Kammerer for Philip H. Nicklin
and Co., Baltimore, Farrand, Mallory and
Co., Boston, Jacob Green, Albany, Edward
Earle and B. B. Hopkins and Co., Philadelphia, 1810);

Odes of Klopstock, from 1747 to 1780, translated by
William Nind (London: Pickering, 1848);

The Poetry of Germany, translated by Alfred Baskerville (New York: Leypoldt & Holt, 1867),
pp. 14-24–includes "Ode to God," "Herman
and Thusnelda," "Morning Song," "Awake
My Heart and Laud," "Henry the Fowler,"
"The Ressurrection [*sic*]";

The Penguin Book of German Verse, edited by Leo-
nard Forster (Baltimore: Penguin, 1969),
pp. 169-172–includes "The Chain of
Roses," "The Graves of Friends Who Died
Young," "Desire for Knowledge";

Anthology of German Poetry through the 19th Century,
edited by Alexander Gode and Frederick
Ungar (New York: Ungar, 1972), pp. 34-35–
includes "The Early Graves."

OTHER: Margareta Klopstock, *Hinterlassne Schriften*, edited by Klopstock (Hamburg: Bohn,
1759);

"Der jezige Krieg," in *Musen Almanach für 1782*,
edited by Johann Heinrich Voß and Leopold Friedrich Günther Goeckingk (Hamburg: Bohn, 1782), pp. 125-128.

PERIODICAL PUBLICATION: "Der Messias,"
*Neue Beyträge zum Vergnügen des Verstandes
und Witzes*, 4, no. 4-5 (1748): 234-378.

Initially celebrated and then quickly forgotten, Friedrich Gottlieb Klopstock appeared on
the arid scene of the mid eighteenth century as
the great innovator of what was to become the
modern literary tradition. His early odes and the
first three cantos of his epic *Der Messias*
(1748-1773; translated in part as *The Messiah*,
1763) were greeted with a burst of enthusiasm by
contemporaries, and Klopstock was recognized as
the first major German writer since Martin
Luther. Poets of the "Göttinger Hainbund"
(Göttingen Grove League) as well as those of the
Sturm und Drang, including the young Johann
Wolfgang Goethe, were inspired by Klopstock,
who also received favorable attention from the

The house in Quedlinburg where Klopstock was born

greatest critics of the time, Gotthold Ephraim Lessing and Johann Gottfried Herder. Klopstock
was, however, soon left behind by the very developments he had inaugurated, and by the last quarter of the century times had changed so much
that his works met with a lack of interest. The nineteenth century virtually ignored Klopstock, and
to modern readers his themes seem lofty and distant, his forms empty and esoteric.

Klopstock was a pioneer in preparing the
way for German Classicism and subsequent developments. His legacy extends from Goethe,
Friedrich Hölderlin, Rainer Maria Rilke, and
Stefan George to contemporary poets such as
Paul Celan and Johannes Bobrowski. Language itself constitutes the center of Klopstock's enterprise, and he stands beside Luther and Goethe as
a reformer and regenerator of German. He was
the first strong poetic personality, and he imbued the position of poet with dignity and divine

calling. Finally, and most important, the status he gave to imagination and emotion engendered a new understanding of the nature of poetry.

Klopstock was born on 2 July 1724 in Quedlinburg, Saxony, the first of seventeen children in the prosperous bourgeois family of Gottlob Heinrich Klopstock and Anna Maria Klopstock, née Schmidt. From his father, a government official, he inherited a strong, self-reliant spirit as well as an athletic prowess which he maintained into old age. He was raised in the Protestant religion, which furnished the framework for a large part of his literary work. The family lived from 1732 to 1736 on a country estate, Friedeburg on the Saale River, where Klopstock acquired a reverence for nature. After three years of schooling in Quedlinburg, Klopstock entered the princely academy in Schulpforta in 1739. There he gained intimate acquaintance with the classical literature of Greek and Latin antiquity. His earliest poetic attempts were made under the influence of Johann Christoph Gottsched's Leipzig school, which advocated the imitation of French Classicism. But he also read the critical writings of the Swiss theoreticians Johann Jakob Bodmer and Johann Jakob Breitinger, which began to appear in the early 1740s; their call for imagination and invention as opposed to imitation and convention shaped his canons of taste and determined his poetic program. In 1745 Klopstock entered the University of Jena; a year later he transferred to the University of Leipzig. He remained there until 1748; then, without completing his degree, he took a position as a tutor in Langensalza, which he held until 1750.

While still in secondary school Klopstock had decided to write a major epic, and in Jena he had begun work on *Der Messias*. Although that work was to be his primary focus for the next twenty-seven years, he also began writing lyric poetry in 1747.

The first three cantos of *Der Messias* appeared in the Bremen journal *Neue Beyträge zum Vergnügen des Verstandes und Witzes* in 1748 and immediately brought fame to the twenty-four-year-old poet. Its visionary Christology is announced in the opening line: "Sing, unsterbliche Seele, der sündigen Menschen Erlösung" (Sing, immortal soul, the redemption of sinful mankind). The first three cantos appeared as a book in 1749, the first five in 1751, and the first ten in 1755; further books of five cantos each were published in 1768 and in 1773, when the epic, comprising

twenty cantos and nearly twenty thousand lines, reached its conclusion. The initial publication in 1748 met with praise as well as criticism, and Klopstock's work immediately became the central issue in literary debates of the time. Its content, form, tone, style, and poetic stance all were felt to be revolutionary.

Even though Klopstock's thematic model was John Milton's *Paradise Lost* (1667), and although the English epic had appeared eighty years earlier, German religious dogma was still more conservative than that in England. Klopstock had to steer a careful course in *Der Messias* between orthodoxy and free thought. Even more innovative than the content was the metrical form of the hexameter, which Klopstock, after early attempts in prose, adopted in 1746 in imitation of Homer and Virgil. Klopstock's work constituted the first sustained attempt to write in the classical meters. His innovation set an important precedent for the subsequent poetic tradition. New also was the poetic expression of fantasy and feeling, in contrast to the rationalistic, descriptive, and didactic poetry of the Enlightenment or the rule-bound Gottschedian poetics. The appeal of Klopstock's verse was to the emotions rather than to the intellect, and thus it called forth criticism of its alleged unclarity, complexity, and "dark" style. To accommodate the new subject of emotion Klopstock invented a new vocabulary, syntax, and style that added an unprecedented dynamic to poetic language. The boldness of the poetic stance was also innovative, as Klopstock consciously and enthusiastically celebrated his divine calling as *vates* (seer). For all of these reasons *Der Messias* was recognized by most critics as the greatest work of art in modern German literature up to its time.

At the center of *Der Messias* is Jesus Christ as the mediator between God and man. The core of the poem comprises the suffering of Christ from his entry into Jerusalem to his Crucifixion and Resurrection. These events of the Passion Week are, however, expanded and intensified by being set in a framework of universal history and cosmic time. Adam and Eve appear as the progenitors of a race in need of redemption, and the Hebrew patriarchs and prophets foreshadow the central event, which will be valid for yet unborn generations until the end of the world. The history of early Christendom is thus embedded in a temporal framework extending from Creation to the Last Judgment. Klopstock unites the biblical conception of heaven and hell with eighteenth-

Der

Meßias

ein

Heldengedicht.

HALLE,
bey Carl Herrmann Hemmerde.
1749.

Title page for the first book publication of the first three cantos of the poem that made Klopstock famous

century science, drawing on the new cosmology for images of stars, planets, and wide regions of the heavens extending into infinity. In spite of the vastness of space, man retains central importance by virtue of his special creation by God.

As in *Paradise Lost*, the chief protagonist and antagonist are God and Satan. Klopstock adapted from Milton the descriptions of heaven and hell and of the angels and devils that inhabit those realms and influence the lives of mortals. Readers of both epics, then as now, found the descriptions of hell particularly intriguing. Abdiel Abbadona, introduced in canto two as the fallen angel who subsequently repented, had a special appeal for eighteenth-century readers; they eagerly awaited publication of further cantos to find out whether the poet would leave the poor soul in hell or give him another chance. (Finally, in canto nineteen, he was saved.) Whereas Milton, following Homer, tends to mythologize and anthropomorphize his three-tiered world, Klopstock tends toward abstraction and spiritualization.

The lack of action in *Der Messias* has been viewed as a central problem: the hero, Jesus

Christ, does not act but suffers. The epic is symmetrically divided, with the Crucifixion occurring in canto ten; and the second half, culminating in the triumphant Messiah's ascension into heaven to take the throne at the right hand of the Father, includes even less action. Some narrative interest is introduced by the actions of the disciples—for example, the denial by Peter and the betrayal by Judas; many peripheral figures appear. But one must conclude that Klopstock did not intend to portray objective actions; and perhaps because of its epical failure the work is a lyrical success.

The main focus of the poem is on the lyrical subject matter of the characters' thoughts and emotions. Descriptions of events are replaced by reports of those events in messages, speeches, dialogues, and songs. The epic is finally transformed into lyric in canto twenty, in stanzas of damnation and fury and of triumph and jubilation. This spiritualization of the universe has been seen as a weakness; Friedrich Schiller complained that Klopstock divested his figures of their bodies in order to make them soul. Although Klopstock adapted from Homer the techniques of simile and recurring formulas, he used them for the opposite effect, namely, to suggest that which is ethereal, disembodied. Perhaps his choice of the epic form was a mistake; but behind this choice lay a new conception of the relationship between intellect and emotion. Although thought and rationality were not excluded, Klopstock viewed feeling as the more adequate vehicle for grasping the essentially spiritual nature of the universe.

This liberation of poetic expression to include the emotions was Klopstock's greatest accomplishment, for it engendered a new understanding of the nature of poetry, a new subjectivity. An important influence was the eighteenth-century movement of Pietism with its nonrational appeal to individual inwardness. In a secularization of religious experience Klopstock transferred the Pietistic language of feeling to the sphere of poetry; and he further brought it together with a conception of the sublime that he had inherited from the classical-humanistic tradition. The very incomprehensibility of the divine gives rise to a new fullness of expression, resulting in an extravagant and high-flown language of ecstasy, rapture, and bursts of exaltation. Whereas this style may appear to modern readers as an inflation of feeling, at the time it was perceived as a great liberation. As Klopstock said in his essay "Von der heiligen Poesie" (On Sacred Poe-

Klopstock in 1757; engraving by J. M. Bernigroth

and with it the convention of rhyme. The unrhymed forms allowed for continuous syntax, and by using new and varied rhythmic patterns and strong enjambment Klopstock introduced an unprecedented dynamic into poetry.

The themes of friendship, love, religion, and nature form the core of his early lyrics. Celebration of friendship was a virtual cult in the Age of Sentimentalism; Klopstock's many poems to and about friends are exemplified by "Auf meine Freunde" (To My Friends, 1747). In this poem Klopstock speaks from personal experience of friendship, a major departure from the literary topoi that dominated seventeenth-century courtly forms of poetry.

This subjectivity is, however, not yet the seemingly spontaneous experience of Goethe's poetry; nor does Klopstock's subjectivity entail individuality, for it is a representative rather than an individual subjectivity. Klopstock's work remains rooted in the humanistic tradition of rhetoric, in which the conception of the sublime served to elevate personal experience. Whereas sublimity and experience may seem to be antithetical notions, Klopstock brought them together, just as he did intellect and emotion, high style and personal confession, tradition and the individual.

The early poems immortalize Klopstock's unrequited love for his cousin Maria Sophia Schmidt, who appears as "Fanny," a name borrowed from the English novelist Henry Fielding. "Die künftige Geliebte" (The Future Beloved, 1747) is far from the coquetry of anacreontic poetry; indeed, it differs from all previous love poems in that it presents the progressive objectification of an unreal situation, whereby time levels are collapsed to enable projection into a perfect future state. That type of fictional visualization is characteristic also of the poems "Der Abschied" (The Farewell, 1748) and "An Fanny" (To Fanny, 1748). The latter poem contains a long conditional clause which extends over five stanzas before arriving at a conception of unity in the hereafter. The notion of life after death, as well as the rhetoric of pathos, bear the marks of Edward Young's *Night Thoughts on Life, Death, and Immortality* (1742-1745), which Klopstock valued highly. The psychological novels of Samuel Richardson also exerted an influence on Klopstock's early work.

The proximity of love and religion in Klopstock's thought is evidenced by the similarity in tone of "An Fanny" to religious poems such as *Ode an Gott* (Ode to God, 1751). Critics at the

try), written as an introduction to the 1755 edition of *Der Messias*, the purpose of sacred poetry is to move the soul. In a departure from the classical-humanistic tradition, which understood the purpose of poetry as being to instruct and delight, *docere et delectare*, Klopstock added a new component, *movere*; and it was that component which made his work unique.

Klopstock's lyric poetry had an equally strong resonance at the time and ultimately had a more lasting appeal than his epic; it also served as an important model for later poets such as Hölderlin. The title of Klopstock's first published poem, "Der Lehrling der Griechen" (The Apprentice of the Greeks, 1747), indicates his departure point: classical antiquity. Although other poets of the time, particularly Jakob Immanuel Pyra and Samuel Gotthold Lange, had experimented with the classical lyric meters, Klopstock is credited with introducing them into German. The primary forms he used were the alcaic, Asclepiadean, and sapphic odes and the elegiac distich. He rejected the alternating meters of the alexandrine, predominant in the preceding century,

Hermanns Schlacht

Ein Bardiet für die Schaubühne

Mit Römischkaiserl. und Churfürstl. Sächsis. allergnädigsten Privilegiis.

Hamburg und Bremen.
Bey Johann Henrich Cramer. 1769.

Title page for the first play in Klopstock's trilogy about the hero who led the Germanic tribes against the Romans in the first century

time took offense at the fact that toward the end of the thirty-two stanzas the poet pleads with God for physical union with the beloved. The love poems as well as the religious lyric reveal the pietistic influence of the language of the heart. In accordance with Klopstock's dictum of Darstellung (presentation) rather than the Beschreibung (description) that was characteristic of Enlightenment verse, the poem presents an effusion of passionate feeling, bold fantasy, and powerful lyrical pathos.

The language of the time was too narrow for the new emotional and enthusiastic content; thus Klopstock had to invent new forms of vocabulary, syntax, and style to express what had not been said before. He is credited with adding many new words and forms to the German language, such as new compounds and derivational forms, plural forms of abstract nouns, and the absolute comparative. In accordance with his doctrine of *movere* he added movement to the language through the use of verbal prefixes indicating directionality, intransitive verbs used as transitives, adverbs of motion, verbal participles used as adjectives, and infinitives used as nouns. Repetition, parallelism, and ellipsis are also characteristic of his style, as are daring syntax with complex embedments and radical inversions. Although there is little external action in

any of Klopstock's works, the dynamism is inherent in the language itself.

In 1750 Klopstock received an invitation from Bodmer to come to Zurich, where he was greeted enthusiastically and celebrated as the leading poet of a new era. One of his most famous poems, "Der Zürcher See" (Lake Zurich, 1750), represents a synthesis of his central themes of friendship, nature, religion, and art. His stern mentor soon took offense at Klopstock's youthful sporting and amorous life-style, and Klopstock left Zurich the following year to accept a position in Copenhagen under the patronage of Bernstorff, the foreign minister at the court of the Danish king Friedrich V. Klopstock was no ordinary court poet, for his independent spirit precluded any form of servility; yet many of his odes and panegyrics testify to his high regard for the king. Klopstock remained in Copenhagen for twenty years with intermittent, sometimes lengthy visits to Germany; and the royal monetary support that was initially offered to enable him to complete *Der Messias* was extended for the remainder of his life.

En route to Copenhagen Klopstock stopped in Hamburg, where he met Margareta (Meta) Moller. They were engaged in 1752 and married in 1754. Their domestic happiness was short-lived, for Meta, herself a talented writer, died in childbirth in 1758. A year later Klopstock published some of her correspondence and literary writings as *Hinterlassne Schriften* (Posthumous Works). Meta is celebrated as "Cidli" in several of Klopstock's odes, and these poems of fulfilled love differ significantly from those arising from his unrequited love for "Fanny." Gone is the high-flown style, convoluted syntax and projection of love into the future. The Cidli poems tell of happiness in the present in relatively simple, natural forms. Most notable among them is "Das Rosenband" (The Chain of Roses, 1753). Klopstock also wrote spiritual poetry, which was published in two volumes as *Geistliche Lieder* (Religious Songs, 1758-1759). These lyrics differ from hymns in the Protestant tradition in that they are not singable.

Klopstock's experimentation with metrical forms led to his invention of German free verse, which incorporated such influences as the Hebrew Psalms and Old Germanic poetry. His free-verse poem "Frühlingsfeier" (Celebration of Spring, 1759) was made famous by Goethe's reference to it in the thunderstorm passage of *Die Leiden des jungen Werthers* (The Sorrows of Young

*Title page for the first authorized collection
of Klopstock's odes*

used for widely anthologized poems such as "Die frühen Gräber" (The Early Graves, 1764) and "Die Sommernacht" (The Summer Night, 1766). A concept that repeatedly appears in Klopstock's theoretical writings is that of Mitausdruck (with-expression), by which he meant an ideal correspondence between meter and meaning in which meter would intensify the semantic message. The new forms allowed for unprecedented possibilities of variation, and "Mannigfaltigkeit" (diversity) became for Klopstock a principle of aesthetic evaluation, in accordance with his conception of imagination as opposed to imitation.

Klopstock's early love of English literature intensified during his first years in Denmark and gave rise to a desire for a German national poetry to rival the English, as allegorically portrayed in the poem "Die beiden Musen" (The Two Muses, 1752). The newly discovered Celtic and Teutonic mythologies were in vogue at the time, as evidenced by the immense popularity of James Macpherson's *Ossian* (1762) and Thomas Percy's *Reliques of Ancient English Poetry* (1765), as well as many German works and translations. In 1767 Klopstock began writing in this mode; he rewrote many of his earlier poems, substituting Nordic and Celtic names for the original figures taken largely from Greek mythology. Poems such as "Hermann" (1767) and "Thusnelda" (1767) were written in this form of Bardendichtung (bardic poetry) in an effort to create a national consciousness. The Germanic past, however, was too little known to serve as a basis for poetry, and the movement has been regarded largely as an aberration.

The vogue of bardic literature also gave rise to a dramatic trilogy focusing on the historical hero Hermann, who led the Germanic tribes against the Romans in the first century A.D. Klopstock's intention was to create a nationalistic drama and thus to free the German theater from dependence on foreign models; the plays may also be read as an expression of his antiabsolutistic political leanings. Of the three dramas—*Hermanns Schlacht* (Hermann's Battle, 1769), *Hermann und die Fürsten* (Hermann and the Princes, 1784), and *Hermanns Tod* (Hermann's Death, 1787)—the last is regarded the best. None of them ever reached the stage.

Klopstock also wrote three Biblical plays: *Der Tod Adams* (1757; translated as *The Death of Adam*, 1763), *Salomo* (1764; translated as *Solomon*, 1809), and *David* (1772). Like the Hermann plays, these dramas were never performed; nor

Werther, 1774), which serves as indication of the powerful effect the poem had on the younger generation. Far from the idyllic or didactic tone of conventional nature poetry, it celebrates the infinity of the universe with spectacular astral imagery. The poem operates on the contrast between the macrocosm and the microcosm, and it metaphorically demonstrates the antithesis between the insignificance and the immortality of man. Creation suffused with divinity is the topic of many hymns in free verse, such as "Dem Allgegenwärtigen" (To the Omnipresent One, 1758) and "Die Gestirne" (The Stars, 1764). Freedom of form is matched by a freedom of expression as the poet speaks in outbursts of ecstatic feeling.

Between 1764 and 1767 Klopstock invented more than sixty stanza forms. Some are used only as illustrations of his theoretical statements; others appear in the triumphal choruses in the twentieth canto of *Der Messias*; still others are were they meant to be. They do not portray actions but the characters and feelings of their heroes; their energy resides in language rather than in external events. Klopstock's understanding of dramatic form is clearly different from that of Lessing, whose dramas began to appear at the same time and were to determine the development of the genre in Germany.

In 1770 Klopstock's patron Bernstorff fell from favor in Denmark; the two men left Copenhagen and moved to Hamburg. Klopstock's odes had appeared over the previous two decades in various editions, some of them pirated; he thus undertook to publish an authorized edition, which appeared in 1771 and was well received. The same year he finally completed *Der Messias*. For the first complete edition, published in 1773, he revised many of the earlier cantos, heightening the level of stylization to differentiate the work further from ordinary prose. A final authoritative edition was published in 1780, although Klopstock again revised parts of the work for publication in his complete works in 1798.

Klopstock was idolized by the younger generation, particularly by poets of the "Göttinger Hainbund." In 1774, on his way to spend a year with the Margrave Karl Friedrich von Baden in Karlsruhe, he visited the poets in Göttingen and also young Goethe in Frankfurt. Klopstock was visited in Hamburg by many prominent writers, including William Wordsworth and Samuel Taylor Coleridge. Although Klopstock was revered, he was out of step with his times, particularly in his opposition to Kantian philosophy–indeed, to any systematic theoretical or critical endeavor. With the advent of the Sturm und Drang and Weimar Classicism, his work appeared outmoded.

Throughout his life Klopstock wrote essays on ethics, aesthetics, linguistics, and metrics. *Die deutsche Gelehrtenrepublik* (The German Intellectual Republic, 1774) presents a bizarre satirical allegory on the state of scholarship in Germany; it was little understood either at the time or later, although Arno Schmidt drew on it for the title of his novel *Die Gelehrtenrepublik* (1957). Other essays contain an odd mixture of insight and error. Most readable today are the aesthetic essays "Von der Sprache der Poesie" (On the Language of Poetry, 1758), "Gedanken über die Natur der Poesie" (Thoughts about the Nature of Poetry, 1759), and "Von der Darstellung" (On Presentation, 1779); some of the ideas about language, style, and meter in these essays were repeated in *Grammatische Gespräche* (Conversations about

Grammar, 1794). In contrast to the imagination and emotion of his poetry, the essays are by and large logical and realistic, in accordance with Klopstock's notion of the difference between poetry and prose. In his later years Klopstock also worked on translations of Homer, Virgil, Horace, and Ovid.

The same impulse to freedom within a disciplined form that characterized Klopstock's writing led him to applaud the French and American revolutions. From 1789 to 1794 he wrote largely political poetry dealing with the French Revolution, as exemplified by "Die États Généraux" (1789). In 1792 the French Republic awarded Klopstock the status of honorary citizen; although he subsequently turned against the revolution because of the Reign of Terror he did not yield to public pressure to renounce the title.

In 1791, after the death of her husband, Klopstock married Johanna Elisabeth von Winthem, Meta's niece, who had been caring for him in his old age; the purpose of the marriage was probably to secure a pension for her. Klopstock died in Hamburg on 14 March 1803 and was buried in nearby Ottensen. He was mourned by an entire nation with a funeral such as no German writer had theretofore received.

Klopstock has suffered the paradoxical fate of the innovator whose works give rise to new standards which then render those works obsolete. If his writings have not met with a favorable reception since his time, it is partly because they have been judged on the basis of criteria that originated in the Romantic era. A new understanding of Klopstock may be provided by the historical-critical edition of his works that is in preparation at the Klopstock Archives at the University of Hamburg; the first volume appeared in 1974, and the complete edition is projected to include approximately thirty volumes.

Letters:

Klopstock und seine Freunde: Briefwechsel der Familie Klopstock unter sich, und zwischen dieser Familie, Gleim, Schmidt, Fanny, Meta und andern Freunden. Aus Gleims brieflichem Nachlasse herausgegeben, 2 volumes, edited by Klamer Schmidt (Halberstadt: Im Bureau für Literatur und Kunst, 1810); translated by Elizabeth Ogilvy Benger as *Klopstock and His Friends: A Series of Familiar Letters, Written between the Years 1750 and 1803* (London: Colburn, 1814);
Auswahl aus Klopstocks nachgelassenem Briefwechsel und übrigen Papieren: Ein Denkmal für seine Ver-

Manuscript for an ode by Klopstock, written in September 1772 for Christian and Friedrich Leopold Grafen zu Stolberg
(from Gustav Könnecke, Bilderatlas zur Geschichte der deutschen Nationallitteratur, *1895)*

ehrer, 2 volumes, edited by Christian August Heinrich Clodius (Leipzig: Brockhaus, 1821);

Kurzer Briefwechsel zwischen Klopstock und Goethe im Jahre 1776 (Leipzig, 1833);

Briefwechsel (Hildburghausen: Bibliographisches Institut, 1842);

Briefe von und an Klopstock: Ein Beitrag zur Literaturgeschichte seiner Zeit. Mit erläuternden Anmerkungen, edited by Johann Martin Lappenberg (Brunswick: Westermann, 1867; reprinted, Bern: Lang, 1970);

Briefwechsel zwischen Klopstock und den Grafen Christian und Friedrich Leopold zu Stolberg. Mit einem Anhang: Briefwechsel zwischen Klopstock und Herder, edited by Jürgen Behrens and Sabine Jodeleit (Neumünster: Wachholtz, 1964);

Es sind wunderliche Dinger, meine Briefe: Meta Klopstocks Briefwechsel mit Friedrich Gottlieb Klopstock und mit ihren Freunden, 1751-1758, edited by Franziska and Hermann Tiemann (Munich: Beck, 1980).

Bibliography:

Gerhard Burkhardt and Heinz Nicolai, *Klopstock-Bibliographie,* in Klopstock's *Werke und Briefe: Historisch-kritische Ausgabe* (Berlin & New York: De Gruyter, 1975).

Biographies:

Carl Friedrich Cramer, *Klopstock: Er; und über ihn,* 5 volumes (Hamburg, Dessau, Leipzig & Altona, 1780-1792);

Franz Muncker, *Friedrich Gottlieb Klopstock: Geschichte seines Lebens und seiner Schriften* (Stuttgart: Göschen, 1888).

*Klopstock in 1798; painting by Anton Hickel
(Staatsbibliothek Hamburg)*

References:

Richard Alewyn, "Klopstock!," *Euphorion*, 73, no. 4 (1979): 357-364;

Alewyn, "Klopstocks Lesser," in *Festschrift für Rainer Gruenter*, edited by Bernhard Fabian (Heidelberg: Winter, 1978), pp. 100-121;

Heinz L. Arnold, ed., *Friedrich Gottlieb Klopstock* (Munich: Edition text + kritik, 1981);

Isaac Bacon, "Pietistische und rationalistische Elemente in Klopstocks Sprache," *Journal of English and Germanic Philology*, 49 (1950): 49-59;

Friedrich Beissner, *Klopstocks Ode "Der Zürchersee": Ein Vortrag* (Münster & Cologne: Böhlau, 1952);

Beth Bjorklund, "Klopstock's Poetic Innovations: The Emergence of German as a Prosodic Language," *Germanic Review*, 56 (Winter 1981): 20-27;

Eric Blackall, *The Emergence of German as a Literary Language: 1700-1775* (Cambridge: Cambridge University Press, 1959);

Paul Böckmann, "Klopstocks neue Ausdruckssprache," in his *Formgeschichte der deutschen Dichtung*, volume 1 (Hamburg: Hoffmann & Campe, 1949), pp. 578-598;

Irmgard Böger, *Bewegung als formendes Gesetz in Klopstocks Oden* (Berlin: Ebering, 1939);

Bernhard Böschenstein, "Klopstock als Lehrer Hölderlins: Die Mythisierung von Freundschaft und Dichtung," in his *Leuchttürme* (Frankfurt am Main: Insel, 1977), pp. 44-63;

Max Freivogel, *Klopstock der heilige Dichter* (Bern: Francke, 1954);

Wilhelm Große, *Studien zu Klopstocks Poetik* (Munich: Fink, 1977);

Karl S. Guthke, *Literarisches Leben im achtzehnten Jahrhundert in Deutschland und in der Schweiz* (Bern & Munich: Francke, 1975);

Hans-Heinrich Hellmuth, *Metrische Erfindung und metrische Theorie bei Klopstock* (Munich: Fink, 1973);

Elisabeth Höpker-Herberg and Rose-Marie Hurlebusch, "Die Hamburger Klopstock-Ausgabe," *Jahrbuch für Internationale Germanistik*, 3, no. 2 (1971): 243-270;

Gerhard Kaiser, " 'Denken' und 'Empfinden': Ein Beitrag zur Sprache und Poetik Klopstocks," *Deutsche Vierteljahrsschrift*, 35 (1961): 321-343;

Kaiser, *Klopstock: Religion und Dichtung* (Gütersloh: Mohn, 1963);

Kaiser, "Klopstocks 'Frühlingsfeyer,' " in *Interpretationen: Deutsche Lyrik von Weckherlin bis Benn*, edited by Jost Schillemeit, volume 1 (Frankfurt am Main & Hamburg: Fischer, 1965), pp. 28-39;

Hans-Henrik Krummacher, "Friedrich Gottlieb Klopstock," in *Deutsche Dichter des 18. Jahrhunderts. Ihr Leben und Werk*, edited by Benno von Wiese (Berlin: Schmidt, 1977), pp. 190-209;

Meredith Lee, "Klopstock's Temple Imagery," *Lessing Yearbook*, 13 (1981): 209-226;

Lee, "A Question of Influence: Goethe, Klopstock, and 'Wanderers Sturmlied,' " *German Quarterly*, 55 (January 1982): 13-28;

Alan Menhennet, "Sentimentalism: F. G. Klopstock," in his *Order and Freedom: Literature and Society in Germany from 1720-1805* (London: Weidenfeld & Nicolson, 1973), pp. 102-115;

Jean Murat, *Klopstock: Les thèmes principaux de son oeuvre* (Paris: Publications de la Faculté des Lettres de l'Université de Strasbourg, 1959);

Helmut Pape, "Die gesellschaftlich-wirtschaftliche Stellung Friedrich Gottlieb Klopstocks," Ph.D. dissertation, University of Bonn, 1962;

Peter Rühmkorf, *Walter von der Vogelweide, Klopstock und Ich* (Reinbek: Rowohlt, 1975);

Klopstock's burial in Ottensen, near Hamburg, 22 March 1803; aquatint by J. F. Friedhof

Gerhard Sauder, "Die 'Freude' der 'Freundschaft': Klopstocks Ode 'Der Zürchersee,' " in *Gedichte und Interpretationen*, volume 2, *Aufklärung und Sturm und Drang*, edited by Karl Richter (Stuttgart: Reclam, 1983), pp. 225-239;

Karl A. Schleiden, *Klopstocks Dichtungstheorie als Beitrag zur Geschichte der deutschen Poetik* (Saarbrücken: West-Ost, 1954);

Arno Schmidt, *Die Gelehrtenrepublik: Kurzroman aus den Roßbreiten* (Karlsruhe: Stahlberg, 1957; reprinted, Hamburg: Fischer, 1971); translated by Michael Horovitz as *The Egghead Republic: A Short Novel from the Horse Latitudes* (London & Boston: Boyars, 1979);

Schmidt, "Klopstock, oder Verkenne Dich Selbst!," in his *Der sanfte Unmensch* (Frankfurt am Main: Ullstein, 1963), pp. 101-132;

Karl Ludwig Schneider, *Klopstock und die Erneuerung der deutschen Dichtersprache im 18. Jahrhundert* (Heidelberg: Winter, 1960);

Gottlieb C. Schuchard, *Studien zur Verskunst des jungen Klopstock* (Stuttgart: Kohlhammer, 1927);

Eberhard W. Schulz, "Klopstocks Alterslyrik," *Euphorion*, 61 (1967): 295-317;

Walter Silz, "On Rereading Klopstock," *PMLA*, 67 (September 1952): 744-768;

Terence K. Thayer, "Klopstock's Occasional Poetry," *Lessing Yearbook*, 2 (1970): 181-212;

Robert Ulshöfer, "Friedrich Gottlieb Klopstock, 'Die Frühlingsfeier,' " in *Die deutsche Lyrik: Form und Geschichte. Interpretationen*, volume 1, edited by Wiese (Düsseldorf: Bagel, 1956), pp. 168-184;

Karl Viëtor, *Geschichte der deutschen Ode* (Hildesheim: Olms, 1961);

Hans-Georg Werner, ed., *Friedrich Gottlieb Klopstock: Werk und Wirkung* (Berlin: Akademie, 1978).

Papers:
Friedrich Gottlieb Klopstock's papers are in the Klopstock Archives at the Staats- und Universitätsbibliothek Hamburg.

Meta Klopstock

(16 March 1728 - 28 November 1758)

Mary Kathleen Madigan
King College (Bristol)

BOOK: *Hinterlassne Schriften von Margareta Klopstock*, edited by Friedrich Gottlieb Klopstock (Hamburg: Johann Carl Bohn, 1759); revised and enlarged edition (Leipzig: Göschen, 1816)–includes "Ein Brief über die Moden."

Edition in English: *Memoirs of Frederick and Margaret Klopstock: Translated from the German*, compiled and translated by Elizabeth Smith (Bath, U.K.: Printed by R. Cruttwell, 1808; Philadelphia: Printed by Fry & Kammerer for Philip H. Nicklin and Co., Baltimore: Farrand, Mallory and Co., Boston: Jacob Green, Albany: Edward Earle and B. B. Hopkins and Co., Philadelphia, 1810).

Called by J. W. Eaton "the model of the intellectual woman" in the Danish society of her time, Meta Klopstock has only begun to be given full recognition as a writer in the twentieth century. In his review of the 1956 edition of her letters, H. T. Betteridge wrote: "In my experience only Goethe's mother and perhaps Bismarck can equal her in making themselves and their surroundings come to life for us." It was not until 1950 that the University of Hamburg acquired an important portion of her work, which was previously held by a private estate.

Margareta Moller was born in Hamburg on 16 March 1728 to Peter Moller, a merchant, and Margarete Moller, née Frieling. She learned to read French, Italian, and English. At a friend's house in 1751 she discovered some torn-up bits of paper intended for use in haircurling; pasted together, they turned out to be a copy of the first part of Friedrich Gottlieb Klopstock's *Der Messias* (The Messiah, 1748-1773). Enthralled but not totally uncritical of the poem, she asked where she could obtain more of it. Shortly thereafter a meeting was arranged with the author himself, who was passing through Hamburg on his way to a royal appointment in Copenhagen.

Once Klopstock met Meta, he had little time for anyone else–including the poet Friedrich von

Meta Klopstock in 1755, painted by D. van der Smissen (Museum für Hamburgische Geschichte, Bildarchiv)

Hagedorn, whom he had originally come to Hamburg to visit. For her part, Meta became so enamored of Klopstock that in order to communicate what had happened, "müßte ich Empfindungen malen können" (I would have to be able to paint feelings). She proceeded to do precisely that: throughout her hundreds of letters the characteristic mode of her writing was the literary depiction of feelings, whether romantic or religious.

At this point in her relationship to Friedrich she still preferred to call "Freundschaft" (friendship) what her suitor called "Liebe" (love): this situation did not change until his next visit to Ham-

160

burg a year later. Then came a period of testing and waiting until Friedrich was accepted as Meta's fiancé; Meta's unconventional view that one should marry for love–a love that is in harmony with and proceeds from one's love of God–and not for money or social status was ahead of her time. Klopstock's position as a professional writer was also unusual, and there was some question about his religious convictions. But after a period of patient waiting, the wedding took place on 10 June 1754. The letters from the happy marriage years in Copenhagen range from themes of domestic concern to Meta's poking fun at Danish high society. In a more serious vein, husband and wife sometimes speculated on which of them would die first; it was Meta's wish, she wrote, to be the one left behind, to spare her husband the pain of bereavement.

During their marriage Friedrich submitted parts of *Der Messias* to Meta for suggestions and dictated parts of the epic to her. At least once he turned to her for information about a particular author because she was able to read the original language.

Meta doubted that she could succeed as a writer, even though Friedrich's literary friends delighted in her letters. But with her husband's encouragement, she began to try her hand at creative writing. Her only drama, *Der Tod Abels* (The Death of Abel), like all of her works, must be considered within the context of Empfindsamkeit (sentimentality), a literary movement that stressed feeling rather than reason and concentrated on the inner experience of the love of God and the intense movements of the soul.

This emotional coloration, combined with direct moral instruction, admonishment, and encouragement, is also present in "Briefe von Verstorbenen an Lebendige" (Letters from the Dead to the Living). In each of ten letters a different deceased person provides a loved one who is still alive instruction in how to become more pleasing to God; the aim of the letters is to make it easier for the reader to believe in God, the immortality of the soul, the redeeming work of Christ, and the beauty and rapture of the afterlife.

Her work also includes two hymns, "Das vergangne Jahr" (The Year Gone By) and "Die Liebe Gottes" (The Love of God). The first begins by lamenting the swift passing of this life but then changes to eager expectation of the next; the second encourages the reader to pray to God as a merciful and loving father. In "Fragment eines Gesprächs" (Fragment of a Dialogue)

Graves of Meta and Friedrich Klopstock at the Christianskirche cemetery in Ottensen (photo by Mary Kathleen Madigan)

Friedrich and Meta discuss motives for writing, such as friendship with readers rather than greed for glory.

In 1758, Meta, expecting a child once more after having suffered several miscarriages, remained in Hamburg after a visit. After delays caused by storms and sickness Friedrich returned from Copenhagen in time to see his wife die in childbirth on 28 November at the age of thirty. The letters written during the separation immediately preceding Meta's death are among the most poignant to be found in their correspondence; they bear moving witness to the Klopstocks' religious faith.

Almost all of Meta Klopstock's works were first published by Friedrich in 1759 as *Hinterlassne Schriften von Margareta Klopstock* (Posthumous Writings of Margareta Klopstock); the witty and humorous essay "Ein Brief über die Moden" (A Letter about Fashions), which had been published in a Hamburg journal, was included in the 1816 edition of *Hinterlassne Schriften* (which forms volume eleven of Friedrich Klopstock's collected works).

Although her career was short, Meta Klopstock's writings merit attention both as models of participation in the literary and religious movements of her time and as independent and original works of art. Despite increasing interest in her creative work, she will probably remain best known for the letters which Friedrich, her family, and her friends so enjoyed receiving and which continue to arouse interest today. A public reading of her letters, with discussion, was presented at the University of Hamburg in the winter of 1988.

Letters:

Meta Klopstock geb. Moller: Briefwechsel mit Klopstock, ihren Verwandten und Freunden, 3 volumes, edited by Hermann Tiemann (Hamburg: Maximilian-Gesellschaft, 1956);

Geschichte der Meta Klopstock in Briefen, edited by Hermann and Franziska Tiemann (Bremen: Schünemann, 1962);

Es sind wunderliche Dinge, meine Briefe, edited by Hermann and Franziska Tiemann (Munich: Beck, 1980).

Biography:

Ludwig Brunier, *Klopstock und Meta* (Hamburg: Nerthes-Besser & Mauke, 1860).

References:

H. T. Betteridge, "Additions and Corrections to the Correspondence of Meta Klopstock," *Modern Language Review*, 54 (October 1959): 518-532;

André Bogaert, *Klopstock: La religion dans la Messiade* (Paris: Didier, 1965);

J. W. Eaton, *The German Influence in Danish Literature in the Eighteenth Century: The German Circle in Copenhagen 1750-1770* (Cambridge: Cambridge University Press, 1929);

Adalbert von Hanstein, *Die Frauen in der Geschichte des deutschen Geisteslebens des 18. und 19. Jahrhunderts*, 2 volumes (Leipzig: Freund & Wittig, 1899);

Elisabeth Höpker-Herberg, "Der Tod der Meta Klopstock: Ein Versuch über des Dichters Auffassungen vom Tode," in *Der Tod in Dichtung, Philosophie und Kunst*, edited by Hans Helmut Jansen (Darmstadt: Steinkopff, 1978), pp. 182-201;

Eva Horvath, "Die Frau im gesellschaftlichen Leben Hamburgs: Meta Klopstock, Eva König, Elise Reimarus," *Wolfenbütteler Studien zur Aufklärung*, 3 (1976): 175-194;

John Louis Kind, *Edward Young in Germany* (London: Macmillan, 1906);

Lieselotte E. Kurth-Voigt, "Existence after Death: Changing Views in Wieland's Writings," *Lessing Yearbook*, 17 (1985): 153-176;

Mary Kathleen Madigan, "Forever Yours: The Sub genre of the Letter from the Dead to the Living with Thematic Analyses of the Works of Elizabeth Singer Rowe and Meta Klopstock," Ph.D. dissertation, University of North Carolina at Chapel Hill, 1988;

Franz Muncker, *Friedrich Gottlieb Klopstock: Geschichte seines Lebens und seiner Schriften* (Stuttgart: Göschen, 1888);

Jean Murat, *Klopstock: les thèmes principaux de son oeuvre* (Paris: Les Belles Lettres, 1959);

Hans Sperber, "Der Einfluß des Pietismus auf die Sprache des 18. Jahrhunderts," *Deutsche Vierteljahrsschrift*, 8 (1930): 497-515;

Terence K. Thayer, "Klopstock and the Literary Afterlife," *Literaturwissenschaftliches Jahrbuch*, new series 14 (1973): 183-208.

Papers:

There is a major collection of Meta Klopstock's manuscripts at the University of Hamburg Library and minor ones at the Goethe House in Frankfurt and the school library of Schulpforta.

Johann Kaspar Lavater

(15 November 1741 - 2 January 1801)

Karl Julius Fink
St. Olaf College

BOOKS: *Der ungerechte Landvogt oder Klage eines Patrioten*, anonymous, by Lavater and Heinrich Füßli (Zurich, 1762);

Zween Briefe an Herrn M. Bahrdt, betreffend seinen verbesserten Christen in der Einsamkeit (Breslau, 1764);

Jesus auf Golgatha: Eine heilige Ode nebst zweyen Oster-Liedern (Zurich: Bürgkli, 1766);

Christliches Handbüchlein oder Auserlesene Stellen der heiligen Schrift: Mit Versen begleitet (Bern: Walthard, 1767); republished as *Morgengebether und Abendgebether auf alle Tage der Woche: Samt einer Zugabe von einigen neuen Gebethern und Liedern* (Zurich: Bürgkli, 1777); enlarged as *Morgen- und Abendgebete auf alle Tage der Woche: Nebst einer Sammlung von Gebeten* (Leipzig: Heinsius, 1787);

Schweizerlieder: Von einem Mitgliede der Helvetischen Gesellschaft zu Schinznach (Bern: Walthard, 1767; revised and enlarged, 1767; enlarged, 1768; revised and enlarged edition, Zurich: Bürgkli, 1788);

Trauungsrede an Heß (Zurich: Orell, 1767);

Aussichten in die Ewigkeit, in Briefen an Herrn Johann Georg Zimmermann, Königlichen Großbrittannischen Leibarzt in Hannover, 4 volumes, anonymous (Zurich: Orell, Geßner, Füßli, 1768-1778; revised, 2 volumes, 1782);

Kurze Lebensbeschreibung Weiland Ihro Hochwürden Herrn Johann Conrad Antistes Wirz, Pfarrer zum großen Münster und Antistes der Züricherischen Gemeine (Zurich: Ziegler, 1769);

Antwort an den Herrn Moses Mendelssohn zu Berlin: Nebst einer Nacherinnerung von Moses Mendelssohn (Berlin & Stettin: Nicolai / Frankfurt am Main: Eßlinger, 1770);

Briefe von Moses Mendelssohn und Johann Kaspar Lavater (N.p., 1770);

Denkmal der Liebe bei dem plötzlichen Hinschied der Jungfrau Anna Schinz (Zurich, 1770);

Nachdenken über mich selbst (Zurich: Bürgkli, 1770);

Ode an Bodmer (N.p., 1770);

Sepia drawing by Wilhelm Tischbein (from Gustav Könnecke, Bilderatlas zur Geschichte der deutschen National litteratur, *1895)*

Ode an den seligen Professor Gellert, anonymous (Zurich, 1770);

Ode an Gott: Für geübtere Leser (Zurich: Orell, Geßner & Füßli, 1770);

Johann Kaspar Lavaters Zueignungsschrift der Bonnetischen Philosophischen Untersuchung der Beweise für das Christenthum an Herrn Moses Mendelssohn in Berlin, und Schreiben an den Herrn Diaconus Lavater zu Zürich von Moses Mendelssohn (Frankfurt am Main: Andreä, 1770);

Die Auferstehung der Gerechten: Eine Cantate (Zurich: Bürgkli, 1771; revised edition, Winterthur: Heinrich & Steiner, 1778);

Einige Briefe über das Basedowsche Elementarwerk, by Lavater and Isaak Iselin (Zurich: Bürgkli, 1771);

Etwas an Bahrdt (Breslau, 1771);

Christliches Handbüchlein für Kinder (Zurich: Bürgkli, 1771); enlarged as *Christliches Handbüchlein oder auserlesene Stellen der Heiligen Schrift: Vermehrt mit einem Anhang erbaulicher Gedanken* (Bad Homburg: Wolf, 1775); enlarged as *Christliches Handbüchlein für Kinder, nebst Gebethen und Liedern* (Frankfurt am Main & Leipzig, 1779);

Fünfzig christliche Lieder (Zurich: Orell, Geßner, Füßli, 1771; revised, 1780);

Historische Lobrede auf Johann Jakob Breitinger, ehemaliger Vorsteher der Kirche zu Zürich (Zurich: Bürgkli, 1771);

Rede bey der Taufe zweier Berlinischen Isrealiten so durch Veranlassung der Lavaterschen und Mendelssohnischen Streitschriften zu wahrem Christenthum übergetreten: Samt einem kurzen Vorberichte (Frankfurt am Main & Leipzig, 1771);

Geheimes Tagebuch von einem Beobachter seiner selbst, 2 volumes, anonymous, edited by Johann Georg Zollikofer (Leipzig: Weidmann & Reich, 1771-1773)–volume 2 published as *Unveränderte Fragmente aus dem Tagebuche eines Beobachters seiner selbst oder Des Tagebuches Zweyter Theil: Nebst einem Schreiben an den Herausgeber derselben;* translated by Peter Will as *Secret Journal of a Self-Observer; or, Confessions and Familiar Letters of the Rev. J. C. Lavater,* 2 volumes (London: Printed for T. Cadell, jun., and W. Davies, 1795); volume 2 of the German version reprinted, edited by Christoph Siegrist (Bern: Haupt, 1978);

ABC- oder Lesebüchlein zum Gebrauche der Schulen der Stadt und Landschaft (Zurich: Bürgkli, 1772);

Erweckung zur Buße und S. Werenfels Abhandlung wider die fleischliche Sicherheit (Frankfurt am Main: Eichenberg, 1772);

Biblische Erzählungen für die Jugend: Altes und Neues Testament, 2 volumes (Zurich: Orell, Geßner, Füßli, 1772-1774);

Christliches Jahrbüchlein oder Auserlesene Stellen der heiligen Schrift auf alle Tage des Jahres: Mit kurzen Anmerkungen und Versen begleitet (Zurich, 1772);

Lieder zum Gebrauche des Waisenhauses in Zürich (Zurich: Ziegler, 1772);

Von der Physiognomik, 2 volumes, edited by Johann Georg Zimmermann (Leipzig: Weidmann & Reich, 1772);

Predigten: Theil I (Breslau, 1772);

Taschenbüchlein für Dienstboten (Zurich: Bürgkli [actually Bern: Haller], 1772);

Predigten über das Buch Jonas: Gehalten in der Kirche am Waysenhause, 2 volumes (Winterthur: Steiner / Frankfurt am Main: Eichenberg, 1773);

Vermischte Predigten (Frankfurt am Main: Brönner, 1773);

Sittenbüchlein für das Gesinde (Frankfurt am Main [actually Leipzig: Gleditsch / Bad Homburg: Göllner], 1773);

Sittenbüchlein für die Kinder des Landvolks (Bad Homburg: Göllner, 1773);

Denkmal auf Johann Felix Heß, weyland Diener göttlichen Wortes (Zurich, 1774);

Fest-Predigten nebst einigen Gelegenheitspredigten (Frankfurt am Main & Leipzig: Brönner, 1774); enlarged as *Festpredigten: Nebst einer Gelegenheitspredigt* (Frankfurt am Main: Brönner, 1784);

Gastpredigten (Frankfurt am Main: Eichenberg, 1774);

Vermischte Gedanken: Manuscript für Freunde. Herausgegeben von einem unbekannten Freunde (Frankfurt am Main: Sommer, 1774);

Christliche Lieder der vaterländischen Jugend, besonders auf der Landschaft gewidmet (Zurich: Ziegler, 1774);

Zwo Predigten, gehalten zu Ems im Juli 1774 (Frankfurt am Main: Eichenberg, 1774);

Vermischte Schriften, 2 volumes (Winterthur: Steiner, 1774-1781);

Physiognomische Fragmente, zur Beförderung der Menschenkenntniß und Menschenliebe, 4 volumes (Leipzig: Weidmann & Reich / Winterthur: Steiner, 1775-1778); translated by George Grenville as *The Whole Works of Lavater on Physiognomy: Translated from the Last Paris Edition,* 4 volumes (London: Printed for W. Butters, 1787);

Freundschaft: Ein Gedicht (Offenbach: Brede, 1775);

Der glücklich besiegte Landvogt Felix Grebel (Arnheim, 1775);

Die wesentliche Lehre des Evangeliums: Die Gerechtigkeit durch den Glauben an Jesum Christum. In sechs Predigten über Apostelgeschichte X, 43. Herausgegeben von einem Schweizer Theologen (Offenbach: Weiss, 1775);

Engraving of Lavater by J. E. Haid, 1774, after a drawing by G. F. Schmoll

Eigentliche Meinung von den Gaben des Heiligen Geistes, 3 volumes (Bremen: Cramer, 1775-1777);

Drey Predigten, gehalten zu Ems und zu Bockenheim bey Frankfurt (Frankfurt am Main & Leipzig, 1775);

Abraham und Isaak: Ein religiöses Drama (Winterthur: Steiner, 1776);

Zweytes Funfzig christliche Lieder (Zurich: Orell, Geßner, Füßli, 1776);

Casualpredigten: Mit einigen einzigen Gedichten (Hamburg: Wolf, 1776);

Hundert christliche Lieder (Zurich: Orell, Geßner, Füßli, 1776);

Zweyte Predigt über die Nachtmahlsweinvergiftung, gehalten den 24. November 1776 über Nahum III, 1 (Zurich, 1776);

Schreiben an seine Freunde: Suche den Frieden und jag' ihm nach. Im März 1776 (Winterthur: Steiner, 1776); revised as *Schreiben an seine Freunde: Nebst K. Pfennigers Appellation an den Menschenverstand* (Frankfurt am Main & Leipzig, 1776);

Der Verbrecher ohne seines gleichen und sein Schicksal: Über Psalm 37, v. 10-15. Den 29. Herbstmonat 1776 auf Hochobrigkeitlichen Befehl bei und Bethtage in der Großmünster-Kirche verübten Gräuelthat der Vergiftung des heiligen Nachtmahlweins (Augsburg: Späth, 1776);

Das gesegnete Andenken des Gerechten: Eine Predigt (Zurich: Füßli, 1777);

Zwo Predigten bey Anlaß der Vergiftung des Nachtmahlweins: Nebst einigen historischen und Poetischen Beylagen (Leipzig: Weidmann & Reich, 1777);

Sämmtliche Werke: Gesammlet, epitomiert und verbessert, edited by B*** (Hamburg: Buchenröder, 1777);

Abschiedspredigt von der Waisenkirche und Antrittspredigt zu dem Diaconat bei der Kirche zu St. Peter (Winterthur: Steiner, 1778);

Anmerkungen zu einer Abhandlung über Physiognomik, nebst denen, die man im Deutschen Museum und Merkur hierüber findet (Leipzig: Weygand, 1778);

Die Bekehrungsgeschichte der Apostel, in einer Predigt (Frankfurt am Main: Eichenberg, 1778);

Predigten über die Existenz des Teufels und seine Wirkungen, nebst Erklärung der Versuchsgeschichte Jesu: Von einem schweitzerischen Gottesgelehrten, 2 volumes, anonymous (Frankfurt am Main & Leipzig, 1778-1781);

Sammlung einiger Gebete auf die wichtigsten Angelegenheiten des menschlichen Lebens (Leipzig: Holle, 1778);

Christliche Lieder: Erstes Hundert. Zweites Hundert, 2 volumes (Zurich: Orell, Geßner, Füßli, 1779-1780);

Jesus Messias oder Die Zukunft des Herrn: Nach der Offenbarung Johannes, anonymous (Zurich: Füßli, 1780);

Die Liebe gezeichnet in vier Predigten und einigen Liedern (Leipzig: Holle, 1780);

Sechszig Lieder nach dem Zürcherischen Catechismus: Der Petrinischen Jugend zugeeignet (Zurich: Füßli, 1780);

Predigt, gehalten den 28. May 1780 nach H. Wasers Hinrichtung über I. Corinther 10. Cap., V. 12.: Wasers des Unglücklichen Briefe an seine Verwandten und einige sein Schicksal betreffende kleine Schriften. Nebst einer Predigt und Gebet über diesen Vorfall (Schaffhausen, 1780);

Johann Kaspar Lavater und eines Ungenannten Urtheile über C. R. Steinbarts System des reinen Christenthums: Mit vielen Zusätzen von J. S. Semler (Halle: Hemmerde & Schwetschke, 1780);

Poesien: Den Freunden des Verfassers gewiedmet, 2 volumes (Leipzig: Weidmann & Reich, 1781);

Pontius Pilatus oder Die Bibel im Kleinen und der Mensch im Großen, 4 volumes (Zurich: Füßli, 1782-1785);

Über den Selbstmord: Eine Predigt (Winterthur: Steiner, 1782);

Reimen zu den biblischen Geschichten des Alten und Neuen Testaments: Für die Jugend (Zurich: Orell, Geßner, Füßli, 1782);

Neue Sammlung geistlicher Lieder und Reimen (Zurich: Orell, Geßner, Füßli, 1782);

Brüderliche Schreiben an verschiedene Jünglinge (Winterthur: Steiner, 1782); republished as *Schreiben an reisende Jünglinge* (Winterthur: Steiner, 1787);

Betrachtungen über die wichtigsten Stellen der Evangelien: Ein Erbauungsbuch für ungelehrte nachdenkende Christen. Nach den Bedürfnissen der jetzigen Zeit, 2 volumes (volume 1, Dessau & Leipzig: Buchhandlung der Gelehrten, 1783; volume 2, Winterthur: Steiner, 1790);

Jesus Christus und Maria Magdalena, anonymous (N.p., 1783);

Jesus Messias oder Die Evangelien und Apostelgeschichte, in Gesängen, 4 volumes (Winterthur: Steiner, 1783-1786);

Lebensregeln für Jünglinge, besonders für diejenigen, welche die hohe Schule beziehen wollen (Basel: Imhof, 1783);

Predigt bei Anlaß der großen Erderschütterungen in Sicilien und Calabrien, gehalten am 30. März 1783 (Zurich: Bürkli, 1783);

Vollkommenheit, des Menschen Bestimmung und Gottes Werk (Offenbach: Weiß & Brede, 1783);

Kleine poetische Gedichte (Winterthur: Steiner, 1784);

Herzenserleichterung oder Verschiedenes an Verschiedene (St. Gall: Reutiner, 1784);

Johann Caspar Lavaters Sämtliche kleinere prosaische Schriften vom Jahr 1763-1783, 3 volumes (Winterthur: Steiner, 1784-1785);

Johann Caspar Lavaters vermischte gereimte Gedichte vom Jahr 1766 bis 1785: Für Freunde des Verfassers (Winterthur: Steiner, 1785);

Predigten über den Brief des heiligen Paulus an den Philemon, 2 volumes (St. Gall: Reutiner, 1785-1786);

Über Jesuitismus und Katholicismus: An Professor Meiners in Göttingen (Winterthur: Steiner, 1786); republished as *Schreiben an Herrn Professor Meiners in Göttingen über Jesuitismus und Katholicismus* (Winterthur: Steiner, 1787);

Lied eines Christen an Christus (Winterthur: Steiner, 1786);

Nathanaél oder Die eben so gewisse als unerweisliche Göttlichkeit des Christenthums: Für Nathanaéle, das ist, für Menschen mit geradem, gesundem, ruhigem, truglosem Wahrheitssinne (Winterthur: Steiner, 1786);

Predigt wider die Furcht vor Erderschütterungen über Psalm 46, v. 2-4: Gehalten Samstagabends den 15. Jenner 1786 (Zurich: Bürkli, 1786);

Rechenschaft an seine Freunde: 1. An meine Freunde über Magnetismus, Cagliostro, geheime Gesellschaften und Nichtchrist, Atheist; 2. Über Jesuitismus und Catholizismus an Herrn Professor Meiners in Göttingen (Winterthur: Steiner, 1786);

Schreiben an seine Freunde im März 1786 (Winterthur: Steiner, 1786);

Predigt nach dem Absterben Herrn Johann Rudolf Freytags, Pfarrers an den Sant Peterskirche in Zürich: Gehalten am Schwörtage Sonntagsmorgens, den 17. Christmonats 1786 (Zurich: Bürkli, 1786);

Briefe von Johann Caspar Lavater, und an ihn und seine Freunde: Nebst einem Briefe an Gaßner (Bremen, 1787);

Lieder für Leidende (Tübingen: Balz, 1787);

Drey Lobgedichte auf den katholischen Gottesdienst und auf die Klosterandachten: Mit Anmerkungen zweier Protestanten (Leipzig: Kummer, 1787);

Drey Pfingst-Predigten über das zweyte Kapitel der Apostelgeschichte (Winterthur: Steiner, 1787);

Zu Bremen gehaltene Predigten, am 2., 4. und 6. Julius 1786: Hinten an ein Lied für die bremischen Fischer (Bremen: Cramer, 1787);

Lavaters Protokoll über den Spiritus Familiaris Gablidone (Frankfurt am Main & Leipzig, 1787);

Vermischte unphysiognomische Regeln zur Selbst- und Menschenkenntniß, 2 volumes (Zurich, 1787); translated by Henry Fuseli as *Aphorisms on Man: Translated from the Original Manuscript of the Rev. Johann Caspar Lavater, Citizen of Zuric* (London: Printed for J. Johnson, 1788; Boston: Printed by I. Thomas and E. T. Andrews, 1790; reprinted, Delmar, N.Y.: Scholars' Facsimiles & Reprints, 1980);

Handbibel für Leidende: Erster Theil (Winterthur: Steiner, 1788);

Predigten über die Versuchung Christi in der Wüste, 3 volumes (Frankfurt am Main: Hermann, 1788);

Christlicher Religionsunterricht für denkende Jünglinge (Winterthur: Steiner, 1788);

Vermischte Gedichte und Verse: Als Manuskript für Freunde gedruckt (Zurich, 1789);

Haussteuer oder Hausrath für meine neu angehenden Eheleute Johann Heinrich und Barbara Lavater (Leipzig: Fleischer, 1789);

Taschenbüchlein für Weise (Basel: Schneider, 1789);

Zween Volkslehrer: Ein Gespräch. Nachgeschrieben, as Jonathan Asahel (Winterthur: Steiner, 1789);

Johann Kaspar Lavaters väterliche Trauungs-Rede an Johann Heinrich Lavater und Jungfrau Anna Barbara Ott: Gehalten zu Klooten, Dienstage, den 17. Wintermonats, 1789 (Zurich, 1789);

Apostolische Ermahnungen, ein Kern der christlichen Sittenlehre: In drey Predigten über Römer 12, 7-21 (Basel: Haas, 1790);

Evangelisches Handbuch für Christen oder Worte Jesu Christi beherzigt (Nuremberg: Raw, 1790);

Hand-Bibliothek für Freunde, 24 volumes (Zurich [actually Winterthur: Steiner], 1790-1793);

Maria, die Mutter Jesum: Predigt, gehalten im Julius 1790 (N.p., 1790);

Antworten auf wichtige und würdige Fragen und Briefe weiser und guter Menschen: Eine Monatsschrift, 2 volumes (Berlin: Rottmann, 1790);

Rede bey der öffentlichen Büchervertheilung an die studierende Zürchersche Jugend (Zurich: Bürkli, 1791);

Auserlesene christliche Lieder zur Erbauung (Basel: Flick, 1791); republished as *Auserlesene christliche Lieder: Ein Handbuch zur Erbauung und zum Nachdenken* (Basel: Flick, 1792);

Philosophische Unterhaltungen von einem französischen und einem schweizerischen Verfasser, anonymous, by Lavater and C. F. de Nelis (Zurich: Ziegler, 1791)–comprises "Der Blinde vom Berg," by de Nelis, translated by Lavater; "Drey Gespräche über Wahrheit und Irrthum, Seyn und Schein," by Lavater;

Etwas über Pfenningern, 6 volumes (Zurich: Näf, 1792-1793);

Worte Jesu, zusammen geschrieben von einem christlichen Dichter, anonymous (Zurich, 1792);

Fragmente von einer Predigt Lavaters über die Kraft des Gebets: Mit Hülfe des Gedächtnisses aufbewahrt und herausgegeben von einem aufmerksamen Zuhörer und aufrichtigen Verehrer, edited by J. G. Maurenbrecher (Copenhagen, 1793);

Regeln für Kinder (Hamburg, 1793);

Reise nach Kopenhagen im Sommer 1793: Auszug aus dem Tagebuch. Durchaus bloß für Freunde (Zurich, 1793);

Jesus auf Golgatha (New York: Amerikanische Tract-Gesellschaft, 1793);

Predigt auf den ausserordentlichen, gemeindsgenoßischen, allgemeinen Beth- und Danktag gehalten Sonntags Morgen den 16. Merz, 1794: Über den vorgeschriebenen Text, aus Psalm CXLVII, v. 12, 13, 14 (Zurich: Bürkli, 1794);

An die Aeltern Hirzel: Am Abend des Begräbnisses ihrer einzigen Tochter Regula, den 3. April 1794 (Zurich, 1794);

Joseph von Arimathia: Ein Gedicht in sieben Gesängen, anonymous (Hamburg: Bachmann & Gundermann, 1794);

Monatsblatt für Freunde: Für das Jahr 1794, 12 volumes (Zurich, 1794);

Christliche Monatsschrift für Ungelehrte, 4 volumes (Zurich: Ziegler & Ulrich, 1794-1795);

Vier und zwanzig kurze Vorlesungen über die Geschichte Josephs, des Sohnes Israels (Zurich: Ziegler & Ulrich, 1794);

Anacharsis oder Vermischte Gedanken und freundschaftliche Räthe, 2 volumes (Zurich: Ziegler, 1795);

Vermischte Erzählungen eines christlichen Dichters von Jesu Christo (N.p., 1795);

Väterliche Trauungsrede über das Gebet des Herrn an Georg Geßner und Anna Lavater, gehalten zu Bassersdorf, Dienstags, den vierzehnten Aprils, 1795 (Winterthur, 1795);

Freundschaftliche Briefe an verschiedene Freunde und Freundinnen: Geschrieben im Juni und Juli 1796 (Zurich, 1796);

Erweckung zur Lobpreisung und zum Vertrauen auf Gott nach abgewendeter Kriegsgefahr, den 30. Oktober 1796: Nach Verlesung eines obrigkeitlichen Manifestes, welches der Predigt vorgedruckt ist (Zurich, 1796);

Geschenkchen an Freunde oder Hundert vermischte Gedanken (N.p., 1796);

Vermischte Lehren an seine Tochter Anna Louisa (Zurich: Ziegler, 1796);

Vermächtniß an seine Freunde: Größtentheils Auszüge aus seinem Tagebuch vom Jahr 1796 (Zurich: Orell, Geßner, Füßli, 1796);

Christliche Belehrungen für Zürich, nach den Bedürfnissen der gegenwärtigen Zeit: Gehalten am ersten Sonntage nach der anerkannten allgemeinen Freyheit und Gleichheit, den 11. Hornung 1798 (Zurich, 1798);

Christliche Erweckungen zur Beherzigung der Güte und des Ernstes Gottes, und zum Gebethe, oder Predigt gehalten Donnerstag Morgens den 6. Herbstmonat 1798: An dem ersten allgemeinen Beth- und Danktag der einen und untheilbaren helvetischen Republik (Zurich: Ziegler & Ulrich, 1798);

Lavater (right) and Gotthold Ephraim Lessing (standing) visit the Jewish philosopher Moses Mendelssohn. Lavater's public challenge to Mendelssohn to convert to Christianity was widely criticized. (lithograph by S. Maier, from a painting by Moritz Oppenheim)

Ein Wort eines freyen Schweizers an die französische Nation, über das Betragen derselben gegen die Schweiz (N.p., 1798); republished as *Johann Caspar Lavater Pfarrer in Zürich an das Direktorium der französischen Republik* (Leipzig: Wolf, 1798); translated anonymously as *Remonstrance Addressed to the Executive Directory of the French Republic, against the Invasion of Switzerland* (London, 1798; New York: Tiebout, 1799);

Predigt über die Pflichten des christlichen Predigers zu der gegenwärtigen Zeit der Staatsumwälzung, gehalten Sonntags den 13. May 1798 (Basel: Dekker, 1798);

Zwey merkwürdige Schreiben: 1. An den Bürger Schauenburg, Obergeneral der fränkischen Armee in der Schweiz; 2. Beschluß der Dankrede im Nahmen der Zürcher Bürgerschaft an den Herrn Bürgermeister Kilchsberger (Zurich, 1798);

Christliches Wochenblatt für die gegenwärtige Zeit, 3 volumes (N.p. 1798);

Johann Kaspar Lavaters Erweckungs-Predigt zur thätigen Barmherzigkeit für die unglüklichen Helvezier im Distrikt Stanz: Gehalten Sonntags Morgen den 28. X. 1798. In der Kirche zum Sankt Peter in Zürich (Zurich: Ziegler & Ulrich, 1798);

Vollständiger Brief-Wechsel zwischen Johann Caspar Lavater und B. Reubell, Mitglied des Direktoriums der französischen Republik: Unterhalten im Jahr 1798. Gesammelt und zusammengetragen zu Nutz und Frommen derer, die gerne Wahrheit hören und verehren (N.p., 1799); enlarged as *Briefwechsel Lavaters und Reubells vom Jahre 1798: Vollständiger und correcter herausgegeben und mit einer Zugabe zweener beziehender Briefe vermehrt* (N.p., 1801);

Predigt von der beglückenden Ueberzeugung: Alles dient dem Freund Gottes zum Besten. Über die Worte aus dem Brief zu die Römer Kap. VIII. v. 28. Gehalten Sonntags Morgen, den 11ten August 1799, in der Münsterkirche zu Basel (Basel: Flick, 1799);

Nachricht von einem fatalen Vorfall den Pfarrer Lavater betreffend: Geschehen Donnerstags Nachmitags, den 26. 9. 1799 (Zurich, 1799);

Schreiben an das helvetische Direktorium: Gedruckt auf Befehl des Vollziehungs-Direktoriums (Zurich: Waser, 1799); republished as *An das helvetische Vollziehungs-Direktorium* (N.p., 1799);

Ansprüche an die Petrinische Gemeinde am Bettage, Sonntag, den 14. Herbstmonats 1800: Nebst zwei kurzen Aufsätzen (Zurich, 1800);

Freymüthige Briefe von Johann Kaspar Lavater über das Deportationswesen und seine eigene Deportation nach Basel: Nebst mancherley Beylagen, Urkunden und der kurzgefaßten Deportationsgeschichte seiner Mitbürger und einiger anderer Schweizer. Zugeeignet allervörderst dem helvetischen Vollziehungsausschuß, sodann allen Feinden der Freyheit und Menschenrechte, 2 volumes (Winterthur: Steiner, 1800-1801);

Drei Psalmen auf den bevorstehenden Bettag: Zum Besten der Hülfsbedürftigen (Zurich, 1800);

Zürich am Ende des achtzehnten Jahrhunderts (Zurich: Bürkli, 1800);

Privatbriefe von Saulus und Paulus (Winterthur: Steiner, 1801); translated anonymously as *Letters of St. Paul the Apostle, Written before and after His Conversion* (London: Printed for J. Johnson, 1805);

Nachgelassene Schriften, 5 volumes, edited by Georg Geßner (Zurich: Orell, Füßli, 1801-1802);

Schreiben an seine Tochter Anna Louisa, welches eine Anweisung zum Briefschreiben enthält: Nebst einem vollständigen Briefsteller (Bregenz: Brentano, 1801);

Zürich am Anfange des neunzehnten Jahrhunderts: Lavaters Schwanengesang (Zurich: Musikalische Gesellschaft in Zürich, 1801);

Sämmtliche christliche Gebete (Bregenz: Brentano, 1802);

Vermischte physiognomische Regeln: Ein Manuskript für Freunde (Leipzig: Jakobäer, 1802);

Simeon oder Unterhaltungen für betagte Christen: Ein nachgelassenes Werkgen (Zurich: Ziegler & Ulrich, 1804);

Die Christus-Religion oder Der feste Christ, der beste Bürger: Neujahrsstück für die musikalische Gesellschaft in Basel 1796 (Berlin, 1812);

Vermischte Gedanken und Räthe der Freundschaft (Ingolstadt: Altenhoven, 1812);

Zur Beherzigung: In Anleitung der fünfundneunzig Sätze von Haras. Eine Predigt, gehalten den 26. Juli 1795 (Hamburg: Perthes & Besser, 1817);

Allgemeine Betrachtungen über Religion und religiöse Physiognomien (Jena: Cröker, 1817);

Sprüche: In 107 Blättern (Tübingen: Laupp, 1819);

Worte des Herzens für Freunde der Liebe und des Glaubens, edited by Christoph Wilhelm Hufeland (Berlin: Dümmler, 1825);

Hundert Sentenzen; Hundert Blättchen (Basel: Schneider, 1827);

Sämmtliche Werke, 6 volumes (Augsburg & Lindau: Kranzfelder, 1834-1838);

J. K. Lavater's Ausgewählte Schriften, 8 volumes, edited by Johann Kaspar Orelli (Zurich: Schultheß, 1841-1844);

Sprüche: Herausgegeben von einem Verehrer des Verfassers (Blaubeuren: Mangold, 1841);

Predigten auf alle Sonn- und Festtage des ganzen Jahres als allgemeines Sonntags-Hausbuch: Säcular-Andenken an Johann Kaspar Lavaters hundertjährigen Geburtstag am 15. November 1841, 2 volumes (Zurich: Hanke, 1842-1845);

Worte Väterlicher Liebe an Anna Louise Lavater auf das heilige Osterfest 1796, als sie das erste Mal zum Tisch des Herrn ging: Zusammengeschrieben in der Charwoche 1796, edited by E. Pasch (Gotha: Perthes, 1856);

Des Freundes Stimme: Worte liebreicher Ermahnung an Jünglinge (Winterthur: Steiner, 1857);

Über Gefängniß-Seelsorge: Ein Vortrag, edited by K. Marthaler (Gotha: Perthes, 1861);

Gottes Vorsehung (Basel: Jaeger & Kober, 1892);

Die Jugendzeit dem Herrn geweiht: Freundesstimmen für Jünglinge und Jungfrauen, edited by J. Biegler (Reutlingen: Enßlin & Laiblin, 1898);

Lavateriana, edited by F. Behrend (Berlin: Literaturarchiv-Gesellschaft, 1916);

J. C. Lavater's Ausgewählte Werke, 4 volumes, edited by Ernst Staehelin (Zurich: Zwingli, 1943).

OTHER: *Der Erinnerer: Monatsschrift,* 3 volumes, edited by Lavater and Johann Heinrich Pestalozzi (Zurich: Heidegger, 1765-1767);

Auserlesene Psalmen Davids zum allgemeinen Gebrauch in deutsche Reimen gebracht, 2 volumes, translated and paraphrased by Lavater (Zurich: Bürgkli, 1765-1768);

Charles Bonnet, *Philosophische Palingenesie oder Gedanken über den vergangenen und künftigen Zustand lebender Wesen: Als ein Anhang zu den letzten Schriften des Verfassers und welcher insonderheit das Wesentliche seiner Untersuchungen über das Christenthum enthält,* 2 volumes, translated by Lavater (Zurich: Orell, Geßner, Füßli, 1769-1770); volume 1 enlarged as *Philosophische Untersuchung der Beweise für das Christenthum: Samt desselben Ideen von der künftigen Glückseligkeit des Menschen. Aus dem Französischen übersetzt, und mit Anmerkungen herausgegeben von Johann Caspar Lavater.*

Manuscript for a poem by Lavater, written in 1790 (from Gustav Könnecke, Bilderatlas zur Geschichte der deutschen Nationallitteratur, 1895)

Nebst dessen Zueignungsschrift an Moses Mendelssohn, und daher entstandenen sämtlichen Streitschriften zwischen Herrn Lavater, Moses Mendelssohn, und Herrn Dr. Kölbele; wie auch der ersten gehaltenen Rede bey der Taufe zweyer Israeliten (Frankfurt am Main: Bayrhoffer, 1774);

Der christliche Dichter: Ein Wochenblatt, 52 issues, edited by Lavater (Zurich: Ziegler, 1782-1783);

Salomo oder Lehren der Weisheit, edited by Lavater (Winterthur: Steiner, 1785);

Christliches Sonntagsblatt, 3 volumes, edited with contributions by Lavater (volumes 1-2, Zurich: Bürgkli; volume 3, Zurich: Ziegler & Weiß, 1792-1793);

Sammlung christlicher Gebether, edited by Lavater (Nuremberg: Raw, 1800).

A religious enthusiast verging on zealotry, Johann Kaspar Lavater lived the life of a pastor in Zurich–counseling prisoners on death row, working in an orphanage, and preaching Sunday sermons. At the same time, he engaged leading intellectuals of his day in debate: he exchanged letters, visits, and ideas first with the new generation of Sturm-und-Drang writers, including Johann Wolfgang Goethe and Johann Gottfried Herder, with whom he shared a passion for life and letters; and later with those of a more rationalistic persuasion, such as Gotthold Ephraim Lessing and Georg Christoph Lichtenberg, who constantly challenged his positions. From the blend of his stable personal and professional life with his controversial intellectual activities came a broad range of writings, from tender expressions of care for children, reasoned advice for adolescents, consoling words for social outcasts, and intuitive statements on character interpretation through the study of facial features, to patriotic songs celebrating his Swiss heritage, odes on the life of Christ, and hymns to Swiss Protestantism. As a poet he was passable and was appreciated mostly by his family, friends, and local admirers; but it was his prose works that attained international attention in his time and remain of value today. Three are of special interest: *Aussichten in die Ewigkeit* (Views of Eternity, 1768-1778), *Geheimes Tagebuch von einem Beobachter seiner selbst* (1771-1773, translated as *Secret Journal of a Self-Observer*, 1795), and *Physiognomische Fragmente, zur Beförderung der Menschenkenntniß und Menschenliebe* (Physiognomical Fragments to Promote the Knowledge and Love of Mankind, 1775-1778; translated as *The Whole Works of Lavater on Physiognomy*, 1787).

Lavater was born in Zurich on 15 November 1741, the twelfth child of Johann Heinrich Lavater, a doctor and member of the city government, and Regula Escher Lavater, who seems to have been the source of Lavater's imaginative and benevolent spirit. He received a classical education at the Collegium Carolinum, where between 1756 and 1762 he was trained in the most up-to-date rationalist theology. He also attracted the attention of the two leading German literary critics who taught there, Johann Jakob Bodmer and Johann Jakob Breitinger. Through them he met leading literary figures, including Christoph Martin Wieland. He also established friendships with the brothers Felix, Jakob, and Heinrich Heß and with Johann Heinrich Füssli. Lavater was ordained in the spring of 1762.

Füssli collaborated with Lavater on the latter's first publication, *Der ungerechte Landvogt oder Klage eines Patrioten* (The Unjust Bailiff or the Complaint of a Patriot, 1762), an anonymous civil complaint against the misdeeds of a local bailiff, Felix Grebel, who was the son-in-law of the mayor of Zurich and was also a member of the city council. Authorship of the complaint came to light, and although the suit was successful and brought them fame beyond the borders of Switzerland (Goethe requested a report on the case), they were severely reprimanded. They decided to follow the suggestion of Bodmer and Breitinger to take an extended trip, along with Felix Heß and under the guidance of the aesthetician Johann Georg Sulzer, to north Germany. There they visited the theologian, Johann Joachim Spalding and met leading writers and intellectuals, including Christian Fürchtegott Gellert, Johann Wilhelm Ludwig Gleim, Moses Mendelssohn, Friedrich Gottlieb Klopstock, Johann David Michaelis, and Abraham Gotthelf Kästner. After a year of travel in Germany, Füssli went on to London, where he changed his named to Henry Fuseli and became a painter. Lavater returned to Zurich on 26 March 1764.

He took a position as a prison chaplain, at the same time continuing visits with leading intellectuals such as Jean-Jacques Rousseau in Geneva. With Johann Heinrich Pestalozzi he founded *Der Erinnerer*, a journal that became a powerful organ against corruption in Switzerland. On 3 June 1766 he married Anna Schinz, with whom he had eight children. In 1769 he was elected deacon at the orphanage church, the Waisenhaus; in 1775 he was appointed pastor. He repeated the same pattern at the St. Peterskirche, becoming deacon in 1778 and first pastor in 1786. He remained in this position until his death. He traveled with Goethe and Johann Bernhard Basedow to Bad Ems and Neuwied in 1774. He also made trips to southwest Germany in 1782; to Göttingen, Weimar, and Bremen in 1786; and to Copenhagen in 1793.

Although the publication of *Schweizerlieder* (Swiss Songs, 1767) brought Lavater some literary recognition, most attention came through his visionary prose writings, beginning with *Aussichten in die Ewigkeit*. The work was initially planned as an ode, reflecting the early influence of Klopstock on the young Lavater; the question of form seemed to inhibit progress on the work until his friend Felix Heß died in 1768, stirring in Lavater emotions and visions about death, dying, and life hereafter. He wrote the work in the form of twenty-five letters, supposedly directed to Johann G. Zimmermann, an acquaintance from Hannover. They are dated from 1 June 1768 to 13 July 1772, and the work was published in three volumes between 1768 and 1773. A fourth volume was added in 1778 in response to reviews and letters.

Title page for the first volume of Lavater's work on the "science" of reading character on the basis of facial features

Inspired by Charles Bonnet's *La Palingénésie philosophique* (1769) and Klopstock's *Der Messias* (The Messiah, 1748-1773) and motivated by his passion to prepare mankind for "das zukünftige Leben" (the future life), Lavater wrote his letters for the "denkende Leser" (thinking reader). He explains in the first three letters that many had speculated about the immortality of the soul, a view which he accepts as given; he extends his vision beyond mere assumption to detailed description of life in eternity, of "die Beschaffenheit des himmlischen Lebens" (the nature of the heavenly life). His approach is to extrapolate the possible from the real, observing the present condition of nature, man, and the individual, and then, by analogy, speculating on the pure forms of each in heaven. The work has four themes: the condition of the soul after the death of the body; the perfection of the body in heaven, including its language and its physical, intellectual, moral, and political powers; the moral government of God; and the eternal continuation of heavenly existence. In the eleventh letter he begins with a quotation from Gottfried Wilhelm von Leibniz which points out that we are still in the earliest stages of scientific development. He then quotes Pet-

rus Musschenbroek's observation that light is so fine that even the smallest hair is at least 5,000,000,000,000,000 times thicker. How much more subtle and perfect would the heavenly light be! Language in heaven, he speculates in the sixteenth letter, will be free of arbitrary sounds, which are unacceptable for that land of truth. He projects "eine allgemeine Sprache" (a general language): a language physiognomic, pantomimic, and musical, a language of "Ruhe und Bewegung" (rest and motion)—each condition communicating expression and meaning. These visions reflect the fascination of the period for the perfectibility of mankind that can also be seen in Lessing's *Erziehung des Menschengeschlechts* (The Education of Mankind, 1780).

In 1770, filled with enthusiasm from translating Bonnet's *La Palingénésie philosophique*, Lavater dedicated the second volume of the translation to Mendelssohn, requesting that the Jewish philosopher publicly accept or reject Bonnet's proofs of Christianity. Lavater's indiscretion generated a host of responses from intellectuals and an extensive exchange of polemical papers, an exchange that illustrates the intensity of his religious passion. Friend and foe alike voiced disappointment, including Bonnet, but Lichtenberg wrote the sharpest criticism in *Timorus* (1773).

For Lavater, the arts and sciences were at man's disposal to advance culture and civilization toward Christ and the life beyond. This search for religious truth through art and science brought Lavater more than once to the cutting edge of intellectual life, particularly in the social and behavioral sciences. In the second letter of *Aussichten in die Ewigkeit* he outlines his approach to extrapolating the possible from the real, to studying science and art for the purpose of discovering the truth about our inner being and our outer condition. The former sort of truth is illustrated in *Geheimes Tagebuch von einem Beobachter seiner selbst* and the latter in his most successful publication, *Physiognomische Fragmente, zur Beförderung der Menschenkenntniß und Menschenliebe*.

Geheimes Tagebuch von einem Beobachter seiner selbst was first published anonymously and without Lavater's permission in 1771 by Johann Georg Zollikofer, a Swiss theologian living in Leipzig; after its authorship was discovered, it was published in an enlarged second edition with Lavater's permission. Responses varied from enthusiastic imitations and the revival of a genre of personalized literature to accusations of

*Lavater in 1789; drawing by Heinrich Lips
(Nationalbibliothek, Vienna)*

works by and letters from contemporaries, and his plans for his own writings, particularly on physiognomy. The work remains a source for the literary critic and the historian of psychology.

Physiognomische Fragmente was Lavater's greatest literary sensation, and it remains his most significant work. Physiognomy was recognized by many of Lavater's contemporaries as a pseudoscience, but the work was appreciated then and remains valuable today as a study in human behavior. The portraits, silhouettes, and caricatures of many contemporary and historical figures and Lavater's descriptions of the illustrations continue to fascinate the reader. The more than eight hundred engravings, most of them by prominent artists such as Daniel Chodowiecki and Johann Heinrich Lips, contribute to the broad and lasting interest in the work. On a theoretical level the book does not claim much attention beyond Lavater's general principles of observation, which seek to relate inner and outer characteristics of the human being. The first volume includes a discussion of the art of physiognomic analysis, that is, reading the inner meaning of lines of expression in the face. Observations are focused on the interaction of solid and mobile features of the face; reading the former is called physiognomy, reading the latter is called pathognomy. Combined, they represent a holistic study of the human being. Despite the hopes of some to establish physiognomy as an experimental science, it remains an art of reading nonverbal expressions, an intuitive skill of "the sixth sense" in which Lavater excelled.

Physiognomy and the art of reading human behavior surfaced in *Aussichten in die Ewigkeit* and remained central to Lavater's writings and observations into his old age. Lavater's talent for reading character contributed to the literary high point reached in his book of aphorisms, *Vermischte unphysiognomische Regeln zur Selbst- und Menschenkenntniß* (Miscellaneous Unphysiognomical Rules for the Knowledge of the Self and of Mankind, 1787), translated into English by his friend Fuseli as *Aphorisms on Man* (1788). The sharp observations and pointed style of the aphorism continued to appear occasionally in Lavater's sermons, essays, and religious and patriotic songs.

Lavater's final testaments, reflecting the chaotic times of the French Revolution, are a letter published without his permission, *Ein Wort eines freyen Schweizers an die französische Nation, über das Betragen derselben gegen die Schweiz* (A Word to the

"Schwärmerei" (zealotry). Although the title emphasized that the book was a testimony to introspection and self-analysis, the publication of such personal materials seemed to imply that it was intended as a prescription for life. The work is valued today for its delicate display of the nuances of inner life. Lavater seems to lay bare his innermost thoughts and feelings, as if in prayer. The work especially gains in merit through the sincerity of Lavater's self-criticism, in a period in which biography was cloaked in idealized forms as much as possible. Although Lavater did not initiate this public display of his innermost feelings, he justified it in the introduction, stating that historians have always complained that they have so little moral material for their histories because they know so little of the "Privatgeschichte" (private history) of their subjects. The book constitutes a record of his daily life: his feelings on the death of his mother, his reactions to confessions of a poverty-stricken woman, his attempts to understand the changes in his moods, his anxieties in presenting sermons and prayers, his reactions to

French Nation on Its Conduct toward Switzerland, 1798; translated as *Remonstrance Addressed to the Executive Directory of the French Republic, against the Invasion of Switzerland*, 1798), and a series of letters (1800-1801) protesting the deportation practices of the French. Lavater himself was arrested on 16 May 1799 and deported to Basel; he returned to Zurich on 16 August of the same year.

These works from Lavater's last years recall the activist posture of his youth. On 26 September 1799, during the second occupation of Zurich, Lavater, after a lifetime of practice in reading character, misjudged the level of belligerence of French soldiers in his attempt to rescue two women on St. Peterskirche square. In a scuffle with the soldiers Lavater received a wound to the abdomen; it was not immediately fatal, but in combination with his rheumatism it was a source of great suffering until his death on 2 January 1801. Lavater's entrance into public life had been the civil complaint against Bailiff Grebel; his exit, too, was an act of protest on behalf of justice.

Letters:

Johann Heinrich Jung-Stilling, *Sequel to Jung-Stilling, Containing Stilling's Old Age, A Fragment; His Last Hours; A Supplement, by His Son-in-law; and Letters to Stilling, from Lavater, Oberlin, Moser, the Baroness von Krudener, Prince Charles of Hesse Cassel*, translated by Samuel Jackson (London: Hamilton, Adams, 1836);

Johann Kaspar Lavater's Briefe an die Kaiserin Maria Feodorowna, Gemahlin Kaiser Pauls I. von Rußland, über den Zustand der Seele nach dem Tode: Nach der Originalhandschrift herausgegeben von der Kaiserlichen öffentlichen Bibliothek zu St. Petersburg (St. Petersburg: Buchdruck der Kaiserlichen Akademie der Wissenschaften, 1858);

Briefwechsel zwischen Lavater und Hasenkamp, edited by Karl C. E. Ehmann (Basel: Bahnmaier, 1870);

Katharina Elisabeth Goethe, *Goethe's Mother: Correspondence of Catharina Elizabeth Goethe with Goethe, Lavater, Wieland, Duchess Anna Amalia of Saxe-Weimar, Friedrich von Stein, and Others*, edited and translated by Alfred S. Gibbs (New York: Dodd, Mead, 1880);

Johann Froitzheim, *Lenz und Goethe: Mit ungedruckten Briefen von Lenz, Herder, Lavater, Röderer, Luise König* (Stuttgart: Deutsche Verlags-Anstalt, 1891);

Aus Lavaters Brieftasche: Neues von Johann Kaspar Lavater. Ungedruckte Handschriften nebst anderen Lavater-Erinnerungen mit Facsimiles, edited by Gustav Adolf Müller (Munich: Seitz & Schauer, 1897);

Briefe Lavaters an seine Bremer Freunde, 1798 (Zurich: Hascher, 1918).

Biographies:

J. A. Näbe, *Johann Kaspar Lavater: Über ihn und seine Schriften* (Leipzig: Gräff, 1801);

Georg Geßner, *Johann Kaspar Lavaters Lebensbeschreibung*, 3 volumes (Winterthur: Steiner, 1802);

Franz Muncker, *Johann Kaspar Lavater: Eine Skizze seines Lebens und Wirkens* (Stuttgart: Cotta, 1883);

Mary Lavater-Sloman, *Genie des Herzens: Die Lebensgeschichte Johann Caspar Lavaters* (Zurich: Morgarten, 1939).

References:

Julius Forssman, *J. K. Lavater und die religiösen Strömungen des achtzehnten Jahrhunderts* (Riga: Plates, 1935);

John Graham, *Lavater's Essays on Physiognomy: A Study in the History of Ideas* (Bern: Lang, 1979);

Reinhard Kunz, "Johann Caspar Lavaters Physiognomielehre im Urteil von Haller, Zimmermann und anderen zeitgenössischen Ärzten," *Zürcher Medizingeschichtliche Abhandlungen*, 71 (1970): 1-44;

Kamal Radwan, *Die Sprache Lavaters im Spiegel der Geistesgeschichte* (Göppingen: Kümmerle, 1972);

Graeme Tytler, *Physiognomy in the European Novel: Faces and Fortunes* (Princeton: Princeton University Press, 1982);

Stiftung von Schnyder von Wartensee, Zurich, *Johann Caspar Lavater, 1741-1801, Denkschrift zur Hundertsten Wiederkehr seines Todestages* (Zurich: Müller, 1902).

Papers:

Unpublished manuscripts and correspondence of Johann Kaspar Lavater are in the Goethe-Museum; Anton- und Katharina-Kippenberg-Stiftung, Düsseldorf; the Freies Deutsches Hochstift, Frankfurter Goethe-Museum, Frankfurt am Main; the Badische Landesbibliothek, Karlsruhe; and the Zentralbibliothek, Weimar.

Gotthold Ephraim Lessing

(22 January 1729 - 15 February 1781)

Gerd Hillen

University of California, Berkeley

BOOKS: *Der Eremite: Eine Erzehlung*, anonymous (Kerapolis [actually Stuttgart: Mezler], 1749);

Die alte Jungfer: Ein Lustspiel in drei Aufzügen, anonymous (Berlin: Voß, 1749);

Tarantula: Eine Poszen Oper, anonymous (Teltow an der Tyber [actually Berlin], 1749);

Weiber sind Weiber: Ein Lustspiel in fünf Aufzügen, anonymous (Berlin, 1749);

Critische Nachrichten aus dem Reiche der Gelehrsamkeit, 2 volumes, anonymous (Berlin: Haude & Spener, 1750-1751);

Palaion: Comédie en un Acte, anonymous (Berlin, 1750);

Kleinigkeiten, anonymous (Frankfurt am Main & Leipzig [actually Stuttgart: Mezler], 1751);

Das Neueste aus dem Reiche des Witzes, anonymous (Berlin, 1751);

Schrifften, 6 volumes (Berlin: Voß, 1753-1755)— volume 6 (1755) includes *Der junge Gelehrte in der Einbildung: Ein Lustspiel in drey Aufzügen, Die Juden, Der Freygeist, Der Schatz, Miß Sara Sampson, Der Misogyne oder Der Feind des weiblichen Geschlechts: Ein Lustspiel in zwey Aufzügen*;

Ein Vade Mecum für den Hrn. Sam. Gotth. Lange, Pastor in Laublingen, in dessen Taschenformate angefertigt (Berlin: Voß, 1754);

Theatralische Bibliothek, 4 volumes (Berlin: Voß, 1754-1758);

Miß Sara Sampson: Ein Trauerspiel in fünf Aufzügen (Berlin: Voß, 1755);

Pope—ein Metaphysiker!, anonymous, by Lessing and Moses Mendelssohn (Danzig: Schuster, 1755);

Philotas: Ein Trauerspiel, anonymous (Berlin: Voß, 1759);

Fabeln: Drey Bücher. Nebst Abhandlungen mit dieser Dichtungsart verwandten Inhalts (Berlin: Voß, 1759); translated anonymously as *Fables: In Three Books* (London: Taylor, 1829); German version republished, edited by Walther Killy (Hamburg: Maximilian-Gesellschaft, 1979);

Painting by O. May, circa 1766 (Gleimhaus, Halberstadt)

Sophokles: Erstes Buch, anonymous (Berlin: Voß, 1760);

Laokoon: Oder Über die Grenzen der Mahlerey und Poesie. Erster Theil. Mit beiläufigen Erläuterungen verschiedener Punkte der alten Kunstgeschichte (Berlin: Voß, 1766); translated by William Ross as *Laocoon; or, The Limits of Poetry and Painting* (London: Ridgway, 1836); translated by Ellen Frothingham as *Laocoon: An Essay upon the Limits of Painting and Poetry* (London: Low, 1874; Boston: Roberts, 1874; reprinted, New York: Noonday Press,

1957); German version republished, edited by Dorothy Reich (London: Oxford University Press, 1965);

Lustspiele, 2 volumes (Berlin: Voß, 1767)–includes *Minna von Barnhelm oder das Soldatenglück*, translated by Fanny Holcroft as *Minna von Barnhelm: A Comedy in 5 Acts*, in *The Theatrical Recorder*, volume 2 (London: Holcroft, 1806), pp. 217-258;

Hamburgische Dramaturgie, 2 volumes (Hamburg & Bremen: Cramer, 1767-1769; reprinted, 1 volume, edited by Friedrich Schröter and Richard Thiele, Halle: Waisenhaus, 1878; reprinted, Hildesheim & New York: Olms, 1979); translated by Helen Zimmern as *Hamburg Dramaturgy*, 1 volume (New York: Dover, 1962);

Brief, antiquarischen Inhalts, 2 volumes (Berlin: Nicolai, 1768-1769);

Wie die Alten den Tod gebildet: Eine Untersuchung (Berlin: Voß, 1769);

Berengarius Turonensis: oder Ankündigung eines wichtigen Werkes desselben, wovon in der Herzoglichen Bibliothek zu Wolfenbüttel ein Manuscript befindlich, welches bisher völlig unbekannt geblieben (Brunswick: Waisenhaus, 1770);

Vermischte Schriften, 14 volumes, edited by Karl Gotthelf Lessing and Johann Joachim Eschenberg (volumes 1-10, 13-14, Berlin: Voß; volumes 11-12, Berlin: Nicolai, 1771-1793);

Sinngedichte (Berlin: Voß, 1771; republished, edited by Helmut Hirsch, Berlin: Der Morgen, 1980);

Trauerspiele: Miß Sara Sampson; Philotas; Emilia Galotti (Berlin: Voß, 1772); *Emilia Galotti* translated by Benjamin Thompson (London: Vernor & Hood, 1800);

Emilia Galotti: Ein Trauerspiel in fünf Aufzügen (Berlin, Voß, 1772);

Zur Geschichte und Litteratur: Aus den Schätzen der Herzoglichen Bibliothek zu Wolfenbüttel, 6 volumes (Brunswick: Waisenhaus, 1773-1781);

Vom Alter der Oelmalerey: Aus dem Theophilus Presbyter, anonymous (Brunswick: Waisenhaus, 1774);

Zwey Lustspiele: Damon; Die alte Jungfer (Frankfurt am Main & Leipzig: Fleischer, 1775);

Über den Beweis des Geistes und der Kraft an den Herrn Director Schumann, zu Hannover, anonymous (Brunswick: Waisenhaus, 1777);

Das Testament Johannis: Ein Gespräch, anonymous (Brunswick: Waisenhaus, 1777);

Anti-Goeze: Das ist, Nothgedrungener Beytrag zu den freiwilligen Beyträgen des Hrn. Past. Goeze, anonymous (Brunswick: Waisenhaus, 1778);

Von den Zwecke Jesu und seiner Jünger: Noch ein Fragment des Wolfenbüttelschen Ungenannten (Brunswick: Waisenhaus, 1778);

Nöthige Antwort auf eine sehr unnöthige Frage des Herrn Hauptpastor Goeze in Hamburg (Wolfenbüttel, 1778);

Der nöthigen Antwort auf ein sehr unnöthige Frage des Herrn Hauptpastor Goeze in Hamburg: Erste Folge (N.p., 1778);

Axiomata, wenn es deren in dergleichen Dingen giebt, wider den Herrn Pastor Goeze in Hamburg, anonymous (Brunswick: Waisenhaus, 1778);

Eine Duplik, anonymous (Brunswick: Waisenhaus, 1778);

Eine Parabel: Nebst einer kleinen Bitte und einem eventualen Absagungsbriefe an Herrn Pastor Goeze, in Hamburg, anonymous (Brunswick: Waisenhaus, 1778); translated by Henry Crabb Robinson as "A Parable from the German of Lessing," *Monthly Repository of Theology and General Literature*, 1 (1806): 183-185;

Neue Hypothese über die Evangelisten als blos menschliche Geschichtschreiber betrachtet (Wolfenbüttel, 1778);

Ernst und Falk: Gespräche für Freymäurer, 2 volumes, anonymous (volume 1, Wolfenbüttel & Göttingen: Dieterich, 1778; volume 2, Frankfurt am Main: Brönner, 1780; republished, Hamburg: Bauhütten, 1980); translated by A. Cohn as *Masonic Dialogues* (London: Baskerville Press, 1927);

Noch nähere Berichtigung des Mährchens von 1000 Ducaten oder Judas Ischarioth dem Zweyten (N.p., 1778);

Nathan der Weise: Ein dramatisches Gedicht in fünf Aufzügen (Berlin: Voß, 1779); translated by William Taylor as *Nathan the Wise* (Norwich, U.K.: Stevenson & Matchett, 1791); translated by Frothingham as *Nathan the Wise* (New York: Holt, 1867); German version republished, edited by Peter Demetz (Frankfurt am Main & Berlin: Ullstein, 1966);

Die Erziehung des Menschengeschlechts (Berlin: Voß, 1780); translated by Frederick William Robertson as *The Education of the Human Race* (London: Smith, Elder, 1858; New York: Collier, 1909); German version republished, edited by Louis Ferdinand Helbig (Bern: Lang, 1980);

Theatralischer Nachlaß, 2 volumes, edited by Karl Gotthelf Lessing (Berlin: Voß, 1784-1786);

The parsonage in Kamenz where Lessing was born in 1749; the house burned down in 1842. Drawing by H. Fröhlich (Pfarrhaus zu Kamenz).

Theologischer Nachlaß, edited by Karl Gotthelf Lessing (Berlin: Voß, 1784);

Analekten für die Litteratur, 4 volumes (Bern & Leipzig: Haller, 1785-1786);

Der Schlaftrunk: Ein Lustspiel in drey Aufzügen von Gotthold Ephraim Lessing, zu Ende gebracht vom Verfasser der Jugendgeschichte Karl und Sophie (Regensburg: Montag, 1785);

Übrige noch ungedruckte Werke des Wolfenbüttlischen Fragmentisten: Ein Nachlaß, edited by C. A. E. Schmidt (N.p., 1787);

Kollektaneen zur Literatur, 2 volumes, edited and enlarged by Johann Joachim Eschenburg (Berlin: Voß, 1790);

Die Matrone von Ephesus: Ein Lustspiel in einem Aufzuge, completed by K. L. Rahbek (Mannheim: Schwann & Götz, 1790);

Sämmtliche Schriften, 32 volumes, edited by Johann Friedrich Schink (volumes 1-28, Berlin: Voß; volumes 29-32, Berlin & Stettin: Nicolai, 1825-1828);

Sämmtliche Schriften, 13 volumes, edited by Karl Lachmann (Berlin: Voß, 1838-1840); revised and enlarged by Franz Muncker, 23 volumes (volumes 1-22, Stuttgart & Leipzig: Göschen; volume 23, Berlin: De Gruyter, 1886-1924; reprinted, Berlin: De Gruyter, 1968);

Werke: Vollständige Ausgabe, 25 volumes, edited by Julius Petersen and Waldemar von Olshausen (Berlin: Bong, 1925-1935; reprinted, Hildesheim & New York: Olms, 1970);

Gesammelte Werke, 10 volumes, edited by Paul Rilla (Berlin: Aufbau, 1954-1958);

Werke, 8 volumes, edited by Herbert G. Göpfert, Karl Eibl, and others (Munich: Hanser, 1970-1979).

Editions in English: *Three Comedies*, translated by J. J. Holroyd (Colchester, U.K.: Totham, 1838)—comprises *The Freethinker, The Treasure, Minna von Barnhelm; or, The Soldier's Fortune;*

Dramatic Works, 2 volumes, translated by Ernest Bell and R. Dillon Boylan, edited by Bell (London: Bell, 1878)—comprises in volume 1 (*Tragedies*), "Memoir," *Miss Sara Sampson, Philotas, Emilia Galotti, Nathan the Wise*; in volume 2 (*Comedies*), *Damon; or, True Friend-*

Lessing (right), age six, with his brother Theophilus; painting by Christian Gottlieb Haberkorn (from Gustav Könnecke,
Bilderatlas zur Geschichte der deutschen Nationallitteratur, *1895)*

ship, *The Young Scholar, The Old Maid, The
Woman-Hater, The Jews, The Freethinker, The
Treasure, Minna von Barnhelm*;

Select Prose Works, translated by E. C. Beasley and
Helen Zimmern (London: Bell, 1879; re-
vised, 1890)—comprises "Laocoön," "How
the Ancients Represented Death," "Dramatic Notes";

Nathan the Wise: A Dramatic Poem in Five Acts, translated and edited by Leo Markun (Girard,
Kans.: Haldeman-Julius, 1926);

Laocoön; Nathan the Wise; Minna von Barnhelm,
translated by William A. Steel and Anthony
Dent, edited by Steel (London: Dent / New
York: Dutton, 1930; reprinted, 1959);

*Nathan the Wise: A Dramatic Poem in Five Acts. Trans-
lated into English Verse,* translated by Bayard
Quincy Morgan (New York: Ungar, 1955; reprinted, 1975);

Theological Writings, translated by Henry Chad-
wick (London: Black, 1956; Stanford: Stanford University Press, 1957);

Emilia Galotti: A Tragedy in Five Acts, translated by
Anna Johanna Gode von Aesch (Great

Neck, N.Y.: Barron's, 1959);

Emilia Galotti: A Tragedy in Five Acts, translated by
Edward Dvoretzky (New York: Ungar,
1962);

*Laocoön: An Essay on the Limits of Painting and Poe-
try,* translated by Edward Allen McCormick
(Indianapolis: Bobbs-Merrill, 1962);

Minna von Barnhelm: A Comedy in Five Acts, translated by Kenneth J. Northcott (Chicago: University of Chicago Press, 1972);

Nathan the Wise, translated by Walter Frank
Charles Ade (Woodbury, N.Y.: Barron's,
1972);

Miss Sara Sampson: A Tragedy in Five Acts, translated by G. Hoern Schlage (Stuttgart: Heinz,
1977);

Philotas, translated by Dvoretzky (Stuttgart:
Heinz, 1979).

OTHER: Crébillon, *Catalina: Ein Trauerspiel. Aus
dem Französischen,* translated anonymously
by Lessing (Berlin, 1749);

Lessing circa 1760; painting by Johann Heinrich Tischbein, Sr. (from Gustav Könnecke, Bilderatlas zur Geschichte der deutschen Nationallitteratur, *1895)*

Charles Rollin, *Römische Historie von der Erbauung der Stadt Rom: Theile 4-6,* 3 volumes, translated anonymously by Lessing (Leipzig & Danzig: Rüdiger, 1749-1752);

Beyträge zur Historie und Aufnahme des Theaters, edited by Lessing and Christlob Mylius (Berlin & Stuttgart: Metzler, 1750);

Pedro Calderón de la Barca, *Das Leben ist ein Traum,* translated anonymously by Lessing (Berlin, 1750);

Titus Maccias Plautus, *Die Gefangenen,* translated by Lessing (Stuttgart: Metzler, 1750);

Voltaire, *Kleinere historische Schriften: Aus dem Französischen,* translated anonymously by Lessing (Rostock: Koppe, 1752);

Juan Huarte de San Juan, *Johann Huarts Prüfung der Köpfe zu den Wissenschaften: Aus dem Spanischen,* translated anonymously by Lessing (Wittenberg & Zerbst: Zimmermann, 1752);

Johann Gotthilf Vockerodt, *An impartial Foreigner's Remarks upon the present Dispute between England and Prussia, in a Letter from a Gentleman at the Hague to his Friend in London: Amerkungen [sic] eines unpartheyischen Fremden über die gegenwärtige Streitigkeit zwischen England*

und Preußen; in einem Brief eines Edelmanns in dem Haag an seinen Freund in London. Aus dem Englischen, translated anonymously from the French by Lessing (Berlin, 1753);

Francois Augier de Marigny, *Geschichte der Araber unter der Regierung der Califen,* volumes 1-2, translated by Lessing (Berlin & Potsdam: Voß, 1753-1754);

Frederick II, *Schreiben an das Publicum: Aus dem Französischen,* translated anonymously by Lessing (Berlin: Voß, 1753);

William Hogarth, *Zergliederung der Schönheit, die schwankenden Begriffe von dem Geschmack festzusetzen: Aus dem Englischen,* translated by Mylius, foreword by Lessing (Berlin & Potsdam: Voß, 1754);

Mylius, *Vermischte Schriften,* edited by Lessing (Berlin: Haude & Spener, 1754);

Elizabeth Rowe, *Geheiligte Andachts-Übungen in Betrachtung, Gebet, Lobpreisung und Herzens-Gesprächen,* translated anonymously by Lessing and Christian Felix Weiße (Erfurt: Nonnen, 1754);

Francis Hutcheson, *Sittenlehre der Vernunft: Aus dem Englischen übersetzt,* 2 volumes, translated anonymously by Lessing (Leipzig: Wendler, 1756);

William Law, *Eine ernsthafte Ermunterung an alle Christen zu einem frommen und heiligen Leben: Aus dem Englischen übersetzt,* translated anonymously by Lessing (Leipzig: Weidmann, 1756);

James Thomson, *Sämtliche Trauerspiele: Aus dem Englischen übersetzt,* translated by a scholarly society in Stralsund, foreword by Lessing (Leipzig: Weidmann, 1756);

Bibliothek der schönen Wissenschaften und der freyen Künste, 3 volumes, edited by Lessing, Moses Mendelssohn, and Friedrich Nicolai (Leipzig: Dyck, 1757-1758);

Samuel Richardson, *Sittenlehre für die Jugend in den auserlesensten Aesopischen Fabeln mit dienlichen Betrachtungen zur Beförderung der Religion und der allgemeinen Menschenliebe vorgestellt,* translated by Lessing (Leipzig: Weidmann, 1757);

Johann Wilhelm Ludwig Gleim, *Preußische Kriegslieder in den Feldzügen 1756 und 1757: Von einem Grenadier. Mit Melodien,* edited by Lessing (Berlin: Voß, 1758);

Briefe, die Neueste Litteratur betreffend, parts 1-4, edited anonymously by Lessing, Mendelssohn, and Nicolai (Berlin: Nicolai, 1759; reprinted, Hildesheim: Olms, 1971);

Minna von Barnhelm,

oder

das Soldatenglück.

Ein Lustspiel in fünf Aufzügen,

von

Gotthold Ephraim Lessing.

Berlin,

bey Christian Friederich Voß.

1 7 6 7.

Title page for the comedy in which Lessing criticizes the aristocratic concept of honor

Friedrich von Logau, *Sinngedichte: Zwölf Bücher. Mit Anmerkungen über die Sprache des Dichters,* edited by Lessing and Karl Wilhelm Ramler (Leipzig: Weidmann, 1759);

Denis Diderot, *Das Theater des Herrn Diderot: Aus dem Französischen,* 2 volumes, translated anonymously by Lessing (Berlin: Voß, 1760; revised, 1781);

Jean-Georges Noverre, *Briefe über die Tanzkunst und über die Ballette: Aus dem Französischen übersetzt,* translated by Lessing and Johann Joachim Christoph Bode (Hamburg & Bremen: Cramer, 1769);

Andreas Scultetus, *Gedichte: Aufgefunden,* edited by Lessing (Brunswick: Waisenhaus, 1771);

Karl Wilhelm Jerusalem, *Philosophische Aufsätze,* edited by Lessing (Brunswick: Waisenhaus, 1776; edited by Paul Beer, Berlin: Behr, 1900; reprinted, New York & Nendeln, Liechtenstein: Kraus, 1966);

Hermann Samuel Reimarus, *Von dem Zwecke Jesu und seiner Jünger: Noch ein Fragment des Wolfenbüttelschen Ungenannten,* edited by Les-

sing (Brunswick: Waisenhaus, 1778);

Pedro Cudena, *Beschreibung des Portugiesischen Amerika: Ein Spanisches Manuskript in der Wolfenbüttelschen Bibliothek,* translated by Christian Leiste, edited by Lessing (Brunswick: Waisenhaus, 1780);

Reimarus, *Fragmente des Wolfenbüttelschen Ungenannten: Ein Anhang zu dem Fragment von Zweck Jesu und seiner Jünger,* edited by Lessing (Berlin: Weber, 1784);

G. E. Lessings Übersetzungen aus dem Französischen Friedrichs des Großen und Voltaires, edited by Erich Schmidt (Berlin: Hertz, 1892; reprinted, Munich: Kraus, 1980).

To the extent that the eighteenth century in Germany was indeed an age of the unfettered critical spirit, as Immanuel Kant assured his contemporaries it was, it found its most articulate voice in Gotthold Ephraim Lessing. As a scholar of classical antiquity he rivals Johann Joachim Winckelmann. In his extended controversy with leading Protestant theologians on the nature of Christianity and the truth of its teachings, a topic of singular importance to the European Enlightenment, he presented the more convincing arguments until he was silenced by ducal decree. But his most significant contribution was the rejuvenation of German literature, especially the drama.

Lessing's devastating attack on Johann Christoph Gottsched's theater reform put an end to the attempt to establish a classicist literature in Germany. Reinterpreting Aristotle's *Poetics,* Lessing subordinated aesthetic "laws" and "rules" to the effect which a specific genre is to have on its recipients, thus replacing the normative poetics that governed French classical literature and that, in turn, were espoused by Gottsched and his followers. The new theoretical orientation, especially in its application to dramatic theory, marks the beginning of "modern" German literature; it led to works which have maintained their place in the canon of German literature ever since. Among them are some of Lessing's own: his plays continue to evoke a considerable amount of critical attention, and his dramatic masterpieces, *Minna von Barnhelm* (1767; translated, 1806), *Emilia Galotti* (1772; translated, 1800), and *Nathan der Weise* (1779; translated as *Nathan the Wise,* 1791), can still be found in the repertoire of the German theater. Lessing reasoned that if the purpose of tragedy is to evoke "Mitleid" (pity), the stoic hero and the related set of aristocratically tinged values cease to be a proper subject for the

The Laocoön sculpture, which became the focal point of an aesthetic controversy between Lessing and Johann Joachim Winckelmann (Vatican, Rome)

drama. Stoic endurance may elicit admiration, but not pity. Witnessing human suffering will evoke pity, and the experience will intensify if the protagonist shares common bonds with his audience. With this argument Lessing opened the stage to the social realities of his time.

Lessing's conviction that pity is the cardinal virtue and the ultimate goal of tragedy did not prevent him from using the theater as an instrument for the more general purposes of the Enlightenment. He attacks anti-Semitism in *Die Juden* (1755; translated as *The Jews*, 1878), exposes cruelty and egocentricity in the guise of patriotism in *Philotas* (1759; translated, 1878), demonstrates the failings of "enlightened" absolutism and bourgeois passivity in *Emilia Galotti*, and crowns his dramatic work with a plea for religious tolerance in *Nathan der Weise*, one of the noblest documents of the European Enlightenment.

Lessing was born in Kamenz, Saxony, on 22 January 1729, the third of twelve children of Johann Gottfried Lessing, a Protestant minister, and Justina Salome Lessing, née Feller. His unusual talents were recognized early. In 1741 he was admitted to St. Afra in Meißen, one of the

elite secondary schools endowed by the dukes of Saxony. In 1746, complying with his father's wishes and equipped with a stipend from his native city, he enrolled as a student of theology at the University of Leipzig. At this center of eighteenth-century scholarship, the unusual alliance of Gottsched, then rector of the university, and Frederike Caroline Neuber, the leader of a theatrical troupe, had given the stage a new respectability. Lessing's lifelong fascination with the theater began in Leipzig. His first play, *Der junge Gelehrte* (1755; translated as *The Young Scholar*, 1878), was performed there in January 1748; it is a comedy in which he lampoons an arrogant young scholar engaged in meaningless philological squabbles totally divorced from real learning, as well as from the world around him. With his friend Felix Weiße, who was to become a minor playwright, Lessing translated Marivaux; wrote poetry in the anacreontic vein; and wrote outlines for several plays, most of which remained fragmentary. Such activities caused his parents some consternation. Although the errant student was allowed to change the focus of his studies to medicine and philology, Lessing left the university in 1748 to seek his fortune in Berlin. In a letter to his mother (20 January 1749), he blames this move on debts he had incurred; it is likely that the bankruptcy of Neuber's troupe in the summer of 1748 was a contributing factor.

Lessing survived in Berlin as a struggling writer. He became review editor of the *Berlinische Priveligierte Zeitung* and received a masters in theology during a stay in Wittenberg in 1751-1752 and gradually built a reputation as a literary critic. He did not eschew formidable targets: he took Friedrich Gottlieb Klopstock to task for his religious fervor, and Samuel Gotthold Lange, Horace translator and respected head of the Halle school of poets, was ridiculed for incompetence in *Ein Vade Mecum für den Hrn. Sam. Gotth. Lange* (A Primer for Mr. Samuel G. Lange, 1754). But although he was a prolific writer–his collected works, *Schrifften* (Writings, 1753-1755), began to appear before he was twenty-five years old–the Prussian capital and the literary market in Germany did not afford him, or any other independent writer, a comfortable existence. The success of his first bourgeois tragedy, *Miß Sara Sampson*, (1755; translated, 1878), increased his stature as a playwright and drew new attention to his early comedies, but it did not alleviate his financial problems. The play depicts Sara's elopement with Mellefont, a young man who finds himself torn be-

Manuscript for the beginning of Lessing's play Emilia Galotti *(from Gustav Könnecke,* Bilderatlas zur Geschichte der deutschen Nationalliteratur, *1895)*

tween her and a former lover. Above all he is motivated by a deep-rooted urge to maintain his personal freedom. The sophistication of Sara's reasoning as to why she cannot accept her distraught father's forgiveness has persuaded critics to interpret the play as a commentary on the Third Commandment. But the indictment of rigid bourgeois morality, specifically with regard to sexual ethics, is equally prominent. The tearful reunion of errant daughter and regretful father, who blames himself and his own strict moralistic stance for Sara's poisoning by Mellefont's former lover, set the stage for domestic tragedies well into the nineteenth century.

The play's English models–Restoration drama–and the London setting had a provocative edge: in no German city was the dominance of French culture felt more keenly than in the Berlin of Frederick II. Yet Lessing's attitude can hardly be called chauvinistic; for while ridiculing

Lessing in 1771; painting by Anton Graff (Karl-Marx-Universität, Leipzig)

Corneille, he praised Diderot, and in Voltaire he admired the philosopher but belittled the playwright. However, his squabble with the great French philosopher over a manuscript Lessing should have returned earlier than he did may well have ruined his chances for an appointment at the Prussian court–if indeed the king needed such a pretext to prefer a French intellectual to a German one. Lessing found support elsewhere. His circle of friends included Moses Mendelssohn, accountant by profession and philosopher by inclination; Friedrich Nicolai, publisher and staunch supporter of Enlightenment causes; and Karl Wilhelm Ramler, author and instructor at the military academy. Travel plans–he had agreed to accompany the son of a rich Leipzig merchant on a tour of Holland, northern Germany, and England–came to an abrupt halt in Amsterdam with the outbreak of the Seven Years' War in August 1756. Lessing returned with his charge from Holland to Leipzig, which was occupied by Prussian troops.

Lessing remained in Leipzig until May 1758, when he returned to Berlin. In Leipzig he barely supported himself by translating works by

Francis Hutcheson (1756), William Law (1756), and Samuel Richardson (1757), and collaborating with Mendelssohn and Nicolai on the journal *Bibliothek der schönen Wissenschaften und der freyen Künste* (Library of Liberal Arts, 1757-1758). But it was not only economically that his position was a tenuous one. Although it was rumored in Berlin that he had written against the interest of the Prussian state, he estranged his Leipzig friends by consorting with officers of the Prussian army who had just levied an extraordinarily heavy tax on the city. A true cosmopolitan, he assured Nicolai that he considered himself neither a Saxon nor a Prussian patriot. And Johann Wilhelm Ludwig Gleim, whose *Preußische Kriegslieder* (Prussian War Songs, 1758) Lessing had edited, was finally taken to task for his blatant nationalism: "Vielleicht zwar ist auch der Patriot bey mir nicht ganz erstickt, obgleich das Lob eines eifrigen Patrioten, nach meiner Denkungsart, das allerletzte ist, wonach ich geitzen würde; des Patrioten nehmlich, der mich vergessen lehrt, daß ich ein Weltbürger seyn sollte" (It is possible that the patriot is also not quite stifled in me, although the reputation as a fervent patriot is the last thing I crave, as a patriot, that is, who makes me forget that I should be a citizen of the world). He also made the price of heroic greatness the theme of a one-act play: the self-sacrifice of the title character in *Philotas* is an indictment of a society that educates its youth to accept death on the battlefield as the ultimate goal and unquestioningly to place the interest of the state over all human concerns. The setting of the play in classical antiquity does not blur the obvious analogy to Prussia's acquisition of Silesia through war.

Despite this anticipation of the spirit that characterized the great minds of the following generation, Lessing was not totally unaffected by the upsurge of pro-Prussian sentiments triggered by the Seven Years' War. He looked forward to his return to Berlin, "wo ich es nicht länger nötig haben werde, es meinen Bekannten nur ins Ohr zu sagen, daß der König von Preußen dennoch ein großer König ist" (where I will no longer be obliged to whisper into my friends' ears that the King of Prussia is a great king in spite of it all), he wrote to Gleim in May 1757.

Among the projects Lessing completed during his second stay in Berlin were an edition of the all but forgotten works of the seventeenth-century poet Friedrich von Logau (1759) and a collection of his own fables, *Fabeln: Drey Bücher*

(1759; translated as *Fables: In Three Books*, 1829).
Of more immediate impact was his *Briefe, die Neueste Litteratur betreffend* (Letters, on the Most Recent Literature, 1759), a journal of literary criticism to which Nicolai and Mendelssohn also contributed. The fictional framework of these "letters"–they are addressed to an officer recovering from wounds received in the battle of Zorndorf–allowed Lessing the elegant informality that characterizes most of his critical writings. Moving beyond the traditional form of reviewing individual publications, he used the journal to exert influence on the entire spectrum of contemporary literature. The famous seventeenth letter (16 February 1759) contains an attack on Gottsched's efforts to reform the German stage. It is based on arguments which were later to be more fully developed by Johann Gottfried Herder: that literary models should be akin to the national character; that indigenous traditions are preferable to imported themes and forms; and that Shakespearean theater is superior to classical French drama, even though the latter adheres to the letter of Aristotelian poetics while the former violates it.

Lessing's theoretical stance placed him between the two established and feuding camps in Leipzig and Zurich. His rejection of Gottsched may have endeared him to the Swiss critics Johann Jakob Bodmer and Johann Jakob Breitinger, but, because their revision of Gottsched's theories was only a modest one, the feeling was not mutual. Lessing saw the danger of forming yet another literary clique. His decision to withdraw from the journal may also have been prompted by his financial situation, which remained as uncertain as ever; he was unable to respond to pleas from Kamenz that he support two of his brothers attending the University of Wittenberg. In September 1760 Lessing resigned; a month later he left for Breslau to join the staff of the Prussian general Bogislaw Friedrich von Tauentzien as regimental secretary.

Less is known about his years in Silesia than about any other part of his life. According to a local schoolmaster, J. B. Klose, he slept late, went to every book auction in town, and, after performing his secretarial duties, attended theatrical performances. Often leaving before the last act, he spent the better part of the night gambling with fellow Prussian officers. Even though Klose's account, cited by Lessing's brother and first biographer Karl Gotthelf, may be slanted, it seems obvious that these were relatively carefree years for Germany's foremost critic.

Eva König, whom Lessing married in 1776

It is unclear what Lessing expected for himself after he proclaimed the end of the long war to the citizenry of Breslau in 1763. But his hopes, hinted at in a letter to his father, were not fulfilled: "Ich warte noch einen einzigen Umstand ab, und wo dieser nicht nach meinem Willen ausfällt, so kehre ich zu meiner alten Lebens Art wieder zurück" (I am only waiting for one decision. Should that be contrary to expectations, then I will return to my old way of life). Von Tauentzien was appointed governor of Silesia, and Lessing returned to his old and rather insecure way of life. But unlike his dramatic figure, the Baltic nobleman Tellheim in *Minna von Barnhelm*, who had also joined the Prussian cause for reasons he finds difficult to explain after his sudden and unjust dismissal, Lessing was not destitute. Although many of his personal effects were lost in transit from Breslau to Berlin, he was able to send a significant amount of money to his family, and his library at this time contained some six thousand volumes.

The literary results of his four years in Silesia were two major works: *Minna von Barnhelm* and *Laokoon: Oder Über die Grenzen der Mahlerey und Poesie* (1766; translated as *Laocoon; or, The Limits of Poetry and Painting*, 1836).

The plot of Lessing's great comedy reflects the aftermath of the war. In a humane and generous gesture, Major von Tellheim had asked for smaller reparations from the defeated Saxons than were expected. When the vanquished proved unable to pay even these at short notice, he advanced them some of his own money to meet the minimum demands of the Prussians. While this selfless deed wins him the love of Minna, an aristocratic Saxon heiress, the Prussian ministry suspects bribery. The play opens with Tellheim dismissed, dishonored, and about to be evicted from his hotel room. It ends with his honor rehabilitated by the king, his fortune restored, and his impending marriage to Minna. Despite this seeming conventionality, Lessing's play is a radical departure from the genre as established on the German stage. More significant than the true-to-life characters and idiosyncratic diction of the dramatis personae was the public discussion of social problems caused by the war and high-handed Prussian administrative measures. Instead of following the traditional pattern of exposing some aberrant form of behavior to ridicule, Lessing subjects the aristocratic concept of honor to scrutiny. When his honor is questioned, Tellheim, although innocent, refuses to marry Minna. When she claims to be dishonored in the eyes of Saxon patriots for loving a Prussian officer, and disinherited as well, he reverses his position; the now-eager suitor is forced to invalidate his own earlier arguments, which Minna quotes back to him. Neither the plausibility of her fictitious misfortune nor the superiority of "Mitleid" over honor as a virtue inspiring moral action could have been lost on the audience. The play rapidly became the most popular of Lessing's dramatic works. Its first performance, in Hamburg on 30 December 1767, was followed before the end of the decade by productions in Frankfurt am Main, Vienna, Leipzig, Berlin, and Breslau. That the king's letter ultimately solves Tellheim's dilemma led to a reading of the play as a glorification of Frederick II; the opposite interpretation points to the arbitrariness of Tellheim's rehabilitation and finds a general indictment of Prussia and its ruler. More recent scholarship has focused on aesthetic and sociopolitical issues.

With *Laokoon* Lessing participated in a larger European debate on the specific differences among the individual arts and the nature of aesthetic perception. His plan was to include music and dance, but the published work is restricted to the pictorial arts (painting and sculpture) and literature. A discussion of theories presented by Joseph Spence in *Polymetis* (1747) and by Anne Claude Philippe de Tubières, comte de Caylus in *Tableaux tirés de L'Iliade* (1757) precedes the introduction of his true target: Winckelmann. In his *Gedanken über die Nachahmung der griechischen Werke in der Malerei und Bildhauerkunst* (On Imitating Greek Artworks in Painting and Sculpture, 1755) Winckelmann analyzed the Laocoön sculpture and concluded that the Greeks avoided the artistic expression of extreme emotions: the priest and his sons, about to be strangled by snakes, display only muted and controlled suffering. This stoic ideal was diametrically opposed to Lessing's own views; yet he disputes Winckelmann's famous dictum that no inner turmoil would disturb the Greeks' "edle Einfalt und stille Größe" (noble simplicity and calm grandeur) not on moral but on aesthetic grounds. Since Homer and Sophocles allow their heroes to scream, he argues, different laws must apply for the writer and the sculptor. In his search for these laws he establishes several principles which have proved to be extraordinarily fruitful for all subsequent theory in this area, among them the structural analysis of the medium to determine its representational possibilities, the distinction of natural and arbitrary signs, and the participatory role of the reader or viewer. Literature uses successive signs in time; the pictorial arts employ coexisting figures and colors in space. Therefore, the proper subject of literature is "Handlungen" (action) while "Körper" (objects) are the most adequate subjects for the painter and the sculptor. Limited to re-creating a single moment in time, the artist must select one that leaves the most latitude for the imagination. It is not the pinnacle of an emotion but an earlier or later stage that allows viewer participation. For this reason Laocoön is depicted as suffering, but not screaming. Lessing concludes that literature is superior to pictorial art because it can represent the entire spectrum of human emotions. It achieves its highest form by translating its arbitrary signs into natural signs, by turning words into the spoken dialogue of drama.

The impact of the work was considerable. Even Winckelmann's great admirer Goethe remembered in his autobiography "daß dieses Werk uns aus der Region eines kümmerlichen Anschauens in die freien Gefilde des Gedankens

Nathan der Weise.

Ein

Dramatifches Gedicht,

in fünf Aufzügen.

Jntroite, nam et heic Dii funt!

APVD GELLIVM.

Von

Gotthold Ephraim Lessing.

1779.

*Title page for the play in which Lessing attacks
religious intolerance*

hinriß" (that this work lifted us from the level of meager perception to the unencumbered regions of thought). But Lessing had to defend himself in *Brief, antiquarischen Inhalts* (Letters on Classical Matters, 1768-1769) against an attack by Christian Adolf Klotz, a professor of rhetoric in Halle; the entire first volume of Herder's *Kritische Wälder* (Critical Essays, 1769) was a critique of *Laokoon*—by and large Herder sided with Winckelmann; and Goethe presented his own views as a third position in the journal *Propyläen* in 1798.

Lessing's hopes for employment as royal librarian in Berlin or at the art gallery in Dresden ended in disappointment. In the spring of 1767 he accepted a position as theater critic at the newly founded German National Theater in Hamburg. He may well have shared the high expectation embodied in the idea of a national theater; his involvement in a similar venture in Mannheim in 1776 and his interest in plans for a national academy in Vienna to be presided over by Friedrich Gottlieb Klopstock would point in that direction. But regional interests and petty rivalries and intrigues foiled all of these attempts to es-

tablish an intellectual center of national significance. The Hamburg enterprise, underfunded and mismanaged, folded before the end of the year. Lessing stayed to complete his contribution: the *Hamburgische Dramaturgie* (1767-1769; translated as *Hamburg Dramaturgy*, 1962).

It is not a systematic work. When the original plan to review each play, all of the actors, and every performance had to be abandoned because of personal sensitivities, Lessing broadened his theme to include all matters pertaining to the contemporary debate on drama: the nature of the tragic hero—he is to be "vom gleichen Schrot und Korn" (of like kind) as the audience in order to affect them; the concept of genius; and the problem of historical accuracy in drama are among the issues treated. An overriding concern is the critique of French classical drama, and Shakespeare is used to substantiate its devaluation. But the greatest attention is devoted to a reinterpretation of Aristotle's comments on tragedy. In the light of modern scholarship Lessing's reading of the crucial passage may be faulty: he translates *eleos* and *phobos* as *Furcht* (fear) and *Mitleid* (pity), declares *Furcht* to be pity we feel for ourselves, and sees both emotions as the object of the cathartic experience of tragedy.

Eminently sociable, Lessing acquired a large circle of friends in Hamburg. With Johann Bode he entered into a short-lived publishing business; in the house of the merchant Engelbert König he met his future wife, Eva, who was then married to König; the children of Hermann Samuel Reimarus, professor of oriental languages, provided him with the manuscript of their father's radically deistic "Apologia oder Schutzschrift für die vernünftigen Verehrer Gottes" (Apology or Defense of the Rational Worshipers of God). He became acquainted with Carl Philipp Emanuel Bach, then musical director of the Hamburg parish, and played chess with Klopstock. He also met Johann Arnold Ebert, professor at the Carolinum in Brunswick, who secured for him his last position: the librarianship at the ducal library in Wolfenbüttel, then and now one of the most significant libraries in Europe.

Financial difficulties and poor health delayed his departure from Hamburg, and he did not assume his new duties until May 1770. His years in Wolfenbüttel were overshadowed by the provinciality of the duchy of Braunschweig-Lüneburg and the social and intellectual isolation in which he found himself. Although his relationship with the court in Brunswick was strained from the beginning, he was not treated ungenerously. His prolonged absences from Wolfenbüttel were tolerated, and he was asked to accompany a member of the ducal family on a tour of Italy from April to December 1775; the duke also exempted his publications from censorship and approved his plan to make the treasures of the library available to the public. Lessing's work on Berengar of Tours (1770) and the six-volume *Zur Geschichte und Litteratur: Aus den Schätzen der Herzoglichen Bibliothek zu Wolfenbüttel* (On History and Literature: From the Collections of the Ducal Library in Wolfenbüttel, 1773-1781) are efforts in this direction. Most of his commentaries on rare or forgotten texts take the form of righting an old wrong. Thus he defends the heretic Berengar against his orthodox critics, Leibniz against the accusation of religious hypocrisy, and the sixteenth-century apostate Adam Neuser as a victim of religious intolerance. The third volume of *Zur Geschichte und Litteratur* (1774) includes the first of a series of fragments from Reimarus's "Apologie," which were to involve Lessing in an extended theological controversy with the Hamburg theologian Johann Melchior Goeze and others, and which culminated in the publication of *Nathan der Weise* in 1779.

But before the quarrel over the "Reimarus Fragments" dominated his life, he was able to complete *Emilia Galotti*. In a letter to his brother, Lessing describes the play as "eine modernisierte, von allem Staatsinteresse befreite *Virginia*" (a modernized *Virginia*, devoid of all political concerns). He provided his ducal employer with a similar description, and it is likely that he deemphasized the play's sociopolitical content to avoid censorship. *Emilia Galotti* is an indictment of an immoral prince, Hettore Gonzaga. The prince's designs on Emilia, who is unaccustomed to the amorality of the court and unable to defend herself against it, seem to leave her no alternative but to seek her own death. On her wedding day she finds herself trapped at the prince's retreat after her bridegroom has been murdered. The prince, indirectly the perpetrator of this crime, now acts as judge and orders a full investigation, thus preventing Emilia's escape. That Emilia is less afraid of the political and judicial power of the prince than of the power of seduction has inspired many psychological analyses. That her father, Odoardo, urged by Emilia, kills her and spares the prince seems to expose the passivity and frustrations of the middle class.

The play was hailed as the prototype of a German drama with true-to-life characters, but Matthias Claudius found the heroine's fear of her own sensuality difficult to understand; Goethe called the play a masterpiece yet found it "nur gedacht" (too contrived); and Friedrich Schlegel, who influenced future commentaries on Lessing by praising the philosopher at the expense of the poet, described the play as "ein großes Exempel der dramatischen Algebra" (a great example of dramatic algebra).

Even though more recent commentaries have deemphasized the play's sociopolitical edge, it is clear that Lessing's view of the Prussian state, which during his lifetime had emerged as a major military power in Europe, had undergone considerable change. In response to an ironic remark by Nicolai regarding censorship in Vienna, Lessing belittled a presumed freedom of the press that allows inane attacks on religion but excludes all critical review of social and political conditions. In this respect, he calls Prussia "das sklavischste Land Europas" (the most slavish country in Europe). Having joined the Freemasons in Hamburg, and possibly disappointed by the "secrets" imparted to him at his initiation, he published *Ernst und Falk: Gespräche für Freymäurer* (1778; translated as *Masonic Dialogues*, 1927). The work maps out the duties of the citizen in an imperfect state.

In 1771, after the death of her husband, Eva König had become engaged to Lessing. Returning from his Italian journey, he intensified his efforts to have his position upgraded, for he considered his own financial independence an essential prerequisite to marriage, despite Eva's considerable fortune. Embittered by delays, Lessing was ready to resign when his conditions were finally met. A few months later, on 8 October 1776, the wedding took place on the estate of friends near Hamburg. Lessing's marital life was short. His son Traugott survived for only one day after a difficult birth, from which the mother never fully recovered. Eva Lessing died on 10 January 1778.

In his grief, Lessing submerged himself in the increasingly polemical debate triggered by his second installment of segments from the Reimarus manuscript. The first portion, "Von der Duldung der Deisten" (On Tolerating Deists) in 1774, had gone widely unnoticed; but the radical questioning of the New Testament accounts of Christ's death and resurrection in *Vom dem Zwecke Jesu und seiner Jünger* (On the Purpose of

Lessing's death mask (Gustav Könnecke, Bilderatlas zur Geschichte der deutschen Nationallitteratur *1895)*

Jesus and His Disciples, 1778) triggered a vociferous response from the already embattled orthodox Protestant camp. Its main spokesman, Goeze, was no match for Lessing's satirical pen, but he succeeded in rousing the established ecclesiastic and secular hierarchies into action. Lessing's publisher, the Waisenhaus-Buchhandlung in Brunswick, was ordered by ducal decree to halt the distribution of all writings pertaining to the controversy; and Lessing, whose efforts to persuade the court otherwise were ignored, was advised to cease all further publications on matters of religion.

To shield Reimarus's children from public wrath, Lessing had presented Reimarus's text as "Fragmente eines Ungenannten" (Fragments by an unnamed author). Furthermore, he had introduced the deistic arguments with counterarguments of his own. Despite these precautions, he was soon publicly suspected of being himself the "unnamed" author. In defiance of his ducal employer's order, Lessing published simultaneously in Hamburg and Berlin; his penultimate response to the ultraconservative Goeze then turned to his old forum, the theater, to present his last word on the matter.

A posthumously published preface to *Nathan der Weise* says: "daß der Nachteil, welchen geoffenbarte Religionen dem menschlichen Geschlechte bringen, zu keiner Zeit einem vernünftigen Manne müsse auffallender gewesen sein, als zu den Zeiten der Kreuzzüge" (the disadvantage which revealed religions bring to mankind can never have been more obvious to a rational man than at the time of the Crusades). The play shows intolerance and inhumanity to be the result of the conviction that a single religion is the sole recipient of transcendental truth. But the principal representatives of the warring factions–a young Templar captured and pardoned by Saladin (the Muslim ruler of Jerusalem), and the wise Jewish merchant Nathan–overcome their religious as well as their political and racial differences. Even before the play's utopian ending, which reveals that they are related to each other, they become friends. This friendship is brought about by several educational processes which permeate the play and culminate in the famous Parable of the Rings. Questioned by Saladin regarding the truth which all religions claim, Nathan responds with Lessing's adaptation of one of Boccaccio's tales from the *Decameron* (1353). Under the veil of allegory Nathan allows all revealed religions the same degree of "truth." They are indistinguishable from one another in that they all base their claims on reported historical events; such "historical proofs" are judged to be insufficient in the court of reason, and therefore their mutually exclusive claims would have to be rejected. But the judge in Nathan's parable moves beyond this deist position; instead of a judgment, he offers advice: although the validity of religious beliefs cannot be demonstrated, their value can be established through the virtuous life of the believer. The absence of transcendental certainty becomes the incentive to strive toward moral autonomy.

In *Die Erziehung des Menschengeschlechts* (1780; translated as *The Education of the Human Race*, 1858) Lessing seems to provide a more definitive answer regarding his stand toward Christianity. He sent the manuscript to his publisher, Voß, with the condition that his authorship be withheld; instead, he was described on the title page as the book's editor. The work describes the Old and New Testaments as schoolbooks that have served their purpose in the continuing progress of mankind toward ultimate enlightenment; Christianity is an imperfect but necessary stage along the way. The work does not focus on the irrelevance or the absence of divine guidance in the education of mankind, however, but on those accomplishments which man, individually or collectively, has achieved for himself. It ends with the conviction that the ultimate goal, the moral autonomy of man, will be reached: "sie wird gewiß kommen, die Zeit der Vollendung, da der Mensch . . . das Gute tun wird, weil es das Gute ist" (the time of perfection will surely come, when man . . . will act virtuously for virtue's sake).

Lessing died in Brunswick on 15 February 1781, in the presence of his stepdaughter Amalie and his friend Alexander Daveson.

Letters:

Briefe von und an Gotthold Ephraim Lessing: In fünf Bänden, volumes 17-21 of *Gotthold Ephraim Lessings sämtliche Schriften*, edited by Karl Lachmann, third edition, edited by Franz Muncker (Berlin & Leipzig: De Gruyter, 1904-1907; reprinted, Berlin: De Gruyter, 1968);

Lessings Briefwechsel mit Mendelssohn und Nicolai über das Trauerspiel: Nebst verwandten Schriften Nicolais und Mendelssohns, edited by Robert Petsch (Leipzig: Durr, 1910; reprinted, Darmstadt: Wissenschaftliche Buchgesellschaft, 1967);

Lessings Briefe in einem Band, edited by Herbert Greiner-Mai (Berlin: Aufbau, 1967);

Briefwechsel über das Trauerspiel: Gotthold Ephraim Lessing, Moses Mendelssohn, Friedrich Nicolai, edited by Jochen Schult-Sasse (Munich: Winkler, 1972);

Briefe Lessings aus Wolfenbüttel, edited by Günter Schulz (Bremen & Wolfenbüttel: Jacobi, 1975);

Meine liebste Madam!: Gotthold Ephraim Lessings Briefwechsel mit Eva König, 1770-1776, edited by Günter and Ursula Schulz (Munich: Beck, 1979);

Dialog in Briefen und andere ausgewählte Dokumente zum Leben Gotthold Ephraim Lessings mit Eva Catharina König: Zur 200. Wiederkehr des Todestages von Gotthold Ephraim Lessing am 15. Februar 1981, edited by Helmut Rudloff (Kamenz: Lessing-Museum, 1981).

Bibliography:

Siegfried Seifert, *Lessing Bibliographie* (Berlin: Aufbau, 1973).

Biographies:

Karl Gotthelf Lessing, *Gotthold Ephraim Lessings Leben, nebst seinem noch übrigen Nachlasse* (Berlin: Voß, 1793);

Erich Schmidt, *Lessing: Geschichte seines Lebens und seiner Schriften* (Berlin: Weidmann, 1899);

Henry B. Garland, *Lessing, the Founder of Modern German Literature*, second edition (London & New York: St. Martin's Press, 1962);

Wolfgang Drews, *Gotthold Ephraim Lessing in Selbstzeugnissen und Bilddokumenten* (Reinbek: Rowohlt, 1962);

Kurl Wölfel, *Lessings Leben und Werk in Daten und Bildern* (Frankfurt am Main: Insel, 1967);

Gerd Hillen, *Lessing Chronik: Daten zu Leben und Werk* (Munich: Hanser, 1979).

References:

Henry E. Allison, *Lessing and the Enlightenment: His Philosophy of Religion and its Relation to Eighteenth-Century Thought* (Ann Arbor: University of Michigan Press, 1966);

Ehrhard Bahr and others, eds., *Humanität und Dialog: Lessing und Mendelssohn in neuer Sicht* (Detroit: Wayne State University Press / Munich: Edition text & kritik, 1982);

Wilfried Barner, *Produktive Rezeption: Lessing und die Tragödien Senecas* (Munich: Beck, 1973);

Barner and Albert M. Reh, eds., *Nation und Gelehrtenrepublik: Lessing im Europäischen Zusammenhang* (Detroit: Wayne State University Press / Munich: Edition text + kritik, 1984);

Barner and others, eds., *Lessing: Epoche, Werk, Wirkung*, fourth edition (Munich: Beck, 1981);

Martin Bollacher, *Lessing: Vernunft und Geschichte. Untersuchungen zum Problem religiöser Aufklärung in den Spätschriften* (Tübingen: Niemeyer, 1978);

Manfred Durzak, *Poesie und Ratio: Vier Lessing-Studien* (Bad Homburg: Athenäum, 1970);

Helmut Göbel, *Bild und Sprache bei Lessing* (Munich: Fink, 1971);

F. J. Lamport, *Lessing and the Drama* (Oxford: Clarendon Press, 1981);

Lessing Yearbook! (1969-);

Volker Nölle, *Subjektivität und Wirklichkeit in Lessings dramatischem und theologischem Werk* (Berlin: Schmidt, 1977);

George Pons, *Gotthold Ephraim Lessing et le Christianisme* (Paris: Didier, 1964);

J. G. Robertson, *Lessing's Dramatic Theory* (Cambridge: University Press, 1939);

Victor A. Rudowski, *Lessing's Aesthetica in Nuce: An Analysis of the May 26, 1769 Letter to Nicolai* (Chapel Hill: University of North Carolina Press, 1971);

Jürgen Schröder, *Gotthold Ephraim Lessing: Sprache und Drama* (Munich: Fink, 1972);

Harald Schultze, *Lessings Toleranzbegriff: Eine theologische Studie* (Göttingen: Vandenhoeck & Ruprecht, 1969);

Hinrich C. Seeba, *Die Liebe zur Sache. Öffentliches und privates Interesse in Lessings Dramen*

(Tübingen: Niemeyer, 1973);

Gisbert Ter-Nedden, *Lessings Trauerspiele: Der Ursprung des modernen Dramas aus dem Geist der Kritik* (Stuttgart: Metzler, 1986).

Papers:

Manuscripts of Gotthold Ephraim Lessing are in various European libraries, notably in the Herzog-August-Bibliothek, Wolfenbüttel, and the Deutsche Staatsbibliothek, Berlin.

Christian Ludwig Liscow

(26 April 1701 - 30 October 1760)

Debra L. Stoudt
University of Toledo

BOOKS: *Kurtze, aber dabey deutliche und erbauliche Anmerckungen, über die klägliche Geschichte von der jämmerlichen Zerstöhrung der Stadt Jerusalem: Nach dem Geschmacke des (S.T.) Herrn M. Heinrich Jacob Sievers verfertiget, und als eine Zugabe zu dessen Anmerkungen über die Paßion, ans Licht gestellet*, as X.Y.Z. (Frankfurt am Main & Leipzig: Herold, 1732);

Briontes der Jüngere, oder Lob-Rede auf den Herrn D. Joh. Ernst Philippi, öffentlichen Professoren der deutschen Beredsamkeit auf der Universität Halle: Gehalten in der Gesellschaft der kleinen Geister, anonymous (N.p., 1732);

Vitrea fracta, oder des Ritters Robert Clifton Schreiben an einen gelehrten Samojeden, betreffend die seltsamen und nachdencklichen Figuren, welche derselbe den 13. Januar styli veteris Anno 1732 auf einer gefrornen Fenster-scheibe wahrgenommen: Aus dem Englischen ins Deutsche übersetzt, anonymous (Frankfurt am Main & Leipzig: Herold, 1732);

Der sich selbst entdeckende X.Y.Z., oder L–C–S H–rm–n B–ckm–rs Rev. Minist. Candid. aufrichtige Anzeige der Ursachen die ihn bewogen, Die Geschichte von der Zerstörung der Stadt Jerusalem mit kurtzen Anmerkungen zu erläutern, und diesen Anmerckungen unter einem falschen Nahmen ans Licht zu stellen, zur Beruhigung und

zum Trost des (S.T.) Hn. Mag. Sievers imgleichen zu Rettung der Unschuld seiner Absichten wider allerhand ungleiche Urtheile und Deutungen zum Druck befördert, anonymous (Frankfurt am Main & Leipzig, 1733);

Unpartheyische Untersuchung der Frage: Ob die bekannte Satyre, "Briontes der Jüngere oder Lob-Rede auf den Herrn D. Joh. Ernst Philippi etc." mit entsetzlichen Religions-Spöttereyen angefüllt und eine strafbare Schrift sey?, anonymous (Leipzig, 1733);

Sottises Champêtres, oder Schäfer-Gedicht des (Tit.) Herrn Professor Philippi seiner Seltenheit wegen zum Druck befördert, anonymous (Leipzig, 1733);

Stand- oder Antritts-Rede, welche der (S.T.) Herr D. Johann Ernst Philippi, öffentlicher Professor der deutschen Wohlredenheit zu Halle, den 21. December 1732 in der Gesellschaft der kleinen Geister gehalten, samt der Ihm darauf, im Namen der ganzen löbl. Gesellschaft der kleinen Geister von dem (S.T.) Herrn B.G.R.S.F.M. als Ältesten der Gesellschaft, gewordenen höflichen Antwort, anonymous (N.p., 1733);

Eines berühmten Medici Glaubwürdiger Bericht von dem Zustande, in welchem Er Herrn Professor Philippi den 20. Junii 1734 angetroffen, anonymous (Merseburg, 1734);

*Christian Ludwig Liscow; engraving by
H. Pfenninger, 1789*

*Die Vortrefflichkeit und Nothwendigkeit der Elenden
Scribenten gründlich erwiesen,* anonymous
(N.p., 1734; edited by Herbert Roch, Ber-
lin: Bott, 1939);

*Anmerkungen in Form eines Briefes über den Abriß
eines neuen Rechts der Natur, welchen der Hr.
Prof. Mantzel zu Rostock in einer Kleinen
Schrift der Welt mitgetheilet,* anonymous (Kiel,
1735);

*Bescheidene Beantwortung der Einwürffe, welche ei-
nige Freunde des . . . Philippi . . . wieder die Nachricht von Dessen Tode gemacht haben,* anonymous (Halle, 1735);

Sammlung Satyrischer und Ernsthafter Schriften, 2 volumes (Frankfurt am Main & Leipzig: He-
rold, 1739);

Liscovs [sic] *Lob der schlechten Schriftsteller, von
einem gebeugten schlechten Schriftsteller seinen
Mitbrüdern zu Gemüthe geführt,* edited by J. J.
Stolz (Hannover: Ritscher, 1794);

*Über die Unnöthigkeit der guten Werke zur Seligkeit:
Eine bescheidene und wohlgemeinte Epistel an
Hrn. M. L. Hg. aus Liscows hinterlassenen Papie-*

ren, edited by Deginhard Pott (Leipzig:
Gräff, 1803);

Christian Ludwig Liscov's [sic] *Schriften,* 3 volumes,
edited by Carl Müchler (Berlin: Himburg,
1806; reprinted, Frankfurt am Main: Athenäum, 1972);

*Werke: Auswahl. Zur 200. Wiederkehr seines Geburtsta-
ges,* edited by August Holder (Halle: Hendel, 1901);

*Vortrefflichkeit und Notwendigkeit der elenden Skriben-
ten und andere Schriften,* edited by Jürgen
Manthey (Frankfurt am Main: Insel, 1968).

OTHER: *Dionysius Longin vom Erhabenen: Grie-
chisch und Deutsch,* translated by Carl Heinrich Heineken, preface by Liscow (Dresden:
Walther, 1742);

*Papiere des Kleeblattes oder Ecksteiniana, Brandiana,
und Andresiana,* edited by Liscow (Meldorf &
Leipzig: Boie, 1787).

Christian Ludwig Liscow was the author of
some of the most biting satires of the first half of
the eighteenth century. The targets of his attacks
were respected scholars in their day but have
now largely been forgotten; accordingly, Liscow,
too, has been relegated to a position of obscurity.
But his treatises, written anonymously or under a
pseudonym, appeared at a time when the nature
of satire was being reexamined; thus Liscow contributed substantially to a new understanding
and broadening of the definition of satire–to include less idealism, more realism and irony–in
eighteenth-century literature.

Little is known of Liscow's early years. At
the time of his birth in Wittenburg on 26 April
1701 his father, Joachim Friedrich Liscow, was a
minister; until two years earlier he had held a
court position in Grabow. Liscow's mother was
Margarethe Catharina Liscow, née Hausvoigt.
During Liscow's youth the family moved to
Lübeck, where the boy attended secondary
school. Liscow began his theological training in
1718 in Rostock but later switched to law; he continued his studies at the University of Jena and
probably in Halle. After a brief visit to France,
he settled in Lübeck as a private tutor in 1729.

While in Lübeck Liscow published his first
satires, most of which were directed against
Heinrich Jacob Sivers, a lecturer at Rostock and
later a clergyman in Lübeck; and Johann Ernst
Philippi, professor of rhetoric at the University
of Halle. Liscow knew neither man personally

but singled them out because of what he considered their self-praising, bombastic writing.

In 1732 Sivers, who had recently been inducted into the Prussian Academy of Sciences in Berlin, published *Leiden und Sterben Christi* (The Suffering and Death of Christ). Sivers's pompous style had already come under scrutiny, and the book was strongly criticized in several newspapers. The author blamed Liscow for one of the negative reviews, and this accusation, combined with Liscow's distaste for the work, prompted him to write *Kurtze, aber dabey deutliche und erbauliche Anmerckungen, über die klägliche Geschichte von der jämmerlichen Zerstöhrung der Stadt Jerusalem* (Brief, but Thereby Clear and Edifying Remarks on the Wretched Story of the Deplorable Destruction of the City of Jerusalem, 1732) under the pseudonym X.Y.Z. Later that year Sivers's *Descriptio lapidis musicalis* (Description of Musical Stones) appeared: having turned his attention to natural sciences, Sivers had discovered some stones on a beach of the Baltic Sea; on careful examination he found that they bore marks which appeared to be musical notation. In his treatise he attempted to decipher them. This work of dubious scholarly value was the impetus for Liscow's *Vitrea fracta* (Broken Windows, 1732). Adopting the persona of Robert Clifton, an English nobleman, Liscow tells how on a cold winter's day he noticed that frost had formed on the windowpane, producing various figures; he proceeds to expound on what these figures might be. The Latin title of the piece has a second meaning, "trifles," which is most appropriate for Liscow's satirical purposes. Liscow does not mention Sivers by name but refers to him as "Mr. Makewind." Sivers continued to publish works of doubtful merit, providing Liscow with a third opportunity for parody, *Der sich selbst entdeckende X.Y.Z.* (The Self-Discovering Mr. X.Y.Z., 1733).

In the meantime Liscow's friends brought to his attention the works of Philippi, who had been chosen over Johann Christoph Gottsched in 1731 as the first professor of rhetoric in Germany. Liscow published five satires directed against Philippi; the first three were literary parodies; the last two were almost exclusively personal attacks. Philippi's *Sechs deutsche Reden* (Six German Orations, 1732) provided Liscow with the basis for *Briontes der Jüngere* (Briontes the Younger, 1732); "Briontes" was Philippi's epithet as a member of the Merseburg Patriotische Assemblée. In this work Liscow depicts the "Gesellschaft der kleinen Geister" (Society of Small Minds), a group that produces inferior writing. Liscow's comparison of the society with the Church brought about accusations of religious satire; in later works he was careful to avoid anticlerical references. Philippi suspected Gottsched as the author of *Briontes der Jüngere*; almost immediately, in retaliation, he wrote "Sieben neue Versuche" (Seven New Essays) and "Gleiche Brüder, gleiche Kappen" (Like Pot, Like Cover–a proverb which means birds of a feather flock together). Philippi was unable to have the works published, but friends of Liscow in Hamburg and Leipzig obtained the manuscripts and passed them on to the satirist. Without Philippi's permission, excerpts from the manuscripts appeared in Liscow's next two works: in *Unpartheyische Untersuchung* (Impartial Inquiry, 1733) Liscow defends his method of satire and attacks Philippi's "Gleiche Brüder, gleiche Kappen"; *Stand- oder Antritts-Rede* (Harangue or Inaugural Address, 1733) includes a speech from "Sieben neue Versuche" and continues the satire on learned societies. Like Sivers, Philippi was undaunted by Liscow's attacks. In *Eines berühmten Medici Glaubwürdiger Bericht* (Reliable Report of a Famous Physician, 1734) Liscow, in the guise of a medical doctor, relates that after being struck on the head Philippi recognized the inferiority of his writing and then died. A short time later Philippi, whose students had begun reading the satires in class, became involved in a brawl while trying to defend his scholarly integrity and lost his professorship. Liscow did not relent in his attacks on Philippi; in 1735 he reaffirmed Philippi's death in *Bescheidene Beantwortung* (Modest Response). Wandering from city to city, unable to find work, Philippi eventually lost his mind; perhaps out of remorse, Liscow provided Philippi with financial support during the latter's final years.

In 1734 Liscow published his most famous work, *Die Vortrefflichkeit und Nothwendigkeit der Elenden Scribenten gründlich erwiesen* (The Superiority and Necessity of Miserable Writers Thoroughly Proved). Here Liscow sets forth his views on the role of the satirist: whereas the clergy is to educate and improve the "elende Scribenten," the satirist is to expose their bogus erudition and false reasoning. The personal attacks that characterize most of Liscow's works are absent; perhaps for this reason critics have viewed this satire more favorably than the rest.

In the fall of 1735 Liscow was employed as embassy secretary by Duke Carl Leopold of

Mecklenburg-Schwerin. Carl Leopold had recently been expelled from the country, and Liscow undertook a trip to Paris in 1736 to secure French assistance for his reinstatement. Liscow was never even received at the French court, however; and with the failure of his mission the duke terminated his service, leaving him stranded in Rotterdam. With the financial help of friends Liscow returned to Hamburg, where his brother Joachim Friedrich lived. In 1738 he became secretary to the superintendent von Blome at the Preetz monastery in Holstein, a position he held until 1739. Liscow was also active as a journalist, writing articles for several Hamburg newspapers. His brother and the poet Friedrich von Hagedorn, with whom Liscow corresponded, often wrote favorable reviews of Liscow's works for the newspapers.

In 1739 Liscow published anonymously an incomplete collection of his works. Among the works not included was *Über die Unnöthigkeit der guten Werke zur Seligkeit* (On the Futility of Good Works for Salvation), first published in 1803. In this satire in epistolary form Master Sebastian Zänker tries to teach Master Lange the true Lutheran doctrine regarding good works.

For several months in 1741 Liscow was the Prussian embassy secretary in Mainz. He then went to Dresden as private secretary to Count Heinrich von Brühl, prime minister of Saxony under August III. Liscow's predecessor as secretary was his friend Carl Heineken. An outgrowth of their friendship was Liscow's last published work, the anonymous preface to the second edition of Heineken's translation of the pseudo-Longinus treatise on the sublime. Here he finally challenged a worthy opponent: he sided with the Swiss critics Johann Jakob Bodmer and Johann Jakob Breitinger in their dispute with Gottsched and his followers on the nature and function of poetry.

Liscow eventually became a cabinet secretary and finally minister of war in Saxony. In 1745 he married Johanna Catharine Christine Mylius von Buch, widow of the court treasurer; they had two daughters and three sons. In 1749 Bruhl's mismanagement of funds led to a plot by his officers to expose his incompetence; although Liscow was not one of the conspirators he was implicated in the plot. On 30 December 1749 he was dismissed from his court positions and briefly incarcerated. In April 1750 he retreated to his wife's estate near Eilenberg, in the vicinity of Leipzig. There he died of apoplexy at age fifty-nine on 30 October 1760. Few of his unpublished works are extant; on his arrest in 1749 some of his papers had been confiscated, and it has been reported that after his death a priest destroyed others of his papers on religious grounds.

Liscow's satires can be understood only in relation to the works that were the objects of his satire, most of which have long since been forgotten. Liscow has frequently been criticized: some of his satires often appear to be unduly personal and harsh, and most of his targets were unworthy of his talent. In some of his attacks he used unpublished manuscripts written by his opponent; such unscrupulousness cast doubt on his integrity. One of the most scathing criticisms is found in part 2, book 7 of Johann Wolfgang von Goethe's *Dichtung und Wahrheit* (Truth and Fiction, 1812). Liscow is frequently compared to his contemporary Wilhelm Rabener, who was also a satirist; Rabener, however, did not attack his adversaries personally, and the didactic strain of Rabener's works has made them more durable. Liscow is also often likened to Jonathan Swift; although it is probable that Liscow had read Swift's works, which had been translated into German, there is little demonstrable influence of the Englishman on Liscow.

Liscow's satires were not originally intended to be published but merely to be circulated among his friends. When he finally did publish the works, he chose to do so anonymously–not out of fear of reprisal, he claimed, but so that the works might be judged on their own merit. Despite the personal nature of the satires, Liscow achieved his goal: he forced the public and other writers to look more critically at style and scientific method.

Biographies:

Karl Gustave Helbig, *Christian Ludwig Liscow: Ein Beitrag zur Literatur- und Kulturgeschichte des 18. Jahrhunderts. Nach Liscows Papieren im Königlichen Sächsischen Haupt-Staats-Archiv und andern Mittheilungen* (Dresden & Leipzig: Arnold, 1844);

Georg Christian Friedrich Lisch, *Liscows Leben nach den Acten des großherzogl.-mecklenburg. Geheimen- und Haupt-Archivs und anderen Originalquellen* (Schwerin: Stiller, 1845);

Johannes Classen, *Über Liscows Leben und Schriften* (Lübeck: Schmidt, 1846);

Berthold Litzmann, *Christian Ludwig Liscow in seiner litterarischen Laufbahn* (Hamburg & Leipzig: Voß, 1853).

References:

Jürgen Brummack, "Vernunft und Agression: Über den Satiriker Liscow," *Deutsche Vierteljahrsschrift für Literaturwissenschaft und Geistesgeschichte*, 49 (1975): 118-137;

Brummack, "Zu Begriff und Theorie der Satire," *Deutsche Vierteljahrsschrift für Literaturwissenschaft und Geistesgeschichte*, 45 (June 1971): 275-377;

Alken Bruns, "Christian Ludwig Liscows Lübekker Satiren," *Zeitschrift des Vereins für Lübeckische Geschichte und Altertumskunde*, 61 (1981): 95-127;

Winfried Freund, "Christian Ludwig Liscow: 'Die Vortrefflichkeit und Notwendigkeit der elenden Scribenten,' Zum Verhältnis von Prosasatire und Rhetorik in der Frühaufklärung," *Zeitschrift für deutsche Philologie*, 96 (June 1977): 161-178;

Friedrich Griese, "Christian Ludwig Liscow," *Goethe-Kalender*, 32 (1939): 68-88;

Griese, "Der mecklenburgische Satiriker Christian Ludwig Liscow," *Carolinum*, 27, no. 34 (1961): 67-72;

Jürgen Jacobs, "Zur Satire der frühen Aufklärung: Rabener und Liscow," *Germanisch-romanische Monatsschrift*, 18 (January 1968): 1-13;

Klaus Lazarowicz, "Liscow," in his *Verkehrte Welt: Vorstudie zu einer Geschichte der deutschen Satire* (Tübingen: Niemeyer, 1963), pp. 28-71;

Albert Leitzmann, "Liscows Zitate," *Zeitschrift für deutsche Philologie*, 50 (1926): 79-92;

Fritz Mauthner, "Liscow," in his *Der Atheismus und seine Geschichte im Abendlande*, volume 3 (Berlin & Stuttgart: Deutsche Verlagsanstalt, 1922), pp. 305-316;

Johannes Müller, "Liscow und die Bibel," in *Festschrift zum siebzigsten Geburtstage Oskar Schade dargebracht von seinen Schülern und Verehrern* (Königsberg: Hartung, 1896), pp. 187-228;

Thomas P. Saine, "Christian Ludwig Liscow," in *Deutsche Dichter des 18. Jahrhunderts: Ihr Leben und ihr Werk*, edited by Benno von Wiese (Berlin: Schmidt, 1977), pp. 62-83;

Saine, "Christian Ludwig Liscow: The First German Swift," *Lessing Yearbook*, 4 (1972): 122-156;

Arnold Schirokauer, "Zur Datierung des Liscowschen Schrift 'Anmerkung in Form eines Briefes,'" *Euphorion*, 22 (1915): 663-671;

Jörg Schönert, *Roman und Satire im 18. Jahrhundert: Ein Beitrag zur Poetik* (Stuttgart: Metzler, 1969);

Karl Schröder, "Zur Christian Liscows Jugend," *Euphorion*, 13 (1906): 556-557;

Christian Schwarz, "Spötter und Scribenten: Untersuchung zu Strategie und Struktur frühaufklärischer Satire bei Christian Ludwig Liscow," Ph.D. dissertation, University of Würzburg, 1977;

John James Stickler, "Christian Ludwig Liscow: A Precursor of Modern Irony," Ph.D. dissertation, Michigan State University, 1974;

Maria Tronskaja, "Die Satire Christian Ludwig Liscows," in her *Die deutsche Prosasatire der Aufklärung*, translated by Brigitta Schröder (Berlin: Rütten & Loening, 1969), pp. 17-40;

Ludolf Wienbarg, "Der größte ironische Schriftsteller Deutschlands," *Hamburger literarische und kritische Blätter*, 9 (January 1845): 65-68.

Papers:

After Christian Ludwig Liscow's death a large portion of his papers was evidently destroyed; however, some correspondence survived. Most of it is in the Hauptstaats-Archiv in Dresden. The Universitätsbibliothek in Kiel has three letters by Liscow, and the Universitätsbibliothek in Leipzig possesses a letter from Liscow to Gottsched.

Moses Mendelssohn

(6 September 1729 - 4 January 1786)

Liliane Weissberg

University of Pennsylvania

BOOKS: *Philosophische Gespräche* (Berlin: Voß, 1755);

Über die Empfindungen (Berlin: Voß, 1755);

Pope, ein Metaphysiker!, by Mendelssohn and Gotthold Ephraim Lessing (Danzig: Schuster, 1755);

Logica R. Moses Maimonidis, cum explicatione R. Samson Kalir atque Censura Amplissimae Facultatis Philosophae Academiae Francofurtanae (Frankfurt am Main: Grillo, 1761);

Philosophische Schriften, 2 volumes (Berlin: Voß, 1761; revised, 1771; revised, 1777; reprinted, Brussels: Culture et civilisation, 1968);

Abhandlung über die Evidenz in metaphysischen Wissenschaften, welche den von der Königlichen Academie der Wissenschaften in Berlin auf das Jahr 1763 ausgesetzten Preis erhalten hat (Berlin: Haude & Spener, 1764; reprinted, Brussels: Culture et civilisation, 1968);

Phaedon oder Über die Unsterblichkeit der Seele in drey Gesprächen (Berlin & Stettin: Nicolai, 1767); translated by Charles Cullen as *Phaedon; or, The Death of Socrates* (London: Printed for the author by J. Cooper, 1789; reprinted, New York: Arno Press, 1973); German version reprinted (Hamburg: Meiner, 1979);

Sefer Megillat Kohelet 'im Biur (Berlin: Speyer, 1770);

Schreiben an den Herrn Diaconus Lavater zu Zürich (Berlin & Stettin: Nicolai, 1770); translated by Frederick Henry Hedge as *Letter of Moses Mendelssohn, to Deacon Lavater* (New York: Kingsland, 1821);

Antwort an den Herrn Moses Mendelssohn zu Berlin von Johann Caspar Lavater: Nebst einer Nacherinnerung von Moses Mendelssohn, by Mendelssohn and Johann Kaspar Lavater (Berlin & Stettin: Nicolai, 1770);

Ritualgesetze der Juden, betreffend Erbschaften, Vormundschaftssachen, Testamente und Ehesachen, in so weit sie das Mein und Dein angehen (Berlin: Voß, 1778);

Oil painting on wood by Johann Christoph Frisch, 1786 (Staatsbibliothek Preußischer Kulturbesitz, Berlin)

Jerusalem oder Über religiöse Macht und Judentum (Berlin: Maurer, 1783); translated by M. Samuels as *Jerusalem: A Treatise on Ecclesiastical Authority and Judaism* (London: Longman, Orme, Brown & Longmans, 1838); translated by Isaac Lesser as *Jerusalem: A Treatise on Religious Power and Judaism* (Philadelphia: Sherman, 1852); German version reprinted (Brussels: Culture et civilisation, 1968); translated by Allan Arkush as *Jerusalem: Or On Religious Power & Judaism*, edited by Alexander

Altmann (Hanover, N.H. & London: University Press of New England for Brandeis University Press, 1983);

Abhandlung von der Unkörperlichkeit der menschlichen Seele (Vienna: Hartl, 1785);

Morgenstunden oder Vorlesungen über das Daseyn Gottes: Erster Theil (Berlin: Voß, 1785; revised, 1786; reprinted, Brussels: Culture et civilisation, 1968; edited by Dominique Bourel, Stuttgart: Reclam, 1979);

Moses Mendelssohn an die Freunde Lessings: Ein Anhang zu Herrn Jacobi Briefwechsel über die Lehre des Spinoza, edited by Johann Jakob Engel (Berlin: Voß, 1786);

Abhandlungen über das Kommerz zwischen Seele und Körper: Aus dem Hebräischen übersetzt, translated by Salomon Anschel (Frankfurt am Main, 1788);

Moses Mendelssohns kleine philosophische Schriften: Mit einer Skizze seines Lebens und Charakters von D. Jenisch, edited by J. G. Müchler (Berlin: Vieweg, 1789);

Moses Mendelssohn's sämmtliche Werke, 12 volumes (Ofen: Burian, 1819-1820);

Moses Mendelssohn: Sammlung theils noch ungedruckter, theils in andern Schriften zerstreuter Aufsätze und Briefe von ihm, an und über ihn, edited by Jeremiah Heinemann (Leipzig: Wolbrecht, 1831);

Moses Mendelssohn's sämmtliche Werke: Ausgabe in einem Bande als Nationaldenkmal (Vienna: Schmidl & Klang, 1838);

Moses Mendelssohn's gesammelte Schriften: Nach den Originaldrucken und Handschriften herausgegeben, 7 volumes, edited by Georg Benjamin Mendelssohn (Leipzig: Brockhaus, 1843-1845; reprinted, Hildesheim: Olms, 1976);

Moses Mendelssohn's Schriften zur Philosophie, Aesthetik und Apologetik: Mit Einleitungen, Anmerkungen und einer biographisch-historischen Charakteristik Mendelssohns, 2 volumes, edited by Moritz Brasch (Leipzig: Voß, 1880; reprinted, Hildesheim: Olms, 1968);

Moses Mendelssohn: Ungedrucktes und Unbekanntes, von ihm und über ihn, edited by M. Kayserling (Leipzig: Brockhaus, 1883);

Gesammelte Schriften: Jubiläumsausgabe, 13 volumes, edited by Ismar Elbogen, Julius Guttmann, Eugen Mittwoch, and others (Berlin: Akademie-Verlag, 1929-1932; Breslau: Marcus, 1938); reprinted and continued, 22 volumes to date, edited by Alexander Altmann and others (Stuttgart-Bad Cannstatt: Frommann, 1974-   );

Ästhetische Schriften in Auswahl, edited by Otto F. Best (Darmstadt: Wissenschaftliche Buchgesellschaft, 1974);

Selbstzeugnisse: Plädoyer für Gewissensfreiheit und Toleranz, edited by Martin Pfeideler (Tübingen & Basel: Erdmann, 1979).

Editions in English: *Jerusalem and Other Jewish Writings*, translated and edited by Alfred Jospe (New York: Schocken, 1969);

Moses Mendelssohn: Selections from His Writings, edited and translated by Eva Jospe (New York: Viking Press, 1975).

OTHER: Jean-Jacques Rousseau, *Abhandlung von dem Ursprunge der Ungleichheit unter den Menschen, und worauf sie sich gründe: ins Deutsche übersetzt mit einem Schreiben an den Herrn Magister Leßing und einem Briefe Voltairens an den Verfasser vermehret*, translated by Mendelssohn (Berlin: Voß, 1756);

Hartog Leo, *Danklied Ueber den rühmlichen Sieg, welchen der HERR Unserm allergnädigsten Könige und Herrn, FRIEDRICH II. am Sabbath den 5. November 1757 bey Roßbach in Sachsen verliehen*, translated by Mendelssohn (Berlin, 1757);

Leo, *Danklied Ueber den Herrlichen und glorreichen Sieg, Welchen Se. Majestät unser alldergnädigster König, den 5. December 1757 bey Leuthen in Schlesien erfochten*, translated by Mendelssohn (Berlin, 1757);

Leo, *Dankpredigt Ueber den Herrlichen und glorreichen Sieg, welchen Se. Majestät unser allgergnädigster König, den 5. December 1757 'bey Leuthen in Schlesien erfochten; Gehalten von Daniel Hirschel Fränkel, Oberland-Rabinner*, translated by Mendelssohn (Berlin: Birnstiel, 1757);

Bibliothek der schönen Wissenschaften und der freyen Künste, 4 volumes, edited by Mendelssohn and Friedrich Nicolai (Leipzig: Dyk, 1757-1760);

Briefe, die Neueste Litteratur betreffend, 24 volumes, edited by Mendelssohn, Lessing, and Nicolai (Berlin: Nicolai, 1759-1765);

Leo, *SCHIR SCHALOM: Friedenslied . . . auf den großen Tag, an welchem . . . auf dem Schloße Hubertusburg . . . Friede geschlossen wurde*, translated by Mendelssohn (Berlin: Rellstab, 1763);

Aron Mosessohns Friedenspredigt in der Synagoge zu Berlin, edited by Mendelssohn (Berlin: Nicolai, 1763);

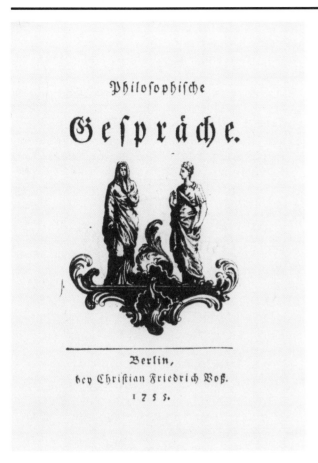

Title page for Mendelssohn's first book, a series of philosophical conversations reflecting the influence of Gottfried Wilhelm von Leibniz, Christian von Wolff, and Lord Shaftesbury

Lesebuch für Jüdische Kinder. Zum besten der Jüdischen Freyschule, edited by Mendelssohn and David Friedländer (Berlin: Voß, 1779);

Sefer Netibot Ha-Schalom, 5 volumes, translated by Mendelssohn, Hartwig Wessely, Salomon Dubno, Aaron Jarolslaw, and Herz Homberg (volume 1, Göttingen: Dieterich, 1780; volumes 2-5, Berlin: Starcke, 1783);

Thomas Abbt, *Thomas Abbts vermischte Werke: Dritter Theil, welcher einen Theil seiner freundschaftlichen Correspondens enthält: Neue und mit Anmerkungen von Moses Mendelssohn vermehrte Auflage*, edited by Mendelssohn (Berlin & Stettin: Nicolai, 1782; reprinted as Thomas Abbt's *Vermischte Werke*, volume 2 (Hildesheim: Olms, 1978);

Manasseh Ben Israel, *Rettung der Juden: Aus dem Englischen übersetzt. Als ein Anhang zu des Herrn. Kriegsraths Dohm Abhandlung: Ueber die bürgerliche Verbesserung der Juden*, translated by Marcus Herz, foreword by Mendelssohn (Berlin & Stettin: Nicolai, 1782);

Die Psalmen, translated by Mendelssohn (Berlin: Maurer, 1783);

Megillat Schir Ha-Schirim, meturgamat aschkenasit al . . . Mosche ben Menachem, translated by Mendelssohn (Berlin: Druck der Jüdischen Freyschule, 1788).

In 1774 Johann Jacob Spiess, the editor of the *Brandenburgische historische Münzbelustigungen*, a popular numismatic publication, asked Moses Mendelssohn to supply him with some biographical data; a coin with Mendelssohn's portrait had just been issued, and Spiess wanted to introduce him to the public. Mendelssohn, however, had doubts in regard to this undertaking: "Meine Lebensumstände sind von so geringer Erheblichkeit, daß ich Ihren Lesern keine sonderliche Unterhaltung versprechen kann; mir selbst haben sie so unwichtig geschienen, daß ich nicht das Mindeste davon aufgezeichnet habe" (The circumstances of my life are of such little importance that I cannot promise your readers any special diversion; to myself they have appeared so insignificant that I have not bothered to note down the least of them).

Mendelssohn proceeded, nevertheless: "Ich bin im Jahre 1729 (den 12 Ellul 5489 nach jüdischer Zeitrechnung) zu Dessau geboren. Mein Vater war daselbst Schulmeister und Zehngebotschreiber, oder Sopher. Unter Rabbi Fränkel, der damals in Dessau Oberrabbiner war, studierte ich den Talmud. Nachdem sich dieser gelehrte Rabbi, durch seinen Commentar über den hierosolymitanischen Talmud, bei der jüdischen Nation großen Ruhm erworben, ward er etwa im Jahre 1743 nach Berlin berufen, wohin ich ihm noch in demselben Jahre folgte. Allhier gewann ich durch den Umgang mit dem nachherigen Doctor der Arzneigelartheit, Herrn Aron Gumperz (der vor einigen Jahren zu Hamburg verstorben), Geschmack an den Wissenschaften, dazu ich auch von demselben einige Anleitung erhielt. Ich ward hierauf in dem Hause eines reichen Juden Informator, hernach Buchhalter, und endlich Aufseher über desselben seidene Waaren-Manufactur, welches ich noch auf diese Stunde bin. In meinem drei und dreißigsten Jahr habe ich geheiratet, und seitdem sieben Kinder gezeugt, davon fünfe am Leben. Übrigens bin ich nie auf einer Universität gewesen, habe auch in meinem Leben kein Collegium lesen hören. Dieses war eine der größten Schwierigkeiten, die ich übernommen hatte, indem ich alles durch Anstrengung und eigenen

Fromet Mendelssohn, née Gugenheim, whom Mendelssohn married in 1762; miniature painting by "Dr. R. S.," 1767 (Collection of Fanny Kistner-Hensel and Dr. Cécile Lowenthal-Hensel, Berlin)

Fleiß erzwingen mußte. In der That trieb ich es zu weit, und habe mir endlich durch Unmäßigkeit im Studiren seit drei Jahren eine Nervenschwäche zugezogen ..." (I was born in the year 1729 [Ellul 12, 5489 according to the Jewish calendar] in Dessau. My father was a school-teacher there and a scribe of the Ten Commandments, or *Sopher*. Under Rabbi Fränkel, who was the chief rabbi in Dessau at the time, I studied the Talmud. This learned rabbi gained a great reputation in the Jewish nation because of his commentary on the Jerusalem Talmud, and he was called to Berlin about 1743; I followed him in the same year. There I became acquainted with the future doctor of pharmacy, Aaron Gumpertz [who died several years ago in Hamburg], and I gained a taste of the sciences, in which he provided me some guidance. Thereafter I became a tutor in the house of a rich Jew, then his accountant, and finally overseer for his manufacture of goods, which I am to this day. I married in my thirty-third year, and I have fathered seven children, of which five are still alive. I have never, by the way, attended any university, nor did I ever hear a *collegium* being read. This was one of

the greatest difficulties that I have taken upon me, that I have had to force everything by effort and my own diligence. Indeed, I have gone too far, and have finally, through the immoderation of my studies, contracted a weakness of the nerves ...). This short tale of a self-made career and the dangers of diligence describes the life of a man who was not only a prominent Enlightenment philosopher but a founder of modern German Judaism as well.

Mendelssohn was born in Dessau on 6 September 1729 to the scribe Mendel Heymann and Bela Rahel Sara. In accordance with the Jewish custom of the time his place of birth was used as his surname, so that he was known as Moses Dessau. As a youth he showed great interest and talent in religious and philosophical studies. Under the guidance of Rabbi David Fränkel he pursued the study of the Bible and the Talmud and read Moses Maimonides' *More nevukhim* (The Guide of the Perplexed, 1190).

When Fränkel left for Berlin in 1743, Mendelssohn followed him. Much has been made of Mendelssohn's entrance into the city, which has been seen as a symbolic step in the history of German Jews. Jews were only allowed to enter Berlin through special gates and were taxed like cattle. According to the legend, Mendelssohn entered the city through the Rosenthaler Gate, stating that the purpose of his stay in Berlin was to learn. Soon he would speak up for the equality of all human beings and become an important voice for Jewish emancipation.

Mendelssohn enrolled in Fränkel's Talmud Academy but also began to learn Latin, English, French, and German. Soon he was reading John Locke's *An Essay Concerning Human Understanding* (1690) in Latin and studying the philosophical writings of Gottfried Wilhelm von Leibniz–especially the *Essais de Théodicée* (1710)–and of Christian Wolff with Aaron Gumpertz, a doctor who became his mentor. Locke, Leibniz, and Wolff introduced Mendelssohn to problems in ethics and metaphysics to which he later responded in his own books. Wolff had published his *Vernünfftige Gedancken von Gott, der Welt und der Seele des Menschen* (Reasonable Thoughts on God, the World, and the Human Soul, 1719) and *Vernünfftige Gedancken von der Menschen Tun und Lassen* (Reasonable Thoughts on Human Actions, 1720) in German, rejecting the customary Latin. For orthodox Jews of the time, German was a secular language that was to be shunned; for Mendelssohn, however, it was far superior to his native

Frontispiece and title page for Mendelssohn's reworking of Plato's dialogue Phaedo

Western Yiddish, which he came to regard as a corrupted dialect. Much of Mendelssohn's work can be understood as a messianic plea for Jews to adopt the German language. He thought that the existence of the Jewish community would not be endangered thereby, but that the Jews would at last be able to enter into a dialogue with the Christian culture surrounding them. This dialogue, he believed, would finally draw attention to the peculiar social situation of the Jews.

At the time of Mendelssohn's arrival in Berlin the Jewish community did not have a defined ghetto. The oldest Jewish families were wealthy descendants of Viennese refugees who had been admitted to the city in the late seventeenth century on the condition that they use their fortunes to help the Prussian economy. These Jews had been followed by other wealthy merchants, as well as by many poor Jews who were barely tolerated in the city and who lived under the constant threat of expulsion. Citizenship did not extend to Jews; letters of protection were rare and often included only an oldest child, leaving the other children and sometimes even the widow without legal rights. Taxes were high and had to be paid frequently. Since Mendelssohn was an unprotected Jew, his residence in the city was precarious. While a student in Fränkel's academy he earned his living by copying texts and received charity. In 1750 he became a tutor in the house of Isaak Bernhard, a silk merchant who received the right to found a factory (Manufaktur) in 1752. In 1754 Mendelssohn became Bernhard's accountant and then his assistant. After Bernhard's death in 1768 Mendelssohn became a part owner of the factory, running it with Bernhard's widow. His success as a businessman made his philosophical endeavors possible.

In 1753 Mendelssohn met Gotthold Ephraim Lessing–according to the story, over a game of chess. Lessing had begun to make a name for himself as a critic and a dramatist; in the following years he guided Mendelssohn in his readings of German literature, helped form

Mendelssohn in 1767; miniature painting on ivory by "Dr. R. S." (Collection of Dr. Felix Gilbert, New York)

his views on aesthetics, and introduced him to Friedrich Nicolai, a critic who became the most important publisher of Enlightenment texts in Berlin. Mendelssohn's anonymously published letter speaking favorably of Lessing's drama *Die Juden* (The Jews, 1755) appeared in the *Theatralische Bibliothek* in 1754. A year later Mendelssohn and Lessing wrote the satirical *Pope, ein Metaphysiker!* (Pope, Metaphysician!). While Lessing functioned largely as a mentor in these early years, he was much taken by Mendelssohn's intelligence and knowledge of philosophy. The title character of Lessing's drama *Nathan der Weise* (Nathan the Wise, 1779) is believed to have been inspired by Mendelssohn.

Mendelssohn's *Philosophische Gespräche* (Philosophical Conversations) and *Über die Empfindungen* (On Sensations), both published in 1755, document the influence of Wolff, Leibniz, and Shaftesbury. These philosophers spoke for the existence of eternal truths, which Leibniz named *vérités de raison* (truths of reason) in contrast to *vérités de fait* (truths of fact). Like Shaftesbury, Mendelssohn chose the dialogue form of

presentation. In *Über die Empfindungen*, he discusses Johann Georg Sulzer's aesthetics, especially the notion of Vergnügen (pleasure) that stands at its center.

Mendelssohn published essays on aesthetics in Enlightenment journals and founded the *Bibliothek der schönen Wissenschaften* with Nicolai in 1757. Nicolai, Mendelssohn, and Lessing began their weekly, *Briefe, die Neueste Litteratur betreffend* (Letters Concerning the Newest Literature), in 1759.

In 1756 Mendelssohn had translated Jean-Jacques Rousseau's *Discours sur l'origine et les fondements de l'inegalité parmi les hommes* (Essay on the Origin of Inequality, 1755). The following year he and Nicolai decided to learn Greek, and in 1760 Mendelssohn began translations of Plato's *Republic* and *Phaedo*. His book on Maimonides' logic in 1761 gives further evidence of his great knowledge of the writings of that medieval philosopher; it was followed by many other works on Jewish law and philosophy.

In 1761 Mendelssohn published *Philosophische Schriften* (Philosophical Writings). He revised the work thoroughly for the editions of 1771 and 1777, expanding his treatment of aesthetics and shifting from an objective account of artistic rules to a subjective "Gefühl des Schönen" (sense of the beautiful). The development of his aesthetics can also be witnessed in his many reviews. That same year Mendelssohn traveled to Hamburg, where he met Fromet Gugenheim; they were married on 22 June 1762. Mendelssohn had still not been able to gain a letter of protection, but the Marquis d'Argens interceded on his behalf, and Mendelssohn was declared an "Außerordentlicher Schutzjude" (Extraordinary Protected Jew) in 1763. The status, however, did not extend to his children. Because of his achievements, the Jewish community freed Mendelssohn from its taxes in the same year and soon gave him several honorary posts.

Throughout this period, Mendelssohn's stature as a philosopher continued to rise. He gained a small victory over the most famous Enlightenment philosopher of his time, Immanuel Kant, in 1763: Mendelssohn's essay *Abhandlung über die Evidenz in Metaphysischen Wissenschaften* (Essay on Evidence in the Metaphysical Sciences) received the first prize from the Prussian Academy; Kant's essay received only the second prize. Mendelssohn was elected to the Berlin Academy in 1771, but because he was a Jew his election was not confirmed by King Frederick II. In 1777

Mendelssohn stopped in Königsberg on a business trip to Memel and met Kant and the aesthetician Johann Georg Hamann.

In 1767 Mendelssohn published *Phaedon oder Über die Unsterblichkeit der Seele* (translated as *Phaedon; or, The Death of Socrates*, 1789). Rather than a translation of Plato's *Phaedo*, the work is a rewriting of the dialogue. Mendelssohn stresses the philosopher's dedication to spending his life pursuing wisdom, learning about death, and embracing truth. *Phaedon* is an important document of eighteenth-century thought, especially in regard to the contemporary discussion of the immortality of the soul. It was Mendelssohn's most successful work and has been translated into many languages.

In 1763 the Swiss clergyman Johann Kaspar Lavater had visited Mendelssohn. Seven years later he published a German translation of Charles Bonnet's 1769 treatise *La Palingénesie philosophique, ou Idées sur l'état passé et sur l'état future des êtres vivants* (Philosophical Palingenesis; or, Ideas on the Past and Future State of Living Beings), which upheld the truth of Christianity. Lavater dedicated the second volume of the translation to Mendelssohn and challenged him either to refute Bonnet or to convert to Christianity. Mendelssohn answered with his *Schreiben an den Herrn Diaconus Lavater zu Zürich* (1770; translated as *Letter of Moses Mendelssohn, to Deacon Lavater*, 1821), in which he rejects conversion without insisting on a hierarchy of religions. After his exchange with Lavater he felt increasingly responsible for the Jewish nation and was frequently called upon for advice. In response to an appeal from Mendelssohn, Lavater helped to improve the situation of Swiss Jews in 1775. Mendelssohn also mediated on behalf of the Jews in Alsace, Saxony, and Königsberg.

In 1780 Mendelssohn and four other scholars published the first volume of their translation of the Torah, the five books of Moses, on which Mendelssohn had been working since 1774. The *Sefer Netibot Ha-Schalom* consists of the Hebrew text with a German translation and Hebrew commentary. No other work has been as important for the reformation of the Jewish community in Germany. It introduced German not as a language that would desecrate a holy text but as one that would make discussion of different religious texts possible. It served as well as a reader and helped to make German the primary secular language for German Jews. The translation of the Torah was completed in 1783.

Mendelssohn's idea of opening the Jewish community to its German environment had a great influence on educational reform. In 1778 David Friedländer and Isaac Daniel Itzig, members of prominent Jewish families, founded the Jüdische Freyschule (Jewish Free School) in Berlin. The school, which opened its gates in 1781, was structured according to Mendelssohn's concepts, and Mendelssohn collaborated on a textbook. For the first time, German was used as a language of instruction in a Jewish school.

While Friedländer would later propose the conversion of the whole Jewish community to a secularized Protestantism in the spirit of the Enlightenment–an offer rejected by the king–Mendelssohn continued to work for reform within the community and for reform of the social status of the Jews. Christian Wilhelm Dohm, the Prussian secretary of war and royal archivist, published *Ueber die bürgerliche Verbesserung der Juden* (On the Civic Reform of the Jews) in 1781; Dohm's work relied on Mendelssohn's comments and was important in the fight for Jewish emancipation. In 1783 Mendelssohn completed *Jerusalem oder Über religiöse Macht und Judentum* (translated as *Jerusalem: A Treatise on Ecclesiastical Authority and Judaism*, 1838). The book deals with the relationship of religion and church and elaborates on the importance of the law for the Jewish religion.

In 1784 Mendelssohn published his essay "Ueber die Frage: was heißt aufklären?" (In Regard to the Question: What Does Enlightenment Mean?) in the *Berlinische Monatsschrift*, a monthly that published many articles on this issue by various prominent philosophers. The essay was first presented at the Mittwochsgesellschaft (Wednesday Society), a group of philosophers, writers, and publicists, of which he had become an honorary member in 1783. Mendelssohn's essay is almost a counterpart to Kant's famous essay on the Enlightenment, which was written at about the same time and which refers to Mendelssohn's piece. In contrast to Kant's investigation of free will and action, Mendelssohn speculates on the definitions of the bourgeois and of culture. "Ueber die Frage: was heißt aufklären?" is one of the most important texts investigating and summarizing concepts of the Enlightenment.

With Lessing's death in 1781, Mendelssohn lost not only a close friend but also his most important link to the non-Jewish environment. A dispute with the writer Friedrich Heinrich Jacobi, who claimed that Lessing questioned the Judeo-

Pen drawing of Mendelssohn by Daniel Chadowiecki (Herzog August Bibliothek, Wolfenbüttel)

Christian idea of God and turned into a follower of Spinoza in his later years, as well as Mendelssohn's private lectures to his son Joseph and Joseph's friends, resulted in *Morgenstunden oder Vorlesungen über das Daseyn Gottes* (Morning Hours; or, Lectures Concerning the Existence of God, 1785). Mendelssohn's most systematic philosophical work, *Morgenstunden* refutes Jacobi's claim and combines a defense of Lessing as a "geläuterter Spinozist" (modified Spinoza student) or, as he later writes, modified pantheist with an attempt to deduce the existence of God scientifically. Religion is shown to be rational.

Mendelssohn died on 4 January 1786, after having caught a cold while delivering the manuscript of what can be seen as the second part of *Morgenstunden, Moses Mendelssohn an die Freunde Lessings* (Moses Mendelssohn's Address to Lessing's Friends, 1786) to his publisher. His oldest surviving daughter, Dorothea, was the author of the novel *Florentin* (1801); she became the wife of the Romantic philosopher Friedrich Schlegel. Her sons from her first marriage, Philipp and Jonas Veit, became painters of the Nazarene school. Mendelssohn's son Abraham was the father of Felix Mendelssohn-Bartholdy, the pianist and composer. With the exception of Joseph, all of Mendelssohn's children converted to Christianity.

Letters:

Gotthold Ephraim Lessings Briefwechsel mit Karl Wilhelm Ramler, Johann Joachim Eschenburg und Friedrich Nicolai, nebst einigen Anmerkungen über Lessings Briefwechsel mit Moses Mendelssohn (Berlin & Stettin: Nicolai, 1794);

Lessings Briefwechsel mit Mendelssohn und Nicolai über das Trauerspiel. Nebst verwandten Schriften Nicolais und Mendelssohns, edited by Robert Petsch (Leipzig: Dürr, 1910; reprinted, Darmstadt: Wissenschaftliche Buchgesellschaft, 1967);

"Briefe von, an und über Mendelssohn," edited by Ludwig Geiger, *Jahrbuch für jüdische Geschichte und Literatur*, 20 (1917): 85-137;

Brautbriefe, edited by Haim Borodianski (Berlin: Schocken, 1936; reprinted, Königstein: Jüdischer Verlag, 1985);

Neuerschlossene Briefe Moses Mendelssohns an Friedrich Nicolai, edited by Alexander Altmann and Werner Vogel (Stuttgart-Bad Canstatt: Frommann-Holzboog, 1973);

Briefwechsel der letzten Lebensjahre, edited by Altmann (Stuttgart-Bad Canstatt: Frommann-Holzboog, 1979).

Bibliographies:

Hermann M. Z. Meyer, *Moses Mendelssohn Bibliographie* (Berlin: De Gruyter, 1965);

Michael Albrecht, "Moses Mendelssohn: Ein Forschungsbericht 1965-1980," *Deutsche Vierteljahrsschrift für Literaturwissenschaft und Geistesgeschichte*, 57 (March 1983): 64-159.

Biographies:

Meyer Kayserling, *Moses Mendelssohn. Sein Leben und seine Werke. Nebst einem Anhange ungedruckter Briefe von und an Moses Mendelssohn* (Leipzig: Mendelssohn, 1862; reprinted, Hildesheim: Gerstenberg, 1972);

Alexander Altmann, *Moses Mendelssohn: A Biographical Study* (University: University of Alabama Press, 1973; Philadelphia: Jewish Publication Society, 1973).

References:

Michael Albrecht, *Moses Mendelssohn 1729-1786: Das Lebenswerk eines jüdischen Denkers der deutschen Aufklärung* (Weinheim: Acta Humaniora, 1986);

Alexander Altmann, *Moses Mendelssohns Frühschriften zur Metaphysik* (Tübingen: Mohr, 1969);

Altmann, "Moses Mendelssohns Kindheit in Dessau," *Bulletin des Leo Baeck Instituts*, 10 (1967): 237-275;

Altmann, *Die trostvolle Aufklärung: Studien zur Metaphysik und politischen Theorie Moses Mendelssohns* (Stuttgart-Bad Canstatt: Fromann-Holzboog, 1982);

Bertha Badt-Strauß, *Moses Mendelssohn: Der Mensch und das Werk. Zeugnisse / Briefe / Gespräche* (Berlin: Welt, 1929);

Ehrhard Bahr, Edward P. Harris, and Laurence G. Lyon, eds., *Humanität und Dialog: Lessing und Mendelssohn in neuer Sicht. Beiträge zum Internationalen Lessing-Mendelssohn-Symposium, veranstaltet im November 1979 in Los Angeles, Kalifornien. Beiheft zum Lessing Yearbook* (Detroit: Wayne State University Press / Munich: text + kritik, 1982);

Karol Bal, "Aufklärung und Religion bei Mendelssohn, Kant und dem jungen Hegel," *Deutsche Zeitschrift für Philosophie*, 27 (August 1979): 1248-1257;

Isaac Eisenstein Barzilay, "Moses Mendelssohn (1729-1786)," *Jewish Quarterly Review*, 52 (1961/1962): 69-93, 175-186;

Schalom Ben-Chorin, "Jüdische Bibelübersetzungen in Deutschland," *Leo Baeck Institute Yearbook*, 4 (1959): 311-331;

Dominique Bourel, "Les Exigences du libéralisme de Mendelssohn," *Recherches de science religieuse* (1978): 517-532;

Bourel, "La purification du Spinozisme chez Mendelssohn," *Archivo di Filosofia*, no. 1 (1978): 133-145;

Bourel, "Les réserves de Mendelssohn: Rousseau, Voltaire et le Juif de Berlin," *Revue internationale de Philosophie*, 32 (1978): 309-326;

Eva Engel, "The Emergence of Moses Mendelssohn as Literary Critic," *Leo Baeck Institute Yearbook*, 24 (1979): 61-82;

Johanna-Maria Geyer-Kordesch, "Die Psychologie des moralischen Handelns: Psychologie, Medizin und Dramentheorie bei G. E. Lessing, Moses Mendelssohn und Friedrich Nicolai," Ph.D. dissertation, University of Massachusetts, 1977;

Arnold Heidsieck, "Der Disput zwischen Lessing und Mendelssohn über das Trauerspiel," *Lessing Yearbook*, 11 (1979): 7-34;

Norbert Hinske, ed., *Ich handle mit Vernunft . . . Moses Mendelssohn und die europäische Aufklärung* (Hamburg: Meiner, 1981);

Jacob Katz, "The German-Jewish Utopia of Social Emancipation," in his *Emancipation and Assimilation: Studies in Modern Jewish History* (Westmead: Gregg, 1972), pp. 91-110;

Heinz Knobloch, *Herr Moses in Berlin: Auf Spuren eines Menschenfreundes* (Berlin: Der Morgen, 1979);

Edward Richard Levenson, "Moses Mendelssohn's Understanding of Logico-Grammatical and Literary Construction in the Pentateuch: A Study of His German Translation and Hebrew Commentary," Ph.D. dissertation, Brandeis University, 1972;

Jean-Paul Meier, *L'esthétique de Moses Mendelssohn (1729-1786)* (Paris: Champion, 1978);

Erich H. Metzing, "Moses Mendelssohn's Bible Translation Methods, with Special Attention to the Book of Deuteronomy," Ph.D. dissertation, University of Leeds, 1968;

Barouch Mevorah, "Johann Kaspar Lavaters Auseinandersetzung mit Moses Mendelssohn über die Zukunft des Judentums," *Zwingliana*, 14 (1977): 431-450;

Paul H. Meyer, "Le Rayonnement de Moïse Mendelssohn hors d'Allemagne," *Dixhuitième Siècle*, 13 (1981): 63-78;

Moshe Pelli, *The Age of Haskalah: Studies in Hebrew Literature of the Enlightenment in Germany*, Studies in Judaism in Modern Times, 5 (Leiden: Brill, 1979);

Nathan Rotenstreich, "Enlightenment between Mendelssohn and Kant," in *Studies in Jewish Religious and Intellectual History: Presented to Alexander Altmann On the Occasion of His Seventieth Birthday*, edited by Sigfried Stein and Raphael Loewe (University: University of Alabama Press, 1979), pp. 263-279;

Rotenstreich, *Jewish Philosophy in Modern Times: From Mendelssohn to Rosenzweig* (New York: Holt, Rinehart & Winston, 1968);

Rotenstreich, "On Mendelssohn's Political Philosophy," *Leo Baeck Institute Yearbook*, 11 (1966): 28-41;

Hans Joachim Schneider, "Moses Mendelssohns Anthropologie und Ästhetik (Zum Begriff der Popularphilosophie)," Ph.D. dissertation, University of Münster, 1970;

Selma Stern, *Der preußische Staat und die Juden: Dritter Teil. Die Zeit Friedrich des Großen* (Tübingen: Mohr, 1971);

Frederick Will, "Cognition through Beauty in Moses Mendelssohn's Early Aesthetics," *Journal of Aesthetics and Art Criticism*, 14 (September 1955): 97-105;

Sylvain Zac, "Les prix et la mention (Les Preis-
schriften de Mendelssohn et de Kant),"
Revue de Métaphysique et de Morale, 79
(October-December 1974): 473-498.

Papers:
Manuscripts and documents concerning the Men-
delssohn family are collected in the Mendelssohn-
Archiv, Staatsbibliothek Preußischer Kulturbesitz,
Berlin. Documents are also located in the archi-
ves of the Leo Baeck Institute, New York, which
has copies of the material in the Mendelssohn-
Archiv.

Justus Möser

(14 December 1720 - 8 January 1794)

Gloria Flaherty
University of Illinois at Chicago

BOOKS: *Ihrem hochansehnlichen Präsidenten Hrn.
J. M. Gesner Bewies am 1. Heumonat 1743 bey
Antretung der academischen Regierung die deut-
sche Gesellschaft ihre schuldigste Hochachtung
durch Justus Möser aus Osnabrück* (Göttingen:
Hager, 1743);

*Jubelode womit ihren gnädigsten Obervorsteher den
Hochgebornen Grafen und Herrn Herrn Heinrich den Eilften ältere Reuß des H. R. R. Grafen
und Herrn von Plauen, Herrn zu Greiz, Kranich-
feld, Gera, Schaiz und Lobenstein etc. etc. etc. am
18ten März 1743 als an dero hohen Geburts- Hul-
digungstage unterthänigst besinget die Deutsche
Gesellschaft in Göttingen* (Göttingen: Hager,
1743);

*Die weise und tapfre Regierung Seiner königlichen Ma-
jestät in Preußen und Kurfürstlichen Durchlaucht zu Brandenburg Friedrichs besungen,* as
M. O. Reise (N.p., 1743);

*Die Gerechten und siegreichen Waffen seiner Majestät
königlichen Majestät in Großbritannien und Kurfürstlichen Durchlaucht zu Hannover Georgs des
Andern besungen in Namen der Deutschen Gesellschaft in Göttingen* (Göttingen: Hager, 1743);

*Seinem Lieben Bruder Itel Ludewig Möser Welcher den
27. Jan. 1745 im 19ten Jahr seines Alters sanft
und selig entschlief* (Osnabrück: Kißling,
1745);

*Versuch einiger Gemählde von den Sitten unsrer Zeit:
Vormahls zu Hannover als ein Wochenblatt ausge-
theilet* (Hannover: Schmid, 1747);

Arminius: Ein Trauerspiel (Hannover & Göttingen:
Schmid, 1749);

*De veterum Germanorum et Gallorum theologia mystica
et populari* (Osnabrück: Kißling, 1749);

*Sendschreiben an Voltaire über den Charakter des Dr.
Martin Luther* (Göttingen, 1752);

*Der Wehrt wohlgewogener Neigungen und Leidenschaf-
ten* (Hannover: Schmid, 1756; revised edition, Bremen: Cramer, 1777);

*Unterthänigste Vorstellung und Bitte Mein Joseph Par-
tridgen Generalentrepreneur der Winterquartiers-
lustbarkeiten, bey der hohen Alliirten Armee,*
anonymous (N.p., 1760);

Harlekin, oder Vertheidigung des Groteske-Komischen,
anonymous (Hamburg, 1761); translated by
Joachim Andreas Friedrich Warnecke as *Harlequin; or, A Defence of Grotesque Comic Performances* (London: Nicoll, 1766); German version revised, as Möser (Bremen: Cramer,
1777);

*Schreiben an den Herrn Vicar in Savoyen, abzugeben
bey dem Herrn Johann Rousseau,* anonymous
(Hamburg & Leipzig, 1765); translated by
Warnecke as *A Letter to the Reverend Vicar of
Savoy: To Be Left at J. J. Rousseau's, Wherein
Mr. Rousseau's Emilius, or Treatise on Educa-
tion Is Humourously Examined and Exploded*
(London: Dodsley, 1765); German version
revised (Bremen: Cramer, 1777);

*Rechtliche Behauptung derer Gründe, worauf die von
Sr. Kgl. Majestät von Großbritannien . . . in Anse-*

Mezzotint by J. G. Huck, based on a now-lost charcoal drawing executed in July 1788 by Caroline Rehberg

hung der osnabrückischen Bischofs-Wahl und der Regierungs-Einrichtung im Stifte, während der Minderjährigkeit des erwählten Herrn Bischofs Kgl. Hoheit, genommenen Massregeln gebauet sind (Osnabrück, 1767);

Osnabrückische Geschichte, allgemeine Einleitung (Osnabrück: Schmid, 1768; revised and enlarged edition, 2 volumes, Berlin & Stettin: Nicolai, 1780);

Patriotische Phantasien, 4 volumes, edited by Johanne Wilhelmine Juliane von Voigts (Berlin: Nicolai, 1775-1776; revised and enlarged, 3 volumes, 1778-1786; revised and enlarged, 1804; revised, 1820);

Kleine Schriften, 5 volumes (Bremen: Cramer, 1777);

Schreiben an Herrn Aaron Mendetz da Costa, Oberrabbinern zu Utrecht ueber den leichten Uebergang von der pharisäischen Sekte zur christlichen Religion (Bremen: Cramer, 1777);

Ueber die deutsche Sprache und Litteratur (Hamburg: Hoffmann, 1781); enlarged as *Ueber die deut-*

sche Sprache und Litteràtur: Schreiben an einen Freund nebst einer Nachschrift die National-Erziehung der alten deutschen betreffend (Osnabrück: Schmid, 1781; edited by Carl Schüddekopf, Berlin: Behr, 1902; reprinted, Nendeln, Liechtenstein: Kraus, 1968);

Der Coelibat der Geistlichkeit, anonymous (Osnabrück & Leipzig: Schmidt, 1783);

Vermischte Schriften von Justus Möser: Nebst dessen Leben, 2 volumes, edited by Friedrich Nicolai (Berlin: Nicolai, 1797-1798);

Sämmtliche Werke, 8 volumes (Berlin & Stettin: Nicolai, 1797-1798; revised and enlarged, 10 volumes, edited by Bernard Rudolf Abeken, Johanne Wilhelmine Juliane von Möser, and Nicolai, Berlin: Nicolai, 1842-1843);

Die Tugend auf der Schaubühne oder Harlekins Heirath: Ein Nachspiel in einem Aufzuge (Berlin & Stettin: Nicolai, 1798);

Osnabrückische Geschichte, 3. Theil: Urkunden. Aus dem Nachlaß, edited by C. Stüve (Berlin & Stettin: Nicolai, 1824);

Gesellschaft und Staat: Eine Auswahl aus seinen Schriften, edited by Karl Brandi (Munich: Drei Masken, 1921);

Justus Mösers sämtliche Werke: Historisch-kritische Ausgabe, 14 volumes, edited by the Akademie der Wissenschaften zu Göttingen (Oldenburg, Berlin & Hamburg: Stalling, 1944-1968);

Ausgewählte pädagogische Schriften, edited by Heinrich Kranz (Paderborn: Schöningh, 1965);

Harlekin: Texte und Materialien mit einem Nachwort, edited by Henning Boetius (Bad Homburg: Gehlen, 1968);

Anwalt des Vaterlands: Wochenschriften, Patriotische Phantasien, Aufsätze, Fragmente, edited by Friedemann Berger (Leipzig & Weimar: Kiepenheuer, 1978);

Patriotische Phantasien, ausgewählte Schriften, edited by Wilfred Ziegler (Leipzig: Reclam, 1986).

OTHER: *Ein Wochenblatt*, 50 issues, edited by Möser (Hannover: Schmid, 1746);

Wöchentliche Osnabrückische Intelligenzblätter, edited by Möser (1766-1782);

"Deutsche Geschichte," in *Von deutscher Art und Kunst: Einige fliegende Blätter*, edited by Johann Gottfried Herder (Hamburg: Bode, 1773), pp. 165-182.

Justus Möser occupies an important position in the history of Western European civilization. Throughout his life he scrutinized the basic assumptions of the reigning philosophes and warned about the dangers of considering rationalism a panacea for all peoples of all times. A poet, dramatist, journalist, historian, pedagogue, jurist, statesman, observer of political institutions, and student of the incipient social sciences, Möser stood firmly in opposition not to enlightened thought but to the Enlightenment as a program that could not be contested. While Möser appreciated the phenomenal artistic contributions of France, he rejected all attempts at French intellectual and cultural hegemony. He also opposed revisionist policies elsewhere–such as those of Catherine the Great, who, under the guise of rational scientific exploration, ordered the suppression of aboriginal tribal customs so as to shape the Russian Empire into an Enlightened state on the pre-Revolutionary French model. Möser's worldview remained a pluralistic one that welcomed variations; he was equally opposed to Jean-Jacques Rousseau's one-sided emphasis on emotion and François-Marie Arouet Voltaire's exclusive emphasis on reason. Möser's writings also rejected the prevalent Europocentric views about other cultures and historical periods. He always worked inductively rather than deductively.

Möser was born in Osnabrück, Westphalia, on 14 December 1720 to Johann Zacharias, a chancellory director, and Regina Gertrud Elverfeld Möser. Growing up in a North German middle-class environment that was typical for the times, Möser studied French both at home and at school. He avidly read the masterpieces of France but could not avoid matters Anglo-Saxon: he showed great interest in England because that country was ruled by the House of Hanover, which continued to have a political presence in Osnabrück. He graduated from the local gymnasium on 28 August 1740; on 7 October 1740 he enrolled at the University of Jena to study jurisprudence. On 16 October 1742 he transferred to the University of Göttingen, where he studied various subjects before leaving without a degree at the end of 1743. That same year he had become a member of the Deutsche Gesellschaft (German Society), a society primarily devoted to the proper use and refinement of the German language. Returning to Osnabrück, he became a lawyer in 1744. On 25 October 1746 he married Regina Juliana Elisabeth Brouning; they had a daughter, Johanne Wilhelmine Juliane (Jenny), born in 1751, and a son, Johann Ernst Justus, born in 1753. (Johann was killed in a duel in 1773 while a student in Göttingen; Jenny, who

married the lawyer Just Gerlachs von Voigts in 1768, later edited some of her father's writings.)

Möser observed community planning in his native Westphalia and connected those observations to reports about the area's ancient inhabitants. The small differences he noted led him to believe that combinations of forces, including diet, climate, and geography, helped mold cultures and traditions. Social institutions evolved to enable people to deal with their problems: religion helped with the mysteries of birth, life, and death; law solved everyday disagreements; education bolstered the common identity by preparing for the future according to the collective experience of the past. The family, the clan, the tribe, and the nation developed, according to Möser, because of psychological as well as social needs. There seemed to be something inherent in human psychology that made individuals want to feel part of a greater whole. Communication was crucial at all levels of social organization, so Möser was especially interested in language, nonverbal as well as verbal. That interest encompassed everything from maternal speech patterns, journalism, and formal rhetoric to hand signs, music, and acting.

Möser's mastery of communications skills was reflected in a long career in government that progressed to positions of ever greater diplomatic responsibility and political sensitivity. In 1762 he became councillor and justice of the criminal court. He negotiated on behalf of Osnabrück during the Seven Years' War, and from August 1763 until April 1764 he was in London on a diplomatic mission involving the regency of Frederick of York. On returning to Osnabrück he was made advocate at the government. In 1783 he was named privy barrister and privy councillor of justice. He died on 8 January 1794 after a short illness.

Möser's style was logical yet poignantly spiced with imagery directed to the audience he wished to reach. His early poetic experiments emulated the nature poetry of Albrecht von Haller, a renowned medical researcher and professor at Göttingen, and the pastoral convention of Friedrich von Hagedorn, the Hamburg anacreontic poet and fabulist. The moral weeklies that Möser published in the late 1740s already reveal his divergence from the canon upheld by arbiters of taste such as the Leipzig academician Johann Christoph Gottsched.

Möser believed that contemporary German culture remained disparate at best, negligible at worst, because the common mythological basis that supported unification had been ebbing away for centuries. Although the ancient Romans never conquered all of the German-speaking lands, they enjoyed a victory of sorts when, in the humanist era, the German language was forced into a Latinate mold, and German classrooms, churches, and eventually courts of law succumbed to Roman models. By the time French culture became the touchstone of taste in the seventeenth century the Germans had been so divided, conquered, and demoralized that little was left of the original culture except among the Lower Saxon peasantry. Möser frequently mentioned that the French political philosopher Montesquieu had singled out the Saxons as having invented the best aspects of general freedom: civil as well as political rights (for propertied males). The contradictions in contemporary native character derived, Möser thought, from the assimilation process the Germans had been forced to undergo.

Möser's concern about these problems was so intense that he produced a series of works dealing with them. Among the earliest was his 1749 examination of pre-Roman Germanic beliefs, *De veterum Germanorum et Gallorum theologia mystica et populari* (The Popular and Mystical Theology of the Ancient Germans and Gauls). He concludes that religion has always served such intangibles and that it can never, by definition, be based on reason. Instead of giving the word *Aberglaube* (superstition) negative connotations, like most of his contemporaries, he interprets it as Germanic man's acknowledgment of a universal divine essence or God. Möser confronts the basic assumptions of the Enlightenment, especially the popularizing version of Bernard le Bovier de Fontenelle, when he defends primordial cave worshipers as having managed to ritualize the mysteries in ways that gave them the comfort they needed to survive in their circumstances. Subsequent essays repeatedly take up the human inclination toward miracles, spirits, ghosts, and the extraordinary. In *Schreiben an den Herrn Vicar in Savoyen, abzugeben bey dem Herrn Johann Rousseau* (1765; translated as *A Letter to the Reverend Vicar of Savoy: To Be Left at J. J. Rousseau's, Wherein Mr. Rousseau's Emilius, or Treatise on Education Is Humourously Examined and Exploded*, 1765) Möser contends that attributing all such paranormal occurrences to superstition is an over-facile solution. He insists that the roots of the ineffable cannot be destroyed because they are so all-

Title page for Möser's defense of the grotesque in comedy

pervasive. Möser continued to defend ancient Germanic beliefs throughout the Enlightenment. In 1790 he was still trying to comprehend why the great thinkers of the age persisted in misunderstanding the obvious underlying sense and importance of rituals, myths, riddles, fairy tales, songs, and other such glorious manifestations of the human imagination.

Another work treating the clash of German and Roman culture appeared in 1749: a tragedy about the great warrior Arminius, whose annihilation of three Roman legions in the Teutoburg Forest in A.D. 9 had come to symbolize the glories of the Germanic past when heroes, along with their wives and families, preferred death to slavery. In its preface Möser warns his contemporaries about the dangers of exposing audiences solely to foreign heroes, contending that each folk needs to be flattered by the knowledge that it, too, could produce a magnificent hero of its own; consequently, he demands equal treatment and equal rights for German heroes. This unflinching campaign on behalf of his heritage made Möser a living legend among the younger generation. It was so highly regarded that Johann Gottfried Herder solicited for his own collection of essays on German manners and arts, *Von deutscher Art und Kunst* (Of German Kind and Art, 1773), the programmatic introduction Möser provided for his history of Osnabrück (1768). Herder's collection, to which Johann Wolfgang Goethe also contributed, was received like a revolutionary manifesto.

Möser, whom contemporaries often likened to Benjamin Franklin, was gifted in many fields. While poetry and drama might not have been the strongest among them, he did possess the kind of aesthetic acumen that produced pathbreaking works dealing with critical theory and applied criticism. Since he considered pleasure as crucial for human existence as sustenance, comfort, and laughter, it had to be the main goal of the arts. Believing that every artistic rule had to derive from a happy–that is, successful–experience, he encouraged experimenting to determine what worked with audiences.

The ideas Möser propounded about genius influenced the writers of the Sturm und Drang–although, as it turned out, they did not fully understand his ideas. Möser claimed that there are no lawmakers for geniuses, that nobody could prevent the genius from transgressing against all manmade rules. Using the image of the eagle daring to soar higher and higher, he argued that there are always certain considerations, trade-offs, or intrinsic rules that have to be obeyed if the eagle wanted neither to be shot by hunters nor burned by the sun.

Harlekin (Harlequin, 1761), an essay defending the grotesque comic in which Harlequin takes on his erudite detractors, represents the best summation of Möser's ideas on theater and the performing arts. Academics are criticized as too speculative, too given to making scholarly pronouncements without consulting all the facts. They base their authority on the rule books composed by their careerist predecessors. They cite artistic categories, species, and theories as evidence of the inferiority of certain theatrical works, rather than attending actual performances of those works before live audiences. The harlequin-

Painting of Möser by Ernst Gottlob (Gleimhaus, Halberstadt)

ade, like the opera, is not permissible in their estimation. In his defense, Harlequin says that he does not wish to chase Pierre Corneille and Jean Baptiste Racine from the stage but simply to claim a small, unobtrusive place for himself. He recommends the plenitude of a nature comprising diverse forms because he thinks that sameness produces nothing but monotony and boredom. He claims that he, like so many people, would rather be his own individual self than the proud lion denigrated with the designation of cat. All theatrical works, Harlequin goes on to say, are representations of possible worlds made believable by performers who know how to appeal directly to the imagination and captivate it. Here as elsewhere Möser boldly stresses that the healing medicine of pleasure or fun, not moral improvement, is most important in art. Pleasure appeals to the weary spirit, helping re-create it and ready it for the serious duties of real life. Harlequin explains that he provides pleasure by using exaggerated caricature to incite laughter and thereby bring about a release of tensions. Agreeing–in this instance–with the opera opponent Saint-Evremond that Miguel de Cervantes was the right physician for melancholy souls, Harlequin speculates as to whether or not his own sword, the emblem of his artistry, lay near Don Quixote's helmet at the beginning of all creation. Intuitive recognition of stereotypes through masks, costumes, and other nonverbal means of communication is as old as art itself. Furthermore, improvised theater still succeeds where drama written according to aesthetic rules does not, because the players can read from the spectators' behavior their actual level of comprehension.

When Frederick II's treatise on the inferiority of Germanic languages and literatures appeared in 1780, Möser rallied with a speedy defense. *Ueber die deutsche Sprache und Litteratur* (On German Language and Literature, 1781) centers on the image of the mighty German oak being manicured by a small French gardener, since Frederick, who thought of Shakespeare and Goethe as barbarous writers worthy of contempt by all but the savages of Canada, proposed reforms to bring German literature into strict line with the Franco-Roman neoclassical code. The Germans, Möser argues, are not French. They live in a harsh climate and derive from sturdy stock that produced different feelings, attitudes, and customs. All of these factors necessitate different artistic styles. Everything in this world, Möser continues, can only be relatively beautiful and relatively great; nothing is ever absolute. Goethe's drama *Götz von Berlichingen* (1773) is to be commended as a noble and beautiful product of the local soil rather than summarily condemned, for it accomplishes its intentions: it presents a collection of scenes depicting the rigorous interaction of German and Roman culture in the early modern period.

Never failing to admit the eminent accomplishments of France, Möser insists that basic cultural differences are too vast to permit the French model to be universally emulated in the German lands. The French sacrifice everything for beauty and regularity while the Germans, like their English relatives, prefer diversity and change. This difference can even be seen in formal French and the studied informality of English gardens. Möser believed that his countrymen, like all other peoples, could achieve greatness without minimizing or deprecating the efforts of other lands, and without copying them. If indigenous artistic products are to be ennobled, he concludes, aspiring young Germans will

have to look to their own rich heritage and to England for models. Of all of these young Germans, he thought Goethe showed the greatest promise for leadership. Once again, Justus Möser proved correct.

Letters:

Justus Mösers Briefe, edited by Ernst Beins and Werner Pleister (Hannover: Selbstverlag der Historischen Kommission für Hannover, Oldenburg, Braunschweig, Schaumburg-Lippe und Bremen, 1939);

"Neue Möserbriefe," edited by Beins, *Mittheilungen des Vereins für Geschichte und Landeskunde von Osnabrück,* 59 (1939): 45-56.

Biographies:

Friedrich Nicolai, *Das Leben Justus Mösers* (Berlin & Stettin: Nicolai, 1797);

Winold Stühle, *Ueber Möser und dessen Verdienste ums Vaterland, nebst verschiedenen Bemerkungen über Staatsverfassung* (Osnabrück, 1798);

Erwin Hölzle, "Justus Möser, 1720-1794," in his *Männer der deutschen Verwaltung: 23 biographische Essays* (Cologne: Grote, 1963), pp. 11-21.

References:

Ludwig Bäte, *Jenny von Voigts: Eine vergessene Freundin Goethes* (Olten: Vereinigung Oltner Bücherfreunde, 1951);

Bäte, *Justus Möser, Advocatus Patriae* (Frankfurt am Main & Bonn: Athenäum, 1961);

Hans Baron, "Justus Mösers Individualitätsprinzip in seiner geistesgeschichtlichen Bedeutung," *Historische Zeitschrift,* 130 (1924): 31-57;

Hermann Bausinger, "Justus Möser," in *Deutsche Dichter des 18. Jahrhunderts,* edited by Benno von Wiese (Berlin: Schmitt, 1977), pp. 176-189;

Bausinger, "Konservative Aufklärung–Justus Möser vom Blickpunkt der Gegenwart," *Zeitschrift für Volkskunde,* 68 (1972): 161-178;

H. Banniza von Bazan, "Ahnenliste von Justus Möser," *Mitteilungen des Vereins für Geschichte und Landeskunde von Osnabrück,* 66 (1954): 181-196;

William J. Bossenbrook, "Justus Möser's Approach to History," in *Medieval and Historiographical Essays in Honor of James Westfall Thompson,* edited by James Lea Cate and Eugene N. Anderson (Chicago: University of Chicago Press, 1938), pp. 397-422;

Karl Brandi, "Justus Möser," *Preußische Jahrbücher,* 227 (1932): 54-69;

Brandi, "Justus Möser und Goethe," *Forschung und Fortschritt,* 8 (1932): 79-80;

Friedrich Buchholz, *Justus Mösers Gedanken über Erziehung: Ein Beitrag zur Pädagogik der Sturm- und Drangzeit,* Sammlung wissenschaftlicher Arbeiten, 33 (Langensalza: Wendt & Klauwell, 1914);

Eberhard Crusius, "Möser als Rezensent, zu Suchier, 'Über einige bisher unbekannte Arbeiten Justus Mösers,'" *Mitteilungen des Vereins für Geschichte und Landeskunde Osnabrücks,* 67 (1956): 233-245;

Robert Reinhold Ergang, "Möser and the Rise of National Thought in Germany," *Journal of Modern History,* 5 (June 1933): 172-196;

Bernhardine Fiebig, "Justus Mösers Staatslehre," Ph.D. dissertation, University of Cologne, 1953;

Gloria Flaherty, "Justus Möser: Pre-Romantic Literary Historian, Critic, and Theorist," in *Traditions and Transitions: Studies in Honor of Harold Jantz,* edited by L. E. Kurth, W. H. McClain, and H. Homann (Bad Windsheim & Munich: Delp, 1971), pp. 87-104;

R. Gösling and Harold Schoeller, "Zur Ahnenliste Justus Mösers, Ergänzungen," *Mitteilungen des Vereins für Geschichte und Landeskunde von Osnabrück,* 68 (1959): 391-397;

Paul Göttsching, "Geschichte und Gegenwart bei Justus Möser," *Mitteilungen des Vereins für Geschichte und Landeskunde von Osnabrück,* 83 (1977): 94-116;

Göttsching, *Justus Mösers Entwicklung zum Publizisten: Mösers Schrifttum 1757-1766,* Frankfurter Quellen und Forschungen zur germanischen und romanischen Philologie, 9 (Frankfurt am Main: Diesterweg, 1935; reprinted, Hildesheim: Gerstenberg, 1973);

Erich Haarmann, "Über Mösers Art zu schaffen, Mit einer Bemerkung über B. R. Abekens editorische Tätigkeit," *Historische Zeitschrift,* 140 (1929): 87-99;

Haarmann, "Wie sah Möser aus?," *Mitteilung des Vereins für Geschichte und Landeskunde Osnabrücks,* 59 (1939): 1-44;

Otto Hatzig, *Justus Möser als Staatsmann und Publizist,* Quellen und Darstellungen zur Geschichte Niedersachsens, 27 (Hannover: Hahn, 1909);

Ernst Hempel, "Justus Mösers Wirkung auf seine Zeitgenossen und auf die deutsche Geschichtsschreibung," *Mitteilungen des Vereins für Geschichte und Landeskunde Osnabrücks,* 54 (1933): 1-76;

Walter Hinck, *Das deutsche Lustspiel des 17. und 18. Jahrhunderts und die italienische Komödie* (Stuttgart: Metzler, 1965);

Wolfgang Hollmann, *Justus Mösers Zeitungsidee und ihre Verwirklichung,* volume 40 of *Zeitung und Leben: Schriftenreihe,* edited by Karl d'Ester (Munich: Zeitungswissenschaftliche Vereinigung, 1937);

Heinrich Kanz, "Der Ganzheitsbegriff im pädagogischen Denken von Justus Möser," *Bildung und Erziehung, Monatsschrift für Pädagogik,* 10 (1957): 385-403;

Kanz, *Der humane Realismus Justus Mösers Bildungsanalyse* (Wuppertal, Ratingen & Kastellann: Henn, 1971);

Peter Klassen, *Justus Möser,* Studien zur Geschichte des Staats- und Nationalgedankens, 2 (Frankfurt am Main: Klostermann, 1936);

Friedrich v. Klocke, *Justus Möser und die deutsche Ahnenprobe des 18. Jahrhunderts,* Flugschriften für Familiengeschichte, 32 (Leipzig: Zentralstelle für Deutsche Personen- und Familiengeschichte, 1941);

Jonathan B. Knudsen, *Justus Möser and the German Enlightenment* (Cambridge: Cambridge University Press, 1986);

Werner Kohlschmidt, *Mösers Almanachgedichte,* Nachrichten von der Gesellschaft der Wissenschaften in Göttingen, new series 2 (Göttingen: Vandenhoeck & Ruprecht, 1938);

Kohlschmidt, "Neuere Möser-Literatur," *Göttingische Gelehrte Anzeigen,* 102 (June 1940): 229-247;

F. A. Kreyszig, *Justus Möser* (Berlin: Nicolai, 1857);

Bruno Krusch, "Justus Möser und die Osnabrükker Gesellschaft," *Mitteilungen des Vereins für Geschichte und Landeskunde von Osnabrück,* 34 (1910): 271-281;

Richard Kuehnemund, *Arminius or the Rise of a National Symbol in Literature (From Hutten to Grabbe),* University of North Carolina Studies in the Germanic Languages and Literatures, 8 (Chapel Hill: University of North Carolina Press, 1953);

A. Laging, "Mösers Prosa: Eine sprachlich-stilistische Untersuchung," *Mitteilungen des Vereins für Geschichte und Landeskunde von Osnabrück,* 39 (1916): 1-142;

Rudolf Lenzing, *Von Möser bis Stüve: Ein Jahrhundert Osnabrücker Pressegeschichte als Spiegel des Bürgertums* (Osnabrück: Schöningh, 1924);

Ulrich Lochter, *Justus Möser und das Theater: Ein Beitrag zur Theorie und Praxis im deutschen Theater des 18. Jahrhunderts*, Osnabrücker Geschichtsquellen und Forschungen, 10 (Osnabrück: Wenner, 1967);

Justus Friedrich Günther Lodtmann, *Genealogie der Möserschen Familie* (Osnabrück: Meinders, 1866);

Brigitte Lorenzen, "Justus Mösers Patriotische Phantasien: Studien zur Erzählkunst," Ph.D. dissertation, Göttingen University, 1956;

Pia-Angela Lorenzi, "Die ökonomische Geschichtsauffassung und Justus Möser: Eine soziologische Studie," Ph.D. dissertation, Heidelberg University, 1958;

Friedrich Meinecke, *Über Justus Mösers Geschichtsauffassung: Einleitende Bemerkungen* (Berlin: De Gruyter, 1932);

Horst Meyer, "Bücher im Leben eines Verwaltungsjuristen: Justus Möser und seine Bibliothek," in his *Buch und Sammler, Private und Oeffentliche Bibliotheken im 18. Jahrhundert* (Heidelberg, 1979), pp. 149-158;

Julius Alfred Möbius, *Darstellung und Beurteilung der pädagogischen Ansichten Justus Mösers* (Berlin, 1932);

Jean Moes, "Les revues publiées par Justus Möser dans sa jeunesse (1746-1747)," in *L'Allemagne des lumières: périodiques, correspondances, témoignages*, edited by Pierre Grappin (Paris: Didier-Erudition, 1982), pp. 103-161;

Virgil Nemoianu, "Alternatives to Revolution: Textual and Political Decentralization in Möser and Rivarol," *Stanford Literature Review*, 2 (Spring 1985): 85-102;

Werner Pleister, "Die geistige Entwicklung Justus Mösers," *Mitteilungen des Vereins für Geschichte und Landeskunde von Osnabrück*, 50 (1929): 1-89;

Hans Reiss, "Goethe, Möser and the Aufklärung: The Holy Roman Empire in *Götz von Berlichingen* and *Egmont*," *Deutsche Vierteljahrsschrift für Literaturwissenschaft und Geistesgeschichte*, 60 (December 1986): 609-644;

Reinhard Renger, "Justus Mösers amtlicher Wirkungskreis," *Mitteilungen des Vereins für Geschichte und Landeskunde von Osnabrück*, 77 (1970): 1-30;

Edmund Richter, *Justus Mösers Anschauungen über Volks- und Jugenderziehung im Zusammenhang mit seiner Zeit*, Pädagogisches Magazin: Abhandlungen von Gebieten der Pädagogik und ihrer Hilfswissenschaften, 367 (Langensalza: Beyer, 1909);

J. Riehemann, "Der Humor in den Werken Justus Mösers," *Mitteilungen des Vereins für Geschichte und Landeskunde von Osnabrück*, 26 (1901): 1-106;

Joachim Runge, *Justus Mösers Gewerbetheorie und Gewerbepolitik im Fürstbistum Osnabrück in der zweiten Hälfte des 18. Jahrhunderts*, Schriften zur Wirtschaft und Sozialgeschichte, 2 (Berlin: Duncker & Humblot, 1966);

Ludwig Rupprecht, *Justus Mösers soziale und volkswirtschaftliche Anschauungen in ihrem Verhältnis zur Theorie und Praxis seines Zeitalters* (Stuttgart: Cotta, 1892);

Heinrich Schierbaum, "Justus Mösers Stellung in den deutschen Literaturströmungen während der ersten Hälfte des 18. Jahrhunderts," *Mitteilung des Vereins für Geschichte und Landeskunde von Osnabrück*, 33 (1908): 167-216;

Schierbaum, "Justus Mösers Stellung in den Literaturströmungen des 18. Jahrhunderts, II Teil," *Mitteilung des Vereins für Geschichte und Landeskunde von Osnabrück*, 34 (1909): 1-43;

Ludwig Schirmeyer, "Das Möserbild nach neuen Briefen," *Mitteilung des Vereins für Geschichte und Landeskunde von Osnabrück*, 59 (1939): 57-98;

Peter Schmidt, *Studien über Justus Möser als Historiker Zur Genesis und Struktur der historischen Methode Justus Mösers*, Göppinger Akademische Beiträge, 93 (Göppingen: Kümmerle, 1975);

Karl-Egbert Schultze, "Zur Ahnenliste Justus Mösers: Ergänzungen," *Mitteilung des Vereins für Geschichte und Landeskunde von Osnabrück*, 69 (1960): 127-128;

Hans Ulrich Scupin, "Justus Möser als Westfale und Staatsmann," *Westfälische Zeitschrift: Zeitschrift für vaterländische Geschichte und Altertumskunde*, 107 (1958): 135-152;

Scupin, "Volk und Reich bei Justus Möser," *Zeitschrift für öffentliches Recht*, 19 (1939): 561-639;

Roland Seeberg-Elverfeldt, "Zur Ahnenliste Justus Mösers: Ergänzungen," *Mitteilungen des Vereins für Geschichte und Landeskunde von Osnabrück*, 69 (1960): 128-129;

Ulrike Sheldon and William Sheldon, *Im Geist der Empfindsamkeit: Freundschaftsbriefe der Mösertochter Jenny von Voights und die Fürstin von Anhalt-Dessau, 1780-1808*, Osnabrücker Geschichtsquellen und Forschungen, 17 (Osnabrück: Wenner, 1971);

William F. Sheldon, *The Intellectual Development of Justus Möser: The Growth of a German Patriot,* Osnabrücker Geschichtsquellen und Forschungen, 15 (Osnabrück: Wenner, 1970);

Sheldon, "Patriotismus bei Justus Möser," in *Deutsche patriotische und gemeinnützige Gesellschaften,* edited by Rudolf Vierhaus, Wolfenbütteler Forschungen, 8 (Munich: Kraus, 1980), pp. 31-49;

N. Horton Smith, "Justus Möser and the British," *German Life and Letters,* new series 5 (1951): 47-56;

Wilhelm Spael, *"Common Sense" oder gesunder Menschenverstand und sein Ausdruck bei Justus Möser* (Essen: Wibbelt, 1947);

Georg Stefansky, "Justus Mösers Geschichtsauffassung im Zusammenhang der deutschen Literatur des 18. Jahrhunderts," *Euphorion,* 28 (1927): 21-34;

Horst Steinmetz, *Der Harlekin: Seine Rolle in der deutschen Komödientheorie und -dichtung des 18. Jahrhunderts* (Groningen: Wolters, 1965);

Wolfram Suchier, *Über einige bisher unbekannte Arbeiten Justus Mösers* (Osnabrück: Schöningh, 1954);

Albert Wiedemann, *Geistesgeschichtlicher Querschnitt durch Justus Mösers Erziehungsideen, orientiert an der Philosophie John Lockes und A. Shaftesburys* (Ochsenfurt: Fritz & Rappert, 1932);

Hans M. Wolff, "Rousseau, Möser und der Kampf gegen das Rokoko," *Monatshefte für den deutschen Unterricht,* 34 (March 1942): 113-125;

Heinz Zimmermann, *Staat, Recht und Wirtschaft bei Justus Möser: Eine einführende Darstellung* (Jena: Fischer, 1933).

Papers:
Unpublished materials from Justus Möser's political, administrative, and literary career are at the Niedersächsisches Staatsarchiv Osnabrück, the Städtisches Museum Osnabrück, and the Niedersächsische Staats- und Universitätsbibliothek Göttingen.

Johann Karl August Musäus

(29 March 1735 - 27 October 1787)

Barbara Carvill
Calvin College

BOOKS: *Grandison der Zweyte oder Geschichte des Herrn von N***, in Briefen entworfen*, 3 volumes, anonymous (Eisenach: Griesbach, 1760-1762); revised as *Der deutsche Grandison: Auch eine Familiengeschichte*, anonymous, 2 volumes (Eisenach: Wittekindt, 1781-1782);

Das Gärtnermädchen: Eine komische Oper in drey Aufzügen, anonymous (Weimar: Hoffmann, 1771);

Physiognomische Reisen, voran ein physiognomisch Tagebuch, 4 volumes, anonymous (Altenburg: Richter, 1778-1779); translated by Anne Plumptre as *Musaeus's Physiognomical Travels, Preceded by a Physiognomical Journal: With His Life by Kotzebue*, 3 volumes (London: Longman & Rees, 1800);

Volksmährchen der Deutschen, 5 volumes, anonymous (Gotha: Ettinger, 1782-1786); translated by William Beckford as *Popular Tales of the Germans*, 2 volumes (London: Murray, 1791); German version edited by Christoph Martin Wieland as *Die deutschen Volksmährchen*, 5 volumes (Gotha: Ettinger, 1804-1805); original German version republished, 1 volume, edited by Norbert Miller (Munich: Winkler, 1976);

Freund Heins Erscheinungen in Holbeins Manier, anonymous (Winterthur: Steiner, 1785);

Moralische Kinderklapper für Kinder und Nichtkinder: Aus dem Französischen des Herrn Monget, anonymous (Gotha: Ettinger, 1787; edited by Rudolf Dietze, Leipzig: Edition Leipzig, 1968);

Nachgelassene Schriften des verstorbenen Professor Musäus, edited by August von Kotzebue (Leipzig: Kummer, 1791);

Märchen und Sagen, 2 volumes, edited by Hans Marquardt (Munich: Kösel, 1972).

Editions in English: "Dumb Love," "Libussa," "Melechsala," translated by Thomas Carlyle in his *German Romance: Specimens of Its Chief Authors*, volume 1 (Edinburgh & London: Tait, 1827; Boston: Munroe, 1841), pp. 1-215;

Johann Karl August Musäus (engraving by M. Steinla after a painting by Johann Ernst Heinsius)

Legends of Rubezahl, and Other Tales, translated by Clara de Chatelain and William Hazlitt (London: Cundall, 1845)—comprises "The Books of the Chronicles of the Three Sisters," translated by Chatelain; "Legends of Rubezahl," "The Hen with the Golden Eggs," translated by Hazlitt;

Select Popular Tales, from the German of Musäus, translated anonymously (London: Lumley, 1845)—comprises "Mute Love," "The Nymph of the Fountain," "Peter Bock; or, The Treasure-Seeker of the Harz," "The Three Sisters," "Richilda," "Roland's Squires," "Legends of Rubezahl," "The Princess's Flight,"

"The Rescued Lover," "The Countryman and His Family";

Libussa, Duchess of Bohemia; also, The Man without a Name, translated anonymously (London: Macdonald, 1852);

The Three Sons-in-law: A Free Version from the German of Musäus, translated by A. F. Frere (London & New York: Nelson, 1861);

Legends of Number Nip, edited by Mark Lemon (London: Macmillan, 1864);

Roland's Squires: A Legend of the Time of Charlemagne. After the German of Musaeus, translated by Harriet Pinckney Huse (New York: Jenkins, 1891).

OTHER: *Straußfedern: Erster Band,* edited by Musäus (Berlin & Stettin: Nicolai, 1787).

Johann Karl August Musäus is known today primarily as the author of the *Volksmährchen der Deutschen* (1782-1786; translated as *Popular Tales of the Germans,* 1791), a collection of popular German tales that is still widely read. He is recognized as one of the most talented humorists and wittiest narrators in eighteenth-century German literature.

Born on 29 March 1735 into a family of renowned theologians and lawyers in Jena (Thuringia), Musäus was educated by his uncle, a Lutheran church official in Eisenach. At the age of nineteen Musäus began his studies of theology at the University of Jena, graduating as a candidate for the Christian ministry in 1758. But his appointment as pastor to the church in Farnroda, a Thuringian village, was canceled by the church council when it was reported that Musäus had been seen dancing in public.

After the setback Musäus decided against a theological career, resolving to try his luck as a man of letters. As a student he had been a member of the Teutsche Gesellschaft (German Society), a literary society whose goal was to promote the production of original German literature of high quality. It was in the spirit of this society that the unemployed Musäus wrote his first novel, *Grandison der Zweyte* (The Second Grandison, 1760-1762).

Epistolary in form, *Grandison der Zweyte* develops a theme which had become popular in European comic fiction since Miguel de Cervantes' *Don Quixote* (1605-1615): the clash between poetic illusion and prosaic reality brought about by novel-reading fools. In *Grandison der Zweyte* two heroes are depicted: a pretentious, unenlightened boor from a German backwater town; and his adviser, a vainglorious, pedantic schoolmaster. Both eagerly devour Samuel Richardson's *History of Sir Charles Grandison* (1753-1754) and try unsuccessfully to imitate the moral heroism and delicate virtue of the English aristocrat Sir Charles, who is the perfect model of the enlightened Christian gentleman. Musäus, like Henry Fielding, used the mock-heroic mold to parody the sentimental novel and to question whether high pathos and exultation of virtue are appropriate to the modern novel, which aims to present a nonidealized view of human nature. In *Grandison der Zweyte* he mocks his German contemporaries for their admiration of Richardson's epistolary novel, which they considered the most edifying work ever printed, next to the Holy Scriptures. Although uneven in quality, Musäus's first work is of considerable importance for German literary history because it is strikingly realistic, set in a typically German milieu, portraying indigenous characters and satirizing contemporary German manners and foibles.

In 1763 the duchess of Weimar, Anna Amalia, a fervent supporter of German literature, drew Musäus to her court as poet and instructor of the court pages. In 1768 he wrote for the duchess the libretto for the comic opera *Das Gärtnermädchen* (The Maiden Gardener, 1771), which enjoyed considerable success in Germany.

Impressed by Musäus's contribution to the deplorable state of the German novel in the 1760s, the prominent Berlin publisher Friedrich Nicolai engaged him to review new fiction for his journal, the *Allgemeine Deutsche Bibliothek.* To the end of his life Musäus reviewed novels for the journal and in so doing provided a model of an educated, enlightened reader who employs sound standards for judging the quality of a literary work. Musäus also used his reviews to give advice to inexperienced novelists who often produced substandard fiction for the hungry German reading public. Musäus wanted to impress on his contemporaries that the novel had to be taken seriously and that it demanded careful craftsmanship and aesthetic integrity. Through his reviews, which are masterpieces of witty, pithy literary criticism, Musäus made a noteworthy contribution to the education of eighteenth-century German novelists and their readers.

In 1769 the duchess established for Musäus a professorship at the Weimar Gymnasium, where he was to teach Latin, history, rhetoric, and creative writing. A year later he married

Juliane Krüger, the daughter of a Brunswick merchant; she was also the aunt to August von Kotzebue, who, partly through Musäus's guidance, became a successful playwright at the end of the century. The pay he received from the duchess was too low to enable Musäus to provide for his wife and their two sons; it was only one-tenth the amount earned by Christoph Martin Wieland, who tutored the duchess's sons. To supplement his income from teaching and from his book reviews, Musäus took student boarders into his small quarters, gave private lessons at court, and wrote occasional poetry for the Weimar citizenry.

When the Weimar castle–and with it the court theater–was destroyed by fire in 1774, aristocrats and commoners joined forces to form an amateur theater group. Musäus became one of the group's most successful actors. His most notable performance was as the innkeeper in Gotthold Ephraim Lessing's *Minna von Barnhelm* (1767).

Soon, however, the intellectual climate changed. In 1775 Duke Karl August took over the government and brought the famous Johann Wolfgang Goethe to Weimar. Musäus, who distrusted both the fashionable adulation of the Sturm und Drang "genius" and the tearful, depressing sentimentalism that followed in the wake of Goethe's *Die Leiden des jungen Werthers* (The Sorrows of Young Werther, 1774), withdrew to the fringes of Weimar society and assumed the role of the skeptical, good-natured humorist and poor schoolmaster. His only remaining contact with the elite was through rehearsals and performances of the amateur theater, which had been placed under the direction of Goethe.

This situation changed when Musäus's second novel, *Physiognomische Reisen* (1778-1779; translated as *Musaeus's Physiognomical Travels*, 1800), made him a celebrity in Germany overnight. *Physiognomische Reisen* was written in opposition to Johann Kaspar Lavater's then well-known theories of physiognomy, which had become a fad all over Europe. Lavater claimed in his *Physiognomische Fragmente* (Physiognomical Fragments, 1775-1778) to have discovered a new science which not only taught how to interpret the character of a person from his facial features but also suggested a way to renew society on the basis of the deep love for one's fellowman that would result from such interpretation. In Musäus's satirical novel a true believer in Lavater's gospel undertakes a journey to meet other members of the invisible church of physiognomists. But after many unpleasant encounters, in the course of which he is deceived and robbed, his faith in physiognomy as a way of truly knowing another person is seriously shaken. He returns home disappointed; the experiences of his journey have turned the physiognomical fundamentalist into a liberal skeptic. Taking Laurence Sterne's *A Sentimental Journey through France and Italy* (1768) as his model, Musäus spices the musings of his physiognomical traveler with many digressions about such topics as the German book market, sentimentalism, the Sturm und Drang, new discoveries in science, medical quackery, and the shortcomings of the German educational and legal systems. The great success of Musäus's novel, which went into a third edition in 1781, was partly due to the whimsical and witty nature of these critiques of the follies and eccentricities of his contemporaries. The Romantic writer Johann Paul Friedrich Richter (Jean Paul) took over and further developed Musäus's narrative strategy of larding the text with references to obscure and quaint publications and events. These playful allusions to long-forgotten books and events make Musäus's work a fascinating cultural document of the German Zeitgeist of the 1770s.

Encouraged by his success, Musäus decided to revise his first novel to make it conform with the changed literary scene of 1780. This new version appeared in 1781-1782 with the title *Der deutsche Grandison* (The German Grandison). Musäus kept the basic plot of the first version but added hilarious new scenes and abolished, to a great extent, the epistolary form. He introduces a narrator who, in the role of a merciless editor, points out the weakness and clumsiness of the first version. Thus, *Der deutsche Grandison* can be read as an extended review of Musäus's first novel. Although Musäus kept the main theme of the first version about how two blundering fools are misled by a naive reading of fiction, the tenor of the book has changed: he has softened his satirical attack considerably and offers his readers cheerfulness and laughter, the only effective antidote to the pervasive melancholy that is, according to the author, the major disease of his time. *Der deutsche Grandison*, however, was not a success. The novel does contain some brilliant comical passages, but it lacks cohesiveness.

In the following years Musäus turned his back on novel writing altogether, devoting himself instead to the five-volume *Volksmährchen der Deutschen*. This work established his European fame. The collection consists of stories drawn from the German and European fairy-tale tradition. Musäus did not rely only on written sources; long before the Grimm brothers, he had children and older men and women tell him their favorite fairy tales. But in contrast to the Romantic collectors, he did not try to preserve the naive and seemingly artless tone of the tales. On the contrary, he retold them in his inimitably witty style for the amusement of the educated adult reader who might suffer from melancholia. Musäus took great pains to create a playful, ironic distance from the supernatural and miraculous in the fairy-tale plots by embroidering the stories with many witty side remarks and allusions to the cultural and political life of the 1780s, new discoveries, and the latest scandals. By placing his tales in a specific historical time and actual German locations he highlighted the whimsical incongruity between the fantastic and the ordinary. "Legenden von Rübezahl" (Legends of Rubezahl), for instance, is set in the Silesian mountains and tells of the mischievous encounters of a ghostly giant with many different people, among them a countess who is one of Voltaire's ardent disciples.

Musäus's contemporaries were enchanted by his treatment of folktales. Wieland, who published a slightly revised edition of the collection in 1804-1805, applauded the originality of Musäus's style. The Romantics, however, taking the fairy tales of the Grimm brothers as their standard, found fault with Musäus's tales and cleansed them of all witty adornments. In this purged form the tales enjoyed enormous popularity in nineteenth-century Germany. By 1900 more than fifty different editions had been published, and the twentieth century has seen nearly thirty editions of Musäus's tales. The advent of a new appreciation of Enlightenment literature that began in the 1970s has led to the republication of the original version of 1782-1786.

Of all of Musäus's European neighbors, it was the English who most loved the tales. William Beckford translated *Volksmährchen der Deutschen* in 1791, and in 1827 Thomas Carlyle opened his anthology *German Romance* with his translations of three of the tales: "Dumb Love" ("Stumme Liebe"), "Libussa," and "Melechsala." During the nineteenth century about twenty more English translations appeared, attesting to the extraordinary popularity of Musäus's work.

Volksmährchen der Deutschen made Musäus one of the attractions of Weimar. Many visitors dropped in to talk to the cheerful professor in the little cottage outside the city walls to which he often withdrew to do his writing.

Because of ill health Musäus never was able to enjoy the financial fruits of his literary labor. His cherished dream of visiting his friend Nicolai in Berlin never came true, since he had to use all his extra income for medical expenses. In October 1787, at the age of fifty-two, Musäus died of a heart attack. The poet Christian Friedrich Daniel Schubart wrote an obituary of Musäus in his newspaper, the *Vaterländische Chronik*: "Keiner in Deutschland schrieb unsere Sprache schöner als er. Wie ein Glockenspiel klangen seine Perioden zusammen, und doch–war's nicht dem Ausland abgehorchte, sondern echt deutsche National melodie, was sein Glockenspiel tönte. Meiner Meinung nach hat noch nie ein Deutscher besser, hinreißender erzählt als Musäus" (No German wrote our language more beautifully than he did. His sentences sounded like harmonious chimes, and the tune of these chimes was not copied from abroad but rather was an authentic national melody. In my opinion, there never was a better, more enchanting German storyteller than Musäus).

Bibliography:

Karl Goedeke, "Musäus," in *Grundriß zur Geschichte der deutschen Dichtung*, volume 4, part 1 (Dresden: Ehlermann, 1916), pp. 579-580.

Biography:

Moritz Müller, *Johann Karl August Musäus: Ein Lebens- und Schriftstellercharakter-Bild* (Jena: Mauke, 1867).

References:

Barbara Carvill, *Der verführte Lesser: J. K. A. Musäus Romane und Romankritiken* (New York & Bern: Lang, 1985);

Gontier-Louis Fink, *Naissance et apogée du conte merveilleux en Allemagne 1740-1800* (Paris: Les Belles Lettres, 1966);

Jürgen Jacobs, *Prosa der Aufklärung: Moralische Wochenschriften, Autobiographie, Satire, Roman. Kommentar zu einer Epoche* (Munich: Winkler, 1976), pp. 298-304;

Erwin Jahn, *Die Volksmärchen der Deutschen* (Leipzig: Voigtländer, 1914);

Volker Klotz, "Dahergelaufene und Davongekommene: Ironisierte Abenteuer in Märchen von Musäus, Wieland und Goethe," *Euphorion*, 79 (1985): 322-334;

Liselotte Kurth, *Die zweite Wirklichkeit: Studien zum Roman des 18. Jahrhunderts* (Chapel Hill: University of North Carolina Press, 1969);

Alfred Richli, *Johann Karl August Musäus: Die Volksmärchen der Deutschen* (Zurich: Atlantis, 1957);

Guy Stern, "A German Imitation of Fielding: Musäus' *Grandison der Zweite*," *Comparative Literature*, 10 (Fall 1958): 335-343.

Papers:

The manuscript for Johann Karl August Musäus's unpublished "Gartendiarium" (Garden Journal), which he kept from 1785 to 1787, is at the Goethe- und Schiller-Archiv, Weimar. Letters from Musäus to Friedrich Nicolai are in the Nicolai papers, Staatsbibliothek Preußischer Kulturbesitz, Berlin.

Friedrich Nicolai

(18 March 1733 - 8 January 1811)

Peter Mollenhauer
Southern Methodist University

BOOKS: *Untersuchung, ob Milton sein Verlohrnes Paradies aus neuern lateinischen Schriftstellern ausgeschrieben habe: Nebst einigen Anmerckungen über eine Recension des Lauderischen Buchs von Miltons Nachahmung der neuern Schriftstellern*, anonymous (Halle: Schwetschke, 1753);

Briefe über den itzigen Zustand der schönen Wissenschaften in Deutschland (Berlin: Kleyb, 1755; reprinted, edited by Georg Ellinger, Berlin: Paetel, 1894);

Sammlung vermischter Schriften zur Beförderung der schönen Wissenschaften und der freyen Künste, 6 volumes (Berlin: Nicolai, 1759-1763);

Ehrengedächtniß Herrn Ewald Christian von Kleist, anonymous (Berlin: Nicolai, 1760);

Ehrengedächtniß Herrn Thomas Abbt: An Herrn D. Johann George Zimmermann (Berlin & Stettin: Nicolai, 1767);

Beschreibung der königlichen Residenzstädte Berlin und Potsdam und aller daselbst befindlicher Merkwürdigkeiten: Nebst einem Anhange, enthaltend die Leben aller Künstler, die seit Churfürst Friedrich Willhelms des Großen Zeiten in Berlin gelebet haben, oder deren Kunstwerke daselbst befindlich sind (Berlin: Nicolai, 1769; revised, 2 volumes, 1779; revised, 4 volumes, 1786; reprinted, 3 volumes, Berlin: Haude & Spener, 1968);

Liebreiche Anrede an alle seine Mitbürger, as Simon Ratzeberger, Jr. (Altona, 1772);

An den Magum in Norden Haussäßig am alten Graben No. 758 zu Königsberg, in Preußen (N.p., 1773);

Das Leben und die Meinungen des Herrn Magister Sebaldus Nothanker, 3 volumes, anonymous (Berlin & Stettin: Nicolai, 1773-1776); translated by Thomas Dutton as *The Life and Opinions of Sebaldus Nothanker*, 3 volumes (London: Printed by C. Lowndes, sold by H. D. Symonds, 1798); German version edited by Fritz Brüggemann, 1 volume (Leipzig: Reclam, 1938; reprinted, Darmstadt: Wissenschaftliche Buchgesellschaft, 1967);

Freuden des jungen Werthers, Leiden und Freuden Werthers des Mannes: Voran und zuletzt ein Gespräch, anonymous (Berlin: Nicolai, 1775; reprinted, edited by Curt Grützmacher, Munich: Fink, 1972);

Widerlegung der falschen Nachricht, als ob Herr Theodor Gülcher in Amsterdam ein Bräutigam sey, anonymous (Berlin, 1776);

Eyn feyner kleyner Almanach Vol. schoenerr echterr liblicherr Volckslieder, lustigerr Reyen, unndt kleglicherr Mordgeschichte, gesungen von Gabriel Wunderlich weyl. Benkelsengernn zu Dessaw, herausgegeben von Daniel Saeuberlich, Schusternn tzu Ritzmück ann der Elbe, 2 volumes,

Painting by Anton Graff, circa 1795 (Karl-Marx-Universität, Leipzig)

anonymous (Berlin & Stettin: Nicolai, 1777-1778);

Einige Zweifel über die Geschichte der Vergiftung des Nachtmahlweins, welche zu Zürich 1776 geschehen seyn soll: Nebst einigen Anmerkungen betreffend Herrn Ulrichs und Herrn Lavaters Predigten über diesen Vorfall, anonymous (Berlin & Stettin: Nicolai, 1778);

Ein paar Worte betreffend Johann Bunkel und Christoph Martin Wieland (Berlin & Stettin: Nicolai, 1779);

Noch ein paar Worte betreffend Johann Bunkel und Christoph Martin Wieland (Berlin & Stettin: Nicolai, 1779);

Bescheidene und freymüthige Erklärung an das Deutsche Publikum betreffend das Verbot der allgemeinen deutschen Bibliothek und vieler sonst allgemein erlaubter Bücher in den kaiserl. königl. Erblanden, anonymous (Berlin, 1780);

Verzeichniß einer Handbibliothek der nützlichsten deutschen Schriften zum Vergnügen und Unterricht, wie auch der brauchbarsten Ausgaben der klassischen Autoren, welche um beygesetzte Preise zu haben sind (N.p., 1780); revised and enlarged as *Verzeichniß einer Handbibliothek der nützlichsten deutschen Schriften zum Vergnügen und Unterrichte, wie auch der brauchbarsten Ausgaben der lateinischen und griechischen klassischen Autoren, und der in Deutschland gedruckten ausländischen Bücher, welche in preußischen klingendem Kurrante, um beigesetzte Preise zu haben sind* (Berlin, 1811);

Versuch über die Beschuldigungen welche dem Tempelherrenorden gemacht worden, und über dessen Geheimniß; nebst einem Anhange über das Entstehen der Freymaurergesellschaft, 2 volumes (Berlin & Stettin: Nicolai, 1782);

Beschreibung einer Reise durch Deutschland und die Schweiz, im Jahre 1781: Nebst Bemerkungen über Gelehrsamkeit, Industrie, Religion und Sitten, 12 volumes (Berlin & Stettin: Nicolai, 1783-1796);

Nachricht von der wahren Beschaffenheit des Instituts der Jesuiten (Berlin & Stettin: Nicolai, 1785);

Des Herrn und der Madame Nicolai in Berlin fünf und zwanzigjähriger Ehe- und Haus-Kalender ans Licht gestellt am 11. Dezember 1785 (N.p., 1785);

Nachricht von den Baumeistern, Bildhauern, Kupferstechern, Malern, Stukkaturern, und anderen Künstlern welche vom dreyzehnten Jahrhunderte bis jetzt in Berlin sich aufgehalten haben (Berlin & Stettin: Nicolai, 1786);

Untersuchung der Beschuldigungen des Herrn Professor Garve wider meine Reisebeschreibung durch Deutschland und die Schweiz: Nebst einigen Erläuterungen die nützlich auch wohl gar nöthig seyn möchten (Berlin & Stettin: Nicolai, 1786);

Vorbericht zu der Schrift der Frau Elisa von der Recke: Nachricht von des berüchtigten Cagliostro Aufenthalte in Mitau, im Jahre 1779, und von dessen dortigen magischen Operationen (Berlin & Stettin: Nicolai, 1787);

Öffentliche Erklärung über seine geheime Verbindung mit dem Illuminatenorden; Nebst beyläufigen Digressionen betreffend Hrn. Johann August Stark und Hrn. Johann Kaspar Lavater (Berlin & Stettin: Nicolai, 1788);

Anekdoten von König Friedrich dem Zweyten von Preußen und von einigen Personen, die um ihn waren; nebst einigen Zweifeln und Berichtigungen über schon gedruckte Anekdoten, 6 volumes (Berlin & Stettin: Nicolai, 1788-1792);

Vorbericht zu Elisa von der Recke: Etwas über des Herrn Oberhofpredigers Johann August Stark Vertheidigungsschrift nebst einigen andern nöthigen Erläuterungen (Berlin & Stettin: Nicolai, 1788);

Nöthige kurze Erklärung über eine Aufforderung des Herrn Oberhofprediger Stark und eine denselben betreffende Korrespondenz (Berlin & Stettin: Nicolai, 1789);

Letzte Erklärung über einige neue Unbilligkeiten und Zunöthigungen in dem den Herrn Oberhofprediger Stark betreffenden Streite (Berlin & Stettin: Nicolai, 1790);

Patriotische Phantasien eines Kameralisten, anonymous (Berlin: Nicolai, 1790);

Freymüthige Anmerkungen über des Herrn Ritters von Zimmermann Fragmente über Friedrich den Großen von einigen brandenbergischen Patrioten, 2 volumes (Berlin & Stettin: Nicolai, 1791-1792);

Zwanzig ernsthafte . . . Vermahnungen an Herrn . . . Marcard, anonymous (N.p., 1792);

Geschichte eines dicken Mannes: Worin drey Heurathen und drey Körbe nebst viel Liebe, 2 volumes (Berlin & Stettin: Nicolai, 1794; reprinted, 1 volume, Weimar: Kiepenheuer, 1972);

Anhang zu Friedrich Schillers Musen-Almanach für das Jahr 1797 (Berlin & Stettin: Nicolai, 1797);

Leben Justus Mösers (Berlin & Stettin: Nicolai, 1797);

Leben und Meinungen Sempronius Gundibert's, eines deutschen Philosophen: Nebst zwey Urkunden der neuesten deutschen Philosophie (Berlin & Stettin: Nicolai, 1798);

Beispiel einer Erscheinung mehrerer Phantasmen nebst einigen erläuternden Anmerkungen: Vorgelesen in der Akademie der Wissenschaften zu Berlin den 28. Hornung 1799 (Berlin, 1799);

Ueber meine gelehrte Bildung, über meine Kenntniß der kritischen Philosophie und meine Schriften dieselbe betreffend, und über die Herren Kant, J. B. Erhard und Fichte: Eine Beylage zu den neun Gesprächen zwischen Christian Wolff und einem Kantianer über Kants metaphysische Anfangsgründe der Rechtslehre und der Tugendlehre (Berlin & Stettin: Nicolai, 1799; reprinted, Brussels: Culture et civilisation, 1968);

*Vertraute Briefe von Adelheid B** an ihre Freundinn Julie S***, anonymous (Berlin & Stettin: Nicolai, 1799);

Ueber die Art wie vermittelst des transcendentalen Idealismus ein wirklich existirendes Wesen aus Princi-pien konstruirt werden kann: Nebst merkwürdigen Proben der Wahrheitsliebe, reifen Ueberlegung, Bescheidenheit, Urbanität und gutgelaunto Großmuth des Stifters der neuesten Philosophie (Berlin & Stettin: Nicolai, 1801);

Über den Gebrauch der falschen Haare und Perrucken in alten und neuern Zeiten: Eine historische Untersuchung (Berlin & Stettin: Nicolai, 1801);

Sammlung der deutschen Abhandlungen, welche in der Königl. Akademie der Wissenschaften zu Berlin vorgelesen wurden in den Jahren 1801-1802 (Berlin: Decker, 1805);

Christ. Fr. Nicolais Bildniss und Selbst-Biographie, edited by M. S. Lowe (Berlin: Starcke, 1806);

Einige Bemerkungen über den Ursprung und die Geschichte der Rosenkreuzer und Freymaurer, veranlaßt durch die sogenannte historisch-kritische Untersuchung des Herrn Hofraths Buhle über diesen Gegenstand (Berlin & Stettin, 1806);

Gedächtnißschrift auf Johann Jakob Engel (Berlin & Stettin: Nicolai, 1806);

Sammlung der deutschen Abhandlungen, welche in der Königl. Akademie der Wissenschaften zu Berlin vorgelesen wurden in den Jahren 1803-1804 (Berlin: Decker, 1806);

Gedächtnißschrift auf Dr. Wilhelm Abraham Teller (Berlin & Stettin: Nicolai, 1807);

Philosophische Abhandlungen: Größtentheils vorgelesen in der Königl. Akademie der Wissenschaften zu Berlin, 2 volumes (Berlin & Stettin: Nicolai, 1808; reprinted, Brussels: Culture et civilisation, 1968);

Gedächtnißschrift auf Johann August Eberhard (Berlin & Stettin: Nicolai, 1810);

Leben und literarischer Nachlaß, edited by Leopold Friedrich Günther von Göckingk (Berlin: Nicolai, 1820);

Gesammelte Werke, 8 volumes to date, edited by Bernhard Fabian and Marie-Luise Spiekermann (Hildesheim, Zurich & New York: Olms, 1985-   ).

OTHER: *Bibliothek der schönen Wissenschaften und der freyen Künste*, 4 volumes, edited by Nicolai and Moses Mendelssohn (Leipzig: Dyck, 1757-1760);

Briefe, die neueste Litteratur betreffend, edited by Nicolai, Mendelssohn, and Gotthold Ephraim Lessing, 24 volumes (Berlin & Stettin: Nicolai, 1759-1765);

Allgemeine deutsche Bibliothek, 118 volumes plus 21 index volumes, edited by Nicolai (Berlin: Nicolai, 1765-1796);

Thomas Abbt, *Vermischte Werke*, 3 volumes, edited by Nicolai (Berlin & Stettin: Nicolai, 1768-1771);

Thomas Amory, *Leben, Bemerkungen und Meynungen Johann Bunkels, nebst dem Leben verschiedener Frauenzimmer: Aus dem Engländischen übersetzt*, 4 volumes, translated by Nicolai (Berlin: Nicolai, 1778);

Neue allgemeine deutsche Bibliothek, 107 volumes plus 10 index volumes, edited by Nicolai (volumes 1-55, Kiel: Bohn, 1793-1800; volumes 56-107, index volumes, Berlin: Nicolai, 1801-1806);

Gotthold Ephraim Lessing, *Briefwechsel mit Karl Wilhelm Ramler, Johann Joachim Eschenburg und Friedrich Nicolai: Nebst einigen Anmerkungen über Lessings Briefwechsel mit Moses Mendelssohn*, edited by Nicolai (Berlin & Stettin: Nicolai, 1794);

Johann Christoph Schwab, *Neun Gespräche zwischen Christian Wolff und einem Kantianer über Kants metaphysische Anfangsgründe der Rechtslehre*, foreword by Nicolai (Berlin & Stettin: Nicolai, 1798);

Neue Berlinische Monatsschrift, 24 volumes, edited by Nicolai (Berlin, 1799-1810);

Neue allgemeine Bibliothek, 51 volumes, edited by Nicolai (Berlin, 1801-1806);

Johann Georg Sulzer, *Lebensbeschreibung von ihm selbst aufgesetzt: Aus der Handschrift abgedruckt mit Anmerkungen*, annotations by Nicolai and J. B. Merian (Berlin & Stettin, 1809).

The growing recognition that Friedrich Nicolai was the catalyst of the Prussian Enlightenment and one of its important satirists indicates that he should no longer be discussed under the category of Dichtung (the poetic arts) but under the heading of literary, cultural, and religious criticism. It was largely through his satirical works that Nicolai became the whipping boy of nineteenth-century literary historians, who—while occasionally acknowledging his merits as publisher, critic, and historian—displayed only slightly veiled contempt for his literary output. Echoing Johann Wolfgang von Goethe's and Friedrich Schiller's attacks on Nicolai, they established a tradition that continued well into the twentieth century of branding him the sworn enemy of German Innerlichkeit (inwardness). Today, the reassessment of the Prussian Enlightenment has resulted in a concomitant revision of Nicolai's reputation. This man of letters wrote no fewer than forty-five books and as many articles on a wide range of literary and cultural subjects, edited and published the monumental *Allgemeine deutsche Bibliothek* (General German Library, 1765-1796) and other important journals, reported on the cultural and economic life of southern Germany, Austria, and Switzerland in a twelve-volume travel account (1783-1796), and left a voluminous correspondence. Living in Berlin most of his life, Nicolai acquired an exhaustive knowledge, if not always a profound understanding, of the literary currents of his time. His truth was of the rationalist age: a call to arms against orthodox theology, against obtuse abstract thinking and muddled language, against what he thought was an exaggerated cult of feeling. He fought a lifelong battle against intolerance, only to open himself to charges of being intolerant of the intolerant.

Grandson of a former mayor of Wittenberg and the son of the Berlin bookseller Christoph Gottlieb Nicolai and Amalie Nicolai, née Zimmermann, Christoph Friedrich Nicolai was born in Berlin on 18 March 1733. His youth and prime working years fell into the reign of Prussia's King Frederick II (Frederick the Great). He lost his mother when he was five. His unsuccessful stint in the Joachimsthal Gymnasium in Berlin in 1746, as well as an agonizing period from May 1747 to May 1748 in the Pietist Latin School of the Francke Endowments in Halle, subjected him to ultrarigid educational practices. These early experiences produced a lifelong aversion to educational straitjacketing, religious dogma, and fanatical enthusiasm. A year in Johann Julius Hecker's new Realschule in Berlin was much more to his liking because of the more practical subjects taught there. From 1749 to 1751 Nicolai apprenticed with a bookseller in Frankfurt an der Oder, studying English, classical authors, and history during the night and frequently skipping breakfast so that he could afford the oil for his lamp. In 1752 he returned to Berlin to join the family business, which, after the death of his father in the same year, was managed by his older brother Gottfried Wilhelm. Nicolai left the business in 1757, planning to spend the rest of his life on his literary projects; but in 1758 the death of his brother forced him to assume responsibility for the firm. He built it into a flourishing publishing and bookselling enterprise, establishing a branch in Stettin in 1765.

During the 1750s Nicolai wrote his first critical pieces, began friendships with Gotthold Ephraim Lessing and Moses Mendelssohn, and

Nicolai with his family; painting by Anna Dorothea Therbusch (from Gero von Wilpert, Deutsche Literatur in Bildern, *1965)*

started the first two of the major literary journals that were to be vehicles of his tireless efforts to encourage publishing in Germany and to mediate between conflicting literary views: the *Bibliothek der schönen Wissenschaften und der freyen Künste* (Library of Belles-Lettres and of the Fine Arts, 1757-1760) and the *Briefe, die neueste Litteratur betreffend* (Letters concerning the Most Recent Literature, 1759-1765). All of the publications of Nicolai's firm bore the image of the bust of Homer on the title page, as if to herald the coming of a new Golden Age for literature. As a publisher, Nicolai reaped handsome profits from these ventures; but the journals he launched during the decade would probably not have succeeded without the support of a well-established business. In these early years Nicolai complained to his friends that the burden of running a large company was keeping him from becoming more prolific as a creative writer, but the sheer quantity of his writings indicates that he managed to combine the duties of a successful publisher with the task his missionary zeal as an enlightener imposed upon him. Not counting the 139 volumes of the *Allgemeine deutsche Bibliothek*, Nicolai was the publisher of some 550 works; with new editions the number of volumes published by his

firm amounted to 1,117. If there were many contemporaries who admired Nicolai's courageous effort to put Germany and Prussia on the map as literary nations, there were others–on the receiving end of Nicolai's criticism or satire–who belittled his accomplishments by claiming that the desire for profit was the motive for his writing and publishing endeavors. Schiller wrote this distich in the "Xenien" (1796), on which he collaborated with Goethe: "Hast du auch wenig verdient um die Bildung der Deutschen / Fritz Nicolai, sehr viel hast du dabey doch verdient" (You have done little for the cultivation of Germany / Fritz Nicolai, you have still earned well in the effort).

Nicolai married Elisabeth Makaria Schaarschmidt in 1760. The marriage was happy and produced eight children, five of whom–Samuel, Karl August, David, Charlotte Makaria, and Wilhelmine–survived childhood. Nicolai survived his wife and all of his children; the son and daughter of Wilhelmine and her husband Friedrich Parthey carried on their grandfather's publishing efforts after his death.

Volumes 1 to 118, plus twenty-one index volumes, of the *Allgemeine deutsche Bibliothek* were published by Nicolai from 1765 to 1796. It was the most comprehensive critical review journal of its time, with a circulation of more than twenty-five hundred copies at the end of the 1770s. Because of pressure from Prussian censors Nicolai had to move the journal to the Hamburg / Kiel bookseller Carl Ernst Bohn, who published fifty-five volumes from 1793 to 1800 under the name *Neue allgemeine deutsche Bibliothek* (New General German Library). Volumes 56-107 of the *Neue allgemeine deutsche Bibliothek* were published in Berlin by Nicolai from 1801 to 1806, but by then the journal's reputation was on the decline. During the first twenty-five years of its existence *Allgemeine deutsche Bibliothek* was Germany's central literary and intellectual organ, and it bestowed powers on Nicolai that were frequently resented. The *Allgemeine deutsche Bibliothek* and the *Neue allgemeine deutsche Bibliothek* reviewed more than eighty thousand titles from 1765 to 1805. During its first fifteen years the *Allgemeine deutsche Bibliothek* placed heavy emphasis on theological articles and books; thereafter the emphasis shifted to literary, philosophical, and scientific topics. In 1769 the journal had some fifty reviewers, including Johann Gottfried Herder, Justus Möser, and Thomas Abbt; in 1805 this number had tripled.

In 1769 Nicolai published his *Beschreibung der königlichen Residenzstädte Berlin und Potsdam und aller daselbst befindlicher Merkwürdigkeiten* (Description of the Royal Cities Berlin and Potsdam and All the Curiosities to be Found Therein), a work of inestimable value to the cultural historian. The work appeared in expanded editions in 1779 and 1786.

The three decades from 1770 to 1800 were marked by Nicolai's satires directed against what he felt to be religious, literary, and philosophical abuses. In 1771 he wrote to Lessing that the public was not yet capable of seeing certain truths "ganz nackend" (in their naked state). This statement characterizes the true satirist, who is convinced that he walks on the path of righteousness and knows that to the majority of people the truth becomes comprehensible and palatable only when it is dressed in the garb of playful distortion.

Nicolai's unquestioned masterpiece among his six major satirical works is *Das Leben und die Meinungen des Herrn Magister Sebaldus Nothanker* (1773-1776; translated as *The Life and Opinions of Sebaldus Nothanker*, 1798). The book met with immediate success and was translated into several languages. Nicolai explained in his autobiography

Title page for Nicolai's parody of Goethe's Die Leiden des jungen Werthers

that it was his intention in the novel "die Verfolgungssucht hartherziger Orthodoxen ... durch das ridendo dicere verum in ihrer Verächtlichkeit darzustellen, und dagegen Geistesfreiheit und Toleranz ... zu empfehlen" (to depict the despicable persecution mania of unfeeling orthodox ministers by saying the truth in a laughing manner, and instead ... to recommend freedom of thought and tolerance). Sebaldus Nothanker is a country parson who is dismissed from office because of his unorthodox beliefs and loses his wife and youngest daughter as a result of his impoverishment. Roaming through Germany and Holland he experiences intolerance, hypocrisy, cruelty, and abuse in his dealings with Pietists, members of the orthodox clergy, and to a lesser degree the nobility; but he finds kindness and common sense in ordinary people, some of whom are superbly characterized. Ideal characters such as the Major and the bookseller Hieronymus represent Nicolai's position.

Nicolai's second major satire was a parody of Goethe's *Die Leiden des jungen Werthers* (The Sorrows of Young Werther, 1774). *Freuden des jungen Werthers, Leiden und Freuden Werthers des Mannes: Voran und zuletzt ein Gespräch* (Joys of Young Werther, Sufferings and Joys of Werther the Man: In the Beginning and at the End a Discussion, 1775) is directed against the exaggerated enthusiasm Goethe's work evoked in young hotheads, which supposedly led to many suicides. Albert, the businessman who acts responsibly in the "real world," is the positive character; Werther, the undisciplined, irresponsible, and soppy "genius," is the negative one. Two other characters, Martin and Hans, carry on a discussion in a prologue and epilogue; functioning as Nicolai's persona, Martin stages the parody and makes Albert reflect his own as well as Nicolai's point of view. In the end Nicolai's Werther shoots himself as Goethe's Werther did, but his pistol is loaded with capsules containing chicken blood. Here and in his other satires Nicolai strives to emancipate a productive citizenry from the demands and assumptions of an effete and sentimental upper class.

Nicolai's struggle against the Sturm und Drang movement came to a conclusion with his parody *Eyn feyner kleyner Almanach* (A Fine and Tiny Almanac, 1777-1778). Nicolai felt this literary movement was using sentimental slogans, authoritative buzzwords, and effusive speculations for the promulgation of an artistic ideal that was not in harmony with the general educational level of society. Ammunition for the satire was provided by Gottfried Bürger's essay "Aus Daniel Wunderlich's Buch" (From Daniel Wunderlich's Book) in the journal *Deutsches Museum* (May 1776), especially by a section in it titled "Herzenserguß über Volkspoesie" (Heartfelt Effusions on Folk Poetry). If Bürger and others in the Sturm und Drang movement had dreams of making folk poetry and folk songs the quintessential expression of all art, Nicolai saw in such poetics no more than an archaistic and disingenuous attempt to empathize with the innermost feelings of the lower classes. The speaker of this short diatribe is the shoemaker-poet Daniel Seuberlich, whose name alludes to Bürger's Daniel Wunderlich. What makes this parody so gro-

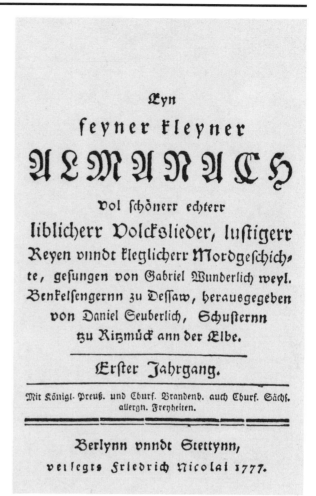

Title page for Nicolai's satirical attack on the Sturm und Drang movement

tesquely effective is its distorted orthography and use of sixteenth-century language.

No major satires were produced in the 1780s, but in this decade Nicolai began to publish the findings of the journey through South Germany, Austria, and Switzerland that he had undertaken in 1781. Therein he launched his attacks against Catholicism–specifically against the Jesuits–and against secret societies.

In the 1790s Nicolai returned to satire with *Geschichte eines dicken Mannes* (Story of a Fat Man, 1794), which is mainly an attack on philosophical systems, especially Immanuel Kant's critical philosophy, but also on Catholicism. Structured as a two-volume developmental novel in forty-two sections that bear titles in picaresque fashion, this work is readable only for a few of its humorous episodes. The protagonist, Anselm Redlich, studies medicine and Kant's philosophy but fails in everything because of his lack of purpose and his tendency

Page from a letter from Nicolai to Hans Caspar Hirzel, 21 September 1786 (Zentralbibliothek Zürich) to engage in fruitless philosophical speculation. Philipp and Herr von Reitheim serve as Nicolai's mouthpieces. The satire in this novel must be considered a failure since the reader gets the impression that the protagonist is stymied not because of his dogged adherence to abstract ideas but as a result of a basic character flaw.

Nicolai's best satire after *Das Leben und die Meinungen des Herrn Magister Sebaldus Nothanker* was *Leben und Meinungen Sempronius Gundibert's eines deutschen Philosophen* (Life and Opinions of Sempronius Gundibert, a German Philosopher, 1798). In this book Nicolai satirizes with special forcefulness the lack of conceptional and linguistic clarity on the part of the disciples of Kant and Johann Gottlieb Fichte, as well as the unclear and exorbitantly elevated prose of Schiller, Friedrich Wilhelm Joseph von Schelling, and the Schlegel brothers. Moreover, Nicolai pits his own utilitarian ethics against the rigid deontological ethics of Kant. While the latter called for people to ignore their inclinations when making moral decisions, Nicolai demands that inclinations be taken into account because "ohne sie wären wir nicht Menschen" (without them we would not be human beings). The novel has three parts: Nicolai's ironic introductory remarks; the story of Gundibert; and the critical apparatus, which contains annotated quotations from contemporary authors. The plot is meant to prove the arguments in the introduction that abstract philosophical ideas cannot be applied to practical situations. Nicolai frequently blends quotations from the critical apparatus into the story so that the reader can have no doubt that the material used is from "the real world." Much of the satirical effect is achieved on the language level: the author uses Kant's or Fichte's terminology in incongruent contexts or degrades the lofty appearance of philosophical terms by using loan translations such as "die vonvornige und vonhintige Philosophie" (the frontal [a priori] and the rear [a posteriori] philosophy). Sempronius Gundibert, the son of a weaver, studies critical philosophy and then embarks on a journey during which he rigidly applies his philosophical jargon to his activities as a teacher and as an administrator. Naturally, he fails miserably in everything he undertakes and ends in a mental institution after a physician overhears one of his sermons on Fichte's philosophy. He is "cured" and returns home to resume his work as a weaver. What did he learn? Herr von Schorndorf, Nicolai's persona, quotes Samuel Butler's *Hudibras* (1668-1673): "He knew what's what, and that's as high / As Metaphysic wit can fly."

Nicolai's epistolary novel *Vertraute Briefe von Adelheid B** an ihre Freundin Julie S*** (Confidential Letters of Adelheid B** to Her Friend Julie S**, 1799) constitutes his last–and by and large unsuccessful–attempt at satire. The novel contains sixty-two letters of a highly personal and often touching nature; the satirical segments cover many of the themes from the two preceding novels while focusing on the relations of the Romantics to society and to the literary scene in general. The incongruence of these two literary endeavors gives the book a peculiarly hybrid character. What is noteworthy, though, is the remarkable sensitivity the hard-nosed old satirist Nicolai displays when he depicts the emotional depth of his protagonist. An educated woman, she functions here as the torchbearer of his program of enlightenment.

A member of the Berlin Academy of Sciences, Nicolai continued to attend its meetings and gave lectures until the end of his life. In addition, he remained an active member of the renowned Montagsklub (Monday Club), to which he had been introduced by Lessing in 1755, and of the Mittwochsgesellschaft (Wednesday Association), which was founded in 1783 and whose existence was only known to its members. Respected and despised, this influential son of the Prussian Enlightenment died in his sleep on 8 January 1811. By then his truths had finally come of age, but they also showed signs of aging.

Bibliographies:

Horst Möller, *Aufklärung in Preußen. Der Verleger, Publizist und Geschichtsschreiber Friedrich Nicolai* (Berlin: Colloquium, 1974), pp. 593-612;

Marie-Luise Spieckermann, "Bibliographie der Werke Friedrich Nicolais," in *Friedrich Nicolai, 1733-1811: Essays zum 250. Geburtstag,* edited by Bernhard Fabian (Berlin, 1983), pp. 257-304.

Biography:

Gustav Sichelschmidt, *Friedrich Nicolai: Geschichte seines Lebens* (Herford: Nicolai, 1971).

References:

Ernst Altenkrüger, *Friedrich Nicolais Jugendschriften* (Berlin: Heymann, 1894);

Karl Aner, *Der Aufklärer Nicolai* (Gießen: Töpelmann, 1912);

Peter Joerg Becker, *Friedrich Nicolai: Leben und Werk* (Berlin, 1983);

Bernhard Fabian, ed. *Friedrich Nicolai, 1733-1811: Essays zum 250. Geburtstag* (Berlin, 1983);

Ernst Kaeber, "Friedrich Nicolais Reise durch Deutschland im Jahre 1781: Ein Beitrag zu seiner Charakteristik," *Der Bär von Berlin: Jahrbuch des Vereins für die Geschichte Berlins*, 6 (1956): 29-76;

Adolf Lasson, "Friedrich Nicolai im Kampf gegen den Idealismus," *Archiv für Litteraturgeschichte*, 22 (1862): 257-286;

Peter Mollenhauer, "Friedrich Nicolai: Catalyst of the Prussian Enlightenment," *Schatzkammer der deutschen Sprachlehre, Dichtung und Geschichte*, 10, no. 2 (1984): 19-25;

Mollenhauer, *Friedrich Nicolais Satiren: Ein Beitrag zur Kulturgeschichte des 18. Jahrhunderts* (Amsterdam: Benjamins, 1977);

Horst Möller, *Aufklärung in Preußen: Der Verleger, Publizist und Geschichtsschreiber Friedrich Nicolai* (Berlin: Colloquium, 1974);

Edith Nahler, "Der Toleranzbegriff bei Friedrich Nicolai und Moses Mendelssohn," Ph.D. dissertation, University of Leipzig, 1962;

Günther Ost, *Friedrich Nicolais allgemeine deutsche Bibliothek*, Germanische Studien, 63 (Berlin, 1928);

Gustav Parthey, *Die Mitarbeiter an F. Nicolais Allgemeiner Deutschen Bibliothek nach ihren Namen und Zeichen . . . geordnet* (Berlin: Nicolai, 1842);

Franz Carl August Philips, *Friedrich Nicolais literari-sche Bestrebungen* (Zalt-Bommel: Van de Garde, 1925);

Paul Raabe, *Friedrich Nicolai 1733-1811: Die Verlagswerke eines preußischen Buchhändlers der Aufklärung 1759-1811* (Weinheim: Verlagsgesellschaft MbH, 1983);

Gustav Rümelin, *Nicolai und sein Reisewerk über Schwaben*, in his *Reden und Aufsätze* (Freiburg, 1881), pp. 407-442;

Richard Schwinger, *Friedrich Nicolais Roman "Sebaldus Nothanker": Ein Beitrag zur Geschichte der Aufklärung* (Weimar: Felber, 1897);

Martin Sommerfeld, *Friedrich Nicolai und der Sturm und Drang: Ein Beitrag zur Geschichte der deutschen Aufklärung* (Halle: Niemeyer, 1921);

Walter Strauß, *Friedrich Nicolai und die kritische Philosophie: Ein Beitrag zur Geschichte der Aufklärung* (Stuttgart: Kohlhammer, 1927).

Papers:

Most of Friedrich Nicolai's papers, including an alphabetical index of individuals who corresponded with him, are in the Staatsbibliothek Preußischer Kulturbesitz, West Berlin, and the Deutsche Staatsbibliothek, East Berlin. Smaller collections of manuscripts and letters are in the Freies Deutsches Hochstift, Goethe Museum, Frankfurt am Main; the Österreichische Nationalbibliothek, Vienna; the Literaturarchiv der Staatsbibliothek Hamburg; and the Herzog-August Bibliothek Wolfenbüttel.

Karl Wilhelm Ramler

(25 February 1725 - 11 April 1798)

Barbara Carvill
Calvin College

BOOKS: *Ankündigung eines Collegii der schönen Wissenschaften und eines Collegii der Rechte* (Berlin: Kunst, 1752);

Ode an Herrn Gleim und Mademoiselle Mayerin am Tage ihrer Vermählung (N.p., 1753);

Der Tod Jesu: Eine Kantate in die Musik gesetzt von C. H. Graun, music by Carl Heinrich Graun (Berlin: Litfaß, 1756); translated by John Troutbeck as *The Passion of Our Lord* (London, 1800);

Der May: Eine musikalische Idylle (Berlin: Birnstiel, 1758);

Die Hirten bey der Krippe zu Bethlehem: Ein musikalisches Gedicht (Berlin: Winter, 1758);

Geistliche Kantaten (Berlin: Voß, 1760);

Die Auferstehung und Himmelfahrt Jesu (Hamburg: Piscator, 1760);

Ode an den Fabius: Nach der Schlacht bey Torgau, den 3. November 1760 (N.p., 1760);

Ode an die Feinde des Königes: Den 24. Jenner 1760 (N.p., 1760);

Ode auf ein Geschütz, wodurch, am Tage der Belagerung Berlins, eine Kugel, bis mitten in die Stadt getrieben wurde, anonymous (Berlin, 1760);

Ode an Hymen: Dem Herrn Ludewig von Gask an Seinem Vermählungsfeste . . . zugeeignet (Berlin, 1760; revised, 1763);

Ode an die Stadt Berlin, den 24. Jenner 1759, anonymous (Berlin, 1760);

Lied der Nymphe Persanthëis: Kolber den 24ten September 1760 (N.p., 1761);

Ode an Herrn C. G. Krause: Berlin, den 3ten Junius, 1762 (Berlin: Winter, 1762);

Ode an seinen Arzt, Berlin, den 24. Jenner 1762, anonymous (Berlin, 1762);

Friedens-Lieder auf den Einzug und die Wiederkunft des Königs zu Berlin den 30. Martii 1763, by Ramler and S. C. Lappenberg (Schwabach: Mizler, 1763);

Ode an die Göttinn der Eintracht: Berlin, den 24. Jenner 1763 (Berlin, 1763);

Ode auf die Wiederkunft des Königes: Berlin, den 30. März 1763 (Berlin, 1763);

Painting by Anton Graff, 1771 (Karl-Marx-Universität, Leipzig)

Ode an die Muse: Berlin den 18. Jenner 1764 (Berlin, 1764);

Ino: Eine Kantate, anonymous (Berlin, 1765);

Ptolomäus und Berenice: Berlin, den 15ten des Julius 1765 (Berlin, 1765);

Glaukus Wahrsagung: Als die französische Flotte aus dem Hafen von Brest nach Amerika segelte, anonymous (Berlin: Voß, 1765);

Gedichte, edited by Johann George Scheffner (Königsberg, 1766);

An den Herrn Joh. Joach. Quanz: Berlin, den 30ten Januar, 1766 (Berlin: Winter, 1766);

Karl Wilhelm Ramlers Oden (Berlin: Voß, 1767);

Hymne an die Liebe: Breslau, im Augustmonat 1768 (Breslau, 1768);

Pygmalion: Eine Kantate (N.p., 1768);

Ode an den Kaiser Joseph den Zweyten, anonymous (Berlin: Voß, 1769);

Ode an die Venus Urania: Den 2. November 1770 (Berlin: Voß, 1770);

Auf den Tod des preußischen Prinzen Friedrich Heinrich Karls 1767, anonymous (Berlin & Stettin: Nicolai, 1770);

Lyrische Gedichte (Berlin: Voß, 1772);

Das Opfer der Nymphen: Ein Vorspiel. Am Geburtsfeste des Königs von Preußen, den 24. Januar 1774 auf dem Deutschen Theater zu Berlin aufgeführet (Berlin: Winter, 1774);

Cephalus und Prokris: Ein Melodrama (Berlin: Dekker, 1778);

Kriegslieder für Josephs und Friedrichs Heere, anonymous (N.p., 1778);

Cyrus und Kassandra: Ein Singspiel (N.p., 1786);

Auf die Huldigung des Königs von Preußen Friedrich Wilhelms (Berlin: Voß, 1786);

Dankopfer für den Landesvater, eine Davidische Kantate, anonymous (Berlin: Unger, 1787);

An den König von Preußen Friedrich Wilhelm II., als Derselbe die Buchdruckerei besuchte, die mit den Werken des höchstseligen Königs beschäftigt war (N.p., 1787);

Die Krönung des Königes Friedrich Wilhelm des Zweyten: Eine Kantate, bey Gelegenheit der Jahresfeier des Preuß. Krönungsfestes, music by B. Wessely (Berlin: Unger, 1787);

Rede am Geburtsfeste des Kronprinzen von Preußen Friedrich Wilhelm, gehalten auf dem Nationaltheater in Berlin, den 3. August 1787 (Berlin: Decker, 1787);

Allegorische Personen zum Gebrauche der bildenden Künstler (Berlin: Akademische Kunst- und Buchhandlung, 1788);

Rede am Geburtsfeste I. M. der Königin Friderike Luise von Preußen, anonymous (Berlin: Dekker, 1788);

Die Bruderliebe, eine Alcäische Ode, dem Könige Friedrich Wilhelm II. bei Gelegenheit des Besuches der Erbstatthalterin der Vereinigten Niederlande gewidmet (Berlin, 1789);

An der regierenden Königinn von Preußen Majestät, als Dieselbe die Sternwarte der Akademie der Wissenschaften besuchte (Berlin, 1789);

Kurzgefaßte Mythologie oder Lehre von den fabelhaften Göttern, Halbgöttern und Helden des Alterthums, 3 volumes (Berlin: Maurer, 1790-1791);

Rede am Geburtsfeste des Kronprinzen von Preußen, gehalten auf dem kgl. Nationaltheater zu Berlin, den 3. August 1790 (N.p., 1790);

Auf die Zurückkunft des Königes von Preußen Friedrich Wilhelm II. nach der Friedensvermittlung, vorgelesen in der Akademie der Künste und mechanischen Wissenschaften den 25. September 1790 (Berlin: Decker, 1790);

Beiträge zur deutschen Sprachkunde, 2 volumes (Berlin: Matzdorf, 1794-1796);

Über die Bildung der Deutschen Nennwörter und Beywörter (Berlin: Maurer, 1796);

Gedächtnisrede auf Bernhard Rode (Berlin: Maurer, 1797);

Kurzgefaßte Einleitung in die schönen Künste und Wissenschaften (Görlitz: Anton, 1798);

Karl Wilhelm Ramlers poetische Werke, 2 volumes, edited by Leopold Friedrich Günther von Goeckingk (Berlin: Sander, 1800-1801; reprinted, 1 volume, Bern & Las Vegas: Lang, 1979);

Auserlesene Gedichte (Heilbronn, 1825);

Alte Tier Fabeln: Mit Steinzeichnungen von Aug. Gaul (Berlin: Cassirer, 1919);

Ramlers Anakreontische Poesie im Briefwechsel aus seinen letzten Lebensjahren 1792-1797, edited by Arnold Charisius (Leipzig, 1921).

OTHER: *Critische Nachrichten aus dem Reiche der Gelehrsamkeit*, edited by Ramler and Johann Georg Sulzer (Berlin: Haude & Spener, 1750);

Marcus Hieronymus Vida, *Das Schachspiel: Ein Heldengedicht*, translated by Ramler (Berlin, 1753);

Charles Batteux, *Einleitung in die Schönen Wissenschaften: Nach dem Französischen des Herrn Batteux mit Zusätzen vermehret*, 4 volumes, translated by Ramler (Leipzig: Weidmann & Reich, 1756-1758; revised, 1763; revised, 1769; revised, 1774);

Friedrich von Logau, *Sinngedichte: Zwölf Bücher. Mit Anmerkungen über die Sprache des Dichters*, edited by Ramler and Gotthold Ephraim Lessing (Leipzig: Weidmann & Reich, 1759);

Ewald von Kleist, *Sämmtliche Werke*, 2 volumes, edited by Ramler (Berlin: Voß, 1760);

Magnus Gottfried Lichtwer, *Herrn M. G. Lichtwers auserlesene, verbesserte Fabeln und Erzählungen*, edited by Ramler (Greifswald & Leipzig: Weitbrecht, 1761);

John Dryden, *Alexanders Fest oder Die Gewalt der Musik: Eine Kantate auf den Tag der Cäcilia, der Erfinderinn der Orgel*, music by George Frideric Handel, translated by Ramler (Berlin: Spener, 1766);

Sammlung der besten Sinngedichte der deutschen Poeten, edited anonymously by Ramler (Riga: Hartknoch, 1766);

Lieder der Deutschen, edited anonymously by Ramler and C. G. Krause (Berlin: Winter, 1766; reprinted, Stuttgart: Metzler, 1965);

Lieder der Deutschen mit Melodien, 4 volumes, edited anonymously by Ramler and Krause (Berlin: Winter, 1767-1768);

Lyrische Bluhmenlese, 2 volumes, edited by Ramler (Leipzig: Weidmann & Reich, 1774-1778);

Horace, *Horazens Dichtkunst übersetzt*, translated by Ramler (Basel: Flick, 1777);

Christian Wernicke, *Christian Wernikens Überschriften: Nebst Opitzens, Tschernings, Gryphius und Olearius epigrammatischen Gedichten*, edited by Ramler (Leipzig: Weidmann & Reich, 1780);

Fabellese, 4 volumes, edited by Ramler (volumes 1-3, Leipzig: Weidmann & Reich; volume 4, Berlin: Maurer, 1783-1797);

Johann Nikolaus Götz, *Vermischte Gedichte*, edited by Ramler (Mannheim: Schwan, 1785);

Salomon Geßner, *Salomon Gessners auserlesene Idyllen in Verse gebracht*, edited by Ramler (Berlin: Unger, 1787);

Oden aus dem Horaz: Nebst einem Anhang zweier Gedichte aus dem Katull und achtzehn Liedern aus dem Anakreon. Mit Anmerkungen, translated and edited by Ramler (Berlin, 1787);

Valerius Martialis in einem Auszuge, lateinisch und deutsch: Aus den poetischen Uebersetzungen verschiedener Verfasser gesammelt, 6 volumes, edited by Ramler (Leipzig: Weidmann & Reich, 1787-1791);

Fabeln und Erzählungen aus verschiedenen Dichtern, edited by Ramler (Berlin: Maurer, 1797);

Anakreons auserlesene Oden und die zwey noch übrigen Oden der Sappho, revised by Ramler (Berlin: Sander, 1801);

Götz, *Vermehrte Gedichte*, 3 volumes, edited by Ramler (Mannheim: Schwan, 1807).

Karl Wilhelm Ramler is one of the background figures on the literary stage of eighteenth-century Germany. He is known as a fine poetic craftsman, an editor and anthologist, a translator of Horace, and a composer of heroic odes in praise of the Prussian royalty.

Ramler was born on 25 February 1725 in Kolberg, Pomerania, to the bank inspector Wilhelm Nikolaus Ramler and Elisabeth Ramler, née Fiddechow. Ramler went to the Latin school in Stettin and later to the famous Waisenhaus gymnasium in Halle, founded by the Pietist H. A. Francke. In these schools Ramler received a thorough training in classical languages, and it was there that his keen philological sense and his love for Roman literature were developed. After a year of listless study of theology at the University of Halle, Ramler went to Berlin in 1743. He became the protégé of Johann Ludwig Gleim, who introduced him into the literary circles of Berlin when that city was becoming the center of intellectual and cultural life in northeastern Germany under Frederick II. In 1747 Ramler was hired by the court to be a professor of philosophy and rhetoric at the Corps de cadets, the officer training school of the Prussian army. Ramler held this post for forty-two years, even though, for most of that time, it provided him with no more than a starvation salary. One of Ramler's most famous students at the Corps de cadets was the officer and author Karl von Knebel, in later years the educator of the Weimar princes and friend of Johann Wolfgang von Goethe.

Ramler earned his first public success as a poet with the text of an Easter cantata, *Der Tod Jesu* (The Death of Jesus, 1756; translated as *The Passion of Our Lord*, 1800), which he composed at the order of Princess Amalia, the sister of Frederick II. Carl Heinrich Graun, the royal concertmaster, set Ramler's text to music, and on 25 March 1755 the first performance took place in the Berlin cathedral with Carl Phillip Emanuel Bach at the harpsichord. *Der Tod Jesu* was performed many times during the nineteenth century and is still a popular piece of Protestant church music during the Lenten and Easter season.

Ramler's other literary productions are largely forgotten today. He did not write much, and in his letters to Gleim he admits that his concern with formal perfection often paralyzed his poetic creativity. Nevertheless, he felt called to write heroic odes, a genre which, since Martin Opitz in the seventeenth century, was considered the highest and most noble literary form. He composed his odes in the Horatian style as far as diction, meter, and themes are concerned. Ramler's odes are occasional poems in the classical sense, celebrating contemporary occurrences, political events, and birthdays and deaths of the members of the Prussian royal house. They are carefully

```
━━━━━━━━                    57
Großmüthige!  macht keine der
Ist möglich?  machen euch so viel Ge-
                                    fahren,
Womit ihr oft
Mit welchen ihr  ihn ringen faht,
Der Kronen keine,
So viele Kronen,  die mit Blut zu kaufen
                                    waren;
Macht keine
So manche  Götterthat,

Kein glorreich übermannter
So manch von ihm zertretnes  Unge-
                                    heuer
Euch endlich
Nicht wieder  zur Verföhnung Luft?

So lange loderte der Rache fchwarzes
                                    Feuer
In keines Gottes Bruft.


 Als Herkuls Arm den Löwen erft er-
                                    drückte,

Der in Nemäens Felfen lag,

Und, mit der Panzerhaut bedeckt', fein
                                    Rachfchwerdt zückte,

Und fchnell, und Schlag auf Schlag
```

Page from Ramler's ode "An die Feinde des Königs" (To the Enemies of the King) in his Lyrische Gedichte, *with revisions by Ramler, who continually polished his works (from Gustav Könnecke,* Bilderatlas zur Geschichte der deutschen Nationallitteratur, *1895)*

crafted, formally impeccable, learned poems which owe much of their "poetic" and elevated character to their many allusions to classical mythology.

During the Seven Years' War Ramler joined Gleim and Ewald von Kleist in writing patriotic poetry celebrating the military exploits of Frederick II in a war which was far from glorious and which caused enormous suffering and hardship in northern Germany. Ramler's patriotic odes glorify the Prussian king as Augustus, Alexander the Great, and Caesar. To the modern reader the attempt to eulogize eighteenth-century Prussia in terms of heroic classical antiquity seems anachronistic and false. Ramler himself sensed that his odes were somewhat out of step with his time because much of the classical erudition with which he larded his verses was unfamiliar to the average reader, and he had to explain the allegorical and mythological references of his poems in extensive and often pedantic footnotes. Nevertheless,

many of Ramler's contemporaries who had good classical educations and respect for meticulous craftsmanship appreciated his odes. The poets of the Göttinger Hainbund (Göttingen Grove League), for instance, would start their regular meetings with a festive recitation of one of Ramler's odes.

Ramler soon became a popular figure on the Berlin literary scene. He collaborated with Johann Georg Sulzer and later with Gotthold Ephraim Lessing, and he became the literary consultant and adviser of Salomon Geßner, Anna Louisa Karsch, Moses Mendelssohn, Kleist, and many others. He acted as literary agent and editor for Johann Nikolaus Götz, a poet in the anacreontic vein who, as a Protestant clergyman, chose to publish his works anonymously. Ramler was also a founding member of the Montagsklub (Monday Club), where the intellectual elite of Berlin gathered to discuss literary and cultural affairs.

Ramler's understanding of poetry and poetic production was shaped by classicist views which originated in Renaissance humanism. According to those views all norms for poetic beauty are rooted in reason and nature. Rules exist for making good poetry, and these rules can be learned from good models–especially from the ancients, who have set timeless examples of beauty. A good poet writes for an audience which can appreciate his erudition, understands the mythological allusions, savors the play with traditional elements, and perceives poetic creativity as a skillful combination of the old with the new.

Ramler found in Horace his great model and poetic inspiration. He advocated Horatian norms of beauty, harmony, simplicity, clarity, correctness, formal perfection, and elegance; he was called by his friends "der deutsche Horaz" (the German Horace). He became an authority on versification and poetic diction, and many Berlin authors submitted their work to his editorial scrutiny before sending it off for publication. Lessing, for instance, gladly accepted Ramler's editorial suggestions for his plays *Minna von Barnhelm* (1767) and *Nathan der Weise* (Nathan the Wise, 1779). Ewald von Kleist submitted his poem *Der Frühling* (The Spring, 1749) to Ramler for advice on versification; but instead of making some stylistic and metrical improvements, as Kleist expected, Ramler reworked the text so substantially that Kleist was unable to publish Ramler's revision as his own work. After Kleist's death in 1759 Ramler, who was responsible for

Kleist's literary estate, published a heavily revised edition of Kleist's writings (1760). Many contemporaries did not approve of these high-handed editorial initiatives. Daniel Chodowiecki, the graphic artist, circulated in Berlin a satirical picture which showed Ramler as barber shaving the corpse of Kleist. The caption read: "Lasset die Toten ungeschoren" (Leave the dead unshorn). The controversy over Ramler's editorial interventions became stronger in 1761 when he published anonymously an unauthorized "verbesserte" (improved) edition of the fables of Magnus Gottfried Lichtwer, who was still alive. The literary journals then debated the prerogatives and limitations of the editor of a literary work. Ramler, as a representative of the old school, thought that a literary text can have two "authors," the second author–the editor–having the task of polishing and perfecting the work according to universally valid standards of beauty. The more progressive writers, for whom Heinrich Wilhelm von Gerstenberg was the spokesman, held that an artwork is the product of an original genius and has its own standards of perfection, which are to be fully respected by an editor. Ramler never changed his position on this point, and, despite the criticism of many readers, his editorial liberties became more and more daring. August Wilhelm von Schlegel spoke for many when he said that Ramler had "die ungesegnete Hand eines poetischen Chirurgen" (the bungling hand of a poetic surgeon).

Ramler was known not only for his revised and "improved" editions of works by Kleist, Geßner, and Götz but also for his anthologies. His purpose was a pedagogical one: the reading public was to be educated with good German examples of various literary genres, and authors needed good models to emulate. Ramler's first anthology was Friedrich von Logau's *Sinngedichte* (Epigrams, 1759), a somewhat modernized collection of epigrams by the seventeenth-century poet which he published in cooperation with Lessing. His anthology *Lieder der Deutschen* (Songs of the Germans, 1766) is considered the most extensive collection of German Rococo poetry. Ramler revised these anacreontic Lieder, improved the quality of the rhymes, made stylistic changes, and printed the emended poems without the names of their authors. He also published *Sammlung der besten Sinngedichte der deutschen Poeten* (Collection of the Best Epigrams by German Poets, 1766) and *Fabellese* (Collection of Fables, 1783-1797). With these anthologies Ramler established him-

Ramler and the Muse; engraving by B. Rode after a drawing by E. Henne

self as the collector and authoritative editor of eighteenth-century German literature in the neoclassical tradition–a tradition which, by the end of the century, had become outmoded.

Ramler's gift for versification, his love of working with the texts of other authors, and his formalistic talents made him exceptionally well suited for being a translator. His great affinity for and admiration of Horace led him to set out to translate the Roman author's poetry as closely, faithfully, and poetically as possible. He worked at this project all his life, hoping to create a poetic German language with Horatian beauty, economy, fluidity, and urbane elegance. His ambition was also to develop the most appropriate German rendering of the Latin verse, rhythm, and Horatian stanza form. The classical quantifying meter had to be transposed into German, an accentuating language which uses stressed and unstressed syllables. In spite of his often pedantic scansion and rather mechanistic imitation of antique meters, Ramler made an important contribution in bringing classical meters and stanza forms into the German lyrical arsenal, a process which was further developed and brought to mastery by Friedrich Gottlieb Klopstock, Goethe, Johann Heinrich Voß, and Friedrich Hölderlin. Ramler published not only several revised editions of his translations of the odes of Horace but also translations of Catullus, Valerius Martialis, and Anacreon. Much admired was his translation of the Anacreontic ode "Loblied auf die Cikade" (Song of Praise to the Cicada), which appeared in his anthology *Lyrische Bluhmenlese* (Lyrical Collection, 1774-1778). Ramler also translated from the French; Charles Batteux's neoclassical *Cours de belles-lettres ou principes de la littérature* (1753) appeared as *Einleitung in die Schönen Wissenschaften* (Introduction to Belles Lettres, 1756-1758), with many examples of original German poetry as normative models to imitate.

After the death in 1786 of Frederick II, whose neoclassical French orientation had led him to ignore German literature, Ramler finally received the attention and respect of the Prussian court. The new king, Frederick Wilhelm II, gave him an adequate salary at the officers' school; he also appointed Ramler to the Berlin Academy of Sciences and as codirector of the royal theater in Berlin, charges which Ramler faithfully executed until his retirement in 1796. He died two years later. He never married.

Even during his lifetime Ramler's contribution to the world of letters was disputed. Lessing, Mendelssohn, Friedrich Nicolai, Goethe, and Voß valued most of his work; Gerstenberg, Sulzer, and Schlegel discredited Ramler because of his Neoclassical formalism and his lack of sensibility for the original genius of a literary work. Most nineteenth- and twentieth-century literary historiography, based on a Romantic understanding of poetics, presents Ramler as cold, pedantic, and anachronistic. More recent studies that have reevaluated German Rococo literature and its classicist origins, however, treat Ramler more appreciatively.

Letters:
Briefwechsel zwischen Gleim und Ramler, 2 volumes, edited by Carl Schüddekopf (Tübingen: Litterarischer Verein in Stuttgart, 1906-1907).

Bibliographies:
Carl Schüddekopf, *Karl Wilhelm Ramler bis zu sei-*
ner *Verbindung mit Lessing* (Wolfenbüttel: Zwissler, 1886), pp. 56-84;
Karl Goedeke, *Grundriß zur Geschichte der deutschen Dichtung*, third edition (Dresden: Ehlermann, 1910-1916), volume 4, part 1, pp. 178-183.

Biographies:
Franz Muncker, "Karl Wilhelm Ramler," in *Deutsche National-Litteratur,* volume 45 (Stuttgart: Union Deutsche Verlagsgesellschaft, 1894), pp. 201-220;
Wilhelm Eggebrecht, "Karl Wilhelm Ramler," in *Pommersche Lebensbilder,* volume 4 (Cologne: Böhlau, 1966), pp. 153-167.

References:
Alfred Anger, "Nachwort," in *Lieder der Deutschen*, edited by Ramler (Stuttgart: Metzler, 1965);
A. G. de Capua, "Karl Wilhelm Ramler: Anthologist and Editor," *Journal of English and German Philology*, 55 (1956): 355-372;
Elias Erasmus (Paul Otto), "Der Fall Lichtwer-Ramler," *Blätter für den deutschen Buchhandel*, 95 (1928): 134-156;
Günter Fleischhauer, "Karl Wilhelm Ramler's musikalische Idylle *Der May* in den Vertonungen Georg Philipp Telemanns und Johann Friedrich Reichardts," in *Dichtung und Musik*, edited by Siegfried Bimberg (Halle: Martin-Luther-Universität at Halle-Wittenberg, 1982), pp. 23-39;
Hans Freydank, *Goethe und Ramler* (Halle: Graeger, 1928);
Wolf Hobohm, "Telemann und Ramler," in his *Telemann und seine Dichter* (Magdeburg: S. N., 1978), pp. 61-80;
Reinhard Hossfeld, "Die deutsche horazische Ode von Opitz bis Klopstock," Ph.D. dissertation, Cologne University, 1961;
Albert Pick, "Über Karl Wilhelm Ramlers Änderungen Hagedornscher Fabeln," *Archiv für das Studium der neueren Sprachen*, 73 (1885): 241-272;
August Sauer, "Über die Ramlersche Bearbeitung der Gedichte E. C. v. Kleists," *Sitzungsberichte der königlichen Akademie der Wissenschaften zu Wien*, 97 (1880): 69-101;
Carl Schüddekopf, *Karl Wilhelm Ramler bis zu seiner Verbindung mit Lessing* (Wolfenbüttel: Zwissler, 1886);

Johann Heinrich Voß, *Über Götz und Ramler: Kritische Briefe* (Mannheim: Schwan & Goetz, 1809);

Herbert Zeman, *Die deutsche anakreontische Dichtung* (Stuttgart: Metzler, 1972).

Papers:

Karl Wilhelm Ramler's papers are in the Goethe-und Schillerarchiv, Weimar; the Nachlaß Johann Georg Zimmermann, Landesbibliothek Hannover; the Literaturarchiv der Akademie der Wissenschaften der DDR, Berlin; the Nachlaß Friedlich Nicolai in the Staatsbibliothek Preußischer Kulturbesitz, Berlin; and the Bibliotheka Jagiellonska, Krakow, Poland.

Christian Friedrich Daniel Schubart

(24 March 1739 - 10 October 1791)

Debra L. Stoudt
University of Toledo

BOOKS: *Nänie auf das Erdbeben in Lissabon* (Schwabach, 1755);

Der gute Fürst, eine Ode auf Antonius Ignatius, Probst zu Ellwangen, anonymous (N.p., 1762);

Der Tod Franciscus des ersten römischen Kaisers (Ulm: Bartholomäi, 1765);

Den Tod eines ehrenvollen Greisen . . . Georg Friedrich Hörners . . . sollte besingen dessen Enkel Christian Friedrich Daniel Schubart (Ulm: Wagner, 1765);

Die Baadcur (Ulm: Bartholomäi, 1766);

Ode auf des Grafen von Degenfeld-Schomburg Hochgräfliche Excellenz (Ulm: Wagner, 1766);

Ode auf den Tod des Herrn Hof- und Regierungsrath Abbt in Bükeburg (Ulm: Bartholomäi, 1766);

Zaubereien (Ulm: Bartholomäi, 1766);

Todesgesänge (Ulm: Bartholomäi, 1767); excerpts published as *Todesgesänge: Geringere, zum Besten des gemeinen Mannes veranstaltete Ausgabe* (Ulm: Bartholomäi, 1767);

Ein Brautlied auf die Klettische und Mannerische Verbindung, welche zu Geißlingen den 27ten September 1768 vergnügt vollzogen wurde, gesungen von einem alten Nachbar, anonymous (Ulm: Wagner, 1768);

Empfindungen bey der Wahl des Hochwürdigsten Fürsten Antonius Ignatius gefürsteten Probsten und Herrn zu Ellwangen, zum Fürsten und Bischoffe

Christian Friedrich Daniel Schubart

233

des hohen Bißtums Regensburg (Ulm: Wagner, 1769);

Würtembergs Genius: Am Höchsten Geburtsfest des Durchlauchtigsten Herzogs (Ludwigsberg: Cotta, 1772);

Deutsche Chronik, 2 volumes (volume 1, Augsburg: Stage, 1774; volume 2, Ulm: Wagner, 1775); continued as *Teutsche Chronik*, 2 volumes (Ulm: Wagner, 1776-1777); reprinted, edited by Hans Krauss as *Deutsche Chronik*, 4 volumes (Heidelberg: Schneider, 1975);

An Herrn Diakonus Hoyer in Aalen, am Tage seiner Vermählung mit meiner Schwester Jungfer Jacobina Dorothea Schubart (Augsburg: Bils, 1774);

*Der Geist Klemens XIV. samt einer Lobrede auf diesen großen Pabst und dem Schreiben des Herzogs von Kumberland aus Rom an die Lady ** in London . . . als ein Anhang zum Leben Pabsts Klemens XIV.*, anonymous (London [actually Nuremberg: Raspe], 1775);

An Herrn StadtAmman Häkhel beym Tode seines Vaters des Reichs-Stadt-Ulmischen Caßiers Herrn Häkhels den 10. Jänner 1775 (Ulm: Wagner, 1775);

Rabners Mantel: Als Herr Wolbach die Jungfer Frikinn freite (Ulm: Wagner, 1775);

Neujahrsschilde in Versen, ausgehängt im Jenner 1775, anonymous (Augsburg: Von Jenisch, 1775);

Threnodie auf den Tod des Herrn Stadtammann Häckhels in Ulm (Ulm: Wagner, 1775);

Neueste Geschichte der Welt oder Denkwürdigste aus allen vier Welttheilen . . . auf das Jahr 1775: Vierter Theil, anonymous (Augsburg: Stage, 1776);

Leben des Freyherrn von Ikstadt Churfürstlichen Bairischen Geheimden Raths (Ulm: Stettin, 1776);

Lied des berühmten Zettelträgers und Tambours Friedrich, anonymous (Ulm: Wagner, 1776);

Thalias Opfer: Ein Vorspiel (Ulm: Wagner, 1776);

Prolog für Demoiselle Reichard, als Emilia Galotti (N.p., 1776);

Kurzgefaßtes Lehrbuch der schönen Wissenschaften von Herrn Professor Schubart: Herausgegeben von einem seiner ehemaligen Zuhörer, edited by Christian Gottlob Ebner (Münster: Perrenon, 1777); excerpts published as *Vorlesungen über Mahlerey, Kupferstecherkunst, Bildhauerkunst und Tanzkunst von Herrn Professor Schubart: Herausgegeben von einem seiner ehemaligen Zuhörer* (Münster: Perrenon, 1777); original edition republished as *Vorlesungen über die schönen Wissenschaften für Unstudierte von Herrn Professor Schubart: Herausgegeben von einem sei-*

ner ehemaligen Zuhörer (Münster: Perrenon, 1777); revised and enlarged as *Kurzgefaßtes Lehrbuch der schönen Wissenschaften: Zwote ganz umgearbeitete und vermehrte Auflage* (Münster, Osnabrück & Hamm: Perrenon, 1781);

Originalien (Augsburg: Bartholomäi, 1780);

Todengesang ihrem Vater und Führer dem Hochwohlgebohrnen Herrn, HERRN Philipp Friedrich von Rieger, Herzoglich-Würtembergischen Generalmaior, Befehlshaber eines Infanteriebatallion, Kommendanten der Vestung Hohenasperg und Rittern des St. Karlordens, in tiefster Rührung geweiht von den sämtlichen Offiziers seines Batallions, anonymous (Stuttgart: Erhard, 1782);

Etwas für Clavier und Gesang (Winterthur: Steiner, 1783);

Klaggesang an mein Klavier auf die Nachricht von Minettens Tod: Herausgegeben und den Liebhabern des Gesanges gewidmet von Ch. F. W. Nopitsch (Augsburg: Stage, 1783);

Grabgesang Sr. Hochwohlgebohrn Herrn Jacob von Scheeler Herzoglich Wirtembergischen General-Major, Chef eines Infanterie-Regiments und Ritter des St. Karlordens: Der am 23sten März plötzlich am Schlage starb, von sämtlichen Offiziers seines Regiments, anonymous (Stuttgart: Cotta, 1784);

Klage der Wehmuth am Grabe Des zärtlichsten Gemahls und besten Vaters Herrn General-Majors von Scheeler (Stuttgart: Cotta, 1784);

Gedichte aus dem Kerker (Zurich: Orell, Geßner & Füßli, 1785);

C. F. D. Schubarts Sämtliche Gedichte: Von ihm selbst herausgegeben, 2 volumes (Stuttgart: Buchdrukkerei der Herzoglichen Hohen Carls-Schule, 1785-1786);

Nachricht ans Publikum (N.p., 1785);

Friedrich der Einzige: Ein Obelisk (Stuttgart: Buchdruckerei der Herzoglichen Hohen Carls-Schule, 1786);

Friedrich der Große: Ein Hymnus (Berlin, 1786);

An Friedrich Wilhelm den Zweiten (Dillingen: Kälin, 1786);

Die Gruft der Fürsten (Berlin, 1786);

Christian Friedrich Daniel Schubarts Musicalische Rhapsodien, 3 volumes (Stuttgart: Buchdrukkerei der Herzoglichen Hohen Carls-Schule, 1786);

Vaterländische Chronik (Stuttgart: Verlag des kaiserlichen Reichspostamtes, 1787); continued as *Vaterlandschronik*, 2 volumes (Stuttgart: Verlag des kaiserlichen Reichspostamtes, 1788-1789); continued as *Chronik*, 2 volumes (Stuttgart: Verlag des kaiserlichen Reichspostamtes, 1790-1791);

Der Durchlauchtigsten Herzogin Franciska, an Ihrem Wiegenfest geweiht (Frankfurt am Main, 1787);

Zwey Kaplieder (N.p., 1787);

Neujahrswünsche für das Jahr 1788 (Stuttgart: Mäntler, 1787);

Danubius et Nekrinos ein Bardenhymenäus (Vienna: Wappler, 1788);

Die Stunde der Geburt: Ein Prolog auf das Geburtsfest des Herzogs von Wirtemberg (N.p., 1788);

Treize Variations pour le Clavecin ou Pianoforte (Spire: Bossler, 1788);

Der Greis: Ein Prolog mit Gesang. Am Höchsten Namensfeste Unsers Durchlauchtigsten Herzogs Karl (N.p., 1789);

Der schön Herbst-Tag: Auf das Namensfest der Herzogin Franzisca von Würtemberg. Eine Poesie (N.p., 1789);

Neujahrswünsche für das Jahr 1790 (Stuttgart, 1789);

Dem General von Bouwinghausen (N.p., 1790);

Lied einer Mutter: Musikalischer Potpourri, für Liebhaber des Gesangs und Klaviers (Stuttgart, 1790);

Die gute Mutter, auf das Geburtsfest der Herzogin Franziska von Wirtemberg (N.p., 1790);

Oper an dem großen Nationalfest der Krönung Kaiser Leopold's des Zweyten: In drey Gedichten (Frankfurt am Main, 1790);

Prolog am Namensfeste Unsers Durchlauchtigsten Herzogs Carl von Wirtemberg (Stuttgart: Herzogliche Akademische Buchdruckerei, 1790);

Der Tempel der Dankbarkeit: Ein Opfer. Am höchsten Geburtsfeste des durchlauchtigsten Herzogs Karl (N.p., 1790);

Schubart's Leben und Gesinnungen: Von ihm selbst, im Kerker aufgesetzt, 2 volumes, volume 2 edited by Ludwig Schubart (Stuttgart: Mäntler, 1791-1793; edited by Claus Träger, Leipzig: Deutscher Verlag für Musik, 1980);

Nekrine: Ein Prolog auf das Namensfest Der Durchlauchtigsten Herzogin Franziska von Wirtemberg (Stuttgart: Herzogliche Akademische Buchdruckerei, 1791);

Neujahrsvision an General Bouwinghausen (N.p., 1791);

Schubart's Vatersegen, an seiner Tochter Juliane Kaufmann, fünfundzwanzigstem Geburtstage (N.p., 1791);

Wetteifer der Liebe, Freundschaft und Hochachtung am Tage Franziskas: Eine Kantate (Stuttgart: Herzogliche Akademische Buchdruckerei, 1791);

Herrn Christian Friedrich Schubart's Abschied an seine Gattin in einer Krankheit auf der Feste Hohenasperg: Zum Singen beym Klavier durchaus in Musik gesetzt (Bregenz: Brentano, 1800);

Gedichte, 2 volumes, edited by Ludwig Schubart (Frankfurt am Main: Hermann, 1802);

Christ. Fried. Dan. Schubart's Ideen zu einer Ästhetik der Tonkunst, edited by Ludwig Schubart (Vienna: Degen, 1806; reprinted, Leipzig: Reclam, 1977);

Vermischte Schriften, edited by Ludwig Schubart, 2 volumes (Zurich: Geßner, 1812);

Sämmtliche Gedichte von Christian Friedrich Daniel Schubart, 3 volumes, edited by W. E. Weber (Frankfurt am Main: Hermann, 1825);

Ausgewählte Gedichte, Cabinets-bibliothek der deutschen Classiker, 63 (Hildburghausen: Bibliographisches Institut, 1834);

C. F. D. Schubart's, des Patrioten, gesammelte Schriften und Schicksale, 8 volumes, edited by Ludwig Schubart (Stuttgart: Scheible, 1839-1840; reprinted, 4 volumes, Hildesheim & New York: Olms, 1972);

Sämtliche Gedichte, 2 volumes (Stuttgart: Scheible, Rieger & Sattler, 1842);

Gedichte: Historisch-kritische Ausgabe, edited by Gustav Hauff (Leipzig: Reclam, 1884);

Gedichte, edited by Heinrich Solger (Halle: Hendel, 1900);

Schuldiktate Schubarts während seiner Wirksamkeit an der Geislinger Schule 1763-69, edited by G. Fehleisen (Tübingen: Verlag des Schwäbischen Albvereins, 1929);

Schubarts Werke in einem Band, edited by Ursula Wertheim and Hans Böhm (Berlin & Weimar: Aufbau, 1959);

C. F. D. Schubart, Strophen für die Freiheit. Eine Auswahl aus den Werken und Briefen, edited by Peter Härtling (Stuttgart: Deutsche Verlags-Anstalt, 1976);

Gedichte: Aus der "Deutschen Chronik," edited by Ulrich Karthaus (Stuttgart: Reclam, 1978).

OTHER: J. F. Herel, *Drey Satiren: Aus dem Lateinischen*, translated by Schubart (Altenburg, 1767);

Herel, *Auszug aus Herrn Herels kritischen Sendschreiben an Herrn Meusel in Halle die Aufnahme seiner Satiren in Moropolis betreffend: Aus dem Lateinischen*, translated by Schubart (Altenburg, 1768);

Friedrich Gottlieb Klopstock, *Kleine poetische und prosaische Werke*, 2 volumes, edited by Schu-

bart (Frankfurt am Main & Leipzig: Verlag
der Neuen Buchhändlergesellschaft, 1771);

C. H. Korn, *Leben Klemens des XIV. Römischen
Pabsts*, introduction by Schubart (Berlin &
Leipzig, 1775);

Der wahre Priester: Pardon all but thyself, edited by
Schubart (N.p., 1775);

L. Foch, *Abhandlung vom Straß enbau*, foreword by
Schubart (Augsburg, 1776);

L. P. Hahn, *Der Aufruhr zu Pisa: Ein Trauerspiel in
fünf Aufzügen*, foreword by Schubart (Ulm:
Wohler, 1776);

Eberhard Friedrich Hübner, *Franz von der Trenk,
Pandurenobrist: Dargestellt von einem Unparthei-
ischen*, 3 volumes, preface by Schubart (Stuttgart: Mäntler, 1788-1790);

*Ueber die Vereinigung der christlichen Religionspar-
teyen: Von einem altchristlichen Wahrheitsfor-
scher. Mit einem Vorbericht*, edited by Schubart
(Stuttgart, 1788);

P. Anfossi, *Die glücklichen Reisenden: Eine Operette
aus dem Italienischen*, revised by Schubart
(Stuttgart: Buchdruckerei der Herzoglichen
Hohen Carls-Schule, 1789);

J. F. Schlotterbeck, *Fabeln und Erzählungen nach
Phädrus, und in eigener Manier: Erstes Bändchen*, foreword by Schubart (Stuttgart: Buchdruckerei der Herzoglichen Hohen Carls-
Schule, 1790).

Christian Friedrich Daniel Schubart is important to eighteenth-century German literature less
for his own literary output than for his influence
on other writers and on the German people as a
whole. This influence took both a literary and a
political form: for writers of his period Schubart
served as a literary critic and the source of dramatic themes; to the German people he gave the
impetus for the awakening of national pride.
Schubart has been described as a poet, a journalist, a musician, and a rebel. He is most famous as
the prisoner in the fortress Hohenasperg, but as
the editor of and sole contributor to the *Deutsche
Chronik* (1774-1777), a journal established as a
commentary on the current political scene, he
gained acclaim and achieved success as a writer.

Schubart was born in Obersontheim in Fran-
conia on 24 March 1739, the eldest of five children. His father, Johann Jacob Schubart, was a
teacher and musician. Within a year of Schubart's
birth the family moved to Aalen, in Swabia,
where his father accepted the positions of preceptor and music director.

*Title page for the journal in which Schubart commented on
the current political scene*

In 1753 Schubart went to Nördlingen to attend the Latin school. In Nördlingen he became
acquainted with the works of Friedrich Gottlieb
Klopstock, especially the odes, which had a profound influence on Schubart's early poetic efforts. In 1756 Schubart moved to Nuremberg to
continue his studies. The political upheaval of
the time and the beginning of the Seven Years'
War awakened Schubart's national consciousness
and kindled his great admiration for Prussia, particularly for King Frederick II.

To follow in his father's footsteps and prepare for the ministry, Schubart was to study theology in Jena; but because of the war he went instead to Erlangen in 1758. There his dissolute
life-style led to debts, for which he was imprisoned, and within two years he was forced to return to Aalen for financial as well as health reasons. From 1760 to 1763 he was employed as
a preacher, composer, organist, and private
teacher in and around Aalen. In October 1763
he applied for and was granted a teaching posi-

tion in Geislingen, where he met and married Helen Bühler. They had five children, two of whom–Ludwig and Julie–survived to adulthood. The marriage was a stormy and unhappy one.

The position in Geislingen was unremunerative, and the work was not to Schubart's liking. He became more involved in literary activities, publishing his first poems and contributing to the weekly political journal *Der Neue Rechtschaffene* (The New Honest Man). In 1769 an increased interest in music and dissatisfaction with his teaching position led Schubart to move to Ludwigsburg, where he became the organist and music director at the court of Duke Karl Eugen of Württemberg. Although he was renowned for his fine organ playing, Schubart's success was short-lived. Imprudent remarks led to disputes with the church superintendent, Sebastian Zilling, and a satirical poem and a parody on the litany as well as his moral laxity brought Schubart into conflict with other religious officials at the court. He was jailed on a charge of adultery but released after his wife intervened on his behalf. On 21 May 1773 Schubart was banished from Württemberg. His wife and children returned to Geislingen, and Schubart journeyed to various cities in southern Germany. In Mannheim a Bavarian envoy offered him a position in Munich on the condition that he convert to Catholicism. Schubart accepted and spent several months at the court of Freiherr von Leyden, but his failure to convert and the arrival of news from Württemberg regarding his exploits at that court brought about his abrupt departure from Munich.

In 1774 Schubart traveled to Augsburg, where he began work on the *Deutsche Chronik* with the publisher Konrad Heinrich Stage. Because of censorship problems, publication of the journal was transferred to Ulm in May 1774; by the end of the year Schubart had moved to Ulm, primarily because of his opposition to the Jesuits, and in 1775 his family joined him there. In the following two years the *Deutsche Chronik* gained in popularity, but Schubart continued to come into conflict with those in authority. His attacks on the former Jesuit priest J. J. Gaßner increased the tension between Schubart and that religious order, which, although banned in 1773, still wielded great influence in Augsburg and Ulm.

On 22 January 1777 a monastic official named Scholl invited Schubart to visit Blaubeuren, near Ulm. Once on Württemberg soil Schubart was arrested; on 24 January he was placed in the fortress Hohenasperg near Stuttgart. The motive behind his imprisonment remains unclear. In his autobiography Schubart emphasizes the role of the Austrian ambassador to Ulm, Baron von Ried, whom he had offended. The more probable instigator was the duke himself, who, since Schubart's days in Ludwigsburg, had harbored ill will toward the musician-poet. Karl Eugen's purpose, apparently, was to make an example of Schubart, thereby demonstrating the consequences of personal attacks on the duke. Although Karl Eugen granted Schubart his freedom in 1784, the writer was not released for another three years. The confinement was quite austere at first, but Schubart was granted more and more liberty in the course of his imprisonment. In the final years of his incarceration the Ducal Academy even published several editions of his poems.

On his release Schubart went to Stuttgart, where he became the director of the court theater and the opera; by employing Schubart in Stuttgart, Karl Eugen was able to keep a watchful eye on him. The new theater director also revived his journal, renaming it the *Vaterländische Chronik*. Schubart died of apoplexy on 10 October 1791.

Schubart was a man of many talents, but he did not possess the resoluteness to bring his plans to fruition; thus, many of his major undertakings remained fragments, and few of his works were published during his lifetime. His earliest works were poems written in Aalen from 1760 to 1763 and in Geislingen, and are largely of two types: odes which betray the influence of Klopstock, and simpler poems, usually characterized as folk songs. In 1771 Schubart published a collection of Klopstock's odes; Klopstock, who himself had not yet had the works published, was quite displeased, since several of the odes were not genuine and there were many printing errors.

Schubart wrote *Die Gruft der Fürsten* (The Tomb of the Princes, 1786) and *Friedrich der Große* (Frederick the Great, 1786) during his imprisonment. The former, a denunciation of princes who abuse their power, contributed to the extension of Schubart's incarceration; the latter, a panegyric to the recently deceased Prussian king, helped obtain the poet's release. One of the poems in *Zwey Kaplieder* (Two Cape Songs, 1787) is a commentary on the sale by the duke of a Württemberg regiment to the Dutch East India Company; the soldiers bid farewell to their home-

Schubart's arrest, probably at the instigation of Duke Karl
Eugen of Württemberg, in January 1777; he spent the next
ten years as a prisoner in the fortress Hohenasperg,
near Stuttgart

land as they are sent to the Cape of Good Hope. Only a few short collections of Schubart's poems, most of which deal with politics and religion, were published during his lifetime.

It has been suggested that Schubart experienced a spiritual conversion in Hohenasperg, since religion played such an important role in the autobiography he began in the fortress in 1788. At first denied pencil and paper, Schubart dictated his thoughts to a fellow prisoner. Four years after his release, in the year of his death, Schubart published the first volume of *Schubart's Leben und Gesinnungen* (Schubart's Life and Opinions); his son published the second volume in 1793. The first volume deals with Schubart's life until his imprisonment, the second with the years in Hohenasperg. In addition to his autobiography, Schubart's letters offer insight into his charac-

ter; these were edited and published in 1849 by David Friedrich Strauß.

Schubart's creative genius turned to several themes which, although they remained undeveloped or underdeveloped by him, flourished in the hands of other artists. Perhaps the best-known adoption is Friedrich Schiller's use of Schubart's "Zur Geschichte des menschenlichen Herzens" (Concerning the Story of the Human Heart) as the basis for his play *Die Räuber* (The Robbers, 1781). "Der ewige Jude" (The Eternal Jew), a brief but popular lyric poem, was translated and published twice in England in the first decade of the nineteenth century; both Lord Byron and Percy Bysshe Shelley employed the theme of the wandering Jew is their own works. The Russian dramatist Denis Fonvizin borrowed several fables which appeared in the *Deutsche Chronik*. In music Schubart's name may be linked with that of one of his most famous contemporaries, Franz Schubert. The composer set to music several of Schubart's poems, among them "Die Forelle" (The Trout), "An den Tod" (To Death), and "An mein Klavier" (To My Piano).

Schubart himself set several of his poems to music, including "Die Forelle," as well as several works by Gottfried August Bürger; in all, he composed some eighty songs, as well as several sonatas, an opera, and a cantata. His widespread acclaim won him the position as court organist in Ludwigsburg; in his autobiography Schubart claims that the congregation came only to hear him play, leaving before the sermon. Between court or teaching positions Schubart supported himself by giving private music lessons, and even during his imprisonment he was permitted to give lessons to the officers' daughters and to direct performances by the soldiers. His posthumously published *Ideen zu einer Ästhetik der Tonkunst* (Ideas toward an Aesthetics of Music, 1806) is a collection of essays rather than a coherent treatise. The first section offers a sketch of the history of music; in the second section Schubart introduces the foundations of harmony and describes each instrument and its musical characteristics. The work closes with a brief discussion of song, musical genius, and musical expression.

Of Schubart's many abilities, his talents as a journalist were his greatest strength. The publisher Stage had just suffered the failure of the *Schwäbisches Journal* when he approached Schubart with the idea of founding a new journal; it had been Schubart's dream to start a

Pastel drawing of Schubart, artist and date unknown (Schiller-Nationalmuseum, Marbach am Neckar)

paper which would inform all of Germany about political and literary events, and he eagerly accepted Stage's offer to write the *Deutsche Chronik*. The chronicle appeared twice weekly from 1774 to 1777. Schubart wrote all the entries himself, using newspapers, books, and other periodicals as his sources; indeed, some of the early articles were copied verbatim from these sources. Schubart refers to several correspondents, but many of these were fictitious. The *Deutsche Chronik* was a mosaic of reports on political events, reviews of literature and music, and lyric and prose pieces by Schubart himself. Among the literary works reviewed by Schubart were several by Christoph Martin Wieland and Johann Wolfgang Goethe's *Götz von Berlichingen* (1773), *Die Leiden des jungen Werthers* (The Sorrows of Young Werther, 1774), *Clavigo* (1774), *Iphigenie auf Tauris* (Iphigenia on Tauris, 1787), and *Torquato Tasso* (1790). The stated goal of the paper was to comment on the German political scene, but the focus soon broadened to include France, England, Russia, Poland, and America. The reports were totally subjective, revealing Schubart's great love of his homeland and calling for national unity and freedom. The *Deutsche Chronik* included articles on Schubart's religious views as well, especially his condemnation of the Jesuits. With Schubart's arrest in 1777 Konrad

Friedrich Köhler and Johann Martin Miller took over the journal; Köhler left after a short time, but Miller continued from January 1777 until the fall of that year, at which time the circulation had dwindled to six hundred, and another editor took over. Publication ceased soon afterward.

In June 1787, six weeks after his release from prison, Schubart obtained permission to begin work on the *Vaterländische Chronik*. Subscriptions soon rose to four thousand, a remarkable number for the time; indeed, Schubart was one of the few eighteenth-century journalists who was able to support himself from work on a periodical. In 1788 he changed the name of the journal to *Vaterlandschronik*. By that time the journal had become almost exclusively political in nature and was embroiled in controversy, with the state of Pfalz-Bayern banning it in March 1788. In May 1791 Karl Eugen imposed a censorship decree on the *Chronik*, as the periodical was then called. After Schubart's death in October 1791 his son Ludwig and Gotthold Friedrich Stäudlin assumed editorship, but shortly thereafter Ludwig obtained a position in Nuremberg. Stäudlin continued as editor until April 1793, when publication ended.

Christian Friedrich Daniel Schubart was a controversial and contradictory figure, whose actions were at times the cause of personal misfortune. Through his poetic works and critical reviews Schubart influenced some of the greatest writers of his day, and through his journalistic endeavors he contributed to the awakening of the German national consciousness.

Letters:

Christian Friedrich Daniel Schubart's Leben in seinen Briefen, 2 volumes, edited by David Friedrich Strauß (Berlin: Duncker, 1849; revised edition, Bonn: Strauß, 1878; reprinted, Königstein: Scriptor, 1978);

Schubart und seine Tochter Julie: Mit ungedruckten Briefen und Versen, edited by Rudolf Krauß (N.p., 1900);

"Neue Briefe von Schubart I: Briefe Schubarts an seine Gattin von Asperg nach Stuttgart," edited by Krauß, *Euphorion*, 8 (1901): 77-102;

"Neue Briefe von Schubart II: Briefe Schubarts an seinen Sohn Ludwig," edited by Krauß, *Euphorion*, 8 (1901): 285-300;

Schubarts Briefe, edited by Ursula Wertheim and Hans Böhm (Munich: Beck, 1984).

Schubart in 1789; painting by Friedrich Oelenhainz (Gemälde-galerie, Stuttgart)

Bibliography:

Winfried B. Lerg, "Neue Schubartiana–Quellen und Literatur," *Publizistik*, 31 (1986): 237-242.

Biographies:

Ludwig Schubart, *Schubarts Karakter, von seinem Sohne* (Erlangen, 1798);

Gustav Hauff, *Schubart in seinem Leben und seinen Werken* (Stuttgart: Kohlhammer, 1885);

Eugen Nägele, *Aus Schubarts Leben und Wirken: Mit einem Anhang: Schubarts Erstlingswerke und Schuldiktate* (Stuttgart: Kohlhammer, 1888);

Karl Maria Klob, *Schubart: Ein deutsches Dichter- und Kulturbild* (Ulm: Kerler, 1908);

Siegfried Nestriepke, *Schubart als Dichter: Ein Beitrag zur Kenntnis C. F. D. Schubarts* (Pössneck: Feigenspan, 1910);

Hermann Hesse and Karl Isenberg, eds., *C. F. D. Schubart: Dokumente seines Lebens* (Berlin: Fischer, 1926);

Konrad Gaiser, *C. F. D. Schubart; Schicksal, Zeitbild, ausgewählte Schriften* (Stuttgart: Steinkopf, 1929);

Ulrich Bertram Staudenmayer, ed., *Christian Friedrich Daniel Schubart–ein schwäbischer Rebell. C. F. D. Schubarts Leben und Gesinnungen*, Schwäbische Lebensläufe, 1 (Heidenheim: Heidenheimer Verlagsanstalt, 1969);

Wilfried F. Schoeller, ed., *Schubart: Leben und Meinungen eines schwäbischen Rebellen, den die Rache seines Fürsten auf den Asperg brachte. Mit einer Auswahl seiner Schriften* (Berlin: Wagenbach, 1979);

Kurt Honolka, *Schubart: Dichter und Musiker, Journalist und Rebell. Sein Leben, sein Werk* (Stuttgart: Deutsche Verlagsanstalt, 1985).

References:

Bernhard Bosch, "Schubart und Schiller," *Schwäbischer Schillerverein Marbach-Stuttgart*, 37 (1932-1933): 13-69;

W. Brüstle, *Klopstock und Schubart: Beziehungen in Leben und Dichten* (Augsburg: Reichel, 1917);

Jean Clédière, "La *Deutsche Chronik* de Schubart," *Etudes germaniques*, 33 (January-March 1978): 70-72;

Clédière, "Ideal cosmopolite, vertus allemandes et image de la France dans la 'Deutsche Chronik' de Schubart," *Revue d'Allemagne*, 18 (1986): 674-691;

Walther Dürr, "Schuberts Lied 'An den Tod' (D518): zensiert?" *Österreichische Musikzeitschrift*, 38 (1983): 9-17;

E. Ebstein, "Schubart und Bürger: Ein neuer Beitrag zu Bürgers Gedichten in der Musik," *Zeitschrift für Bücherfreunde*, 12 (April 1908): 34-39;

Wilhelm Feldmann, "Christian Schubarts Sprache," *Zeitschrift für deutsche Wortforschung*, 11 (1907): 97-149;

Guy Stanton Ford, "Two German publicists on the American Revolution," *Journal of English and Germanic Philology*, 8 (1909): 145-176;

Konrad Gaiser, "Christian Friedrich Daniel Schubart," in *Schwäbische Lebensbilder*, volume 1, edited by Hermann Haering and Otto Hohenstatt (Stuttgart: Kohlhammer, 1940), pp. 492-509;

Gaiser, "Schubart im Exorzistenstreit," *Euphorion*, 28 (1927): 564-595;

H. Grasshoff, "Eine deutsche Parallele der *Lisica-koznodej* (Fonvizin und Schubart)," *Zeitschrift für Slawistik*, 7 (1962): 167-174;

R. W. Harpster, "Genius in the 18th Century: C. F. D. Schubart's 'Vom musikalischen Genie,'" *Current Musicology*, 15 (1973): 73-77;

Peter Härtling, "Ein Rebell im Rokoko: Über Christian Friedrich Daniel Schubart," *Der Monat*, 20 (October 1968): 59-66;

Peter Hoffmann, "Unbeachtete Äusserungen Ch. F. D. Schubarts über den Bauernkrieg in Rußland 1773-1775," *Zeitschrift für Slawistik*, 15 (1970): 900-910;

Ernst Holzer, *Schubart als Musiker*, Darstellungen aus der Württembergischen Geschichte, 2 (Stuttgart: Kohlhammer, 1905);

Holzer, "Schubartiana," *Württembergische Vierteljahresheft für Landesgeschichte*, 15 (1906): 558-571;

Hans-Wolf Jäger, "Von Ruten: Über Schubarts Gedicht 'Die Forelle,' " in *Gedichte und Interpretationen*, volume 2, edited by Karl Richter (Stuttgart: Reclam, 1983), pp. 372-385;

M. Roxana Klapper, *The German Literary Influence on Shelley*, Romantic Reassessment, 43 (Salzburg: Institut für englische Sprache und Literatur, Universität Salzburg, 1975);

Hans Gerd Klein, "Deutsche Chronik (1774-1793)," in *Deutsche Zeitschriften des 17. bis 20. Jahrhunderts*, edited by Heinz-Dietrich Fischer, Publizistik-historische Beiträge, 3 (Munich: Verlag Dokumentation, 1973), pp. 103-113;

Gerard Kozielek, "Das Polenbild in Schubarts 'Deutscher Chronik,' " *Weimarer Beiträge*, 29 (1983): 2175-2182;

Hans Joachim Krämer, "Schubart und Ludwigsburg," *Ludwigsburger Geschichtsblätter*, 33 (1981): 25-40;

Rudolf Krauß, "Schubart als Stuttgarter Theaterdirektor," *Württembergische Vierteljahrshefte für Landesgeschichte*, 19 (1901): 252-279;

Michael Mann, "Die Turmbesteigung: Notizen zu Chr. Fr. D. Schubart," in *Festschrift für Bernhard Blume: Aufsätze zur deutschen und europäischen Literatur*, edited by Egon Schwarz, Hunter G. Hannum, and Edgar Lohner (Göttingen: Vandenhoeck & Ruprecht, 1967), pp. 76-80;

Eduard Metis, "C. F. D. Schubart als Journalist," *Neue Jahrbücher für das klassische Altertum, Geschichte und deutsche Literatur und für Pädagogik*, 19 (1916): 609-612;

Günter Moltmann, "Schubarts *Kaplied* von 1787 und die Entstehung des weltlichen Auswandererliedes in Deutschland," *Yearbook of German-American Studies*, 22 (1987): 21-37;

Hartmut Müller, *Postgaul und Flügelroß: Der Journalist C. F. D. Schubart (1739-1791)*, Europäi-

sche Hochschulschriften, 846 (Frankfurt am Main: Lang, 1985);

Walter E. Schäfer, "Anekdotische Erzählformen und der Begriff Anekdote im Zeitalter der Aufklärung," *Zeitschrift für deutsche Philologie*, 104, no. 1 (1985): 185-204;

Erich Schairer, *C. F. D. Schubart als politischer Journalist* (Tübingen: Mohr, 1914);

Schairer, "C. F. D. Schubart 1739-1791," in *Deutsche Publizisten des 15. bis 20. Jahrhunderts*, edited by Heinz-Dietrich Fischer (Munich & Berlin: Verlag Dokumentation, 1971), pp. 118-128;

Wilfried F. Schoeller, *C. F. D. Schubart. Dichter und Staatsmann* (Berlin: Wagenbach, 1978);

Christhard Schrenk, *Schubart-Sammlung* (Aalen: Stadtarchiv, 1985);

Jürgen Schröder, "Facit iracundia versum. C. F. D. Schubart: 'Die Fürstengruft,' " in *Geschichte im Gedicht: Texte und Interpretationen (Protestlied, Bänkelsang, Ballade, Chronik)*, edited by Walter Hinck (Frankfurt am Main: Suhrkamp, 1979), pp. 59-73;

Carl Schüddekopf, "Schubart und Gleim," *Euphorion*, 2 (1895): 571-578;

Wolfgang Suppan, "Zum Problem der Trivialisierung der Volkslieder im Volksmund," in *Das Triviale in Literatur, Musik und bildender Kunst*, edited by Helga de la Motte-Haber (Frankfurt am Main: Klostermann, 1972), pp. 148-162;

Eduard Thorn, "Christian Schubart und seine Tochter Julchen, nach ungedruckten Briefen," *Der Kreis*, 7 (1930): 329-337;

Werner Volke, "Christian Friedrich Daniel Schubart," in *Literatur im deutschen Südwesten*, edited by Bernhard Zeller (Stuttgart: Theiss, 1987), pp. 59-71;

John A. Walz, "Three Swabian Journalists and the American Revolution," *Germanic American Annals*, 1 (1903): 209-224, 257-274, 347-356, 406-419, 593-600;

Albert Walzer, *Katalog des Heimats- und Schubartmuseums Aalen* (Aalen: Heimat- und Schubart-Museum, 1936);

F. I. Wiener, "Schubart's Conversion," *German Life and Letters*, 8 (1954-1955): 273-284;

Adolf Wohlwill, "Beiträge zur Kenntniss C. F. D. Schubarts," *Archiv für Literaturgeschichte*, 6 (1877): 343-391;

Wohlwill, "Neue kleine Beiträge zur Kenntniss C. F. D. Schubarts," *Archiv für Literaturgeschichte*, 15 (1887): 21-36, 126-159;

Wohlwill, "Schiller und Schubart," *Marbacher Schillerbuch* (1904): 269-282;

Wohlwill, "Schubartiana," *Archiv für das Studium der neueren Sprachen und Literaturen*, 87 (1891): 1-32;

Wohlwill, "Schubartiana," *Euphorion*, 2 (1895): 798-806;

Wohlwill, "Zur Schubart-Biographie," *Euphorion*, 16 (1909): 349-360;

Wolfgang Zorn, "Reichs- und Freiheitsgedanken in der deutschen Publizistik des ausgehenden achtzehnten Jahrhunderts," in *Darstellungen und Quellen zur Geschichte der deutschen Einheitsbewegung im 19. und 20. Jahrhundert*, volume 2: *Männer und Zeiten des Vormärz*, edited by Paul Wentzcke (Heidelberg: Winter, 1959), pp. 34-39.

Papers:

Most of Christian Friedrich Daniel Schubart's papers are in the Schiller-Nationalmuseum Marbach / Deutsches Literaturarchiv. Other important documents are in the Heimat- und Schubart-Museum in Aalen and the Württembergische Landesbibliothek in Stuttgart.

Moritz August von Thümmel

(27 May 1738 - 26 October 1817)

John Van Cleve
Mississippi State University

BOOKS: *Willhelmine, oder Der vermählte Pedant: Ein prosaisches comisches Gedicht*, anonymous (Leipzig, 1764; reprinted, Nendeln, Liechtenstein: Kraus, 1968);

Die Inoculation der Liebe: Eine Erzählung, anonymous (Leipzig, 1771);

Sinngedichte (Frankfurt am Main & Leipzig: Schwickert, 1771);

Kleine poetische Schriften (Frankfurt am Main & Leipzig: Schneider, 1782);

Reise in die mittäglichen Provinzen von Frankreich im Jahr 1785 bis 1786, 10 volumes, anonymous (Leipzig: Göschen, 1791-1805); abridged translation by William Combe as *Journal of Sentimental Travels in the Southern Provinces of France, Shortly before the Revolution* (London: Ackermann, 1821);

Poetische Schriften (Vienna: Schrämbl, 1792);

Sämmtliche Werke, 7 volumes (Leipzig: Göschen, 1811-1819);

Taschenbuch für Damen, 3 volumes (Leipzig: Brockhaus, 1817-1819);

Der heilige Kilian und das Liebes-Paar, edited by Friedrich Ferdinand Hempel (Leipzig: Brockhaus, 1818).

Moritz August von Thümmel participated in the literary Rococo, a tendency in style and theme that recurred in various forms from the 1730s through the first decade of the nineteenth century. The Rococo offered a playful, worldly alternative to the sober rationalism of the dominant movement, the Enlightenment. The erosion of Thümmel's literary reputation during the twentieth century can be attributed in part to fluctuations in the popularity of the Rococo and to the rise in the esteem accorded Christoph Martin Wieland, a writer who is now seen as eclipsing the movement to which he belonged. That rise was well underway by 1909, when a German encyclopedia, *Meyers Konversations-Lexikon*, asserted that Thümmel surpassed Wieland as an observer of society but lagged behind him in stylistic elegance. The article goes on to predict that Thümmel's powers of observation and description, combined with his penchant for frivolity and sensuality, will guarantee a lasting resonance within the reading public. This prophecy has proven incorrect, but familiarity with Thümmel can still lead to a better understanding of the Rococo, of Wieland, and of the beginnings of popular literature. In addition, those interested in the history of taste can learn from the early response to Thümmel. The two titans of Weimar set the stage with brief but positive evaluations. Friedrich Schiller found Thümmel to be a keen analyst of his fellowman both as an individual and as a social creature but found his oeuvre wanting in aesthetic dignity. Johann Wolfgang von Goethe saw in Thümmel an example of the preference of the contemporary reading public for satire that included representatives of the upper classes. Although Goethe's opinion of such satire is ambivalent, he commends Thümmel's comic prose epic *Willhelmine, oder Der vermählte Pedant* (Willhelmine; or, The Pedant Wedded, 1764) as pleasant, bold, and imaginative and notes its great popularity. Thümmel did provide business for publishers: at least a dozen editions of his collected works, several editions of his selected writings, and many printings of individual titles appeared during the nineteenth century.

Thümmel was born into the Saxon aristocracy at the family estate of Schönefeld near Leipzig. He attended the University of Leipzig, where he studied jurisprudence and met several men who were to toil in the trenches, if not lead the charge, for the Enlightenment: Christian Fürchtegott Gellert, Ewald Christian von Kleist, Gottlieb Wilhelm Rabener, and Christian Felix Weiße. In 1761 he took a position as gentleman-in-waiting to the prince of Saxony-Coburg. His career at court was made in 1768 when he was named minister and privy councillor to the new regent of Saxony-Coburg-Gotha, Duke Ernst Friedrich. During the 1770s Thümmel traveled extensively both to serve his ruler and to satisfy his own curiosity. In addition to tours of Austria and Italy, he made two extensive sojourns in France and the Netherlands. In 1779 he married the widow of one of his brothers, and in 1783 he withdrew from public life to devote himself to the maintenance of his estate and to the use of his creative talents.

From Wieland and Laurence Sterne came the themes and narrative structures employed by Thümmel. His first published prose took the form of the comic epic, whose mixture of satire, sensuality, and wit had contributed to Wieland's great popularity. Later Thümmel turned to the subjective travelogue to write the "sentimental journey" of a young Berliner who seeks a cure for debilitating hypochondria. His practice of using the successful formulas of his predecessors indicates a keen interest in popularity, an interest that was becoming a force in German letters during the 1760s and 1770s. It was during those decades that German literature began to divide into parallel traditions: one that retains the original commitment to the edification of the reader in a form harmonious with great literature of the past, modern as well as classical; and another that concerns itself primarily with the entertainment needs of a rapidly growing readership and with the profit margins of the book trade. Prose forms such as the novel and the tale came to dominate the latter tradition, which has been designated "Trivialliteratur" (popular literature). Thümmel stands at the beginning of this literature for mass production and mass consumption, but, with his tie to Wieland, he still has one foot in the earlier tradition.

At age twenty-six Thümmel became an overnight sensation with *Willhelmine*. This short epic or epyllion consists of six "cantos" in rhythmic prose. The central character is Master Sebaldus, the pious, pedantic, naive pastor of a small village not far from the splendid residence of a prince. For four years Sebaldus has pined for Willhelmine, a beautiful, innocent member of his congregation who was carried off to the sophisticated palace by a lascivious seneschal. He has a dream in which Cupid announces that Willhelmine will visit her father the following day, New Year's Day. Cupid advises the pastor to declare his true feelings in the most touching fashion he can devise. The visit is paid; the advice is followed. Willhelmine has the dress and the air of an experienced lady-in-waiting. (Like Wieland, Thümmel devotes special attention to the swelling breasts of his heroines.) She consents to Sebaldus's proposal of marriage and offers as an engagement token a diamond whose setting is a flaming heart. Far from questioning his beloved's possession of such a ring, Sebaldus is enraptured. The couple rushes back to the palace, where they receive the seneschal's blessing to be married immediately. The unsuspecting pastor takes no notice of the mocking laughter that follows his every expression of gratitude. One courtier after another lays costly presents in the bride's lap, and the seneschal himself presents a necklace whose diamond-encrusted cross tumbles into her yawning décolletage. When the wedding guests tarry too long at the pastor's reception Cupid starts a small fire in the pastor's kitchen, and the celebrants flee for their lives. The demigod triumphantly reports his stratagem for saving the bridal night to his mother, whose approbation is supported by that of the Muses.

The rural idyll, the mythological figures, the mild eroticism, and the playful juxtaposition of the naive and the all too experienced are typical of the Rococo. Thümmel uses them with relative restraint to satirize both the aristocracy and the middle class. Within the latter are found both willing tools of the nobility, such as Willhelmine, and fools whose education has produced a pedant's inability to see the forest for the trees and whose piety is an easy target for sophisticates. But Thümmel hardly can be charged with sparing his own class: their insensitivity to the demands of common decency in relations with members of other classes; their voluptuous, decadent life-style; and their sneering, leering lechery make the aristocratic characters decidedly less attractive than the comical couple. This harsh representation is noteworthy because of its relatively early date; not until the 1770s did such portrayals become commonplace. Humor, not consciousness-raising, however, is the writer's objective; the energy and anger of the Sturm und Drang movement are nowhere in evidence. Instead, Thümmel offers the wry detachment of the late Enlightenment, with its cosmopolitan awareness of the limits of reason and virtue.

Thümmel's other major work is the ten-volume *Reise in die mittäglichen Provinzen von Frankreich im Jahr 1785 bis 1786* (1791-1805; translated in abridged form as *Journal of Sentimental Travels in the Southern Provinces of France, Shortly before the Revolution*, 1821), a travelogue written over a decade after the author's own sojourn in France. It is an epistolary novel that purports to be the travel journal that a young Berliner named Wilhelm is keeping for his friend Eduard. To cure his debilitating hypochondria Wilhelm packs his clothes, his books, his servant, and his dog into a coach and sets out for southern France. The journal records his observations, thoughts, and feelings during the journey. Weary of the chaos of big-city life, the painfully sensitive nobleman spends only two days in Paris; but Thümmel's descriptions of the misery endured by the lower classes in the city did much to legitimize the early phases of the French Revolution for German readers. There is little else that a reader would expect of a travelogue. Cities and customs are less important to Wilhelm than self-analysis. Sterne's *Sentimental Journey* (1761) echoes on every page. The traveler loses much of his melancholia on the road, although his infatuation

in Avignon with the duplicitous adventuress Klärchen does expose him to the same treachery in human relations that caused him to flee his many acquaintanceships in Berlin. Still, Wilhelm becomes progressively less egocentric and more involved in the lives of others–and in his own physical nature. Thümmel pokes fun at his hero by having Wilhelm become a gastronome. The traveler's first question about the next stop on the itinerary often concerns the availability of a first-class dining establishment; his depression decreases as his body weight increases. Toward the end of the journey he is drawn to the sweet, loving Agathe; but love and family are not to be Wilhelm's path of escape from self-involvement. When he returns to Germany, melancholia and hypochondria attend him once again.

Thümmel follows Jean-Jacques Rousseau in the perception that modern civilization is an evil to be avoided. Wilhelm, however, responds with a psychic withdrawal that has emotionally and intellectually corrosive results. The only relief to be found is contact with simple, provincial forms of society. Unfortunately for him, Wilhelm's monomaniacal self-absorption filters his impressions of the outside world to such an extent that direct contact with reality beyond self is impossible. This degree of solipsism is reminiscent of Goethe's hero in *Die Leiden des jungen Werthers* (The Sorrows of Young Werther, 1774). But whereas Werther's intellectual and emotional isolation is progressive, self-destructive, and–from the perspective of the reader–tragic, Wilhelm's egocentrism is cyclical, benign, and bathetic. Whether or not he intended to do so, Thümmel casts this representative of his own class as a self-indulgent, if well-intentioned, fool who has nothing better to do than travel about inserting his complex emotional perturbations into the lives of others. The inordinate popularity enjoyed by *Reise in die mittäglichen Provinzen von Frankreich im Jahr 1785 bis 1786* suggests that he found a combination of themes that had broad appeal. Middle-class readers could enjoy the chance to observe a member of the aristocracy at close quarters day after day, an opportunity that is all the more enjoyable when those days bring embarrassing situations and piteous confessions. Aristocratic readers would want to test the verisimilitude of Wilhelm's personality and actions. The work also satisfied nonclass-specific predilections for sensuality; for exposés of the scandalous living conditions endured by many; and for descriptions of foreign places, especially prerevolutionary France. When the comic element is taken into account, the status of *Reise in die mittäglichen Provinzen von Frankreich im Jahr 1785 bis 1786* as an archetype for the popular novel can be appreciated. Its greatest weakness is its length; the modern reader will weary of Wilhelm, whose tale offers no timeless truths to the late twentieth century. The novel is significant as an early work in the tradition that subsequently has produced detective novels, romances, science fiction, and other types of literature produced according to set formulas with proven mass appeal.

More significant than either the man or the oeuvre is Thümmel's popularity. Potential popularity in the literary marketplace soon came to be a consideration for all participants in literary life—publishers, editors, authors, and critics. Moritz August von Thümmel, with his ability to produce highly marketable variations on themes created by other writers, was one of a new breed. Its emergence is a significant development in the history of German culture.

Biography:

Horst Heldmann, *Moritz August von Thümmel: Sein Leben. Sein Werk. Seine Zeit. Erster Theil: 1738-1783* (Neustadt / Aisch: Degener, 1964).

References:

Rolf Allerdissen, "Moritz August von Thümmel," in *Deutsche Dichter des 18. Jahrhunderts: Ihr Leben und Werk*, edited by Benno von Wiese (Berlin: Schmidt, 1977), pp. 412-428;

Allerdissen, *Die Reise als Flucht: Zu Schnabels "Insel Felsenburg" und Thümmels "Reise in die mittäglichen Provinzen von Frankreich"* (Bern & Frankfurt am Main: Lang, 1975);

Dieter Kimpel, *Der Roman der Aufklärung* (Stuttgart: Metzler, 1967), pp. 110-112;

Helmut Kreuzer, "Trivialliteratur als Forschungsproblem: Zur Kritik des deutschen Trivialromans seit der Aufklärung," in his *Veränderungen des Literaturbegriffs: Fünf Beiträge zu aktuellen Problemen der Literaturwissenschaft* (Göttingen: Vandenhoeck & Ruprecht, 1975);

Gerhard Sauder, *Der reisende Epikureer: Studien zu Moritz August von Thümmels Roman "Reise in die mittäglichen Provinzen von Frankreich"* (Heidelberg: Winter, 1968);

Manfred Windfuhr, "Empirie und Fiktion in Moritz August von Thümmels 'Reise in die mittäglichen Provinzen von Frankreich,'" *Poetica*, 3 (January-April 1970): 115-126.

Papers:

Moritz August von Thümmel's papers are in the Staatsarchiv Coburg.

Johann Peter Uz

(3 October 1720 - 12 May 1796)

Herbert Rowland
Purdue University

BOOKS: *Lyrische Gedichte*, anonymous (Berlin: Weitbrecht, 1749); enlarged as *Lyrische und andere Gedichte*, as Uz (Ansbach: Posch, 1755; revised, Leipzig: Weitbrecht, 1756; enlarged, Ansbach & Leipzig: Posch, 1767);

Der Sieg des Liebesgottes: Eine Nachahmung des Popischen Lockenraube, anonymous (Stralsund, Greifswald & Leipzig: Weitbrecht, 1753);

Schreiben des Verfassers der Lyrischen Gedichte an einen Freund, anonymous (N. p. , 1757);

Versuch über die Kunst stets fröhlich zu sein (Leipzig: Dyck, 1760);

Sämmtliche poetische Werke, 2 volumes (Leipzig: Dyck, 1768);

Poetische Werke von Johann Peter Uz: Nach seinen eigenhändigen Verbesserungen, edited by Christian Felix Weiße (Vienna: Degen, 1804);

Sammlung von zum Theil noch ungedruckten Dichtungen des Ansbacher Dichters über Römhild, und dessen Briefen an Johann Peter Grötzner, edited by Hermann Trapp (Römhild, 1866);

Sämtliche poetische Werke, edited by August Sauer (Stuttgart: Göschen, 1890; reprinted, Nendeln, Liechtenstein: Kraus, 1968).

OTHER: *Die Oden Anakreons in reimlosen Versen: Nebst einigen andern Gedichten*, translated by Uz and Johann Nikolaus Götz (Frankfurt am Main & Leipzig, 1746);

Ode an die Weisheit: Aus dem Englischen, translated by Uz (Berlin [actually Ansbach], 1757);

Johann Friedrich von Cronegk, *Schriften*, 2 volumes, edited by Uz (Anspach & Leipzig: Posch, 1760-1761);

Horace, *Die Werke des Horaz, aus dem Lateinischenübersetzt*, 3 volumes, translated by Uz, Johann Zacharias Leonhard Junckheim, and Georg Ludwig Hirsch (Ansbach: Haueisen, 1773-1775);

Neues Anspachisches Gesangbuch, edited by Uz and Junckheim (Ansbach: Messerer, 1781);

Horace, *Oden und Epoden: Lateinisch und Deutsch*, translated by Uz and Christian Friedrich

Painting by J. M. Schwabeda, 1780, from a pastel drawing by G. O. May (Gleimhaus, Halberstadt)

Karl Herzlieb, edited by Walther Killy and Ernst A. Schmidt (Zurich: Artemis, 1981).

Johann Peter Uz is best known in German literary history for his translation of Anacreon with Johann Nikolaus Götz and his original endeavors in the style associated with the Greek poet. His philosophical and religious poetry has on the whole been unduly neglected, for it is here that he did much of his most successful and historically most significant work; his achievement in reflective poetry earned him a prominent position

246

in a tradition which culminated in the Ideenlyrik (philosophical poetry) of Friedrich Schiller.

Uz was born on 3 October 1720 in Ansbach, southwest of Nuremberg in northern Bavaria. The son of a moderately wealthy goldsmith, he studied law from 1739 to 1743 at the University of Halle, where he heard lectures in philosophy by three of the most influential figures of the German Enlightenment—Georg Friedrich Meir, Alexander Baumgarten, and Christian Wolff. His later work clearly attests to his familiarity with Baumgarten's aesthetics and his assimilation of Wolff's brand of Leibnizian rationalism.

Early during his stay in Halle, Uz went to a bookstore to purchase a copy of a book by Johann Jakob Bodmer, only to find it out of stock. The young poet Johann Wilhelm Ludwig Gleim happened to be present and offered Uz the use of his own copy, thus initiating both a lifelong friendship and an influential literary relationship. Under the guidance of the more mature Gleim, Uz and their mutual friend Götz read the works of the ancients and their own contemporaries, particularly the formally refined, Stoic-Epicurean wisdom of Friedrich von Hagedorn and the pseudoclassical poetry of Immanuel Jacob Pyra; together they undertook translations of Homer and Pindar. More consequentially, Uz collaborated with Götz on a translation of lyrics attributed to Anacreon and thus became one of the founders of Anacreonticism in Germany.

As trifling as these mytho-pastoral songs of wine and love may seem today, they were of substantial historical importance. Into a literary landscape still dominated by baroque pomp they helped introduce additional, lighter antique art forms and aesthetic values such as simplicity and regularity, thereby marking the advent of the Classical era in Germany. In their emphasis on form over content they suggested the possibility of a union of the aesthetic and utilitarian, of aristocratic Epicureanism and bourgeois moral earnestness. Uz was angered by Götz's highhanded decision to publish the songs in 1746, perhaps less because of the collapse of their friendship four years earlier than because of his concern over the unpolished state of the pieces. He had nothing to do with the second edition of 1760. Meanwhile, the translation had its effect: Anacreontic poetry was cultivated by almost every poet of stature, including the young Johann Wolfgang von Goethe in the early 1770s.

Uz experienced a deep sense of personal and intellectual isolation following Gleim's departure from Halle in 1741, especially after his wish to follow his friend to Berlin was thwarted by his widowed mother. Much against her will he spent the spring semester of 1743 in Leipzig. There, almost penniless, withdrawn, and bereft of contact with literary figures save Christian Fürchtegott Gellert, with whom he took meals at an inn for a time, he endured the most miserable period of his life. Ultimately, he yielded to the insistence of his family that he return home, where he remained without a position for five years, writing and receiving intellectual and artistic sustenance from his correspondence with Gleim and, through him, with the poets Karl Wilhelm Ramler and Ewald von Kleist. In 1748 he accepted an unsalaried position as secretary to a councillor of justice.

Long pressed by Gleim, Uz agreed in 1749 to have his friend arrange for publication of his poetry under the title *Lyrische Gedichte* (Lyric Poems). The opening piece, "Die lyrische Muse" (The Lyrical Muse), announces the program of the volume in the line "Denn nur von Lust erklingt mein Saitenspiel" (For my lyre resounds with naught but pleasure). Accordingly, around half of the poems exhibit the dallying shepherds and shepherdesses and mythological figures typical of Anacreontic poetry. Aside from particular felicitous images and turns of phrase their success, like that of all the pieces, derives from their expert craftmanship and musicality. Throughout his life Uz polished his works tirelessly, often consulting Gleim and others for advice. Many of the lyrics of his early period became popular songs, and all of the religious poetry of his maturity was set to music. In light of the strident defense of rhymeless poetry by most Anacreontics it may come as a surprise that only one piece in the collection—indeed in Uz's lifework—is unrhymed. But this piece, "Der Frühling" (Spring), is significant both as a response to James Thomson's *The Seasons* (1726-1730) and for its influence on Kleist's more important *Der Frühling* (1749).

In several poems, such as "Die Zufriedenheit" (Contentment), the pastoral landscape serves a more serious purpose: to reflect Uz's view that the marriage of pleasure and virtue according to the golden mean is a moral ideal. In others Uz casts a critical glance at certain aspects of contemporary poetry. He scoffs in "An Venus" (To Venus) at poor imitations of Anacreon and in "Magister Duns" (Schoolmaster

Dunce) at the use of unpoetic, rationalistic language in the lyric. He jibes at the insincerity of much occasional poetry in "Die Muse bei den Hirten" (The Muse among the Shepherds). The volume was accorded a generally favorable reception, not least from the young Gotthold Ephraim Lessing.

Uz appears to have accepted his lot in Ansbach with characteristic good cheer. In 1752 he took an unsalaried position as secretary to Ansbach's emissary to an imperial commission charged with settling disputed claims to the township of Römhild in Thuringia. In Römhild he began a lifelong friendship with the court councilor Johann Peter Grötzner and fell in love with his sister Elisabeth Johanna, the Climene of his poems. Although his affection was unreciprocated, the year and a half in Römhild proved to be the happiest time of his life. He later had another fleeting romance but never married, choosing to live with his mother and two spinster sisters.

The year 1753 brought Uz's return to Ansbach and also the publication of his *Der Sieg des Liebesgottes* (The Victory of Cupid), which also found Lessing's approval. Reminiscent of Alexander Pope's *The Rape of the Lock* (1712), the work satirizes the Germans' slavish subservience to the French in matters of taste and poor German imitations of fashionable English authors.

In 1755 an enlarged edition of Uz's first book was published in Ansbach under the title *Lyrische und andere Gedichte* (Lyric and Other Poems). Dissatisfied with the appearance of the volume, he had a nearly identical edition published the following year by his original publisher, who had moved from Berlin to Leipzig. Anacreontic poems comprise less than half of the new pieces, which are combined with the old into four books. In "An die Scherze" (To the Amoretti) Uz bids a premature but prophetic farewell to the style of his youth. "Die Nacht" (Night) is a mood piece which reveals an unwonted, almost Romantic side of the poet. Perhaps the majority of the poems belong to a more serious type of ode, a reflective lyric influenced by the revered Horace that draws its themes from morality, philosophy, and religion. Representative of this genre is the lengthy "Theodicee" (Theodicy), the most famous of the poems and one of the outstanding poetic expressions of Gottfried Wilhelm von Leibniz's view of this as the best of all possible worlds.

Following the poems there appear four "Freundschaftsbriefe" (Letters of Friendship), epistles—in verse or verse and prose—of a kind which originated in the sentimental cult of friendship. Uz's letters are remarkably unsentimental for the time. His description of the beauties of the area surrounding Römhild and his attempt to console Gleim over the dissolution of his engagement are marked by Anacreontic grace and wit. In letters to Johann and Elisabeth Grötzner, written during and after the period in Römhild, his playful rococo style elegantly conceals quite sober disappointment and sadness. In one he gives himself over to the literary polemics that had begun to engulf him a few years earlier.

The translation of Anacreon and the *Lyrische Gedichte* of 1749 had made Uz a figure to be reckoned with. Despite his turn to more serious themes in the early 1750s he became the target of accusations of immorality by the so-called seraphic writers, particularly Bodmer and the young Christoph Martin Wieland—all the more so since the criticism in *Der Sieg des Liebesgottes* and other poems was directed in part at them. Lasting for much of the decade and frequently ugly, the quarrel was at base a clash between a rationalist Neoclassicism inspired by the French and a religiously colored sentimental modernism on the English model. Uz responded most cogently in a verse epistle, *Schreiben des Verfassers der Lyrischen Gedichte an einen Freund* (Letter from the Author of the Lyric Poems to a Friend), which he addressed to Gleim in 1757. Here he draws a distinction common prior to Romanticism between the ethos of a genre and the personal integrity of the poet, defending both Anacreonticism and his own character, and resumes his attack on the irregularity, bombast, and emotionalism of the Swiss. At Uz's request Gleim solicited the aid of Lessing and Friedrich Nicolai, whose influence finally ended the controversy in Uz's favor.

The year 1760 yielded Uz's most ambitious work since *Der Sieg des Liebesgottes*. *Versuch über die Kunst stets fröhlich zu sein* (Essay on the Art of Being Ever Cheerful) is an extensive didactic poem in the manner of Lucretius's *De rerum natura* (On the Nature of Things) and represents an almost systematic exposition of the philosophy of life found in many of the earlier pieces. What appeared progressive in the ode form seemed conventional or even regressive in the familiar Alexandrine poems, however, and most observers agreed with Moses Mendelssohn's assessment that

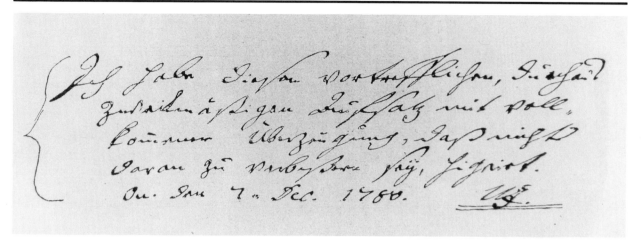

Note in Uz's handwriting (from Joseph Kürschner, ed., Deutsche National-Litteratur, *volume 45, n.d.)*

the work failed to meet Uz's customary high standard.

Versuch über die Kunst stets fröhlich zu sein was to be one of the last products of Uz's muse. In 1763 he was named assistant judge at the imperial court in Nuremburg and adviser to the margraves of Ansbach and Kumlbach. This position entailed a substantial and much-needed increase in income: while his works sold well, Uz received no honoraria due to the unregulated publishing conditions of the time. But his advancement severely limited his leisure for writing. In a verse epistle to the dramatist Christian Felix Weiße in 1767 he formally retired from poetry, citing both his new responsibilities and the fact that he no longer had anything new to say.

Weiße directed the publication of a two-volume edition of Uz's works, titled *Sämmtliche poetische Werke* (Collected Poetic Works), in Leipzig in 1768. In the midst of the polemics over his Anacreontic poetry Uz had been working more and more exclusively in the genre of the serious ode and had turned from moral philosophy to religion for his subject matter. The previously unpublished poems comprising the fifth book of the *Sämmtliche poetische Werke* still display a diversity of theme. In certain of the pieces Uz manifests an unaccustomed topicality, looking beyond Ansbach to the Seven Years' War. Although representing a poetic vision of Petrarch's beloved, "Laura" is his least conventional and most compelling love poem. His "An die Freude" (Ode to Joy) stands together with Hagedorn's work of the same title in a line leading to Schiller's famous poem.

The sixteen pieces that constitute the sixth book, on the other hand, all deal with God or

Christ, as indicated by titles such as "Gott, der Gesetzgeber" (God the Lawgiver) and "Der Erlöser" (The Redeemer). Of particular interest is "Gott im Frühlinge" (God in the Spring), in which the bucolic motifs of Anacreonticism are used in a Christian context. The volume closed with four Freundschaftsbriefe, among them the two to Gleim containing Uz's defense of his character and farewell to poetry.

On the whole Uz stood by his decision to withdraw from the world of letters. After 1767 he wrote two religious pieces, a couple of verses for the albums of friends, and three occasional poems for members of the local nobility. None was included in the 1772 edition of the *Sämmtliche poetische Werke*, which was a new impression of the preceding one and the last edition to appear during Uz's lifetime. Wednesday evenings with his friends Johann Zacharias Leonhard Junckheim and Georg Ludwig Hirsch led eventually to a complete prose translation of Horace, which was published in 1773-1775 and republished, despite sharp criticism of the first edition, in 1797. Uz and Junckheim were later commissioned to edit the *Neues Anspachisches Gesangbuch* (New Ansbach Hymnal, 1781).

Uz's later years were interspersed with pleasant reminders of his fame in the form of visits from Goethe's friend Karl Ludwig von Knebel as well as the writers Nicolai, Wilhelm Heinse, Johann Gottfried Herder, and the young Romantic Wilhelm Heinrich Wackenroder. He received recognition from figures as varied as Jakob Michael Reinhold Lenz, the long-reconciled Wieland, and Goethe himself. He found his loudest echo in Schiller, however, who, even during his tempestuous youth, considered Uz one of his favorite

Painting of Uz by an unknown artist (from Gero von Wilpert, Deutsche Literatur in Bildern, *1965)*

poets and for a time contemplated doing for the philosopher Immanuel Kant what Uz had done for Leibniz in "Theodicee."

Despite his reputation among his literary colleagues Uz's renown long failed to reach the ears of his own ruler. Margrave Carl Alexander learned of his distinguished subject only during a visit to Rome in 1770, when Pope Clement XIV congratulated him on having a poet whose excellence was recognizable even in the Italian translation (Uz's works were also translated into Dutch, Spanish, and French). On returning home, Carl Alexander immediately had Uz presented to him and often showed him his favor over the following years. In 1771 Uz was appointed to the local board of education, and in 1790 he was named privy councilor and director of the board of councilors. Political events forced Uz into an unwanted retirement the next year, but he returned to the judicial arena in 1796 as privy councilor of justice. He died on 12 May of that year from complications of a stroke.

Letters:

Briefe an einen Freund aus den Jahren 1753-82, ed-

ited by August Henneberger (Leipzig: Brockhaus, 1866);

Briefwechsel zwischen Gleim und Uz, edited by Carl Schüddekopf (Tübingen: Litterarischer Verein in Stuttgart, 1899).

Biographies:

Henriette Feuerbach, *Uz und Cronegk: Zwei fränkische Dichter aus dem vorigen Jahrhundert. Ein biographischer Versuch* (Leipzig: Engelmann, 1866);

Peter Khaeser, *Johann Peter Uz: Ein Lebensbild* (Erlangen: 1973).

References:

Bernhard Dombart, "Anfang und Ausgang des Streites zwischen Uz und Bodmer," *Jahrbuch des Historischen Vereins für Mittelfranken,* 46 (1898): 3-24;

August Ewald, "Uz und Goethe," *Euphorion,* 20 (1913): 613-640;

Armin Human, "Johann Peter Uz und dessen Freundschaftsverhältnis mit Hofadvokat Rat Johann Peter Grötzner in Römhild," *Schriften des Vereins für Sachsen-Meiningische Geschichte und Landeskunde,* 23 (1896): 137-148;

Friedrich Wilhelm Kantzenbach, "Johann Peter Uz und sein Ansbacher Freundeskreis in frömmigkeitsgeschichtlicher Sicht," *Zeitschrift für bayrische Kirchengeschichte,* 33 (1964): 109-116;

Heino Kuhlmann, "Die Sprache der Musen: Zum Gebrauch der Mythologie in den Gedichten von Johann Peter Uz. Ein Beitrag aus Anlaß seines 250. Geburtstages," *Jahrbuch des Historischen Vereins für Mittelfranken,* 86 (1971-1972): 277-301;

Erich Petzet, "Die deutschen Nachahmungen des Popeschen 'Lockenraubs': Ein Beitrag zur Geschichte des komischen Epos in Deutschland," *Zeitschrift für vergleichende Litteraturgeschichte,* new series 4 (1891): 409-433;

Petzet, "Der Einfluß der Anakreontik und Horazens auf Johann Peter Uz," *Zeitschrift für vergleichende Litteraturgeschichte,* new series 6 (1893): 329-392;

Petzet, *Johann Peter Uz,* edited by Thomas Stettner (Ansbach: Brügel, 1930);

Petzet, "Das Uzische Frühlingsmetrum," *Zeitschrift für vergleichende Litteraturgeschichte,* new series 10 (1896): 293-299;

Hellmuth Rössler, "Markgraf und Bürger: Carl Alexander, Johann Peter Uz," in his *Fränki-*

scher Geist, deutsches Schicksal: Ideen, Kräfte, Ge-
stalten in Franken 1500-1800 (Kulmbach: Bau-
mann, 1953), pp. 275-289;

Thomas Stettner, "Uz, ein stilles Dichterleben,"
in his *Aus Ansbachs und Frankens vergangenen
Tagen* (Ansbach: Brügel, 1928), pp. 9-43;

Newell E. Warde, *Johann Peter Uz and German Anacreonticism: The Emancipation of the Aesthetic*
(Frankfurt am Main: Lang, 1978);

Helena Rosa Zeltner, "Johann Peter Uz : Von der

'Lyrischen Muse' zur Dichtkunst," Ph.D dissertation, University of Zurich, 1973.

Papers:

Johann Peter Uz apparently destroyed most of
his papers. The largest collection appears to be
Uz's correspondence with Friedrich Nicolai,
housed at the Staatsbibliothek Preußischer Kulturbesitz, Berlin.

Christian Felix Weiße

(28 January 1726 - 16 December 1804)

Bruce Duncan
Dartmouth College

SELECTED BOOKS: *Scherzhafte Lieder* (Leipzig:
Weidmann & Reich, 1758; edited by Alfred
Anger, Stuttgart: Metzler, 1965);

Beytrag zum deutschen Theater, 5 volumes (Leipzig:
Dyck, 1759-1768)—comprises in volume 1,
*Eduard der Dritte; Die Poeten nach der Mode;
Die unerwartete Zusammenkunft, oder der Natu-
raliensammler; Wälder; Richard der Dritte;* in vo-
lume 2, *Die Matrone von Ephesus; Die Haushäl-
terinn; Amalia; Rosemunde; Mustapha und
Zeangir;* in volume 3, *Die Mißtrauische gegen
sich selbst; Krispus; Großmuth für Großmuth,
Die Befreyung von Theben;* in volume 4, *Der
Projektmacher; Weibergeklatsche, oder ein Quid
pro quo; Atreus und Thyest;* in volume 5, *Die
Freundschaft auf der Probe; List über List;
Romeo und Julia;* enlarged (1765-1771); volume 1 revised (1771);

Amazonenlieder (Leipzig: Weidmann & Reich,
1760);

*Kleine Lieder für Kinder, zur Beförderung der Tu-
gend, mit Melodien zum Singen beim Clavier*, 2
volumes (Flensburg: Korte, 1766-1767); enlarged as *Lieder für Kinder: Mit neuen Melodien von A. Hiller* (Leipzig: Weidmann,
1768); translated anonymously as *Moral
Songs for Children* (London: Searle, 1789);

Komische Opern, 3 volumes (Leipzig: Dyck, 1768-
1772)—comprises in volume 1, *Lottchen am
Hofe; Die Liebe auf dem Lande;* in volume 2,
*Die verwandelten Weiber, oder Der Teufel ist los;
Der lustige Schuster; Der Dorfbalbier;* in vol-
ume 3, *Die Jagd; Der Aerntekranz;*

*Neues ABC-Buch, nebst einigen kleinen Übungen und
Unterhaltungen für Kinder* (Leipzig: Crusius,
1772);

Kleine lyrische Gedichte, 3 volumes (Leipzig: Weidmann & Reich, 1772);

*Armut und Tugend, ein kleines Schauspiel in einem Auf-
zuge: Zum Besten der Armen* (Leipzig: Dyck,
1772);

Die Jubelhochzeit, eine komische Oper in 3 Aufzügen
(Leipzig: Dyck, 1773);

Trauerspiele, 5 volumes (Leipzig: Dyck, 1776-
1780);

Lustspiele, 3 volumes (Karlsruhe: Schmieder,
1778);

Lustspiele, 3 volumes (Leipzig: Dyck, 1783);

Selbstbiographie, edited by Christian Ernst Weiße
and Samuel Gottlob Frisch (Leipzig: Voß,
1806).

OTHER: *Bibliothek der schönen Wissenschaften und
der freyen Künste*, 86 volumes, edited by
Weiße (Leipzig: Dyck, 1759-circa 1789)—title

Painting by Anton Graff, 1769 (Universitätsbibliothek Leipzig)

changed to *Neue Bibliothek der schönen Wissenschaften und der freyen Künste* in 1765;

Der Kinderfreund, 24 volumes, edited by Weiße (Leipzig: Crusius, 1775-1782);

Briefwechsel der Familie des Kinderfreundes, 12 volumes, edited by Weiße (Leipzig: Crusius, 1784-1792);

Johann Peter Uz, *Poetische Werke von Johann Peter Uz: Nach seinen eigenhändigen Verbesserungen*, edited by Weiße (Vienna: Degen, 1804).

Christian Felix Weiße was probably the most popular writer of the German Enlightenment. His prodigious output of successful tragedies, comedies, operetta librettos, poetry, and children's literature; his editorship of the most widely read literary journal of his day; and his friendships with almost every important writer of the time put him at the center of German literary life, especially in the 1760s and 1770s. Today he is largely forgotten, a victim of both the ease

with which he wrote and the historical developments that passed him by. Concerning Weiße's facility with the pen, Moses Mendelssohn echoed a common judgment when he wrote to him, "Sie scheinen mir mit gar zu großer Leichtigkeit zu dichten. Boileau hat den Racine gelehrt, sich die Verse sauer werden zu lassen. Ich wünsche Ihnen einen Boileau" (You seem to me to write with much too great a facility. Boileau taught Racine to let his verses come painfully. I wish you a Boileau). More important, Weiße's works, conservative in form, did not fit well into the developments that have come to define the eighteenth-century literary canon. His best tragedies, which sought a middle ground between French and English influences, pleased audiences but put off critics who were intent on redefining dramatic conventions. Similarly, his comedies seemed too rooted in the Italian traditions from which German theater was struggling to break free. Ironically, if modern audiences could see Weiße's comedies staged, they would probably, like eighteenth-century theatergoers, find them far more appealing than the canonical "Saxon comedies" of the period. Finally, those genres in which Weiße *did* pioneer, namely children's literature, the operetta libretto, and popular song lyrics, fell outside the realm of high literature. Johann Wolfgang von Goethe in his autobiography speaks for his whole generation when he reports that he and other students in Leipzig valued Weiße's person and enjoyed his plays enormously but considered his works poor models to follow.

Weiße was born in Annaberg in Saxony on 28 January 1726 to Christian Heinrich Weiße and Christiane Elisabeth Weiße, née Cleemann. His father, a philologist and school director, died when the boy was three years old and was replaced by a despised stepfather. Weiße's affection for his twin sister, however, seems to have sustained him and made his childhood reasonably happy. After completing studies at the Altenburg Gymnasium in 1745 he began further studies–ostensibly theology–in Leipzig and formed friendships with almost all the young writers who gathered in this "Little Paris": Christian Friedrich von Blankenberg, Johann Friedrich von Cronegk, Karl Christian Gärtner, Christian Garve, Christian Fürchtegott Gellert, Abraham Gotthelf Kästner, Friedrich Gottlieb Klopstock, Christlob Mylius, Gottlieb Wilhelm Rabener, Johann Elias Schlegel, Moritz August von Thümmel, Friedrich Wilhelm Zachariä, and Georg Jochim Zollikofer. From 1747 until August 1748 he was especially close to the young Gotthold Ephraim Lessing, who shared his passion for the theater. Always short of money for tickets, the two scrounged food and lodging as best they could and finally turned to translating first French and then English plays for the theater of Caroline Neuber. The stage success of Lessing's *Der junge Gelehrte* (The Young Scholar) in 1748 inspired Weiße to rework *Die Matrone von Ephesus* (The Matron of Ephesus), a comedy he had first written four years before, and then to try his hand at other genres, including tragedy and light verse.

In 1750 Weiße became the private tutor and companion of the somewhat younger Count von Geyersberg, a position that allowed him to remain in Leipzig and form further friendships with such writers as Johann Wilhelm Ludwig Gleim, Johann Peter Uz, Ewald von Kleist, and Heinrich Wilhelm von Gerstenberg, as well as to spend six months in Paris. At the end of that stay, in August 1761, Count Schulenburg von Burgscheidungen invited him to serve as his companion at the young nobleman's estate and at the court of Gotha until the beginning of 1762.

In 1759 Friedrich Nicolai prevailed upon Weiße to take over the editorship of the *Bibliothek der schönen Wissenschaften und der freyen Künste* (Library of Belles Lettres and the Liberal Arts). Officially a quarterly, this journal appeared in practice somewhat less regularly. Each issue contained announcements and approximately ten reviews of new publications. For the next thirty years (it is not clear just when he stopped) Weiße struggled with deadlines and reluctant contributors in return for an emolument that failed to cover postage. He seems to have been motivated by a sense of duty and by the opportunity for contact with other writers. Conciliatory by nature, he had no stomach for literary quarrels, which he avoided largely by failing to commission reviews of controversial works. With the *Bibliothek*, however, Weiße inherited a bitter feud with the Swiss critic Johann Jakob Bodmer, which for many years was fought by proxy among their acquaintances.

His duties as tutor, and later as editor, still afforded him the opportunity to write, and the 1750s and early 1760s saw the composition of some of his best-known theatrical works. Charles Coffey's 1732 "ballad opera," *The Devil to Pay; or, The Wives Metamorphos'd*, had already been translated for the Berlin stage in 1743, but Gottfried Heinrich Koch's theater troupe commissioned Weiße to create a different version with new

music by Johann C. Standfuß. *Die verwandelten Weiber, oder Der Teufel ist los*, published in Weiße's *Komische Opern* (Comic Operas, 1768-1772), had astonishing success, as evidenced both by its many performances and the vigor with which Johann Christoph Gottsched attacked it. His vitriolic broadsides assailed the musical's disregard for the three unities, its use of dialect, its implausible situations (including ghosts), its implied improvisations and invitations for audience participation, and its frivolous sensuality. Weiße went on to create a sequel by adapting Coffey's *The Merry Cobbler* as *Der lustige Schuster*, this time with music by Johann Adam Hiller, who remained his usual musical collaborator. *Der lustige Schuster* was also published in *Komische Opern*.

The first of Weiße's tragedies to reach the stage was *Richard der Dritte* (Richard III). He began work on the play in the spring of 1758 and finished it a year later. Weiße subscribed to the Enlightenment idea that artistic production is subject to rules, and he regularly sent his manuscripts to friends so that they could point out his errors; but his impending trip to Paris and a publication deadline allowed him enough time to consult only Rabener. The text appeared in 1759 in volume 1 of the first edition of Weiße's *Beytrag zum deutschen Theater* (Contribution to the German Theater, 1759-1768) and was successfully performed in Hamburg the same year by Koch's troupe. Hans Konrad Dieterich Ekhof, a friend who also played the lead role, wrote the author in 1761 with his criticisms. Weiße immediately revised the piece, which appeared in its new form in the second edition of *Beytrag zum deutschen Theater* in 1765. Koch brought this version to the Leipzig theater two years later. The third edition of *Beytrag zum deutschen Theater* (1771) contained further changes, as did the collected *Trauerspiele* (Tragedies) in 1776. These frequent revisions testify to Weiße's modesty, as does his introduction, in which he claims not to have remembered Shakespeare's play while writing his tragedy. Should he suffer too much in the comparison, he hastens to add, he hopes that the reader will at least give him credit for not having committed plagiarism, even if it might have been better for him to have done so. The play's reception set the pattern for many of Weiße's works. It went through many performances and editions throughout the rest of the century. Conservative voices, such as the *Allgemeine deutsche Bibliothek* (Universal German Library), pronounced it an excellent example of verse drama as late as 1789.

But progressive critics, such as Lessing in 1769, while acknowledging a certain raw power, took the play to task for not conforming to new Enlightenment principles. Today, *Richard der Dritte* is best known for Lessing's attack on it in the *Hamburgische Dramaturgie* (Hamburg Dramaturgy, 1767-1769). Weiße, as always, took these critical objections to heart, demurring only by pointing out that some of his shortcomings, such as the use of alexandrine verse, should be seen in historical context. Germans, he complained, tended to be so taken with a new masterpiece that they dismissed all previous works that did not anticipate it in form. Modern critics would be unlikely to side with Lessing, who considered the evil Richard an inappropriate hero for tragedy and felt that Weiße's fascination with unrepentant wickedness violated the moral imperative Lessing believed drama should have.

In 1762 Weiße was appointed tax collector, a position which, while no sinecure, provided a steady income and sufficient leisure for him to engage in his literary activities in Leipzig for the rest of his life. He carried out his bureaucratic responsibilities conscientiously and seems to have been as popular as a tax collector can be, especially one who had to begin by administering the heavy Prussian levies in the Seven Years' War. Once settled into his position, he set about starting a family, and for the rest of his life he would be remembered by everyone as a kind and generous paterfamilias. On 6 June 1763 he married the younger sister of his friend Friedrich Platner. The union produced three daughters and two sons, who inspired his contributions to children's literature. Dissatisfied with the songs that their nurse sang to them, he published *Kleine Lieder für Kinder* (Little Songs for Children) in 1766-1767. Six years later he became unhappy with the available readers and wrote *Neues ABC-Buch* (New ABC-Book, 1772). Both works were enormously popular, and many editions appeared on into the next century. His magazine *Der Kinderfreund* (The Children's Friend) started out in 1775 as a weekly but for economic reasons soon became a quarterly. It presents the continuing story of a family loosely modeled on Weiße's own, headed by a patriarch named "Mentor." It was so popular (even with the British royal household) that the whole Weiße family achieved celebrity. Twenty-four volumes appeared between 1775 and 1782 in five authorized editions and at least three pirated ones; one Viennese pirated edition had a printing of fifteen thousand copies. A Dutch trans-

lation went through three editions, and imitators sprang up in various languages. Weiße continued to reflect his children's progress in the *Briefwechsel der Familie des Kinderfreundes* (Correspondence of the Children's Friend's Family), whose twelve volumes from 1784 to 1792 had only somewhat less popular success. Here Mentor's children, grown to young adulthood, continue their stories through letters.

Weiße's income from writing and, in 1790, an inheritance from his wife's family supplemented his already comfortable salary, so that he was able to travel often and to provide for his large household and frequent guests. By the mid 1770s his plays had ceased to command much critical respect, and he had all but given up writing new dramas; but the popularity of the old ones continued, his reputation as a children's author had spread all over Europe, and his editorship of the *Bibliothek* kept him in touch with the literary world. Weiße used his resulting influence generously. He encouraged and found publishers for young authors such as Johann Paul Friedrich Richter (Jean Paul), arranged scholarships and tutoring positions, and assisted intellectuals such as the philosopher Johann Gottlieb Fichte when they ran afoul of authority.

Only illness marred Weiße's domestic idyll. Never physically robust, he suffered periodically from erysipelas and other ailments. His wife was also frequently ill. His younger son died suddenly in 1773, and all of Weiße's children had dangerous bouts of scarlet fever and measles. Weiße estimated that his family never experienced a two-month period in which they were entirely free from serious afflictions. Worst of all was the painful nervous disease that befell his daughter Karoline in 1786. The family spent the following years vainly searching for a way to relieve her agony. His youngest daughter, Dorothea, became similarly afflicted in 1803.

Despite these difficulties, Weiße and all who knew him counted his life a fortunate one. He lived out his last years in the company of his family and many admirers, who showered him with affection. His posthumously published autobiography (1806) lists with understandable pride the many authors who entrusted their works to him for revision and publication, some of the special occasions on which he was honored, and the many books that were dedicated to him. The honors continued after his death on 16 December 1804, and his funeral was attended by all classes, including royalty. Hundreds of schoolchildren preceded the casket, and hundreds of university students followed it. For some time afterward theaters presented special performances of his works.

Wholly a man of his time, Weiße could not hope to have his fame continue far into the future. Nevertheless, he deserves an important position among the writers of his generation.

Letters:
"Briefe aus Christian Felix Weißes Nachlaß," edited by Jakob Minor, *Archiv fur Litteraturgeschichte*, 9 (1880): 453-462.

References:

Eckehard Catholy, *Das deutsche Lustspiel: Von der Aufklärung bis zur Romantik* (Stuttgart, Berlin, Cologne & Mainz: Kohlhammer, 1982), pp. 50-56;

Gertrud Fankhauser, " 'Der Kinderfreund' (1775-1784): Die Kinderzeitschrift von Christian Felix Weiße als Spiegelbild der Erziehungs- und Gesellschaftsideale des deutschen Bürgertums am Ende des Aufklärungszeitalters," Ph.D. dissertation, New York University, 1975;

Robert R. Heitner, *German Tragedy in the Age of Enlightenment* (Berkeley & Los Angeles: University of California Press, 1963), pp. 232-278;

Bettina Hurrelmann, *Jugendliteratur und Bürgerlichkeit: Soziale Erziehung in der Jugendliteratur der Aufklärung am Beispiel von C. F. Weißes "Kinderfreund" 1776-1782* (Paderborn: Schöningh, 1974);

Jakob Minor, *Christian Felix Weiße und seine Beziehung zur deutschen Literatur des achtzehnten Jahrhunderts* (Innsbruck: Wagner, 1880);

Walter Pape, "Der ästhetische Erzieher: Christian Felix Weiße oder die bürgerliche Utopie," in his *Das literarische Kinderbuch: Studien zur Entstehung und Typologie* (Berlin & New York: De Gruyter, 1981), pp. 129-235;

Friedhelm Radandt, *From Barock to Storm and Stress* (New York: Barnes & Noble, 1977), pp. 70-72;

Albert R. Schmitt, "Christian Felix Weißes 'Jean Calas'–Dokumentarisches Theater im 18. Jahrhundert," in *Aufnahme–Weitergabe: Literarische Impulse um Goethe. Festschrift für Heinz Moenkemeyer zum 68. Geburtstag* (Hamburg: Buske, 1982), pp. 2-30;

S. Etta Schreiber, *The German Woman in the Age of Enlightenment: A Study in the Drama from Gottsched to Lessing* (New York: Kings Crown, 1948), pp. 167-213;

Alison Scott-Prelorentzos, *The Servant in German Enlightenment Comedy* (Edmonton: University of Alberta Press, 1982), pp. 88-122.

Papers:
Christian Felix Weiße's papers are widely scattered. At his request, all letters in his possession were returned after his death. The greatest concentration is in the Goethe-Schiller Archiv in Weimar, which possesses 109 letters to Karl Wilhelm Ramler, but that represents only a tiny fraction of his correspondence.

Christoph Martin Wieland
(5 September 1733 - 21 January 1813)

Thomas C. Starnes
Tulane University

SELECTED BOOKS: *Die Natur der Dinge in sechs Büchern,* anonymous (Halle: Hemmerde, 1752 [actually 1751]; revised edition, Zurich: Geßner, 1753);

Lobgesang auf die Liebe, anonymous (Halle: Hemmerde, 1751);

Zwölf moralische Briefe in Versen, anonymous (Frankfurt am Main & Leipzig [actually Heilbronn]: Eckebrecht, 1752);

Anti-Ovid, oder die Kunst zu lieben: Mit einem Anhang Lyrischer Gedichte, anonymous (Amsterdam [actually Heilbronn: Eckebrecht], 1752);

Erzæhlungen, anonymous (Heilbronn: Eckebrecht, 1752);

Der Fryhling, anonymous (Tübingen: Löffler, 1752);

Hymne, anonymous (N.p., 1752);

*Schreiben an HERRN *** von der Würde und der Bestimmung eines schönen Geistes,* anonymous (Zurich: Geßner, 1752);

Abhandlung von den Schönheiten des Epischen Gedichts Der Noah, von dem Verfasser des Lehrgedichts "Über die Natur der Dinge," anonymous (Zurich: Geßner, 1753);

Briefe von Verstorbenen an hinterlassene Freunde, anonymous (Zurich: Orell, 1753);

Gebet eines Deisten: Veranlaßt durch das Gebet eines Freygeistes, anonymous (Berlin [actually Zurich: Orell & Geßner], 1753);

Gebet eines Christen: Von dem Verfasser des Gebets eines Deisten, anonymous (Berlin, 1753);

Plan, Von einer neuen Art, von Privat-Unterweisung, anonymous (N.p., 1753);

Der gepryfte Abraham: Ein Gedicht in vier Gesängen, anonymous (Zurich: Orell, 1753); translated anonymously as *The Trial of Abraham: In Four Cantos* (London: Becket & de Hondt, 1764; Boston: Perkins, 1764);

Hymnen: Von dem Verfasser des gepryften Abrahams (Zurich: Orell, 1754);

Erinnerungen an eine Freundin, anonymous (Zurich: Orell, 1754);

Christoph Martin Wieland; painting by Friedrich August Tischbein, 1799 (Bremer Kunsthalle)

Ode auf die Auferstehung Jesu, anonymous (Zurich: Geßner, 1754);

Ode auf die Geburt des Erlösers, anonymous (Zurich: Geßner, 1754);

Ankündigung einer Dunciade für die Deutschen: Nebst dem verbesserten Hermann, anonymous (Frankfurt am Main & Leipzig, 1755);

Betrachtungen: Uber [sic] den Menschen: Nebst einer allegorischen Geschichte der menschlichen Seele, anonymous (Zurich: Geßner, 1755);

Fragmente in der erzählenden Dichtart von verschiedenem Innhalte: Mit einigen andern Gedichten, anonymous, by Wieland and Bodmer (Zurich: Orell, 1755);

Hymnen auf die Allgegenwart und Gerechtigkeit Gottes, anonymous (Zurich: Orell, 1756);

Sympathien, anonymous (Zurich: Geßner, 1756); translated by F. A. Winzer as *The Sympathy of Souls* (London: Bladon, 1787);

Empfindungen eines Christen, anonymous (Zurich: Orell, Geßner, 1757);

Ode zum dankbaren Andenken eines Erlauchten und Verdienstvollen Staatsmanns in der Republick Zürich, anonymous (Zurich: Geßner, 1757);

Auf das Bildniß des Königs von Preußen von Herrn Wille, anonymous (Zurich: Geßner, 1758);

Lady Johanna Gray, oder Der Triumph der Religion: Ein Trauer-Spiel (Zurich: Heidegger, 1758);

Plan einer Academie, zur Bildung des Verstandes und Herzens junger Leute: Nebst Gedanken über den patriotischen Traum, von einem Mittel, die veraltete Eidgenoßschaft wieder zu verjüngen, anonymous (N.p., 1758);

Sammlung einiger prosaischen Schriften, 3 volumes (Zurich: Orell, 1758); republished as *Sammlung prosaischer Schriften*, 2 volumes (Zurich: Orell, Geßner, 1763-1764); republished as *Prosaische Schriften*, 2 volumes (Zurich: Orell, Geßner, Füßli, 1771-1772);

Cyrus (Zurich: Geßner, 1759);

Araspes und Panthea: Eine moralische Geschichte in einer Reyhe von Unterredungen (Zurich: Orell, 1760); translated by John Richardson as "Araspes and Panthea; or, the effects of love," in his *Dialogues from the German of M. Wieland* (London: Printed for S. Leacroft, 1775);

Clementina von Poretta: Ein Trauerspiel. Von dem Verfasser der Lady Johanna Gray (Zurich: Orell, 1760);

Poetische Schriften, 3 volumes (Zurich: Orell, Geßner, 1762; revised, 1770);

Der Sieg der Natur über die Schwärmerey oder die Abentheuer des Don Sylvio von Rosalva, Eine Geschichte, worinn alles Wunderbare natürlich zugeht, anonymous (Ulm: Bartholomäi, 1764); republished as *Die Abentheuer des Don Sylvio von Rosalva*, 2 volumes (Leipzig: Weidmann & Reich, 1772); translated, probably by John Richardson, as *Reason triumphant over fancy, exemplified in the singular adventures of Don Sylvio de Rosalva: A history in which every marvelous event occurs naturally*, 2 volumes (London: Printed for J. Wilkie, Leacroft & Heydinger, 1773); revised by Ernest A. Baker as *The Adventures of Don Sylvio de Rosalva* (London: Routledge/New York: Dutton, 1904); German version republished as *Der Sieg der Natur über die Schwärmerei oder*

Die Abenteuer des Don Sylvio von Rosalva (Berlin: Aufbau, 1984);

Comische Erzählungen, anonymous (Zurich: Orell, Geßner, 1765; revised, 1768);

Geschichte des Agathon, anonymous, 2 volumes (Frankfurt am Main & Leipzig [actually Zurich: Orell, Geßner], 1766-1767); revised and enlarged as *Agathon*, anonymous, 4 volumes (Leipzig: Weidmann & Reich, 1773); revised and enlarged as *Geschichte des Agathon*, 3 volumes (Leipzig: Göschen, 1794); translated by Richardson as *The History of Agathon*, 4 volumes (London: Cadell, 1773); original German version republished as *Geschichte des Agathon*, 1 volume (Stuttgart: Reclam, 1979);

Musarion, oder die Philosophie der Grazien: Ein Gedicht in drey Büchern, anonymous (Leipzig: Weidmann & Reich, 1768; revised, 1769); republished, edited by Alfred Anger (Stuttgart: Reclam, 1964);

Idris: Ein heroisch-comisches Gedicht. Fünf Gesänge, anonymous (Leipzig: Weidmann & Reich, 1768);

Die Geschichte der Biribinkers (Ulm: Bartholemäi, 1769);

ΣΩΚΡΑΤΗΣ ΜΑΙΝΟΜΕΝΟΣ *oder die Dialogen des Diogenes von Sinope: Auseiner alten Handschrift*, anonymous (Leipzig: Weidmann & Reich, 1770); translated by Wintersted as *Socrates out of his Senses, or dialogues of Diogenes of Sinope* (London: Davies, 1771; reprinted, Newburgh, N.Y. & New York: Denniston & Fellow, 1797); German version republished as *Sokrates Mainomenos oder Die Dialogen des Diogenes von Sinope*, edited by Peter Fix (Leipzig: Dietrich, 1984);

Beyträge zur Geheimen Geschichte des menschlichen Verstandes und Herzens: Aus den Archiven der Natur gezogen, anonymous, 2 volumes (Leipzig: Weidmann & Reich, 1770);

Combabus: Eine Erzählung, anonymous (Leipzig: Weidmann & Reich, 1770);

Die Grazien: Ein Gedicht in sechs Büchern, anonymous (Leipzig: Weidmann & Reich, 1770); translated by Sarah Taylor Austin as *The Graces: A Classical Allegory, Interspersed with Poetry, and Illustrated with Explanatory Notes: Together with a Poetical Fragment Entitled Psyche among the Graces* (London: Whittaker, 1823);

Der neue Amadis: Ein comisches Gedicht in achtzehn Gesängen, anonymous, 2 volumes (Leipzig: Weidmann & Reich, 1771);

Aurora: Ein Singspiel in einem Aufzug auf das höchste Geburtsfest der Durchlauchtigsten Herzogin Regentin von Sachsen-Weimar und Eisenach, anonymous (N.p., 1772);

Gedanken über eine alte Aufschrift, anonymous (Leipzig: Weidmann & Reich, 1772);

Kleine Schriften (Amsterdam: Auf Kosten der Gesellschaft, 1772);

Der goldne Spiegel oder die Könige von Scheschian, eine wahre Geschichte: Aus dem Scheschianischen übersetzt, anonymous (Leipzig: Weidmann & Reich, 1772);

Alceste: Ein Singspiel in fünf Aufzügen, anonymous (N.p. [actually Weimar: Hoffmann], 1773; republished, with music by Anton Schweitzer, Leipzig: Weidmann & Reich, 1773);

Die Abderiten, eine sehr wahrscheinliche Geschichte (Weimar: Hoffmann, 1774); revised as *Geschichte der Abderiten,* 2 volumes (Leipzig: Weidmann & Reich, 1781); translated by Henry Christmas as *The Republic of Fools: Being the History of the State and People of Abdera in Thrace,* 2 volumes (London: Allen, 1861); German version republished, edited by Emil Steiger (Frankfurt am Main: Fischer, 1961);

Der verklagte Amor: Ein Gedicht in vier Büchern (Weimar: Hoffmann, 1774);

An Psyche, anonymous (N.p., 1774);

Neueste Gedichte vom Jahre 1770 bis 1777, 3 volumes (Weimar: Hoffmann, 1777-1779);

Rosamund: Ein Singspiel in drei Aufzügen, music by Anton Schweitzer (Weimar: Hoffmann, 1778);

Oberon: Ein Gedicht in vierzehn Gesängen, anonymous (Weimar: Hoffmann, 1780); translated by William Sotheby as *Oberon: A Poem from the German,* 2 volumes (London: Cadell & Davies, 1798; Newport, R.I.: Rousmanier / Boston: Belcher, 1810; reprinted, New York: Garland, 1978); translated by John Quincy Adams as *Oberon: A Poetical Romance in Twelve Books,* edited by A. B. Faust (New York: Crofts, 1940);

Clelia und Sinibald: Eine Legende aus dem zwölften Jahrhundert (Weimar: Hoffmann, 1784);

Auserlesene Gedichte, 7 volumes (Leipzig: Weidmann & Reich, 1784-1787);

Kleinere prosaische Schriften, 2 volumes (Leipzig: Weidmann & Reich, 1785-1786);

Gedanken von der Freyheit über Gegenstände des Glaubens zu philosophieren (Leipzig: Göschen, 1789);

Vermischte Erzählungen (Leipzig: Weidmann & Reich, 1791);

Geheime Geschichte des Philosophen Peregrinus Proteus, 2 volumes (Leipzig: Göschen, 1791); translated by William Tooke as *Private History of Peregrinus Proteus, the Philosopher* (London: Johnson, 1796);

Neue Götter-Gespräche (Leipzig: Göschen, 1791); excerpts translated by William Taylor as *Dialogues of the Gods, originally written in German* (London: Johnson, 1795);

Sämmtliche Werke, 45 volumes (Leipzig: Göschen, 1794-1811);

Agathodämon in sieben Büchern (Leipzig: Göschen, 1799);

Aristipp und einige seiner Zeitgenossen, 4 volumes (Leipzig: Göschen, 1800-1801);

Taschenbuch für 1804: Menander und Glycerion (Tübingen: Cotta, 1803);

Krates und Hipparchia: Ein Seitenstück zu Menander und Glycerion von C. M. Wieland. Zum Neujahrs-Geschenk auf 1805 (Tübingen: Cotta, 1804); translated by Charles Richard Coke as *Crates and Hipparchia: A Tale in a Series of Letters* (Norwich & London: Longmans, 1823);

Euthanasia: Drey Gespräche über das Leben nach dem Tode, veranlasst durch D.J.K. W**Ls Geschichte der wirklichen Erscheinung seiner Gattin nach ihrem Tode (Leipzig: Göschen, 1805);

Das Hexameron von Rosenhain (Leipzig: Göschen, 1805);

Sämmtliche Werke, 63 volumes (Vienna: Doll, 1811-1813);

Ueber das Fortleben im Andenken der Nachwelt (N.p., 1812);

Sämmtliche Werke, 53 volumes, edited by Johann Gottfried Gruber (Leipzig: Göschen, 1818-1828);

Werke, 16 volumes, edited by Heinrich Düntzer (Berlin: Hempel, 1879-1880);

Gesammelte Schriften, 23 volumes to date, published by the German Commission of the Prussian Academy of Sciences (after 1954 by the Academy of Sciences of the German Democratic Republic), edited by Bernhard Seuffert, Hans Werner Seiffert, and others (Berlin: Weidmann, 1909-1954; Berlin: Akademie-Verlag, 1954-).

OTHER: *Sammlung der Zürcherischen Streitschriften zur Verbesserung des deutschen Geschmackes wider die Gottschedische Schule von 1741 bis 1744,* 3 volumes, preface by Wieland (Zurich: Orell, 1753);

Johann Jakob Bodmer, *Die Syndflut: Ein Gedicht in fynf Gesängen*, preface by Wieland (Zurich: Heidegger, 1753);

Bodmer, *Gedichte in gereymten Versen*, foreword by Wieland (Zurich: Orell, 1754);

Friedrich Gottlieb Klopstock, *Der Tod Adams: Ein Trauerspiel*, introduction by Wieland (N.p., 1757);

William Shakespeare, *Theatralische Werke: Aus dem Englischen übersezt*, 8 volumes, translated by Wieland (Zurich: Orell, Geßner, 1762-1766);

Sophie von La Roche, *Geschichte des Fräuleins von Sternheim: Von einer Freundin derselben aus Original-Papieren und anderen zuverläßigen Quellen gezogen*, 2 volumes, edited by Wieland (Leipzig: Weidmann & Reich, 1771);

Johann Georg Sulzer, *Allgemeine Theorie der Schönen Künste*, 2 volumes (Leipzig: Weidmann & Reich, 1771-1774)–includes in volume 1, "Hirtengedichte," pp. 537-540, in volume 2, "Naiv," pp. 803-809, by Wieland;

Der teutsche Merkur, 68 volumes, published and edited by Wieland (Weimar: Verlag der Gesellschaft, 1773; Weimar: Hoffmann, 1774-1789);

Horace, *Briefe, aus dem Lateinischen übersetzt und mit historischen Einleitungen und auch nöthigen Erläuterungen versehen*, 2 volumes, translated with commentary by Wieland (Dessau: Verlagskasse und Buchhandlung der Gelehrten, 1782);

Horace, *Satyren, aus dem Lateinischen übersetzt und mit Einleitungen und erläuternden Anmerkungen versehen*, 2 volumes, translated with commentary by Wieland (Leipzig: Weidmann & Reich, 1786);

Dschinnistan oder Auserlesene Feen- und Geister-Mährchen, theils neu erfunden, theils neu übersetzt und umgearbeitet, 3 volumes, edited by Wieland (Winterthur: Steiner, 1786-1789);

Allgemeine Damen Bibliothek: Eine freye Übersetzung des französischen Werkes dieses Namens, 6 volumes, edited by Karl Leonhard Reinhold, introductions by Wieland (Leipzig: Weidmann & Reich, 1786-1789);

Lucian, *Sämmtliche Werke, aus dem Griechischen übersetzt und mit Anmerkungen und Erläuterungen versehen*, 6 volumes, translated with commentary by Wieland (Leipzig: Weidmann & Reich, 1788-1789);

Johann Heinrich Meister, *Von der natürlichen Moral: Aus dem Französischen des Herrn M** von Hrn. Sch** übersetzt*, translated by Jo-

hann Georg Schultheß, edited by Wieland (Leipzig: Göschen, 1789);

Marguerite de Lussan, *Thessalische Zauber- und Geistermährchen aus dem Französischen*, 2 volumes, translated by J. S. G. Schorcht and Samuel Baur, introduction by Wieland (Zittau & Leipzig: Schöps & Göschen, 1789);

Der neue teutsche Merkur, 60 volumes published by Wieland, edited by Wieland until 1796 (Leipzig & Weimar: Göschen, 1790-1799; Weimar: Gädicke, 1800-1802; Weimar: Landes-Industrie-Comptoir, 1803-1810);

Historischer Calender für Damen für das Jahr 1790, edited by Wieland and Johann Wilhelm von Archenholtz (Leipzig: Göschen, 1790)–includes Wieland's "Die Pythagorischen Frauen," pp. 190-247; "Aspasia," pp. 248-285; "Julia," pp. 286-328;

Historischer Calender für Damen für das Jahr 1792, edited by Friedrich Schiller, introduction by Wieland (Leipzig: Göschen, 1792);

Das attische Museum, 4 volumes, edited by Wieland (Zurich: Geßner, 1796-1804);

Taschenbuch auf das Jahr 1804, edited by Wieland and Johann Wolfgang Goethe (Tübingen: Cotta, 1803)–includes Wieland's "Zwey Erzählungen aus dem Pentameron von Rosenhain";

Johann Karl August Musäus, *Die deutschen Volksmährchen*, 5 volumes, edited by Wieland (Gotha: Ettinger, 1804-1805);

Ludwig Wieland, *Erzählungen und Dialogen*, 2 volumes, edited by Wieland (volume 1, Leipzig: Göschen, 1803; volume 2, Zurich: Geßner, 1805);

Das neue attische Museum, 3 volumes, edited by Wieland, Johann Jakob Hottinger and Friedrich Jacobs (Zurich & Leipzig: Geßner & Wolff, 1805-1811);

La Roche, *Melusinens Sommer-Abende*, edited by Wieland (Halle: Verlag der Neuen Societäts-Buch- und Kunsthandlung, 1806);

Friedrich Ludwig Dulon, *Dülons des blinden Flötenspielers Leben und Meynungen von ihm selbst bearbeitet*, 2 volumes, edited by Wieland (Zurich: Geßner, 1807-1808);

Marcus Tullius Cicero, *Sämmtliche Briefe, übersetzt und erläutert*, 4 volumes, translated with commentary by Wieland (Zurich: Geßner, 1808-1812).

PERIODICAL PUBLICATIONS: "Briefe an einen Freund über das deutsche Singspiel 'Alceste,'" 2 installments, *Der teutsche Merkur*

(January 1773): 34-72; (March 1773): 223-243;

"Der Geist Shakespears," *Der teutsche Merkur* (September 1773): 183-195;

"Stilpon oder über die Wahl eines Oberzunftmeisters von Megara, eine Unterredung," *Der teutsche Merkur* (September 1774): 295-337;

"Das Urtheil des Midas: Ein komisches Singspiel in einem Aufzug," *Der teutsche Merkur* (January 1775): 3-19;

"Geschichte des Philosophen Danischmende," 9 installments, *Der teutsche Merkur* (January 1775): 29-66; (February 1775): 97-132; (March 1775): 211-244; (April 1775): 42-45; (May 1775): 105-108; (June 1775): 209-230; (July 1775): 16-36; (August 1775): 110-135; (November 1775): 115-133;

"Der Mönch und die Nonne, auf dem Mittelstein," 2 installments, *Der teutsche Merkur* (March 1775): 193-305; (April 1775): 3-15;

"Unterredungen zwischen W** und dem Pfarrer zu ***," 5 installments, *Der teutsche Merkur* (April 1775): 70-96; (June 1775): 243; (September 1775): 251-268; (October 1775): 61-74; (December 1775): 263-271;

"Titanomachia, oder das neue Heldenbuch: Ein bürleskes Gedicht in so vielen Gesängen als man will," *Der teutsche Merkur* (October 1775): 9-15;

"Liebe um Liebe," 6 installments, *Der teutsche Merkur* (May 1776): 121-146; (June 1776): 217-230; (July 1776): 38-57; (August 1776): 97-111; (November 1776): 149-161; (December 1776): 193-211;

"Bonifaz Schleicher: Ein biographisches Fragment," 3 installments, *Der teutsche Merkur* (June 1776): 249-261; (August 1776): 136-150; (September 1776): 220-232;

"Geron der Adelich, eine Erzählung aus Konig Artus' Zeit," 2 installments, *Der teutsche Merkur* (January 1777): 3-16; (February 1777): 105-142;

"Betrachtung über die Abnahme des menschlichen Geschlechts," *Der teutsche Merkur* (March 1777): 209-246;

"Das Sommermährchen oder Des Maulthiers Zaum: Eine Erzählung aus der Tafelrunde-Zeit," 2 installments, *Der teutsche Merkur* (July 1777): 3-21; (August 1777): 97-121;

"Gedanken über die Ideale der Alten," 3 installments, *Der teutsche Merkur* (August 1777): 121-169; (September 1777): 198-228; (October 1777): 69-80;

"Über das göttliche Recht der Obrigkeit oder: Über den Lehrsatz, daß die höchste Gewalt in einem Staat durch das Volk geschaffen sei; an Herrn P. D. in C.," *Der teutsche Merkur* (November 1777): 119-145;

"Hann und Gulpenhee, oder: Zuviel gesagt ist nichts gesagt: Eine morgenländische Erzählung," *Der teutsche Merkur* (February 1778): 103-114;

"Der Vogelsang, oder Die drei Lehren," *Der teutsche Merkur* (March 1778): 193-211;

"Schach Lolo," *Der teutsche Merkur* (May 1778): 97-130;

"Zergliederung des Buchs, genannt: Leben, Bemerkungen und Meynungen Johann Bunkels," 5 installments, *Der teutsche Merkur* (July 1778): 75-90; (August 1778): 165-172; (October 1778): 55-75; (November 1778): 158-173; (December 1778): 248-260;

"Pervonte, oder Die Wünsche," 3 installments, *Der teutsche Merkur* (November 1778): 97-110; (December 1778): 193-201; (January 1779): 3-18;

"Unmaasgebliche Gedanken eines Laien über Herrn D. Carl Friedrich Bahrdts Glaubensbekenntnis," 2 installments, *Der teutsche Merkur* (August 1779): 170-179; (September 1779): 218-262;

"Über eine Anekdote von J. J. Rousseau," 2 installments, *Der teutsche Merkur* (April 1780): 74-90; (May 1780): 112-151;

"Nachtrag zur Anekdote von J. J. Rousseau," 2 installments, *Der teutsche Merkur* (August 1780): 146-156; (October 1780): 25-67;

"Athenion, genannt Aristion, oder das Glück der Athenienser unter der Regierung eines Philosophen," 2 installments, *Der teutsche Merkur* (September 1781): 3-22; (October 1781): 140-170;

"Gespräche über einige neueste Weltbegebenheiten," 3 installments, *Der teutsche Merkur* (May 1782): 154-178; (June 1782): 253-279; (July 1782): 19-46;

"Briefe an einen jungen Dichter," 3 installments, *Der teutsche Merkur* (August 1782): 129-157; (October 1782): 57-85; (March 1784): 228-253;

"Über die Frage: Was ist Hochteutsch," 3 installments, *Der teutsche Merkur* (November 1782): 145-170; (December 1782): 193-216; (April 1783): 1-30;

"Die Aëropetomanie oder die neuesten Schritte der Franzosen zur Kunst zu fliegen," *Der teutsche Merkur* (October 1783): 69-96;

"Die Aëronauten, oder Fortgesetzte Nachrichten von den Versuchen mit der aërostatischen Kugel," 2 installments, *Der teutsche Merkur* (January 1784): 69-96; (February 1784): 140-170;

"Über die Rechte und Pflichten der Schriftsteller in Absicht ihrer Nachrichten, Bemerkungen, und Urtheile über Nationen, Regierungen und andre politische Gegenstände," *Der teutsche Merkur* (September 1785): 193-207;

"Gedanken aus Veranlassung eines Briefes des Herrn D. Bicker in Bremen an Herrn Hofrath Baldinger über Lavater's Magnetismus," 2 installments, *Der teutsche Merkur* (January 1787): 82-96; (February 1787): 172-185;

"Gedanken von der Freyheit über Gegenstände des Glaubens zu philosophieren," 4 installments, *Der teutsche Merkur* (January 1787): 77-93; (March 1787): 195-221; (June 1787): 549-567; (July 1787): 3-28;

"Eine Lustreise in die Unterwelt," 2 installments, *Der teutsche Merkur* (August 1787): 108-141; (October 1787): 3-28;

"Peregrin, ein Auszug aus Lucian's Nachrichten von dem Leben und Ende dieses Schwärmers," *Der teutsche Merkur* (July 1788): 61-96;

"Das Geheimniß des Kosmopolitenordens," *Der teutsche Merkur* (August 1788): 97-115; (November 1788): 121-143;

"Peregrin und Lucian: Ein Dialog im Elysium," *Der teutsche Merkur* (August 1788): 176-190;

"Ein paar Worte für die Jesuiten," *Der teutsche Merkur* (January 1789): 208-220;

"Über die Rechtmäßigkeit des Gebrauchs, welchen die französische Nation dermalen von ihrer Aufklärung und Stärke macht," *Der teutsche Merkur* (September 1789): 225-262;

"Kosmopolitische Adresse an die französische Nationalversammlung von Eleutherius Philoceltes," *Der teutsche Merkur* (October 1789): 24-60;

"Faustina, ein Seitenstück zu Aspasia und Julia im Historischen Kalender für Damen 1790," *Der neue teutsche Merkur* (January 1790): 19-26;

"Unpartheiische Betrachtungen über die dermalige Staatsrevolution in Frankreich," 2 installments, *Der neue teutsche Merkur* (May 1790): 40-69; (June 1790): 144-164;

"Zufällige Gedanken über die Abschaffung des erblichen Adels in Frankreich," *Der neue teutsche Merkur* (August 1790): 392-424;

"Ausführliche Darstellung der in der französischen Nationalversammlung am 26. und 27. November 1790 vorgefallenen Debatten nebst Epilogus des Herausgebers," 2 installments, *Der neue teutsche Merkur* (January 1791): 1-80; (February 1791): 123-169;

"Erklärung des Herausgebers des T.M. über die im 6ten Monatsstück des T. Merk. 1791 auf der letzten Seite befindliche Note," *Der neue teutsche Merkur* (October 1791): 113-149;

"Sendschreiben des Herausgebers des T.M. an Herrn P** zu ****," *Der neue teutsche Merkur* (January 1792): 64-112;

"Das Merkwürdigste aus der Session der französischen Nationalversammlung vom 25. December 1791," *Der neue teutsche Merkur* (February 1792): 146-159;

"Betrachtungen über des Herrn Condorcet Erklärung, was ein Bauer und Handarbeiter in Frankreich sei," *Der neue teutsche Merkur* (May 1792): 19-58;

"Schreiben an einen Correspondenten in Paris," *Der neue teutsche Merkur* (October 1792): 192-223;

"Die französische Republik," *Der neue teutsche Merkur* (November 1792): 275-329;

"Betrachtungen über die gegenwärtige Lage des Vaterlandes," *Der neue teutsche Merkur* (January 1793): 3-55;

"Über teutschen Patriotismus: Betrachtungen, Fragen und Zweifel," *Der neue teutsche Merkur* (May 1793): 3-21;

"Die Cyklopenphilosophie und das Cyklopenrecht in nuce, aus dem 'Cyklops' des Euripides," *Der neue teutsche Merkur* (June 1793): 199-203;

"Kurze Darstellung der innerlichen Verfassung und äußerlichen Lage von Athen in dem Zeitraum, worin Aristophanes seine noch vorhandenen Komödien auf die Schaubühne brachte," *Der neue teutsche Merkur* (January 1794): 19-49;

"Über Krieg und Frieden," *Der neue teutsche Merkur* (June 1794): 181-201;

"Versuch einer metrischen Übersetzung der Acharner des Aristofanes," 3 installments, *Der neue teutsche Merkur* (August 1794): 350-388; (September 1794): 3-45; (October 1794): 113-171;

"Die Wasserkufe oder der Einsiedler und die Seneschallin von Aquilegia," *Der neue teutsche Merkur* (March 1795): 239-270;

Isocrates, "Die Panegyrische Rede des Isokrates," translated by Wieland, *Das attische Museum*, 1, no. 1 (1797): i-xl, 1-110;

Aristophanes, *Die Ritter oder Die Demagogen des Aristophanes*, translated by Wieland, *Das attische Museum*, 2, no. 1 (1798): iii-xxxii, 1-144;

"Gespräche unter vier Augen," 5 installments, *Der neue teutsche Merkur* (February 1798): 105-129; (March 1798): 259-288; (April 1798): 355-383; (May 1798): 3-48; (July 1798): 201-222;

"Fragment eines Gesprächs zwischen einem ungenannten Fremden und Geron," *Der neue teutsche Merkur* (October 1798): 101-116;

Aristophanes, *Die Wolken des Aristophanes*, 2 installments, translated by Wieland, *Das attische Museum*, 2, no. 2 (1798): 49-174; no. 3 (1798): 1-124;

"Versuch über die Frage: Ob und wiefern Aristofanes gegen den Vorwurf, den Sokrates in den Wolken persönlich mißhandelt zu haben, gerechtfertigt oder entschuldigt werden könne?," *Das attische Museum*, 3, no. 1 (1799): 57-100;

Xenophon, "Sokratische Gespräche aus Xenofons denkwürdigen Nachrichten von Sokrates," 2 installments, translated by Wieland, *Das attische Museum*, 3, no. 1 (1799): 101-168; no. 2 (1799): 296-336;

"Meine Erklärung über einen im St. James Chronicle, January 25, 1800, abgedruckten Artikel, der zur Überschrift hat: Prediction concerning Bounapart, mit dem Beysatz: the following Dialogue is now circulating in the higher Circles; the observations are of the pen of a foreign Minister," *Der neue teutsche Merkur* (March 1800): 243-276;

Xenophon, "Xenofons Gastmahl," translated by Wieland, *Das attische Museum*, 4, no. 1 (1802): 65-148;

"Versuch über das Xenofontische Gastmahl als Muster einer dialogisirten dramatischen Erzählung betrachtet," *Das attische Museum*, 4, no. 2 (1802): 99-124;

Euripides, *Ion: Eine Tragoedie des Euripides*, translated by Wieland, *Das attische Museum*, 4, no. 3 (1803): 3-166;

"Grundriß und Beurtheilung der Tragödie Ion von Euripides," *Das neue attische Museum*, 1, no. 1 (1804): 3-46;

Euripides, *Helena: Eine Tragödie von Euripides*, translated by Wieland, *Das neue attische Museum*, 1, no. 1 (1804): 47-158;

Aristophanes, *Die Vögel des Aristofanes*, 2 installments, translated by Wieland, *Das neue attische Museum*, 1, no. 3 (1805): 51-158; no. 2 (1806): 107-163;

"Grundriß und Beurtheilung der Helena des Euripides," *Das neue attische Museum*, 2, no. 2 (1806): 1-90.

Christoph Martin Wieland's literary career spanned six decades. During a large part if not all of that period he was the most widely known and most popular writer of the German language. The prominence was gained, in the opinion of some, by his overemphasis of the erotic (it was Wieland who introduced the word *erotisch* into German). These critics felt that he ignored the traditional concepts of a literary artist's moral obligations, and he admitted that he never allowed his unmarried daughters to read his writings. He added further fuel to the fire when he questioned from time to time the moral rectitude of other poets, and this issue, along with his mercurial and sometimes combative nature, kept him at or near the center of controversy throughout his life. Negative criticism and contention notwithstanding, a clear majority of his colleagues in the German literary community considered him the most learned, most talented, and most skillful of their number, and throughout Europe he was regarded as his nation's most prominent writer. Before he was forty years old he was called the German Voltaire, for his genius appeared to be no less universal than that of the great Frenchman, and his attitudes toward the institutions of society seemed just as irreverent. This man, so highly esteemed by his own age, was, however, during the course of the nineteenth century subjected in literary histories to such repeated accusations of salaciousness and of a cosmopolitanism alien to the true Germanic spirit that he slipped first into disrepute and then into near oblivion. Only recently have critics and historians begun to discover in his works major contributions to the evolution of German literature. The rehabilitation has been carried to the point that Wieland is now often seen as the key figure for any real understanding of the eighteenth century in Germany, since for over half a century it was he who set the standard for German Rococo and set the stage for both Classicism and Romanticism. He was the first German translator of Shakespeare's dramas (1762-1766), and his annotated translations of Horace and Lucian are still regarded as among the most successful ever made into German; his

Lady Johanna Gray (1758) can be considered the first German drama in blank verse; his *Geschichte des Agathon* (1766-1767; translated as *The History of Agathon,* 1773) was the first modern German novel of psychological development; his *Alceste* (1773) was the first modern opera with a German libretto; his critical review *Der teutsche Merkur* was the first successful general literary journal in German; and his reasoned reporting of events in France during and after the revolution represents the only systematic commentary about those momentous events by a German poet. For literary history, moreover, his life is almost as significant as his works. For over half a century he maintained personal contact with almost all the major writers of the German language, worked together with many of them, helped some begin their careers, and directly influenced countless others in their style, philosophy, and choice of subject matter. As the editor of and leading contributor to the *Merkur* he became the arbiter of style and taste in literary matters for all of southern Germany (a conclusion drawn by no less an authority than Johann Wolfgang von Goethe). He and his publisher Georg Joachim Göschen became involved in litigation which set precedents within German jurisprudence protecting authors and artists from exploitation by the book trade. Younger poets frequently attracted attention by questioning the writings and the person of Wieland, the one author most surely known by the public they addressed.

Wieland, like so many other German writers of the eighteenth century, was the son of a Lutheran minister. At the time of his birth on 5 September 1733 his father, Thomas Adam Wieland, was the pastor in Oberholzheim, a village owned by the Heilig-Geist-Spital (Holy Ghost Hospital) in the imperially chartered Swabian city of Biberach and located some twenty-three kilometers northeast of the city. His mother, Regina Catherina Wieland, née Kick, was the daughter of a military officer in the service of the margrave of Baden. Both sides of the family had been residents of Biberach for many generations; the Wielands had been particularly prominent, having provided the city with clergymen, merchants, attorneys, and, in the seventeenth century, a mayor. Christoph Martin was a precocious child; his proud but stern father, a former student of the famed theologian August Hermann Francke at Halle, provided him the best education available, first in personally conducted tutorials and then in the public schools of Biberach.

The boy was a prodigious reader and an astoundingly facile learner whose capacities, it was soon seen, exceeded the qualifications of his teachers. He later recalled that as a child he could complete his lessons with ease and then devote the remainder of his time to studying "unaufhörlich" (ceaselessy) a popular guidebook to the art of poetry by Johann Christoph Gottsched and to the delectation of long didactic verses from his favorite poet, Barthold Hinrich Brockes. His own writing of verse began before he was three years old. The predilection was frowned upon by his father but encouraged by his mother, even though some of the verses he wrote about his teachers were more than slightly impertinent. At thirteen he was sent far north to one of the most prestigious boarding schools of the age, Klosterbergen, located just outside the walls of Magdeburg. There, too, his genius was quickly appreciated by his teachers, but the youth continued to exhibit a hard-to-control independence of thought and a sense of humor a bit too irreverent for the pious headmaster of the school. But Wieland overcame his difficulties with administrators and certain teachers, satisfied the academic requirements of the institution, and read voraciously beyond the assignments set for him. His tastes were universal and ranged from Christian Wolff's philosophy to Pierre Bayle's *Dictionnaire historique et critique* (1697) and the major French materialists and even to French translations of Samuel Richardson's sentimental English novels. In less than two years he left the school, having learned all that he could be taught and having acquired for himself the unsavory reputation of being a freethinker.

The next fifteen months Wieland spent in the home of Johann Wilhelm Baumer, a physician and professor of medicine, chemistry, and philosophy at the University of Erfurt and a brother-in-law of Wieland's maternal uncle. There he worked diligently, reading widely under Baumer's supervision but focusing his attention on the writings of Gottfried Wilhelm von Leibniz, Bayle, and Johann Jakob Bruckner. In May 1749 he enrolled at the university, but the only academic experience of which he spoke in later years was a series of lectures given him privately by Baumer on Miguel de Cervantes' novel *Don Quixote* (1605-1615).

In the spring of 1750 Wieland returned for the first time in three years to the home of his parents. There he met a distant cousin from Augsburg, Marie Sophie Gutermann; the girl had fled to relatives in Biberach after her Protestant father forced her to break her engagement to a Catholic. Wieland found in this beautiful, well-read, and profoundly unhappy young woman all the moral splendor of one of Richardson's heroines, and he became so transported in his love for her that Platonic raptures replaced the cool, rational world he had constructed from his readings and musings. Sophie responded to the virtuous eloquence of her new friend, and soon the two were engaged. The extent of her influence on him at this time can scarcely be exaggerated; his later declaration that he would never have become a poet had she not entered his life is quite possibly an accurate self-assessment. Their bliss, however, was as brief as it was intense; in October the new young idealist had to depart for Tübingen to begin a course of study in jurisprudence upon which he and his parents had agreed.

Wieland soon discovered that the law held little attraction for him. He found poetry his true calling and, in his opinion, the noblest of all the arts. It appears that he stopped attending most lectures and spent much of his time alone, devoting his energies to literary compositions. He exchanged verses with Sophie, but in the main he concentrated on preparing and composing a didactic poem, *Die Natur der Dinge* (The Nature of Things, 1751), an ambitious refutation, forty-one hundred lines long, of the Epicurianism in Lucretius's *De rerum natura*. In May 1751 he was inspired by Sophie to write *Lobgesang auf die Liebe* (Hymn to Love, 1751), in which he stressed the divine quality of his affections but also blended into the verses more traditional and popular Anacreontic depictions of his beloved's intoxicating charms. During the following summer he undertook an epic on the subject of the ancient German hero Arminius or Hermann, sent *Die Natur der Dinge* to Halle for evaluation and publication, and initiated a correspondence with one of the most prolific writers and most outspoken literary polemicists of the day, Johann Jakob Bodmer of Zurich. Within a year this exchange of letters led Bodmer to suggest that the young man come to Zurich as a poet's apprentice. Before that invitation was extended Wieland had completed another large group of odes, most of them for Sophie but one addressed to his new patron in Switzerland, and three books. Two of the books, *Zwölf moralische Briefe in Versen* (Twelve Moral Epistles in Verse, 1752) and *Erzæhlungen* (Tales, 1752), he produced to demonstrate the suitability

Sophie Gutermann, to whom Wieland became engaged in 1750. Three years later, during Wieland's prolonged sojourn in Zurich, she married Georg Michael La Roche; but she and Wieland remained friends until her death in 1807. Drawing by an unknown artist (Schiller-Nationalmuseum, Marbach am Neckar).

of the German language for the kind of religiously sentimental writing popular at the time in England and, to a degree, in France as well; the third, *Anti-Ovid, oder die Kunst zu lieben* (Anti-Ovid; or, The Art of Loving, 1752), was an attempt to prove his theory that Anacreontic techniques and humor were adaptable to literary works with high moral purpose.

In October 1752, following a brief reunion with his fiancée in Biberach, Wieland traveled to Zurich. The trip was supposed to last only a few weeks, during which Sophie had agreed to wait at his parents' house for his return. The few weeks in Switzerland were to turn into eight years, and the engagement was not to survive. The loss of his beloved was a great disappointment for Wieland, but the Swiss sojourn, the first twenty months of which he spent in Zurich as

Bodmer's houseguest, brought him great rewards. He gained much of the experience and knowledge he had hoped to acquire and found more fame than he had envisioned.

Bodmer had experimented before with the role of mentor to budding young genius. In 1750 he had brought into his house the gifted north German poet Friedrich Gottlieb Klopstock, but he had been dismayed to discover that the author of the lofty biblical epic *Der Messias* (The Messiah, 1748-1773) was too easily distracted from serious study by such activities as dancing, ice-skating, and horseback riding in the company of people his own age. To avoid repetition of such disappointment Bodmer set a regimen for Wieland which kept the new pupil occupied almost uninterruptedly for the next year and a half with a program of reading and discussions with the city's leading intellectuals, but above all with exercises at the writing desk. Bodmer was quickly satisfied that his protégé was sufficiently docile, and he became so impressed with the young man's philosophical and philological talents that he declared that Wieland had been born to become Germany's next Leibniz. The young poet, in turn, seemed content within the limitations imposed by his mentor and passed his time mostly in the company of his elders, two notable exceptions being close friendships with the young pastor Johann Heinrich Schinz and with the painter-poet Salomon Geßner.

Despite all appearances, the relationship between Wieland and his patron was not ideal. Bodmer was a learned man, an inspiring and able teacher, but at the same time he was a demanding master who may well have misused the eager pupil. Wieland's first assigned exercise was an analysis of the aesthetic qualities in Bodmer's epic poem *Noah* (1752); he was then called on to participate in the literary polemic Bodmer had been waging intermittently for two decades against the literary community in Leipzig and its leader, Professor Gottsched, the scholar who had so influenced Wieland during his childhood. A collection of old partisan writings from assorted Swiss critics was edited and published as a volume for which Wieland provided a preface. Matters became more acrimonious in 1755, when Wieland announced anonymously a new "Dunciad" for the Germans after the model of Alexander Pope. The work would chastise dunces in general but particularly the Antichrist Gottsched, the lawgiver whose rigid insistence that literature be cleansed of all irrational elements had erected barriers between poetry and its most natural subject matter, the wonders of religion. The most intemperate of his efforts to please Bodmer by doing battle with secular literature came, however, in his *Empfindungen eines Christen* (Sentiments of a Christian, 1757). The preface, written as an open letter to the Prussian Court pastor August Friedrich Wilhelm Sack in Berlin, was a diatribe against the Anacreontic poets of the day, whose celebrations of wine, women, and song made them, in Wieland's reeducated eyes, preachers of lust and debauchery. The verses of Johann Peter Uz were singled out as an insult to Christianity: any true Christian would prefer the poorest verses in any hymnal to the best poems of an Uz! Wieland quickly rued his hasty comments and was so contrite that for a second edition of the book in 1758 he wrote a new preface in which he apologized to Uz. The young poet's desire to make peace was thwarted, however, by his Swiss mentors—Bodmer and particularly Bodmer's confidant Martin Künzli—who convinced him of the implausibility and undesirability of any retraction or apology.

Letters from Biberach had made clear as early as the late fall of 1752 that Sophie felt neglected by her betrothed and was miserable in her parents' home. Wieland opted to do nothing, hoping that matters would resolve themselves. Even after he received reports the following year that Sophie was regularly attending social events at the nearby castle in Warthausen, the residence of the distinguished and highly cultivated Count Friedrich Stadion, he took no steps to save his engagement. Still, when the news arrived that on 27 December 1753 Sophie had married Georg Michael La Roche, Stadion's illegitimate son and amanuensis, he was inconsolable. He denounced all young females as mindless butterflies, forswore their company, and sought out older and wiser matrons, widows, and spinsters, who became his admirers and members of what came to be called his "Serail" (seraglio). In response to their extravagant praise for his verses he produced a series of sentimental works such as *Briefe von Verstorbenen an hinterlassene Freunde* (Letters from the Deceased to Friends Left Behind, 1753), *Empfindungen eines Christen*, and *Sympathien* (1756; translated as *The Sympathy of Souls*, 1787), all of which emphasized the inevitability of suffering and the need for steadfast religious faith during periods of travail. An even more pious chord was struck in a series of hymns he wrote between April and December 1755. Bodmer praised the sublimity of these poems but was displeased with his pupil's new life-style and contended that the women's uncritical admiration would have an adverse effect on the quality of Wieland's work. The sometimes caustic remarks made by Bodmer to the young man about his chosen company led Wieland to feel increasingly the need for some degree of independence. Although he was careful to avoid a total rupture in the relationship, he resolved to leave Bodmer's house. One of the feminine admirers, Verena Grebel, a widow some fifteen years Wieland's senior and the object of his most tender affections, helped him find a way out. Frau Grebel's sister-in-law was the mother of two boys for whom a tutor was being sought; other affluent families in Zurich provided four additional pupils, and Wieland began the career as a private tutor that was to be his principal source of income for the next six years.

From September 1754 until he left Zurich in June 1759 Wieland juggled his duties as preceptor and his role as Bodmer's protégé in a more or less satisfactory fashion. He accompanied his mentor on trips to Trogen in Appenzell to meet the physician Lorenz Zellweger, to Neftenbach to visit Pastor Johann Caspar Heß, and, perhaps most important, to Winterthur, where he was introduced to Johannes Wolfgang Dietrich, and Johann Georg Sulzer. At Bodmer's suggestion he began a correspondence with the philosopher and physician Johann Georg Zimmermann in Brugg; Zimmermann was to become Wieland's most important confidant for at least the next five years. Bodmer and these new acquaintances encouraged his writing and, to support that nonremunerative calling, sought to help him become established as a pedagogue as well.

For his part Wieland labored assiduously, producing in 1757-1758—in additon to his vast output of lyric and narrative verse—one of the most noteworthy efforts of his early period: *Lady Johanna Gray*, a dramatic account of the reign and martyrdom of England's nine-day queen. Although the tragedy was derided by the highly respected north German critic Gotthold Ephraim Lessing, who found the characters tiresomely virtuous and accused Wieland of plagiarizing Nicholas Rowe's *The Tragedy of Lady Jane Grey* (1715), the play is remarkable for several reasons. The title character, a young woman who cannot be untrue to her convictions however dire the consequences, whose instincts are in complete harmony with her perceptions of duty, and who accepts harsh fate and can still recognize nature

as just, is clearly a forerunner of Goethe's and Friedrich Schiller's later classical heroines. Equally important, the drama is the first successful German work in blank verse, the form of choice for all the great dramatists of the nation over the next half century. Wieland wrote the drama as he did because of his growing interest in and knowledge of English literature; he had not only read Rowe's play but had begun to read and think about the works of Shakespeare. The gleanings from his study he put to use in *Lady Johanna Gray*; his employment of typically English metrical forms, his English subject matter, and his high pathos combined to give the piece a measure of novelty on account of which it enjoyed some success throughout German-speaking Europe over the next two decades, Lessing's criticism notwithstanding. The drama played to highly appreciative and responsive audiences in Winterthur and Schaffhausen with the distinguished actress Sophie Ackermann in the title role.

By the end of 1758 Wieland realized that he had little more to expect from his stay in Zurich. His relationship with Bodmer was strained—even the success of *Lady Johanna Gray* had become a cause for dissension. Still, Bodmer continued to help the younger man search for a good position as a teacher. Wieland's successes as an author had attracted the attention of all Germany. From Lessing and from Friedrich Nicolai had come criticism that Wieland's religion seemed affected and posturing, and fear as well as distrust were expressed by those he had attacked at Bodmer's behest; but among more traditionally oriented theologians and pedagogues Wieland had been received far more positively. As a consequence he received many offers of employment. To improve his chances further, he created a poetic work more manly in tone than most of those he had produced over the preceding five years: *Cyrus* (1759), an epic celebration of the valorous deeds and noble character of a great national leader. His title hero was a Persian monarch, but his model and inspiration was the idol of the day, the Prussian soldier-king Friedrich II. Still more directly addressed to his purposes was a treatise on the aims and methods of pedagogy (1758), stressing the role of education in developing intellectual and spiritual integrity along with social utility. The essay was designed to appeal particularly to the Swiss and to procure a vocation for him in Basel. Although the work failed to obtain the intended results, a wealthy Bern official, Friedrich von Sinner, offered him a position as a private tutor; on 1 June 1759 Wieland left Zurich.

Wieland was welcomed warmly by the leading citizens of Bern, but he quickly discovered that his acceptance of employment by the Sinner family had been a mistake. Within a month he left his position to teach a group of boys from several different families. His failure, however, to establish a satisfactory relationship with his first employer cost him the respect and goodwill of most of the patricians who had welcomed his arrival. Among the few influential men of the city who defended and continued to befriend him were the pastor Daniel Stapfer and the wealthy landowner and author Bernard Vinzenz Tscharner. More important for him than either of these friendships, however, were the bonds which soon linked him to Julie von Bondeli, Bern's most famous female intellectual. Although their initial meeting was less than cordial, each came quickly to respect the other's ability, and within two months Wieland had declared his love for her. Julie helped him form the new attitudes toward which he had been groping after the loss of Sophie and in the vacuum created by his rejection of the absolute authority of his mentor, Bodmer. Julie was a decidedly practical individual, and this side of her personality left its mark on her fiancé. She is credited with playing an important role in his overcoming the excesses of idealism and enthusiasm that had characterized most of his behavior and writing for nearly a decade. With her counsel and approval he completed a short novel he had begun in Zurich, *Araspes und Panthea* (1760; translated as "Araspes and Panthea," 1775), contrasting the irresistible and destructive effects of erotic passions on human behavior to the ennobling emotions of loyalty and devotion. Love and the dilemmas produced by it were also the themes of the drama *Clementina von Porretta* (1760), which he wrote hurriedly in response to the success of *Lady Johanna Gray*. The new play, based on Richardson's novel *The History of Sir Charles Grandison* (1753-1754), focuses on the episode in which the true devotion of Sir Charles for Clementina is frustrated because of the difference in their faiths: the Catholic girl is forbidden to marry a Protestant, a tragedy which uncannily foreshadows Wieland's own experiences a few years later.

In spite of his fondness for Julie and his contentment in her company, Wieland knew that his position in Bern was even less tolerable than the one in Zurich had been. An opportunity for escape was provided by his native city: when he was nominated for membership on the inner council of Biberach, he lost no time in accepting the post. In July 1760 he returned home, once again leaving a fiancée behind but promising to send for her as soon as his financial conditions might permit marriage.

Any refuge from controversy Wieland had hoped to find was not to be. On returning home he became involved almost immediately in a difficult campaign for Protestant mayor of the city being waged by Johannes von Hillern, the brother-in-law of Sophie La Roche. Sophie's sister and her husband quickly won Wieland as an ally, even though the choice meant that he had to oppose the very senators who had just elected him to the council. Nonetheless, he joined the political fray enthusiastically, just as he had readily participated in Bodmer's literary feuds eight years earlier. Once again, he was to find his eagerness costly. When he was nominated by the new Mayor von Hillern to become director of the municipal chancellery, he was challenged by the enemies he had created for himself on the grounds that, as neither a member of the nobility nor the holder of an earned academic degree, he was unqualified for the office. Another issue soon surfaced: according to the laws of parity for the city established by the Treaty of Westphalia, the chancellorship had traditionally belonged to the Protestant party; now, however, the Catholics wanted to gain the lucrative office, and with disunity among their opponents about the candidate the stage was set for a protracted and bitter battle. First, Wieland's appointment was disputed; then, after he was elected, his salary was sequestered for more than three years while litigation pended in various imperial courts.

Wieland's personal life, meanwhile, was no less turbulent. His beloved Sophie, now a mother, had returned with her husband from Mainz to Warthausen in the entourage of Count Stadion. The reunion forced the poet to face emotions which he had suppressed for years. He sought to supplant them in a love affair with Christina Hogel, the nineteen-year-old daughter of a Catholic sexton in Biberach. "Bibi" Hogel was a singer by whom Wieland had first become enchanted at a concert; Sophie encouraged the relationship, for she hoped that it might cure him of his love for her and put him in touch with reality. Thus Bibi became an instrument of therapy and the former fiancée a consultant in a curative process which is described in part in Wieland's novel *Der Sieg der Natur über die Schwärmerey, oder Don Sylvio von Rosalva* (1764; translated as *Reason triumphant over fancy, exemplified in the singular adventures of Don Sylvio de Rosalva: A history in which every marvelous event occurs naturally*, 1773). The book is a multifaceted work whose Don Quixotelike hero searches through a world of fairies and other supernatural creatures for the blue butterfly of contentment, a quest which includes blithely candid considerations of the physical side of romantic love. Because *Don Sylvio*, as it is generally known, is an unabashedly comic novel, German critics were long reluctant to accord the work serious attention; but in recent years scholars have discovered great significance in it. It is now considered by some to be the "first modern German novel" because of a new kind of intrusive role assumed by its narrator. Whether or not Wieland in this particular respect deserves credit as an innovator, *Don Sylvio* represents a milestone in the Age of Enlightenment's battle about the admissability of the marvelous in a work of art; and the novel appeared at a critical point when this new form of epic was beginning to acquire a measure of respectability in the eyes of literary arbiters.

In later years Wieland confessed that while writing *Don Sylvio* he was far less motivated by literary considerations than by a compelling need of money for Bibi. In order that he might spend more time with his beloved he hired her as his housekeeper and shortly thereafter moved her into his quarters at the chancellery. Many people in Biberach and elsewhere viewed the affair merely as an indiscreet, youthful self-indulgence, but there is no doubt about the sincerity of Wieland's feelings for Bibi. He made repeated efforts to marry her, all of which were frustrated, even after she had borne him a child. The lovers were thwarted by her parents and the Catholic Church—and possibly also, behind the scenes, by Wieland's father, who in March 1761 had become the senior Lutheran pastor in the city and who apparently preferred an illegitimate grandchild to a son in a marriage of mixed confessions. A consequence of the turmoil was the loss of Wieland's fiancée Julie, who had long exhibited a tolerant attitude toward the affair.

Wieland's municipal office did not involve time-consuming duties that interfered with his literary pursuits. He was quite serious about his career as a writer and did not let even the long legal battles to secure his election and obtain his salary deter him from his main purpose. Shortly after his arrival in Biberach he had begun translating the dramas of Shakespeare, a project he had contemplated before leaving Zurich. When he was delegated by the council to supervise the city's "evangelische Comödianten-Gesellschaft" (Protestant Actors' Society), the oldest continuous theatrical organization in Germany, he decided to combine the assignment with his work on Shakespeare. Under his direction the actors performed in September 1761 *The Tempest*, translated as *Der Sturm oder der erstaunliche Schiffbruch* (The Storm; or, The Amazing Shipwreck), the first staging of a Shakespearean play in German. Soon thereafter Wieland resigned his post as the company's director; but he continued his work on Shakespeare, completing twenty-two translations which were published from 1762 to 1766 in Zurich by Orell, Geßner and Company. Isolated as he was from learned companionship, however, and lacking even the most basic library resources, he found the task almost insurmountably difficult. His attitude toward the original texts, was, moreover, ambivalent; in his preface he claimed to admire Shakespeare's work despite its many flaws, one of which was language too crude for refined tastes. In translating, Wieland altered or simply eliminated whatever he found offensive and in so doing became Shakespeare's first notable bowdlerizer. The critic Heinrich Wilhelm von Gerstenberg condemned this abuse of the original text, and over the following years the criticism was echoed by an angry new generation of impatient and outspoken poets. These young men, later labeled Sturm-und-Drang writers, saw in Shakespeare the quintessence of modern poetic genius, and they were outraged by Wieland's failure to show adequate respect for their master. Still, however negatively the Sturm-und-Drang generation may have spoken about the translator, most of its members came to know Shakespeare basically as Wieland presented him. Goethe, the most prominent of that generation's representatives, surveyed a half century later the many options open to him for reading Shakespeare's dramatic works, including the highly acclaimed Schlegel-Tieck translation (1797-1810) as well as the original English texts, and declared that whenever he wished to read the plays for pure enjoyment he always turned to Wieland's version.

On the recommendation of Sophie and Georg La Roche, Wieland was introduced into Count Stadion's salon at the Castle Warthausen. It was a world completely new to the young writer; the count had been the "Großhofmeister" for the Archbishop of Mainz, in essence the head of government for one of the seven electoral princes of the Holy Roman Empire, and had associated with the great and near-great men of the age, including Voltaire. Wieland was fascinated and captivated by this graceful and truly cultivated aristocrat, so different from anyone he had ever met. Stadion, in turn, was impressed by the poet, considered him an interesting companion, and quickly proved to be a useful friend. The count counseled Wieland in his disputes with the senators of Biberach and may, through contacts with imperial authorities in Vienna, have provided more concrete assistance. In return, Wieland produced new literary works for Stadion's entertainment, adapting his subject matter and style to the tastes and attitudes he encountered at Warthausen. He found the adjustment easy. The earnest religiosity of his earlier verses had been on the wane since 1756, and it disappeared altogether as he regaled his courtly audience with a series of verse narratives as frivolous and suggestive as any French Rococo poetry. The seigneur was not only amused but was amazed that the German language could be used so deftly and with such wit. When Wieland began to publish his efforts in this vein–a collection appeared in 1765 under the title *Comische Erzählungen* (Comic Tales)– aristocratic and cultured bourgeois circles which had ignored German writers responded with similar enthusiasm. From other quarters, however, the new tone of writing evoked horrified criticism: the pious saw in the metamorphosed Wieland an apostate, not only an affront but a menace to public morality. Patriotic zealots were no less appalled, for they found the verses a pandering to foreign tastes and a desertion of Germanic traditions. The poet himself marveled at the chameleonlike ease with which he had adapted to his new environment.

On 5 January 1762 Wieland wrote his friend Zimmermann that he had several months earlier begun a fictionalized but essentially true autobiography which he called *Geschichte des Agathon*, whose hero he would in the end make as happy and fortunate as the author himself hoped ultimately to be. Since the story is in essence an account of Wieland's psychological development from naïveté to maturity, it is not surprising that in later years he regarded the edition of 1766-1767, written when he was thirty-four years old, incomplete and chose to amend the work in 1773 and again in 1794. It is, however, the first version which is the most compelling, for it pre-

sents in the clearest fashion the competing forces, the diametrically opposed systems of thought and attitudes toward life, on account of which Agathon is subjected to a series of successive disasters. The hero is a foundling reared by priestesses in the ideal surroundings of the Delphic temple, where he is kept totally ignorant of the realities of the world. The idyllic nature of his existence is made even sweeter by the presence of the beautiful young Psyche. The consummation of Agathon's love for her seems to be inevitable, but the idyl is broken by an overamorous and not-too-honorable priestess and then shattered by pirates who abduct and bear Agathon and Psyche off to separate fates. Agathon is sold as a slave to Hippias of Smyrna, a highly cultivated sophist who quickly recognizes the talents of his new property and attempts in philosophic disputation to subvert the young Platonist. After repeated failures, Hippias employs the beautiful hetaera Danae to achieve his ignoble purposes. The woman's charms overwhelm the young man, but the purity of his soul proves irresistible to her; and so the seduction intended by Hippias becomes instead a pure and beautiful evolution of love. Unfortunately, Agathon does not realize how profoundly he has affected Danae, so when his master reveals that the hetaera had been employed to test his virtue his despair is absolute. He flees to the court of Dionysius in Syracuse, where he again impresses all who come to know him. He finds favor, obtains high office, and attempts to do good by leading a political life in accordance with his instincts and the principles of his first education, only to find that uncompromising pursuit of ideals leads to failure. He finally perceives that he must somehow seek a path more attuned to the realities of the world, a conclusion forced upon him not only by the disaster of his political experiences but also by the chance discovery that Psyche, his only true love, is in fact a sister from whom he was separated at birth: his abduction by pirates had saved him from following his virtuous instincts into the cruel fate of unwitting incest. Although Agathon does not reach a state of wisdom in this first version of his history, he is set in motion toward it, and Wieland defines in the novel the nature of the quest. It lies in overcoming innate tendencies toward "Schwärmerei" (impractical and excessive enthusiasms), in blending the restraints of cold reason and the urges of warmer passion, in resolving the conflicting calls of head and heart. Preventing idealism from becoming visionariness and finding a middle road between rationality and sentiment is not only a mission for Agathon-Wieland; it becomes the basic task of humanity. With the appearance of *Geschichte des Agathon* Wieland acquired the reputation of Germany's premier philosopher-poet. The book is—as Lessing, the foremost German critic of the age and Wieland's sometime foe, characterized it—the first German novel written to appeal to a thoughtful reader with classical tastes.

Pressed by his parents to begin his own family and sensing a need for domestic tranquillity and financial security, Wieland decided to take a wife. In his search he turned to Sophie La Roche for counsel. She introduced him to Anna Dorothea von Hillenbrand, the daughter of a wealthy merchant in Augsburg, and advised him during negotiations concerning the dowry. As a wedding gift Count Stadion conferred on the poet the title "Comes Palatinus" (Count Palatine), granting him such powers and privileges as the certifying of notaries, the legitimatizing of children born out of wedlock, and the awarding of diplomas to baccalaureates and masters of the free arts. The marriage ceremony took place in Biberach on 21 October 1765, with Wieland's father officiating. Over the following months Wieland sometimes made light of the institution of matrimony and even of his bride: he had, he wrote Geßner in Zurich, taken a foolish step; he had simply let himself be bedded, he declared to a second friend. His spouse was a simple woman, he wrote on yet another occasion, who would never be able to understand his writing. Still, she was an "artiges Weibchen" (good little wife) to whom he was devoted from the beginning, and over the years the bonds between the two were strengthened. Anna Dorothea was to bear fourteen children, twelve of whom survived infancy: Sophie Katharine Susanne, Maria Carolina Friederica, Regina Dorothea, Amalia Augusta, Charlotte Wilhelmine, Ludwig Friedrich August, Carl Friedrich, Philipp Siegmund Albrecht, Wilhelm August, Juliane Caroline Dorothea, Wilhelmine Frederike, and Maria Louisa Charlotte. Wieland once commented that no other writer had ever produced so many books and such a large number of children simultaneously.

Not even the new wife, however, replaced Sophie La Roche in Wieland's private and public worlds. During the first half year of his marriage he composed his Rococo masterpiece, the verse narrative *Musarion, oder die Philosophie der Grazien* (Musarion; or, The Philosophy of the Graces,

1768). Its title character, the incarnation of beauty, charm, and wisdom, was, he later confessed in print, inspired by Sophie. In this poem Wieland continued to employ the entertaining style and somewhat risqué wit of his *Comische Erzählungen*, but with an obviously more moral and serious purpose. The costume is Greek, but the story is of the poet's own maturation; and the process entails, as it had in *Geschichte des Agathon*, overcoming the excesses found in rationalism on the one hand and in sentimentalism on the other and a blending of the competing forces. The hetaera Musarion points the way to a resolution of the dilemma; she leads the newly destitute and discontented young hedonist Phanias away from two philosophic pedants who have accompanied him into retreat and vie with each other to convert him to Pythagorism or Stoicism. The clever girl is a more effective mentor than either sage; with her help Phanias recognizes that each philosophy has its merits, but that disciples of idealistic philosophic schools are no less subject to frailties of the flesh than any other human being. The best appreciation of life's purposes is to be gained from Musarion herself; this mortal goddess employs the wiles and wisdom of love to teach him a "Philosophie der Grazien" (philosophy of the graces), a spiritual as well as intellectual Epicureanism which enjoys pleasure in serene moderation. The poem was a best-seller and a highly influential literary artwork; among its impressed readers was Goethe, who later declared in his autobiography that he gained his first real insights into the culture of antiquity from Wieland's *Musarion*.

Since Wieland composed *Musarion* while he was still writing *Geschichte des Agathon*, it is not surprising that the poem and the novel are thematically related. Both works, Wieland's two most serious literary efforts during his years in Biberach, are essentially autobiographical in nature, and the two couples, Phanias-Musarion and Agathon-Psyche, provide two views of the poet and Sophie which make it clear that during the year 1766-1767 his analysis of her role in his life underwent a change. The ideal relationship achieved by Phanias and Musarion in the poem is replaced in the novel by acceptance of the fact that fate, which had apparently so cruelly snatched Psyche from Agathon, had instead saved the hero from a terrible turn of events. The revelation that Psyche had never been an acceptable partner for Agathon surely represents conclusions drawn by Wieland about the loss of his first fiancée.

Wieland and his family; painting by G. Melchior Kraus, 1775 (Landesbibliothek, Weimar)

In 1767 Wieland chose a project which would take him into uncharted poetic waters: he decided to create a verse epic following the model of Ludovico Ariosto. By subjecting himself to the challenge and discipline of ottava rima in a comicheroic narrative some ten cantos long, he intended to discover how far his talents for rhyme and meter extended. In *Idris* (1768) his hero is again a Platonic enthusiast in search of a fairy queen; Idris must share the story with a rank hedonist counterpart, but he appears to have found the way to wisdom when he comes to know a pair of lovers living in idyllic happiness isolated from the grand world. Thus the content of the work seems a revised and modified version of *Musarion*, but in *Idris* both plot and ethical considerations are subordinated to the joy of pure fantasy, to the relishing of adventure in a fairy world of pure sensation. Wieland, however, never finished the poem; his wife suffered a miscarriage late in her first pregnancy, and the loss of the child and the near loss of Anna Dorothea herself made it impossible for him to continue

writing in so playful a vein. He decided a few years later to leave the poem a fragment forever.

The years 1766 and 1767 were further marred for Wieland by a bitter dispute between Count Stadion and the city of Biberach. The poet spoke out, in his capacity as a municipal official, in defense of democratic principles–too loudly and passionately in the opinion of the offended aristocrat, who responded by declaring him persona non grata at the Castle Warthausen. Thus Wieland was deprived of the most pleasant diversions in his life by being separated from Sophie and the other people of taste and wit in Stadion's retinue, all of whom were forbidden any contact with him. In 1768 a reconciliation was brought about, largely because Sophie once again undertook to play her familiar role of mediator in the poet's life. This time, however, her efforts were to little practical purpose, for when the two men finally met again the old count was only weeks away from death.

A topic of conversation for Stadion and Wieland before the estrangement had been the likelihood of finding an environment more suitable for a creative artist than the distinctly unintellectual atmosphere of a small Swabian imperial city. Stadion's influence at the court in Mainz made one solution to the problem feasible: the city and university of Erfurt belonged to the archbishopric, and the Electoral Prince Emmerich Joseph was determined to reform the once famous academy and restore its eroded reputation. The prestige of the institution could only be enhanced by the addition of Wieland to its faculty. After Stadion's death the plan was set in motion; from Mainz and Wetzlar the campaign was coordinated by the associate justice of the imperial chancery court, Franz Wilhelm Loskant, a former secretary to the count, and from Erfurt by Professor Friedrich Justus Riedel, a well-known philosopher and literary critic, who in December 1767 had initiated a correspondence with Wieland. It was not difficult to overcome whatever reluctance the poet might have felt about leaving his parents and his native city; he clearly recognized a need to relocate. In May 1769 he lay down his duties at the municipal chancellery to accept an appointment as first professor of philosophy in Erfurt. He took with him to Erfurt an amanuensis; his wife; a six-month-old daughter named after Sophie La Roche; and his former fiancée's son, Fritz, whose education the new professor was to supervise.

Although the terms of his appointment would have permitted him a near total freedom from teaching, Wieland in his first semester lectured eight hours per week on Isaac Iselin's history of humanity and assorted other subjects bearing on the consequences of ignorance and unenlightenment. He soon became one of the faculty's most popular teachers, one whose lecture halls were not large enough to accommodate his auditors. He attracted not only the curious, but serious young talent as well. Johann Jakob Wilhelm Heinse, Friedrich August Clemens Werthes, C. G. Büler, Friedrich Wilhelm Ludwig von Beulwitz, Joseph Schwarz, and Tobias Brandmüller, most of them future writers, were among the students who enjoyed special relationships with Wieland and a cordial reception in his house. Wieland recognized talent and came to its aid; thus he let his verse narrative "Der verklagte Amor" (Amor Indicted) be published along with Werthes's *Hirtenlieder* (Pastoral Songs, 1772) so that the young poet might attract a larger audience for his first major public offering; Heinse was permitted to include in his *Erzählungen für junge Damen und Dichter* (Tales for Young Ladies and Poets, 1775) three of Wieland's narratives: "Aurora und Cephalon," "Endymion," and "Nadine."

Wieland's academic reputation spread across the land; between 1769 and 1776 he was offered professorships at the universities in Halle, Leipzig, and Jena. He was considered for professorship at Gießen, but it was not extended because the university felt itself unable to make an offer financially attractive enough to obtain so distinguished a scholar. (In 1776, four years after his departure from Erfurt, he would be invited to return to the university as its director.) In spite of his successes, or perhaps because of them, Wieland never felt completely at home in Erfurt. The fame he was acquiring across the nation and the adulation of his students could not compensate for the attitudes of his academic colleagues. Most of his elders were conservatively Catholic, totally opposed to the program of modernization decreed in Mainz. Wieland's attempts, along with those of his principal ally Riedel, to help implement Emmerich Joseph's reforms produced resentment that often erupted into conflict. The contest was bitter, and the almost inevitable result was that Wieland, once again doing essentially the bidding of others, became the center of controversy. Many on the faculty looked on their archbishop's favored professor as a freethinker and a sometimes-frivolous poet, an interloper with no academic credentials. He, in turn, did not take long to realize that the university was no less provincial than Biberach. Less than half a year after his arrival he described the people of Erfurt as crude, mindless, heartless, and tasteless.

For all the open and covert hostility within the faculty Wieland felt secure behind the aegis of the electoral prince, and this feeling was reflected in the content and tone of his writing. His novel ΣΩΚΡΑΤΗΣ ΜΑΙΝΟΜΕΝΟΣ *oder die Dialogen des Diogenes von Sinope* (1770; translated as *Socrates out of his Senses, or dialogues of Diogenes of Sinope,* 1771) is tongue-in-cheek praise for the cynicism of Diogenes, to which the author is attracted, as he declares, because he lacks the financial means to become a proper Epicurean and is still too young to become a Stoic; he is therefore glad to eschew the possessions of the world, the greatest misuse of which is probably to be found in the Catholic church. Wieland's literary output during his first year at Erfurt was prodigous: in addition to ΣΩΚΡΑΤΗΣ ΜΑΙΝΟΜΕΝΟΣ he sent

Idris, the fragment written in Biberach, to the publisher. He also composed *Die Grazien* (1770; translated as *The Graces,* 1823), a longish pastoral of prose mixed with verse, set in classical antiquity and designed to elaborate on the "philosophy of the Graces" enunciated in *Musarion.* Using the Middle Ages as his setting he wrote the verse narrative *Der neue Amadis* (The New Amadis, 1771), a comic treatment of traditional chivalric themes in eighteen long cantos. Even more frivolous and risqué was his narrative poem *Combabus* (1770), an oriental tale of a loyal courtier who, anticipating that a commission from his monarch might lead to charges of misconduct with the queen, is prompted both by a sense of virtue and a sense of self-preservation to castrate himself before the event and is thus able later to disprove the accusations he so accurately foresaw. While working on *Combabus* Wieland also wrote a peculiar mixture of essays and satirical fiction under the title *Beyträge zur Geheimen Geschichte des menschlichen Verstandes und Herzens* (Contributions to the Secret History of the Human Mind and Heart, 1770), intended as a moderating balance to the era's fevered enthusiasm for Jean-Jacques Rousseau's praise of all things primitive. Wieland's position is summarized at the end of the first tale, where he concedes that a search for the joys of eternal childhood is almost irresistibly appealing but insists that human beings were not created to remain children; rather they were intended to progress from the natural innocence of childhood through tortuous stages of error and self-deception until they finally achieve their higher potential. In addition to producing all of this original writing Wieland spent considerable time correcting the text of Sophie La Roche's novel *Geschichte des Fräuleins von Sternheim* (Story of Miss von Sternheim), which appeared in two volumes in May and September 1771 with his introduction and annotations.

The highlights of Wieland's three-year tenure at Erfurt occurred when he traveled in May 1771 to visit Sophie and Georg La Roche at their new home in Coblenz, where La Roche had entered the service of the electoral prince of Trier. There Wieland made the acquaintance of Georg and Friedrich Heinrich Jacobi, who had journeyed there expressly to meet the lion of German letters and who then invited him to visit them in Düsseldorf and to view the art gallery in that city. He was received in Coblenz by Archbishop Clemens Wenzeslaus, and at Mainz-Höchst he was accorded by Archbishop Emmerich Joseph the honor of a one-and-one-half-hour private audience. Returning to Erfurt after a four-week absence he was greeted by his wife and a second daughter, Caroline, who had been born while he was away.

In spite of Wieland's strong feelings of loyalty toward his patron in Mainz, he realized that he would ultimately have to seek greener pastures. The most likely spot appeared to be Vienna, for just as Emmerich Joseph was bent on bringing a measure of enlightenment to his archbishopric, so did Emperor Joseph II seem resolved to introduce the new age into the hereditary lands of the Hapsburgs. A commission had been appointed to reform the educational system and was recruiting throughout German-speaking Europe the most prestigious and competent educators, without regard to religious affiliations. Wieland and other professors at Erfurt were under consideration. Riedel was called early on and left for Vienna to prepare a place for his friend. To call attention to his particular fitness for civil service Wieland wrote a new novel of statecraft in which he addressed the issues of monasticism, absolutism, and political freedom. Taking his inspiration from Montesquieu and, to a lesser extent, from Albrecht Haller's political novels, he created *Der goldne Spiegel* (The Golden Mirror, 1772), a chronicle of successive generations of rulers in the Asian kingdom of Scheschian. The work is yet another attempt by Wieland to counter the themes of cultural pessimism introduced into European literature by Rousseau. It issues no call to revolution; instead, it offers a contemplative discussion of the social, religious, and political arguments of the day. The ideal political program it proposes differs little from the practical goals of the eighteenth century's enlightened absolute monarchs. The book was a great success and found its intended readers in Vienna, including Joseph II himself; but it did not have the anticipated results, for Joseph's mother, Maria Theresa, acting on the advice of her most pious confidante about the nature and tone of some of Wieland's verse narratives, expressly forbade an offer to him.

The failure to obtain a suitable position in Vienna did not mean that Wieland's campaign had been totally unsuccessful, for it had drawn attention to him in quarters much closer to home. Anna Amalia, the dowager duchess of Saxe-Weimar, faced with supervising the final education of her sixteen-year-old son Karl August before he was invested with sovereign authority, found in the author of *Der goldne Spiegel* a thinker to her liking, and she proposed that he become the prince's tutor in philosophy. A release from Mainz was secured, and Wieland departed Erfurt on 18 September 1772 to assume his new responsibilities. In a letter to Sophie La Roche he claimed to view the assignment as an opportunity to do something truly useful for the welfare of mankind.

Wieland's instructional duties, which during his first months in Weimar included lectures on the philosophy of history, on Adam Ferguson's moral philosophy, and on aesthetic theory, filled about ten hours of each week. As the private tutor to the prince his presence was also frequently required at the ducal table. He found, moreover, that as the resident poet he was expected to provide a certain amount of literary diversion for the court. Since Duchess Anna Amalia was particularly devoted to the stage and maintained a good theatrical company at her court, and since Wieland, with *Clementina von Poretta* and *Lady Johanna Gray*, had won a reputation as one of Germany's notable dramatists, he made contributions primarily for the theater. He cooperated in the adaptation of his *Idris* for a ballet and collaborated with Weimar's court composer Anton Schweitzer to produce a libretto for the singspiel *Aurora* (1772). By far the most ambitious undertaking, however, was his effort, again with Schweitzer, to create a new musical work based on Euripides' *Alcestis*. Wieland's attempt to render this drama of antiquity more realistic and modern while he simultaneously, and perhaps paradoxically, idealized and refined the humane qualities of its heroine places *Alceste* together with *Lady Johanna Gray* among the most important milestones along the way toward classical German drama. The work has also been called the first modern German opera. Whether the designation is completely appropriate or not, staging a work consisting in its entirety of arias and recitatives all sung in German seemed in 1772 a revolutionary undertaking, and Wieland's preparations for the premiere were highly publicized. The project drew the attention and praise of Christian Felix Weiße, the best-known librettist of German operettas; the prominent author and publisher Friedrich Nicolai came from Berlin to observe rehearsals and attend the first performance. Among those present at the premiere there was consensus that the work marked the beginning of a new era, and theatrical schedules from all parts of Germany show that *Alceste* remained for at least a decade a frequently staged work. The title character, the wife who offers her own life so that her husband may live, is Wieland's tribute to Anna Dorothea and her complete and selfless devotion to him and their children.

Teaching, appearances at court functions, and theatrical projects notwithstanding, Wieland found enough time and energy to resurrect a long-cherished plan: the editing and publishing of a general literary journal. In May 1771 he had discussed his concepts with Friedrich Heinrich and Georg Jacobi; thirteen months later the matter was introduced into their correspondence. Both Jacobis endorsed the project enthusiastically and pledged their cooperation; at the suggestion of Friedrich Jacobi the new journal was christened *Der teutsche Merkur,* an admission that it was conceived as a German version of the century-old *Mercure de France.* In December 1772, after a mere three months of planning, the publication was announced in all major papers, and two and one-half months later the first numbers were mailed. Public response to the *Merkur* was so positive that the initial printing of two thousand copies had to be supplemented by an additional press-run, an impressive success made even more phenomenal by the appearance of at least two pirated printings of the journal during its first few years of existence. Although contributions to the early issues came from various parts of Germany—from Carl Anton Maria von Dalberg, the stadtholder in Erfurt and future leader of Napoleon's Rhine Confederation; from the physician Marcus Herz in Berlin; from the historian Johann Christian Maier in Jena; and from several poets in Halberstadt—the principal writers for the *Merkur* were Wieland and the two Jacobis. Soon to become another of the most important collaborators was the young Friedrich Justin Bertuch, later famed as the translator of *Don Quixote* (1775) and as the mercantile genius of Weimar. As well as becoming a regular contributor to the journal, Bertuch quite early in its history took over much of the management of its business affairs; he continued to provide that service for some twelve years.

The enthusiastic public response to *Alceste* prompted Wieland to write "Briefe an einen Freund über das deutsche Singspiel 'Alceste'" (Letters to a Friend concerning the German Lyrical Drama "Alceste") for the January and March 1773 issues of the *Merkur.* The essays are significant in literary history because of Wieland's views on adapting the outgrown attitudes and values of

Drawing of Wieland by Johann Wolfgang Goethe, 1776
(Goethe-Nationalmuseum, Weimar)

antiquity to the tastes of a modern society; they are perhaps just as important for musicology because of their consideration of the need to integrate music and libretto. The letters are marred, however, by the author's too obvious satisfaction at his own grand accomplishment. The tone irritated the younger literary generation, which was no less offended by what it perceived as Wieland's condescending remarks about Euripides than it had been earlier by his offhand comments about flaws in the writing of Shakespeare. There was a loud polemic reaction, the most memorable responses coming from Johann Michael Reinhold Lenz, Friedrich Maximilian Klinger, Friedrich Müller, and Goethe. The latter's satirical playlet *Götter, Helden und Wieland* (Gods, Heroes, and Wieland, 1774) contended that the true spirit of antiquity–particularly the heroism of Euripides' Hercules–was perceived by Wieland as passé because it was simply beyond the comprehension of anyone mired in the decadence of the Rococo.

Criticism of Wieland as a writer inadequately religious and too wanton, frivolous, and fashionably francophile came not only from Goethe and Goethe's friends in Frankfurt, Mannheim, and Strasbourg but from other areas and groups as well. One widely reported expression of scorn came from the "Hainbund" (Grove League) in Göttingen, a coterie of young poets who particularly venerated the great master of religious and patriotic verse, Klopstock. On 4 August 1773, celebrating the birthday of their idol, members of the group trampled Wieland's *Idris* underfoot, used pages from the book to light their pipes, and then burned the text in its entirety, inveighing against Wieland and Voltaire in a single breath.

Wieland was often offended by these highly publicized criticisms of his person and work, but, having already experienced in Zurich the dangers of polemical campaigns, he restrained as best he could his impulses to respond in kind. He wrote instead for the *Merkur* the effectively temperate essay "Unterredungen zwischen W** und dem Pfarrer zu ***" (Conversations between W[ieland] and the Parson at ***, 1775), in which he explained his participation in earlier literary feuds and defended his personal and literary morality. He also employed his journal on three separate occasions to review works by Goethe; with great skill he praised the obvious talents of the young writer and so tactfully censured excesses of enthusiasm that he succeeded in silencing this most dangerous of his adversaries.

In the late fall of 1774 Wieland completed his duties as Karl August's tutor. The salary he had received for his services, one thousand talers per year, was continued as a pension on the condition that he maintained his residence in Weimar. Shortly before the end of the year the prince set out on his grand tour, the principal destination of which was Paris. During the journey this pupil of the renowned Wieland was the object of much curiosity. Poets, philosophers, lords, ladies, and statesmen were eager to see him. In Karlsruhe the seventeen-year-old prince favorably impressed the great Klopstock; earlier in Frankfurt he had won the friendship of the twenty-five-year-old Goethe, who had accepted an invitation to visit Weimar the following year. On 7 November 1775 Goethe arrived at Karl August's court; immediately he was introduced to Wieland, and all earlier animosities were forgotten. Although Goethe's reported drinking and wenching exploits with the duke were to become the scandal of the nation over the next months, the celebrated young rebel was also during that time a frequent guest in Wieland's house. Goethe looked on the relative serenity within a family circle as a welcome escape from the more hectic aspects of his life, and the peaceful atmosphere there may have contributed to his desire to outgrow and bring to an end his Sturm-und-Drang period. Certainly Goethe's evolution into a classical poet was influenced by the opinions of his older colleague; it was Wieland who encouraged Goethe's work on *Iphigenie auf Tauris* (Iphigenia on Tauris, 1787), a drama remarkably similar in tone to *Alceste*, and later persuaded him to polish the rough prose version of the piece into its final metrical form. Years later Goethe still called on Wieland from time to time for counsel about works in verse, such as *Reinecke Fuchs* (Reynard the Fox, 1794).

Eighteenth-century Germans frequently complained about their lack of a national capital, a mecca for artistic talent and a hub of creative activity comparable to London or Paris. Because Goethe and Wieland, the most celebrated writers of their respective generations, both lived in Weimar, the notion began to surface that this small ducal residence, the earlier source of patronage for such artistic giants as Lucas Cranach and Johann Sebastian Bach, might become a center of literary culture. A major step in that direction was made when Wieland suggested that Goethe persuade his friend Johann Gottfried Herder, the theologian and noted literary critic, to accept a position as superintendent of the Lutheran church in Weimar. When Herder arrived on 11 October 1776 his first call was on Wieland. Although the two men were opposite personalities and found the early years of their acquaintance difficult, Herder became a valued contributor to the *Merkur* and, some twenty years later, Wieland's closest literary ally in Weimar.

Obtaining adequate suitable material for the *Merkur* was a never-ending tribulation for Wieland. In 1774 he decided to fill several issues by printing in installments a work which he later considered one of his greatest literary accomplishments, *Der Abderiten, eine sehr wahrscheinliche Geschichte* (The Abderites: A Very Probable Story, 1774; revised as *Geschichte der Abderiten* [1781]; translated as *The Republic of Fools*, 1861). Setting his scene in Abdera, antiquity's home of quintessential folly, Wieland impishly satirizes the inanities of the eighteenth century. The misadventures of Democritus, Euripides, and Hippocrates among the Abderites and the absurdities in thea-

ters, temples, and courts of law in that city are only thin disguises that allowed Wieland to dissect with impunity the fools and knaves of his own day. Politicians and academicians unable to grasp truths, performers and audiences ignorant of the essence of theatrical art, religious leaders oblivious to all issues other than the preservation of power and perquisites, lawyers motivated solely by the joys of disputation and profit—all felt the sting of his pen as the poet-philosopher revenged himself on senators in Biberach, on attorneys throughout the Holy Roman Empire of the German Nation, on self-serving professors in Erfurt, on pretentious young dramatists of the Sturm und Drang movement, and on ladies who acquired in bedrooms the power to interfere in matters of state—in short, on all who had frustrated and irritated him for so many years. The five episodes of his "history" produced laughter in every corner of German-speaking Europe but also evoked roars of indignation as one prominent person after the other claimed to see himself ridiculed by the persiflage.

The Middle Ages, which Wieland had come to know well while working with Bodmer in Zurich and which he had treated many times in a generally comic fashion in narrative verses, furnished subject matter in 1779 for a project of a more serious nature. For half a year he devoted his energies almost exclusively to composing the poem *Oberon* (1780; translated, 1798). The epic, initially published as the sole text of the first issue of the *Merkur* for 1780, is a peculiar mixture of the adventures of Charlemagne's paladin Huon of Bordeaux with the marital tribulations of Oberon and Titania, the king and queen of the fairies, borrowed from Shakespeare's *Midsummer Night's Dream*; there is also a character of Wieland's own invention, the old hermit Don Alfonso, whose longing for reunion with his deceased family provides the point of departure for an exposition on spiritualization of the individual in nature, the source of solace and moral truth. The plot Wieland concocts to accommodate such disparate elements is one in which the true love of two young, noble, but humanly frail people is put to a bitter test of abstention before they can be rejoined in a normal relationship. It is a poem in which Goethe claimed to find the genius of Wieland as a consummate storyteller; he is said to have read the entire sixteen long cantos, some three hundred pages, without being able to put down the text. On *Oberon*—a mixture of knight-errantry and fairy wonders with a single-minded striving toward the noble goal of pure love–rests a large part of Wieland's claim to being one of the forerunners of Romanticism. To the young English poets William Sotheby; John Keats; George Gordon, Lord Byron; Percy Bysshe Shelley; and Samuel Taylor Coleridge, Wieland was the writer to be emulated and recognized as the founder of the European Romantic movement. Critical acclaim for *Oberon* prompted Wieland to draft a new version of the Tristan legend and to collect source materials for other similar works from the Middle Ages. None of the plans, however, came to fruition.

Perhaps poetically exhausted by *Oberon*, and admittedly fatigued by the editing and publishing of a popular periodical, Wieland turned away from creative writing and directed most of his attention for nearly six years to translating. The correspondence and business affairs of the *Merkur* he dropped into the willing hands of Bertuch, who became a partner in the operation. Wieland continued to read the articles that were published in the journal, though probably only in proof; many of them he annotated, some copiously. Apart from these notes, from some samples of his translations, and from a few occasional poems, he contributed little to the *Merkur* from 1781 through 1786. He was, nonetheless, literarily quite active. By mid 1781 he had made considerable progress on his project of translating and annotating the letters (1782) and satires (1786) of Horace. Then he translated and published in four volumes (1788-1789) the collected writings of the Greek satirist Lucian of Samasota. In these ambitious undertakings Wieland remained true to his enlightened view of the purposes of translation: to remove the language barrier and make important works accessible in versions true to the spirit of the original but adapted to the tastes and moral standards of the translator's nation and age. In the cases of both Horace and Lucian, Wieland's theories proved appropriate to the task at hand. Two hundred years later his renderings of the works of these writers are still being reprinted, and modern scholars rank them among the best available to German readers.

As a form of relaxation from his labors with Lucian and Horace, Wieland turned to fairy tales. The impulse came from Paris, where the first volume of an enormous collection of tales, the *Cabinet des fées*, had appeared in 1785. Wieland had always considered fairy tales a significant literary subgenre, provided that they were re-

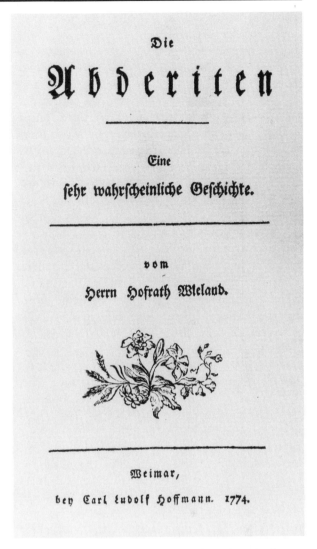

Title page for the novel in which Wieland satirizes what he considered the absurdities of eighteenth-century German society

told with taste and skill so that the marvelous and natural elements were successfully blended; such tales were compatible with the convictions and goals of Enlightenment because of their suitability for painless moral instruction and their universal and timeless appeal. He was favorably impressed with the new French edition of stories and decided to use it as the starting point for a collection for German readers. The results were published in three volumes as *Dschinnistan oder Auserlesene Feen- und Geister-Mährchen, theils neu erfunden, theils neu übersetzt und umgearbeitet* (Dschinnistan; or, Selected Fairy Tales and Ghost Stories, in Part Newly Invented, in Part Newly Translated and Revised, 1786-1789). His son-in-law Johann August Jakob Liebeskind and his friend Friedrich Hildebrandt von Einsiedel, chamberlain to Duchess Anna Amalia, collaborated on volumes two and three.

During his years of intensive translation activity Wieland became closely associated with yet another project of more than passing significance for his era. He had never shared the attitude of many eighteenth-century gentlemen of letters that a writer must not expect monetary reward. As time passed he became ever more aware that it was not the public which benefited from such auctorial benevolence; it was, instead, the businessmen who manufactured and sold books at a handsome profit. From time to time Wieland made rather bitter comments about his early publishers in Zurich; some of the edge was removed from his irritation by relatively large honoraria he later received for works published by Weidmanns Erben und Reich in Leipzig, but Wieland never ceased to believe that authors were preyed upon by merchants. In early 1783 he addressed the problem directly by investing and participating in a publishing cooperative in Dessau called the "Buchhandlung der Gelehrten" (Publishing Firm of Scholars) or the "Dessauer Verlagskasse" (Dessau Publishers' Account Office). The enterprise had been established in 1781 to print and distribute new works and to pay the authors two-thirds of all revenues from sales. As a sign of good faith Wieland contracted to have his translation of Horace's satires published by the society. The organization was plagued, however, by misfortune, due in part to efforts by the booksellers' association to sabotage the project. Even though it went out of existence within five years after its inception, the undertaking had considerable impact on the subsequent financial lot of authors and artists.

In July and August 1784 Wieland joined his old associatte Bertuch and Professor Christian Gottfried Schütz in Jena as an investor in and cofounder of the *Allgemeine Litteraturzeitung,* which quickly became and long remained the most highly respected organ of review in the German language. Although Wieland severed his connection with the journal just as its first numbers began to appear, his early association with the project contributed greatly to its initial success. The wide range of Wieland's contributions to the scholarly community continued to be recognized throughout the land. He was elected to membership by more than a dozen learned organizations, including the German Society in Mannheim, the Academy of Practical Sciences in Erfurt, and, in December 1786, by the Prussian Academy of Sciences in Berlin.

On 1 May 1784 an unusual young Austrian apostate arrived on Wieland's doorstep. Karl Leonhard Reinhold, a Jesuit novice who had become a Barnabite priest and lecturer in philosophy at the seminary in Mistelbach after the suppression of the Society of Jesus, had decided to renounce his vows and seek asylum beyond the reach of Hapsburg authorities. Aided by Freemasons in Vienna, Reinhold found his way to Weimar and to Wieland. Since the young man came with high recommendations and with some journalistic experience, he was taken in not only as a reviewer and essayist for the *Merkur* but as a houseguest as well. Reinhold was an almost ideal associate; he was tactful and patient in the face of Wieland's occasional temperamental explosions; and his energies served as a catalyst for the older man, who began again to write regularly for his own journal and to believe that it might be revitalized and regain some of its lost luster. Wieland was so impressed with Reinhold's character and talents that he chose the young man to become his first son-in-law, pressing his oldest daughter Sophie, eighteen years old and romantically involved with an actor unacceptable to her parents, to marry the promising journalist-philosopher. With Reinhold a part of the family, Wieland persuaded Bertuch to withdraw from the *Merkur* so that this partner's share of the revenues might provide a basic income for the new couple. Reinhold proved to be a son-in-law of whom the poet could be proud. The young man's interest in the philosophy of Immanuel Kant and gift for clear writing made him, in time, Kant's most effective exegete and popularizer. Substantial portions of his critical elucidation of Kant's works appeared in the *Merkur*, enhancing the reputation of the journal in philosophic circles though not adding greatly to its readership. Reinhold's growing academic reputation, however, was to lead him away from the journal, for in the spring of 1787 he received an appointment as a lecturer in philosophy at the university in Jena. He continued to write for the *Merkur* after his move away from Weimar, but the number of his articles gradually decreased; and in 1794, when he accepted a professorship at the university in Kiel, his collaboration came to an end.

Only five weeks after Reinhold's departure for Jena another young man of great promise, Friedrich Schiller, appeared in Weimar. The new

Wieland in 1779; painting by Georg Oswald May (Wieland-Museum, Biberach)

arrival had already acquired considerable fame as a member of the Sturm und Drang movement. Schiller had come to meet Wieland as a peer and never attempted to ingratiate himself as had Reinhold. He was nonetheless received with great warmth, for the older poet respected the younger one's talent and wanted him as a colleague to replace Reinhold. Perhaps Wieland also hoped to find a suitable husband for another of his maturing daughters, a possibility to which Schiller alluded in correspondence. Though never a son-in-law, the young man did become a collaborator and provided the *Merkur* in 1788 and 1789 with short essays; excerpts from his history of the Netherlands; critical commentary concerning his drama *Don Carlos* (1787); as well as the poems "Die Götter Griechenlands" (The Gods of Greece) and "Die Künstler" (The Artists), both of which were completed with the encouragement and advice of Wieland. It was announced with considerable fanfare in the fall of 1788 that Schiller would become a coeditor and publisher of the journal the following year, but

the plan to tie him ever more closely to the *Merkur* did not materialize, in part because he, like Reinhold before him, received an appointment at the university in Jena.

The phenomenon of men who appeared throughout the eighteenth century claiming to possess supernatural powers or arcane wisdom had long fascinated and repelled Wieland. In such individuals, as well as in such secret organizations as the Rosicrucians, the Illuminati, and the Freemasons, he saw threats to the goals of the Age of Enlightenment. He proposed in place of closed societies an open order of cosmopolites for all men of clear thought and goodwill, persons who would require no symbols to recognize each other. The issue of the miraculous and the supernatural in general as well as the growing numbers and influence of wonder-workers was addressed regularly by the *Merkur,* especially during the 1780s. Wieland wrote essays on faith, miracles, and reason within the framework of the Christian religion and on occult sciences, apparitions, and mesmerism, as well as articles about such problematic individuals as Count Allesandro di Cagliostro, Emanuel Swedenborg, Johann Kaspar Lavater, and the medieval adept Nicolaus Flamel. By the end of the decade he had come to distinguish various degrees of charlatanry–that of the maliciously fraudulent and that of the deceivers who misled themselves as much or more than they did their followers–and he was ready to contemplate the question in a long narrative work entitled *Geheime Geschichte des Philosophen Peregrinus Proteus* (1791; translated as *Private History of Peregrinus Proteus, the Philosopher,* 1796). The novel, first published in installments in the *Merkur,* is in the form of a series of long conversations between the second-century itinerant philosopher and thaumaturge Peregrinus and one of his early biographers, the Greek skeptic and satirist Lucian. Peregrinus is a student of the occult and for a time an apostle of the Christian movement; his power to perform miracles wins many converts for the group. In time, however, he becomes disillusioned by the organization of the infant church and leaves it. He forms his own sect, in which he attempts to combine the simple ascetic virtues of the early Cynics with those of the first Christians. When he perceives that he can no longer hold a following, he resolves to regain the public's attention by immolating himself in fire before a crowd of witnesses. The novel is basically an attempt to rehabilitate Peregrinus's reputation; but Wieland later confessed that the views he expressed about the ancient Greek were equally applicable to his contemporary, the Swiss theologian, physiognomist, and magnetic healer Lavater, another honest "Schwärmer" (fanatic).

All Germans of the eighteenth century were attentive to cultural, scientific, and political developments in France, none more so than Wieland. To some of his countrymen, indeed, his interest was excessive. Whatever the merits of this criticism, Wieland's understanding of French culture and its influence on neighboring peoples prepared him better than anyone else in the German literary community to observe, analyze, and even forecast the unfolding developments of France's great revolution. In 1787 and 1788, even before hostilities erupted, he had written articles predicting the cataclysm, voicing skepticism about the suitability of democratic government for a major modern state, and warning that democracy could lead to despotism more oppressive than any monarchy it might replace. After the die was cast, however, he adopted a more positive attitude. In articles and annotated translations for the *Merkur* he reported on all major occurrences, and in *Neue Götter-Gespräche* (New Conversations of the Gods, 1791), dialogues modeled after those of Lucian he provided commentary on the philosophical implications and practical consequences of the successive stages of the revolution. He urged his countrymen to maintain a benevolent neutrality toward what was transpiring west of the Rhine but simultaneously warned the French to exercise restraint and caution. He applauded the National Assembly's efforts to correct social evils, as, for example, in its decrees suppressing religious orders. He repeatedly defended the great social experiment against its conservative detractors even in the face of periodic outbreaks of fanaticism, explaining that the French had been subjected to far greater abuse from the aristocracy than Germans could ever comprehend. Not even the excesses of the Jacobins made him give up his hope that the good set in motion by the search for freedom would ultimately outweigh all darker forces. Mirabeau's death, the beheading of Louis XVI, and the defection to the Austrians by General Dumouriez, however, forced Wieland at last to conclude that the revolution had become a great apocalyptic whore and that the establishment of order and justice in France was a more compelling need than the continued pursuit of liberty and equality. In mid 1794 he stopped writing his running reports for the *Merkur*; but four years later he published

there "Gespräche unter vier Augen" (Conversations in Private), in which he betrayed an ever-increasing skepticism about the events in Paris. He concluded that nothing less than an absolute ruler could end the chaos and found only one man on the French scene with the ability and will to act effectively: Napoleon Bonaparte.

During the 1790s Wieland faced once again the task of defending his rights as an author–this time in a major legal contest, the outcome of which represents a landmark in the history of German letters. The energetic young publisher and bookseller in Leipzig, Georg Joachim Göschen, whom Wieland first came to know at the writers' cooperative publishing society in Dessau and who had later taken over distribution of the *Merkur*, had suggested in 1787 that the poet consider the financial needs of his large family and attempt to secure its future; a few months later Göschen proposed specifically that Wieland capitalize on his popularity by publishing his collected works in a major new edition. Wieland liked the idea and agreed to review and partially rewrite many of his works so that the new edition might reflect the thoughts and skills of the mature artist. Almost immediately the project encountered obstacles. Weidemanns Erben und Reich, the firm in Leipzig that had published most of Wieland's writings from 1768 through 1792, sought to dissuade the author from the undertaking, first with counteroffers and then with threats and intimidation. Finally the firm Reich brought suit in chancery court against Göschen and Wieland, contending that republication would represent a breach of contract and would deprive the company of revenue from legally acquired property. In early December 1793 the jury found for the defendants and went on to specify in its judgment that an author retains a natural and incontrovertible right of property to the works of his creation. Weidemanns und Reich immediately sought a reversal of the ruling in an appeal to the faculty of jurisprudence at the university in Leipzig, but one year later the panel reaffirmed the original decision.

The litigation completed, Wieland was able to focus his energies on the revision of his works. He did not complete the task, however, until 1802, when the last of the originally planned thirty-six volumes, along with six supplements, were finally published. Even that was not the end, for later writings were added to the collection; the final volume, number thirty-nine, did not appear until 1811. The first tomes of the

Wieland in 1794; drawing by Anton Graff (Schiller-Nationalmuseum, Marbach am Neckar)

Sämmtliche Werke (Collected Works) had been distributed with great ceremony in August 1794. Göschen had announced his intention to produce the works of Germany's greatest writer as a masterpiece of the printer's art, an unparalleled example of typographical artistry and accuracy. The collected works appeared in four simultaneously issued formats: a quarto "Fürstenausgabe" (Princes' Edition) printed on the highest quality paper available and embellished with lavish illustrations from the most celebrated artists and engravers of the era; a second edition in large and a third in small octavo; and finally a fourth edition in small octavo on common printing paper, a "wohlfeile Ausgabe" (bargain edition) so inexpensive that financial considerations should deter no friend of fine literature from acquiring Wieland's complete writings! So ambitious an undertaking was unprecedented, but subscription lists indicate that Göschen had assessed the market correctly: orders came from all major courts of German Europe, and subscriptions from well-

to-do bourgeois circles were even more plentiful. The project initially promised handsome returns, but its implementation extended over such a long period that profits were eroded by the deaths of original subscribers and then more significantly by the financial disruptions of a decade of general European war. In the beginning stages of the venture the exuberance of the publisher infected Wieland as well. He became so carried away in his zeal that he wrote a rather ill-considered general preface to volume one, noting that the appearance of his works in such splendid costume might well mark the end of an era: he had, he declared, begun his literary career at a time when it seemed the sun was rising on a golden age of German letters, and now he was closing it as that sun appeared to be setting.

Wieland's tactless reference to a German literary culture in decline annoyed Goethe and Schiller, as their correspondence clearly reveals. Schiller was particularly irate; Goethe, Wieland's longtime friend, tended to be conciliatory. The latter's essay "Literarischer Sansculottismus" (Literary Sansculottism) in Schiller's periodical *Die Horen* (May 1795) commended the diligence with which Wieland had revised early texts for his collected works and suggested that it might even be possible to derive a theory of literary good taste by studying his techniques of revision. In an essay by Schiller in the same journal five months later, "Über naive und sentimentalische Dichtung" (On Naive and Sentimental Poetry), however, Wieland was taken publicly to task: Schiller acknowledged a natural and superior quality in Wieland's work but implied that an all-pervading detached rationality in tone spoiled it irreparably. In letters and conversations Schiller continued to display his irritation—sometimes tastelessly, as in his observation that Wieland would probably look on the death of the philosopher Christian Garve as the loss of another member of the Golden Age; but at times with wit and humor, as in the assertion that Wieland would at any time detour from any chosen philosophical pathway to ogle a hetaera at her bath.

Whatever Schiller's negative attitudes may have portended, Wieland's fame was in 1795 at its zenith. During this year his private life was also marked by a high point of happiness: Salomon Geßner had been Wieland's closest friend in Zurich, and in June 1795 Geßner's son Heinrich came to Weimar to wed Charlotte Wieland, the poet's third and perhaps favorite daughter. Wieland was deeply touched by the ceremony, which was performed by Herder, and so ecstatic about the union of the two families that he promised to overcome his aversion to travel and to visit his daughter in Zurich. A year later he kept his word. The trip took him away from Weimar from 23 May through 11 September 1796; for three months he sojourned with his wife some distance from the center of Zurich in a comfortable villa provided by the Geßner family. The experience delighted him and reawakened his old dream of leading the kind of rural existence praised by his favorite poet, Horace. On the other hand, his hope that the trip might enable him to relive his youth in Zurich was dashed: the few old acquaintances he found still alive were for the most part only disappointing shadows of his memories. There were, however, compensations: the stay brought new friendships, and at least three of them–with Johann Jakob Hottinger, Johannes Tobler, and Johann Heinrich Pestalozzi– were to prove important. The advancement of Pestalozzi's pedagogical reform movement became a major objective for the *Merkur,* where excerpts from his longer writings were published as well as regular reports about his experimental schools and those of his followers. The clergyman Tobler became one of the most prolific contributors to the *Merkur* over the next ten years, continuing in essays and poems for the journal the traditions of the moral philosophers of an earlier era. With the theologian and philologist Hottinger, Wieland planned a new periodical, *Das attische Museum,* which he had conceived both to indulge his predilection for Greek antiquity and to provide business for his son-in-law Heinrich, the manager of the Geßner family's publishing house.

Toward the end of 1796 Wieland was forced to endure what he considered a totally unwarranted attack on his person. Goethe and Schiller, annoyed by reactionary criticism of themselves and their programmatic works, replied with a broadside against the world of letters at large. They did so in Schiller's *Musenalmanach auf das Jahr 1797* with a collection of distiches they called "Xenien." Among the hundreds of dartlike insults they hurled were several directed at Wieland, the "zierliche Jungfrau" (dainty old maid) of Weimar, the absentee messenger of the gods (that is, the editor of the *Merkur* who no longer wrote for his own journal), the writer who had, to be sure, chastised fools but from time to time had plagued the wise as well. Reaction throughout Germany to the "Xenien" was heated; Wie-

land was also irked by the impertinence of the two poetic titans and was urged by some of his friends, particularly by the Herders, to join in a traditional polemic battle. Greater than his irritation, however, was his fear for the reputation of the entire literary community should its members begin exchanging insults. To help forestall such a war of words he wrote in January 1797 for the *Merkur* a long and temperate review of all the new year's major literary almanacs, including the offending one. In an urbane and detached tone he put the turmoil in proper perspective, crediting Goethe and Schiller for their wit while faulting them for their arrogance, and expressing the hope that he might be spared from ever hearing again of the mischievous little verses.

Partly in reaction to his growing estrangement from Goethe and Schiller and partly to satisfy a lifelong desire for escape to the peace of the countryside, Wieland decided during the winter of 1797 to purchase a farm and leave Weimar. Such a move had been made financially feasible by the honoraria earned and still expected from his collected works. After weighing several options, including leaving the Grand Duchy of Weimar altogether, he ignored his financial counselors and bought an old, large, and expensive baronial estate on the banks of the Ilm River near the village of Oßmannstedt, a four-hour carriage ride from the city to where he had lived for a quarter of a century. On 25 April 1797 he moved his family of thirteen onto his new property, which was mortgaged to the hilt. The difficulties of facing up to debt, coping with an agricultural enterprise, and adjusting to a totally new style of life far removed from the city merely served to invigorate him, and he returned to his writing with renewed zest.

Religion and its charismatic luminaries were once again Wieland's topic in 1798 and 1799 as he wrote his novel *Agathodämon* (1799) for publication in *Das attische Museum.* The title figure, the "beautiful spirit," is the second-century magus Apollonius of Tyre. A foe of anthropomorphic polytheism who is convinced that man can find salvation only within himself, Apollonius establishes an order dedicated to the improvement of uncultured humankind. To achieve his noble ends he uses all arts of manipulation at his disposal, including trickery and outright deception, for he realizes that the great masses of mankind must be treated as children until they attain their majority. As the apostles of Christianity invade Apollonius's sphere of influence he contemplates

Wieland's country estate near Oßmannstedt, where he lived from 1797 until 1803

their teachings and methods, accepting the ethics of their gospel but rejecting the miracles of Christ's resurrection and ascension. He foresees a progressive contamination of the Christian church as it becomes an established social institution but holds that even in the periods of its greatest future decay it will, as the single most effective force against barbarism, do more good than harm. He predicts further that at some much later, unspecified date society will reach the cultural pinnacle for which it is destined and that the institutional church will then wither away, leaving religion a private matter for each individual. After he completed the novel Wieland declared that it expressed the most devout convictions of his personal philosophy.

In August 1799 Wieland was subjected to yet another assault on his reputation, the most clamorous and the most damaging of all. August Wilhelm and Friedrich Schlegel printed at the end of the third issue of their periodical *Athenäum* a short paragraph under the heading "Citatio edictalis" in which they summoned all authors living and dead from whose works Wieland had too liberally borrowed to attend a creditors' bankruptcy hearing. The Schlegels' disrespectful

jest was itself not very original; the notice is reminiscent of accusations made nearly thirty years earlier by Heinrich Wilhelm von Gerstenberg at a time when Klopstock and Lessing were also charging Wieland with literary misdeeds ranging from uncritical eclecticism to outright plagiarism. There was, however, something more ominous in this new attack by the young Romanticists: in their private and public utterances there was a fanatic zeal never present before. The brothers Schlegel, their spouses, and their friends spoke of the annihilation of Wieland's reputation as an indispensible first step in establishing a foothold for a new, progressive generation of writers. Soon Wieland heard himself scorned openly as outdated and irrelevant by such young authors as Ludwig Tieck, Friedrich Schleiermacher, and Clemens Brentano. Perhaps the bitterest aspect of the polemic was that Wieland's son Ludwig, an aspiring journalist and poet in his own right, considered himself a member of the new Romantic school and shared its negative attitudes toward his father.

In his rural retreat Wieland ignored as best he could the impertinences of the new generation; honors continued to come his way, perhaps

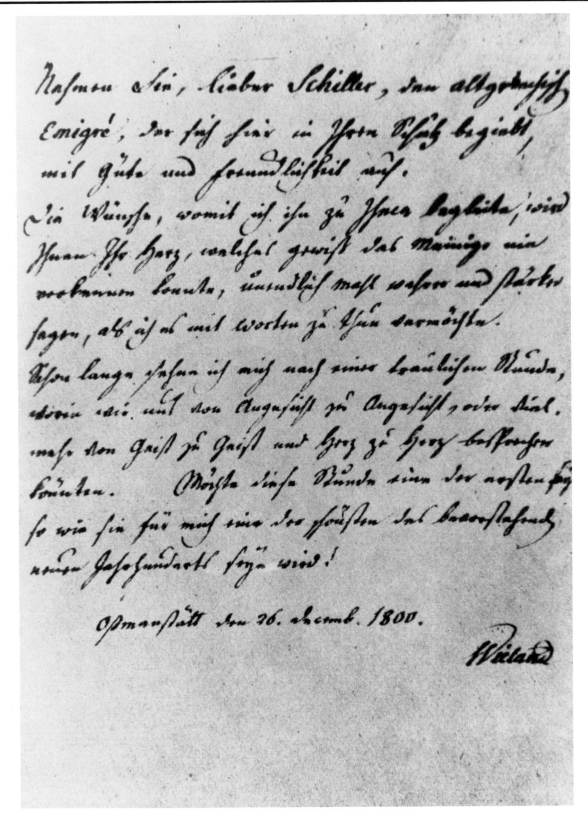

Last page of a letter from Wieland to Friedrich Schiller concerning Wieland's Aristipp und einige seiner Zeitgenossen
(Schiller-Nationalmuseum, Marbach am Neckar)

the most notable being his election to membership in the National Institute of France. He continued writing, turning again to a project he had first considered almost five decades earlier: an epistolary novel in which he would depict for the eighteenth-century German reader the classical Greece he knew so well. Wieland's goal was a true depiction of the Socratic world, and for his central character he selected Aristippus of Cyrene, one of Socrates' pupils and a forerunner of Epicurus. The painstaking detail with which Wieland tried to re-create this ancient society and the issues which preoccupied it is illustrated by his characters' one-hundred-twenty-page-long dissection of Plato's *Republic*. More interesting, perhaps, for those who read the four volumes of *Aristipp und einige seiner Zeitgenossen* (Aristippus and Some of His Contemporaries, 1800-1801) were the ruminations about pleasure and happiness reflected in the relationship between the sensualist Aristippus and the beautiful hetaera Lais.

Wieland's withdrawal to the countryside did not mean that he had taken up a life of endless and lonely labor. His existence, at least during the first two years at Oßmannstedt, was comfortable and pleasant enough; he received regular visits from his close friends in Weimar, most frequently from Carl August Böttiger and Johann Daniel Falk. Goethe was so impressed by Wieland's new life-style that he imitated it by purchasing an estate of his own at the nearby village of Oberroßla. Many notable travelers came to talk with Wieland at his Horatian "Sabinum" on the Ilm, including the historian and diplomat Christian Dohn, the journalist and critic Garlieb Merkel and the philologist Karl Morgenstern. Friedrich David Gräter, the Germanist and mythologist from Schwäbisch-Hall, was a houseguest for a week, during which Wieland persuaded him to become a regular contributor to the *Merkur*. Johann Paul Friedrich Richter (Jean Paul) paid several calls and, like other writers before him, apparently contemplated the role of son-in-law to Germany's most celebrated author. Heinrich von Kleist remained some six weeks as a houseguest, receiving badly needed encouragement to continue his literary career and becoming emotionally involved with Wieland's youngest daughter, fourteen-year-old Louise. Perhaps the most remarkable visit was one paid in July and August 1799 by the widowed Sophie, now Sophie von La Roche (her husband having been awarded a patent of nobility before his death), who brought with her to Oßmannstedt her granddaughter Sophie Brentano. For Wieland the encounter with his sentimental and too garrulous former fiancée was at best a mixed pleasure, but in her beautiful and unhappy young companion he found a kindred spirit who was as much attracted to him as he was to her. The girl had a rejuvenating effect on the old writer, and from him she gained a degree of immortality as the model for Lais in *Aristipp und einige seiner Zeitgenossen*. In late July 1800 Sophie Brentano returned alone to Oßmannstedt and there fulfilled her expressed wish to spend the rest of her life with the poet. The remainder of her life proved to be a mere two months, but the closeness of the friendship generated over so short a time is revealed in the fact that, at her request and over the objections of her family, she was buried in a plot at Oßmannstedt which later became the resting place for Anna Dorothea and finally for Wieland himself.

The end of the idyl in Oßmannstedt began when Wieland could not longer ignore the fact that his estate had drained his financial resources almost to their limit and that the health of his wife was deteriorating. In desperation he pushed Göschen to agree to plans for even more works to be written or edited in Oßmannstedt, one journalistic project to be a joint effort with his son Ludwig (with whom Wieland made repeated, though generally unsuccessful, efforts at reconciliation). The death of Sophie Brentano on 20 September 1800 made him far less certain about the joys of his country existence, but it was the loss of Anna Dorothea a year and a half later that finally shattered his dreams. Without the support of his wife his retreat was no longer tolerable; he realized that he needed the regular companionship of old friends in Weimar, but they were separated from him by a long and fatiguing carriage ride. Near the end of 1802 he agreed with those of his children who had urged him to rid himself of the increasingly oppressive burdens of debt and isolation. With the help of his son-in-law Karl Wilhelm Constantin Stichling he found a buyer for his estate, a wealthy merchant from Hamburg named Christian Johann Martin Kühne. When the transaction was completed in April 1803 Wieland returned to Weimar to take up a relatively comfortable life surrounded and tended to by daughters and granddaughters in a large apartment near the palace of Anna Amalia. The duchess made the transition even more pleasant for him by giving him a key to her garden, through which he had direct access to her quarters.

The house in Weimar in which Wieland lived for the last ten years of his life; engraving by E. Lobe

The sale of his estate had not only freed Wieland from debt but also provided money for investment, the interest from which, along with his ducal pension and periodic honoraria from his publishers Georg Göschen and Friedrich Cotta, left him without financial worries. Literary projects which he had proposed in desperation to subsidize his unprofitable farm he simply dropped; works he had begun because of their appeal to him he continued. The novellas *Menander und Glycerion* (1803) and *Krates und Hipparchia* (1804; translated as *Crates and Hipparchia*, 1823), which he published in successive years in Cotta's pocket almanacs, are works with themes particularly close to his heart. Both represent a return to a theme dominant in his earlier writings: the force of eros. *Menander und Glycerion*, about the Greek comedian and a flower maiden, attempts, for all its costume of antiquity, to analyze a relationship Wieland believed he had discerned between his daughter Louise and Kleist. The story is essentially a depiction of readiness for selfless sacrifice on the part of a totally devoted young woman. *Krates und Hipparchia* tells of the woman who loved the cynic philosopher Crates so absolutely that she was willing at his request to consummate

the relationship publicly; the story shows how complete devotion can, under certain circumstances, be just as debasing as it can be ennobling. It was, however, a third work written after Wieland's return to Weimar which was for the old poet most important. In 1804 a book by J. K. Wözel was published in Chemnitz; in it the author claimed to have established visual and spiritual contact with his deceased wife. Wieland considered the book a menace to all the goals of Enlightenment—and perceived also that it contained a personal challenge. His response, *Euthanasia: Drey Gespräche über das Leben nach dem Tode* (Euthanasia: Three Conversations about Life after Death, 1805), sought to disprove Wözel's claims, partly on the grounds that if anyone could return from the dead to comfort the bereaved then most certainly Wieland's own sorely missed Alceste, his Anna Dorothea, would do so. At about the same time Wieland put together a collection consisting of novellas that had appeared between 1800 and 1802 in various almanacs and pocketbooks. The collection, *Das Hexameron von Rosenhain* (1805), shows considerable artistic skill in a poet seven decades old. In the summer of 1806, at the request of Sophie von La Roche, he wrote a preface and annota-

Wieland's encounter with Napoleon on 6 October 1808;
engraving by V. H. Schnorr, 1809

tions for her book *Melusinens Sommer-Abende* (Melusine's Summer Evening, 1806). By rendering this service to his old friend he acquired the distinction of having edited both the first and the last works of eighteenth-century Germany's best-known female author.

During the years following, his return to Weimar Wieland suffered additional painful losses. Schiller's death in May 1805 touched him; even more disturbing was the news in late February 1807 that Sophie had died. Most distressing of all was the passing of Anna Amalia on 10 April 1807. With her he lost one of his life's requisites: association with a talented and intelligent woman. The feeling of bereavement was eased somewhat by an extensive correspondence with Countess Elisabeth of Solms-Laubach. In their letters the two shared the tribulations of parenthood as well as anxieties about Germany's future, and he recounted for her his most interesting experiences at home, at court, and in the theater. For the visitors who flocked to Weimar he contin-

ued to play his role as the most accessible of the city's great men. Many were merely curious to see the "dean of the German Parnassus"; but those with more serious purposes included such phrenologists, prelates, philosophers, journalists, poets, painters, and composers as Franz Josef Gall, Henri Gregoire, Arthur Schopenhauer, Johann Gruber, Franz Passow, Friedrich Rochlitz, Franz Anton von Sonnenberg, Bettina Brentano, Johannes Schulz, Achim von Arnim, Madame de Staël, Johann Ernst Wagner, Henry Crabb Robinson, Wolf Graf Baudissin, Christine Westphalen, Franz Xaver Bronner, Christian Friedrich Tieck, Gerhard von Kügelgen, Johann Gottfried Schadow, Jakob Wilhelm Christian Roux, and Carl Maria von Weber.

The most publicized of Wieland's encounters with the world at large was with Napoleon Bonaparte. The emperor, in Thuringia for the Congress of Erfurt, asked to meet the famous German writer who had predicted his ascendency to supreme authority over the French nation. For an hour and a half on the evening of 6 October 1808, during a ball held at the court of Duke Karl August, the two men held an uninterrupted conversation. French and German diplomats standing nearby overheard and recorded portions of the discussion. Perhaps the most interesting thoughts expressed were Napoleon's comments about the nature of the origins of Christianity, views to which Wieland took exception. Surely the most daring remark of the evening was prompted by the emperor's observation that Julius Caesar had erred by showing too much leniency toward his enemies: the poet rejoined that a Bonaparte would surely not make a similar mistake. Instead of taking offense, within the week Napoleon bestowed upon Wieland the Legion of Merit; the gesture was promptly matched by Czar Alexander of Russia, who conferred upon the writer the Cross of Saint Anna.

Wieland's contacts were not limited to travelers. His circle of friends was large: Schiller's widow Charlotte, Herder's daughter Louise, and the city's most celebrated hostess, Johanna Schopenhauer, were particularly attentive to him; Maria Palovna, the daughter of the czar and the consort of Weimar's Prince Carl Friedrich, summoned him frequently to the palace for conversation and for instruction in the history of her new land. Two active young members of Weimar's literary community, Johann Stephan Schütze and Carl Bertuch, courted the women in his house and kept him informed about local affairs. In

April 1809 Wieland altered his lifelong attitude toward closed organizations and became a Freemason. During the three years following his initiation he prepared three papers reflecting on the ideals of Masonry, two of which he read before the members of the Amalia lodge.

As Wieland watched Europe lurch toward the end of the Napoleonic Era, he became increasingly aware of the similarities between the early nineteenth century and the end of the Roman Republic. Since he felt that the best characterizations of that period of antiquity were to be found in the epistles of Marcus Tullius Cicero, he undertook, a few weeks after the battle of Jena and at the age of seventy-three, the demanding task of translating and annotating the documents. He hoped that they might serve as a kind of oracle to warn those who seemed doomed to relive a tragic history being ignored. Before he died on 21 January 1813 he had published five volumes of the letters. The project was completed in 1818 with a sixth volume prepared from his notes by Friedrich David Gräter.

A wake was held for Wieland at the palatial home of his oldest friend in Weimar, Friedrich Justin Bertuch. There the poet lay in state with his imperial French and Russian decorations on display. Following Masonic ceremonies he was buried between his wife and Sophie Brentano on the grounds of his former estate, Oßmannstedt.

Letters:

Auswahl denkwürdiger Briefe von C. M. Wieland, 2 volumes, edited by Ludwig Wieland (Vienna: Gerold, 1815);

Ausgewählte Briefe von C. M. Wieland an verschiedene Freunde in den Jahren 1751. bis 1810. geschrieben und nach der Zeitfolge geordnet, 4 volumes, edited by Heinrich Geßner (Zurich: Geßner, 1815-1816);

C. M. Wieland's Briefe an Sophie von La Roche, nebst einem Schreiben von Gellert und Lavater, edited by Franz Horn (Berlin: Christiani, 1820);

Aus klassischer Zeit: Wieland und Reinhold. Original-Mittheilungen als Beiträge zur Geschichte des deutschen Geisteslebens im XVIII. Jahrhundert, edited by Robert Keil (Leipzig & Berlin: Friedrich, 1885);

Neue Briefe Chr. Mart. Wielands, vornehmlich an Sophie von La Roche, edited by Robert Hassencamp (Stuttgart: Cotta, 1894);

Wielands Briefwechsel, 5 volumes to date, published by the Institute for German Language and Literature of the Academy of Sciences of the German Democratic Republic, edited by Hans Werner Seiffert (Berlin: Akademie-Verlag, 1963-).

Bibliographies:

Julius Steinberger, *Bibliographie der Wieland-Übersetzungen* (Göttingen: Selbstverlag, 1930);

Gottfried Günther and Heidi Zeilinger, *Wieland-Bibliographie* (Berlin & Weimar: Aufbau, 1983);

Hansjörg Schelle, "Nachträge und Ergänzungen zur Wieland-Bibliographie," *Lessing Yearbook,* 16 (1984): 253-261; 17 (1985): 209-215: 18 (1986): 227-237; 19 (1987): 287-294; 20 (1988): 293-299.

Biographies:

Johann Georg Gruber, *C. M. Wielands Leben,* volumes 50-53 of Wieland's *Sämmtliche Werke,* edited by Gruber (Leipzig: Göschen, 1828);

Victor Michael, *C. M. Wieland: la formation et l'évolution de son esprit jusqu'en 1772* (Paris: Boivin, 1938);

Friedrich Sengle, *Wieland* (Stuttgart: Metzler, 1949);

Thomas C. Starnes, *Christoph Martin Wieland: Leben und Werk. Aus zeitgenössischen Quellen chronologisch dargestellt,* 3 volumes (Sigmaringen: Thorbecke, 1987).

References:

Derek Maurice van Abbé, *Christoph Martin Wieland (1733-1813): A Literary Biography* (London, Toronto & Wellington: Harrap, 1961);

Werner Beyer, *The Enchanted Forest* (New York: Barnes & Noble, 1963);

Beyer, *Keats and the Daemon King* (New York: Oxford University Press, 1947);

Eric A. Blackall, "The Culture of Wit and Feeling," in his *The Emergence of German as a Literary Language* (Cambridge: Cambridge University Press, 1959), pp. 387-425;

Elizabeth Boa, "Sex and Sensibility: Wieland's Portrayal of Relationships between the Sexes in the *Comische Erzählungen, Agathon,* and *Musarion,*" *Lessing Yearbook,* 12 (1980): 189-218;

Boa, "Wieland's 'Musarion' and the Rococo Verse Narrative," in *Periods in German Literature,* edited by James M. Ritchie, volume 2 (London: Wolff, 1969), pp. 21-41;

Wolfram Buddecke, *C. M. Wielands Entwicklungsbegriff und die Geschichte des Agathon* (Göttingen: Vandenhoeck & Ruprecht, 1966);

Charlotte Craig, *Christoph Martin Wieland as the Originator of the Modern Travesty in German Literature* (Chapel Hill: University of North Carolina Press, 1970);

Max Dufner, "The Tragedy of Lais in C. M. Wieland's 'Aristipp,'" *Monatshefte*, 52 (January 1960): 63-70;

Charles Elson, *Wieland and Shaftesbury* (New York: Columbia University Press, 1913; reprinted, New York: AMS Press, 1966);

Albert Fuchs, *Les apports français dans l'oeuvre de Wieland de 1772 à 1789* (Paris: Champion, 1934);

Fuchs, *Geistiger Gehalt und Quellenfrage in Wielands Abderiten* (Paris: Société d'édition "Les belles lettres," 1934);

Hans Herchner, "Die Cyropädie in Wielands Werken," *Neue Jahrbücher für Philologie und Pädagogik*, 66 (1896):199-208;

Edith Harn, *Wieland's "Neuer Amadis"* (Göttingen: Vandenhoeck & Ruprecht, 1928);

Karl Hoppe, *Der junge Wieland: Wesensbestimmung seines Geistes* (Leipzig: Weber, 1930);

Wolfgang Kayser, "Die Anfänge des modernen Romans im 18. Jahrhundert und seine heutige Krise," *Deutsche Vierteljahrsschrift für Geistesgeschichte und Literaturwissenschaft*, 28, no. 4 (1954): 417-446;

Wilhelm Kurrelmeyer, *Die Doppeldrucke in ihrer Bedeutung für die Textgeschichte von Wielands Werken* (Berlin: Verlag der Königlichen Akademie der Wissenschaften, 1913);

Liselotte E. Kurth-Voigt, *Perspectives and Points of View: The Early Works of Wieland and Their Background* (Baltimore: Johns Hopkins University Press, 1974);

Kurth-Voigt, "The Reception of C. M. Wieland in America," in *The German Contribution to the Building of the Americas: Studies in Honor of Karl J. R. Arndt*, edited by Gerhard K. Frieseri and Walter Shatzberg (Worcester, Mass.: Clark University Press, 1977), pp. 97-133;

George Leuca, "Wieland and the Introduction of Shakespeare into Germany," *German Quarterly*, 28 (November 1955): 247-255;

Fritz Martini, "Christoph Martin Wieland: Zu seiner Stellung in der deutschen Dichtungsgeschichte im 18. Jahrhundert," *Deutschunterricht*, 8, no. 5 (1956): 87-112;

K. Otto Mayer, "Die Feenmärchen bei Wieland," *Vierteljahrsschrift für Litteraturgeschichte*, 5 (1892): 374-408, 497-533;

John A. McCarthy, *Christoph Martin Wieland* (Boston: Twayne, 1979);

James A. McNeely, "Historical Relativism in Wieland's Concept of the Ideal State," *Modern Language Quarterly*, 22 (1961): 269-282;

Frederick William Meisnest, "Wieland's Translation of Shakespeare," *Modern Language Review*, 9 (January 1914): 12-40;

Jan-Dirk Müller, *Wielands späte Romane: Untersuchungen zur Erzählweise und zur erzählten Wirklichkeit* (Munich: Fink, 1971);

Klaus Oettinger, *Phantasie und Erfahrung: Studien zur Erzählpoetik Christoph Martin Wielands* (Munich: Fink, 1970);

Ernst Pasqué, "Alceste von Wieland und Schweitzer: Die erste deutsche Oper der neuen Zeit," *Recensionen und Mittheilungen über Theater und Musik*, 7 (1861): 35-37;

Wolfgang Paulsen, "Die emancipierte Frau in Wielands Weltbild," in *Die Frau als Heldin und Authorin: Neue kritische Ansätze zur deutschen Literatur*, edited by Wolfgang Paulsen (Bern & Munich: Lang, 1979), pp. 153-174;

Allesandro Pellegrini, *Wieland e la classicit à tedesca* (Florence: Olscki, 1968);

Manfred A. Poitzsch, *Zeitgenössische Persiflagen auf C. M. Wieland und seine Schriften* (Bern & Frankfurt am Main: Lang, 1972);

Wolfgang Preisendanz, "Wieland und die Verserzählung des 18. Jahrhunderts," *Germanisch-Romanische Monatsschrift*, 12 (1962): 17-31;

Herbert Rowland, *"Musarion" and Wieland's Concept of Genre* (Göppingen: Kümmerle, 1975);

Bernhard Seuffert, "Der junge Goethe und Wieland," *Zeitschrift für deutsches Alterthum und deutsche Litteratur*, 26 (1882): 252-287;

Seuffert, "Wielands Pervonte," *Euphorion*, 10 (1903): 76-90;

Cornelius Sommer, *Wieland* (Stuttgart: Metzler, 1971);

Hansjörg Schelle, ed., *Christoph Martin Wieland* (Darmstadt: Wissenschaftliche Buchgesellschaft, 1981);

Violet Amie Alice Stockley, *German Literature as Known in England: 1750-1830* (Port Washington, N.Y. & London: Kennikat Press, 1929), pp. 77-106;

Martin Swales, *The German Bildungsroman from Wieland to Hesse* (Princeton: Princeton University Press, 1978), pp. 38-56;

Hans Tribolet, *Wielands Verhältnis zu Ariost and Tasso* (Bern: Francke, 1919; reprinted, Nendeln, Liechtenstein: Kraus, 1970);

Wolfgang von Ungern-Sternberg, *Ch. M. Wieland und das Verlagswesen seiner Zeit: Studien zur Entstehung des freien Schriftstellertums in Deutschland* (Frankfurt am Main: Buchhändler-Vereinigung, 1974);

Jürgen Viering, *Schwärmerische Erwartung bei Wieland, im trivalen Geheimnisroman und bei Jean Paul* (Cologne & Vienna: Böhlau, 1976);

Bernd Weyergraf, *Der skeptische Bürger: Wielands Schriften zur Französischen Revolution* (Stuttgart: Metzler, 1972);

John Whiton, "Sacrifice and Society in Wieland's 'Abderiten,'" *Lessing Yearbook*, 2 (1970): 213-234;

Daniel W. Wilson, *The Narrative Strategy of Wieland's "Don Sylvio von Rosalva"* (Bern, Frankfurt am Main & Las Vegas: Lang, 1981).

Papers:

Christoph Martin Wieland's manuscripts including letters written by him, are scattered in more than three dozen libraries and archives in Europe and North America; the principal collections, accounting for over ninety-five percent of his known papers, are held by five institutions: in the Federal Republic of Germany by the Wieland-Archiv, Biberach, and the Germanisches National-museum, Nuremburg; in Switzerland by the Zentralbibliothek Zurich; and in the German Democratic Republic by the Goethe-Schiller-Archiv of the National-Gedenk- und Forschungs-stätten der klassischen deutschen Literatur, Weimar, and the Sächsische Landesbibliothek, Dresden.

Johann Joachim Winckelmann

(9 December 1717 - 8 June 1768)

James Hardin
University of South Carolina
and
Renate Wilson

BOOKS: *Gedancken über die Nachahmung der Griechischen Wercke in der Mahlerey und Bildhauer-Kunst* (N.p., 1755; enlarged edition, Leipzig & Dresden: Walther, 1756); translated by Henry Fusseli as *Reflections on the Painting and Sculpture of the Greeks* (London: Millar, 1765); German version reprinted (Baden Baden: Heitz, 1962); translation reprinted, (Menston, U.K.: Scolar Press, 1972);

Description des pierres gravées du feu Baron de Stosch dédiée à son Eminence Monseigneur le Cardinal Alexandre Albani par M. l'abbé Winckelmann bibliothécaire de son éminence (Florence: Bonducci, 1760);

Anmerckungen über die Baukunst der Alten (Leipzig: Dyck, 1762; reprinted, Baden Baden: Heitz, 1964);

Sendschreiben von den Herculanischen Entdeckungen: An den hochgebohrnen Herrn, Herrn Heinrich Reichsgrafen von Brühl (Dresden: Walther, 1762); translated anonymously as *Critical Account of the Situation and Destruction by the First Eruptions of Mount Vesuvius, of Herculaneum, Pompeii, and Stabia; the Late Discovery of Their Remains; the Subterraneous Works Carried on in Them; and the Books, Domestick Utensils, and Other Greek and Roman Antiquities Thereby Happily Recovered; the Form and Connection of the Ancient Characters Being Faithfully Preserved, in a Letter (originally in German) to Count Bruhl of Saxony, from the Celebrated Abbé Winckelmann; Illustrated with Notes, Taken from the French translation* (London: Printed for T. Carnan and F. Newbery, jun., 1771); German version reprinted (Baden Baden: Heitz, 1964);

Abhandlung von der Fähigkeit der Empfindung des Schönen in der Kunst, und dem Unterrichte in derselben (Dresden: Walther, 1763);

Johann Joachim Winckelmann; painting by Anton Raphael Mengs (The Metropolitan Museum of Art, New York)

Geschichte der Kunst des Alterthums, 2 volumes (Dresden: Walther, 1764); translated by G. Henry Lodge as *The History of Ancient Art* (4 volumes, Boston: Osgood, 1849-1873; 2 volumes, London: S. Low, Marston, Searle, & Rivington, 1881); German version reprinted (Baden Baden: Heitz, 1966); translation reprinted, 2 volumes (New York: Ungar, 1968);

Nachrichten von den neuesten Herculanischen Entdek-kungen: An Hn. Heinrich Füssli aus Zürich (Dresden: Walther, 1764);

Versuch einer Allegorie, besonders für die Kunst (Dresden: Walther, 1766; reprinted, Baden Baden: Heitz, 1964; New York: Garland, 1976);

Anmerkungen über die Geschichte der Kunst des Alterthums, 2 volumes (Dresden: Walther, 1767; reprinted, Baden Baden: Heitz, 1966);

Monumenti antichi inediti spiegati ed illustrati, 2 volumes (Rome: Published by the author, 1767);

Werke, edited by Karl Ludwig Fernow, Heinrich Meyer, Johannes Schulz, Karl Gottfried Siebelis, and F. Förster, 12 volumes (volumes 1-9, Dresden: Walther; volumes 10-12, Berlin: Schlesinger, 1808-1825);

Sämtliche Werke: Einzige vollständige Ausgabe, 12 volumes, edited by Joseph Eiselein (Donaueschingen: Verlag Deutscher Classiker, 1825-1835; reprinted, Osnabrück: Zeller, 1965);

Werke: Einzige rechtmäßig Original-Ausgabe, 2 volumes (Stuttgart: Hoffmann, 1847);

Kleine Schriften und Briefe, edited by H. Uhde-Bernays, 2 volumes (Leipzig: Insel, 1925);

Werke in einem Band, edited by Helmut Holtzhauer (Berlin & Weimar: Aufbau, 1969);

Kunsttheoretische Schriften: Zehn kleinere Schriften (Baden Baden: Koerner, 1971);

De ratione delineandi Graecorum artificum primi artium seculi ex nummis antiquissimis dignoscenda, edited by Klaus-Peter Goethert (Wiesbaden: Steiner, 1974).

Edition in English: *Writings on Art*, edited by David Irwin (London: Phaidon, 1972).

PERIODICAL PUBLICATIONS: "Erinnerung über die Betrachtung der Werke der Kunst," *Bibliothek der schönen Wissenschaften und der freyen Künste*, 5, no. 1 (1762): 1-13;

"Von der Grazie in Werken der Kunst," *Bibliothek der schönen Wissenschaften und der freyen Künste*, 5, no. 1 (1762): 13-23;

"Nachrichten von dem berühmten Stoßischen Museo in Florenz von dem Herrn Winckelmann an den Herrn L. R. v. H.," *Bibliothek der schönen Wissenschaften und der freyen Künste*, 5, no. 1 (1762): 23-33;

"Beschreibung des Torso im Belvedere zu Rom," *Bibliothek der schönen Wissenschaften und der freyen Künste*, 5, no. 1 (1762): 33-41; translated by Thomas Davidson as "Description

of the Torso of the Hercules of Belvedere in Rome," *Journal of Speculative Philosophy*, 2 (1868): 187-189;

"Anmerkungen über die Baukunst der alten Tempel zu Girgenti in Sizilien," *Bibliothek der schönen Wissenschaften und der freyen Künste*, 5, no. 2 (1762): 223-242.

Profoundly influenced by his immersion in the art, literature, culture, and philosophy of ancient Greece, Johann Joachim Winckelmann brought about a revolutionary reevaluation of the art of the ancient world that had enormous impact on the aesthetic sensibilities of his own time and that is still felt today. Henry Hatfield suggests that as the founder of German Hellenism Winckelmann was, aside from Frederick II of Prussia, the most famous German between Gottfried Wilhelm von Leibniz and Johann Wolfgang von Goethe. His contributions to the development of new disciplines such as art history and archaeology are well known, but he also influenced the course of literature, music, and plastic art not only in Germany but also in the rest of Europe. He influenced the writing of history and changed the course of German literature by urging the primacy of ancient Greek rather than Roman models. Even the prose style of his writings was influential: his "classic" style, a lofty idealism combined with great simplicity of expression, had a distinctive impact on expository writing in German. His works were instrumental in awakening the growing interest of the German educated public in classical antiquity.

Winckelmann was born in Stendal on 9 December 1717, the only child of Martin and Anna Maria Winckelmann, née Meyer. His father was a cobbler, his mother the daughter of a weaver and cloth merchant. Winckelmann attended the local Lateinschule (grammar school), helping to offset the cost of his education by singing in a choir that performed at funerals, weddings, and other important functions; he sometimes accompanied the choir on the organ. In 1734 he became director of the choir, receiving one-fourth of the income from its engagements. Winckelmann also tutored fellow students and acted as the factotum of the principal, who was blind. In addition to all these duties, Winckelmann helped administer the school library, where he first became acquainted with the art of Greek antiquity. The curriculum of the grammar school consisted of religious studies, Latin, history, and some Greek. Instruction was in Latin, which gave Winckelmann a good command of that language; but even then he had a preference for Greek.

In 1735 he became a student at the Köllnische Gymnasium in Berlin. There, Christian Tobias Damm, one of the first German scholars to argue the superiority of Greek literature to Latin, furthered his knowledge of Greek. In Berlin he also met Johann Leonhard Frisch, a noted Latin scholar and naturalist and the director of the famous Gymnasium zum grauen Kloster. In 1738 Winckelmann enrolled at the University of Halle. He wanted to study medicine but could not afford to do so; instead, he chose theology, which was subsidized by the state and the church.

The Prussian city of Halle had little of the worldly sophistication of nearby Leipzig, but the intolerance of church and educational authorities in Saxony had caused many eminent scholars to leave Leipzig for Halle, most notably the philosopher and jurist Christian Thomasius. One of Winckelmann's teachers in Halle was the prominent aesthetician Alexander Gottlieb Baumgarten. But Winckelmann was not completely submerged in his studies while in Halle; he liked to frequent inns, where he enjoyed conversing with the local citizenry about their travels. He was forced to earn money by tutoring, and only infrequently attended lectures in theology. Winckelmann preferred to read in his room in the morning before going to the university library. The library, far from providing the resources needed by a scholar, contained fewer than ten thousand volumes and was open only from 1:00 P.M. to 2:00 P.M., three days a week. He also read at the library of the Francke Orphanage. He increased his own collection by copying books verbatim or by buying them at auctions. Perhaps the most significant influence on Winckelmann in Halle was Johann Heinrich Schulze: his lectures on Greece and Rome, which made extensive use of his collection of ancient coins, kindled Winckelmann's interest in classical antiquity even more than before. In early 1740 he became a private tutor to the oldest son of the patrician soldier Georg Arnold Grolmann in Osterburg, making social contact for the first time with an educated upper-class milieu. In the winter of 1740-1741 he developed an interest in English, French, and Italian, possibly encouraged by Frau Grolmann, an educated woman with many interests. This position provided him with sufficient financial resources to enable him to matriculate in 1741 at the University of Jena as a student of medicine instead of continuing his theological studies.

He studied with Georg Erhard Hamberger, a proponent of a mechanistic view of medicine who required his students to learn physics as well as anatomy and medicine. These studies were later to help Winckelmann in the anatomical description of statues. He planned to complete his studies with the *erudita peregrinatio*, a traditional academic journey sometimes undertaken in lieu of writing a thesis in the seventeenth century and still common in the eighteenth. Winckelmann's academic journey was to have taken him to Paris, but he had to interrupt the trip in Gelnhausen because he feared being impressed into the army—the Austrian War of Succession had brought about ruthless recruitment practices—and because he had exhausted his funds. He made his way to Fulda, and in 1742 he found yet another position as a tutor—this time to Friedrich Wilhelm Peter Lamprecht, the fourteen-year-old son of a prominent government official who lived in Hadmersleben, near Halberstadt. Winckelmann held this position for one and a half years, and his pupil—with whom he had formed a romantic attachment—followed him when he became associate director of the school in Seehausen in April 1743. When Lamprecht left Winckelmann in 1746, the latter suffered a severe emotional crisis.

For a meager salary Winckelmann taught Hebrew, geography, logic, history, Latin, and Greek; he also sang and gave private lessons. Sometimes he was even responsible for church sermons. Among his private students was Friedrich Ulrich Arwed von Bülow, whose family owned Castle Schönberg near Seehausen and with whom Winckelmann—whose tutorial relationships always seemed to include elements of emotional attachment—shared a passionate friendship. He traveled to Leipzig, Magdeburg, Halle, Brunswick, and other places to purchase books, especially on Greek literature, and used the libraries of pastors and noblemen in the vicinity of Seehausen. He spent his days teaching at the school, taught his private pupils in the evenings, and used most of the night for his own studies, leaving only four hours for sleep in an armchair. Winckelmann remained in Seehausen for more than five years, a period marked by problems with his students, who felt he placed excessive demands on them. During this time Winckelmann experienced many professional disappointments, the greatest of which was probably caused by Johann Friedrich Wilhelm Jerusalem, the father of the young man whose suicide was made notorious in Johann Wolfgang Goethe's *Die Leiden des jungen Werthers* (The Sorrows of Young Werther, 1774): Jerusalem was too busy to receive Winckelmann and consider him for a teaching position at the Collegium Carolineum in Brunswick, one of the most progressive schools in Germany.

In September 1748 Winckelmann became a research assistant and librarian for Heinrich von Bünau, a distinguished statesman who had retired to his estate at Nöthnitz to write historical works. Bünau's library, containing some forty-two thousand volumes, was one of the foremost private collections in Europe. One of his colleagues at Nöthnitz was Johann Michael Francke, who was to become his lifelong correspondent; another was Christian Gottlieb Heyne, who was later to become professor of archaeology in Göttingen and to recommend that Winckelmann be inducted into the Royal Academy of Sciences in Berlin. As Bünau's librarian, Winckelmann had access to the books of such writers as Bolingbroke, John Milton, John Dryden, William Congreve, Alexander Pope, Voltaire, Montesquieu, La Rochefoucauld, and Jean de La Bruyère. Thus he was exposed to–and clearly influenced by–the prevailing religious skepticism of the Enlightenment.

Among the many visitors to whom Winckelmann showed the treasures of the library was the ambitious papal nuncio to the Saxon court in Dresden, Alberigo Archinto. Archinto told Winckelmann that the Vatican librarian, Domenico Cardinal Passionei, was looking for a custodian for the library of more than three hundred thousand volumes; Winckelmann would not necessarily be expected to convert to Catholicism, Archinto told him, although such a step– a mere formality that could be done privately–would be advantageous. Archinto also flattered Winckelmann by saying that it would be a great honor to bring such a noted scholar into the church. After several years' hesitation Winckelmann finally converted under the guidance of the Dresden court chaplain, Leo Rauch, in July 1754, and in October of the same year he left Nöthnitz. His conversion was rewarded by a stipend from the Saxon court, which had converted to Catholicism to enable the Elector of Saxony to assume the crown of Poland. This stipend allowed Winckelmann to live comfortably in Dresden for the next several months, devoting his time to the study of the arts. Dresden had become the art capital of Germany, and Winckelmann had access to the rich holdings of the Dresden galleries and museums

as well as to the men who administered them. He rented a room from and studied drawing with the painter Adam Friedrich Oeser, who later taught the young Goethe to draw. Oeser's influence is evident in Winckelmann's appreciation for the art of antiquity and rejection of contemporary art: intaglios and cameos, among the earliest collected ancient art objects, were used extensively by Oeser in his instruction. In Dresden, Winckelmann also became acquainted with Philipp Daniel Lippert, a collector of antique cut gems who developed a practical method of producing prints of them.

Early in 1755 Winckelmann made preparations for the journey to Rome. In the same year he published his epochal *Gedancken über die Nachahmung der Griechischen Wercke in der Mahlerey und Bildhauer-Kunst* (translated as *Reflections on the Painting and Sculpture of the Greeks*, 1765); virtually overnight he became an intellectual force in Germany. Gilbert Highet contends that the beginning of the "German Renaissance"–which came two hundred years later than in England, Spain, and France–was signaled by the publication of this work. Victor Lange calls the forty-page pamphlet "the key document of the emerging European Neo-Classicist Movement" and argues that this "most influential of his publications, indeed, his credo" contains in a nutshell the ideas that he would develop in much greater detail and with perquisite scholarly apparatus in his later works. At the heart of Winckelmann's conception of Greek art is that "modern" art, to achieve greatness, must imitate the aesthetic conceptions of antiquity: "Der einzige Weg für uns groß, ja, wenn es möglich ist, unnachahmlich zu werden, ist die Nachahmung der Alten" (The only way for us to become great, indeed, if it is possible, to become inimitable, is the imitation of the Ancients).

Winckelmann does not advocate the slavish imitation of Greek art. He points out that Greek masterpieces do not merely copy nature in the manner of Dutch landscape or genre painters but are imbued with an idealized, heightened Platonic beauty that combines the sensual and spiritual. The modern artist must imitate the *manner* of the Greeks. Winckelmann, like Friedrich Schiller after him, finds a direct link between beauty and that which is morally good. Austere upbringing, physical exercise, and health, as embodied in young Spartan athletes, provide an outer beauty that is perfectly mirrored in the best classical statuary. Thus, even the human models for ancient artists were superior to those of the modern era:

"Man nehme einen jungen Spartaner ... der in der Kindheit niemals in Windeln eingeschränkt gewesen, der von dem siebenten Jahre an auf der Erde geschlafen und im Ringen und Schwimmen von Kindesbeinen an war geübt worden. Man stelle ihn neben einen jungen Sybariten unserer Zeit: und alsdann urteile man, welchen von beiden der Künstler zu einem Urbilde eines jungen Theseus, eines Achilles ... nehmen würde" (Let one take a young Spartan ... who in his youth was never restrained in diapers, who has slept on the earth from the time he was seven and had been trained in wrestling and swimming from the earliest time. Place him next to a young sybarite of our time: and then let one judge which of the two the artist ... would take as the model for a young Theseus, an Achilles).

Here as elsewhere Winckelmann idealizes the culture of ancient Greece, and this one-sided view of a healthy, untroubled, beautiful people persisted until well into the nineteenth century. More important from an aesthetic viewpoint is his theory as to what made Greek art superior to that of his time: the tendency of its best artists to form "gewisse allgemeine Begriffe von Schönheiten sowohl einzelner Teile als ganzer Verhältnisse der Körper" (certain general concepts of beauty both of individual parts of the body as well as of relationships of one part to the other). In this the Greeks were followed by the greatest of the moderns, Raphael. Winckelmann cites a letter from the latter to Count Baldassare Castiglione: "Da die Schönheiten unter dem Frauenzimmer so selten sind, so bediene ich mich einer gewissen Idee in meiner Einbildung" (Since beauty is so rare among women, I make use of a certain idea [of beauty] in my imagination). Winckelmann's view of the physical beauty of the Greeks does not conflict with his contention that Greek art contains a Platonic element: "Die sinnliche Schönheit gab dem Künstler die schöne Natur, die idealische Schönheit die erhabenen Züge; von jener nahm er das Menschliche, von dieser das Göttliche" (Beautiful nature gave the artist sensual beauty; ideal beauty gave him sublime features. From the former he took that which is human; from the latter the divine). Modern art attempts only to imitate nature without portraying the underlying ideal. Winckelmann criticizes the great Baroque sculptor Lorenzo Bernini on this count: "Das Studium der Natur muß also wenigstens ein längerer und mühsamerer Weg zur Kenntnis des vollkommenen Schönen sein, als es das Studium der Antiken ist, und Bernini hätte jungen Künstlern, die er allezeit auf das Schönste in der Natur vorzüglich wies, nicht den kürzesten Weg dazu gezeigt" (The study of nature must therefore at the very least be a longer and more toilsome path to knowledge of perfect beauty than is the study of the Ancients, and Bernini would not be showing young artists the shortest way by always pointing to the most beautiful aspects of nature). The art of ancient Greece contains the concentrated essence of beauty and proportion that is indiscriminately scattered throughout nature. Only Michelangelo's sculptures approached the greatness of classical statuary; and only his strong, muscular figures did so—certainly not the tender, youthful ones; or the females, who, under his hand, become Amazons.

Winckelmann's final and most often cited tenet in the essay is one he took from his teacher, Oeser: "Das allgemeine vorzügliche Kennzeichen der griechischen Meisterstücke ist ... eine edle Einfalt und eine stille Größe, sowohl in der Stellung als im Ausdruck" (The general and predominant mark of Greek masterpieces is ... a noble simplicity and a quiet grandeur, both in posture and in expression). In this connection he discusses at length the *Laocoön* group, depicting the destruction of Laocoön and his two sons by sea serpents; this work was executed around 25 B.C., long after the golden age of Greek plastic art. Winckelmann stresses the dignified, stoic nature of the portrayal: the pain, although revealed in the contorted muscles of his body, does not cause Laocoön's face to be distorted by a scream. In this way the sculptor reveals the greatness of soul of his subject. In modern art Winckelmann finds a similar expression of "edle Einfalt und stille Größe" in Raphael's *Attila* painting, which represents the legendary meeting between Pope Leo I and Attila in 452. The pope is pictured quietly and with dignity, without baroque gesticulation and tension.

Such examples illustrate Winckelmann's conception of good taste in art, a view that—taken up by Gotthold Ephraim Lessing, Goethe, and others—was of immense influence in the aesthetics of German Classicism. The main theme of the book was not new, having been touched on by writers such as Montesquieu and La Bruyère; but the concise, almost aphoristic style of the work as well as its bold criticism of still prevailing Baroque and Rococo art forms captivated the German educated public. A small initial printing increased demand for the book, which became something of a rarity.

In 1753 Archinto had been recalled from the court in Dresden to Rome, where he was elevated to cardinal and made the *governatore* of Rome, a powerful position that combined control of the Vatican police and judiciary. Father Rauch and the Dresden court physician Giovan Lodovico Bianconi arranged a royal stipend for Winckelmann to go to Rome for two years to study Roman art and antiquities; in return, he was to provide firsthand reports on the recent fascinating discoveries of the treasures of Pompeii and Herculaneum. In the fall of 1755 Winckelmann traveled to Rome in the company of a Jesuit priest. Shortly after his arrival he befriended Monsignore Michelangelo Giacomelli, translator of Aristophanes. Giacomelli arranged Winckelmann's first meeting with the liberal, Francophile Cardinal Passionei. Archinto wanted Winckelmann to take a position in his or Passionei's service; but Winckelmann rented a room in the artists' quarter, which was quite a distance from the Vatican. There he was surrounded by such celebrated artists as the dramatist Carlo Goldoni, the architect and painter Giambattista Piranesi, and the Dresden painter Anton Raphael Mengs, with the last of whom he developed a close friendship. Bianconi arranged a private audience with Pope Benedict XIV on 17 January 1756, at which Winckelmann received permission to view the Greek manuscripts in the Vatican library. Frederick II occupied Saxony in August 1756, cutting off the Dresden court's subsidiaries to Winckelmann; the expatriate found himself obliged after all to become librarian to Cardinal Archinto, who had meanwhile become secretary of state in the Vatican, after the pope the most important position in the papal states. Winckelmann received an apartment in the Palazzo della Cancelleria and in 1757 assumed the dress and title of an abbé, although without consecration. His duties required that he make a cursory inventory of Archinto's library, but he concentrated his efforts on art history and began work with Mengs on a series of essays on the taste of sculptors of antiquity and the restoration of statues. Winckelmann wrote in one of his letters that Rome would have been a wasteland had it not been for Mengs, Mengs's Italian wife, and their family. Winckelmann was at first put off by noise in the Roman streets at night and by the food at local inns, but he learned to appreciate the bewildering variety and natural beauty of the city, writing in one of his letters that one loves Rome more as one gets to know it better. Passionei invited Winckelmann to his country estate in Camaldoli atop the ruins of Cicero's Tusculum, where he found himself in Francophile circles he did not much care for. He wrote to his friend Hieronymus Dietrich Berendis at this time of a friendship with a handsome Roman youth "mit dem ich von Liebe rede" (with whom I talk of love).

Several of Winckelmann's descriptions of various Roman art treasures were eventually published in *Geschichte der Kunst des Alterthums* (1764; translated as *The History of Ancient Art*, 1849-1873); his essay "Beschreibung des Torso im Belvedere zu Rom" (1762; translated as "Description of the Torso of the Hercules of Belvedere in Rome," 1868) was published separately. The Belvedere is a terrace in the Vatican consisting of an octagonal court with a fountain. Four of the works of art that were displayed there and in adjoining rooms attracted Winckelmann's particular attention: the *Apollo*, the *Antinous*, the *Laocoön*, and the *Torso*. On examination of the *Torso* he concluded that the creative hand can turn the material into the spiritual: in the immobility and quietude of the body is revealed the great mind of the man who exposed himself to danger for the love of justice. In *Geschichte der Kunst des Alterthums* Winckelmann postulates that the great works of the fourth and fifth centuries B.C. had an educational and moral effect on their viewers, creating a lifelong receptivity for the genuine and true. In the spring of 1758 Winckelmann went to Naples to observe the excavations at Herculaneum; his correspondents in Germany, France, and Switzerland had collected money to make the trip possible. Winckelmann had solicited letters of recommendation from his friends and acquaintances in the Catholic church and at the Dresden court, but he had failed to establish ties with the archaeologists and antiquarians in Naples; viewing all outsiders with suspicion, they denied Winckelmann access to many of their excavations, but he was allowed to examine fragile ancient Greek papyri discovered in a patrician villa. Father Antonio Piaggio, who was painstakingly attempting to unroll these delicate papyri without causing further damage, taught Winckelmann about technical aspects of writing in antiquity. Winckelmann also undertook an excursion to Paestum, whose temples made a profound impression on him.

Upon the publication of *Gedancken über die Nachahmung der Griechischen Wercke in der Mahlerey*

Johann Winckelmanns,
Präsidentens der Alterthümer zu Rom, und Scrittore der Vaticanischen Bibliothek,
Mitglieds der Königl. Englischen Societät der Alterthümer zu London, der Maleracademie
von St. Luca zu Rom, und der Hetrurischen zu Cortona,

Geschichte der Kunst
des Alterthums.

Erster Theil.

Mit Königl. Pohlnisch- und Churfürstl. Sächs. allergnädigsten Privilegio.

Dresden, 1764.
In der Waltherischen Hof-Buchhandlung.

Title page for the first volume of Winckelmann's history of ancient art

und Bildhauer-Kunst Winckelmann had sent a copy of the book with a flattering letter to Baron Philipp von Stosch, a retired diplomat and secret agent who had spent his retirement in Florence collecting carved stones and writing a respected work on signed intaglios. A lively correspondence ensued, in which Stosch shared his knowledge and scholarly advice with Winckelmann and invited him to Florence; but Stosch died in 1757, before Winckelmann was able to visit him. When Winckelmann returned from Naples in 1758 he learned that Benedict XIV had died and that his patrons Archinto and Passionei were among the leading candidates to become pope. When neither was elected, Winckelmann decided to accept the invitation to Florence of Baron von Stosch's nephew, Wilhelm von Muzel-Stosch. Muzel-Stosch wanted to publish a sale catalog of the collection he had inherited from his uncle. French was chosen as the language for the catalog because the most active collectors at that time were

French. Winckelmann listed every piece, limiting his commentary to the more important ones. The catalog appeared in the spring of 1760 under the title *Description des pierres gravées du feu Baron de Stosch dédiée à son Eminence Monseigneur le Cardinal Alexandre Albani par M. l'abbé Winckelmann bibliothécaire de son éminence* (Description of the Intaglios of Baron de Stosch, Dedicated to His Eminence Cardinal Alexandre Albani by Abbé Winckelmann, Librarian of His Eminence). As a result of his contribution to Etruscan studies in the Stosch catalog, Winckelmann became a member of the Academy of Cortona in 1760; in the same year he was admitted to the Academy of St. Luke in Rome and to the Society of Antiquaries in London. In a letter to Bianconi he mentions falling in love with a Florentine youth named Niccolò Gastellini and with the young painter Franz Stauder, a student of Mengs. He also mentions his infatuation with a twelve-year-old ballerina and ironically refers to the loss of his virginity.

In 1758 Winckelmann had received a letter from Alessandro Cardinal Albani asking him to become the cardinal's private secretary and librarian. On 18 July 1759 Winckelmann moved into Albani's Palazzo alle Quattro Fontane, which remained his residence until his death. Albani's extensive collection of drawings of antique subjects represented a valuable resource for Winckelmann.

In 1762 when Winckelmann made a second journey to Naples; he was accompanied by the young Count Brühl, son of the Saxon prime minister. Winckelmann's visit made it clear to him that the excavations of Pompeii and Herculaneum were not being conducted with proper care for the objects being unearthed, and that opportunities to study the past were being lost because of the arbitrary dismantling and restoration of works of art. In 1762 he published his highly critical *Sendschreiben von den Herculanischen Entdeckungen: An den hochgebohrnen Herrn, Herrn Heinrich Reichsgrafen von Brühl* (Letter Concerning the Discoveries in Herculaneum: To the Noble Peer, Imperial Count von Bruhl). A French translation of the work reached Naples, resulting in Winckelmann's temporary ban from the Kingdom of the Two Sicilies. In 1763 he undertook a third journey to Naples, on which he based his *Nachrichten von den neuesten Herculanischen Entdeckungen* (News of the Latest Discoveries in Herculaneum, 1764). In this work, in his letter to Brühl, and in other publications Winckelmann eloquently established the prominent role of Pompeii and Herculaneum in the archaeological reconstruction of ancient civilization, further developed his theories on the relationship between Greek art and society, and revealed the irreparable damage to scholarship caused by careless excavations whose purpose was to unearth treasures for display, not to reconstruct the past.

On 16 April 1763 Pope Clement XIII named Winckelmann "Commissario delle Antichità della Camera Apostolica" (antiquarian to the pope). This appointment combined a modest salary with considerable social standing, since one of his duties was to act as guide for prominent visitors. He also gained a following of youthful enthusiasts who came to Rome to learn from him and promoted his ideas after his death. Among them were Friedrich Reiffenstein, who was inspired by Winckelmann to remain in Rome and become an art historian; Friedrich Wilhelm von Erdmannsdorff, who became the architect of Wörlitz Castle for Prince Leopold III of Anhalt-Dessau; and Johann Hermann von Riedesel, whose *Reise durch Sizilien und Großgriechenland* (Journey through Sicily and Greece, 1771) owes much to Winckelmann and was consulted by Goethe on his Italian journey. On 2 May 1763 Winckelmann was made "Scriptor Linguae Teutonicae" (scribe in the German language); in this position he worked directly under Cardinal Albani, supervising the disposition of German manuscripts in the Vatican library and passing on applications of researchers who wanted to view the manuscripts. The nominations as antiquarian and scriptor to the pope in his forty-sixth year marked the apex of Winckelmann's career.

In 1763 Winckelmann published a treatise titled *Abhandlung von der Fähigkeit der Empfindung des Schönen in der Kunst, und dem Unterrichte in derselben* (Treatise on the Capability of Experiencing the Beautiful in Art, and Instruction Therein). His characterization of the lover of art in this work is based on Friedrich Reinhold von Berg, a young baron from the Baltic area for whom he had developed great affection during Berg's visit to Rome in 1762 and whose departure apparently caused him considerable sorrow. According to Winckelmann, the appreciation of beauty is given to all rational creatures, but in varying degrees. Those who are themselves beautiful and have leisure to devote to the arts are capable of greater appreciation of beauty, but their appreciation must be developed and honed through instruction in the arts. In 1763 Winckelmann made

the acquaintance of the young painter Angelika Kauffmann, who painted a famous portrait of him in 1764 and who, under Winckelmann's guidance, became one of the first of her generation to embrace the principles of classicism.

In 1764 Winckelmann published his monumental *Geschichte der Kunst des Alterthums* (translated as *The History of Ancient Art*, 1849-1873), on which he had been working since shortly after his arrival in Rome. If *Gedancken über die Nachahmung der Griechischen Wercke in der Mahlerey und Bildhauer-Kunst* had established his reputation in Germany, *Geschichte der Kunst des Alterthums* founded his European fame. In the preface he states his aim to teach the origin, growth, change, and decline of art in conjunction with the different outlooks of peoples, times, and artists. His own qualifications, as he puts it, are a thorough knowledge gained from personal study of ancient works of art, a lifelong love of art, and willingness to use deductive reasoning to infer the essentials of art. The treatise reveals a profounder knowledge of ancient history, and is less naive about the nature of life in ancient Greece, than his first book. He sees distinctly, in somewhat Spenglerian terms, the rise and fall of ancient Greek culture. In short, Winckelmann now views Greek civilization less as an aesthetic phenomenon and more as a historical organism. Still, the connection with central ideas in his first work are obvious: the Greeks were favored by a temperate climate and by a system of governance that encouraged freedom (climate was linked in the thought of the Enlightenment with political system: in this view intemperate climates encouraged tyrannical regimes). And freedom lay at the heart of their great art: "Durch die Freiheit erhob sich, wie ein edler Zweig aus einem gesunden Stamme, das Denken des ganzen Volks. Denn wie der Geist eines zum Denken gewöhnten Menschen sich höher zu erheben pflegt im weiten Felde oder auf einem offenen Gange, auf der Höhe eines Gebäudes als in einer niedrigen Kammer und in jedem eingeschränkten Orte, so muß auch die Art zu denken unter den freien Griechen gegen die Begriffe beherrschter Völker sehr verschieden gewesen sein. Herodot zeigt, daß die Freiheit allein der Grund gewesen von der Macht und Hoheit, zu welcher Athen gelangt ist. . . . Die Redekunst fing an aus ebendem Grunde allererst in dem Genusse der völligen Freiheit unter den Griechen zu blühen; daher legten die Sizilianer dem Gorgias die Erfindung der Redekunst bei.

Die Griechen waren in ihrer besten Zeit denkende Wesen, welche zwanzig und mehr Jahre schon gedacht hatten, ehe wir insgemein aus uns selbst zu denken anfangen ... ” (Through freedom arose, like a noble limb from a healthy trunk, the thought of the entire people. For just as the spirit of a man who is accustomed to thinking tends to rise to loftier heights in the open field or in an open corridor, on the heights of a building than in a low room and in any oppressive place, just so must the free Greeks' way of thinking have appeared very different in contrast with other peoples. Herodotus shows that freedom alone was the reason for the power and glory that was achieved by Athens.... For the same reason eloquence and rhetoric among the Greeks began to blossom in the enjoyment of complete freedom; and for that reason the Sicilians attributed to Gorgias the invention of rhetoric. In their best period the Greeks were thinking creatures, who had been thinking for twenty and more years before we generally begin to think independently ...). Winckelmann's book helped to define two new disciplines: archaeology and art history. He writes that the origin of art cannot be found in a single country but in many regions at varying times. Originally, it was an expression of religious impulses. Greek art developed later than the art of the Middle East and independently from it, though both arose from attempts to render a likeness of the gods symbolically. Sculpture lost its stiffness in the course of time and started to express movement. Differences in the art of various peoples, Winckelmann contends, can be traced to climatic conditions which help determine the degree of bodily perfection and the linguistic and cultural development of a people.

Winckelmann maintains that Egyptian art has never departed very much from its oldest style. He attributes this lack of development to the lack of music and poetry in the backward Egyptian society and the fact that artists did not enjoy much prestige. Furthermore, the prevailing cult of the dead prevented anatomical studies; only gods and animals could be shown in somewhat realistic style. The Persians have left only a few carved stones; none of them show an unclothed body because religious laws forbade it. The same is true of the art of the Hebrews and the Parthians. The old monarchies of the Near East lacked the religious tolerance and social interaction necessary for the arts to flourish. Winckelmann assumes that the Etruscans must have en-

joyed a certain degree of freedom; that their art lags behind Greek art can be explained by their melancholy, somewhat violent and superstitious nature.

The chapter on art of the Greeks is the longest and most important in the book. The intellectual climate that awakened the Greek sense of beauty was made possible by a system of government that allowed philosophy and rhetoric to develop and art and wisdom to be respected, and that regarded art not only as the handmaiden of religion but as an appropriate reward for great civic and athletic accomplishments. As is often the case in Winckelmann's writings, he implies criticism of social and political values of his own period. He finds the goal and essence of art to be the creation and portrayal of beauty. Beauty is for Winckelmann the pure form of the sculpted, nude human body, which is, in turn, a reminder of the divine. He criticizes the notion that beauty is not universal and devised a scale of beauty that ranges from the realistic to the idealized representation of human form, to heroes, demigods, and finally gods, who unite the most exalted perfection of the human body with ethical perfection. In addition to unity and simplicity, Winckelmann considers the absence of individuality–in other words, an emphasis on the universal–an essential element of beauty. Ideal beauty is created by selecting beautiful parts from many individuals and harmoniously uniting them in one figure. No expression should be so strong as to disturb the gentle repose of perfect form. Strong sentiments should be frozen at the time of their occurrence. Winckelmann considers in succeeding chapters the beauty of various parts of the human body, and says that Mengs has been able to incorporate in his work all of the perfections of the ancients.

Winckelmann distinguishes several periods and styles of Greek art. The older style has survived only on coins and carved stones. Its lines are severe and powerful but without grace. As many of these earliest works of art depict violence, they contain more expression than is compatible with beauty. While in the beginning the older style shows a similarity with Egyptian and Etruscan works, in its flowering shortly before Phidias and Polyclitus it reveals a relaxation of the archaic effects. Movement becomes more harmonious; stormy emotions subside. The works of the grand style of the Golden Age under Pericles display monumental refinement and grandeur. The beautiful style, which followed the grand style and is characterized by grace and flowing

Winckelmann in 1764; painting by Angelika Kauffmann
(Kunsthaus, Zurich)

lines, lasted until the rule of Alexander the Great. The final style was that of the imitators. Art had to regress, having reached such heights. The imitator was condemned always to lag behind the art he imitated. Winckelmann does not have a high opinion of Roman art, considering it derivative first of Etruscan and then of Greek art. In the second part of the work Winckelmann summarizes chronologically the development of ancient art. Winckelmann's superb descriptions of the *Laocoön*, the *Torso Belvedere*, and the *Apollo Belvedere* give special interest to this section, although it is dated because many important works of ancient art had not yet been discovered at the time he was writing.

In 1765 Winckelmann was offered a position as director of antiquities at the court of Frederick II, but an agreement on salary could not be reached. In his *Versuch einer Allegorie, besonders für die Kunst* (Essay on Allegory, Especially for Art, 1766) Winckelmann develops the idea that originality in choosing a topic had not yet kept pace

with the technical development of painting. In 1767 he made his fourth journey to Naples, accompanied by the young Baron Johann Hermann von Riedesel.

The two-volume *Monumenti antichi inediti spiegati ed illustrati* (Unpublished Ancient Monuments, Explained and Illustrated) appeared in 1767 with two hundred twenty-six copper plates. The term *unpublished* refers to coins, intaglios, statues, and other works of ancient art that had either never before appeared in an illustrated work or, if reproduced, had been misinterpreted. The book was written under the auspices of Cardinal Albani, who had provided financial backing as well as expert advice. Winckelmann is at pains to correct two misunderstandings: first, the tendency to exaggerate the role of history and to underestimate the importance of mythology as a source for the motifs and themes of antiquity; second, the exaggerated role of imagination in classical art. Even seemingly naturalistic renderings such as images of daily life as found in Pompeii and Herculaneum can surprisingly often be traced back to scenes that are better known from mythological lore; and the ancients only rarely showed scenes that sprang from their imagination. Although the book is primarily concerned with individual works of art, art history assumes a prominent role.

In 1768 Winckelmann traveled to Germany to visit friends; he was accompanied by the Roman sculptor Bartolomeo Cavaceppi. Their trip took them to Munich and then to Regensburg, where Winckelmann became depressed and decided to return to Rome. But Cavaceppi persuaded him to continue their journey to Vienna, where Winckelmann delivered important papers from Albani to Empress Maria Theresa and her chancellor Prince Kaunitz. Cavaceppi went on alone while Winckelmann, after a few days at a Viennese hospital, turned back to Rome. On 1 June 1768 he arrived in Trieste and took lodgings in the elegant forty-room Locanda Grande. He spent considerable time during the next few days with a fellow lodger, Francesco Arcangeli, while waiting for a ship to continue his journey to Rome. Arcangeli spoke the Trieste dialect and knew his way around the city. Winckelmann showed Arcangeli coins given to him by Maria Theresa; Arcangeli said later that the coins were the reason he first thought of murdering Winckelmann and claimed that he suspected him of being a Lutheran, a Jew, or a spy. On 8 June 1768 Arcangeli attacked Winckelmann in his room, attempting to strangle him with a rope. Failing to overpower Winckelmann, Arcangeli stabbed him repeatedly but fled when a servant who heard the struggle arrived on the scene. Winckelmann died several hours later, after identifying his assailant and dictating his will. Arcangeli was arrested, confessed to the murder, and was publicly executed on the wheel. Winckelmann was buried in Trieste. The many expressions of the sense of loss felt by scholars, literary men, and even his critics were a measure of Winckelmann's prestige among his contemporaries.

Much in Winckelmann's writings is hopelessly outdated. He saw only a few examples of Greek art from the period of its great efflorescence; archaeology was a new quasi science, virtually founded by him, and he did not live to see the great discoveries of the following century. Art historians and archaeologists of the nineteenth and twentieth centuries are somewhat perplexed, therefore, as to what attitude to take toward him. Although some have lamented the lack of a critical edition of his works, others say that his writings have only antiquarian interest. Scholarly opinion concedes his enormous impact on his time and points out that many of his conclusions about classical art–reached more by intuition than by observation–were borne out by discoveries made long after his death. Scholars continue to pay homage to Winckelmann, who was early canonized by Goethe, but as an inspired seer rather than as a scholar and scientist. His presumed ahistorical view of classical antiquity made him a cult hero after World War I to the circle around Stefan George, who saw him as a symbol for the search for timeless norms. But for the academic world, his enthusiasm; his associative, essayistic style; his immediate reaction to his beloved subject matter were embarrassing. In the increasingly positivistic, abstract, "objective," and mechanistic world of late nineteenth-century scholarship, Winckelmann's idealism seemed hopelessly old-fashioned. The intertwining in his works of aesthetics and art history was another mark against him in an age of increasing specialization. But it is his belief in Platonic norms and absolutes, and his tendency to make value judgments based on them, that appeared to positivistic science–all too often unaware of its own prejudices–as the fatal flaw in his thought. Recent studies of Winckelmann take a more balanced view, suggesting that his great achievement be regarded in its historical context and that modern scholarship emulate, not imitate him, by admitting that mere facts presented without connection and within the context of a value system are lifeless.

Letters:

Briefe, 3 volumes, edited by F. Förster, volumes 10-12 of Winckelmann's *Werke*, edited by Karl Ludwig Fernow and others (Berlin: Schlesinger, 1824-1825);

Briefe, 4 volumes, edited by H. Diepolder and Walther Rehm (Berlin: De Gruyter, 1952-1957);

Aus Joh. Jac. Winckelmanns Briefen, edited by Richard Meszlényi (Nendeln, Liechtenstein: Kraus, 1968).

Bibliography:

Hans Rupert, "Winckelmann-Bibliographie," *Winckelmann-Gesellschaft Stendal* (1942): 5-50.

Biographies:

Carl Justi, *Winckelmann und seine Zeitgenossen*, 2 volumes (1866; reprinted, Hildesheim, Zurich & New York: Olms, 1983);

Wolfgang Leppmann, *Winckelmann* (New York: Knopf, 1970); published in German as *Winckelmann: Ein Leben für Apoll* (Bern & Munich: Propyläen, 1971).

References:

Walter Bosshard, *Winckelmann: Ästhetik der Mitte* (Zurich: Artemis, 1961);

Todd Adam Britsch, "Winckelmann and Romanticism: Study of Eighteenth-Century Shift in Aesthetic Sensibility," Ph.D. dissertation, Florida State University, 1966;

E. M. Butler, *The Tyranny of Greece over Germany* (Cambridge: University Press, 1935);

Glen Dolberg, *The Reception of Johann Joachim Winckelmann in Modern German Prose Fiction*, Stuttgarter Arbeiten zur Germanistik, 31 (Stuttgart: 1976);

M. Kay Flavell, "Winckelmann and the German Enlightenment," *Modern Language Review*, 74 (1979): 79-96;

Thomas W. Gaehtgens, ed., *Johann Joachim Winckelmann 1717-1768*, Studien zum Achtzehnten Jahrhundert, 7 (Hamburg: Meiner, 1986);

Johann Wolfgang von Goethe, "Winckelmann und sein Jahrhundert," in *Goethes Werke*, volume 12, edited by Erich Trunz (Hamburg: Wegner, 1948-1964), pp. 96-128;

Berthold Häsler, ed., *Beiträge zu einem neuen Winckelmann-Bild* (Berlin: Aufbau, 1973);

Henry Hatfield, *Aesthetic Paganism in German Literature: From Winckelmann to the Death of Goethe* (Cambridge, Mass.: Harvard University Press, 1964);

Hatfield, *Winckelmann and His German Critics, 1755-81: A Prelude to the Classical Age* (New York: King's Crown Press, 1943);

Gilbert Highet, *The Classical Tradition: Greek and Roman Influences on Western Literature* (Oxford: Oxford University Press, 1949);

Victor Lange, *The Classical Age of German Literature 1740-1815* (New York: Holmes & Meier, 1982);

Hans Mayer, *Außenseiter* (Frankfurt am Main: Suhrkamp, 1975); translated by Denis M. Sweet as *Outsiders: A Study in Life and Letters* (Cambridge: MIT Press, 1982);

Horst Rüdiger, "Winckelmanns Geschichtsauffassung: Ein Dresdner Entwurf als Keimzelle seines historischen Denkens," *Euphorion*, 62 (1968): 99-116;

Eberhard Wilhelm Schulz, "Winckelmanns Schreibart," in *Studien zur Goethezeit*, edited by Hans-Joachim Mähl and Eberhard Mannack (Heidelberg: Winter, 1981);

Hinrich C. Seeba, "Johann Joachim Winckelmann: Zur Wirkungsgeschichte eines 'unhistorischen' Historikers zwischen Ästhetik und Geschichte," *Deutsche Vierteljahrsschrift*, 56 (September 1982): 168-201;

Walter Eckehart Spengler, *Der Begriff des Schönen bei Winckelmann: Ein Beitrag zur deutschen Klassik*, Göppinger Arbeiten zur Germanistik, 17 (Göppingen: Kümmerle, 1970);

David Turner, "Johann Joachim Winckelmann," in *German Men of Letters: Literary Essays*, volume 6, edited by Alex Nathan and Brian Keith-Smith (London: Wolff, 1972), pp. 265-292;

Ludwig Uhlig, "Klassik und Geschichtsbewußtsein in Goethes Winckelmannschrift," *Germanisch-Romanische Monatsschrift*, 31 (1981): 143-155;

Winckelmann 1768/1968 (Bad Godesberg: Inter Nationes, 1968).

Papers:

The Bibliothèque Nationale Paris has many of Johann Joachim Winckelmann's papers. There are letters in the Zentralbibliothek Zürich.

Friedrich Wilhelm Zachariä

(1 May 1726 - 30 January 1777)

Armin P. Sinnwell
University of South Carolina

BOOKS: *Gedicht dem Gedächtnisse Des Herrn von Hagedorn gewidmet*, anonymous (Brunswick: Schröder, 1754);

Scherzhafte Epische Poesien nebst einigen Oden und Liedern, anonymous (Brunswick & Hildesheim: Schröder, 1754; revised, 1761)—comprises "Der Renommiste," "Verwandlungen," "Das Schnupftuch," "Phaeton," "Oden und Lieder";

Die Poesie und Germanien: Ein Gedicht, anonymous (Berlin, 1755);

Die Tageszeiten: Ein Gedicht, In vier Büchern (Rostock & Leipzig: Koppe, 1756; revised, 1757; revised, 1767);

Die Pilgrime auf Golgatha: Ein musikalisches Drama (Brunswick: Schröder, 1756);

Der Tempel des Friedens (Brunswick: Schröder, 1756; revised, 1762);

Lagosiade, oder Die Jagd ohne Jagd: Ein scherzhaftes Heldengedicht (Leipzig, 1757);

Murner in der Hölle: Ein scherzhaftes Heldengedicht (Rostock: Koppe, 1757; revised, 1767); translated by Rudolf Erich Raspe as *Tabby in Elysium: A Mock Poem* (London: Printed for the translator by H. Goldney, 1781);

Die vier Stufen des Weiblichen Alters: Ein Gedicht in vier Gesängen (Rostock: Koppe, 1757; revised, 1767);

Die Schöpfung der Hölle: Nebst einigen andern Gedichten (Altenburg: Richter, 1760; revised, 1767);

Sammlung Einiger Musikalischen Versuche, 2 volumes (Brunswick, 1760-1761);

Poetische Schriften, 9 volumes (Brunswick, 1763-1765);

Cortes: Erster Band (Brunswick: Waisenhaus, 1766);

Der Adel des Herzens, oder Die ausgeschlagene Erbschaft: Ein Nachspiel in einem Aufzuge (Hamburg & Bremen: Cramer, 1770);

Musikalische Versuche in deutschen Arien (Brunswick, 1770);

Fabeln und Erzehlungen: In Burkard Waldis' Manier (Frankfurt am Main & Leipzig, 1771);

Friedrich Wilhelm Zachariä; painting by E. Bekly, 1757 (Gleimhaus, Halberstadt)

Zwey schöne Neue Mährlein: Als I. Von der schönen Melusinen; einer Meerfey. II. Von einer untreuen Braut, die der Teufel hohlen sollen der lieben Jugend, und dem ehrsamen Frauenzimmer zu beliebiger Kurzweil, in Reime verfasset, anonymous (Leipzig, 1772);

Tayti, oder Die glückliche Insel (Brunswick: Waisenhaus, 1777);

Hinterlassene Schriften, edited by Johann Joachim Eschenburg (Brandenburg: Waisenhaus, 1781);

Zwei polemische Gedichte (1754-1755), edited by Otto Ladendorf (Berlin: Behr, 1903; reprinted, Nendeln, Liechtenstein: Kraus, 1968);

Der Renommiste; Das Schnuptuch: Mit einem Anhang zur Gattung des komischen Epos, edited by Anselm Maler (Stuttgart: Reclam, 1974).

OTHER: Adrien Richer, *Neuere Geschichte der Chineser, Japaner, Indiander, Persianer, Türcken und Russen &c. Als Fortsetzung der älteren Geschichte von Rollin*, translated by Zachariä (Berlin, 1755);

John Milton, *Das Verlohrne Paradies: Aus dem Englischen Johann Miltons in Reymfreye Verse übersetzt, und mit eignen sowohl als andrer Anmerkungen begleitet*, 2 volumes, translated by Zachariä (Altona: Iversen, 1760-1763; volume 1 revised, 1762);

Die schöne Russinn oder Wunderbare Geschichte der Azema, translated by Zachariä (Brunswick: Waisenhaus, 1766);

Auserlesene Stücke der besten deutschen Dichter von Martin Opitz bis auf gegenwärtige Zeiten: Mit historischen Nachrichten und kritischen Anmerkungen versehen, 2 volumes, edited by Zachariä (Brunswick: Waisenhaus, 1766-1771);

Gottlob Sebastian von Lucke, *Olint und Sophronia: Ein Gedicht in drey Gesängen; nebst einem Anhange einiger andern Gedichte*, edited by Zachariä (Brunswick: Waisenhaus, 1767);

Robert Paltock, *Die Fliegenden Menschen oder Wunderbare Begebenheiten Peter Wilkins*, translated by Zachariä (Brunswick: Vieweg, 1767);

Eberhard Friedrich Freiherr von Gemmingen, *Poetische und prosaische Stücke von dem Freyherrn von G ****, edited by Zachariä (Brunswick: Waisenhaus, 1769);

Johann Nikolaus Meinhard, *M. Johann Nic. Meinhard Versuche über den Charakter und die Werke der besten Italiänischen Dichter*, preface by Zachariä (Brunswick, 1774).

"Du bist uns kaum entwichen, und schwermütig ziehen / Aus dumpfen Höhlen ... Verdruß und Langeweile" (You have only just disappeared, and heavily rise / Frustration and boredom ... from musty caves). Johann Wolfgang Goethe wrote these emphatic lines about Friedrich Wilhelm Zachariä after meeting him in Leipzig in 1767. Goethe implicitly refers to the kind of literature for which Zachariä was known and appreciated in his time: light, entertaining poems and mock-heroic epics in the Rococo style. Zachariä's works were successful, and some of them underwent many reprints and translations. Today he would be forgotten if it were not for his first work, the mock-heroic poem "Der Renommiste" (The Braggart, 1744), which made this genre extremely popular in mid-eighteenth-century Germany.

Friedrich Wilhelm Zachariä was born in Frankenhausen, Thuringia, the third child of Friedrich Sigismund Zachariä, the chamber secretary of the prince of Schwarzenberg and government secretary, and Martha Elisabeth Zachariä, née Müller. Both his grandfather and his father were locally renowned for their poems composed for particular occasions. Throughout his life Zachariä continued this tradition and wrote poems for birthdays, anniversaries, promotions, expressions of thanks, and the like.

After attending the Princely Landschule (village school) of his native town, Zachariä matriculated at the University of Leipzig on 22 May 1743. Although he was studying law, he began participating in the literary life of Leipzig, which was at that time dominated by Johann Christoph Gottsched. Zachariä attended Gottsched's lectures on literary history and poetics and adopted Gottsched's rationalistic approach to literature.

Under Gottsched's influence Zachariä wrote "Der Renommiste," which was first published in the journal of Gottsched's disciple Johann Joachim Schwabe, the *Belustigungen des Verstandes und Witzes* (Entertainment for Reason and Wit) in 1744. "Der Renommiste" is a mock-heroic poem in the tradition of Nicolas Boileau-Despréaux's *Le lutrin* (1676) and Alexander Pope's *The Rape of the Lock* (1712). Gottsched, who had published a translation of part of *Le lutrin* in 1730, promoted this genre in Germany and devoted an entire chapter of his *Versuch einer Critischen Dichtkunst* (Attempt at a Critical Poetics, 1729) to the mock-heroic poem, defining it as "Nachahmung einer lächerlichen That ... die der Dichter in eine solche Erzählung einkleidet, daraus das Auslachenswürdige derselben auf eine spaßhafte und doch lehrreiche Art erhellet" (Imitation of a ridiculous action ... which the poet couches in a narrative such that the ridiculousness of the action is revealed in a funny and instructive way). His definition focuses on two aspects, the ridiculous action itself and the treatment of the action; the latter emphasizes the ridiculousness of the action by describing petty things in lofty terms and sublime things in common language.

The ridiculous action in "Der Renommiste" is carried out by the two protagonists, who stand for two different life-styles: Raufbold represents the coarseness and depravity of students in Jena, while Sylvan is symbolic of the effeminate manner of high society in Francophile Leipzig. Directed by their tutelary spirits and a mass of allegorical gods and goddesses ("Mode" [Fashion], "Gallanterie" [Gallantry], and so on) who try to defend the principles their names stand for, Raufbold and Sylvan clash over a local beauty. They fight a duel, in consequence of which Raufbold has to leave Leipzig.

As Gottsched postulated, the comic effect arises both from the action itself and from the application of epic elements (invocation of the Muses, announcement of the action, heroic speeches, lofty description of battles, directing gods, sublime comparisons and allegories, and so on) to unimportant people (students), everyday topics (carouses, the morning after, dance, fashion), and trivial conflicts. An example is the following passage:

Des Phöbus Wagen lief den Sonnenweg herab.
Mit Keuchen stolperte der Pferde müder Trab;
. . . .
Als auf dem müden Gaul ein jenischer Student
Im stolpernden Galopp durch bunte Wiesen rennt.

(Apollo's chariot drove down the way of the sun.
Panting exhaustedly, the horses stumble along;
. . . .
As on a tired mare a Jena student
In a broken gallop races over gay meadows).

After Zachariä had broken with Gottsched he revised "Der Renommiste." This revision, which was published in his collection *Scherzhafte Epische Poesien nebst einigen Oden und Liedern* (Comical Epic Poems with Some Odes and Songs, 1754), is significant because it reveals a move from a strictly rationalistic, "enlightened" literature to the playfulness of the Rococo. Zachariä weakens the satirical elements, expands the description of idyllic details, reduces the allegorical figures, individualizes the rather typical characters, and increases the number of literary allusions. In short, the mock-heroic poem becomes a merely comical epic; the pleasure of description overcomes the urge of criticism. Characteristic is the change of the ending. In the first version Raufbold is not really defeated: he leaves Leipzig, but he is in good spirits. The second version leaves no doubt about the victory of Rococo gallantry:

Mit Herrlichkeit umringt und Lorbeern stolz
    umlaubt
Erhob die Mode nun mit neuer Pracht ihr Haupt.
. . . .
Und die Gallanterie ging nach der jen' schen Saale.
Da wurden Stutzer reif an ihrem holden Strahle,
So artig, so geputzt, als Leipzigs Stutzer ist;
In ew'ge Schande fiel der Name Renommist.

(Crowned with splendor and laurels
Fashion raised her head with glory.
. . . .
And Gallantry went to Jena upon Saale.
The fops there became mature through her golden
    sheen,
As nice, as adorned, as fops in Leipzig are;
The name braggart, however, fell in eternal dis-
    grace.)

"Der Renommiste" was highly popular and frequently imitated in the eighteenth century. Goethe called it "ein schätzbares Dokument woraus die damalige Lebens- und Sinnesart anschaulich heraustritt" (a valuable document which vividly reveals the way of life and thinking of that time). One reason for its popularity was probably the implicit criticism of the ideal of the courtly hero. The character of Raufbold is endowed with everything suitable for a satirical depiction of the impertinence and hollowness of this ideal. In the nineteenth and first half of the twentieth centuries "Der Renommiste" did not receive much critical attention. If read at all, it was seen as a source of cultural history and local color. Recent scholarship has emphasized the poem's genre-specific features and its social criticism.

Zachariä's second major work, the comical epic "Verwandlungen" (Metamorphoses), was also written in Leipzig and shows Gottsched's influence. It is a satire on typical representatives of contemporary society: gentlemen and ladies, servants and maidens, fashionable Frenchmen, officers, occasional poets, and so on. Drawing on Ovid's *Metamorphoses*, it exhausts itself in satirical descriptions of unrelated people turned into animals by a jealous lover. First published in 1744 in the *Bremer Beiträge*, which was to become the forum for authors dissatisfied with Gottsched's dogmatism, this epic marks a turning point in Zachariä's literary career. In the wake of the literary feud between Gottsched, on one side, and Johann Jakob Bodmer and Johann Jakob Breitinger, on the other, Zachariä gradually turned against his former champion.

Moving to Göttingen in May 1747 to continue his studies, he came under the influence of the Rococo style. This change is manifest in his many Anacreontic poems, in his fiery eulogy on the Anacreontic poet Friedrich von Hagedorn (which led to a public quarrel between Gottsched and Zachariä), in the revision of "Der Renommiste," and in his third comical epic, "Das Schnupftuch" (The Handkerchief, 1754). The latter obviously draws on *The Rape of the Lock*, from which it borrows names, allegories, the central topic, and even entire sentences. The plot lacks the satirical edge that is essential to "Der Renommiste." The central conflict is of a private nature: the goddess Discord uses a handkerchief to create quarrels between two lovers but is finally overcome by a sylph, and the lovers are reconciled. The epic is critical of private weaknesses, not of life-styles in general. It is a gallant, playful, and apparently approving depiction of the social life of the aristocracy in the eighteenth century.

A third phase in Zachariä's literary development was initiated on 18 April 1748, when he was appointed preceptor at the Collegium Carolinum, an educational institution between the gymnasium and the university, in Brunswick. This appointment was made possible by the recommendation of Johann Christian Claproth, the chairman of the Deutsche Gesellschaft (German Society) at Göttingen, which had accepted Zachariä as a member shortly after the first publication of "Der Renommiste." Zachariä stayed in Brunswick for the rest of his life. On 30 January 1761 he was promoted to regular professor at the Collegium Carolinum. He taught poetics, mythology, and a course called "Zeitungscollegium" (newspaper lectures) in which he provided background information about current events. He held various other positions which made him the best-paid member of the teaching staff at the Carolinum. In 1762 he was appointed supervisor of the bookstore and printery of the princely orphanage in Brunswick. He also edited the *Braunschweigische Anzeigen* (Brunswick Announcements) and its weekly supplement, the *Gelehrte Beyträge* (Learned Contributions), and in 1768 he began editing the *Neue Braunschweigische Zeitung* (New Brunswick Newspaper). These positions provided perfect outlets for publishing almost everything he wrote, edited, or translated, from poems to book reviews to books. In his capacity as supervisor of the bookstore and printery Zachariä went to the Leipzig Easter Fair in 1767 to in-

crease business contacts. It was on this occasion that he met the young Goethe, who was a student at the University of Leipzig.

In Brunswick Zachariä developed a taste for the literary trend of "Empfindsamkeit" (Sensibility). He corresponded with Christian Fürchtegott Gellert, one of the champions of Sensibility; he became friends with Gotthold Ephraim Lessing; he read Ewald von Kleist's *Der Frühling* (Spring, 1749), Friedrich Gottlieb Klopstock's *Der Messias*, (The Messiah, 1748-1773), Albrecht von Haller's enthusiastic hymns on nature, and, most important of all, John Milton's *Paradise Lost* (1674). In most of his later works he tried to imitate these authors.

The comical epics "Phaeton" (Phaëton, 1754) and *Murner in der Hölle* (Murner in Hell, 1757) transcend mere satire on human weaknesses as well as the playfulness of the Rococo epic. Touching scenes and idyllic descriptions of family and country life replace the derision of ridiculous attitudes and actions as well as the previous abundance of episodes, characters, and allegorical figures. Following Milton and Klopstock, Zachariä wrote these works in hexameter, a meter Gottsched despised.

Zachariä's descriptive poems reveal the influence of the Sensibility even more. With *Die Tageszeiten* (The Times of the Day, 1756) he obviously drew on Klopstock, Kleist, James Thomson, and Edward Young. In the four parts of the poem Zachariä muses about the discrepancy between the simple but happy country life and the luxurious yet unhappy life in the city. This contrast gives him the opportunity to deal with a variety of literary, artistic, and political problems, the realistic treatment of which makes the poem still readable. Zachariä did not avoid taking issue with contemporary grievances: in blunt descriptions of recent wars he shows what endangers the happiness of mankind. And he criticizes Frederick II, the hero of the German Enlightenment, for neglecting poetry, art, and music.

The works Zachariä wrote later are considered second-rate. An attempt at imitating Klopstock and Milton with a religious epic failed. Zachariä soon gave up the project, but he published fragments under the title *Die Schöpfung der Hölle* (The Creation of Hell, 1760). His plan to write a historical epic about the conquest of Mexico also exceeded his poetical genius; he never finished the work but published the first four cantos under the title *Cortes* (Cortez, 1766). Definitely damaging to Zachariä's reputation was the publication of his translation (1760-1763) of *Paradise Lost*. Zachariä could not match Milton's powerful language and sublime emotiveness; his verses appear clumsy and unharmonious. Contemporary critics, including Friedrich Nicolai, blamed Zachariä for his negligence and superficiality. Nevertheless, as Momme Mommsen has pointed out, this translation and Zachariä's Miltonian poems had an impact on Goethe when he was working on the "Prolog im Himmel" (Prologue in Heaven) and the "Geisterchor" (Choir of Spirits) sections of *Faust I* (1808) in 1799.

In short, Zachariä was not able to keep up the poetical élan of his early works. Partly because of his position in Brunswick he wrote and published a great deal, but his contemporaries saw that he was too prolific for his relatively limited creativity.

The last years of his life passed uneventfully. On 6 January 1773 he married the thirty-eight-year-old Henriette Sophie Elisabeth Wegener. The marriage was childless. After Zachariä quit his supervisory and editorial posts in 1774 the duke bestowed a canonship on him, an indication that he enjoyed a considerable reputation in his community. In 1775 Zachariä began suffering from a chronic fever; he died of edema and consumption on 30 January 1777. Johann Joachim Eschenburg edited his posthumous works in 1781.

References:

Otto Bessenrodt, *Friedrich Wilhelm Zachariä* (Mühlhausen: Urquell, 1926);

Hermann Kaspar, *Die komischen Epen von Friedrich Wilhelm Zachariä: Beitrag zur Geistesgeschichte des 18. Jahrhunderts* (Breslau: Priebatsch, 1935);

Otto Hermann Kirchgeorg, *Die dichterische Entwikklung J. F. W. Zachariäs* (Greifswald: Abel, 1904);

Fritz Meyen, *Bremer Beiträger am Collegium Carolinum in Braunschweig: K. Chr. Gärtner, J. A. Ebert, F. W. Zachariä, K. A. Schmid* (Brunswick: Waisenhaus, 1962);

Momme Mommsen, "Zur Entstehung und Datierung einiger Faust-Szenen um 1800," *Euphorion*, 47 (1953): 295-330;

Franz Muncker, "Friedrich Wilhelm Zachariä: Einleitung," in *Bremer Beiträger*, 2 volumes, edited by Muncker, Deutsche National-Litteratur, 43-44 (Berlin & Stuttgart: Spemann, 1889), II: 243-260;

Johannes Hermann Tisch, " 'Paradise Lost' in der vollen Pracht des deutschen Hexameters: Observations on the Milton Translation by Friedrich Wilhelm Zachariä and Simon Grynäus," *Seminar*, 9 (October 1973): 187-201;

Hans Zimmer, *Zachariä und sein Renommist: Ein Beitrag zur Litteratur- und Kulturgeschichte des 18. Jahrhunderts* (Leipzig: Roßberg, 1892);

Paul Zimmermann, *Friedrich Wilhelm Zachariä in Braunschweig* (Wolfenbüttel: Zwissler, 1896).

Papers:

There is an unpublished manuscript in the Niedersächsische Staats- und Universitätsbibliothek Göttingen, containing the opera "Günther, oder die Schwarzburgische Tapferkeit auf dem Kayserthrone" (Günther; or, The Schwarzburg Braveness on the Emperor's Throne) and a treatise on the singspiel.

Appendix

The German Transformation from the Baroque to the Enlightenment

P. M. Mitchell
Cornell University

While every era may be considered to be the resultant of forces from foregoing eras and thus part of a continuum, there are certain junctures in the course of history that indicate more abrupt changes and are imbued with a special poignancy. Such a period of transition can be discerned in the first half of the eighteenth century for Western culture in general and for German literary culture in particular. It can be characterized as the shift from the Baroque to the Enlightenment but also as the change from a theologically based Weltanschauung to an age of secularization. It was a time when nonfunctional ornamental design gave way to less decorativeness in architecture and dress as well as in speech. It was a time when indigenous tongues began to supersede Latin as a means of expression both learned and literary, when rationalism rather than faith and traditional beliefs became a common touchstone. Moreover, the culture of the eighteenth century is still basically our culture: the philosophical and political concepts of the late eighteenth century remain our concepts today. The later eighteenth century, which does not seem distant or foreign to us today, is unthinkable without the first half of that same century. If we are to understand what is blithely called the Age of Goethe and might equally well be called the Age of Kant, we cannot disregard the base from which Johann Wolfgang von Goethe, Immanuel Kant, and their contemporaries sprang, just as we must have some knowledge of the antecedents of the American and the French revolutions if we are to understand them and the forces that brought them about.

Many of the influential ideas that struck root in the disorganized mass of German-speaking states around 1700 had already made themselves felt elsewhere somewhat earlier: notably in France and in England, both of which were political powers in a way that Germany—which comprised more a linguistic than a political unit—was not. France had a theater that could boast of brilliant playwrights such as Molière and Pierre Corneille, and England enjoyed the freedom of the press, while the Netherlands was a haven for independent thinkers seeking religious liberty. The Germans were to learn from all their neighbors, but the progressive ideas that those neighbors cultivated could not be introduced swiftly in any all-embracing fashion. Nevertheless, by the end of the century Germany had achieved a serious theater, had produced thinkers and writers who commanded an international as well as a domestic audience, and had achieved a degree of tolerance that was spiritually removed from the narrow theocratic convictions that obtained less than a century before—although the dream of German political unity was, for better or for worse, unrealized.

If one were to seek the single most important strand of thought that was generated in the seventeenth century and still permeated the early eighteenth century, it would be found to be a philosophical-religious one that can be more narrowly defined as the expanding concept of teleology. The vibrant nerve of philosophical discussion around the year 1700, this concept is identified on the one hand with Pierre Bayle in his radical, if not revolutionary, encyclopedic work, *Dictionaire historique et critique* (1697), and on the other hand with Gottfried Wilhelm Leibniz in his *Essais de théodicée* (1710). Although they were superficially religious antagonists, both Bayle and Leibniz were indebted to René Descartes for some of their liberal views. Cautious in the text of the main entries, but bold in the sometimes contradictory footnotes, Bayle's dictionary was widely read by inquisitive minds at the turn of the century. The liberal views found in some of the footnotes were enough to put the work on the Index of the Roman Church, but in libraries that did not feel constrained by the Index, the book was much used. The Danish historian and dramatist Ludvig Holberg (1684-1754) tells in his memoirs of students waiting for Cardinal Mazarin's library to open and then racing to be the first to obtain Bayle's encyclopedia. Although written in French, the best-known response to Bayle came from Germany: Leibniz's theodicy was a defense of the divine order of the world and was meant to refute Bayle's dangerous skepticism. It did in fact provide an apology for the future of the natural sciences. Scientific research, according to Leibniz, was not undertaken to overturn traditional ecclesiastical teaching (although in practice it did) but to determine the pattern of the universe, that is, a divine pattern. It is not too much to claim that this principle still obtains for the natural and physical sciences, for the teleological assumption is still made, and the theory of an orderly patterned universe rather than inexplicable chaos is basic to scientific investigation. This nucleus of thought lies at the basis of the intellectual phenomenon we call the Enlightenment and marks the transition to the modern times of which we are a part today.

Congruent with this altered philosophy was the rise of a distinctly secular culture that in many fields of endeavor extracted itself from ecclesiastical domination. By mid century there were substantial works of architecture, art, belles lettres, and music that enjoyed independent existence in an increasingly secular society which, although it did not feel itself divorced from an established church, nevertheless sensed a disjunction between theological admonitions and the realities of daily life. To be sure, there was clearly an element of such disjunction in the worldly poetry of the Baroque, but in the seventeenth century, wordliness and especially the erotically frivolous were more a pose than a reflection of everyday existence. Such lighthearted poetry took on somewhat altered form in the early eighteenth century among those poets whom we identify as Anacreontic. Their poetry of wine, women, and song—poetry that was but vaguely related to its Greek source of inspiration—was not an outgrowth of a new philosophical conviction, but neither was it out of place in an age of the secularization of society.

There was a need for new orientation in all realms of the spirit—in philosophy, law, oratory, linguistic usage, and art. These many needs were met—some in part, some more thoroughly; some sooner, some later; some by recasting principles of classical antiquity, some by the exploitation of indigenous tradition—so that by about 1750 there

had come about a noticeable alteration and a shift of emphasis as well as a revaluation in many disciplines. The sum of all these changes can be looked upon as the achievement of the Enlightenment, an achievement that provided the basis for what was to be known as German Classicism.

The term *Classicism* itself suggests an orientation based upon the thought and cultures of Greece and Rome; the suggestion is accurate in two ways. First, there was a reassessment of classical antiquity, its monuments and its literature. Second, there was a conscious effort to create parallels to the achievements of classical antiquity in Western Europe and specifically in Protestant Europe, which had sloughed off many of the bonds to the past that the Church of Rome preserved. In part, then, one can say that the efforts of the eighteenth century to create a new culture, while drawing on the pagan past, were not without religious overtones. What had been abandoned or lost required replacement. The Enlightenment had cast off the restrictions of the parochial; it had emancipated philosophy, but at the same time it had created lacunae that required replenishment.

In retrospect, a key to the new culture of the eighteenth century that is also part of our culture in the West today is the preeminence of the vernacular. In the eighteenth century Latin remained the language of learning and of scholarship and of much intercultural communication. Indeed, the importance of Latin was clear to anyone who would achieve the "klassische Bildung" (the classical education) that was an ideal in several countries and particularly in Germany until the second half of the present century. The disengagement was slow everywhere. A lance had nevertheless been broken for the vernacular as the language of learning toward the end of the seventeenth century, but it was many decades later before the use of German at German universities could be said to have become the norm. Even the champions of the vernacular, whether in German, French, Danish, or some other Western tongue, realized the usefulness of an international language to allow one to be read beyond the borders of one's own country—as is often shown today by the use of English (which is, in effect, something of a throwback to the use of Latin rather than a mark of total success for the vernacular). The use of the vernacular nevertheless spread and contributed to the rise of a nationalism that came to be identified with language in the nineteenth and twentieth centuries.

In any case, the use of the vernacular for belles lettres made for richer national literatures and created a pluralistic literary awareness that was to further the cause of translation.

In Germany–that is, the many states that had the bond of a common language–the reassessment of the indigenous past and the rise of a critical literature in the vernacular is to be identified above all with Johann Christoph Gottsched (1700-1766), who holds an ambiguous place in most histories of German literature. He is the leading figure on practically all fronts until into the 1740s, but he is best known because of Gotthold Ephraim Lessing's intemperate attack on him in the "siebzehnter Literaturbrief" (seventeenth letter on literature) in *Briefe die neueste Litteratur betreffend* (Letters on the Most Recent Literature) in 1759. With a hyperbole that damaged Gottsched's reputation for all time, Lessing disputed even Gottsched's incontrovertible contributions to the advancement of the theater in Germany. In the popular mind, however, Gottsched is identified even today chiefly with the stage and is often viewed with the ridicule engendered by Lessing's biting criticism.

Despite the historical ambivalence of Gottsched's position, he was for two decades the central figure of popular philosophy and of literary criticism in Germany and may therefore be taken as representative of the first half of the century. There is no aspect of literature in which he did not play a role. Gottsched had come to Leipzig, the cultural center of Germany at the time, to escape from being impressed into military service in east Prussia. He had taken a master's degree at the University of Königsberg before he and his brother found their way to Saxony. Within a short time he became a confidant and librarian of the renowned scholar and book collector J. B. Mencke (1674-1732) as well as an unsalaried lecturer at the University of Leipzig and the "senior" in the Deutsche Gesellschaft (German Society), a literary association that he renamed and remolded according to his own ideas and that became the model for some sixteen other groups, from Königsberg to Vienna, that adopted the same name. Despite the fact that at least two of them, in Königsberg and in Göttingen, could add the appellation *königliche* (Royal) to their names, these societies were bourgeois institutions. There had been similar societies for the cultivation of the German language in the seventeenth century, the so-called Sprachgesellschaften (Language Societies), but

Gottsched encouraged the production of poetry and criticism in German with the perceptible ideal of the Académie Française in view. Although Gottsched urged many of his contemporaries to write odes and elegies and instilled in many poetasters a new sense of pride in the use of the vernacular, the Deutsche Gesellschaften did not produce poets of consequence. That so many societies were founded on the Leipzig model suggests that Gottsched had struck a sensitive nerve of the time and had disseminated a positive plan as to what might be done to further the cause of secular, vernacular literature.

In the second and third decades of the century new impulses came from without, especially from Great Britain. There was a rapid spread of interest in contemporary English literature–but also in John Milton, Lord Shaftesbury, Alexander Pope, and Edward Young, who were much admired and were translated energetically into German. Both Shaftesbury and Pope were articulate speakers for a rationalism that was the soul of the Enlightenment. So, too, was Bernard Mandeville in his *The Fable of the Bees* (1714). It was as if every aspect of English intellectual activity found an echo in Germany–and nowhere more clearly than in Göttingen, which became a center of Anglo-German activity with the founding of the new university (1734) and by virtue of the personal union that bonded the Electorate of Hannover and the British crown.

The literary forms that exfoliated in England, in particular the moral weekly and the novel, were avidly read in translation and widely imitated. Both of these genres that reflected the daily life of the bourgeoisie were born of the Enlightenment and spread a common-sense philosophy. The breadth and depth of interest in English belles lettres and humaniora can be determined by a perusal of the bibliographies of Lawrence and Mary Bell Price (in the University of California Publications in Modern Philology, volumes 9, 17, 37, and 44, 1919-1955). For the years 1700 to 1730 alone, the Prices located on the average seventy-five translations from the English annually–although few of these were belletristic; belletristic items increased rapidly in the following decades.

The moral weekly that had begun in England with Joseph Addison and Richard Steele's *Tatler* and made a still greater name for itself with the *Spectator* (1711-1712) was to have an immeasurable and lasting impact despite its short life. The imitations of the *Spectator* were innumerable–in Germany alone there were several hundred. Two of the earliest, intrinsically important though not of widespread distribution, were the Hamburg *Patriot*, the moving spirit of which was B. H. Brockes (1680-1749), and the Swiss *Discourse der Mahlern* (1721-1723), written by Johann Jakob Bodmer (1698-1783) and his collaborator in several literary ventures, Johann Jacob Breitinger (1701-1776). Bodmer and Breitinger championed not only the English moral weekly but, subsequently, Milton and also Shakespeare, whose genius was not readily admitted by all German critics. Among the most influential German "Spectator" weeklies were two written almost entirely by the young Gottsched: *Die vernünftigen Tadlerinnen*, originally issued in 1725-1727 (and republished in 1726, 1738, 1745, and 1748), and *Der Biedermann*, produced in 1728-1729 at the request of a publisher because of the success of Gottsched's first moral weekly. The titles of the two journals are not necessarily self-explanatory. It is noteworthy that the nominal authors of *Die vernünftigen Tadlerinnen* were all supposed to be women–a reminder that Gottsched was an early feminist who agitated for the establishment of a university for women and whose lifework was bound up with the collaborative efforts of his wife, Luise Adelgunde Victoria Kulmus (1713-1762), after their marriage in 1735 (that is, after Gottsched had been made a full professor with an adequate salary). The title of Gottsched's first journal literally means "The Rational Women Critics," but it is possible that Gottsched thought that the cognate *Tadler* (negative critic) was identical with one of the meanings of the English *tatler*. The term *Biedermann*, which is related to the term *Biedermeier* employed later in art criticism, suggests the upright, staid burgher. The titles were at least original; many other German weeklies called themselves *Spektator* or *Zuschauer*–the latter term simply a translation of the English *spectator*. Incidentally, Frau Gottsched translated the English *Spectator* into German under the title *Der Zuschauer* from 1739 to 1743 (reprinted between 1749 and 1751).

After these beginnings, the "Spectator" literature multiplied rapidly in Germany. The moral weeklies were clever and entertaining periodicals that in altered form have survived to the present day. A principal characteristic of the moral weekly is the tendency to make fun of the irrational in daily life and to support a traditional morality. The same spirit informed the most success-ful of English novels, Daniel Defoe's *Robinson Crusoe*, first published in 1719 and translated into German the following year. The enthusiasm for *Robinson Crusoe* rivaled that of the moral weekly, which is not altogether surprising in that they were contemporary, bourgeois publications with moralizing tendencies, although Defoe's novel was superficially a tale of adventure. In the course of several decades many imitations of Defoe's novel–some written as children's books–appeared in German as well as in other languages. Among the best known are *Robinson der Jüngere* (Robinson the Younger, 1777-1780) by Joachim Heinrich Campe (1746-1818) and *Der Schweizerische Robinson* (Swiss Family Robinson, 1812-1827) by Johann David Wyss (1743-1818).

Although the Deutsche Gesellschaften and the moral weeklies provided a practical answer to the question of what could be done, there was a corresponding need for a theoretical discussion of literature and a basis and point of view from which it could be viewed. The young, ambitious, enterprising, energetic, and well-organized Gottsched was lecturing on multiple aspects of imaginative literature at the university and soon transmuted his lectures into a volume of comprehensive poetics, first published in the autumn of 1729 (with the imprint 1730) as *Versuch einer critischen Dichtkunst vor die Deutschen* (Attempt at a Critical Poetics), a work which was to undergo revision in three subsequent editions in 1737, 1742, and 1751. The third edition can be viewed as canonical; it is upon this edition that Joachim Birke based his text for volume 6 (1973) of Gottsched's *Ausgewählte Werke* (Selected Works).

Although Gottsched claimed to be a disciple of Martin Opitz and to be basing his work on Opitz's *Buch von der deutschen Poeterey* (Book of German Poetry, 1624), he was in fact writing in a different spirit and with different goals from his Baroque predecessor. The subtitle of Gottsched's poetics establishes his principles: *Darinnen erstlich die allgemeinen Regeln der Poesie, hernach alle besondere Gattungen der Gedichte, abgehandelt und mit Exempeln erläutert werden, überall aber gezeiget wird daß das innere Wesen der Poesie in einer Nachahmung der Natur bestehe. Anstatt einer Einleitung ist Horatii Dichtkunst in deutsche Verse übersetzt, und mit Anmerckungen erläutert ...* (In Which First the General Rules for Poetry, Thereafter All the Particular Kinds of Poetry Are Treated and Illustrated by Examples, Everywhere, However, Is Shown That the Inner Nature of Poetry Is the Imitation of Nature. Instead of an Introduction Horace's Poetics Is Translated into German Verse and Explained in Notes . . .). That is, on the one hand, Gottsched believed that the rules for imaginative writing could be derived from the state of the natural world–again the teleological assumption–and, on the other, he felt the rules could be deduced from the masterpieces of earlier, classical writers. Although there were other efforts to offer poetical guidance in the early eighteenth century, Gottsched's *Critische Dichtkunst*, as it is generally known, actually had no competition for more than a decade. Then Gottsched's judgments began to be called into question by more liberal critics who were more willing to admit fantasy and to disregard the dicta of traditional poetic categories with clearly recognizable patterns of verse form or dramatic structure. This important difference explains Gottsched's unwillingness to recognize the genius of Shakespeare, although his dislike of Milton was engendered rather by a rejection of the Baroque metaphor that Gottsched felt had been superseded at the beginning of the eighteenth century. For Gottsched, Milton represented an acceptance of outdated, exaggerated figures of speech.

The disagreement about the significance of the two English writers led to the clash between "the Swiss," that is, Bodmer and Breitinger, and "Leipzig," that is, Gottsched and his followers. In reality, the two Swiss critics and their Leipzig contemporary had much in common and earlier had carried on a friendly correspondence, with Bodmer even contributing to the first of Gottsched's several critical journals. As was to be the case in the mid 1750s between Lessing and Gottsched, the adversaries actually shared a goal (in the latter case the creation of a national theater) but were in sharp disagreement about how the goal was to be reached. In both cases antagonism caused personal invective to guide the arguments. When Breitinger published his own poetics in 1740 he entitled it, with unmistakable irony, *Critische Dichtkunst*. Although traditionally literary historians have tended to view the Swiss as the victors in the great literary feud of the 1740s, Breitinger's poetics did not measure up to Gottsched's in general acceptance and use, nor did it have a second edition.

There was at first an intrinsic flaw in Gottsched's poetics: examples to illustrate the kinds of poetry that he was describing and for which he was agitating belonged to the present and future rather than to the past. As a consequence most of his examples were taken from writers from the beginning of the eighteenth century (and often before) or were written by Gottsched himself. While Gottsched was the leading critic of the day, that he was not an inspired poet is shown by the large amount of occasional verse that he–like so many of his contemporaries and predecessors–produced, in part as a source of additional income. On the whole his occasional poetry not only has no appeal to the twentieth-century reader but is generally overlooked, despite the role it once played and despite its testimony to the taste of an earlier time and the formal qualities of its verse. Although in later editions of his poetics Gottsched replaced his own work with examples from other writers, all four editions furnish evidence of the trends of the times, that is, of the "early modern" viewed from the standpoint of both theory and practice. Aside from their importance per se, the discursive publications of Gottsched and the Swiss are a demonstration of the desire to create a new literature with its philosophical basis in its own time and with freedom from the verbal ornamentation and other excesses of the poetry that had gone before. These younger critics considered the work of the so-called court poets from the turn of the century, such as Friedrich von Canitz, to be acceptable (although Canitz had not lived into the eighteenth century, having died in 1699).

There is, to be sure, a partial poetic carryover from the late seventeenth into the early eighteenth century. Its extent can be measured simply by examining the index of Gottsched's *Critische Dichtkunst*, where there are multiple references to the work of Christian Weise (died 1708), Johann Christian Günther (died 1723), Benjamin Neukirch (died 1729), Johann Ulrich König (died 1744), and Barthold Heinrich Brockes (died 1747). Christian Weise could be viewed as an acceptable model because of his didactic school dramas from around the year 1700; he was almost alone as a representative of plays that were neither bombastic (like many earlier dramatic works of the seventeenth century) nor frivolous (like the Hans-Wurst or harlequin comedies of popular entertainment).

In view of the fact that Neukirch was the editor of the so-called Hofmannswaldau anthology (1695-1727), which contained a large amount of erotic, if not pornographic, verse, it seems strange that the straitlaced Gottsched would draw upon him for examples that eighteenth-century writers might follow and, in addition, would have edited a collection of Neukirch's poetry in 1744. The explanation must be sought not in a lack of conviction on Gottsched's part but rather in Neukirch's own ambivalence. Like many other writers of the late seventeenth century, Neukirch displayed a dual nature: he was on the one hand secular and worldly and on the other conservative and courtly. In any case, he wrote verse that corresponded to the young Gottsched's convictions about the rules according to which poetry should be composed.

Of the several poets on whom Gottsched drew for illustrative and instructive examples, Günther was the youngest; at his death he was only forty-three years old. He was more modern in spirit and form than the others; moreover, he was more dedicated to poetry as a profession than his predecessors and contemporaries on the German literary scene. In fact his poetry was not really a carryover from the previous century but rather the beginning of a body of more personal and emotional verse that would be identifiable throughout the new century.

König was important not only for his poetry but also for his edition of the work of Freiherr von Canitz and the essay he appended to the edition: "Über den guten Geschmack" (On Good Taste), a discourse that may be viewed as evidence of a critical juncture in the development of literary attitudes in Germany. The concern with taste, the attempts to define and to delimit it, but at the same time the desire to cultivate it, was a pan-European phenomenon. The terms *gout, taste, Geschmack*, all of which derive from a physiological function, were discussed vigorously in an attempt to abstract an aesthetic equivalent capable of general and fixed application. Artistic absolutes, supported by an established church for centuries, had faded, and new standards were needed by which works of art could be judged. The discussion has, of course, never ceased, and we would not expect to establish a universal standard today. The eighteenth century, however, still assumed that such a standard might be found. An entire chapter of part 1 of Gottsched's *Critische Dichtkunst* is devoted to the matter of good taste among poets.

Brockes, finally, the author of the multivolume *Irdisches Vergnügen in Gott* (Earthly Pleasure in God, 1721-1748), was the imaginative writer most clearly exemplifying the teleological principle of a divinely ordered natural world. The entire eighteenth century drew on this principle, which provided the basic assumption for the

systematic philosophers of the time. The most widely read was for many years Christian Wolff's valuable and able disciple, Gottsched. Brockes himself was, however, retrospective and must be classified as belonging to the late Baroque.

While Gottsched showed poor judgment in his rejection of Milton and Shakespeare, he took an indefensible position vis-à-vis the brightest new star on the German literary horizon: Friedrich Gottlieb Klopstock. In 1748 the young Klopstock published the first three cantos of his verse epic *Der Messias* (The Messiah)–in the style of Milton–in the so-called *Bremer Beiträge*, a periodical that was founded by young critics who were dissatisfied with Gottsched's autocratic inflexibility in literary matters. To make matters worse, judged from Gottsched's standpoint, Klopstock seemed at first to ally himself with Bodmer and Breitinger, for he accepted their invitation to visit them for an extended stay in the wake of the enthusiasm that the first cantos of *Der Messias* had evoked throughout Germany. Gottsched could scarcely be expected to be other than offended at this state of affairs. His own reputation could but suffer by his going against the current of the enthusiastic acceptance of Klopstock, who clearly provided the answer to the German prayer for a verse epic that might be looked upon as a parallel to the epics of Homer and Milton. Gottsched, however, continued to treat with reserve the acclaimed younger poet, who was to enjoy royal patronage in Denmark for nineteen years to complete *Der Messias*. Gottsched and others who were attempting to establish a standard German literary language and standard orthography must also have looked askance at Klopstock's willingness to accept the phonetic spelling–such as *y* for *ü*–of the Swiss.

Klopstock was trying, willy-nilly, to be a German Milton and, perhaps subconsciously, to produce the German epic for which the German literary world longed. As a German Milton, though, he could be viewed as a phenomenon of the late Baroque. No wonder, then, that the enthusiasm for *Der Messias* had died by the time it was completed (1773), two decades after it had been begun and at a time when Klopstock's appeal to the reading public derived from his Neoclassical odes and, to a lesser extent, from his dramatic works that drew on German legend and early history.

To comprehend the major currents in the literature of the time one must recognize the centrality of Gottsched's position from approximately

1725 to 1745. Protestant Germany sought during this period to produce moral weeklies and to provide a new critical and theoretical basis for belletristic endeavor. It also sought to establish a viable theater; to formulate and systematize the pervasive ideas of Leibniz and Wolff into a formal philosophy; to standardize written German with regard to structure and orthography; and to found critical organs that could evaluate recent and contemporary publications. In all these efforts Gottsched set the pace and accomplished most, despite his being superseded in the realm of the drama in the 1750s.

Soon after coming to Leipzig, Gottsched evinced interest in the improvement of the theater, which at the time was in the hands of traveling companies that moved from court to court or from city to city but played regularly in Leipzig when the fairs took place. The foremost of these theatrical groups was led by Frau Caroline Neuber (called "die Neuberin"), and the young Gottsched made the unusual move of joining forces with her to improve the contemporary theater and to overcome the domination of the stage by slapstick comedy and Italian opera. The theater was to have a more elevated function and was to be governed by reason; it was not to be merely a conglomeration of ephemeral humor and extravagant stage effects. Gottsched wanted in particular to rid the stage of the Hans Wurst figure–a clownish character who, for the sake of evoking laughter, might interrupt the course of action in a play. Gottsched won the confidence of Neuber, but theorist and stage director were confronted by a seemingly insoluble problem: there was no body of plays in German that fitted their needs and corresponded to their ideal. They had the choice either of translating plays that satisfied their ideal and provided models they hoped German playwrights would follow or of producing original German plays. Both options were taken, but the early emphasis was on translation–especially from the French, since the French stage was on a high level and could draw on the oeuvre of dramatists who had distinguished themselves on the European, and not only the French, scene. Gottsched was urging his countrymen not to take over the French stage (as sometimes was claimed) but to learn primarily from the French in order to create a comparable and if possible superior body of dramatic literature in German. Gottsched also looked for models to Denmark, which had overcome a similar situation by engaging the university professor and satirist Ludvig

Holberg to produce comedies for the newly established Danish stage in the early 1720s.

Because of the lack of a repertoire, German theatrical companies had little to draw upon before the publication of *Die Deutsche Schaubühne* (The German Stage), which Gottsched edited in six volumes between 1741 and 1745. The title was somewhat misleading in that it did not mean that the plays contained in the collection were of German origin (although some were) but rather that they could be given on German stages. The first two volumes contained only translations from the French and the Danish. The original German plays that later were included were not of consequence save that they were in German. Gottsched himself tried his hand both at play writing and translating. His one successful play, *Sterbender Cato* (Dying Cato, 1732), which was republished several times, was a reworking of material used by Joseph Addison in his *Cato* (1713). That *Die Deutsche Schaubühne* appeared in a second edition speaks for the usefulness of Gottsched's venture. Even the young Lessing, who later was to denounce Gottsched so bitterly, had an early play of his given by Frau Neuber's players when he was a student at the University of Leipzig.

On two counts Gottsched did not succeed in his own time: there were no important playwrights who had him as a mentor, and there was still no established theater. Late in his career he published a reference work on extant German plays, *Nöthiger Vorrath zur Geschichte der deutschen Dramatischen Dichtkunst* (Essential Source for the History of German Dramatic Art, 1757-1765), but the book was solely of historical value. The great German drama was yet to come, but the efforts of Gottsched and lesser lights, both in the realm of theory and in practice, were a necessary fermentation that preceded the flowering of a distinctly bourgeois native drama in the 1770s.

While the philosophy of Christian Wolff was dominant in the early eighteenth century, there was a need to organize Wolff's ideas and make them comprehensible to the general public. This was a demanding task, considering the many facets of eighteenth-century philosophy, but Gottsched–who taught philosophy at the University of Leipzig–undertook to present a comprehensive philosophy in a methodical way and in a manner understandable to the educated layman. In so doing, he became Wolff's leading interpreter. Gottsched's philosophy, *Erste Gründe Der gesamten Weltweisheit* (First Principles of a Complete Philosophy), which presumably to a large extent evolved from his university lectures, was published in 1733-1734 and was well received. There were no fewer than seven editions of the lengthy work during the author's lifetime, and an eighth edition appeared eleven years after his death.

To examine Gottsched's philosophy cursorily is to acquire some understanding of Wolff's concepts of cosmography, of the role of man in the universe, and of the desired organization of daily life and of the ideal state. In his introduction Gottsched deplores the fact that university students often lack a basic understanding of philosophy and its importance. He stresses their need of more than a superficial acquaintance with philosophy if they are to be successful in the advanced faculties of theology, medicine, and law. Of signal importance is that Gottsched is writing in German as a matter of principle: he avoids Greek and Latin terminology in his text, providing the traditional classical terms in marginal notes.

After giving a brief historical background, Gottsched furnishes definitions for the terms that he employs, such as *Erklärung* (explanation) and *urtheilen* (to judge). He is as clear and unequivocal as possible—something that probably explains the widespread acceptance of the book. He introduces the reader to traditional logic and adduces a large number of true and false syllogisms. After explaining the value of reason (Vernunft) Gottsched describes characteristics of the physical world and the distinguishable bodies in the world, then touches briefly on the supernatural versus the natural. Little space is expended on the supernatural, as one might expect from a rationalistic thinker in the eighteenth century.

There follows a series of discussions about disciplines that we now would identify as elementary physics, mechanics, astronomy, geology, and anatomy. Gottsched then turns to meteorology, fire, electricity, plants, animals, and, finally, the human body. The last topic leads to a discussion of the senses, the emotions, and the nature of the soul. The volume concludes with a proof of the existence of God and an enumeration of divine characteristics and with brief mention of the recurrent problem of the existence of evil in a world of godly design.

The second volume of the *Weltweisheit* comprises the so-called practical philosophy, beginning with the necessary condition for the achievement of happiness, the contrast between virtue and vice, and the duties of the human being to God, society, and the government. Gottsched ad-

dresses the problems of daily life, of the family, and of marriage—with a cautious treatment of sexual intercourse and the need for chastity. We smile when we read the puritanical admonition "man lese keine Liebesgeschichte, und andere unzüchtige Schriften der Poeten" (one should read no love story or other lascivious writings of the poets) or the advice that the most effective means of preserving one's chastity is "wenn man mäßig im Essen und Trinken ist" (when one is temperate in eating and drinking). There is positive evaluation of diligence, economy, generosity, friendship, and uprightness. The final section of the practical philosophy is nominally devoted to "Staatslehre," or what might be called political science, but it deals with the institution of marriage, the upbringing of children, and the organization of one's home, as well as the requirements for the ideal ruler and the ideal state.

This outline of the most widely read philosophy of its time suggests the dominant worldview and the accepted set of prescriptive ethics in the early eighteenth century and therewith a different and clearly more secular interpretation of physical and moral existence than had prevailed in the previous century. Gottsched's magnum opus was a summary product of the Enlightenment, a monument of rationalism that could provide a basis for the understanding and acceptance of existence and that would provide a key to the solution of questions about the realms of the physical and the spiritual—or even the suppositional.

As mentioned before, a matter of great consequence in eighteenth-century Germany was the development of a standard literary language with standard grammar and orthography. Here again Gottsched played a leading role—if not the leading role—with the publication of his *Grundlegung einer Deutsche Sprachkunst* (Basics of the German Language), a book that today would be identified as a German grammar, although it was more extensive and more inclusive than are grammars as we know them today. No book by Gottsched had a more protracted genesis—but no book by him was ultimately more widely used. The first edition did not appear until 1748, although Gottsched had been preparing the work for two decades (and had announced its forthcoming publication more than once). There were five editions of the grammar during Gottsched's lifetime, but the Gottsched bibliography in volume 12 (1987) of the *Ausgewählte Werke* records more than 120 other editions, translations, and revisions of Gottsched's work, through the year 1852. Gottsched had indeed met a need and produced a standard reference tool. It was an exhaustive book of such a nature that it scarcely could be read in toto, but it could and did serve as a reference work. The book is detailed and thorough, from the pronunciation of the letters of the alphabet down to idiomatic usage and dialectical differences. In an effort to leave no loose ends, Gottsched evolved hundreds of such pragmatic rules as one for determining the genders of nouns according to their endings (but also listing exceptions), and others covering every aspect of structure and usage. There are also extensive lists of metaphors and idioms.

In keeping with the tenet that the native, rather than foreign, terminology should be used, Gottsched employed many linguistic neologisms, including some of his own coinage. Fortunately, he furnished a list of classical terms and their German equivalents. Thus ablative is "die sechste, oder Nehmendung," participles are "Mittelwörter," prepositions are "Vorwörter," and syncope is "die Verbeissung." Some of the puristic terms have been accepted into the language (for example, "Beywort," now written *Beiwort* for adjective), but others, such as "die Abänderung" for declension, have not. There is no question that Gottsched's efforts contributed much to the standardization of modern German and established the usage of Saxony as a model—to the detriment of Low German in the North and Swiss usage in the South. An important goal had been reached, however: there was an accepted German literary language and at the same time there was greater pride in that language as a means of communication on all levels. French continued as the language of the court, however, and as the language of diplomacy (the latter function lasting into the twentieth century), while Latin was the language of scholarship. The stage was now set, though, for a flowering of a new, indigenous literature that would incorporate the idea of a literary level comparable to that of France. The language of the Baroque had been overcome, and rational thought prevailed.

A genre that enjoyed especial popularity in the eighteenth century and that harmonized with the ideal of a new German literature was the fable and particularly the animal fable in verse. To be sure, the animal fable is an ancient genre identified with the name of the Greek slave Aesop, but the fable was given a new lease on life through the work of Jean La Fontaine (1621-1695), whose sophisticated French versifications caught the public fancy and encouraged many imitators to produce similar poems. La Fontaine's fables distinguish themselves by their elegant wit and cleverness and their ability to depict human failings by masking the actors as animals. Such poetry represented a break with the artificiality of the earlier poetry that we identify as "Baroque"—incidentally a term that did not gain currency until the middle of the eighteenth century.

Germany had its own La Fontaine in Christian Fürchtegott Gellert (1715-1769). After having written a dissertation in Latin on the fable (1744) and, like Gottsched, embracing an academic career at the University of Leipzig, he went on to become the most widely read author in Germany. He was, however, not merely an imitator of La Fontaine. The spirit that informed his work was less elegant and more homely than that of the French poet. No one wrote in German more in the taste of the time than did Gellert; his fables were found in practically every German household and were also widely translated. Another author worth mentioning who also wrote fables was Friedrich von Hagedorn (1708-1754), who had made a name for himself as early as 1729 with his *Versuch einiger Gedichte*. With Wilhelm Ludwig Gleim (1718-1803) and Johann Peter Uz (1720-1796), Hagedorn was a leader of the Anacreontic poets whose lighthearted lyrics gave evidence of a Neoclassical orientation and stood in contrast to the newer strain of serious poetry appreciative of nature, the foremost example of which was the Swiss polymath Albrecht von Haller's "Die Alpen" (The Alps, 1732). The fable and the moral essay were the two leading genres of a florescent literature that employed simple forms, embodied the rational thought and the wit of both English and French writers, and was serious about its mission of improving man and society.

Contemporary with the awareness of the importance of the vernacular was an awakening to the appreciation of an indigenous literature, such as the folk literature that existed in chapbooks, and the still older literature preserved from the Middle Ages that had not been given serious consideration by critics. Gottsched played a role in the rejuvenation of both kinds of literature. With regard to the chapbooks, however, he occupied an ambivalent position. He rejected the *Faust* book as unworthy of renewal, whereas he translated *Reineke Fuchs* (Reynard the Fox) from Low

German into High German. It is difficult to understand why he would reject the one work and accept the other, especially since the *Faust* was subsequently to furnish the raw material for the most influential German epic drama, Goethe's *Faust* (1808-1832). The explanation is to be sought in the role of the supernatural in *Faust* and possibly also its comic element when contrasted with the subtle satire of the fox and the other members of the animal kingdom that reflected human behavior in high places—and to Gottsched suggested a parallel with Homer, albeit only the pseudo-Homeric *Batrachomyomachia*. In any case, there was now some cognizance of folk literature that would increase with time and lead to many discoveries in literary realms that hitherto had been overlooked, if not despised.

Similarly, there was a new view of medieval German literature; but here Bodmer and Breitinger deserve special mention as the rediscoverers and promoters of a lost literature, in particular because of their edition of one of the greatest treasures of the Middle Ages, the Mannesse manuscript (the most important collection of German medieval poetry). Gottsched collected medieval manuscripts and wrote appreciatively of Wolfram von Eschenbach and other masters of Middle High German literature as well as popular literature that employed various international motifs. An entire section of the fourth edition of the *Critische Dichtkunst* is devoted to fables, tales of knights, and works identified as medieval novels.

Of unequivocal and lasting significance for the entrenchment of the Enlightenment was the appearance of critical journals starting at the beginning of the 1730s. Even earlier there had begun to appear scholarly journals such as Jean Le Clerc's several "bibliothèques" in the Netherlands and the *Acta Eruditorum* in Leipzig, but they were given to the reporting of facts about learned publications and academicians and did not undertake to pass critical judgments. The new journals can be said to have a single predecessor in the *Monatsgespräche* (Monthly Conversations) of Christian Thomasius toward the end of the seventeenth century.

The first critical journal in German that was addressed to a more general audience was an outgrowth of Gottsched's Deutsche Gesellschaft: *Beyträge Zur Critischen Historie Der Deutschen Sprache, Poesie und Beredsamkeit* (Contributions to the Critical History of the German Language, Poetry and Rhetoric), published between 1732 and

1745. The *Critische Beyträge*, as the journal is known, marked a new chapter in German literary history. Contributors were expected to write critically and at length or to provide résumés about recent publications. The journal was widely read and was the inspiration for a series of other similar journals. Gottsched himself subsequently published two further journals of like nature, *Neuer Büchersaal der schönen Wissenschaften und freyen Künste* (New Library of Belles Lettres and Liberal Arts, 1745-1750) and *Das Neueste aus der anmuthigen Gelehrsamkeit* (The Latest News of Genial Scholarship, 1751-1762).

The many journals that sprang up served the cause of the Enlightenment. They disseminated new ideas; they upheld the banner of rationalism; they shed light on a multitude of disciplines. Thus they became essential elements of the literary scene and have retained their commanding position until the present day, although it is no longer possible to point to one or the other journal which would give us accurately the pulse of contemporary life and thought. In principle the early journals were not agitating for any particular persuasion, if we except the belief in the virtue of rationalism. They represented several points of view and spoke with many voices—not infrequently contradicting one another. There had been a great change in the course of two decades: from no journals to many journals and from the mere reporting of facts about publications to the vigorous expression of well-founded opinions.

Even in the narrower world of learning there arose a lasting counterpart to the more widely distributed critical journals: the *Göttinger Gelehrte Anzeigen* (Göttingen Scholarly Notices), which is intimately bound up with the name of Albrecht von Haller in its early years and—after having undergone some slight changes of title—is still being published by the Göttingen Academy of Science. There is no more tangible evidence of the interrelation of our own times with the eighteenth century.

It would be incorrect to assume that the dominant rational current of the mid eighteenth century was the only current identifiable in its time. Older religious convictions and literary forms continued, but as subcurrents in a forward-looking and optimistic culture. The language of the young Klopstock as well as his choice of subject matter for his epic or the success of Count Nikolaus Zinzendorf (1700-1760) in propagating Pietism is evidence of attitudes different from and in part antithetical to those held by the historically better-known figures in German literature.

The stage was now set for a new generation to create the literature that we more readily associate with the eighteenth century. Lessing, the dramatist and critic; Christoph Martin Wieland, the novelist and poet; and Friedrich Nicolai, the publicist and didactic writer, were more than ready to take stage center. The year 1766 may be given symbolic significance: it was the year of Gottsched's death, of Lessing's *Laokoon*, and of Wieland's *Agathon*. Nicolai's outstanding critical journal, the *Allgemeine Deutsche Bibliothek* (Universal German Library), had been founded only the previous year. The transformation from the Baroque to the Enlightenment had been completed. German Classicism emerged.

Books for Further Reading

Blackall, Eric A. *The Emergence of German as a Literary Language, 1700-1775*, second edition. Ithaca, N.Y.: Cornell University Press, 1978.

Browning, Robert M. *German Poetry in the Age of the Enlightenment: From Brockes to Klopstock.* University Park & London: Pennsylvania State University Press, 1978.

Bruford, Walter H. *Germany in the Eighteenth Century: The Social Background of the Literary Revival.* Cambridge: Cambridge University Press, 1935.

Cassirer, Ernst. *The Philosophy of the Enlightenment.* Princeton: Princeton University Press, 1951.

Closs, August. *Genius of the German Lyric: An Historical Survey of its Formal and Metaphysical Values*, revised and enlarged edition. London: Cresset, 1962.

Gaede, Friedrich. *Humanisnus, Barock, Aufklärung: Geschichte der deutschen Literatur vom 16. bis zum 18. Jahrhundert.* Bern & Munich, 1971.

Garland, Henry and Mary. *The Oxford Companion to German Literature*, 2nd edition. Oxford & New York: Oxford University Press, 1986.

Gay, Peter. *The Enlightenment: An Interpretation. The Rise of Modern Paganism.* New York: Knopf, 1966.

Graham, Ilse. *Goethe and Lessing: The Wellsprings of Creation.* New York: Harper & Row, 1973.

Guthke, Karl S. *Literarisches Leben im achtzehnten Jahrhundert in Deutschland und in der Schweiz.* Bern & Munich: Francke, 1975.

Hatfield, Henry C. *Aesthetic Paganism in German Literature. From Winckelmann to the Death of Goethe.* Cambridge, Mass.: Harvard University Press, 1964.

Hazard, Paul. *European Thought in the Eighteenth Century, from Montesquieu to Lessing.* New Haven: Yale University Press, 1954.

Hettner, Julius Hermann. *Literaturgeschichte der Goethezeit*, edited by Johannes Anderegg. Munich: Beck, 1970.

Hinck, Walter, ed. *Europäische Aufklärung.* Frankfurt am Main: Athenaion, 1974.

Kieffer, Bruce. *The Storm and Stress of Language: Linguistic Catastrophe in the Early Works of Goethe, Lenz, Klinger, and Schiller.* University Park: Pennsylvania State University Press, 1986.

Lange, Victor. *The Classical Age of German Literature, 1740-1815.* New York: Holmes & Meier, 1982.

Newald, Richard. *Die deutsche Literatur vom Späthumanismus zur Empfindsamkeit, 1570-1750.* Munich: Beck, 1951.

Newald. *Von Klopstock bis zu Goethes Tod*, volume 1: *Ende der Aufklärung und Vorbereitung der Klassik*. Munich: Beck, 1957.

Pasley, Malcolm. *Germany: A Companion to German Studies*, 2nd edition. London: Methuen, 1982.

Prawer, Siegbert. *German Lyric Poetry: A Critical Analysis of Selected Poems from Klopstock to Rilke*. New York: Barnes & Noble, 1952.

Robertson, John George. *A History of German Literature*, 6th edition, edited by Dorothy Reich. Edinburgh & London: Blackwood, 1970.

Saine, Thomas P. *Von der Kopernikanischen bis zur Französischen Revolution: Die Auseinandersetzung der deutschen Früaufklärung mit der neuen Zeit*. Berlin: Schmidt, 1987.

Schöffler, Herbert. *Deutsches Geistesleben zwischen Reformation and Aufklärung: von Martin Opitz zu Christian Wolff*, 3rd edition. Frankfurt am Main: Klostermann, 1974.

Staiger, Emil. *Stilwandel: Studien zur Vorgeschichte der Goethezeit*. Zurich: Atlantis, 1963.

Wellek, René. *The Later Eighteenth Century*, volume 1 of *A History of Modern Criticism 1750-1950*. New Haven: Yale University Press, 1955.

Wiese, Benno von, ed. *Deutsche Dichter des 18. Jahrhunderts: Ihr Leben und Werk*. Berlin: Schmidt, 1977.

Wiese, ed. *Das deutsche Drama vom Barock bis zur Gegenwart*, 2 volumes. Düsseldorf: Bagel, 1958.

Wiese, ed. *Die deutsche Lyrik: Form und Geschichte*, 2 volumes. Düsseldorf: Bagel, 1970.

Zeman, Herbert. *Die deutsche anakreontische Dichtung: Ein Versuch zur Erfassung ihrer ästhetischen und literarhistorischen Erscheinungsformen im 18. Jahrhundert*. Stuttgart: Metzler, 1972.

Contributors

Beth Bjorklund...*University of Virginia*
Barbara Carvill...*Calvin College*
Bruce Duncan ....*Dartmouth College*
Karl Julius Fink ....*St. Olaf College*
Gloria Flaherty..*University of Illinois at Chicago*
James Hardin ....*University of South Carolina*
John L. Hibberd...*University of Bristol*
Gerd Hillen...*University of California, Berkeley*
Erich P. Hofacker, Jr...*University of Michigan*
Meredith Lee ....*University of California, Irvine*
Mary Kathleen Madigan...*King College*
Mark R. McCulloh...*Davidson College*
P. M. Mitchell...*Cornell University*
Peter Mollenhauer.......................................*Southern Methodist University*
Arthur D. Mosher ....*University of South Carolina*
James C. O'Flaherty...*Wake Forest University*
Helene M. Kastinger Riley.......................................*Clemson University*
Herbert Rowland ....*Purdue University*
John B. Rutledge..................................*University of North Carolina at Chapel Hill*
Christoph E. Schweitzer ....*University of North Carolina at Chapel Hill*
Timothy F. Sellner...*Wake Forest University*
Armin P. Sinnwell ....*University of South Carolina*
Robert Spaethling................................*University of Massachusetts-Boston*
Thomas C. Starnes..*Tulane University*
Debra L. Stoudt..*University of Toledo*
John Van Cleve..*Mississippi State University*
Erdmann Waniek ....*Emory University*
Liliane Weissberg ....*University of Pennsylvania*
Renate Wilson...*Columbia, S.C.*

Cumulative Index

Dictionary of Literary Biography, Volumes 1-97
Dictionary of Literary Biography Yearbook, 1980-1989
Dictionary of Literary Biography Documentary Series, Volumes 1-7

Cumulative Index

DLB before number: *Dictionary of Literary Biography,* Volumes 1-97
Y before number: *Dictionary of Literary Biography Yearbook,* 1980-1989
DS before number: *Dictionary of Literary Biography Documentary Series,* Volumes 1-7

A

B

C

F

H

L

N

Surveys of the Year's Poetry

T

U

V

W

Y

Z

(Continued from front endsheets)

71: *American Literary Critics and Scholars, 1880-1900,* edited by John W. Rathbun and Monica M. Grecu (1988)

72: *French Novelists, 1930-1960,* edited by Catharine Savage Brosman (1988)

73: *American Magazine Journalists, 1741-1850,* edited by Sam G. Riley (1988)

74: *American Short-Story Writers Before 1880,* edited by Bobby Ellen Kimbel, with the assistance of William E. Grant (1988)

75: *Contemporary German Fiction Writers,* Second Series, edited by Wolfgang D. Elfe and James Hardin (1988)

76: *Afro-American Writers, 1940-1955,* edited by Trudier Harris (1988)

77: *British Mystery Writers, 1920-1939,* edited by Bernard Benstock and Thomas F. Staley (1988)

78: *American Short-Story Writers, 1880-1910,* edited by Bobby Ellen Kimbel, with the assistance of William E. Grant (1988)

79: *American Magazine Journalists, 1850-1900,* edited by Sam G. Riley (1988)

80: *Restoration and Eighteenth-Century Dramatists,* First Series, edited by Paula R. Backscheider (1989)

81: *Austrian Fiction Writers, 1875-1913,* edited by James Hardin and Donald G. Daviau (1989)

82: *Chicano Writers,* First Series, edited by Francisco A. Lomelí and Carl R. Shirley (1989)

83: *French Novelists Since 1960,* edited by Catharine Savage Brosman (1989)

84: *Restoration and Eighteenth-Century Dramatists,* Second Series, edited by Paula R. Backscheider (1989)

85: *Austrian Fiction Writers After 1914,* edited by James Hardin and Donald G. Daviau (1989)

86: *American Short-Story Writers, 1910-1945,* First Series, edited by Bobby Ellen Kimbel (1989)

87: *British Mystery and Thriller Writers Since 1940,* First Series, edited by Bernard Benstock and Thomas F. Staley (1989)

88: *Canadian Writers, 1920-1959,* Second Series, edited by W. H. New (1989)

89: *Restoration and Eighteenth-Century Dramatists,* Third Series, edited by Paula R. Backscheider (1989)

90: *German Writers in the Age of Goethe, 1789-1832,* edited by James Hardin and Christoph E. Schweitzer (1989)

91: *American Magazine Journalists, 1900-1960,* First Series, edited by Sam G. Riley (1990)

92: *Canadian Writers, 1890-1920,* edited by W. H. New (1990)

93: *British Romantic Poets, 1789-1832,* First Series, edited by John R. Greenfield (1990)

94: *German Writers in the Age of Goethe: Sturm und Drang to Classicism,* edited by James Hardin and Christoph E. Schweitzer (1990)

95: *Eighteenth-Century British Poets,* First Series, edited by John Sitter (1990)

96: *British Romantic Poets, 1789-1832,* Second Series, edited by John R. Greenfield (1990)

97: *German Writers from the Enlightenment to Sturm und Drang, 1720-1764,* edited by James Hardin and Christoph E. Schweitzer (1990)

Documentary Series

1: *Sherwood Anderson, Willa Cather, John Dos Passos, Theodore Dreiser, F. Scott Fitzgerald, Ernest Hemingway, Sinclair Lewis,* edited by Margaret A. Van Antwerp (1982)